The
Power Game

The
Power Game

How Washington Works

Hedrick Smith

Random House
New York

Library of Congress Cataloging-in-Publication Data

Smith, Hedrick.
  The power game.

  1. United States—Politics and government—1945-
2. Politicians—United States. 3. Power (Social
sciences) I. Title.
JK271.S577 1988   320.973   87-42669
ISBN 0-394-55447-7

*Grateful acknowledgment is made to the following for permission to reprint previously
published material:*

Brookings Institution: Excerpts from "The Crisis of Competence in our National
Leadership" by James L. Sundquist which appeared in *Political Science Quarterly* Vol. 95,
No. 2 (Summer 1980) p. 192.

CBS Inc.: Excerpts from a *CBS Evening News* broadcast of October 4, 1984 in which Leslie
Stahl shared her script with the author. Copyright © CBS Inc. All rights reserved.

Harper & Row Publishers, Inc.: Excerpts from *A Different Kind of Presidency* by Theodore
C. Sorensen. Copyright © 1984 by Theodore C. Sorensen, Eric Sorensen, Stephen Sorensen,
and Philip Sorensen. Reprinted by permission of Harper & Row Publishers, Inc.

The New York Times: An excerpt from "Deciding Who Makes Foreign Policy" by Zbigniew
Brzezinski. Copyright © 1983 by The New York Times Company. An excerpt from "The
White House Mystique" by John S. D. Eisenhower. Copyright © 1987 by The New York
Times Company. Excerpts from "The Greening of Washington" by Kenneth Schlossberg.
Copyright © 1986 by The New York Times Company. Reprinted by permission.

The Public Interest: Excerpts from "The Democratic Distemper" by Samuel P. Huntington.
Copyright © 1975 by National Affairs, Inc. Reprinted with permission of the author from
The Public Interest, No. 41 (Fall 1975), p. 27.

Time: Excerpt from "Needed: Clarity of Purpose" by Richard M. Nixon. Copyright © 1980
Time Inc. All rights reserved. Reprinted by permission from *Time.*

WETA Washington: Excerpts from an interview with Elliot Richardson for a PBS-TV
documentary entitled *The Power and the Glory.* Copyright © 1982 by Greater WETA
Educational Telecommunication Association.

To Susan, and the spark of renewal

Acknowledgments

No book is an individual enterprise. This book, like many others, has benefited greatly from the cooperation, assistance, wisdom and generosity of many people—my editor, academic mentors, researchers, news sources, journalistic colleagues, friends, and family.

Four people in particular gave special nourishment and encouragement to this book, for which I am deeply grateful: Kate Medina, my editor at Random House, whose immediate and persistent enthusiasm for the concept and for the reporting, seasoned with insightful and demanding critiques, provided me with both the lift and spur that I wanted and needed; Austin Ranney, my sponsor and friend at American Enterprise Institute, whose gentle coaching and sheer enjoyment of the power game, put fun and reward into the work of writing; Bill Nell, my chief researcher, who poured heart and soul and tireless hours and attention to tasks and facts too numerous to begin to enumerate; and Susan, my wife, whose "reader's reactions" often helped me and whose faith and patience and support nurtured me throughout the writing of this book.

This book would not have been possible without two institutions and their leaders to whom I feel and owe special thanks. Over the past twenty-five years *The New York Times* has given me the rich opportunity of having a fifty-yard-line seat at the power game, and of getting to know so many government officials and congressional politicians at close hand. I am especially grateful to Publisher Punch Sulzberger, and former Executive Editor Abe Rosenthal for granting me a leave of absence to write the manuscript, and to current Executive Editor Max Frankel, who was understanding when I needed more time.

For one very important year, the American Enterprise Institute for Public Policy Research and its former president, Bill Baroody, Jr., gave me an academic home as a visiting journalist. I am extremely grateful in particular to four senior fellows at AEI—Austin Ranney, Michael Malbin, Norm Ornstein, and John Makin—for their willingness to share so much time and knowledge to educate me. Austin Ranney and Tom Mann of Brookings Institution were generous enough to read the manuscript and give me their insights, and I am deeply in their debt, though obviously I alone bear responsibility for the judgments rendered in this volume.

Many members of Congress and administration officials offered me help or access—some four hundred to five hundred interviews—far too many for me to list them all. And some of the most helpful asked to remain anonymous. I am grateful to Presidents Reagan and Carter for their interviews with me and for similar access to Speakers Tip O'Neill and Jim Wright and Majority Leaders Howard Baker, Bob Dole, and Robert C. Byrd, as well as to scores of members of Congress and several dozen senior Reagan administration officials.

A few people—normally less visible to the public—deserve special mention because they enjoyed analyzing the power game as much as I have and they shared their understanding of the process of governing, and helped me see the patterns more clearly: Richard Darman, who is rich with insights into the levers of power and political dynamics of the presidency, or anywhere on the playing field; Mike Deaver, who has a storyteller's gift for the inside world of the Reagan White House; Ken Duberstein, Kirk O'Donnell and Chris Matthews, who tutored me on the ways of new-breed and old-breed politicians in the House; Tom Griscom, Steve Bell, and Linda Peake, whose expertise lay in the Senate; Dick Conlon, who provided vital "institutional memory" on the congressional reforms; Marty Franks and Joe Gaylord, who have for many elections kept me abreast of the partisan battle for control of the House; Bob Sims, unfailingly helpful, whether at the National Security Council or the Defense Department.

Journalistic colleagues helped on many points, large and small, in providing information and refining my own understanding of events—especially Lou Cannon and Haynes Johnson of *The Washington Post;*

Charles McDowell of the *Richmond Times-Dispatch;* Charles Corddry of the Baltimore *Sun;* Bob Shogan and Jack Nelson of the *Los Angeles Times;* Steve Roberts, Marty Tolchin, Barbara Gamarekian and Jonathan Fuerbringer of *The New York Times;* Leslie Stahl of CBS News; Chris Wallace of NBC News; and Sam Donaldson of ABC News; and Paul Duke, of the Public Broadcasting System.

Important material for many chapters in this book was pulled together by my three consecutive researchers—Bill Nell, Lauren Simon-Ostrow, and Kurt Eichenwald—whose assistance was indispensable to my writing. All three assisted me in many ways: compiling files, doing interviews, preparing memos, relentlessly chasing minutiae. Each brought special reporting and research talents to this project, and I am extremely grateful for their care, skill, and dedication. And we all owe thanks to Nancy Ganahl, the librarian at the Washington bureau of the *Times,* for her willing and thoughtful help.

I am most appreciative, too, for support in many areas from Lynda McAvoy, my efficient and cheerful assistant at AEI. To Randa Murphy, Mildred Edlowitz, Lyn Balthazar, and Penny Dixon goes my gratitude for their careful and patient transcribing of literally thousands of pages of my taped interviews.

Through the auspices of AEI, I was fortunate to have the help, too, of several interns, and I hope they got as much from this project as I did from them. Let me thank John Carpenter, Dave Deluca, Stephen Greene, Kathleen Hynde, Phil Hinz, Carol Monaghan, Debra Piehl, Mark Shaw, and Beate Thewalt.

My thanks, too, to Mitchell Ivers for his hours of patient copyediting of my manuscript, to Olga Tarnowski for so cheerfully shepherding my work through Random House, and to Julian Bach, my literary agent, who got a light in his eye when I first mentioned the power game and who launched the project and put it under Kate Medina's kind and constructive care.

HEDRICK SMITH
Chevy Chase, Maryland
January 15, 1988

Contents

Introduction

We Americans are a nation of game players. From Friday night poker and Sunday bingo to corporate rivalry and the nuclear arms race, Americans are preoccupied with winning and losing. Competition is our creed; it is knit into the fabric of our national life. Sports and game shows are national pastimes. Either we play games ourselves or we take part vicariously. We swim, cycle, jog or play tennis—making it a game by matching ourselves against a rival, against par in golf, or against the stopwatch when we hike or run. Five out of six Americans spend several hours a week viewing football, baseball, boxing, bowling, or some other sport on television. One hundred million people tune into television game shows weekly—forty-three million to *Wheel of Fortune*, appropriately named for a nation almost addicted to games. All over the world, people are playing at commerce on one hundred million sets of Monopoly.

Some people treat life itself as a game, to be won or lost, instead of seeing it in terms of a religious ethic or of some overarching system of values.

In Washington, senators and congressmen talk of politics as a game, and of themselves as "players." To be a player is to have power or influence on some issue. Not to be a player is to be out of the power loop and without influence. The ultimate game metaphors in government are the "war games"—not just the military exercises for fleets of ships or regiments of troops, but those ghostly, computer-run scenarios that our policymakers and nuclear experts use to test their reflexes and our defenses in a crisis: human survival reduced to a game.

So it seems only natural to look at how we are governed—the way Washington *really* works today—as a power game, not in some belittling sense, but as a way of understanding how government actually works and why it does not work better. For the game is sometimes glorious and uplifting, at other times aggravating or disenchanting. It obviously is a serious game with high stakes, one in which the winners and losers affect many lives—yours, mine, those of the people down the street, and of people all over the world.

When I came to Washington in 1962, to work at the Washington bureau of *The New York Times,* I thought I understood how Washington worked. I knew the usual textbook precepts: that the president and his cabinet were in charge of the government; that Congress declared war and passed budgets; that the secretary of State directed foreign policy; that seniority determined who wrote legislation in Congress; and that the power of southern committee chairmen—gained by seniority—was beyond the challenge of junior members; that voters elected one party or the other to govern; and the parties set how the members of Congress would vote—except for the southern Democrats, who often teamed up with Republicans.

These old truisims have been changed dramatically. My years as a reporter have spanned the administrations of six presidents, and over the course of that time, I have watched a stunning transformation in the way the American system of government operates. The Washington power game has been altered by many factors: new Congressional assertiveness against the presidency, the revolt within Congress against the seniority system, television, the merchandising of candidates, the explosion of special interest politics, the demands of political fundraising, the massive growth of staff power—and by changes in voters as well.

The political transformations of the past fifteen years have rewritten the old rules of the game. Presidents now have much greater difficulty marshaling governing coalitions. Power, instead of residing with the president, often floats away from him, and a skillful leader must learn how to ride the political waves like a surfer or be toppled. The old power oligarchy in Congress has been broken up. The new breed of senators and House members, unlike the old breed, play video politics, a different game from the old inside, backroom politics of Congress.

Party labels mean much less now to voters and to many candidates, too.

Altogether, it's a new ball game, with new sets of rules, new ways of getting power leverage, new types of players, new game plans, and new tactics that affect winning and losing. It is a much looser power game now, more wide open, harder to manage and manipulate than it was a quarter of a century ago when I came to town.

My purpose in this book is to take you inside each part of the political process in Washington and to show you how it works. And then, to show you how the whole game of governing fits together—and also to show where it doesn't fit together. My premise is that the games politicians play today—that is, how the power games are played and therefore how Washington *really* works—have unwritten rules, rituals, and patterns that explain why things so often happen the way they do. These political customs, conventions, and predictable patterns of behavior lie behind what Max Lerner once called "the ultimate propulsion of events":[1]

· Why presidents have so much trouble forming the coalitions it takes to govern,

· Why the Pentagon buys so many weapons that cost too much and don't work better,

· Why the secretary of State really can't run foreign policy and keeps getting into fights with the national security adviser, administration after administration,

· How the Democrats keep the Republicans from winning the House of Representatives,

· How the political money game generally helps finance the major deadlocks in government,

· Why some presidents such as Ronald Reagan are able to shed most of their political troubles and others such as Jimmy Carter get mired in them,

· Why the press goes after some politicians and leaves others alone,

· And how Lieutenant Colonel Oliver North wound up with so much power for secret dealings with Iran and underwriting the Nicaraguan *contras*—climbing out on a limb extending from a branch of precedent set by Henry Kissinger.

In using the metaphor of games, I do not mean to imply that politics is child's play. Governing the United States of America is a serious enterprise. Washington is a world where substance matters. Issues matter. Ideas matter. One political party, for example, can gain the

intellectual initiative over the other party, and that is vitally important
in the power game. The Democrats seized the "idea advantage" at the
time of Franklin Roosevelt's New Deal; the Reagan Republicans seized
it in the early 1980s with their idea of cutting government and taxes.

But Washington is a city engaged simultaneously in substance and
in strategems. Principles become intertwined with power plays. For
Washington is as much moved by who's up and who's down, who's in
and who's out, as it is by setting policy. Politicians are serious when they
debate about Star Wars, arms control, a fair tax system, protectionism,
and welfare reform. But they are no less serious when they devise
gambits to throw the other team on the defensive, when they grandstand to milk a hot issue for public relations points and applause. They
pursue the interests of their home team—their constituents. But in the
special world of Washington, they also hotly pursue their highly personal interests in the inside power games—turf games, access games,
career games, money games, blame games—each of which has an inner
logic of its own that often diverts officeholders away from the sin-
gleminded pursuit of the best policy.[2]

Politics in Washington is a continuous contest, a constant scramble
for points, for power, and influence. Congress is the principal policy
arena of battle, round by round, vote by vote. People there compete,
take sides, form teams, and when one action is finished, the teams
dissolve, and, members form new sides for the next issues. Of course,
team competition is our national way of life, but rarely does the contest
take place at such close quarters, among people who rub elbows with
each other, professionally and socially, day in and day out.

The lingo of games rings naturally on the playing fields of political
combat. For analogies, our politicians often turn to the argot of the
sports arena, the track, the boxing ring, the playing field, or the casino.
Richard Nixon, as president, would not dream of operating without "a
game plan." Jack Kennedy, comparing politics to football, told his press
secretary, Pierre Salinger, "if you see daylight, go through the hole."
When Gerald Ford was the House Republican leader, he could not
resist using football clichés; hardly a major vote could take place without Ford's warning that the ball was on the ten-yard line and the clock
was running out. More recently, Ronald Reagan's campaign strategists,
like ring handlers coaching a prizefighter, tapped a "sparring partner"
to warm up Reagan for the 1980 presidential campaign debates. They
chose David Stockman as the person to prep Reagan for debates with
John Anderson and Jimmy Carter. Later, Secretary of State Alexander
Haig was dropped from the Reagan cabinet because the White House

felt that he was not "a team player." Both admirers and critics saw how Henry Kissinger approached our national rivalry with Moscow as a global chess match, with other nations serving as his pawns.

The power game echoes Las Vegas and the daily double. Howard Baker, as Senate majority leader, fashioned the image that Reagan tax-cut economics was a "riverboat gamble." Politicians are forever citing the long odds against them, talking about front-runners and dark horses. Political reporters are kin to sportswriters, indulging in political locker-room talk: We compile "the book" on leading contenders and often devote more attention to the advance handicapping, the pace of the favorite, and the skill of his campaign trainers than to the issues and the national agenda.

But the purpose of this book goes beyond locker-room jargon and game analogies for American politics. The game metaphor helps to explain the patterns and precepts that skilled politicians live by, regardless of party or administration, as well as the consequences in all of this game playing, for all of us. Actually the Washington power game is not one game, but an olympiad of games, going on simultaneously, all over town. My aim is to take that olympiad apart, play by play, game by game, player by player, so that the overall game of governing is revealed.

Seeing the inner workings of Washington as a power game is a way of following the action amidst the babel. It's a metaphor for understanding what makes famous people—and faceless people, unknown but powerful—do what they do. Sometimes it explains why some good people don't play the game better, why they don't win. It helps in spotting the tricks of the political trade used by the winners, for seeing why some politicians succeed and others fail.

Knowing the rules of the game, the right moves and countermoves, is crucial to success. Some politicians like to say that the power game is an unpredictable casino of chance and improvisation—"lightning hitting the outhouse" is the way Senator Alan Simpson puts it. But most of the time politics is about as casual and offhand as the well-practiced triple flips of an Olympic high diver. The appearance of a casual, impromptu performance may add to its political appeal out in the country, as Reagan's TelePrompTer speeches and rehearsed press conferences do. But the real pros, like chess masters, rarely trust true amateurism in politics. They usually have a pretty good feel for how certain policy lines and maneuvers will play out, before they start.

Politicians themselves know that there are advantages for those who understand the rules and the moves, the power realities and the win-

ning gambits, and for those who are savvy about the traps and escape
routes of modern politics. The rules of the game apply from one
administration to the next. To pick just a few examples, a modern
handbook of political tactics would say:

·The smart White House chief of staff knows that you don't let the
president get committed to an all-out fight with Congress unless he
has enough votes in advance for near-certain victory; then you complain constantly about the uphill battle, to disarm the opposition and
to make the president's triumph more dramatic.
·The wise cabinet secretary knows you build a partnership with the
chairmen of the Congressional committees that watch over your
department, even if they come from the opposite party.
·The clever press secretary knows that you dump the really bad news
on Friday night when it's too late for the television networks and sure
to be buried by the print press in lightly read Saturday newspapers.
·The shrewd bureaucrat knows that the best way to control a program is to keep everyone else in the dark about it; then no higher-ups
or Congressional committees will know enough to change the program or challenge the bureaucracy.
·The smart bureaucrat also knows the best way to keep a program
alive is to provoke the loudest political protests: by underestimating
the program's cost, leaking bad news about budget cuts to friendly
members of Congress, and then making the cuts that cause the *most*
political pain—not the least—to the program's constituents.
·The smart legislator knows that the best way to beat an objection-
able piece of legislation is not to take it head-on in an up-or-down
vote on the floor, but to water it down with amendments that
reshape it, and then let it pass.
·The smart legislative staffer knows that if he will just let his boss,
the senator or the House member, take the limelight and get the
credit, the staffer can quietly shape much of the policy.
·The smart lobbyist knows that too.
·The smart lobbyist also knows that the best time to schedule a
political fund-raiser in Washington is right after a Congressional
recess because, as Tommy Boggs, one of the smartest lobbyists, told
me, "Everyone wants to get together and swap the latest gossip
because they haven't seen each other for two weeks."

Some of the most sophisticated people around the country often fail
to understand the rules of the Washington power game, people who

become cabinet members and even presidents and high corporate executives who frequently call at the White House. For instance, in late 1983, Thomas Wyman, former CBS board chairman, came to make a policy pitch to Edwin Meese III, who was then counselor to President Reagan. At the time, the television networks were fighting the Hollywood studios over control of the lucrative syndication rights for movies made for TV. It meant big money. Both sides went to Washington to get their way, and Wyman took his case to Meese, according to someone close to the Reagan inner circle.

As it happened, Meese was unable to keep the appointment because he was caught up in a sudden foreign policy crisis with the president. As a courtesy, Meese had Wyman sent to the office of Craig Fuller, then secretary of the Reagan cabinet and a top White House adviser to Meese. Fuller offered to help Wyman.

"I know something about this issue," Fuller suggested. "Perhaps you'd like to discuss it with me."

But Wyman waved him off, unaware of Fuller's actual role and evidently regarding him as a mere staff man.

"No, I'd rather wait and talk to Meese," Wyman said.

For nearly an hour, Wyman sat leafing through magazines in Fuller's office, making no effort to talk with Fuller, who kept working at his desk just a few feet away.

Finally, Meese burst into Fuller's office, full of apologies that he simply would not have time for a substantive talk.

"Did you talk to Fuller?" he asked.

Wyman shook his head.

"You should have talked to Fuller," Meese said. "He's very important on this issue. He knows it better than any of the rest of us. He's writing a memo for the president on the pros and cons. You could have given him your side of the argument."

Washington insiders know that the staff is often the key on any substantive issue. In this case, they would have known that Fuller, as brain truster for Meese and hence for the president, was the key figure. Fuller had already been thoroughly lobbied for the Hollywood studios by Nancy Reynolds, a former Reagan White House aide and a well-known lobbyist. Not that Fuller would neglect to give Meese both sides of the argument, but Wyman had lost a golden opportunity. Time with Fuller was actually worth more on that issue than time with Meese was, because Fuller was drafting the administration's position.

Wyman's mistake was not unusual. Many people, not understanding how the game is played, are dazzled by political celebrities and feel they have to go to the top: to the president or his right-hand man, to the Treasury secretary, the senator, the committee chairmen. Washington insiders pay far more attention to the power and expertise of staff than outsiders do. The insiders pay their respects to the person with the title and then work the serious issues with less-celebrated staff people who actually draft policy. The wise game player always paves the way to the higher-ups through the staff person.

Wyman's experience was a small incident, but change the names and the issues and it happens hundreds of times every year, from the Carter administration to the Reagan administration to the next administration, not only in the White House but in Congress, at the Pentagon, at the Agriculture Department, all over town. It is not just a matter of understanding staff power; it's also a matter of knowing whose economic figures to trust, which House leaders can pull together coalitions, which senators personally provoke opposition when they sponsor legislation, when to press the attack, and when to lay back and let the normal rhythms of politics pass by.

Washington has its special political culture, its tribal customs, and its idiosyncrasies. These folkways can trip up not only an untutored network boss, but also a new president such as Jimmy Carter, a business titan such as Donald Regan, and sometimes even a government career-ist such as former Secretary of State Alexander Haig. All because these people really didn't know how to play the power game—or, in Haig's case, because he hadn't really absorbed the lessons of his own experi-ence. These three men and others failed to understand the maxim that in political Washington, unlike in the military or industry, power is not hierarchical. Persuasion works better than unilateral policy pronounce-ments. Command is less effective than consensus.

Even as skillful a politician as Ronald Reagan can run into pitfalls when he forgets the basic rules of the game. Reagan was masterful as a political leader in 1981 and as president. During the brilliant launch-ing of his first administration, he understood the game, or he relied on others who did. He followed a near-perfect script for presidential lead-ership, especially in his critical first year, which fixed the country's approving impression of his presidency for six years. So often, early on, Reagan made the right move, whereas Jimmy Carter, in the opening days of his presidency, made the wrong move, which lost his presidency ground that it never regained.

But strangely, after Reagan's reelection to a second term in 1984, he failed to follow his own successful game plan, and in 1985 he began to fare badly. His 1984 landslide with the voters did not, ultimately, have the dramatic consequences that were expected. But the way Reagan played the game did.

Let me emphasize that the outcome in American government does not always depend on game playing. Obviously, the political environment affects the success or failure of presidents. For example, Jimmy Carter was handicapped by skyrocketing world oil prices beyond his control, prices that shot up the rate of inflation in America; whereas Ronald Reagan was helped immensely by the tumbling of those same oil prices, bolstering his campaign against inflation.

Nonetheless, over the past half dozen presidencies, there is ample evidence to suggest that regardless of philosophy or motives, some politicians have played the power game well and largely gotten their way, and others have played it badly and seen their policies falter. Beyond that, there are some political games that are vital to the effective functioning of our system, others that delude us for a time, and still others that tie our government in knots and stall the whole process. There are trivial games and weighty ones—the turf games of a bureaucrat protecting his piece of policy, the image games of the video politician, the "perk" games of access and proximity to the team captain. There is the blame game—dumping responsibility on the other side. There are the "porcupine politics" played by mavericks who derive their power from being prickly, from harassing the majority. And there's the political game that we, as citizens, most need for the players to play—the game of building coalitions.

The examples in this book draw heavily on the past decade, especially on the Reagan period; this period amply illustrates what works well in the power game and what works poorly. It is full of both smart moves and foolish gambits. What is more, this period reflects the larger dynamics of the power game that have driven our system in recent years and are likely to drive it in the coming administrations. I've also drawn on experiences from the presidencies of John F. Kennedy, Lyndon B. Johnson, Richard Nixon, and Jimmy Carter. But the Reagan period was particularly fruitful, not only because it is so fresh and it reflects the most up-to-date power techniques, but also because Reagan himself demonstrated some of the most skillful and triumphant game playing in recent American politics—and some of its most glaring failures. So did members of his cabinet, his staff, and the Congressional leaders during his presidency. Their patterns, their ways of winning, and the pitfalls of losing—the dos and don'ts—are likely to persist well into the next administration and beyond.

In all of this, power is the mysterious quotient. Power is the ability

to make something happen or to keep it from happening. It can spring
from tactical ingenuity and jugular timing, or simply from knowing
more than anyone else at the critical moment of decision. At its most
clear-cut, power is President Reagan's ordering the bombing of Libya
in 1986 or, six months later, tabling a spur-of-the-moment arms-control
proposal in Reykjavík. It is House Speaker Thomas P. "Tip" O'Neill,
Jr., and Senate Majority Leader Howard Baker striking a deal to push
a tax increase through in 1982 and then putting that bill on the agenda
for both houses of Congress. It is the stuff of headline news.

But there are many other less orthodox kinds of power, for power
operates in many indirect, invisible ways. Before presidential decisions
are made or the final congressional votes are taken, their content is
shaped by hidden hands. In Washington, as elsewhere, power does not
always follow organizational charts; a person's title does not necessarily
reflect the power that he or she has.

In Part One, my approach is to look, first of all, at the nature of
power: how different it is from what it appears to be and how the levers
of power have changed dramatically in the past fifteen years. Next, in
Part Two, we look at the playing field on which the power game takes
place. This is the terrain that the players take for granted: the folkways
of Washington, the power networks, the odd couples, the rise of
women in the power game. Then we will follow the various strands of
the power game: the world of the constant campaign in Congress, the
pork-barrel and turf-cartel politics of the Pentagon, the modern techniques of lobbies and the channels of political money, and the hidden
but immense power of staff. All of these together form the backdrop
for the big games of Part Three: presidential agenda setting, the building of coalitions, the strategies of opposition, the making of foreign
policy. And finally, in Part Four, we will look at the basic dilemmas of
our political system and why it doesn't work better: the deadlocks of
divided government, the steep costs of the absence of a majority party,
and the disconnect between our political campaigns and the very process of governing. My purpose, through it all, is to show how the
Washington power game really works, and how it could work better.

PART I

The Nature of Power

I. The Presidency and the Power Float: Our Rotating Prime Ministers

The President . . . is rightly described as a man of extraordinary powers. Yet it is also true that he must wield those powers under extraordinary limitations.[1]
—John F. Kennedy

Let us begin in Huntsville, Tennessee.

It would take years to find a more unlikely command post for an American president than Huntsville. Normally, Huntsville is a sleepy, peaceable mountain town (population 519), a classic slice of rural Americana set in the Appalachian forests of the Cumberland Plateau, nearly three thousand feet above the sea, and a sixty-mile drive northeast from Knoxville on sweeping, curving highways. It is the kind of tight-knit, little country community where, as one frequent visitor noted, "everyone knows when you come into town; and when you leave, they all know what your business was."

For well over a century, this upland neck of eastern Tennessee has been so staunchly Republican and so loyal to the Union that when Tennessee seceded during the Civil War, Scott County seceded from Tennessee. For much of this century, the staples of the local economy were strip-mining, lumbering, and prospecting for oil and natural gas. But the local folks say that environmental regulations have squeezed the life out of these industries and that the best jobs these days are making hardwood parquet floors at Tibbals Flooring, or working for B. F. Goodrich in Oneida, about seven miles up the road.

Huntsville is home to the Scott County government seat but boasts little else. The center of town, "the mall," is not much more than a grassy area surrounded by a two-story brick courthouse, a municipal building, one school, a grocery store, a drug store, one self-service laundry, a filling station, a community center, a motorcycle dealership, and a gazebo. No stoplight; only a blinker when school is in session. And the locals lament with envy that the nearest McDonald's is over in Oneida.

In short, Huntsville has little to distinguish itself from thousands of tranquil towns dotted across this nation—except that it is located just off Howard H. Baker Highway, named for an extremely skilled and amiable hometown lawyer who rose to become majority leader of the United States Senate in 1981, just as Ronald Reagan moved into the White House. The Baker family had crossed the mountains into Tennessee back in the 1790s and achieved some local prominence. Senator Baker's grandfather was elected sheriff of a neighboring county. The Bakers erected the town gazebo in Huntsville. But no one in the Tennessee family tree foreshadowed Senator Baker's eminence as a close confidant and political ally of a president. Nor did anyone dream what their relationship would mean to Huntsville.

Because some months into Mr. Reagan's term, Senator Baker used the occasion of a visit to the White House to propose that the president give a boost to the World's Fair in Knoxville by appearing at its opening in the spring of 1982. Delighted by Mr. Reagan's acceptance, the senator shared the good news with his wife, Joy. But she went him one better. "Well, why don't you go back and ask him if he'll stay with us that night?" she suggested. "That'd be a great thing."

For all their years in politics, the Bakers were a pair of innocents. Neither fully anticipated the logistical tornado that is unleashed by an overnight presidential visit. But something else checked Senator Baker briefly. Like most politicians, he holds the presidency as an institution in considerable awe. That made him initially somewhat shy about actually asking President Reagan into his home. Moreover, since the attempt on the president's life in 1981, the security restrictions on Reagan's movements had been so tight that the president had not spent the night in any private residence.

"I didn't want to do it," the senator confessed, remembering his hesitancy. "But I finally decided I would. I mentioned it to a couple of his aides and they thought it was a great idea. So I worked up my courage and I asked the president, told him I appreciated his coming down, would he and Mrs. Reagan care to stay with us in our home up in the country outside Knoxville that night? And he said, 'Sure, but I tell you what—Nancy's coming in a day early. Could she stay an extra day?' "[2]

The Bakers owned a large rambler-style home, which they had built in the 1950s on the family's secluded landholding. The nearest house was half a mile away, and on three sides, you could see nothing but virgin mountain forests. What the senator had in mind for the Reagans was a four-room guesthouse, about a hundred yards down a grassy knoll from the main house, with a stunning view of the mountains from a ledge overhanging a gorge on the New River. The guesthouse had been fashioned from barn sidings but was lavishly furnished for a cabin, with porches front and back to let visitors drink in the mountain panorama. For many years, the late Senate Republican leader, Everett McKinley Dirksen, who was Mrs. Baker's father, used the guesthouse when he came to see his grandchildren. The quiet of the place was medicinal. From its high perch, one could hear the gurgling of the river, the evening crickets, and the mountain breeze rustling the oaks.

At word of the president's acceptance, Mrs. Baker redecorated the guesthouse and fixed it up fresh. But the White House managers had in mind a much more ambitious overhaul than merely spiffing up the cottage. To the Bakers this might seem just a tranquil overnight interlude for a busy president and his lady, but the White House bureaucracy viewed the Baker homestead as a temporary global command post for the commander in chief. The trappings of power go with the President wherever he goes; they are the instruments of his power.

Automatically, the elaborate machinery of presidential travel geared up preparations for the president's coming—for his safety, his movements, his communications, even his food. Nothing could be left to chance or, indeed, to well-meaning amateurs. From the White House view, it takes an imperial retinue to insure the president's safety, his contact with the rest of the world, his access to staff and to the press.

The first step was to install sufficient links to the president's global communications network so that from the Baker's rustic homestead, Mr. Reagan and his aides could hook up instantaneously with anyone in Tennessee or in Washington or, for that matter, anyplace on earth. And Senator Baker's ordinary telephone service was deemed grossly inadequate.

"They sent a technical crew in there, days ahead of time, and asked for fifty-six telephone circuits into my guesthouse," Senator Baker recalled with a mixture of amusement and irritation. "And the poor little old telephone company out there, which is an independent telephone company, I don't imagine had fifty-six telephone circuits or trunk lines for the whole community. But they dutifully put them in, and they drilled holes in my floor where they ran telephone cables up and which, to this day, are a matter of aggravation to my wife. They brought in a voice encoding machine, you know, one of these secure-line jobs, and put it in the room adjacent to the President's. They set up a tie line, not one, but several direct tie lines to the White House switchboard. They had a direct tie-in to the airport, direct tie-in to the hospital, direct tie-in to the highway patrol."

"The phone people really had nightmares," echoed Larry Crowley, chief of the Huntsville Volunteer Fire Department. "For a little town like us, a small company like us, this was out of the ordinary," said Charlie Welch, who put in the lines for the Highland Telephone Cooperative. "There were phones in places you'd never dream of putting phones, like outside the church."[3]

Then there was a debate over where to put the portable switchboard. The Army Signal Corps, which operates the president's military communications network, arrived with a whole switchboard packed into a communications van, which they wanted to park beside the guesthouse. But Senator Baker, sensing his hospitality about to be desecrated, was adamant against scarring the pastoral setting. "I don't want it there," he declared. So the trailer was duly dispatched to a less prominent site near the senator's dog pens, setting up howls from Mr. Baker's beagle and his Saint Bernard. "The dogs were terribly perplexed by all this," the senator recalled.

Although the Baker home seemed a particularly secluded spot in sparsely settled Huntsville, the Secret Service began throwing its security cloak over a large region about ten days ahead of time. Its agents lined up the Scott County sheriff and his deputies, plus the thirty volunteer firemen, to reinforce sizable detachments brought in from outside. Police dogs were sent to sniff for explosives in the Huntsville Presbyterian Church, where the Reagans were to attend Sunday services. Metal detectors were set up for the congregation. The president's bulletproof limousine was flown to Knoxville and driven up to Huntsville for the short Sunday morning ride from the Baker home to the church. Secure space was set aside for a figure out of *Dr. Strangelove*: the military aide who carries what White House aides call the "football," a briefcase full of secret codes available for ordering a launch of nuclear weapons, kept near the president twenty-four hours a day, 365 days a year.[4]

On the bluff outside the guesthouse, the Secret Service mounted high-intensity floodlights to shine down onto the woods and river below. As May 1, the day of the Reagan's visit, approached, the woods on both sides of the river and all around the Baker property were seeded with heavily armed federal and military security teams. "They had SWAT teams on the mountain, which is more than a mile from the guesthouse," Senator Baker reported. "They had SWAT teams on the road. They had SWAT teams down below the bluff. I never saw so many people."

By the time Saturday May 1 dawned, security barriers had been erected on all approaching roads. The fire department's "attack pumper" truck took a position on the far edge of the Bakers' lawn, the local volunteers flanked by a clutch of Secret Service agents. Some, according to the daily paper in Oneida, were clad in camouflage fatigues "not unlike a SWAT police unit you might see on television."[5]

The real show was about to begin. About forty longtime friends and supporters joined Mrs. Baker and her daughter, Cissy, around the Baker's circular driveway. They were about to be initiated into a scaled-down, informal version of a modern American ritual: the Arrival of the President. It is an event staged in waves.

First, a huge helicopter landed five hundred yards to the east of the Baker home to drop off forty-five White House reporters and photographers, who were trucked to the president's landing site. Next, a smaller helicopter touched down near a big red "pillow" landing marker on the Bakers' front lawn to deposit White House aides. Finally, Marine One, the president's huge white-capped helicopter, came into view, roaring in from the east at treetop level, making a sharp ninety-degree turn and then hovering for a moment before settling on the high ground near the house. Its throbbing rotors kicked up such strong prop stream that not only did it flatten the grass and whip up dust, but the people around the driveway had to lean into its backwind to keep from falling down.

Neil Sexton, the Bakers' longtime handyman, had been fearful all along that the presidential visit would wreak havoc. To his dismay, the helicopter whirlwind blew the lawn furniture down the hill and un-ceremoniously unwrapped Cissy Baker's wraparound skirt. "I knew it," Sexton muttered.

Whatever the inconvenience, Senator Baker recalled that moment with the satisfaction of a country squire extolling his favorite Tennessee walking horses. "I had a yard full of presidential helicopters," Senator

Baker later recalled. "I had three or four of them. Big old things. And
people were more intrigued with that than they were with the president, to tell you the truth. They'd stop and stare at the helicopters
longer than they'd stop and stare at the president."

As soon as the president landed, the senator could not wait to show
off to the Reagans his real pride and joy: the picture-postcard view from
the guesthouse. "I was just chafing at the bit to show the president that
magnificent view off the back porch of the guesthouse, looking over the
river gorge to its unspoiled mountain beauty," he said. At the guesthouse, he said, "I started to raise the blinds, and they wouldn't come
up. I found out the damned Secret Service had nailed them shut."

In rising frustration, the senator whirled on the ranking Secret Service agent. "What have you done?" he demanded. "You've nailed the
blinds to the floor."

"There might be a sniper out there," the agent replied.

The senator dismissed that as ridiculous. "But it's two miles to the
nearest hill!" he protested.

The agent was unmoved. "Yeah," he said, "but we can't afford to
take the chance."

Trapped by security demands even in this tranquil setting, Baker,
who had made a run for the presidency in 1980 and harbored ambitions
for 1988, found doubts suddenly flitting through his mind about
whether he really wanted to be president. "I was beginning to think,
you know, I don't think it's worth being president if you have to live
like a prisoner."

But as those second thoughts preoccupied him, President Reagan
bent over and started pulling the blinds up, ripping the nails right out
of the floor. It was an impulsive act like those of other presidents—
Richard Nixon, Jimmy Carter, or John F. Kennedy plunging into
crowds against the warnings of the Secret Service, determined to assert
their authority and independence. Moreover, it turned out that the
blinds had only been lightly tacked down, giving Senator Baker a
moment of liberation. "The Secret Service was huffing and puffing and
carrying on, but we went outside," he recalled with a broad grin, "and
at that point, I knew this man is sure enough president."

After the Reagans had duly admired the view, Senator Baker played
tennis doubles with some White House aides while the first lady massaged the president's neck and shoulder muscles and the president, in
shirt-sleeves, nibbled on grapes.

Just before dinner, the security forces suffered another setback. Not
only had they closed off all approaching highways and roadways, but

they had theoretically erected a security barrier overhead by ordering all air controllers to close the airspace over the Baker homestead. Even so, Dinah Shore, the singer, who is a Tennessean and a friend of the Bakers, slipped through the net. She arrived for dinner by air, unannounced. "She came flying over in the tiniest helicopter I ever saw, directly over the guesthouse, and landed not fifteen feet from the president's bedroom," the senator explained, "The Secret Service was just apoplectic, but they couldn't do much about it."

With shades of Oriental food tasters, the security precautions for the Reagans even affected the Bakers' barbecue dinner. Several days beforehand, the White House had obtained two place settings of Mrs. Baker's china and her silverware which were flown off to Washington. "They fixed his dinner at the White House *on her china* and brought it down, which created a real problem in our kitchen," the Senator said. "They brought their own White House stewards, and they were dressed just like the caterer that we had. I don't know whether they brought the food down hot or not, but they cooked it in Washington."[6]

By the time dinner was over, things were quite relaxed. Dinah Shore suggested that if the president and Mrs. Reagan didn't "mind some pickup musicians, we'll just play awhile." Governor Lamar Alexander took over the piano, country-western singer Chet Atkins pitched in with a guitar, and the Reagans joined the Tennesseans in a sing-along with Dinah Shore.

Outside in the darkness among the chirping crickets, the Secret Service had assembled an army of about 250 agents, highway patrolmen, military SWAT teams, and local officers. "The irony of the whole goddamned thing," Senator Baker recalled, "is the entire, tiny, town constabulary, which is two or three people, the county sheriff, who had about twenty, and the highway patrol were all gathered up in the intensive security operation for the president, and while the dinner party was going on, somebody robbed one of my neighbor's houses— Ross Faires's—because they knew full well there wasn't a policeman left anywhere around."

Quickly he added, "We had a marvelous time that night."

The Image of Power: The President as John Wayne

The presidential circus that enveloped the Bakers and Huntsville may be a more intimate and amusing glimpse of the chief executive than most people experience. But the Huntsville story fits the public's general image of a Gulliver-sized president. At close range, any president

and his entourage are overwhelming—filling every available room, setting up their global command post, tunneling telephone lines, swarming the woods with SWAT teams, commandeering every local deputy
within miles, flying in hordes of reporters. Action. Power. Even at a
distance, the massive apparatus of the White House radiates the impression of almost limitless presidential power.

But that awesome image of near invincibility is misleading. It exag-
gerates the actual power of the presidency, which is considerably less
than suggested by the public attention which gets focused on the single
figure at the apex of our political system. Indeed, the absence of
hierarchical power in politics baffles and aggravates corporate executives when they come to take political jobs in Washington. Political
power does not work the way they expect. As a nation, we focus
obsessively on the president, out of proportion with other power centers. This happens largely because the president is one person whom
it is easy for television to portray and whom the public feels it can come
to know. Other power centers are harder to depict: The Supreme Court
is an aloof and anonymous body; Congress is a confusing gaggle of 535
people; the bureaucracy is vast and faceless. It is almost as if the
president, most politicians, and the press, especially television, have
fallen into an unconscious conspiracy to create a cartoon caricature of
the real system of power.

There is a strong urge for simplicity in the American psyche, a
compulsion to focus on the single dramatic figure at the summit, to
reduce the intricacy of a hundred power-plays to the simple equation
of whether the president is up or down, winning or losing on any given
day or week. Television and the viewing millions seek to make a simple
narrative of complex events. Television news feeds the public appetite
to treat events as binary—good or bad, up or down, progress or setback,
winners or losers—and to push aside more complex layers of reality.

The temptation is particularly strong to treat the president (especially Ronald Reagan who invites it) as if he were a political John
Wayne, strapping on his trusty six-shooters in the morning and heading
out for a duel in the OK Corral with his latest rival. Typically, the
outcome of the encounter is painted in black and white. If the president strides back down the dusty street alive, the implicit presumption
is that he and the nation were victorious and the audience can sit back
to await the next episode.

While President Reagan has been far more adept at video politics
than his immediate predecessors, the image of president as knight in
shining armor was hardly Reagan's invention. I can remember coming

to Washington as a green reporter in the early 1960s and being captivated by the first press conferences of President John F. Kennedy. Scotty Reston, bureau chief of *The New York Times*, would call a dozen reporters into his office several hours ahead of Kennedy's press conference for a "prayer meeting"—an exercise devoted to debating the most pressing issues and formulating questions with the precise wording deemed most likely to lance President Kennedy's verbal armor. Then, Reston would ship a group of us to the State Department in a rented limousine and sprinkle us around the auditorium for a jousting match with the president. Time and again, we learned that Kennedy was the master of the press conference, the easy victor, the gallant young champion of those encounters.

The image that presidents project when they go abroad to summit meetings or on foreign missions reinforces this public image of the president as the nation's political John Wayne. Rare is the time when a president more totally dominates our political landscape than when he is our leader abroad. These voyages become political sagas that capture the public imagination and arm the presidency with the excitement of new adventure, with the glamor of pomp and ceremony.

Normally, the presidential apparatus is invisible, tucked away in the White House and nearby office buildings. But on a major presidential trip, the entourage—the vast trappings of office—become visible, for when a president moves, legions move with him. In a very real sense, the president never really leaves the White House, he brings most of it with him.

Many times, as I clambered off planes on presidential trips to Paris or Jerusalem or Moscow or Shanghai and glanced over the tarmac at a sea of people struggling with briefcases and shoulder luggage while the president took a welcoming military salute, I thought to myself, this is our modern imperial retinue. In earlier eras, such a bureaucratic army would have been described by historians as the Napoleon's camp followers or Caesar's Roman *impedimenta*, the human train and baggage of the emperor.

For if President Carter heads off for meetings with Western leaders in London or Bonn, or President Reagan treks twenty thousand miles across the Pacific to China, their human convoys can number one thousand more. At the core are three hundred to four hundred government officials: the president's senior staff plus echelons of policy advisers, negotiators, communiqué drafters, military aides, doctors, stewards, personal valets, even the first lady's hairdresser; plus several cabinet members with their lieutenants, specialists, secretaries, spokesmen, and

miscellaneous handlers; and a phalanx of as many as one hundred
Secret Service agents ready to form a human wall, if need be, to insure
the president's physical safety.

Another battalion is the Greek chorus of the press: from two hundred and fifty to one thousand reporters, photographers, television
crews, and technicians lugging cameras and sound systems, enough to
fill one chartered Boeing 747 and sometimes overflow into another.
With us, always, was a vital escort of ten to twenty White House press
officials equipped with photocopying machines and one hundred thousand sheets of paper for a torrent of texts and press releases, many of
them issued in flight against deadlines for instant filing at the inevitable
temporary press center at the next stop.[7]

The logistics of transporting this unwieldy caravan are a nightmare
and make the Huntsville trip seem child's play. The president and his
most elite advisers and assistants travel on *Air Force One,* while second-
ranking officials travel on an identical backup plane and still other
stragglers on commercial aircraft. From the basic aerial convoy something like one thousand pieces of luggage must be carted off and on
at each overnight stop. In advance, two or three huge Air Force C-130
cargo planes carry the heavy gear: communications equipment, voice
scramblers, coding machines, special cars for the Secret Service, and
two bulletproof limousines for the president. In China, for example,
there were two limousines, so that one could ferry President Reagan
around Peking while a second was jumped ahead to his second stop in
Xi'an, whereupon the first one could be leapfrogged ahead to his third
stop in Shanghai.

"When we went to China, Reagan was like a modern-day Marco
Polo with all the technology and everything," commented Michael K.
Deaver, who as White House deputy chief of staff was the impresario
of presidential travel from 1981 to 1985.[8]

Thanks primarily to television, this modern-day-Marco-Polo image
gets fixed in the public mind: the American president, on the move,
buttressed by a huge retinue whose primary function is to amplify his
authority as America's leader. More than at almost any other time, a
president traveling abroad personifies the nation; he engages our national pride.

Near the climax of the Watergate scandal in mid-1974, Richard
Nixon seemed to hope for some rescue in a final summit meeting with
Leonid Brezhnev in the Soviet Crimea. Jimmy Carter's presidency
reached a pinnacle with his Camp David mediation effort in 1978 and
his pilgrimmage a year later to Egypt and Israel to consummate their

peace treaty. For President Reagan, ventures to the Great Wall of China and the commemoration of the D-day landing at Normandy, both in his reelection year, were vaulting political triumphs. The most talented stage managers of presidential travel, such as Mike Deaver, carefully craft itineraries to lift the drama and appeal of presidential diplomacy—to heighten the impression of presidential power.

The power of the presidency as an office is indisputable. No other single governmental office approaches it, either in terms of legal authority or the platform it offers its occupant for persuading Congress and the public. Even so, the presidential hoopla—most of it as contrived as mass advertising—obscures a true understanding of the real workings of power in Washington. It magnifies and distorts the president's actual political leverage most of the time. For example, only a few weeks after his Crimean summit with Brezhnev, Nixon had to resign from office; in spite of Carter's unprecedented negotiating breakthrough at Camp David and the Egyptian-Israeli peace treaty, public confidence in Carter plummeted; Reagan, though a strong president, has repeatedly found his will checked, and the political initiative wrested from him by others, not to mention his being humbled by the Iran-*contra* affair.

In short, politics reduced to the level of John Wayne's Dodge City can be a captivating illusion. It makes for great TV, but it focuses too much attention on the fellow at center stage, while much of the real action in the Washington power game often goes on elsewhere. I myself had to learn that whether the president was Kennedy or Reagan, the glamorous image of medieval jousting or western gun toting simply misses far too much about the fluid, fragmented, and floating nature of political power in Washington.

In April 1986, when President Reagan was riding a crest in the public opinion polls, after the American air attack on Libya and well before the nation knew anything of the Iranian scandal, Al Kingon, Reagan's cabinet secretary, his main staff link to the executive branch, lamented to me that the White House "is the most defensive operation anywhere in government—you're constantly under barrage.

"You'd think on the outside what a fabulous place to work," he went on, curling his stocking feet around the edge of his office coffee table. Then, in Brooklyn accent and with some exaggeration, Kingon declaimed: "Power? There ain't none. What power? I'm being bashed around as I've never been bashed around in my life. Every morning when I come in here, the phone rings. Something happened somewhere, and your reaction is, 'Oh, my God, how do I get out of this one?'

I believe it was Henry Kissinger who said, 'You don't have time to think. All you do is expend all the intellectual capital you've accumulated before.' "[9]

Power Reality: Our Rotating Premiers

The sense of impotence at the very heart of our government has echoes in the past. Harry Truman, Dwight Eisenhower, Jack Kennedy, all gave voice to that complaint. Truman, in his final days, made a famous quip after meeting his successor, General Eisenhower: "He'll sit right here and he'll say, 'Do this. Do that!' And nothing will happen. Poor Ike—it won't be a bit like the Army. He'll find it very frustrating."[10] Truman was talking about the problems any president has in getting his orders carried out by the bureaucracy.

And since the days of Truman, Eisenhower, and Kennedy, organic changes have taken place in the way our nation is governed. Paramount power is now harder to grasp and exercise than it ever has been in our history. Not only has Congress grown much more assertive since the mid-1970s but within Congress itself the old power oligarchy has been broken up by internal reform. Television has given relatively junior members of Congress a platform to become policy entrepreneurs, and the highest ranking leaders on Capitol Hill are sometimes forced to chase after junior back benchers, to find the head of the political parade.

Government has become so complex and the top leaders so daunted by its complexity that they have granted enormous powers to staff aides who labor in the shadows. At times, this shadow government makes policy—most stunningly in the Iran-*contra* affair, when National Security Adviser John Poindexter not only bypassed cabinet secretaries and usurped the authority of the president, but kept them all in the dark. Presidents such as Jimmy Carter and Ronald Reagan are blocked or overturned by special interest lobbies, which build mass support on pet issues. The power of political parties has been eroded by the rise of independent, ticket-splitting voters, who frequently keep presidents from gaining majorities in Congress to pass their programs.

In this final period of the twentieth century, we Americans have a more fluid system of power than ever before in our history. Quite literally, power floats. It does not reside in the White House, nor does it merely alternate from pole to pole, from president to opposition, from Republicans to Democrats. It floats. It shifts. It wriggles elusively, like mercury in the palm of one's hand, passing from one competing

power center to another, with the driving leadership on major policies—from the budget to tax reform to military spending and the MX
missile—gravitating to whoever is daring enough to grab it and smart
enough to figure out the quickest way to make a political score.

Even our high school catechisms about the division of powers in
government, among the executive branch, the legislature, and the
courts, miss the elusive fluidity of power these days. The old notion of
separation of powers implies, for many people, a seesaw power struggle
for primacy, principally between the president and Congress—essentially a variation of the John Wayne metaphor: President wins, Congress loses, or vice versa. Actually, the power float is more like water
polo, where the ball is tossed among players trying to keep their heads
above water, or fast-action basketball, where anyone can steal the ball,
change the flow of the game, and then score from practically anywhere
around the basket.

The old-fashioned seesaw image omits powerful institutions such as
the Federal Reserve Board, the primary influence on interest rates,
monetary policy, and inflation. The simple notion of Congress versus
President overlooks the fact that often, presidents are not challenged
frontally by Congress but rather by powerful political alliances that
bridge across the executive and legislative branches to alter, outflank,
or subvert presidential policy. Jimmy Carter was forced to build an
aircraft carrier he did not want—not by Congress alone, but by an
alliance between his own admirals and pro-Navy members of Congress.
Ronald Reagan had to bow to combined pressures from some officials
within his administration and from most of Congress for some sanctions against South Africa. The simple seesaw idea also ignores the fact
that the powers of Congress and president often mesh and can only be
wielded jointly. As the Harvard University presidential scholar Richard
Nuestadt observed, we have not so much a government of separated
powers as "a government of separated institutions sharing powers."[11]

Case in point: Ronald Reagan built a reputation as a strong president, and at times he clearly took charge: ordering the invasion of
Grenada and air strikes against Libya, pressing budget and tax cuts
through Congress in 1981, naming justices to the Supreme Court, or
suddenly announcing plans for a space-based defense that few others
thought wise or realistic. At these times, especially when dealing with
foreign policy, Reagan clearly combined the functions of chief of state
and prime minister, both of which are inherent in our presidency. His
early legislative victories restored the vigor of the presidency and

revived public confidence in the nation's highest office. Unquestionably, he rekindled the ceremonial majesty of the presidency.

But for other long stretches of time—not just as a late-second-term, lame-duck president, but even in his first term—the power of political initiative floated away from Reagan, despite popularity ratings on a par with Franklin Delano Roosevelt and Dwight Eisenhower. During Reagan's passive periods, policy has been driven not by the president but by others.

This is not unique to Reagan. Eisenhower had to bargain with Democrats Sam Rayburn and Lyndon Johnson. Nixon, Ford, and Carter all found it impossible to grasp and exercise continuous control and deliver on their pet programs. Each wound up on the defensive, with declining popularity. What is so striking and instructive about the Reagan presidency is the peculiar combination of his overwhelming personal popularity and his frequent lack of matching political leverage. It is as if we had unknowingly slipped into operating like a European parliamentary system, with its revolving coalition governments, while our president reigned above it all, a regal symbol of nationhood.

"What you have right now is a constitutional monarchy," asserted Representative Newt Gingrich, a bright Reaganite Republican from Georgia. "What we've done is we've reinvented Hanoverian kingship without reinventing the parliamentary prime ministership. We have this tremendously nice, likable King Victoria. Everybody likes him but where the hell's Disraeli? or Gladstone? What I'm saying is that in the age of television, we now have the television-series equivalent of [rotating] prime ministerships."[12]

Michael Barone, writing in *The Washington Post*, once compared the kaleidoscopic shuffle of political coalitions in the Reagan period to the Italian government, where a relatively small group of politicians shuffle and reshuffle the top government ministries. "Italian politics is often held up to ridicule as comically unstable, with constantly changing ministries, divided responsibility, and splinter parties," he observed. "But how much different, in practice, is ours? . . . Functional responsibility—not necessarily the title, but the real decision-making power—gets passed around here as well, to those strong enough to grab it."[13]

Barone's analogy fits, not only the Reagan years but the modern presidency in general. The president is always part of the power mix but not necessarily the central part. In 1981, when Reagan pressed his budget and tax cuts through Congress, he was at the peak of his power—the prime minister of his own coalition; his leading ministers were his budget director, David Stockman, and his White House chief of staff, James A. Baker III. But by that same fall and into the following year, 1982, the critical role of driving economic policy had passed to Paul Volcker, chairman of the Federal Reserve Board. Volcker's tight money policies were wringing inflation out of the economy and bringing on a painful recession that the president could not prevent; Reagan deficits compounded the problem.

In the spring of 1982, a new political coalition emerged to take over policy leadership, a surprising partnership between Senate Majority Leader Howard Baker and House Speaker Tip O'Neill. They forced the president to backtrack and accept a $98 billion, three-year tax increase in August 1982. They eventually pushed through two jobs bills, and they worked out a Social Security compromise with the president. In the spring of 1983, the MX issue was resolved by a new coalition spearheaded by two congressmen, Les Aspin of Wisconsin and Albert Gore of Tennessee, and Senator Sam Nunn of Georgia. These three Democrats stepped into a foreign-policy vacuum left by Reagan's inability to move Congress. In the election year of 1984, little happened and the nation was left with a caretaker government.

Surprisingly, after his landslide reelection in 1984, Reagan did not reclaim the prime ministership in 1985. His one big policy push was tax reform, but that was slow in coming. The start of Reagan's second term marked a rapid turnover in national political leadership. First came Robert Dole, the new Senate majority leader, who drove the budget process for six months, insisting on austerity for both the Pentagon and Social Security. When the White House pulled the rug out from Dole and toppled his coalition, Representative Dan Rostenkowski, Democratic chairman of the House Ways and Means Committee, took the limelight by rewriting the president's tax-reform bill. Reagan's role was rescuing it from defeat by angered House Republicans.

The public was still giving Reagan high marks for strong leadership, but in fact, leadership was largely coming from below. By fall 1985, two freshman Republican senators, Phil Gramm of Texas and Warren Rudman of New Hampshire, became the driving forces, the new prime ministers, for a five-year plan to balance the budget. In early 1986, the stunning turnaround of Bob Packwood, Senate Finance Committee chairman—and not anything done by President Reagan—revived the dying tax reform bill. On the Philippines, Reagan was pushed into a new policy primarily by Richard Lugar of Indiana, Republican chairman of the Senate Foreign Relations Committee. With public accusations of vote fraud, Lugar made it virtually impossible for Reagan not to break with the Philippine government of Ferdinand Marcos and recognize the election victory of Corazon Aquino. Reagan simply got dragged along, as he did on South African sanctions and trade policy.

When the Iran crisis broke in November 1986, Reagan behaved like a monarch, acting as if he were above the controversy that consumed his aides, ousting chief of staff Donald Regan and others—as if he were a king dismissing a discredited prime minister to spare the crown. By his direction, the national security staff had secretly continued aid to the Nicaraguan *contras*—but at times the staff ran him, not vice versa. In late 1987, yet another prime minister emerged, House Speaker Jim Wright, taking the policy lead and forcing Reagan to go along with a Central American peace plan. To be sure, through it all, Reagan clung to his Star Wars defense, held summit meetings with Soviet leader Mikhail Gorbachev, and signed the medium-range-missile agreement. But what is striking in many other cases is how often the policy initiative came not from the president, but from someone else.

Reflecting on the record, some of Reagan's own domestic policy advisers privately admit how frequently power floats out of the White House.

"Part of it is that Reagan's programmatic agenda is simply not the majority agenda," Richard Darman, a senior first-term Reagan White House aide and later deputy Treasury secretary candidly conceded in 1986. "And the American political system is telling him, 'Look, we like you. You're an icon. You represent almost everything we ever loved about America. You're from the Midwest. You went West. You made money but you're still a small-town boy. You love the girl; the girl loves you. You've been a hero of all these different kinds. You survived an assassination. You sure seem to love our country. You make everybody feel good.' That's Walter Bagehot's nineteenth-century English notion of the monarchy, consistent with the living symbol of the nation's whole history and values and all of that. That's all a plus.

"But the curious thing about Reagan," Darman went on, "is that even though all of this is much loved, his constitutional amendment to ban abortion is opposed seventy to thirty. His constitutional amendment to balance the budget can't get through Congress. His constitutional amendment for prayer in schools runs against the majority feeling. His desire to privatize big hunks of government is not the majority view. All Reagan budgets have been dead on arrival with the exception of the '81 budget. The House of Representatives is particularly in touch with the people. And with power fragmented and information floating widely in the system, anybody anywhere who tries for too long to run against the majority simply will not hold power. To govern, a president has to move toward the middle."[14]

Those observations were true enough, although they pin too much on Ronald Reagan's shortcomings. He has been a president given to delegating great authority to others, undisturbed at allowing chunks of power to slip away, as demonstrated by the bold adventures of Rear Admiral John Poindexter and Marine Lieutenant Colonel Oliver North on the covert Iranian arms deals.

But the root causes of the modern power float lie well beyond Ronald Reagan—in the political transformations of the past fifteen years that have altered the power game and the way our nation is governed. They await the presidents who take their oaths of office through the rest of this century.

2. The Power Earthquake of 1974: The Impact of Reform, Money, and Television

The Washington establishment has been blown wide open.
—Tommy Boggs, lobbyist

The political fault line from the Old Washington power game to the New Washington power game was 1974.

To most Americans, 1974 was the memorable year in which Richard Nixon was driven from the White House by the Watergate scandal. But Watergate is now behind us and what is far less well remembered—even though it is more enduring—is that 1974 was also the year that climaxed a political earthquake. It was an earthquake that shook the established power structure of the American political system.

Forces which had been pulling at the threads of power for several years finally ripped apart the tighter weave of the old power structure. The old political game was shoved aside, and a new game took over. The political context for governing changed. That transformation dramatically altered how power works in Washington. And the impact is still with us today.

After decades highlighted by periods of presidential dominance from Teddy Roosevelt and Woodrow Wilson to Franklin Roosevelt, Congress finally revolted, and not just for the moment: Changes were made that would affect how we are governed for a long time to come.

Angered by Lyndon Johnson's conduct of the Vietnam War, Richard Nixon's intentional confrontations over government spending, and Nixon's abuses of power such as illegal wiretapping and using the Internal Revenue Service to go after political enemies, an assertive Congress rose up to challenge not just Nixon but the presidency as an institution. As *The Wall Street Journal* observed in 1973, Nixon "aroused a snoozing Congress and made it mad."[1]

Congress seized for itself the legal authority and the expertise to insure that its challenge to the chief executive would be permanent. As if that were not upheaval enough, the House of Representatives also assaulted the citadel of the old congressional power system—seniority —and then balkanized its own power: It created scores of "subcommittee governments," each taking charge of a slice of federal policy.

That same fateful year of 1974 also gave rise to a big class of new House Democrats, who shook the foundations further by throwing out several established power barons.

As these three upheavals were happening in Congress, a fourth change was occurring in the basic power system in Washington: The power of political parties, which had provided a critical glue, a vital force for cohesion in American government, was being dissolved by a highly mobile, independent-minded, ticket-splitting electorate.

The weakening of the parties and the trend toward a more wide-open power system was hastened by the mushrooming importance of television—and of its political offspring, a new generation of video politicians whose medium was the tube rather than the political clubhouse.

Finally, the increased fragmentation of governmental power set off a political gold rush among thousands of special interest groups, all of whom were bent on panning the new streams of power for nuggets, and were well enough heeled to buy their way into the New Washington power game.

To be sure, the fundamental structure of the old political system was still standing and many old habits remained. No one had torn up the Constitution. But within the basic framework, the rules of the power game had been rewritten, and the old power relationships had been dramatically shaken up. What emerged was a more fluid system of power, one which made the American political system harder to lead than just a couple of decades ago.

For one thing, the sheer volume and velocity of political activity became staggering. The profusion of activity took a quantum leap since the 1960s and especially in the phenomenal growth decade from the mid-seventies to the mid-eighties. Everyone flocked to Washington:

trade associations, health and welfare groups, labor unions, businesses, environmentalists, lobbyists for cities, counties, states, right-to-lifers and freedom of choice advocates, consumer groups, political consultants, pollsters, public relations firms. They all moved in. Politics became a full-time industry for tens of thousands of people. In addition, millions of grass-roots voters poured into Washington when their pet issues came up. Voters inundated Congress with oceans of mail, and Congressmen sent back their own unbelievable volumes of mail. The growth of activity in every area was exponential—and it swamped the political system.

Watergate was the epicenter of that political earthquake, but the tremors of reform had been rumbling through the political parties and through Congress in the late 1960s and early 1970s. For a decade, a climate of congressional bitterness and mistrust had developed toward the executive branch. It was fed by the Vietnam War; it was confirmed by the confrontations with President Nixon over money—Congress had legally voted to spend money on domestic programs, but Nixon impounded the money and defiantly refused to spend it. This atmosphere of distrust was climaxed by the investigation of the Nixon campaign's criminal break-in at the Democratic headquarters located in the Watergate complex, and by disclosures of the multimillion-dollar Nixon campaign slush funds, financed by wealthy corporations.

In revolt, Congress vigorously asserted its authority and its independence from the White House and then armed itself for a prolonged seige against the executive branch. In reaction to Johnson's escalation of the war in Vietnam without any congressional declaration of war, Congress in 1973 passed the War Powers Resolution requiring any president to obtain congressional approval for commitment of American forces to a combat zone for more than ninety days. Alarmed by Central Intelligence Agency operations such as attempts at assassinating foreign leaders, Congress asserted new oversight authority, requiring notice of all CIA covert operations. To check presidential authority further, Congress demanded that all executive branch agreements with other countries—those below the status of formal treaties—get Senate approval. All these restrictions hemmed in presidential power.

In reaction to the taint of Nixon's corporate campaign slush funds, Congress voted for public financing of presidential elections. In reaction to its own budget conflict with President Nixon, Congress passed the Budget and Impoundment Control Act of 1974, to bar future presidents from refusing to spend what Congress voted. That law also set up a new Congressional budget process and established the Congressional Budget Office (CBO) to produce independent analysis of the economy and budget; Congress no longer had to depend on administration economists.

That single change—an independent Congressional Budget Office—was crucial, and symptomatic. Such congressional power was unthinkable in the era of John Kennedy and Lyndon Johnson. When I arrived in Washington in 1962, Congress simply accepted the administration's economic figures. Arguments were over policy, rarely over the facts. From a distance, the significance may be hard to appreciate. But when Congress got its own economic experts and facts, the executive branch was much more often thrown on the defensive.

"The creation of CBO was of fundamental importance in terms of the way power operates in Washington," insisted Stuart Eizenstat, who felt its power as domestic policy chief in the Carter White House.

"One can trace from the time of the New Deal through the early and mid-parts of the Nixon Administration, a clear, gradual, perceptible increase in presidential power relative to the legislative branch," Eizenstat pointed out. "The creation of CBO began to redress the balance of power. It did that via one fundamental way—it ended the president's monopoly on information, on budget forecasts, on economic forecasts. The fact is that the CBO staff has been consistently more accurate on their economic forecasts, their deficit projections, than the executive branch has.

"What does that mean? It means that the president says, 'Look, I think we're in a four-and-one-half-percent growth year and therefore that leaves room for more spending' or 'that enables us to cut the budget' or 'that enables us to spend more on defense' or, if you're a Democratic president, more on domestic policy. And CBO says, 'No, we think that growth is going to be three percent.' And therefore you've just lost something on the order of $20 billion [in tax revenues for the budget]."[2]

Beyond that, CBO can kill new proposals or force drastic revisions merely by giving realistic cost estimates. Eizenstat recalled that in 1977, Joseph Califano, then secretary of Health, Education and Welfare, proposed modest changes in welfare programs, introducing some new elements and offsetting their costs with efficiencies in existing programs. Overall, Califano reckoned the added cost at about $5 billion in 1978.

One morning after the legislation had gone to Congress, Eizenstat was struck by a newspaper headline: CBO TO CARTER—WELFARE REFORM $17 BILLION. The CBO staff, then led by Alice Rivlin, a liberal

Democratic economist, had dismissed Califano's efficiencies as largely fictional. It pegged the annual cost of Califano's proposals—in full operation—at $17 billion.

"The second I saw that headline," Eizenstat recalled, "I said, 'Our program's over. There's no way the Congress is going to pass what they think is a $17 billion welfare-reform proposal.' "

The same sort of thing happened to Reagan. The CBO constantly challenged White House economic projections that were tilted to make Reagan's budgets look better. On the 1987 budget, CBO accused the Reagan administration of understating what the Pentagon would spend by $15 billion. With the higher CBO figure, congressional Republicans as well as Democrats put a tighter squeeze on the Pentagon. It was a dramatic illustration of how the seemingly innocent capacity to make calculations changed the balance of power between the White House and Congress.

The CBO's new clout epitomized the effort by Congress to build its own expertise on everything from farm programs to Star Wars, because members of Congress did not trust the executive branch to give them the straight story. Congress expanded the personal staffs of individual senators and House members and the committee staffs in both houses; it created the CBO, added to the research service of the Library of Congress, and expanded other support agencies. Overall, congressional staff jumped from about 11,500 to more than 24,000 between 1973 and 1985, as Congress armed itself to lay seige to the executive branch.[3]

But simultaneously, the House of Representatives overturned its own power structure. Mainstream congressional Democrats had bridled for years at the seniority system and the power baronies it gave to conservative committee chairmen from the "Solid South." The Democratic Study Group (DSG), the powerful informal caucus of House liberals, felt squeezed between the committee barons and a president whom they did not trust. According to Dick Conlon, the DSG's executive director, the DSG set a strategy in late 1969 for breaking up the old baronies.

In 1971 and 1973, they pushed through changes in the rules of the House Democratic Caucus, establishing more democratic principles.[4] The reformers took powers from the old oligarchy and turned them over to the Democratic Caucus as a whole, and also to the speaker, secure in the knowledge that with Carl Albert as a weak speaker, they did not have to worry about that post. Then in early 1975, reinforced by seventy-five freshman Democrats elected in 1974, the reformers ousted three long-entrenched committee chairmen: Wright Patman of the Banking Committee, F. Edward Hebert of Armed Services, and W. R. Poage of Agriculture.

Of course, the seniority system did not disappear entirely.[5] In 1986, North Carolina's Jesse Helms won a seniority fight in the Senate. But the system in the House was dramatically altered by the 1974 upheavals. After that, no other power baron could dare to act as dictatorially as in the past. The spirit of '74 flared again in 1985: Les Aspin, a Wisconsin Democrat, led a coalition of mostly younger members to overthrow Mel Price, the Armed Services Committee chairman. Then Aspin leaped over seven senior committee members to take the chairmanship himself. Aspin's own power was challenged two years later. Although he managed to hang on, this challenge and counter challenge reminded all committee chairmen they could not afford to ignore rank-and-file members.

Even more significant for the long run, the House Democrats in 1974 had adopted "the subcommittee bill of rights" which decentralized power in the House, radically changing the way the power game would be played from then until now. In a stroke, it took power that had largely rested with the barons, the chairmen of the twenty-two House standing committees, and parceled out a healthy share of that power to 172 subcommittees. The number of subcommittees suddenly mushroomed in 1975, later to recede. But the more important change was the way things worked. In the old game, the power barons kept choice subcommittees for themselves and parceled out a few subcommittee chairs to allies, usually by seniority. Now, suddenly, junior Democrats, backbenchers, could seek reelection as subcommittee chairmen and then, as chairmen, they could hector the administration, bargain with high officials, push their pet ideas, or simply grab publicity. They could hire staff and run hearings. They had turf to protect and small subgovernments to manage. Many of them were aggressive and freewheeling, no longer under the thumb of full committee chairmen.

Even reformers such as Morris Udall, the veteran congressman from Arizona, sometimes groaned at what they had done. There were so many new subcommittee chairmen that Udall once joked to me that when he passed some junior Democrat whose name he'd forgotten, he would simply say, "Good morning, Mr. Chairman," knowing that roughly half the time, he'd be right, because just about half of the House Democrats were chairs of committees or subcommittees. Power had sprawled that widely.

Less dramatically, but just as surely, the dispersal of power hit the

Senate, too. "We have proliferated the number of committees and subcommittees, the number of staff, the number of floor amendments, the number of cloture votes, the number of roll call votes, the number of fiscal processes," asserted Indiana Republican Senator Dan Quayle, summing up a Senate study in late 1984. Actually, the subcommittee surge had ebbed by then, and the numbers had declined from peak levels in the mid-seventies. But still Quayle, like many others, was dismayed. "We have trivialized the matters with which we are concerned," Quayle charged. "We use our processes more and more to emphasize small issues rather than large ones, and that is turning the Senate away from its historic function as the focus of national debate."[6]

It was more a matter of changing political style than mere numbers. Individual senators had become more aggressive about pursuing their own agendas, disrupting their own leaders. In late 1985, Senator Tom Eagleton, a three-term Democrat from Missouri, protested in exasperation that the Senate was suffering from "unbridled chaos." He objected strenuously to independent-minded members launching so many filibusters—more in the last seventeen years than in the previous 170—and frequently blocking votes on legislation with endless amendments.[7] Quayle objected that one defense-funding bill was subjected to 103 amendments, fewer than ten of which he found "substantive." In his folksy way, Senator David Pryor of Arkansas complained of the paralysis of the Senate. "Being in the Senate," he told my colleague, Steve Roberts of *The New York Times*, "is like getting stuck in an airport and having all your flights canceled."

In sum, proliferation of power in Congress, and loosening discipline, have made it far harder for any administration or any congressional leaders to pull together coalitions to pass major legislation. Votes have to be gathered up much more laboriously; it takes marathon bargaining. The White House cannot count on simply striking a deal with a small coterie or working out a tax compromise, say, with Wilbur Mills, who reigned for years as the lord of tax legislation from his throne as chairman of the House Ways and Means Committee. In the old Washington power game, when Mills gave his word, he could deliver his committee and that virtually assured passage in the House. But in the new Washington power game, committee majorities are far from automatic. A chairman such as Danny Rostenkowski (who now holds Mills's seat) is influential, to be sure. But almost every member of Rostenkowski's committee has to be won over individually, and each member's pet provisions have to be accommodated. That takes months of one-by-one negotiating.

This situation has driven both Democratic and Republican administrations wild. I remember a small private dinner at the White House with President Carter in 1978. Eighteen of us were gathered around the table in the family quarters. Over coffee, President Carter talked about policy. I have a vivid memory of his acute frustration over the entangling ways of Congress. His top priority, his energy legislation, he told us, had to pass through twenty-two different congressional committees and subcommittees. The process had become an impossible legislative steeplechase.

Viewing the new power game from a different angle, Tommy Boggs, a highly successful lobbyist, grinned and said to me, "The Washington establishment has been blown wide open."[8]

Crowds Kill the Old Coziness

The new power game has not only multiplied the centers and circles of power, but it has led to a more piecemeal, jumbled, adversarial brand of politics. The faster tempo, the crowded calendar, and the growth of everything have made members of Congress less familiar to each other and, some argue, less accustomed to the comity and give-and-take that make government work more easily.

"I came here in '61, the last congressman sworn in by Sam Rayburn," recalled Morris Udall, the slender, likable Arizonan who ran second for the Democratic presidential nomination in 1976. "This used to be a small town when I got here. I knew the names of the administrative assistants and key assistants for most of the members. You knew their wives and some of the children. But it's exploded. Now at noon, I'm told, the population on Capitol Hill is twenty-five thousand, and you don't know everybody anymore. You're always running into people you've never met."[9]

It sounds like the nostalgia of old-timers everywhere, except that this time the facts support Udall's memories of dramatic change. Before the jet airplane made travel home quick and easy, Udall contended, members of Congress had more time to talk about policy, time to socialize, time to get to know each other. That familiarity oiled the wheels of compromise and made government workable.

"It used to be that my brother, who held the seat before I did, would drive his car or take a train, which meant that if you were from west of the Mississippi, you were stuck in Washington for five, six months while the session ground on," Mo explained (he is Mo to everyone). "You'd have a party and invite all your committee members and their wives, or the Eighty-seventh Congress Club would have an annual get-together. But now, I would venture that the average member does not know, could not identify half of his colleagues."

The new strangeness, Mo lamented, "tends to provoke confrontation and all the things you have in an impersonal institution." He was reminded of frictions he had seen elsewhere. "I practiced law in Tucson, and I knew every lawyer in town, knew their families. You knew whose word was good. You knew a few guys you couldn't trust. And the courtroom demeanor was always very friendly. I went to Chicago once to extradite somebody when I was the prosecuting attorney, and the opposing lawyers were treated like thieves and crooks. Unpleasant. And you find that tendency here. You find that people are suspicious of each other."

In another arena, Scotty Reston recalled for me the wartime days when he used to visit every morning with Secretary of State Cordell Hull in the old State Department building next to the White House. Sometimes, he said, Byrnes, an old Tennessee politician, would throw a few overnight cables from American ambassadors across his desk and ask Reston, "What d'you think?" The relationship between press and government was relaxed enough in those days that Reston understood it was all off-the-record, not for direct use, and he would hand back the cables after reading them, without stealing secrets.

Henry Brandon, for decades the London *Times*'s correspondent in Washington, recalled traveling with a small White House press corps to Key West, where President Truman relaxed. Truman, who normally wore a corset to tuck in his tummy, would hold bare-chested press conferences in swimming trunks. Even though this exposed a pear-shaped profile, Truman did not flinch at informal snapshot taking. On such trips, the U.S. Navy not only provided billets for reporters but arranged deep-sea fishing excursions for their amusement. Brandon, thinking of the angry confrontation between press and government since Vietnam and Watergate and everyone's sensitivity to buying influence with favors, chuckled quietly, and asked, "Can you imagine either side putting up with that kind of arrangement these days?"[10]

In the early 1960s, when I first came to Washington, it had the easy feel of a southern city. There was still a clubbiness, a close-webbed intimacy within the power establishment. "Washington used to be cozy," observed Barbara Gamarekian, who worked in the Kennedy White House and later became a *New York Times* reporter. "You could go to a party, a reception of a hundred people, and look around and say, 'Well, everybody's here—everybody who counts.' You can't do that anymore. The city has grown big and amorphous. There are so many social circles: the administration people, the corporate crowd, members of Congress, patrons of the arts, the old Kennedy-Johnson crowd, the Reagan Republicans, the Nixon-Ford Republicans. These circles bump up against each other now but it's not one cozy network anymore."[11]

Then more than now, I believe, small power circles dined intimately and debated policy over candlelight and sterling silver or over brandy in the sitting rooms of tastefully rich homes in Georgetown. From those dinners, secretaries of Defense and State or their assistant secretaries would be discreetly summoned, and quietly depart to deal with some distant crisis. In Dean Acheson's vivid phrase, the other diners felt they were "present at the creation" of policy. In that vein, Stewart Alsop titled his vintage account of the power elite in the Johnson presidency simply *The Center*. That book's inside-the-cabinet profiles and its judgment that Congress mattered "less and less" were a revealing record of the time. But from the vantage point of the late 1980s, Alsop's focus on the power apex and his virtual silence about television, political money, the fluidity of modern power, the lobbying and brawling now common to Congress, seems rather quaint.

"The jet airplane wrecked everything," Mo Udall groused. "It used to be when a constituent came in, it was a big deal. You stopped whatever you were doing and hailed this traveler from far-distant Arizona. Now, hell, they come in here by the jetload every morning, educators and businessmen and whatever. Your day is full with Arizona people coming to see you."[12]

For a senator or congressman, the time compression has become unbearable. "I've got two hundred lobbyists pressing to talk to me about the tax bill, each one representing some different interest," Senator David Pryor of Arkansas shrugged helplessly. "And every time there's a change in the tax bill that affects their industry or their group, those lobbyists want to talk to me again."[13]

A look at the numbers shows how overloaded the system has become:

• Lobbyists: Reporting standards are tougher now, but only 365 were registered with Congress in 1961 and 23,011 were registered with the secretary of the Senate in mid-1987 (a ratio of 43 to 1 for each member of the House and Senate).
• Lawyers: The District of Columbia Bar Association listed 12,564 members in 1961 and 46,000 in 1987.
• Journalists: 1,522 were accredited to Congressional press galleries

in 1961 and 5,250 in 1987; the 1980 census showed 12,612 journalists citywide.

When Truman ordered dropping the atomic bomb on Japan in 1945, I was told, he broke the news to the entire White House press corps—twenty-five reporters. By mid-1987, some 1,708 people had regular White House press passes. So enormous had the wider political community grown—lobbyists, lawyers, journalists, policy think tanks, defense or health consultants, and the hotels, offices, accountants, restaurants and the service industries that support them—that by 1979 this whole nongovernmental sector actually outnumbered federal government employees in Washington!

Mail, too, illustrates the exponential growth. Congress is now drowned in a Niagara of constituent letters and postcards, mostly organized by lobbies and mass-generated by computers. In 1972, mail volume to the House of Representatives was 14.6 million pieces a year. But it jumped by 1985 to more than 225 million pieces—an average of more than half a million pieces a year per member.

Sometimes lobby groups target a particularly sensitive date and a key member of Congress and then truck in mass computerized mail all at once for maximum psychological impact. They literally bury a member in one day's mail. In 1984 and 1985, whenever Social Security recipients got worried about some imminent vote to freeze their cost-of-living adjustments, they would inundate House Speaker Tip O'Neill. When American trade negotiators were engaged in ticklish talks with Japan or European countries, then–Majority Leader Jim Wright got swamped more than once by the steel industry and other sectors hit by imports. On several occasions, O'Neill's and Wright's mail ran 5 million or 6 million pieces in a single day. The record, according to Bob Rota, the House postmaster, came in the summer of 1985 when Speaker O'Neill got 15 to 18 million pieces in one day.

"Three big tractor trailers rolled up full of mail," recalled Rota. "Those big trailers, you know, eighteen-wheelers. There was no way we could count it. The freight people weighed it and gave us an estimate of the volume. Those trucks were blocking our whole area up here. We had to find rooms to store the mail and get those big trucks out of there. You wouldn't believe the mail the members receive: car keys from people with notes saying 'Unlock the economy,' pieces of two-by-fours from the homebuilders with the message 'Cut the budget across the board.' One year we had hundreds of thousands of baby chicks from farmers upset about high interest rates."[14]

Money and Razzle-dazzle

Business has led the new political rush to Washington. Obviously
business leaders have worked their influence in Washington for more
than a century. But a new surge of corporate involvement came in the
late 1970s. Initially it was a reaction to the consumer activism of Ralph
Nader and was fired by fear of new regulatory pressures in the environment and the workplace, as well as by Democratic control of government under Carter. Corporate CEOs such as Irving Shapiro of Du
Pont, Reginald Jones of General Electric, Thomas Murphy of General
Motors, and Walter Wriston of Citibank, long critical of Washington
but leery of too close contact, set up the Business Roundtable to
represent corporate leaders in the new Washington.

A real breakthrough for business came in March 1977, when business lobbying helped mobilize the House to defeat organized labor's
highest priority, the common-site-picketing bill. A year later, business
lobbies helped kill President Carter's legislation for a consumer protection agency, a pet Nader project, and helped push through a reduction
in capital gains taxes. The tax turnaround was typical of the new,
wide-open power game. It sprang from a completely unexpected—and
successful—revolt against President Carter's tax bill led by William
Steiger, a mid-rank Republican congressman from Wisconsin. That
surprise victory had an electrifying effect on business.

"The Steiger amendment marked a turning point for the business
community in Washington," commented Arthur Levitt, president of
the American Stock Exchange. "After that, business began to see they
could get some of the things they wanted, and within a couple of years,
you saw Carter's attitudes turn around."[15]

Success brought more bees after the honey. Back in 1968, for instance, only 100 corporations had offices in Washington; by 1978 that
figure had jumped to 500. One business directory listed 1,300 corporations in 1986. By the early 1980s, Washington had surpassed New York
as the trade association capital of America and is now far ahead. By
1986, it had 3,500 trade associations' headquarters, more than triple
the number in 1960, with a work force of roughly 80,000.

But the most stunning indicator of business activism was the skyrocketing growth of corporate political action committees (PACs) to
raise money and make contributions to the election campaigns of
candidates friendly to corporate interests. In 1974, there were eighty-
nine corporate PACs; a decade later, the number had shot up to 1,682.

Paradoxically, the drive to reform campaign funding was what gave business the green light to become more aggressively involved in financing political campaigns. Reform went astray, as often happens in Washington—high-minded reforms have unintended consequences. In this case, the reformers wanted "public financing" of political campaigns—that is, public subsidies from the government to major candidates to eliminate private financing by individuals, corporations, unions, or interest groups. The reformers achieved public financing for the general election campaign for the presidency in 1974, but Congress blocked such taxpayer subsidies for congressional races—leaving that arena open to individual contributions and to PACs. About the same time, court decisions made it legal for government contractors to have PACs (a practice previously barred for fear that the PACs of government contractors would be used to buy influence). The court decision making corporate PACs legal was a watershed.

"It opened the door for the creation of PACs and institutionalized the role of PAC money to buy influence," asserted Fred Wertheimer, president of Common Cause, the public-interest lobby. Any organization or group of people can form a PAC, but Wertheimer pointed out that "the biggest increase [in recent years] was the corporate PACs, because they came from practically nothing and there are so many corporations."[16]

Not only PAC donations but the overall hard cash pumped into congressional campaigns rocketed steeply from 1974 onward. In the campaigns of 1974, for example, a total of $72 million was spent on House and Senate races; by 1986, the figure had multiplied more than six times, to $450 million.[17] At the national level, the national Republican party and its campaign committees raised $254.6 million in the presidential election year of 1984, more than triple the $74.3 million that the rival Democratic committees raised.[18] Political spending was spiraling everywhere, but PACs were the main vehicle of growth. Their number, including all kinds of PACs—business, labor, and other interest groups—jumped from 608 in 1974 to 4,157 in mid-1987, and PAC donations to candidates leapt nearly a multiple of fifteen—from $8.5 million in 1974 to $132.2 million in 1986.

Big money has changed the face of Washington and its life-style. In a decade or less, several billion dollars of investment funds have poured into Washington to finance scores of new luxury office buildings, top-of-the-line hotels, stylish restaurants, and ten significant new art museums that have put glitter into downtown Washington. Texas money. British money. Dutch money. Plus multimillionaire local developers such as Oliver T. Carr and Charles E. Smith are expanding commercial corridors along K Street, the West End, the Potomac Riverfront in Georgetown, and in Virginia.

With its think tanks, consulting firms, lawyers, and lobbyists, Washington is a natural boomtown in an economy driven by the information revolution. By the mid-1980s, it was bolting ahead so rapidly that more new office space was being opened and leased in the capital each year than in New York, Los Angeles, Chicago, or Houston.[19] Between 1976 and 1983, thirty-seven new hotels opened. Two glass-box mini-cities of consulting firms sprouted in Crystal City and Rosslyn across the Potomac River, mainly to serve the Pentagon. Spreading political power has been a catalyst for the real estate surge, but a lot of new money flowed to Washington with modern light industry. A dozen high-rise, high-tech mini-cities have sprung up in the capital's backyard, and in early 1987, Mobil became the first major industrial corporation to choose Washington's Virginia suburbs for its world headquarters.

The city of Washington has become zip-code chic for firms eager to display a capital address but anxious to avoid rising rents downtown. *USA Today* built twin modernistic towers in Arlington, Virginia, but listed its address as "Box 500, Washington, DC 20044." The Mariott Hotel Corporation put its world headquarters in suburban Rockville, Maryland, but listed its address at a mythical "Marriott Drive, Washington, DC 20058."

Pennsylvania Avenue, the political spine of the city, was once the butt of tart complaints from President Kennedy, who bemoaned the seedy combination of liquor stores, souvenir shops, and vacant lots that he saw on his inaugural ride from Congress to the White House in 1961. Since then, Pennsylvania Avenue has been transformed not only with new parks and promenades but a huge burst of investment. Between $1 billion and $1.5 billion in private capital has gone into its renovation: for rescuing the National Theatre and the old Post Office Building from demolition and reviving them; for giving the National Press Building a $47 million face-lift; for a new $35 million Canadian Embassy; much larger sums for several swanky office-hotel complexes between Sixth and Thirteenth streets, with price tags from $125 million to $200 million apiece: and also for Oliver Carr's elaborately authentic $150 million Beaux Arts restoration of the historic Willard Hotel, where Abraham Lincoln and other presidents awaited their inaugurations.

"What's happened to Washington is wealth," suggested Mabel "Muffy" Brandon, former social secretary to Mrs. Reagan and now an impresario of cultural events and parties for corporations. "We were always known as a city of power. But in the last several years wealth has come. It's always been here but very discreetly. This has never been a city of conspicuous consumption. But now the wealth is flagrant in the cars people drive, the clothes they wear, what they spend on real estate."[20]

The new corporate activism has fanned explosive growth and a pell-mell pace. "You bring in the militia [corporate lobbyists] from outside to fight your battles and then you've got to feed them and you've got to house them," Muffy Brandon observed, "and then you've got whole armies of people fighting for visibility. Everybody wants visibility. Everybody wants access. Everybody wants air time. Everybody wants influence time. Our little one-industry village is no longer a quiet southern town."

Corporate millions pour into well-oiled lobbying campaigns, and corporate money underwrites the most elaborate social occasions and cultural events. Except for Katharine Graham, chairman of the Washington Post Company, Pamela Harriman, who runs fund-raising dinners and issue salons for the Democratic Party, and Esther Coopersmith, a bustling political and social activist from nearby Potomac, Georgetown hostesses have not been able to keep up with the social largesse of big business. In the past decade, corporations have openly become the big entertainers. Many politicians used to shy away from open connections with business, but the political climate has changed.

"You just don't hear about the Georgetown cocktail party the way you used to," Jerry terHorst, former press secretary to President Ford and now a vice president of Ford Motor Company, remarked. "It's still there but not as important as it once was. One reason is that an awful lot of corporate leaders can put on a party and have important people come. What they found out was that people in Washington don't mind coming to a party given by a corporate CEO. It's not regarded as being too bourgeois."[21]

"The most elegant dinner parties these days are given at the National Gallery," echoed Sandy McElwaine, a well-connected free-lance writer. She was alluding to the skill of Carter Brown, the National Gallery director, at persuading corporations such as AT&T, Occidental Petroleum, Mobil, and Ford to finance major art shows. In 1985, Ford spent $3 million to $3.5 million to bring a collection of art treasures from the homes of the British aristocracy to the gallery and to underwrite much of the opening-night swirl of parties that featured Prince Charles and Princess Diana. The arrival of royalty and British peerage put democratic Washington into a froth. It brought out more mink and glitter than people had seen since the first Reagan inaugural. On one evening, there were forty-two simultaneous black-tie dinners. Ford billed it as a soft-sell, proud of the cachet and entrée it had won.

Bill Regardie, a bright, brassy, vain, California-casual (though a Washington native) entrepreneur, has capitalized on the new Washington glitz and wealth. In 1980, he unveiled *Regardie's*, a glossy magazine pitched "to the lifestyles of the rich and famous." Six years later, the forty-five-year-old publisher pegged *Regardie's* circulation at fifty-seven thousand. A feature issue in September 1985 listed what *Regardie's* called Washington's one hundred richest people, thirteen with fortunes of more than $300 million, including Katharine Graham, Jack Kent Cooke (owner of the Washington Redskins football team), Joe Allbritton (chairman of Riggs Bank), and the J. Willard Marriott family of motel fame.

Regardie himself is full of theories, some apt, some hyped, about Washington, a city which he says has moved into Alvin Toffler's *Third Wave*, a modern economy based on service, research, and information.[22] Regardie has clearly picked up the new beat of a political city, where David Stockman quit as budget director and signed a $2.4 million contract for a kiss-and-tell insider's book, *The Triumph of Politics*. And where other Reagan aides or campaign strategists set up multimillion dollar influence-peddling operations. In 1984, Reagan's campaign slogan, pitched at the Olympics, was Go for the Gold, but obviously others took that slogan commercially. Bill Regardie's own self-indulgent mockery of the city hangs on a corner coatrack, the official *Regardie's* jacket: silver satin, styled like a car-racing team jacket, embroidered on the back with *Money, Power, Greed.*[23]

This is obviously no longer the relatively quiet town that Mo Udall found in the 1960s. It's a new game. It's as if the Old Washington had the cool, deliberate pace, the quiet sociability, and the predictable carom shots of a game of billiards played in a smoke-filled pool parlor. While the public occasionally hooted disapproval of the old game, at least we understood the shots, we knew the few important players and we could follow the action. But the reform movements of the late 1960s and early 1970s insisted on blowing the smoke and the back-room deals out of the system.

And paradoxically, reform opened up a razzle-dazzle political circus. The old pool-parlor game is now more like a street carnival, with roller coasters, whirling rides, shooting galleries, and a roomful of modern video games, with their gyrating spaceships, rumbling sound effects, and changing scenarios. The action of the new game is much faster and much harder to follow, both for the players and those who watch.

Boss Tube Replaces Boss Tweed

Television is the other major revolutionary ingredient in the new power mix. By now, it is a familiar cliché that television has largely replaced the political parties as the middleman between candidates and voters. In effect, Boss Tube has succeeded Boss Tweed of Tammany Hall, Boss Crump of Memphis, and the Daley machine in Chicago. Television brings politicians right into the living room and lets voters form their own impressions, rather than voters having to depend on what local party bosses, union leaders, church spokesmen, or business chiefs say. The campaign impact of television is undeniable. For many candidates it has replaced going door to door.

And it has also profoundly affected the Washington power game. It has eroded still further the cohesive force of the two parties in Congress, feeding centrifugal forces. Television fuels the independence of individual politicians, and that compounds the problems of congressional leaders in rounding up majorities. The trend in television politics is for candidates to build their personal mass appeal and political organizations, bypassing the regular party apparatus. Once they arrive in Congress, candidates who get elected as political Lone Rangers are less responsive to party leaders.

Television has altered other power relationships, too. In the old days, Arthur Krock, chief correspondent of *The New York Times* in Washington and a premier columnist from Franklin Roosevelt's era to Dwight Eisenhower's presidency, used to host an informal weekly luncheon table at the Metropolitan Club, one of those elite male establishments. When George Tames, the veteran *Times* photographer, retired in 1985, he told me that up to twenty top government officials would show up at Krock's regular lunch table and swap gossip, news, and off-color stories. No senior columnist today commands a similar table. But, illustrating the change, 134 senators and members of Congress showed up one night in October 1985 for Ted Koppel's ABC *Nightline*. Invited in advance, they were vying for a chance, first come, first served, to appear on camera for a minute each—just for the privilege of asking questions of Soviet and American policy experts on the outcome of the Reagan-Gorbachev summit in Geneva.

Television has become the new reality in American politics—in 1960 for the president, in the mid-seventies for other politicians. It has drastically expanded the arena of action. In the past few years, the commercial outlets for political news have mushroomed. On top of established network coverage, change came rapid fire: *The MacNeil-Lehrer Report* opened on public television in 1975, ABC's *Good Morning America* started in 1975, ABC's *Nightline* went four nights a week in 1980, and that same year the Cable News Network was born. A year later, the Sunday morning news shows got a shot in the arm with ABC's *This Week with David Brinkley*.

In 1979, the House began live telecasts of its floor debates. Howard Baker, before retiring as Senate majority leader, kept urging the Senate to follow suit, as a way of getting cameras to focus on the main action rather than on the publicity antics of individual members. "If you don't let them [the senators] do anything on the floor," Baker commented, "they do it on the Capitol steps and somehow there's always a TV camera out there."[24] The Senate followed Baker's advice eighteen months later.

Quite clearly, television has offered a fast track to those with political sex appeal and a knack for personality politics. It has opened the door to celebrities from other walks of life: Jack Kemp, the former Super Bowl quarterback for the Buffalo Bills football team; Bill Bradley, the New York Knicks basketball Hall of Famer; astronaut John Glenn; and regional media personalities such as Jesse Helms, not to mention a Hollywood actor such as Ronald Reagan.

Stephen Hess, a political scientist at the Brookings Institution, contends in his book *The Ultimate Insiders* that network news coverage actually reinforces the established leadership. In 1983, for example, he found that some, though not all, of the Senate leaders and potential presidential contenders got the heaviest coverage on the network evening news and Sunday shows and in five major newspapers.[25] Indeed, the sharpest, most telegenic leaders can use TV to enhance their power; Senate Republican leader Bob Dole is a prime example. But Hess's survey showed that in 1983, some major committee chairmen got less media play than senators with less formal power who were public celebrities, among them John Glenn and Gary Hart. Both were presidential contenders, but their news-celebrity status came not from the slow patient route of seniority and old-fashioned inside politics, but from their skill at the media game or their notoriety.

Moreover, another study in Hess's book made clear that publicity-sharp middle-rank or junior senators (Christopher Dodd of Connecticut, Paul Tsongas of Massachusetts, Arlen Specter of Pennsylvania, Larry Pressler of South Dakota, and Howard Metzenbaum of Ohio) were doing extremely well on the newer television shows.[26] On the House side, some backbenchers have clearly used video politics to magnify their influence.

"The changes in the media," observed political scientist Michael Robinson, "have given younger members and maverick members more political visibility—and hence greater power—than ever before."[27]

The most talented of the new breed have charm and wit on television; some have become substantive legislators, too. This group combines inside savvy with flair for the media game. What put them on the fast track was the happy combination of being telegenic and pithy—the ability to simplify issues and fashion thematic messages. John F. Kennedy, a lackluster senator impatient with inside politics, was the first to market glamour politicking on TV. Some current presidential aspirants (Jack Kemp of New York), welcome Kennedy comparisons. This is not to say that Kennedy and others have lacked substantive achievements; merely that video appeal was central to their rise to prominence. To keep up in the power game, even old-timers such as House Speaker Tip O'Neill have had to learn how to play the game of video politics.

In Congress, the first wave of new-breed politicians who had grown up with television and found it their natural medium was the Democratic class of 1974—bright, articulate, energetic politicians such as Timothy Wirth of Colorado, Thomas Downey and Stephen Solarz of New York, Tom Harkin of Iowa, Robert Edgar of Pennsylvania, Chris Dodd and Toby Moffett of Connecticut. That class of 1974 changed the temper of the Congress, for they were upstart, independent voices, irreverent toward the congressional Establishment. Television helped them get ahead and put their mark on issues. Then in 1978, a big class of new-breed Republicans arrived to be sworn in on the new regular live coverage of the House. Some, such as Newt Gingrich, an outspoken go-getter from Georgia, have used media skills to build their influence.

With the exception of Kemp, none of the new-breed Republicans has garnered the limelight more dramatically than Phil Gramm, a supremely self-confident Reaganite economist from Texas. Gramm is no stereotyped, blow-dried, airhead TV politician; he is not a glamour boy, but a bespectacled ex-professor with thinning locks. Gramm shot to prominence by combining a shrewd sense of timing, brilliant legislative packaging, and a knack for self-promotion and selling his ideas on television. He came to the House of Representatives as a Democrat in 1978. Just three years later he played a central role in the Reagan budget package by leading the defection of southern conservative

Democrats to support Reagan's budget. In 1983, he switched parties
and got elected to the Senate as a Republican in 1984. A year later,
as a freshman Senator—indeed as the ninety-seventh-ranking senator—he emerged as a prime architect (with another freshman Republican, Warren Rudman of New Hampshire) of the highly controversial
plan to balance the budget by 1991 through mandatory annual reductions in the deficit. Gramm's media skills got him wide political notice
and legislative results.

Rather caustically, some old hands branded the flashy new-breed
legislators as "show horses" who chase publicity while the grubby
details of legislation are hammered out in private by the "workhorses."
And in fact, Pete Domenici, the Senate workhorse budget chairman,
had to rework the Gramm-Rudman plan considerably to do what
Gramm and Rudman intended. But in fairness, the most effective
newcomers offer more than the blow-dried look. They have developed
substantive expertise. What has aroused the jealousy of their elders is
the refusal of newcomers to sit back quietly and behave like novitiates.

Television helped break up the policy monopolies of established
committees and throw open the power game. Overshadowing the
grinding "inside" spadework of bill drafting in committee, television
offered shortcuts and a showcase. Kemp and Gramm are prime examples of those who learned how to influence Congress and market their
ideas with their colleagues through the media. Over television, they
sent messages to the voters and generated grass-roots interest that
ricocheted back to Congress. Thus, television offered a marketplace for
all 435 members of the House and one hundred Senators to become
policy entrepreneurs. That is one major reason why Congress seems so
unruly today.

"Congress has become atomistic," remarked Charles Schumer, a
rising young Brooklyn Democrat. "In the House we are 435 little atoms
bouncing off each other, colliding and influencing each other but not
in a very coherent way," he remarked to me. "There used to be much
more structure. But now there is no bonding that holds the atoms
together.

"In a way, this reflects American society," Schumer suggested. "Our
society has become more atomistic. In fact, the thing that has struck
me most about Congress is how the House of Representatives accurately reflects the country, both in terms of philosophy and structure.
The other thing that has amazed me is not just how good the people
are in Congress, but how the institution is screwed up. I think the
pendulum has swung too far away from strong leadership."[28]

Actually, the pendulum has begun swinging back the other way. Tip O'Neill was a strong House speaker, the strongest since the legendary Sam Rayburn died in 1961. Both Howard Baker and Bob Dole were effective Senate majority leaders. All three were able—with great difficulty and only on a few occasions—to assert leadership over the atomistic forces in Congress.

But Charlie Schumer's observations are worth pondering by people who regularly scorn "the mess in Washington." I think he is correct that the House of Representatives does mirror the country well. It is true that Congress has its scoundrels and dullards. But its periodic paralysis and its brawling stalemates do not prove the incompetence or laziness of its members. Often congressional immobility reflects the lack of clear public consensus on major issues. What's more, as an institution, Congress suffers less from too many crooks and dodos, than from too many bright, hyperkinetic, ambitious politicians clamoring for attention and tripping over each other as they compete for airtime, trying to give voice to the competing impulses within the American electorate.

The more open power game provides strong incentives for politicians to play highly individualistic politics. Except for times of genuine crisis, or when some institutional deadline is imminent, both House and Senate often bog down in immobility or mere muddling through. But that is less the fault of poor politicians than it is of the sprawling dispersion of power, of the multitude of competing interests, and of the lack of cohesive forces powerful enough to pull members to work together.

3. The Soft Side of Power: Visibility, Credibility, and Power Surfing

This place depends very heavily on personal relationships and personal credibility.
—Senator Warren Rudman

Integrity is power—I'd put integrity first.
—Bryce Harlow, aide to President Eisenhower

One wintry afternoon, I asked Tom Eagleton, the veteran Missouri Democrat nearing the end of eighteen years in the Senate, what was the most important element of power in Washington, and he shot back without hesitation: "Being in the majority."[1]

Of course, Eagleton was right, as far as he went. It matters greatly who is president, who is speaker, which party is in the majority in the House and Senate, and who are the principal committee chairmen. Eagleton, who had seen a Democratic Senate majority slip away to the Republicans, explained what being the majority meant: fixing the legislative schedule, having first crack at setting the agenda, picking the top committee staff, running hearings, arranging foreign trips, being called to the White House.

But formal titles of power confer less automatic authority than people imagine. That is an enduring lesson of American politics, but one that is especially true in the fluid arena of the new power game.

Across the country, all too often people equate position with power, and overlook the soft sides of power: the intangible ingredients that add up to influence and authority. The formal structures of government are only the scaffolding of power. They do not account for its human chemistry. High office offers leverage, but politicians can either squander or exploit that potential. No power is absolute or guaranteed, for at its heart, our politics is a contest of persuasion. In that contest, the intangibles have always been important, but never more so than in the era of television, which plays up the politics of personality and where impressions and appearances are so crucial to a politician's power.

From recent experience, we know that one president (Ronald Reagan) appears strong and comfortable with power, while another president (Jimmy Carter) seems ill at ease with power and comes across as uncertain and strained. We have seen that a speaker of the House (Tip O'Neill) can be assertive and potent while another (his predecessor, Carl Albert) can seem almost invisible; that some committee chairmen can work their will while others flounder; that as budget director, David Stockman drove the policy process, while his successor, James Miller, was a secondary player whom congressmen kiddingly called "Miller Lite."

In short, the most vital ingredients of power are often the intangibles. Information and knowledge are power. Visibility is power. A sense of timing is power. Trust and integrity are power. Personal energy is power; so is self-confidence. Showmanship is power. Likability is power. Access to the inner sanctum is power. Obstruction and delay are power. Winning is power. Sometimes, the illusion of power is power.

Take visibility: A president has many legally established powers—the power to purge the top echelons of government and put in his own allies; the power to appoint scores if not hundreds of federal judges; the power to issue executive orders and to make administrative decisions; the power to launch planes against Libyan terrorist camps or to make arms proposals to a Soviet leader; the power to reward political friends and punish enemies by approving programs, granting favors, or withholding benefits; and sometimes, the political power to affect the survival of other politicians by throwing his personal weight for or against them in campaigns.

Yet few presidential powers are more central to success than a president's ability to command public attention, or in Theodore Roosevelt's phrase, to mount the "bully pulpit" and preach his cause. No such power is granted in the Constitution. Yet the president can request and usually receive network television time—the coin of the realm in the new power game. As can no one else, the president can attract an audience in the tens of millions to put forward an agenda, to spell out priorities, to use the nation as his sounding board, to move the political system in the direction he wants; in short, to persuade.

Position makes the president preeminent, but it does not grant him a monopoly. We have seen others steal the stage and use it to change the agenda or to redefine reality and thus force the president's hand. I believe it happens more readily in the new game of instant mass communication than it did in the old closed-circuit politics; television gives others a platform and a megaphone that magnifies their power.

One case in point is the change in American foreign policy, to support Corazon Aquino after the Philippine election on February 7, 1986. That change came in no small measure because Indiana Senator Richard Lugar shrewdly worked the leverage of his visibility. President Reagan's sympathies clearly lay with President Ferdinand Marcos, whom he regarded as an old friend, an anti-Communist ally. Reagan tried to cling to Marcos. Before the Philippine election, Lugar had warned that the administration was tying itself too closely to strong-man rulers such as Marcos. As the respected Republican chairman of the Senate Foreign Relations Committee, Lugar went to Manila heading a U.S. delegation to observe the fairness of the election.

At the first reports of fraud by the Marcos side, some American observers discounted it as no worse than a Chicago election. Lugar was more critical. After a very slow count and after computer operators walked out of the election commission charging they had been ordered to change vote counts, Lugar concluded that Aquino had surely won the election. He felt the time had come to change the Philippine government and American policy. Aides said he pressed that argument in a private session with President Reagan on February 11. Reagan suggested there had been fraud on both sides, but Lugar insisted that he had seen it only on the Marcos side.[2] That night, Lugar was stunned to hear Reagan tell a press conference there was "the possibility of fraud . . . on both sides." The next day, Lugar pointedly told reporters the president was "not well informed," and the White House backed down. Reagan went incommunicado—to be unseen by reporters for several days. Lugar filled the vacuum, arguing in television interviews that Marcos "ought to step down."

On Sunday, February 23, Lugar took center stage. He appeared on all three network television interview shows (*Meet the Press, Face the Nation,* and *This Week with David Brinkley*). Other politicians called it the "hat trick," the feat in hockey of scoring three goals in one game. From that television platform, Lugar called on Reagan to telephone Marcos to ask him to resign, and his television appearances had impact. The next day, Senator Paul Laxalt of Nevada—Reagan's close friend and intermediary with Marcos—talked with the Philippine leader by phone and told him to "cut, and cut cleanly." Said Laxalt, "I think the time has come" to resign.

Reagan had been forced to shift. His position had been undermined both by televised scenes of massive fraud and by Lugar's highly visible charges that the election was stolen and Marcos should go.

Similarly, when the tax bill backed by Reagan fell victim to a House Republican revolt in December 1985, Speaker Tip O'Neill put Reagan under the gun by declaring publicly that Reagan would be a "lame-duck" president if he could not muster fifty Republican votes to help a majority of Democrats pass the tax bill. Like Lugar, O'Neill used his visibility to define political reality and the terms of success, forcing the president to respond. On the tax bill, Reagan got the votes. But in the tactics of power, O'Neill, like Lugar, had forced the president's hand. Both of them stole the bully pulpit from Reagan. Their leverage came from appealing to a wider audience.

Visibility sometimes gives junior members of Congress more power than people many years their senior. In 1980 and 1981, it was Buffalo Congressman Jack Kemp's high profile advocacy of a thirty-percent reduction in personal income tax rates that provided the basic outline for Reagan's bill. Kemp's visibility had more impact than did the patiently acquired expertise of the ranking Republicans in Congress on tax matters, Senator Bob Dole and Representative Barber Conable. Indeed, the clashing styles and philosophies of Conable and Kemp offer examples of what Washingtonians now call "inside" and "outside" politics. In recent years, sharp jealousies have developed between the "inside" politicians, whose power derives from their ability to craft and broker legislation, and the "outside" politicians, who exert their influence on policy through publicity and sloganeering.

Conable, who has subsequently become president of the World Bank, was an old-school Republican congressman. By 1981, Conable had seniority in the House, but he had much more. He had earned a reputation as a serious, thoughtful politician who knew the tax code inside out and was a skilled legislative craftsman. Elected first in 1964, Conable had worked up the ladder to become the ranking Republican on the tax-writing Ways and Means Committee. As an orthodox balance-the-budget conservative, Conable showed no enthusiasm for

Kemp-style tax cutting, although he went along when President Reagan adopted it.

Kemp's power base was not seniority but visibility. As a telegenic celebrity politician and former pro football quarterback, he had popularized the supply-side economic theory that cutting tax rates would boost growth and, ultimately, government tax revenues. His star quality and theme politics had given him more clout than the more cautious Conable, especially with the new Reagan team. I was told privately that Conable had complained bitterly at being handed the Reagan tax bill at the last minute by Treasury Secretary Donald Regan and asked to cosponsor it, although it had been conceived and written by others. In subsequent maneuvering, Conable got some vindication: He helped inject into the bill some probusiness breaks that he favored: faster depreciation schedules and a provision to index tax rates to inflation. But Kemp still got the larger public glory.

Again, in Reagan's dramatic 1981 blitzkrieg of Congress, it was David Stockman, as director of the Office of Management and Budget, who stole the limelight, not members of the cabinet who theoretically outranked him. Stockman came from practically nowhere, a mere two-term Michigan congressman, thirty-four years old. But he dazzled Washington. He had answers for the questions practically everyone was then asking.

Knowledge was Stockman's power base. Reagan offered a vision of cutting government, Stockman had the blueprint for how to do it. He was the whiz kid with the razor-sharp mind, master of both the impenetrable arithmetic of the budget and the intricacies of congressional procedure.

In the first blush of what partisans called the Reagan Revolution, Stockman was at peak influence because, in one of Washington's most telltale phrases, he was "ahead of the power curve." Long after, Stockman confessed that neither he nor anyone else knew as much as he had pretended. But in the critical presidential transition of 1980, he knew better than anyone else where he was going, where Reagan wanted to head, and how to get there politically. The others were at sea. That was why people relied on Stockman. It was more than his understanding of the budget. It was his timing, his conviction, his road map. Stockman was bold and sure when others were hesitant, articulate when others stumbled. He sensed the moment to strike, and he showed others how to exploit the power vacuum.

Five years later, Stockman embarrassed Reagan by telling how he had "cooked the books" to make Reagan's budgets look as though they would balance in 1984, and how little Reagan understood of the economic policies he was advocating. But even after Stockman's first disloyal confessions in *The Atlantic* in late 1981, President Reagan did not fire him. Stockman was too indispensable: Knowledge was his power.

Credibility

Washington has many yardsticks for measuring power. Two of the most common are money and people: The more people an official "owns," or commands in his bureaucratic empire, and the larger his budget, the more powerful he is supposed to be. By that measure, the Defense secretary would automatically be the most powerful member of the cabinet. But that fails to explain the changing fortunes of Caspar Weinberger, who was riding high in Reagan's first year or two and then was relentlessly besieged in later years. In part Weinberger fell victim to the shifting public mood toward military spending and the scandalous costs of spare parts. More fundamentally, Congress lost faith in Weinberger's credibility. And in the intangible chemistry of power, no quality matters more than trust.

Credibility—trust—is the most important key to survival and influence. It lies at the heart of political authority, for without credibility a political leader or a high government official cannot make a persuasive case to others. Loss of trust forced Richard Nixon from office; it fatally wounded Lyndon Johnson; it drove Gary Hart out of the 1988 presidential race. As Bryce Harlow, Eisenhower's legislative aide, liked to say: "Integrity is power—I'd put integrity first."[3]

On a less exalted level, in an arena of constant controversy, the advocate who is too parochial, too partisan, or too political to be credible is not heard or heeded as time wears on. "This place depends very heavily on personal relationships and personal credibility— whether people trust and respect your analysis, your intellect, your fairness, and your word" is the way Senator Warren Rudman of New Hampshire put it.[4]

Over the years, for example, presidential estimates on the economy have largely come to be discounted by both houses and parties in Congress, because they are so often politically biased in the president's favor. Over time, such mistrust built up in Congress toward Weinberger, though Reagan relied on him, and even the Republican-led Senate voted 95–0 to impose Pentagon reforms that Weinberger opposed. Even more so, the late William Casey, as director of Central

Intelligence for six years, lost the trust of Congress and some colleagues in the administration—in a position where credibility is crucial.

From many, Casey got high marks for reviving CIA morale and for improving the quality of its intelligence analysis. Especially in the early years, Casey's intelligence budgets grew significantly. But his penchant for aggressive covert military operations in Nicaragua, Angola, and elsewhere polarized Congress and fed running controversies with the Democratic-dominated House Intelligence Committee and with Senate Democrats such as Pat Moynihan of New York and moderate Senate Republicans such as Dave Durenburger of Minnesota. The congressional balance of support for the *contra* war in Nicaragua was always touch and go because of policy disagreements. But several key members of both houses blamed Casey personally for tipping the balance *against* the administration in 1984 and 1985 by showing arrogant disdain for Congress and by giving evasive, deceptive, and dishonest testimony to intelligence committees.

"Casey has a contempt for Congress," Dave McCurdy, an influential, sometimes pro-*contra* Democrat on the House Intelligence Committee, complained in 1985. "Casey's contempt is not even disguised. He feels Congress is interfering in his activity. He says Congress can't keep a secret [although] the intelligence committees have kept plenty of secrets. But then his own credibility is lacking with Congress. He either mumbles when he's not telling the truth or he avoids answering questions."[5]

McCurdy vividly recalled one talk with Casey at CIA headquarters in 1983. "This is when he was telling us in committee that the *contra* aid was just for interdicting the arms flow from Nicaragua into El Salvador," McCurdy told me. "So over breakfast, I asked him, 'What's our policy in Nicaragua?' He said, 'Whatever it takes.' I said, 'What does that mean—overthrowing the Sandinistas?' And he said again, 'Whatever it takes.' So sometimes he slips and says what he really thinks. But after that, I knew I could not believe what he said in committee."

Congressional mistrust of Casey reached a peak in early 1984 when Nicaraguan harbors were mined by Latin American commando teams trained and commanded by American CIA agents. Barry Goldwater, then Senate Intelligence Committee chairman, hotly protested that Casey had never informed his committee of plans for the harbor mining, though that was required by law. "I am pissed off," Goldwater yelped. "Bill, this is no way to run a railroad, and I find myself in a hell of a quandry. . . . The President has asked us to back his foreign policy.

Bill, how can we back his foreign policy when we don't know what the hell he is doing? Lebanon, yes, we all knew that he sent troops over there. But mine the harbors in Nicaragua? This is an act violating international law. It is an act of war. For the life of me, I don't see how we are going to explain it."[6]

Eventually, Casey apologized to Goldwater. But privately, Goldwater fumed to other committee members that "Casey wouldn't tell you if your coat was on fire." Ultimately, the mining episode and Casey's handling of it led to the cutoff of aid to the Nicaraguan *contras* in mid-1984. When nonlethal aid to the *contras* was renewed by Congress in 1985, the legislation passed only on condition that the CIA could not be the channel for the funding. Casey's evasions had so undermined his credibility that some intelligence committees simply did not want to have to deal with him on *contra* aid.

Early on, the intelligence committees came to count on Casey's deputy, Vice Admiral Bobby Inman, to level with them; Inman had a rock-solid reputation for integrity. He became known for a nervous habit of tugging at his socks when Casey was misleading congressional committees. Unable to look committee members in the eye at such moments, Inman would bend over and pull up his socks. Once, during a Senate intelligence hearing, Goldwater made fun of him.

"You're a three-star admiral," he chided Inman. "Can't you afford socks that don't fall down?"

"I can't help it," Inman replied. "It's a nervous habit."

The next time it happened, Goldwater picked up the clue, pressing Casey on the point at hand.

"Bill, can you be a bit more precise about that," Goldwater asked. Casey added some more detail.

At other times, Democrats such as Joe Biden of Delaware and Patrick Leahy of Vermont said they had learned to watch Inman's telltale habit for clues to the veracity of Casey's testimony and would press Inman so say whether he agreed with what Casey was saying.[7]

The mistrust in the Senate Intelligence Committee toward Casey was so imbedded that when Inman resigned in mid-1982, his successor, John McMahon, a career CIA official with a reputation for honesty, encountered deep suspicion of Casey among senators when he made his private courtesy calls on the Senate Intelligence Committee members before his confirmation hearing.

One Democratic Senator told McMahon he had only one question: "If Casey doesn't tell us the truth, will you tell us the truth?"

It was an issue on many minds. "I'll give you the same answer that

I've given to each of the other senators who asked me just one question, the same one as yours," McMahon replied. "My answer is: Yes, I'll tell you the truth."

But mistrust finally caught up with another Casey deputy, William Gates, because some members of Congress suspected Casey and Gates of hiding the Iranian arms deal from Congress, despite Casey's written promise to Goldwater not to play such games. President Reagan nominated Gates to succeed Casey, who was taken fatally ill in early 1987. So angered was the Senate Intelligence Committee by Casey's evasions and Gates's failure to block the Iranian-*contra* deals or inform Congress of them that the committee refused to confirm Gates as CIA director. Reagan had to pull back Gates's name and get someone who had the trust of Congress, former FBI Director William Webster.

The most damning indictment of Casey came not from Congress but from within the Reagan administration, from Secretary of State George Shultz. Not only did Shultz accuse Casey of deception in dealing with other officials but of slanting intelligence to support policies that Casey favored, such as the Iranian arms deals.

"I hate to say it, but I believe that one of the reasons the president was given what I regard as wrong information about Iran and terrorism was that the agency or the people in the CIA were too involved in this [operation]," Shultz told Congress. "Long before this all emerged, I had come to have grave doubts about the objectivity and reliability of some of the intelligence I was getting."[8]

So devastating is that notion—of a CIA director slanting intelligence estimates to favor his pet policies—that Shultz and others advocated separating the function of intelligence estimates from covert operations and policy-making. For not only had Casey destroyed his own credibility in many circles of government, but he had so damaged the intelligence agency that he left others bent on reducing its power.

By contrast with Casey, much of the power of Paul Volcker, during his two terms as chairman of the Federal Reserve Board, derived from his personal credibility—with Congress and with the financial markets. By casting himself as the number-one economic policymaker fighting inflation, one who was unwilling to bow to politics, Volcker enlarged his power and influence. Not only his position as chairman of the Federal Reserve Board, also known as the "Fed," but also widespread trust in Volcker's integrity won him repeated selection as Washington's "second most powerful official" behind the president, in annual reader polls by *US News & World Report.*

Volcker is a towering six-foot seven-and-one-half-inch, 245-pound economist and government banker with a good enough sense of humor to show up at a masquerade party dressed as the "jolly green giant" and with a keen enough conscience to quip that he fits H. L. Mencken's description of bankers as people who have the "haunting fear that someone, somewhere may be happy." He has habitually operated so secretively in the hidden pathways of international finance that a Japanese foreign minister once nicknamed him Ninja, or "the invisible warrior." He would emerge periodically from the Fed's shroud of secrecy to draw a huge crowd at congressional hearings, drawn by respect for Volcker's views. He made his appearances in rumpled pin-striped suits, smoking cheap Antonio y Cleopatra cigars, blowing clouds of smoke, dropping ashes on his lapels and issuing intricate pronouncements on the economy and the monetary policy he was pursuing. Somehow, Volcker managed both to flatter the members of Congress by listening to them and getting them to accept him as an oracle.

John Kennedy was the first president to tap Volcker's talents; he lured Volcker to the Treasury Department as an economist. Every president since then has given Volcker some important economic appointment. With inflation running at fifteen percent, Jimmy Carter summoned Volcker, then president of the New York Federal Reserve Bank, to make him the Fed chairman. Carter chose Volcker, a conservative Democrat, because he was the favorite of Wall Street, the business community, and the international financial markets—groups which had lost faith in Carter's economic policies. Volcker warned Carter that to beat down inflation, he, Volcker, would have to tighten the money supply, a policy which could hurt Carter politically as interest rates rose. Carter gave Volcker the job anyway.

In October 1979 and then again in February 1980, Volcker persuaded the Fed's open market committee to hold down the growth of the money supply. The economy contracted, shooting interest rates up even higher. In August 1980, Volcker tried to ease off but it was too late to help Carter before the election. With Reagan in the White House and inflation rising again, Volcker clamped down even harder on the money supply in 1981. As the prime interest rate soared over twenty percent and thousands of farmers and small businessmen went under for lack of credit, hostility toward Volcker became so great that he was given Secret Service protection. By February 1982, *The Tennessee Professional Builder*, a construction trade magazine, turned its cover into a WANTED poster for Volcker and the six other Fed board members. The magazine charged the Fed with "premeditated and coldblooded murder of millions of small businesses." It was Volcker's willingness to brook all this ill feeling, in order to cure the economy's woes, that won him wide credibility later on. But in the short run, he was castigated.

As the economy plunged into its worst recession since the 1930s, Donald Regan, then Treasury secretary, repeatedly lashed out at Volcker's tight-money policy. While many businessmen endorsed Volcker's painful medicine, Senate Majority Leader Howard Baker and House Majority Leader Jim Wright talked of limiting the Fed's power. But Volcker, seemingly unflappable, charged that the administration shared as much blame as the Fed for the skidding economy: Reagan's tax cuts had run the deficit up above $100 billion, and *that* was keeping interest rates sky-high. Volcker refused to ease up on credit until August 1982, acting only after a major tax increase was enacted to combat the deficit. Then he shrewdly eased off restraints so that the country's economic recovery was well under way before his four-year term ran out, in August 1983.

By then, Volcker's credibility was running high. Inflation was heading down from twelve percent toward five percent and Volcker, Villain of Recession, had become Volcker, Conqueror of Inflation. Secretary Regan and administration conservatives still wanted to get rid of Volcker, but with a good-news economy and the financial markets singing Volcker's praises, President Reagan kept him on for four more years. Subsequently, Volcker's prestige vaulted to the point where he had much more clout and credibility with Congress on economic policy than the president did. In 1985, Volcker said the federal deficit had to be cut by $50 billion, setting the mark for Congress. The financial markets came to see him as their bulwark against a resurgence of inflation and the voice of sound economics amidst the erratic, often conflicting gyrations of administration policymakers. Volcker was "a giant among pygmies," as one high Reagan aide put it.

Nonetheless, his tight money, anti-inflation policies aggravated some administration policymakers who wanted lower interest rates and easier money, to make the economy grow faster. They were also bent on pushing down the value of the dollar to make the prices of American exports more competitive abroad, to curb the soaring American trade deficit. For a while, Volcker joined forces in this effort with Jim Baker, who had taken over as Treasury secretary. However, within a few months Baker wanted to push the dollar down faster and further than Volcker, who was worried that a plunging dollar would shoot up the cost of imports and unravel six years of work fighting inflation.

Secretly, the administration decided to overpower Volcker. With two new Reagan appointments to the Federal Reserve Board, the administration gained a 4–3 majority for the first time in early 1986. In a risky power play, Treasury Secretary Baker privately encouraged the four Reagan appointees to push for lower interest rates.[9] On February 24, the "Reagan Four" revolted against Volcker by voting to cut the discount rate, the interest rate the Fed charges member banks. Volcker opposed this step unless Germany and Japan took similar action, fearing that the American step would cause foreign investors to withdraw funds from the United States and sharply weaken the dollar. The vote challenged Volcker's authority as the Fed boss. It also put the administration's credibility and judgment on the line, because the whole affair became public, raising questions about why the administration was undercutting its respected Fed chairman.

Volcker fought back with a power play of his own, tapping the reservoir of trust he had built up over the years. He went secretly to Secretary Baker and declared, one high official disclosed to me, that "if this was going to be the basis on which things were going to proceed, he might have to resign." That rang an alarm bell. Baker backtracked, recognizing Volcker's importance as a symbol of the American government's credibility to the financial markets. Baker had wanted to pressure Volcker, not to provoke him. By afternoon, Baker sent word to Wayne Angell, a new, swing vote on the Fed Board, to reverse his position. The vote turned 4–3 in Volcker's favor. Ten days later, some other countries lowered their rates as Volcker had wanted. Then he changed his position, so that American interest rates could come down too.

"When push came to shove, the administration knew that if it undercut Volcker, it would disrupt the financial markets and set off inflationary fears that could indirectly hurt the economic recovery," Robert Hormats, vice president of Goldman Sachs investment banking house, commented to me at the time. "It is Volcker's credibility which has given the markets confidence about the future. Volcker has convinced the financial markets that he is committed to fighting inflation even while he juices up the money supply to help keep the economic recovery going. The administration can't afford to shake that confidence."[10]

An even more flattering—and fairly typical—appraisal of Volcker's political skill came from Jack Albertine, former executive director of the American Business Conference, an organization of high-growth companies.

"Paul Volcker is the best bureaucratic player in Washington since J. Edgar Hoover," Albertine told me. "He has forced two presidents to appoint him, despite their reluctance. Jimmy Carter did not want him but had to take him because the economy and his government were collapsing in 1979. And Reagan went with Volcker because he needed him, too. Just as presidents feared J. Edgar Hoover because he had information on everyone, presidents worry about Volcker. If he goes, the bond market collapses. Volcker is a very smart banker and a very smart financial analyst. But that's not why he's successful. He's successful because he's a master politician and people believe in him."[11]

In August 1987, Reagan let Volcker retire after eight years as Fed Chairman, evidently fearful that Volcker's anti-inflation beliefs could produce tight-money policies in 1988 and dampen the American economy, hurting Republican chances in the 1988 elections. Word of Volcker's departure caused such worries in the financial community that the markets dropped quickly. Only by choosing a successor of great credibility with the financial markets—conservative economist Alan Greenspan, who had been chairman of the Council of Economic Advisers to President Ford—did Reagan avoid more serious backlash from Volcker's retirement.

Likability, Light Touch, and Surfing

Take credibility a step further and we are into the politics of personality—important in ways that the public often does not see at work in Washington. Sheer likability, or even a lively sense of humor, can be important ingredients of power, sometimes tipping the balance on substantive issues. Being able to entertain a banquet of several hundred political and business bigwigs with one-liners and anecdotes, can be a more important source of influence for Texas-born Washington lawyer Bob Strauss than mastering budget economics.

Barney Frank, a shrewd, tough-minded liberal Democratic congressman from outside Boston, contends that success in the Washington power game parallels high school politics. Congress has to operate informally, according to Frank, with the kinds of networks and personality politics that work in high school, because Congress has no clear power hierarchy. Leaders lack the corporate executive's power to give commands or to hire and fire.

"In some ways, being in Congress is more like being in high school than anything I've done since high school—I mean the way the structure is," Frank asserts. "Nobody in the House of Representatives can give any other member an order. The speaker is more influential than a new Republican from Texas, but he can't order anybody to do anything. Nobody can fire anybody. So what that means is that you become influential by persuading people, being likable, and having other people respect you but not resent you. That's why it's like high school."[12]

Morris Udall, the popular Arizona congressman, once tested Frank's notion; he learned the names of all new House members. "I carried a little book of names and pictures, and kept it by my bedside," Udall said. "You go up to a guy who's been here a year and call him by name and say, 'I understand you represent Schenectady,' or whatever, and I'd point out something interesting about each person. It pays off. If there's a vote going on and he comes in here and it's my bill, and otherwise the forces are equidistant, pushing him either way, he'd give you the benefit of the doubt because he knows you."[13]

Of course, it takes more than that. You have to be genuinely popular, and Udall is enormously well liked, especially among younger liberals to whom he is a folk hero. Udall's personal popularity foiled an effort in 1984 by Frank and other liberals to stop subsidizing public power in some western states. Udall was sponsoring a bill that would continue the old subsidized rates; Barbara Boxer, a young California liberal working with Frank, wanted power from hydroelectric projects such as the Hoover Dam to be priced at market rates.

"Mo's a public power guy, a westerner, and it was his committee handling the bill," Frank recalled. "The environmentalists were with us; the old system was wasting water. It was bad economics. I talked to some guys on the floor. I said, 'Look, on all the merits of the bill you should be with us.' And they said, 'But how can we vote against Mo?' It was a fairly close vote but we lost. We were opposing Mo Udall, and we love Mo. We lost because of Mo—a good example of personality affecting politics."

More broadly, where Carter failed at likability, it was one secret of Reagan's success. After disclosures of the Reagan administration's secret arms deals with Iran in 1986, majorities of people registered their mistrust of Reagan. He was deeply wounded as president. Other presidents might have been destroyed, but likability helped save Reagan. Voters might mock his claims of ignorance, but they had trouble seeing him as an impeachable villain on a par with Richard Nixon at Watergate.

On lesser problems, Reagan has been rescued at times by the mass appeal of his "aw, shucks" smile, the jaunty little toss of his head, his disarming ability to laugh at himself. Bryce Harlow compared Reagan to his former boss, Dwight Eisenhower.

"Eisenhower liked people so people liked Eisenhower," Harlow reminisced. "Eisenhower trusted people; therefore, they trusted Eisenhower. Eisenhower could fall flat on his *tokhus* out in public, do something very wrong or very stupid, make a big goof, and the American people would rush forward as one and grab him and pick him up and dust him off and say, 'Don't bother at all about that. We like Ike.' And on he'd go. Reagan gets the same treatment. Because he is a man with no internal hangups whatever. He likes people. He likes a charwoman quite as much as a queen. The people react to that."[14]

Reagan has been helped by a couple of other important intangibles; one is grasping power lightly. Bryce Harlow remarked to me that one vital secret for presidents and other top officials is to avoid appearing too hungry to wield power. Both the press and the public, he said, mistrust politicians who lust too obviously for power, as, he pointed out, was the case with Johnson and Nixon. Jimmy Carter, too, created problems by being so eager to exercise power that he became enmeshed in too many fights on too many fronts. Certainly Secretary of State Alexander Haig and White House Chief of Staff Donald Regan suffered from power hunger, as well.

"Reagan is not a power-hungry guy," suggested Lee Atwater, who helped run Reagan's 1984 campaign and later became campaign manager for Vice President Bush. "Nixon was power hungry. Johnson was power hungry. Carter was power hungry. Look at the guys who were run out of town by the media—the guys who were obsessed with power. Reagan stays detached. He's got a Zen approach to power: He doesn't care about power for power's sake alone. Eisenhower is the only other person who had the same detached way of holding power."[15]

Finally, power depends on illusion, on theater, on the appearance of floating above the battle. One of Reagan's trademarks has been staying out of petty battles. Like Tom Sawyer letting others whitewash Aunt Polly's back fence, Reagan's technique is to let others do battle and serve as his lightning rods—Secretary of State Shultz, Interior Secretary James Watt, congressional leaders, even Lieutenant Colonel Oliver North and Rear Admiral John Poindexter. Reagan holds himself aloof, waiting for the few big battles that he cares about and stands a strong chance of winning.

"Standing above the fray has its virtues," Maryland's Senator Charles McC. Mathias, Jr., observed near the end of his twenty-six years in Congress. "Number one, you don't wear out your welcome. And number two, you can judge what's happening in the arena and make sure that you come out with the winners. In the final stages, you can arrange yourself so that you're going to be on the winning side. Winning is very, very important. People love winners."[16]

Reagan has been extremely skillful at appearing more of a winner than he actually has been. Year after year, Reagan submitted budgets that Congress rejected out of hand. By standing back, without fighting hard for his own budgets, Reagan let slip from view what amounted to major defeats. He waited until Congress produced its own budget and then blamed Congress for not meeting his targets. By that time, voters had forgotten that Reagan's budget had died with barely a supporting vote; the same with tax reform. He launched the idea, then stood back ready to blame others if it failed. He waded in at crucial junctures, but only after congressional leaders had done the back-breaking work of preparing majorities. By holding back, Reagan husbanded his power and kept his image of success. His game style will be a model for future presidents.

Indeed, until the Iran-*contra* scandal broke at the end of 1986, Reagan's presidency was an object lesson in cultivating the impression of power. Reagan is among the most skillful of chief executives at knowing how to cut his losses and move deftly to what has become an inevitable outcome and then claiming it as *his* victory. In 1982, for example, Reagan had opposed a tax increase, but both houses and both parties in Congress forced a tax increase on him. Ultimately, he embraced it and took credit for it, holding a victory celebration in the Rose Garden. In 1985, Reagan resisted sanctions against South Africa, but rather than being overriden if he vetoed a congressional sanctions bill, he instituted his own milder sanctions. In the Philippine policy switch, Reagan bowed to pressure and then baldly proclaimed victory for a new policy of opposing dictators of both right and left, as if he had intended that all along.

In short, power depends heavily on the illusion of power. Presidents—past, present, and future—have less power than the country images, but the successful ones convey the impression of power and get reputations as strong presidents by playing down their problems and trumpeting their few clear victories.

Fred Dutton, a White House adviser to President Kennedy and a keen student of politics ever since, made the point to me that there is far less purpose and grand design to what goes on inside the White

House than most people assume. That lesson from Kennedy's time is still valid today, and will be in the future.

"Washington isn't all that thought out," Dutton remarked. "So much of it is improvisation. Too much rationality and planning can be attributed to it. Much of it is trying something, taking a pratfall, and then looking either bad or good when you do. The really shrewd players have their eyes out for the big chance. There are always a lot of cerebral people writing lots of memos to presidents or senators: *Do This, Do That.* But the constant activist cannot bring high drama to events. The constant activist loses perspective. I've got to give Reagan credit for having certain values to guide him. But like the others, he seizes opportunities. And look at the things he lets go by. You've got to do that. You've got to float above events."[17]

The president and players in the power game are like surfers riding the waves of power. Sometimes they are careening at top speed before some giant wave; sometimes they are coasting slowly, looking for a crest. Their success depends on avoiding the thundering surf around them. From time to time, they may have to make those agile sideward shifts that enable the most skilled surfers to escape being crashed beneath the waves. Sometimes they will fall and quickly mount their boards to ride a new crest triumphantly. From the distance on shore, the best surfers appear to have uncanny balance, ever gliding and in control.

"It's a stylistic thing," Dutton said. "Both Kennedy and Reagan have ridden the thing with grace. To look at the presidency purely in terms of congressional wins and losses is a mistake. There's much more to it that that. It's a matter of grace, of looking like you're handling it. I used to think that being an actor was the worst possible background for a president, but it turns out that it's a good background. A president has to keep up appearances to protect his power."

4. *Porcupine Power: The Politics of Being Prickly*

The key is to be a porcupine—have a reputation for being difficult.

—Christopher Matthews, speaker's spokesman

On the political stump, North Carolina's Senator Jesse Helms projects the folksy style of the antebellum South; he's full of stories about ninety-two-year-old Miss Ellie blessing him for fighting for school prayer or grandfathers surprised by how tall he is. With an owlish glance through his horn-rimmed glasses, he can mix homespun anec-dotes with righteous tirades against world Communism and he can paint himself as the innocent defender of freedom victimized by a biased, malicious big media.

In the Senate, his manners are courtly. But his parliamentary tech-niques are telling and crafty. Helms plays the politics of confrontation: stalling, filibustering with marathon speeches, tying the Senate up in knots, frustrating others to achieve his own ends. His aides have proudly nicknamed him Senator No. Helms represents another basic kind of power in Washington: the power of obstruction, a negative power, the power to block and deny, the power of being difficult and prickly. Some call it porcupine power.

Partisan Democrats such as Joseph Biden of Delaware rail against

Helms, but they acknowledge his power and his skill at the tactics of legislative guerrilla warfare. "Helms is the master," was Biden's frank appraisal. "He's the toughest. He's the smartest. He is the three hundred-pound gorilla of the right wing, the godfather of the right-wing network. He's the architect of this notion that if you plant enough cells out there, the revolution will go on."[1]

It was typical of Helms, in October 1983, to protest stormily when most other Republicans and practically all Democrats favored a bill declaring a federal holiday in honor of Martin Luther King, Jr. Howard Baker, then the Senate majority leader, and even strong conservatives such as Idaho's Jim McClure, urged Helms not to provoke a painful and futile battle. Their vote counts showed the measure would pass easily, and they argued that a losing donnybrook on such a racially sensitive issue would only hurt the Republican party nationwide. They asked Helms to play his opposition low key; he ignored them.

On October 4, Helms launched a filibuster to shelve the Martin Luther King bill. Hoping to scotch the embarrassment to Republicans, Howard Baker moved to kill Helms's filibuster, and President Reagan announced he was ready to sign the bill. The next day, Helms dropped the filibuster. But two weeks later, he tried to derail the legislation with four amendments and sharp accusations that secret FBI files would show King's "association with far-left elements and elements in the Communist Party, U.S.A." New York Democrat Daniel Patrick Moynihan threw a bound copy of Helms's charges on the floor, denouncing its contents as "filth" and "obscenities." Ted Kennedy of Massachusetts accused Helms of a reckless "smear campaign" to revive "vestiges of old hatreds." The House had already passed the bill; broad bipartisan support swept it through the Senate, 78–22, leaving other Republicans grumbling about Helms.

But the champion of the New Right knew what he was doing. He had gotten big press play, especially back in North Carolina where polls showed him trailing Democratic Governor Jim Hunt who was out to take away Helms's Senate seat in the 1984 election. Democrat Bill Bradley of New Jersey accused Helms of "playing up to 'old Jim Crow' " back home. Helms and his staff denied the charge. "That had nothing to do with black versus white," one Helms aide insisted to me. "Senator Helms's point was that if you want a black holiday, why pick a black with a background that includes some possible Communist connections." But the reaction back home indicated Bradley was on the mark. When Helms went home after his anti-King maneuver, lily-white crowds cheered him at truck stops and his poll standings turned upward.

"It was a substantial turning point in the campaign," commented Farrell Guillory of the Raleigh *News & Observer.* "The racial cue had great resonance in the state among voters who had not made up their minds."[2]

This was Jesse Helms juicing up his power and appeal with the politics of confrontation. His political base in North Carolina and around the country is his passionate right-wing following and his organizational network. What galvanizes that movement and gives him power leverage in Washington is his calculated practice of the politics of obstruction. Helms has a variety of maneuvers: filibusters, delaying amendments, putting his personal "hold" on legislation so that it cannot be brought up for a vote, or stalling appointments for months on end.

On the Martin Luther King holiday, it did not matter to Helms's strategy that he was doomed to lose the Senate vote. He was playing to the grandstand—trying to fire up his reelection effort. At other times, he has tried to instill fear and caution in the State Department, kill the nominations of ideological foes, bargain for something he wants by taking other senators' bills hostage, or pressuring the Reagan administration to follow the "true conservative faith." Blocking, stalling, and rejecting are the tactics and tools of this brand of power.

Certainly, Helms has no monopoly on porcupine power. There are many subcommittees and fiefdoms all over Capitol Hill—narrow legislative gates through which bills must pass, little sluiceways where the politician in charge of that power station determines just how much money will flow over his part of the federal dam. This is power based on controlling turf, and the favorite chokepoints of turf politicians are the appropriations subcommittees in both houses, which get first crack at deciding how much money gets spent on everything.

For nearly four years, for example, the most powerful figure in Congress on aid to El Salvador was an obscure, eccentric old curmudgeon, a Maryland Democrat named Clarence Long. After "Doc" Long's son served in Vietnam, the congressman became a dove on foreign policy and a strong advocate of human rights. As chairman of the House Appropriations Subcommittee on Foreign Operations, often able to cast the deciding vote, Long regularly extracted pledges from the Reagan administration to take some action against Salvadoran rights abuses, especially the death squads. That was the price for his support. Long would stall legislation and bargain. To get on Long's good side, the administration tried to placate him, once going so far as to persuade the Salvadoran government to name a local Salvadoran school for Long. Year after year, Long practiced the power of obstruction, until he lost his seat in 1984.

According to Christopher Matthews, an experienced legislative aide, the key to the game of negative blocking power is a willingness to offend your colleagues. It requires a purposeful crankiness, especially in the closing days of a legislative session, when time is short. The ideal settings for legislative orneriness are the House and Senate conference committees formed to reconcile the differences in legislation passed by the two houses. Conference committees must produce a single version accepted by a majority of the conferees or else the legislation dies. The bargaining can be tough.

"The key is to be a porcupine—have a reputation for being difficult," Matthews told me. "Don't have a reputation for being a nice guy—that won't do you any good. Everybody knows that the most effective conferees are porcupines. I worked for [former Senate Budget Committee Chairman] Ed Muskie for three years. He was the best of them all, the absolute best, because nobody wanted to tangle with him. You know, why tangle with the guy? Why ruin your day? Most people are generally utilitarian; they try to achieve the greater happiness. So why spend your day being miserable? And Muskie will make you miserable, because he'll outwit you. He'll be gross. He'll smoke a god-awful cigar. He'll just be difficult, cantankerous. That's one of the tricks of being a successful conferee."

"That is why Muskie wrote more legislation than most guys will ever write," Matthews went on. "You know, clean air, countercyclical assistance to communities, public-works-style stuff, and budget resolutions. It's all because he was an extremely difficult guy to deal with, and people would just sort of walk around him, ignore him, try to avoid fights with him. In other words, at the margin, you tend to give the guy slack. . . . I think a bad temper is a very powerful political tool because most people don't like confrontation."[3]

In the late 1950s, Oklahoma's Bob Kerr had a reputation as a senator who got his way by effective bullying, even more than Lyndon Johnson did as majority leader. Nowadays, John Dingell, the pile-driving chairman of the House Energy and Commerce Committee, and Dan Rostenkowski, the relentless chairman of the House Ways and Means Committee, are known for facing down or wearing down more tender souls. Porcupine power also pays a premium for patience when others are in a hurry.

"Muskie's great strength was that he never left the [conference] room," Matthews recalled. "I mean he *never* went to the bathroom. He'd go in at nine o'clock and stay until one. Everybody else was getting hungry. If there was a photo opportunity, congressmen and senators would come in and out, get their pictures taken, say a few things and leave. Muskie would stay—right? That's a great strength. You've got to decide whether you're there to get your picture taken or you're there to get the bill passed. He's there to get the bill passed—*his way*! And if you're hungry and he's not, all the better. He'll wait until one o'clock and if you want to go eat at twelve, fine, leave a proxy. He'll take your proxy, and he'll finish at one-thirty, and he'll have his resolution then."

On the Senate floor, the prime tactic of negative power players is using filibusters or controversial amendments to bog down legislation. Practically every senator occasionally uses such dodges to stop bills he considers anathema. The practice dates back to such legendary masters of legislative blockades as Louisiana's Huey Long, Mississippi's Theodore Bilbo, and Alabama's Jim Allen. It has become much more common in the new power game with its independent-minded players. The Senate is vulnerable to such paralyzing tactics because its rules and procedures are so much looser than those of the House, guaranteeing unlimited debate unless cloture, or a cutoff, is voted by three fifths of the Senate.

When reform-minded senators have tried to change the rules to limit debate and make the Senate more efficient, Helms has led the fight to preserve the old rules granting individual senators maximum leeway against the majority. Helms also used old-fashioned seniority to protect his power. After voluntarily relinquishing his position as ranking Republican on the Foreign Relations Committee in 1985, in order to serve as Agriculture Committee chairman, Helms demanded his ranking post on Foreign Relations back in 1987. In the interim, Dick Lugar of Indiana had been a popular and effective Foreign Relations Committee chairman, and the committee Republicans wanted him to stay on. But Helms appealed to the Senate Republican Conference, all forty-six Republican senators, and won back his position on seniority alone. Enough other Republican senators were fearful of being ousted by abler, younger senators unless they banded together—another example of Helms's politics of obstructing change.

As a Republican gadfly, Jesse Helms has a match on the Democratic side—Howard Metzenbaum, the silver-haired millionaire liberal Ohio businessman whose pet peeve is special breaks for special business interests.

Metzenbaum's most celebrated campaign was his prolonged but vain effort to block President Reagan's nomination of Ed Meese as attorney general. In 1981, Metzenbaum's most stunning filibuster cut in half the multibillion-dollar tax break being granted to independent oil producers. But what has made him a target of his colleagues' scorn—Senator Ted Stevens of Alaska once publicly called him "a pain in the ass"—are Metzenbaum's "watchdog filibusters" in the closing crush of a session. By that time, floor action is like a rugby scrum, everyone pumping through special bills for favored constituents when no one else has time to study the contents. Metzenbaum, a seventy-year-old self-appointed watchdog for taxpayers, maintains a vigil on the floor to block the most egregious favoritism. If Metzenbaum's filibuster is overruled, he switches to strangling bills by amendment. Tenacity is a key to his power, as it is with Helms.

In the lame-duck session of 1982, Metzenbaum later boasted, he blocked twenty-six separate "giveaways to special interests" that would have cost the U.S. Treasury more than $10 billion.[4] Stevens was enraged by Metzenbaum's blocking the sale of a federal railroad to Alaska. Other senators were rankled because Metzenbaum halted lucrative bills that, among other things, would have granted antitrust immunity to the beer and shipping industries and the National Football League, permitted large timber companies to cancel more than $2 billion of government contracts they wanted to escape, made major changes in bankruptcy law; leased oil shale lands, and removed physicians and other professionals from oversight by the Federal Trade Commission. Metzenbaum says he would like to give up his obstructionist game but the unruliness of the Senate leaves him no choice.

Metzenbaum got indirect confirmation from Timothy Wirth, a Colorado Democrat who won a Senate seat in 1986 after serving six terms in the House. In just one month, Wirth told me, he concluded that Senate procedures encourage the negative power game. "In the House, you learn how to get something done by putting together a coalition, counting votes and getting legislation passed," Wirth said. "But in the Senate, people's power arises from their ability to say no, their power to block anything. The people who are really good at legislating are good at knowing how to threaten the use of negative power."[5]

Helms and Jackson: Mirror Images

In the broader political arena, the confrontational politics of Jesse
Helms were paralleled in some ways by those of Jesse Jackson in the
1984 presidential campaign. For Helms and Jackson have worked as
highly symbolic politicians who gain power and leverage by mobilizing
a minority within their own party, and keeping it stirred up, often to
the exasperation of their party leaders. Their philosophies are radically
different, but their tactics have been similar in leading mass movements: Jackson, the blacks; and Helms, the hard right. Just as Helms
angered other Senate Republicans with his attack on the Martin Luther King holiday, Jackson gave heartburn to Democratic party leaders
in 1984 by pitching his campaign at black voters and black pride,
causing a backlash among white voters that later hurt Democratic
presidential nominee Walter Mondale, especially in the South. In the
1988 campaign, Jackson played a more traditional style of politics,
trying to broaden his appeal. But in 1984, Jackson, like Helms, played
an antimainstream strategy.

When party leaders have tried to placate or negotiate with Helms
or Jackson, it has rarely worked. For the porcupine power game depends on being the odd man out, not on building coalitions. In that
game, the battle is usually more important than the victory because the
battle keeps the movement alive and aroused. Helms and Jackson
typically battle for their share of the spoils, using their popular leverage
against their own party leaders. In that game, power stems from drama-
tizing the Cause, forcing new showdowns, stirring again and again the
emotional dynamic of their movement, and in Helms's case, in touching those predictably sensitive nerves that trigger a new flow of financial
contributions. In confrontational politics, there is little incentive to
compromise. For compromising with the power structure dilutes the
force of the symbolic leader's appeal to his most ardent partisans.

In another sense, Jesse Helms has become the 1980's political cult
figure of the right, to replace Senator Edward Kennedy, the 1970's cult
figure of the left. Kennedy had great influence with other congressional
Democrats. His legislative staff network reached into many committees, touching many issues. With the Kennedy family cachet, he could
help other Democrats, and they clustered around him. When Kennedy
moved on an issue, others moved with him, especially as he challenged
Jimmy Carter in 1979 and 1980. The failure of Kennedy's bid for the
presidential nomination, and the defeat of several liberal Democratic

senators in 1980, caused the Kennedy movement to ebb.

In almost mirror image, Helms has been to Reagan as Kennedy was to Carter, except that Helms was smart enough not to tackle Reagan directly. But Helms has been the keeper of the ideological flame, riding partisan shotgun as the "genuine conservative," just as Kennedy had cast himself as the "genuine Democrat" against Carter's watered-down version. Each tried to hold his president's feet to the fire, to bring the president back to the true gospel. The role is well-known in American politics; other presidents have had purists on their flanks: Dwight Eisenhower had Senator Robert A. Taft; Franklin Roosevelt had Henry Wallace. If Ted Kennedy thought Carter was too tightfisted to be a true Democrat, then Helms and company clamored that Rasputins in the White House were poisoning Reagan's pure conservatism. "Let Reagan be Reagan!" they chanted.

Helms's political apparatus is far more structured and extensive than was Kennedy's, and it has given extra muscle to Helms's obstructionist politics. In the Senate, Helms made himself the moving force of the Steering Committee, an informal, secretive band of fifteen to twenty conservative Republicans who lunch weekly on Tuesdays. Their committee has no official standing but it has gained clout by its members' working together, hiring an effective staff, and using filibusters and their senatorial rights to "hold" legislation and appointments. In the Reagan years, Helms's hard core became known as the 4-H Club: Helms, Orrin Hatch of Utah, Gordon Humphrey of New Hampshire, and Chic Hecht of Nevada. Other steering committee regulars were Steve Symms and Jim McClure of Idaho, Malcolm Wallop of Wyoming, Don Nickles of Oklahoma, Robert Kasten of Wisconsin, Jake Garn of Utah, and until they left the Senate in 1986, Jeremiah Denton of Alabama and John East of North Carolina.

An equally potent element of the Helms apparatus is the network of sharply partisan conservative congressional staffers, known as the Madison Group. They are orchestrated by a pudgy, boyish-looking, and politically ingenious attorney from South Carolina named John Carbaugh. Staffers such as Michael Pillsbury, David Sullivan, Margot Carlisle, Quentin Crommelin, Angelo Cordevilla, Debbie DeMoss, and Jim Lucier have often pushed Steering Committee senators to take action. Some of these staff aides joined the Reagan administration, formed a network inside government, and fed information—often classified—to those still on Senate staffs. By publicizing what they saw as Soviet violations of arms treaties, the Madison Group activists put pressure on Secretary of State Shultz and President Reagan to take a

tougher line toward Moscow. Through cleverly coordinated moves
inside and outside the administration, they maneuvered the government into covertly shipping Stinger antitank weapons to Jonas Savimbi,
the Angolan rebel leader.

The core of Helms's North Carolina apparatus is the Congressional
Club, widely regarded as the second most potent fund-raising apparatus
in the country after the Republican Party. Using commercial companies it spawned, the Congressional Club pulls in millions for Helms-
endorsed candidates and causes. Its peak effort produced the most
expensive campaign in Senate history, Helms's $16.4 million reelection
campaign in 1984, a fund-raising feat that caused Howard Baker to call
Helms "the Nelson Rockefeller of political fund-raising."

In Washington, Helms is the godfather of a large network of right-
wing organizations. He inspired the National Conservative Political
Action Committee, a multimillion-dollar PAC which targets liberal
and some moderate politicians nationwide with blistering negative
advertising campaigns. He was a guiding spirit for the Conservative
Caucus and Young Americans for Freedom and a founding father of
the Council on National Policy, the secretive right-wing answer to the
eastern establishment's Council on Foreign Relations. He has his own
bevy of think tanks, The Institute of American Relations (IAR), the
Center for a Free Society, the Institute on Money and Inflation, and
the American Family Institute, as well as a couple of tax-exempt lobbying groups, the IAR Foreign Affairs Council and the Congressional
Club Foundation.

This political machinery has given Helms the ability to mobilize
support to put pressure on others in government, much as mass lobbies
do. "Jesse Helms would never have done as well with his issues without
being able to trigger mail writing and phone calls," observed Chris
Dodd, the Democratic senator from Connecticut. "If Jesse hasn't
convinced you, there's the thought of all those people he can activate."[6]

Others contend that the tail of the Helms apparatus has been wag-
ging the dog and that Helms sometimes has to stir up filibusters and
make big publicity plays, like the Martin Luther King episode, to raise
funds in order to keep his huge apparatus well financed. When Helms,
Don Nickles, and James East forced the Senate to stay in session nearly
to Christmas Eve 1982 by filibustering a bill imposing a gasoline tax
to finance highway improvements, they infuriated other senators. The
normally mild-mannered Republican Whip Alan Simpson denounced
them for an "obdurate and obnoxious performance." The bill passed,

with Helms ridiculed by his colleagues as "Senator Grinch." No matter; Helms's gambit played well with his home crowd and produced a new flow of dollars for his network.

Howard Baker, an aide told me, ventured privately to his staff that Helms had "become a prisoner of the monster apparatus he created," because he constantly needed new issues to keep the donations flowing into the Congressional Club and his foundations. "The question is: Does Jesse Helms run the Congressional Club or does the Congressional Club run him?" one Baker lieutenant said to me. "They thrive on unresolved issues or issues where they can make a big fuss even when they cannot win."

A key objective of Helms's porcupine politics has been to press and harass the Reagan administration into a more aggressively anti-Communist foreign policy, especially to promote guerrilla wars against Marxist regimes in Afghanistan, Nicaragua, and Angola. At a roast in Helms's honor for his sixty-fourth birthday in 1985, Senator Dole called Helms "the Rambo of the Geritol set," playing on the gun-toting, anti-Soviet heroism of the movie *Rambo*. The roast fell on the very night that President Reagan was returning triumphantly from his 1985 summit meeting with Soviet leader Mikhail Gorbachev—a meeting that the right-wing crowd had adamantly opposed. At the Helms dinner, their mood was conveyed in the toastmaster's quip that as door prizes, Helms would pass out copies of "George Shultz's Summit Cookbook: Forty Ways to Eat Crow."

Sometimes, Helms has tried to run his own independent foreign policy, accusing Shultz of being duped by an appeasement-minded Foreign Service and suggesting that even Casey's CIA suffered from "pro-Soviet bias" on arms issues.

When Helms was chairman of the Senate Agriculture Committee in 1985, he sought a personal showdown with the Russians over the case of Miroslav Medved, a Soviet seaman who tried to defect from a Soviet freighter unloading grain near New Orleans. After Medved was examined by American doctors and told them he had changed his mind and now wanted to go home, the White House was prepared to close the incident. But Helms was far from satisfied. He charged Medved was being held against his will. Helms issued a subpoena for Medved and sent a personal emissary, David Sullivan, to serve the subpoena and order Medved to appear in Washington. The Soviet freighter captain refused to let Sullivan on board.

The whole Helms gambit was extraordinary: an Agricultural Committee chairman usurping the normal functions of the State Department or the attorney general. A few weeks later, Secretary Shultz, in a burst of frustration, exploded at a Helms aide during a reception that his senator was a "constitutional ignoramus," implying that Helms did not know what he was doing.

In fact, Helms usually knows precisely what he is after. He just plays a very different game from most senators. Their game is pushing programs, passing legislation, making compromises. Helms's game is the opposite: stalling action or provoking filibusters by making proposals sure to infuriate liberals such as Lowell Weicker of Connecticut and generally gumming up the works.

"Any time they wanted to put a stick in the spokes, Helms would throw in an abortion amendment or a prayer-in-schools amendment, and Lowell Weicker would stand up and solemnly declare he was going to filibuster the rest of his life on this issue," Howard Baker told me one morning. "To tell you the truth, Jesse Helms is a much-maligned politician from a senatorial standpoint because, more than most, if you had to do something for the sake of the Senate or the country or the party, and you went to Jesse, you could cut a deal. . . . Sometimes it took months. Sometimes I had to let it languish there for months, as in some State Department appointments."7

Helms's favorite weapon against Shultz and the State Department has been the legislative "hold," a senatorial courtesy which allows a single senator to delay action on some presidential appointment if he has personal objections. Most senators use the "hold" sparingly, generally when they have not had a chance to meet the nominee or attend a confirmation hearing and want more time. Helms uses it constantly.

In 1981, Helms pressed for a "housecleaning in the Asia bureau" of the State Department and put a five-month hold on a former associate of Henry Kissinger's to force replacement of two other officials. The Kissinger network is a special Helms target; Helms hated Kissinger's promotion of détente with Moscow. In 1982, Helms put such a long hold on two senior Reagan appointees to the Arms Control and Disarmament Agency that their names were eventually withdrawn. In June 1985, Helms put a hold on twenty-nine ambassadorial and high-level appointments by Shultz to try to force six of his own favorites into ambassadorial spots. From July to November, he held up the appointment of a new ambassador to China: Winston Lord, another former Kissinger aide and former president of the Council on Foreign Relations. Helms did not relent until the administration paid his price: pledging not to funnel economic aid to China through the United Nations for a birth-control program that included forced abortions.

Helms and Metzenbaum know that these tactics so anger their colleagues that they face retaliation whenever they want something. They are both usually careful not to offer much that can be held hostage by others. Indeed, Helms's guerrilla strategy left him ill suited as Agriculture Committee chairman for the vital task of lining up votes in both parties to pass farm legislation. He had to lean on Bob Dole, an expert craftsman of compromises and coalition-builder.

"Howard and Jesse are the skilled of the skilled, and both of them carry very few identifiable legislative bills," remarked Alan Simpson, the Republican whip. "I can tell you that other senators go hunting with passion for the bills that Helms or Metzenbaum want. They say, 'Well, Howard held me up,' or 'It came to the end and he stopped me,' or 'Jesse held me up. What have they got? What do they want? I want to go find it. I want to trash it. I want to filibuster it.' And there's not much there. It's just a few vapor trails going through the sky."[8]

But occasionally, other senators spot and grasp at those vapor trails. One example: In early 1986, Helms was pushing a protege, James Malone, for ambassador to Belize. After a long tussle, Shultz nominated Malone only to have two Democrats, John Kerry of Massachusetts and Ed Zorinsky of Nebraska, fight the appointment. They asserted that Malone had "falsely testified" to the Senate Foreign Relations Committee about some of his past dealings, and they implied there had been a conflict of interest in his relations with former clients while he held a State Department post. The committee blocked Malone's nomination, the first such action in this century. Helms squawked that he had been sabotaged by an "anti-Reagan faction" in the State Department, but eventually he had to give up on Malone.

So finally, the porcupine politician met porcupine power on the other side. But not without demonstrating many times that power can derive not only from mustering majorities to pass legislation, but also from the simple ability of a tenacious and cantankerous senator to withhold what large majorities want.

5. The Power Loop: Narrow Access vs. Widening the Circle

There's that old line about flattery . . . it's all right if you don't inhale it, and the pomp and circumstance of public office is like that.[1]

—Former Defense Secretary Elliott Richardson

Robert Strauss is an archetypal Washington figure—never elected to national office, but supremely successful as a power broker. He was national chairman of the Democratic party in its dark days after the debacle of George McGovern's 1972 presidential campaign; he was President Carter's political tutor, Middle East negotiator, special trade representative, and finally, chairman of Carter's unsuccessful 1980 campaign. In spite of his partisanship, Strauss, now a wealthy, silver-haired lawyer, has been nimble enough to stay close to high Republicans and to be tapped for bipartisan commissions by President Reagan. He is a favorite of both press and other politicians because of his political yarns and the irreverent humor he turns on himself and other politicians. Strauss is a high-stakes political player who knows the ins and outs of the power game and can laugh at them even while he's playing the game.

"You know, power is an interesting thing," Strauss grinned at me one day, his face flushed with a mid-winter Florida tan. "I used to think political power was going to a political dinner. And then I thought political power was helping *put on* a political dinner. And then I thought it was being invited to stay at the candidate's hotel in a convention city. And then I used to stand in the hall outside of Sam Rayburn's suite at the political convention, and I thought that was something. And then I got to go into the living room of the candidate's suite, and I thought *that* was something. And then I found out there that the decisions were all made back in the bedroom. And finally, I was invited in the bedroom with the last eight or ten fellas, and then I knew I was on the inside—until I finally learned that they stepped into the john. In the end, just me and Jimmy Carter and Hamilton Jordan made the final decision in the john."[2]

The moral of Strauss's story is one that politicians live by. It is an element of continuity in politics unaffected by the new power game, for among all the yardsticks that Washington has for measuring power, access is primary. That is the law of organizational politics everywhere, more important probably in Washington than elsewhere because influence and persuasion are the currency of the Washington power game. A president cannot reward his top aides with handsome salaries, annual bonuses, or stock options. There is no profit-and-loss statement, no annual output of widgets to measure; that gives diamond value to access. It is both a channel for doing business and a symbol of trust and importance. It is a privilege to be treasured or a right to be jealously protected.

In Strauss's story, the president was at the center of the access maze. But access counts at all levels, in all power pyramids and networks: Congress, Pentagon, Federal Reserve Board, Supreme Court, White House. To politicians, lobbyists, lawyers, journalists, staff aides, and high-level policymakers, access is bread and butter. There is always another circle of power to penetrate; access is the open door, the answered phone call, a couple of minutes with a key player in a corridor or committee room. The pressures of time make access precious; it spells the chance to talk to people who make decisions, draft programs, write legislation. Without it, your case doesn't get heard; you can't be a player in the power game. Obviously that's why corporations, unions, and lobbyists of all sorts pay enormous fees for prestigious Washington lawyers or pump millions into campaigning: They are buying access, if not more.

But access in the power game is not merely physical; it is mental, too. It is not only entry to the inner sanctum; it is being in the power loop—being chosen to receive the most sensitive information, as fresh grist for the policy struggle. Being "cut out" on information, or being "blindsided" as the power lingo has it, can be crippling.

People who think they deserve to be included, some at the very highest levels, are deeply embittered when access is denied, and often its absence is a serious omen. During Gerald Ford's brief presidency, for example, the bad blood between Vice President Nelson Rockefeller and White House Chief of Staff Donald Rumsfeld was an open secret. Rumsfeld kept watch over who went into the Oval Office. That nettled Rockefeller. As the 1976 election approached, frictions mounted because Rockefeller was left in the dark about whether Ford wanted him as a running mate. Separately and privately, Ford and Rockefeller took political soundings about the upcoming campaign with Clifford White, who had masterminded Barry Goldwater's 1964 campaign.

"Nelson would talk to me every once in awhile and get me to pass messages to Ford," White told me. "I'd ride on his private plane back to New York, and we'd talk, mostly politics. He'd raise some issue and say, 'You know, you ought to tell the president that.' He left the impression that he wanted the message passed along, and he was having trouble doing it himself. He was very angry at Rumsfeld because he felt Rumsfeld was blocking him out. Having used staff to protect himself, Rockefeller knew how staff could keep others away. I told Rumsfeld about it, and his response was that Rockefeller should just ask for an appointment. But Nelson did not feel that as vice president, he should have to make appointments to see the president."[3] (An old problem for American vice presidents, one which foreshadowed Ford's later decision to pick another running mate.)

In the Reagan years, Jim Baker, as chief of staff, took care of Vice President Bush. He had run Bush's campaign in 1980, and he wanted to assure Bush clear access to Reagan. So, Baker arranged a private weekly luncheon between Reagan and Bush, with no one else present. It was a rich plum for Bush.

"The president really enjoyed the Bush relationship because he'd sound off on a lot of things to George," a Californian close to Reagan told me. Bush used the weekly luncheon as a vital channel for giving Reagan confidential advice (among other things, I was told, urging Reagan to travel to China in 1984 and to move quickly in 1985 toward a summit meeting with Soviet leader Mikhail Gorbachev). It was also a vital symbol for buttressing Bush's claim—especially to the Republican right wing—that he is the rightful heir to the Reagan mantle in 1988.

Some cabinet officials wangled private sessions with Reagan through subterfuges, to get around the palace guard, the top White House staff.

Attorney General William French Smith and CIA Director William Casey were especially aggressive, citing their need to report privately to Reagan on national security matters, though White House aides suspected them of doing other business, too. "It was important to them and their staffs for them to be seen meeting with the President as often as possible," one Reagan confidant remarked. "So they would think up inane reasons."

This may sound like Trivial Pursuit, but something much more important than ego trips or displays of importance is involved. Access, especially the exclusive access that blindsides other players in the policy game, is a trump card. Access to the president means involvement in major actions and decisions. It is especially important with a president like Reagan with whom policy is affected by who talks to him last—as his top policy advisers have learned from experience. But that kind of access matters in every presidency. Listen to George Reedy, White House press secretary to Lyndon Johnson:

"For . . . White House assistants there is only one fixed goal in life. It is somehow to gain and maintain access to the president. This is a process which resembles nothing else known in the world except possibly the Japanese game of *Go*, a contest in which there are very few fixed rules and the playing consists of laying down alternating counters in patterns that permit flexibility but seek to deny that flexibility to the opponent. The success of the player depends upon the whim of the president. Consequently, the president's psychology is studied minutely, and a working day in the White House is marked by innumerable probes to determine which routes to the Oval Room are open and which end in a blind alley."[4]

Reedy could have extended his comment to cabinet members. Under Reagan, Secretary of State George Shultz insisted on private weekly meetings with the president, and high Pentagon officials accused him of using these private sessions to sell Reagan on questionable policy moves. On one occasion, I was told, Shultz blindsided both Casey and Weinberger by getting Reagan's approval for Shultz to undertake a diplomatic mission to Nicaragua on June 1, 1984. On another occasion, Shultz angered the Pentagon by persuading Reagan to endorse a draft communiqué for the 1985 summit meeting with Gorbachev. Similarly, Donald Regan, as chief of staff, used his one-on-one access with the president in early October 1985 to sell Reagan on the Gramm-Rudman budget-balancing scheme before Shultz and Weinberger could warn Reagan of the jeopardy to Reagan's military buildup.

On a less exalted plane, few things inspired more wild jealousy among lobbyists than Michael Deaver's privilege, after leaving the Reagan White House in 1985, of keeping his White House security pass and getting a daily copy of President Reagan's schedule. Those two perks—symbols of his continued links to the president—were probably worth millions of dollars to Deaver from clients who wanted to buy his access to Reagan. But there was such a public furor about Deaver's access being excessive and improper that he had to surrender his privileges.

Politicians, bureaucrats, and lobbyists covet tokens of access and influence the way Eagle scouts collect merit badges. Senior White House officials scheme and fume over the location of their offices, their parking places, where they ride on *Air Force One,* and whether they have "POTUS phones"—direct lines to the president of the United States (POTUS). Only cabinet secretaries, the Joint Chiefs of Staff, and half a dozen other officials qualify for "porthole to porthole"—daily door-to-door chauffeur service. Other high officials on an A list and a B list, divided by rank, can order government cars for official business.

Three or four top White House officials can have lunch served in their offices by Filipino mess boys, dressed like Yale Whiffenpoofs in blue blazers and gray charcoal slacks. The others, in descending order of rank, can eat in:

1. the executive mess
2. the regular White House mess, or
3. the overflow board room.

There are only slight differences in menu; the decor and the dining compartments convey the pecking order. Only about twenty out of probably two thousand people who work in the Office of the President can use the White House gym. And Jimmy Carter himself decided who could use the tennis court on the South Lawn.

But the size and location of one's office is the main badge of status and a prime indicator of access. In any heirarchy—business, university, or military service—one's office is an important symbol of rank and eminence; in the White House power game, it has acute significance. Proximity to power is crucial for both real and symbolic reasons. Only those closest at hand can readily walk into the Oval Office or be quickly summoned.

However, as most tourists are probably amazed to discover (I was), the White House is pretty small. Only the cream of the power elite can fit into about a dozen well-appointed offices on the first and second floors of the West Wing. In that highly prized terrain, the territorial imperative is as powerful as in the jungle. Most people in the Office of the President do not have offices in the White House; they work across the street in a handsome, baroque structure that was once the State Department and is now known as old Executive Office Building (EOB).

"People will kill to get an office in the West Wing," Mike Deaver told me while he was still Reagan's closest personal aide. "You'll see people working in closets, tucked back in a corner, rather than taking a huge office with a fireplace in the EOB. God help you if you're suddenly moved to the fourth floor of the EOB because that's death row, as they call it over there. That means you're on the way out."[5]

Deaver and I were sitting in his office, adjoining the Oval Office. It is a room handsomely furnished with antiques, several oil paintings by Childe Hassam, a fireplace, and its own private patio. President Carter had made it his study, but Reagan had turned it over to Deaver, the trusted aide he wanted nearest to him. By Deaver's account, the president had taken him into the study after the inauguration ceremonies in 1981.

"I want you to have this office," Reagan told Deaver.

"I can't do that," Deaver demurred. "Where are you going to go if you want to get away?"

Reagan smiled and gestured toward the Oval Office, visible through the open door connecting the two rooms.

"I've been trying to get that round office in there for the last fourteen years," he said. "Why would I want to get away?"

The Access Itch

When the president travels, the "access itch," the urge to be physically close to the president, becomes acute. The fewer people who can fit into a plane, a helicopter, a presidential limousine, the more competitive the inner circle becomes.

"Who rides in the limousine with the president is very important," Deaver said, shaking his head. "People sit on each other's laps. I finally had to make a rule that you couldn't put any more than three people in the president's limousine if the motorcade took more than ten minutes, because the president winds up all scrunched up.

"Jim Baker would always want to be in there as chief of staff. If [then–presidential counselor] Ed Meese was along, he would want to be in there. But if you landed in some state, you had the governor, two United States senators, the mayor, maybe you had a congressman. And you had to do it just from a protocol standpoint—and that would be the governor, who outranks everybody else in the state, and one staff member, and that was usually Baker, and if he wasn't along, it was me."[6]

Long trips touch off a power scramble for choice seating on *Air Force One*, which carries only about twenty officials; nearly half of the plane's forty seats are assigned to Secret Service agents and a press pool. Simply traveling in high-echelon quarters of *Air Force One* is a heady experience for many politicians and visitors. Coming back from an economic summit meeting in Canada aboard *Air Force One* for an interview with Reagan, I remember being impressed by the high-backed luxury-style seats, the fancy service by Navy stewards in blazers, and by having a telephone plugged into the arm of my seat and a signal corps operator asking, "Where would you like to call, sir?" Mentally, I imagined the click of military heels coming to attention at the other end of the line. Like an overawed tourist, I scooped up souvenirs: matchboxes, napkins, swizzle sticks, any item embossed with the presidential seal.

Little tokens of status and power become enormously important to people who live in this hothouse power environment. Some officials squabble over choice seats near the president's cabin. Equally important to some high officials is being seen at the president's side as he gets off the plane. By protocol, only the president and Mrs. Reagan were to use the front exit; everyone else was to use the rear exit. But the TV cameras and welcoming parties were at the front, and the most perk-and-publicity-conscious officials—press spokesman Larry Speakes; Dick Darman, a top presidential aide; National Security Adviser Bill Clark—would violate protocol and get off the front, ahead of the president rather than exit from the rear.

"We tried to temper it by saying that the only person off the front of the plane is the president, or the president and Mrs. Reagan, or Reagan and Secretary Shultz," said Bill Sitman, a Deaver aide whose job was to manage travel arrangements. "You'd see people have a fit. They didn't want to get off from the back door of the plane. After all, what's the point of being on *Air Force One* if people don't see you get off the front of *Air Force One* with the president? Larry Speakes would get off the front; Dick Darman would do it; Bill Clark would always go off the front—he couldn't find the back of the plane if his life depended on it. Senators, congressmen—they'd always get off the plane up front before the president."[7]

The proximity crush becomes far more intense when the president travels on his *Marine One* helicopter. It is a huge Sikorsky VH-3D, but packed with communications gear, it has only ten seats, five taken up by a doctor, Secret Service agents, and military and personal aides to the president. With Mrs. Reagan on board, that left only three empty seats, normally assigned to the chief of staff, the national security adviser, and Speakes or another top White House aide. These arrangements have vexed ego-sensitive politicians looking for a moment in the sun at the president's side, when flying into their own home state and town, or cabinet officers eager for time with "The Chief."

One helicopter trip ended unhappily, and ominously, for former Secretary of State Alexander Haig, and it underscored the importance of the staff's proximity to the president. During Reagan's visit in 1982 to Queen Elizabeth at Windsor Castle, Haig was miffed that he and his wife were left off Reagan's *Marine One* helicopter between London and Windsor. There was not enough room for them because Bill Clark, then National Security adviser, was traveling with Reagan. Throughout Reagan's trip to England and a Western summit meeting in Versailles, Haig and Clark had been feuding, and Clark used the staff man's inside track to take the prerogative of riding with the president to Windsor on Marine One. Haig and his wife were relegated to a second helicopter, larger, slower, less comfortable, with bench seats.

"There were no other cabinet people on that helicopter," Bill Sitman recalled. "John Louis, the American ambassador to Great Britain, was also on that helicopter with his wife. They fly those helicopters with the rear door open. Mrs. Haig seemed to take it all right. I guess she's flown a lot of helicopters, being a military officer's wife. But Haig didn't like being put on that helicopter with other lower officials.

"The last straw came as we were leaving Windsor. It was in the morning at the end of the visit. Haig and Mrs. Haig were walking to their helicopter as *Marine One* was taking off. The backwind blew off Mrs. Haig's hat. Someone went after it, but the hat was gone. So the Haigs got on their helicopter, and as it was taking off, you could see out this open back door, the hat went waffling across the green at Windsor. That was the last straw for Haig. Mrs. Haig was a saint, but Haig blew his top. He was not a happy man on the helicopter leg from Windsor to London Airport."

That episode, like Nelson Rockefeller's lack of access to President Ford, was an ill omen for Haig. At Clark's instigation, Reagan forced

Haig to resign two weeks later, and Haig later howled that one of his biggest problems was the White House staff's blocking his access to the president.

"Are You in the Loop?"

Timely inside information is a special form of access that gives a power player the chance to make his move before competitors can react. Like inside tips in the stock market, it is the lifeblood of the government policy-maker. Without fresh information a policymaker is forever "behind the power curve," scrambling to catch up. The question in this part of the power game is not "Who can you see?" but "What are you allowed to know?"

In the national security power fraternity, the put-down comes in the form of one official asking another: "Are you in the loop?" Translated, that means: "Are you on the short list—in the power loop—for getting the most important documents and hottest information," like the *NID* (*National Intelligence Daily*) or the *FTPO* (*For the President Only*).

Each morning, the Central Intelligence Agency prepares a top-secret *NID*—a précis of the most important overnight "take," or yield, of the intelligence community. It runs about a dozen pages, carries a distinctive red-and-black flag in the upper right corner and a telltale, broad, baby-blue stripe down the side. It comes out six days a week (not on Sunday) and goes only to officials with top-secret clearance or higher, the senior two hundred officials at the White House, Defense Department, State Department, and intelligence agencies.*

I have never read a *NID*. Those who have tell me that it includes the latest intelligence reports from American agents around the world, the "take" from electronic eavesdropping on foreign leaders, the freshest satellite photography. Reagan has particularly liked maps and photos: "after-action" photos from the American bombing raid on Libya, diagrams of the Iran-Iraq war, satellite coverage of East European freighters delivering weapons to Nicaragua, or Soviet missile tests and deployments.

"There's a tremendous impact with visuals, a sort of high-level voyeurism," one *NID* reader said. "If they have a tape of one world leader talking to another world leader and even if it doesn't say something of

---

*The *NID* is more high-powered and selective than *DINSUM*, the *Defense Intelligence Summary*, put out daily by the Defense Intelligence Agency; the *Chairman's Brief*, done by the joint military staff for the chairman of the Joint Chiefs of Staff; or the *Secretary's Morning Summary*, done by the State Department Bureau of Intelligence and Research for the secretary of State.

cosmic significance, they run it anyway. The Agency [the CIA] likes to show off to the president and other top people that they have these things."

Even more rarified, however, is another, smaller intelligence document: the *FTPO—For the President Only*. White cover, normally only four or five pages of even juicier secret items pegged to the president's daily schedule, it is likely to have inside tips on the health of a foreign leader whom the president is meeting, reports on that leader's political troubles at home, or a fresh analysis of some topic due for discussion with a congressional group. Each copy of the *FTPO* is numbered and jealously guarded. It often contains SCI—secret compartmented information—circulated only on a need-to-know basis because it could expose American spies or collection methods. Sometimes officials have to read it with an armed guard standing nearby, ready to take it away when they're finished—no copy for their own files. Only about twenty people qualify to see it: the president, vice president, their chiefs of staff, and the innermost of the national security circle.

In this rarified loop, when officials exchange phone numbers, they don't use normal government extensions. They exchange their three-digit "secure phone" numbers—such as KY 238 or KY 107. These phones are equipped with scramblers: electronic devices that jumble and encode words spoken into a telephone and then ungarble them at the other end. This allows officials to discuss the most sensitive classified information without Soviet electronic eavesdroppers understanding.

Narrowing the Access

Obviously, deciding who gets the most sensitive and essential information also decides who can be a full player in the policy game. Knowledge is power. Some information, such as Oliver North's messages to his agents in the Iranian arms operation and on weapons drops to the Nicaraguan *contras*, is too sensitive even for the *NID* or the *FTPO*. The loop on those operations was extremely small—so small that word was passed orally or on secure private-line computers of the national security staff. Above all, the Iranian episode dramatized the fact that whoever controls information can control policy. For months at a time, National Security advisers Robert McFarlane and John Poindexter kept both Shultz and Weinberger in the dark about the operation and thus unable to object to specific actions. The cabinet secretaries were "information blind."

One stunning shock of the Iran-*contra* operation to most people was that North, Poindexter, and McFarlane, as staff aides, would dare to keep such critically important information secret from cabinet secretaries and the president, deceiving their superiors. Yet however extreme and shocking their behavior, it reflected the game-playing style of career bureaucrats, the established habits of the permanent government, to control policy by operating in secret without fully informing the "in-and-outers"—their politically appointed superiors who move in and out of government. In effect, many careerists are telling their bosses: "You decide the big policies; leave the details to us." But as the saying goes, The devil is in the details.

Policy gets defined just as much by implementing details as it does by deciding the broad sweep; any president or top policymaker who does not know that just doesn't understand the game of governing. To borrow an image from basketball or soccer, bureaucrats engage in *ball control*—controlling policy by tossing the ball among themselves and leaving their superiors out of the loop.

Take the case of the Defense Security Assistance Agency (DSAA), which handles multibillion-dollar arms sales abroad, and the F-16 jet fighters that President Reagan agreed to sell to President Mohammed Zia of Pakistan in 1981. This was a major switch from Carter's cautious policy toward Pakistan, and a big Reagan thank you to Pakistan for channeling military help to anti-Soviet guerrilla fighters in Afghanistan. The White House wanted the arms deal to work smoothly. The DSSA had other ideas, such as cutting costs, taking care of the U.S. Air Force, and protecting its own institutional authority.

A problem developed around a life-and-death gadget inside the F-16, a high-tech item which could detect enemy radar systems as they "lock" onto the American plane. This gadget is the jet fighter's equivalent of a "fuzz buster"; it gives the pilot a chance to evade whatever is being shot at him. When the deal was made, the F-16 had a pretty good fuzz buster known as the ALR-47. By 1983, when the planes were ready for delivery, the Air Force had the much improved ALR-69 model. The old model simply set off a buzzer in the cockpit telling the pilot to start some evasive action, without saying what kind of evasion. The new model, more high tech, guided the pilot on what evasive action to take by flashing little symbols on his radar screen, telling him whether he was being attacked by another jet fighter or a ground-launched missile—a life-and-death difference from the old model.

In the original arms deal, the United States agreed to provide Pakistan with "standard" Air Force electronics on the plane. To DSAA, that meant the old-model fuzz buster, which was "standard" when the deal was made. The new model was more expensive and the Air Force wanted it for American pilots. The Pakistani Air Force felt it was entitled to the new fuzz buster. DSAA refused. No one told the White House or the top Pentagon brass about the dispute. Eventually, Pakistani President Zia blew up, refusing to accept planes with old equipment. The controversy jeopardized Reagan's goodwill gesture of agreeing to supply the planes. It took Reagan's personal action to override the bureaucracy and set his policy back on course.

Even so, the F-16 episode demonstrates how a bureaucracy can set policy—and protect its institutional turf—by keeping others ignorant. Change the issues, and things like that happen frequently in the Agriculture Department, Department of Energy, or other agencies, just as readily as in the Pentagon. In the case of the F-16 fuzz busters, the bureaucrats were uncovered. More often they are not, and they manage covertly to maintain their policy independence and subtly to undermine the policies that presidents think they have decided. The careerists control policy by keeping the power loop small.

Widening the Circle

The opposite power tactic is widening the circle—spreading information to summon political allies within the administration or in Congress, or to rally public opinion. That is the basic dynamic behind most policy news leaks that are a favorite tactic in the power game. Almost invariably, the weaker side in an internal dispute widens the circle to call for help.

The press, especially *The New York Times* and *The Washington Post,* serves as the bulletin board on which insiders post notices to allies elsewhere. All over political Washington, government officials and members of Congress keep track of internal battles in the government by following leaks to the press.

On Wall Street, passing insider information to others is an indictable offense. In Washington, it is the regular stuff of the power game. Everyone does it, from presidents on down, when they want to change the balance of power on some issue. Lyndon Johnson was legendary for leaking information to reporters in off-the-record sessions where he could not be quoted. Usually Johnson was trying to change the slant of Congress or the public on some issue. He did it anonymously to avoid the appearance of special pleading. Sometimes Johnson would later publicly dispute the very same information, to cloak his role as the original source.

In my experience, that sort of practice has taken place in every White House since Johnson. The Reagan team liked to pass information, say on Soviet-built airstrips in Nicaragua or possible Soviet violations of arms treaties, to friendly senators and congressmen, disguising the origin of the information. Such leaks were usually timed to occur during congressional battles over funding for the Nicaraguan *contras* or the Pentagon budget: They were intended to stir up public opinion and use public pressure to influence the power game in Washington.

Some years ago, political scientist E. E. Schattschneider of Wesleyan University spelled out the dynamics of "widening the circle" in a seminal work, *The Semisovereign People*. He contended that in every political conflict there are two parties: the actual participants and the audience irresistibly drawn to the scene. "Nothing attracts a crowd as quickly as a fight," Schattschneider wrote. "Nothing is so contagious. Parliamentary debates, jury trials, town meetings, political campaigns, strikes, hearings, all have about them some of the exciting qualities of a fight; all produce dramatic spectacles that are almost irresistibly fascinating to people."[8]

So far, so normal—but Schattschneider's special insight is that the audience determines the outcome of the fight. He cited the Harlem race riot of 1943, which began as a fistfight between a black soldier and a white policeman and mushroomed into a mob scene with looting, four hundred people injured, and millions of dollars in property damage. Schattschneider's point was that if the audience had not joined the two-man fight, it would not have been a big deal. But as the audience joined in, the nature of the fight changed. Schattschneider's moral: "If a fight starts, watch the crowd because the crowd plays the decisive role."[9]

That insight goes to the heart of scores of Washington power games. One example, mentioned earlier, was President Reagan's policy toward the Philippines in late 1985. He and his White House advisers were content to roll along with President Ferdinand Marcos. But the murder of opposition leader Benigno Aquino and then the massive corruption in the 1986 Philippine election aroused and angered the American public. Senator Richard Lugar of Indiana played up the vote stealing, discrediting Marcos and undermining Reagan's policy. Lugar was allied with people inside the administration, such as Secretary of State George Shultz; in fact, Lugar had been drawn into the power game by the State Department. Lugar's deliberate play to public opin-

ion changed the balance of forces inside the administration and eventually changed the policy. By constantly widening the audience, Lugar
changed the outcome.

Another case study is the CIA's covert war against the Sandinistas
in Nicaragua. Initially, the CIA, like the DSAA in the story about the
F-16s for Pakistan, began secretly to arm the Nicaraguan *contras*. Only
a few people in the government and in Congress knew what the CIA
was doing. Some feared where the policy would lead, but voiced their
arguments in private; CIA Director Casey kept control of policy. By
early 1984, internal critics felt the CIA had overstepped its bounds—
blowing up oil depots, attacking coastal installations, and finally mining
Nicaraguan harbors. Then, à la Schattschneider, these dissenters appealed to a wider audience: Critics inside the government fed information to allies on Capitol Hill. Congressional intelligence committees,
the first of the wider circles, joined the fight. When policy did not
change, the weaker side kept leaking embarrassing disclosures until the
full Congress became involved. House Democrats, fearing a wider war,
blocked further military aid to the Nicaraguan *contras* after July 1984.

As the administration was thrown on the defensive, President Reagan adopted the Schattschneider tactic: He took his case to a still wider
audience, trying to revive aid to the *contras*. All pretense of a covert
war was abandoned: The power game went public. Reagan threatened
congressional opponents with future blame if Central America "went
communist." The fear of a political backlash among voters threatened
enough fence-sitting congressmen to revive military aid in 1986. Politically, the battle followed a Schattschneider scenario: What began as
covert policy and an inside policy dispute escalated into an open confrontation, driven by the logic of the Harlem race riot, each side trying
to gain the upper hand by summoning reinforcements.

This is how Washington works, again and again. Think of the challenge posed to the Reagan military buildup by the furor over scandalously priced Pentagon spare parts and faulty weapons. The Pentagon
rip-off was quietly publicized through press leaks by internal critics.
Public outrage reinforced congressional attempts to slow the growth of
military spending.

Even the final halt in arms dealing with Iran did *not* come with the
first disclosure on November 3 in the Lebanese press, but six weeks
later, on December 16, after Secretary of State Shultz engaged in a
"battle royal" to change policy. He made public protests over a policy
still running loose. National Security Adviser John Poindexter and
Lieutenant Colonel North wanted to maintain secrecy, not only for

self-protection, but also to keep control of policy and to keep their arms channels open to Iran. Shultz went public to put an end to the Iranian arms deals and to wrest control of policy away from them.

Actually, the dynamic action that Schattschneider analyzed dates back in American history to the very formation of our political parties. Inside the Federalist administration, there was sharp debate over Alexander Hamilton's mercantilistic economic policies and his pro-British foreign policy. Thomas Jefferson and his allies opposed Hamilton but realized that Hamilton had the backing to prevail in the cabinet and possibly in Congress. So they began leaking word of the internal debates, seeking to involve a larger public. Eventually, the Jeffersonian faction formed the Democratic-Republican party to contest the 1798 congressional elections and ultimately the presidential election of 1800. The process of leaking, of widening the circle, led to the formation of political parties.[10]

Schattschneider put his finger on one of the central laws of the Washington power game: Those who are in control of policy, whether the president and his top advisers or bureaucrats buried in the bowels of government, will try desperately to keep the information loop small, no matter what the issue; those who are on the losing side internally will try to widen the circle. As the audience grows and the circle is widened, control over policy shifts, the conflict spreads, and the very nature of the game changes. It is a Washington theme, a pattern of the past that will echo in stories and situations throughout this book, and in Washington power game for years to come.

PART II

The Players and the Playing Field

The Players and
the Playing Field

Television news shows, newspaper headlines, and the American public all focus on the big games of Washington politics: titanic battles between White House and Congress over taxes, the president's nominees to the Supreme Court, or aid to the Nicaraguan *contras*.

But most of the time, the vast majority of players in the Washington political community are concerned with less visible games, small but important power games that do not grab the big headlines, but which dramatically affect the way that Washington works.

These games form the political terrain that the big games are played on, the backdrop, the milieu in which political Washington moves and operates. The public senses that this world exists but knows little about it. To the players in the power game, this world is second nature: the networks of power and the odd couples; the survival politics of the constant campaign; the pork-barrel politics and the iron triangles epitomized by the Pentagon cartel; the craft of lobbying and the influence of political money; the enormous and largely hidden power of staff.

It is hard for outsiders to fathom the dynamics of the big games without first understanding this inner world of Washington, the world that power players themselves call "inside the beltway."

6. Life Inside the Beltway: The Folkways of Washington

The longer you stay, you realize that sometimes you can catch more flies with honey than with vinegar.
—Senator Strom Thurmond

When a brand-new member of Congress comes to Washington, he is fresh from the heady experience of winning public acclaim for his politics and victory for himself. Then suddenly, the newcomer is a naked freshman in a world of veterans, a stranger in the political home he has won for himself. Instinct tells him immediately that no individual politician can operate as an atom. He must make his way to clusters of comrades, to small survival groups, to networks of power to which he can attach. He must come to know the folkways of the power city.

Up close, just as from afar, Washington can seem a foreign place, even though its Capitol dome, White House lawn, and Washington Monument are familiar symbols. But to freshly minted political victors, it is suddenly a strange universe. Near the end of 1980, on the very night that Michael Deaver arrived with his family from California to begin work in the Reagan White House, his five-year-old son, Blair, asked in his innocence a question that must silently sit on many adult tongues: "Daddy, is Washington part of this world?"

Eighteen months earlier, at the depths of his political despair in the summer of 1979, President Carter had given his own angry, frustrated answer to that question. Carter openly derided Washington as an island "isolated from the mainstream of our nation's life."

In an era of Washington bashing, this is a theme that many people voice and many politicians exploit: this theme that Washington is disconnected from the country. But it is a misleading notion.

Washington is different, yes; but it is not isolated. With high-speed jets and round-the-clock television news, the capital is closer to being on the same political wavelength as the rest of the country than at any previous time in our history. Congress works a short week in Washington (Monday afternoon to Friday morning), to give members more time with constituents; members are constantly dashing home to maintain the umbilical connection with their voters. In their obsession to keep track of grass-roots sentiment, politicians are forever putting up wet fingers to test the wind. To keep in touch, they have become compulsive consumers of opinion surveys.

More to the point, Washington is surprisingly open to newcomers, even to those it initially intimidates. Practically everyone in political Washington has come from somewhere else. Each new political tide brings in waves of newcomers. In presidential election years, especially when the White House changes hands, the influx is wholesale. The new crowd from Georgia or California take over literally thousands of the choicest jobs in town. Even in midterm elections, one or two dozen new congressmen and senators arrive with fresh messages from the country for the old hands. The Washington political community is "almost absurdly permeable" to outside influence, suggested Nelson Polsby, a keen academic observer of American politics.

"What other community in America," Polsby asked, "regularly accords automatic, immediate, unshakable top status to someone from out of town, even if that someone's public conversation consists mainly of unpleasant statements about the community and attacks on its oldest inhabitants?"[1]

Indeed, Washington regularly takes in newcomers, absorbs them and makes them its own. Those who arrive to serve in Congress learn to live in two worlds—in their hometowns and states, and in the special world of the capital. The longer they stay in Washington, the more they become Washingtonians, buying homes, raising children, worrying about parking places and street crime, some even rooting for the Washington Redskins football team against their home-state teams.

Newcomers arrive full of idealism and energy only to discover what a tiny fragment of power they grasp. To expand that fragment, they make alliances, join groups, get appointed to committees, make contacts with the press, find friends in the administration. Before they know it, they become caught up in Washington's internal politics, involved in the rivalries of Congress and administration, consumed by their committee work, their personal specialties, their Washington careers—the clout they develop in Washington and the amount of attention they can command in the Washington power game.

In short, people who come here to serve in the executive branch or Congress catch "Potomac fever"—the incurable addiction of wielding political power or feeling at the political center. When their president leaves office or they lose their congressional seats, very few politicians go home to retire or make money. Most stay in Washington and become lawyers, lobbyists, or consultants, because they've grown accustomed to Washington's ways and to thinking of themselves as movers and shakers, and no other place has quite the same excitement and allure.

Power, of course, is the aphrodisiac—the special brand of federal power that is Washington's monopoly. New York and Los Angeles have enormous financial muscle. Houston, Chicago, Pittsburgh, and Detroit have industrial and commercial might. Silicon Valley outside San Francisco is at the leading edge of high-tech science and electronics. Hollywood and Broadway create stardom. But Washington is where the nation's destiny is set. The incomparable titillation for politicians and government officials is doing the public's business and feeling that the nation is paying close attention.

Political Washington is a special community with a culture all its own, its own established rituals and folkways, its tokens of status and influence, its rules and conventions, its tribal rivalries and personal animosities. Its stage is large, but its habits are small-town. Members of Congress have Pickwickian enthusiasm for clubs, groups, and personal and regional networks to insure their survival and to advance their causes. They love the clubbiness of the member's dining rooms and such Capitol Hill watering holes as the Monocle or the Democratic Club. And downtown, politicians, lobbyists and journalists like to rub shoulders and swap stories at Duke Zeibert's, Mel Krupin's, or Joe and Mo's, where the movers and shakers have regulsr tables.

Political parties have a social impact; most politicians fraternize mainly with colleagues from within their own party. But when I first came to the city, I did not realize how personal relationships often cut across party and ideological lines, so that conservative lions and liberal leopards who roar at each other in congressional debates play tennis on the weekends or joke together in the Capitol cloakrooms. And yet, for all their backslapping gregariousness, politicians strike me as a lonely crowd, making very few deep friendships because almost every relationship is tainted by the calculus of power: How will this help me?

Above all, Washington is a state of mind. I'm not talking about the 3.5 million people who live in the Washington metropolitan area: the hospital administrators, shopkeepers, schoolteachers, and the people who inhabit the middle-class city of Washington and its Virginia and Maryland suburbs; rather, I'm referring to the hundred thousand or so whose life revolves around government, especially the few thousand at the peak who live and breathe politics. To the people of that world, this is the hub, the center, the focus of what Henry Adams once called "the action of primary forces."[2] The conceit of this Washington is not all that different from the conceit of Paris or Moscow.

Example: The city and its suburbs are encircled by a sixty-four-mile freeway loop known as the beltway (U.S. 495). The political community of Washington talks as if that beltway formed a moat separating the capital from the country. "Inside the beltway," political Washington's favorite nickname for itself, is a metaphor for the core of government. Hardly a dinner or a meeting goes by without someone observing that the mood inside the beltway on Iran or a new Soviet-American summit or on protectionist measures is running ahead of the country, or that the president, any president, is in trouble inside the beltway but not "out there," with a wave of the hand toward the boondocks.

The distance between Washington and the rest of the country is partly a matter of language. Jargon is a vital element of the Washington game. Washington jargon is impenetrable and often deliberately so, to exclude all but the initiated.

For starters: Unless you're President Reagan, you can't be a major player in budget politics unless you know the difference between constant dollars and current dollars, between outlays and obligations, between the baseline and the out-years; you can't enter the arena of arms control without some grasp of launchers, throwweight, and RVs.* If you're an insider, you will have mastered such trivia as knowing that the shorthand for the Department of Housing and Urban Development is pronounced "HUD," but that the nickname for the Depart-

---

*Constant dollars are economic figures adjusted for inflation; figures in current dollars are not adjusted. Outlays are actual government funds spent, but obligations are funds authorized for spending, perhaps in later years. The baseline is the cost of the current level of government services and programs, and the out-years are projections for future years. Launchers are bombers and missiles; throwweight is the overall payload a missile can heave aloft; and RVs are re-entry vehicles, or the nuclear warheads and decoys on a ballistics missile.

ment of Transportation is pronounced "D-O-T" and never "dot." You will also know that bogeys are the spending targets the secretary of Defense gives the armed services and that beam-splitters are the nearly invisible TelePrompTers that flash the text of a speech to the president as he turns his head from side to side.

The split between capital and country also reflects a different awareness of how Washington really works. The veterans know that the important, knock-down, drag-out battles in Congress usually come on amendments to a piece of legislation, not on final passage of the bill. They understand that when some member rises on the floor of the House or Senate and says that a piece of legislation is a "good bill" and that he wants "to offer a perfecting amendment," he is really getting ready to gut the legislation. Sometimes an amendment is a complete substitute bill with quite different impact and meaning, known in the trade as a "killer amendment." That's the way the legislative game is played.

In many other ways, political perceptions differ sharply inside the beltway and out in the country. For example, Thomas Foley of Washington State, the House majority leader, is hardly a household word. But in the Washington political community, Republicans as well as Democrats respect him as an effective leader with sound judgment who can hold northern liberals and southern conservatives in a Democratic coalition and also work well across party lines. A large comfortable Saint Bernard of a man, Foley has on occasion shrewdly blunted the force of Republican attacks and at other times steered Democrats toward compromises with Reagan.

Conversely, New York State Congressman Jack Kemp has made a national splash with his tax issue, but political insiders regard him as generally less influential with other House Republicans than Trent Lott of Mississippi, the House Republican whip. "Lott swings plenty of votes," one Reagan White House strategist confided to me. "You can't count on Kemp to bring that many members with him." Over in the Senate, Jesse Helms is the booming public voice of the New Right but when it comes to working major issues with other Republicans, James McClure of Idaho, a quieter legislator, is given more credit as the leader of Senate conservatives. In 1984, McClure, not Helms, was the conservatives' candidate for majority leader. In short, Kemp and Helms are the national figures with mass appeal; Lott and McClure are rated by their peers as more solid performers. The most striking modern case of a politician who was no great shakes as a congressman or senator but who won a mass following—and the presidency—was Jack Kennedy.

A City of Cocker Spaniels

What really sets Washington apart, of course, is the heady brew of
power and prominence. Washington combines the clout of the corporate boardroom and military command with the glamour of Hollywood
celebrities and Super Bowl stars. That magnetism and the stakes of the
battle are what draw armies of politicians, lobbyists, lawyers, experts,
consultants, and journalists to Washington. It is a self-selected group,
ambitious and aggressive, marked by collective immodesty. Politicians
love to be noticed, and they take their notices very seriously, assuming
their own importance and grasping for daily confirmation in the attention of the press and television.

Many people treat the word *politician* as a synonym for hypocrisy,
but I believe most politicians come to Washington largely motivated
by a sense of public service, and usually with a deeper interest in policy
issues than is felt by people back home. Most politicians really want
to contribute to the public weal, as protectors of their home districts
or exponents of some cause; their early motiviation is the ideal of better
government. Most people who make a career of government could earn
a good deal more money in other walks of life. And they toss into the
bargain the loss of personal privacy for themselves and for their families. Not all politicians are that self-sacrificing, but I believe a majority
are; only a small minority seem charlatans. Their agendas differ greatly,
but if one urge unites them all—and really makes Washington tick—it
is the urge for that warm feeling of importance.

That ache for applause and recognition shows in the weighty tread
of senators moving onto the floor and glancing upward for some sign
of recognition from the galleries. It shows in the awkward jostling for
position as a group of congressmen approach the television cameras and
microphones outside a hearing room, or after a White House session
with the president. I have marveled at it in the purgatorial patience of
politicians with endless handshakes, speeches, receptions. I have sensed
it, too, in the flattered eagerness of corporate executives arriving at a
White House dinner in their limousines. And I have felt it in the smug
satisfaction of a select group of columnists and commentators called to
a special briefing from the president in the family theater of the White
House. None of us is completely immune to that siren song of being
made to feel important.

"Washington is really, when you come right down to it, a city of
cocker spaniels," Elliott Richardson once remarked. Richardson, a

Republican Brahmin from Boston, held four cabinet positions in the Nixon and Ford administrations and after a few years out of the limelight felt the ache for attention badly enough to make an unsuccessful try for the Senate.

"It's a city of people who are more interested in being petted and admired than in rendering the exercise of power," Richardson contended. "The very tendency of the cocker spaniel to want to be petted and loved can in turn mean that to be shunned and ignored is painful, and there is a tendency in Washington to turn to the people who are in the spotlight and holding positions of visibility at a given time."[3]

In their collective vanity, the power players are willing to endure long hours of boredom to bathe in the roar of the crowd. Talking with me in his Senate study one rainy afternoon about the vanity of the political breed, Senator Charles McC. Mathias, the Maryland Republican, recalled an incident at an American Legion dinner in Washington years ago. As Mathias arrived, he saw two fellow Republican warhorses—Leverett Saltonstall of Massachusetts with his arm in a sling and Everett Dirksen hobbling on crutches.

"It was one of those many functions which you attend but where your absence might not even be noted," Mathias observed. "Saltonstall and Dirksen had valid excuses [to stay away], but they came anyway. And I thought: Is there never surcease from this demand and this compulsion to get out to these things? But of course, they would be put at the head table and introduced, and the spotlight would fall upon them, and the people from Massachusetts and Illinois would wave their napkins in the air when their names were mentioned, and the band would play their state anthems. It is all utterly meaningless, and yet those two wanted to be part of the act, and the applauders wanted the act, too."[4]

Narcissism is not too strong a label for the Washington syndrome. Political Washington is consumed with its own doings: Who's up, who's down, did you hear what the president said over an open mike, how's the tax bill doing, should we have bombed Libya, what's next? Surely ranchers in Texas, car makers in Detroit, textile executives in South Carolina, or doctors and lawyers anywhere are equally self-absorbed. But Washington, rivaled perhaps by Hollywood, allows itself the collective vanity of assuming that people elsewhere are fascinated with its doings.

"The capital, with its curious mixture of high ideals and hard work and base ambition and blind vanity, becomes the universe: If I am so famous that *The* [*Washington*] *Post* is writing about me, then, of

course, the whole world is reading it," observed former Secretary of
State Alexander Haig,[5] with the wry detachment of hindsight, once he
was out of office.

"Going into the White House every day to work, seeing the iron
gates open and then the iron gates shut, you're in an almost-unreal
world," Carter White House aide Stuart Eizenstat commented.
"There is something almost unnatural about the way in which people
treat you. There's a certain unnatural deference. You have microphones thrust in your face and cameras watching you when you make
a speech. You begin to think, perhaps, you're more important than you
thought you were when you came into the job. All of these things have
the potential, if you're not careful, to make you again feel that you have
the kind of unbridled influence to do that which you will, that somehow
you're a voice of wisdom. And I think that one has to fight against that
feeling."[6]

Washington is a city mercurial in its moods, short in its attention
span, and given to fetishes. Events flash and disappear like episodes in
a soap opera, intensely important for a brief period and then quickly
forgotten. Like a teenager, the political community lurches from one
passion to the next, seized for a season by the Gramm-Rudman budget-
balancing act, later consumed by a battle with Japan over trade sanctions, or gossiping madly over the millionaire antics of White House
officials turned lobbyists.

But whatever the twist and turns, the themes are invariably political.
People visiting from New York or Los Angeles complain that Washington is a guild town with just one industry and one preoccupation. New
York has the intensely self-preoccupied worlds of Wall Street, Broadway, publishing, and advertising, and Chicago with its corporate headquarters, grain trade, steel industry, and distribution centers. Each city
has variety, while Washington, in spite of its growing world of art,
theaters, opera and symphony, has only one passion.

"It's a one-subject town," lamented Austin Ranney, a political scientist from California who spent a decade at the American Enterprise
Institute in Washington. "I don't know how many dozens or hundreds
of dinner parties I went to, largely as an outsider, an observer, and yet
I almost never had a conversation about music, about novels, or very
briefly about anything except the weather. It was always politics, politics, politics, of the insider variety."[7]

Hugh Newell Jacobson, a prominent Washington architect, protested to Barbara Gamarekian, a *New York Times* colleague of mine,
"This is the only city where you can go to a black-tie dinner [in a private

home], and there at the foot of the table is a television set up to catch a press conference!"[8]

In Washington, people take their own importance so much for granted that their first instinct with a new book is to turn immediately, not to the first page, but to the index to see whether they are mentioned. Yet very few politicians will admit in print how much they hunger for public recognition. Paradoxically, one who did was Paul Tsongas, a Massachusetts Democrat, who had impressed me during his ten years in the House and Senate as less driven by vanity than most. Tsongas had voluntarily retired for family and health reasons. But after retirement, he confessed to me what "heady stuff" it was to win the title of U.S. Senator. His mind flashed back to the moment on election night 1978 when over the radio in his car came the first word that he was the likely winner, and a campaign aide blurted out, "The goddamned senator!"

"It was so overwhelming to have that word next to my name," Tsongas said, a bit of wonder in his quiet voice even years later. "It just seemed so unlikely to everybody in the car, and yet from that moment on, that title attaches. And the respect accorded to that title, irrespective of person, is enormous, and you begin to think of yourself in those terms. To a lot of senators that title is life. I've seen people who have been defeated and who basically never got over having lost the title."[9]

In a very different vein, Newt Gingrich, a voluble, publicity-prone junior Republican from Georgia, admits to the exultation of making it to Washington. "There are very few games as fun as being a congressman," he gushed one evening over a Chinese dinner. "Talk to guys who spent Christmas break traveling the world. Talk to people who landed on an aircraft carrier or went to see the space shuttle launched or had dinner at the White House or got to talk to people from *The New York Times*. There's a sense of being at the center of things. This is the great game!"[10]

Congress: High School Networks

Great game or not, the individual congressman is often isolated and feeble. Without the echo and support of like-minded young Republican conservatives, Gingrich would be less exultant. In self-defense, politicians naturally band together in power networks, either within the executive branch, on Capitol Hill, or bridging the two. Obviously, the two main political parties are the basic networks of power. But the weak, loose structure of American political parties makes other networks essential. In Congress, individual members are far less creatures of party than are their counterparts in European legislatures, whether the British Parliament, the French National Assembly, or the Canadian House of Commons, where parties provide strong organizational spine. Despite a bit of a comeback in Congress in this decade, American parties are more amorphous than they have been earlier in our history. And so, members make up their own alliance games.

"Almost everyone in government, whether he works on Capitol Hill or in the bureaucracy, is primarily concerned with his own survival," observed Charles Peters in a knowledgeable little book, *How Washington Really Works*, which describes the webs that politicians spin for their own safety and advancement. "He wants to remain in Washington or in what the city symbolizes—some form of public power. Therefore from the day these people arrive in Washington they are busy building networks of people who will assure their survival in power."[11]

The most natural networks are the product of generations, not the normal twenty-year generations but political generations based on when each new batch of politicians arrived in the city. California political scientist Nelson Polsby compares the Washington political community to a formation of geological strata, each new political generation layering on top of the preceding ones, each providing identity and a network of connections to its members.[12] It is an apt image. The sediment of old generations hardens because so many politicians remain in Washington. Today, there are networks of older Democrats from the Kennedy and Johnson years, Republicans from the Nixon and Ford administrations, Carter Democrats and more recently the new generation of Reaganite and New Right Republicans with their conservative caucuses, think tanks and political action committees.

These generational clusters are neighborhoods in the political city. Lasting alliances get forged in the crucible of political campaigns or service in the battles between one administration and its Congress. "You have a special connection with people who are alumni of the various political wars you have fought in," remarked Dennis Thomas, former legislative strategist in the Reagan White House. Ed Rollins, another Reagan political strategist, underscored the need for such networks for sheer survival, citing Anne Burford, Reagan's first environmental director, as someone who lost her job because she had no network of allies.

"You just really need the network, which means, in essence, that you've got to give up a little bit of your independence, a little bit of your turf and not make wars over every little issue," Rollins explained. "Sooner or later, you're going to need the support of some entity or another. Anne Burford is an example of people who have gotten wiped out by not having allies. She came here as a conservative, carried out Reagan's agenda. When she got in trouble, there was no one to come to her rescue. She had not built coalitions with White House staffers. She had not built coalitions with people on the Hill. She had not built coalitions with the conservative movement. She didn't build relations within her agency."[13]

In the power fraternity, political alliances are vital not only for survival but to promote policies, to lobby former colleagues, or to play the more personal game of "careers," advancement up the ladder for the in-and-outers who ride the ebb and flow of partisan politics upward with each generation.

Many of the most potent networks are factions of the two parties. Senator Jesse Helms and his right-wing Republican colleagues use the Steering Committee as their network to push issues or pet nominees for top administration positions, or to block the legislative initiatives of moderate Republicans or Democrats. The Steering Committee, and other networks like it, are called prayer groups, so nicknamed because they are not official arms of the Senate, just as prayer groups are usually not official arms of the church. In the House, Republicans have political fraternities, such as The Chowder and Marching Society and S.O.S. (the initials are secret). But the rough policy counterpart to the Steering Committee among House Republicans is the Conservative Opportunity Society, formed by partisans of supply-side, tax-cutting economics and less government. Moderate Republicans join the Wednesday Club, which lunches on Wednesday.

House Democrats have their own splinter groups. The liberal wing of the House Democratic Caucus gravitates to the Democratic Study Group and the Arms Control Caucus. Conservative southern Democrats (who call themselves boll weevils because, like the cotton weevil, they bore from within the boll) have formed the Conservative Democratic Forum. The list of networking groups goes on—many of them crossing party lines: the black caucus, women's caucus, Hispanic caucus, automotive caucus, footwear caucus, space caucus, military-reform caucus, textile caucus, even the mushroom caucus.

But for most members of Congress, the most important initial networks are the freshmen classes—the legislators who arrive in Congress in the same year, especially if their first election came during a political high tide. Among Democrats, the biggest and most potent freshman

class in recent years was the class of '74, the year when Watergate
helped elect seventy-five new Democrats to the House. Among Republicans, the big years were the class of '78, when the pendulum began
to swing back toward the GOP, bringing thirty-six new Republicans
into the House, and the class of '80, when the Reagan sweep helped
lift sixteen new Republicans into the Senate and fifty-two into the
House.

Cutting across these freshmen-class layers are state and sectional ties.
The big state delegations—California, New York, Texas, Pennsylvania,
Illinois—marshall their troops for issues of local importance, whether
military contracts or pet provisions in tax legislation. Significantly,
whole state delegations, Republicans and Democrats, liberals and conservatives, work together for parochial interests. The big states demand,
and usually get, a set share of seats on the most powerful committees
that deal with spending and taxes: Appropriations and Ways and
Means in the House; Appropriations and Finance in the Senate. Then,
there are broader regional coalitions, the Northeast-Midwest Caucus,
or the looser clustering of western and Sunbelt politicians.

The kind of regional splits that now divide Snowbelt (Midwest and
Northeast) and Sunbelt (South and West) date back in American
history to Jeffersonian times. Historian James Sterling Young has written that back then, members of Congress lived together for months in
boarding houses arranged along sectional lines. Those "boarding house
fraternities," as Young called them, enforced an iron social and political
discipline that would be the envy of congressional leaders today. Sectional ties are still strong, but they lack the raw power of social ostra-
cism used in the Jeffersonian era to whip members into line.[14]

For many decades, congressional committees have been important
hubs of power, focusing the work of their members. Farm-state senators and congressmen gravitate to the agriculture committees; Rocky
Mountain politicians want to be on the interior committees that affect
land use and environment; those from big cities head for labor and
education; and so on. Sitting side by side on those committees, parceling out funds from the federal pork barrel, committee members form
alliances.

The committees become the members' power bases for larger struggles with other power groups. Each committee forms the anchor of an
"iron triangle": the committee members and their staffs, the government agencies which the committee oversees, and the interest groups
and lobbyists interested in issues which the committee handles (banking, labor, health, etc.). Sometimes the legs of the triangle clash, but

more often all three legs work things out to forge policy in their area and then combine forces to battle other special interest communities and their committees over slicing up the budget and setting priorities. The committees are the hubs of the political action.

The congressional networks evoke those in high school, as Barney Frank suggested. "Everybody's got the same networks—your class, the people you were elected with. That's like your high school class," Frank observed. "Then the people from your region, they're like the people whose neighborhood you live in. And then, the people whose committee you're on, they're like the other students you used to go to class with. Those are the three networks that everybody has. And you may be able to pick up some over and above that."[15]

One of the most important informal networks that has developed is among younger House members who play sports or work out together in the House gym. Located in the subbasement of the Rayburn Office Building, the gym is a hideaway for members; they alone can use it. It is barred to their staffs, reporters, constituents, and most lobbyists (former members turned lobbyists can enter, but can do no serious lobbying on the premises). Senators have their own "baths." The House gym is not large; it has a sixty-foot pool, $28,000 in Nautilus equipment, a half-length basketball court which doubles for paddleball, as well as steam, massage, and locker rooms. Some members do little more than take a steam bath, shave, shower, and go back to work refreshed; others work out daily.

But many find that playing sports with political adversaries eases the wounds of political combat. "Ours is a very conflict-ridden profession," Frank remarked. "I vote against you. I think you're wrong. I mean, people in other professions are able to muffle that better. We are forced daily to conflict with each other. The gym promotes some stability, which is very important. But also, it's an information kind of thing. You get to know what people are like, what's important to them. You get information about what's going on with this, what's going on with that. It's that kind of chatter. And occasionally you will talk about some specific bill."[16]

Frank, a Jewish bachelor in his late forties whose pudgy cheeks once bulged around horn-rimmed glasses, lost seventy pounds through strict dieting and weight lifting. Now, at two hundred pounds, he has shoulders like a New England Patriots tackle. He mixes with the other side: One of his weight-lifting partners is Vin Weber, a staunch Republican right-winger from Minnesota and from the far end of the ideological spectrum. That is typical of the gym. The regular pickup basketball games are bipartisan: plenty of hard-court razzing goes on, but serious partisanship is left off the court. "Republicans and Democrats play together," says Thomas Downey, a Long Island Democrat with a snappy jump shot. "It's a great way to release tension."

Political Odd Couples

In my years of reporting in Washington, one of the more intriguing discoveries has been the number of warm political relationships that develop across party lines and across ideological disagreements. Sometimes such relationships are nurtured by common home state or other special interests; other links are more personal. The way we talk and think about most politicians is too stereotyped to account for people's fluidity and practicality. The fiery rhetoric of political campaigns and the shorthand of many press reports encourages the popular assumption that Democrats have virtually no use for Republicans and that liberals and conservatives are constantly at each other's throats. Some of that is for show; in fact, inside the beltway, political labels are frequently transcended. Some party scraps are genuine and passionate, but just as often, tolerance and partnership work extremely well across party or philosophical lines.

To a degree, this reflects the mentality of professional politicians, who know that with different issues, people change sides so that there is no point in making permanent enemies of anyone. "Most people think of politics as dirty and cutthroat," Henry Waxman, a California liberal, remarked to me one afternoon. With a gesture beyond the beltway, he added: "People out there don't understand that politicians can disagree and still get along personally. They don't understand the attitude we have toward each other as professionals."[17]

In short, the best politicians know they have to deal with a spectrum of conflicting views and that personal comity is a vital lubrication to the governmental process. Occasionally, friendships develop from simple human chemistry. Edward Kennedy of Massachusetts and Paul Laxalt of Nevada, from the left and right ends of the Senate, sometimes play tennis together and enjoy each other as friends. In other cases, amicable relations develop from professional respect. Other political opposites enjoy close friendships, such as conservative columnist Robert Novak and liberal humorist Art Buchwald, staunch Republican Al Haig and ardent Democrat Joseph A. Califano, conservative writer William Safire and left-of-center commentator Daniel Schorr. Former House Speaker Tip O'Neill and House Republican leader Bob Michel were longtime golfing partners.

Sometimes personal relationships develop from the fact that people at the peak of the power pyramids inevitably must deal with one another, regardless of differing views and clashing functions. The bond that has developed between Nancy Reagan and Katharine Graham, chairman of The Washington Post Company, is an example. Every president since John Kennedy, except Richard Nixon, has dined at Mrs. Graham's house. She was one of the first people in Washington to entertain Ronald Reagan after his election in 1980. But her personal relationship with Mrs. Reagan dates back to Reagan's time as governor of California.

"Nancy and I had a mutual friend who said we would like each other and then I met them [the Reagans] at a governors' conference where I was at one of those press seminars," Katharine Graham told me. "I saw them there in California two or three or four times, and said, wouldn't they call when they came to Washington. One of the times they came, I did say, 'Would you and the governor come to dinner since you're going to be here?' And she said, 'No, we can't because Ronnie's giving a speech that night.' And I said, 'Oh, well, that's too bad. Would you like to come anyway, and I'll have some people for you?' And she, being in this old-fashioned mold, somebody's wife, thinks you never want to see *her,* said, 'Oh, no, let's not do that—you don't want me.' And I just laughed and said, 'Nancy, we're supposed to get over that. Now, of course I want you. You come to dinner and then if Ronnie wants to come after the speech, fine. It doesn't matter.' And so she came and I gave a dinner for her."[18]

That episode, Mrs. Reagan's friends say, created a bond, and the two women have lunched half a dozen times a year during the Reagan presidency, in spite of the *Post*'s endorsements of Jimmy Carter and Walter Mondale and periodic fusillades between Mrs. Graham's paper and the Reagan White House.

"Celebrity women, powerful women have a common bond—of vulnerability, of concern for their families, of being treated unfairly by the press, of being survivors," remarked Nancy Reynolds, a longtime friend of the Reagans who worked for several years for Mrs. Reagan, both in California and in the White House. "And I think Nancy admires Kay Graham, but with a caveat that Nancy knows the *Post* is going to write a lot of things Nancy isn't going to like. And she accepts that and knows, I think, or feels that Kay is separate from all the negative things that the *Post* might write."[19]

The relationship has not been without scars. In 1982 after Colman McCarthy, a liberal *Post* columnist, wrote a biting review of Mrs. Reagan's ghostwritten book on the foster grandparents program,

Graham sent the first lady a "note of sympathy." During the 1984 reelection campaign, they fell out of touch over some misunderstanding and not until the summer of 1985 did they get back together. With some nudging from Mike Deaver, Mrs. Reagan's closest confidant in the White House, the first lady spent a weekend at Graham's summer cottage on Martha's Vineyard with other celebrities, and the two women went walking together on the beach.

In Congress, "odd couples" are fairly common. Capitol Hill's slashing rhetoric is sometimes little more than political soap opera, or what Senator Alan Simpson of Wyoming colorfully calls "doing the goddamned sage-chicken dance," a ritual mating dance where the sage cock inflates his chest with air, a nice image for politics. But even when the battles are genuine and leave feelings raw, the best politicians take them philosophically, always careful in victory not to wound their foes so badly that there is a residue of bitterness. They temper their disagreements with civility. For one of the main axioms of the power game is to keep the lines open, because you may need your foes of today as allies tomorrow.

Rarely has that axiom been more graphically illustrated than in the spring of 1986, by Senator Bob Packwood of Oregon. In one of the most dramatic political reversals in recent congressional history, Packwood did a U-turn on the tax-reform bill. He went from a bill that protected loophole after loophole for special business interests to one that slammed shut a lot of loopholes on personal tax shelters and radically reduced the top tax rates. His somersault literally turned his alliances upside down. He left a nucleus of supporters from oil-and-gas states (Lloyd Bentsen of Texas, Russell Long of Louisiana, David Boren of Oklahoma), and shifted to a proreform nucleus of moderates (Bill Bradley of New Jersey, Daniel Patrick Moynihan of New York, and John Chaffee of Rhode Island).

"What you discover is that there are no permanent friends, no permanent enemies—just temporary alliances," Packwood pragmatically admitted. "It just doesn't do you any good to bear grudges in this business. The person who may be against you this week, you're going to need next week."[20]

As a moderate Republican, Packwood has not been a tough point man against Democrats; that made his turnaround easier politically. But other politicians with more partisan reputations—Senate Democrats such as Gary Hart of Colorado, Alan Cranston of California, and Joseph Biden of Delaware—have also quietly developed bipartisan partnerships that are little known and more intriguing. Sometimes odd couples are deliberately created; sometimes they are fused in the suddenness of events.

Alan Simpson, a Republican whose fund of humor has made him a modern Will Rogers, recalls arriving in 1979 as a freshman senator from Wyoming and being immediately thrust into three political odd couples. He served on three Senate subcommittees opposite three liberal Democrats with presidential ambitions: Cranston, Hart, and Ted Kennedy.

"I suddenly thought, 'My God, I could be washed away in this process,' " he recalled, rubbing his chin. " 'Here's three guys who want to be president.' I went to each one of them and said, 'Look—don't you use this committee for your quest, and I won't use it to embarrass you in any way.' "21

Simpson had to deal with Kennedy on immigration issues, Cranston on veterans issues, and Hart on the Three Mile Island nuclear accident. His partnership with Cranston became so effective that as the rival Republican and Democratic whips in the Senate since 1981, they have defused many partisan showdowns.

Fate gave Simpson time to feel his way with Kennedy and Cranston, but not with Hart.

Ten weeks after Simpson had arrived in the Senate, the Three Mile Island nuclear accident occurred. Hart and Simpson, respectively the chairman and ranking opposition member of the Senate Subcommittee on Nuclear Regulation, were quickly flown by helicopter to Harrisburg, Pennsylvania.

On the helicopter, Simpson eyed Hart, wondering whether Hart was going to seize on the nuclear accident and exploit it to build his presidential bid. "Are you going to make a circus out of this nuclear thing?" he asked Hart.

"Now, who told you that?" Hart replied.

"I don't know," Simpson parried. "But I'm brand new here, and I'm not ready for a circus. I don't even know what this issue is. I don't even know where the hell I'm going today.

"Well," Hart began reassuringly, "why don't you watch and see how I do it, and I'll bet you won't be embarrassed in the process. 'Cause you and I are going to be in this deep."

By Simpson's account, Hart was good to his word and a wonderful companion, even though other senators call Hart a loner. "He's pleasant to work with," Simpson said. "He loves a good joke, has a very infectious belly laugh. He practically gets tears in his eyes when he gets into one. And then he'll tell one himself."

On substance, Simpson found Hart bending over backward to keep him informed and to make the subcommittee report thorough and accurate. "But Gary called me every time he had an interview or went on *Meet the Press,*" Simpson recalled. "Every time we were on the data link with the Nuclear Regulatory Commission, he included me in everything. He never put stuff in front of the committee that was totally political. He and I managed bills on the floor together, worked closely together." Sometimes, Hart would let Simpson take the lead. "Instead of his just sitting off and sniping," Simpson observed, "we actually got our work done."[22]

An even more unlikely political pair are Joseph Biden, a passionate Democratic liberal, and Strom Thurmond, the South Carolina Dixie-crat who became a Republican two decades ago. Thurmond, of course, won his spurs fighting for Dixie, stalking out of the 1948 Democratic convention under the banner of states' rights, leading his own presidential splinter ticket. Biden, four decades younger and first elected to the Senate in 1972, got his own reputation for brashness, a quick lip, and rough-and-tumble battling. On many issues they began poles apart—provisions of the 1982 Voting Rights Act and Senate approval of Ed Meese as attorney general and Bradford Reynolds as his deputy among them. But their disagreements have been clean and courteous, and they have cooperated on important legislation.

When Strom Thurmond became chairman of the Senate Judiciary Committee in 1981, Biden, as the committee's ranking Democrat, went to him privately and offered a deal: no parliamentary tricks, no savage sallies or gambits to embarrass Thurmond, in return for a solid chance for both sides to air the issues. Biden also gave Thurmond a ninety-page draft of a crime bill that Biden and his staff had developed, offering to let Thurmond become its main sponsor. That was not only courtesy to a committee chairman but an act of political pragmatism, because Biden knew that no crime bill would pass without Thurmond's backing. Initially, Thurmond was distrustful.

"He just sat, you know, very cautious, and listened," Biden recalled. "Then he finally figured out I was serious, that he could work with me. I told him—and I told my Democratic colleagues—'I'll make a deal: If you keep your right-wing guys from killing this bill, I'll keep the liberals off the bill. And if you and I stand fast and agree on what we can agree on and just hold firm, we can pass this thing.' From that point on, Strom Thurmond has never, never, never once suckered me or done any of the old chicanery stuff. And I don't play around with him. I kid him, but he knows I do it with affection."[23]

The version from the Thurmond side is much the same. Thurmond thinks so highly of Biden that he has invited Biden to appear at Thurmond's testimonials. Their toughest moment probably came on the night before the final Senate voting on the 1981 crime legislation. A Thurmond aide said the two men worked all night alone, hammering out final compromises.

"When I arrived in the morning, there they were, the two of them in their shirt-sleeves, still working, still dealing," the aide told me. "It's much harder to deal, to compromise, than to stand up and shout, 'This far and no further.' It's hard to sit across the table from your adversary and say, 'Okay, neither one of us is going to have everything we want. Now what can we work out.' "

Thurmond speaks of Biden with the affection of an eighty-five-year-old father talking about a forty-five-year-old son whose views bewilder him. In his soft South Carolina drawl, Thurmond instructed me on his philosophy, mellowed by the years:

"Some people feel that because of different philosophies, they have to be antagonistic. I take the position that you have to work with people even if they have a different philosophy—if they're sincere. Biden and I get along. Biden is a nice fellow. He's a high-quality man. He's an excellent speaker. He's impressive. He's articulate. He's flexible. He's a good family man. And I say, the longer you stay here, the more you realize there's more than one side to the question, the more you realize that compromise and courtesy are necessary. The longer you stay, you realize that sometimes you can catch more flies with honey than with vinegar."[24]

Workaholics: The Lonely Crowd

From afar, politicians appear as disembodied villains or cardboard celebrities. The demands of televised image making for blow-dried breeziness and self-assured opinions on any subject under the sun often disguise their humanity and vulnerability. The common perception often misses the mark.

I have frequently run into the popular assumption that politicians work less hard and have an easier life than people in the private sector. My experience is the opposite: People coming into government from private life are shocked at the compulsive intensity and workaholic ethic of Washington, in Congress or high in the executive branch.

Not surprisingly, the White House is such a pressure cooker that after a year as cabinet secretary and aide to Reagan, Al Kingon, the former Wall Streeter and publisher of *Saturday Review* magazine, confessed to me that he had found the workload "overwhelming— beyond my wildest dreams." Normal days found him starting work at seven A.M. and ending late at night, with many a cold or canceled dinner. The late Malcolm Baldrige told me that he worked fifty-percent longer hours as secretary of Commerce than he did as chief executive officer of Scovill Manufacturing Company. As a corporate number one, he used to make speeches saying that any business leader who was working more than an eight-hour day wasn't delegating enough to subordinates. But in Washington, Baldrige said, "I found eight hours isn't enough—I need twelve. And I stopped making those speeches."[25] People leaving high government positions say the pressure is less on the outside. David Gergen, former White House communications director, told me he found the pace less frantic as editor of *US News & World Report.*

For senators and members of Congress, the pressures are unrelent- ing. Days are a kaleidoscopic jumble: breakfasts with reporters, morn- ing staff meetings, simultaneous committee hearings to juggle, back-to-back sessions with lobbyists and constituents, phone calls, briefings, constant buzzers interrupting office work to make quorum calls and votes on the run, afternoon speeches, evening meetings, receptions, fund-raisers, all crammed into four days so they can race home for a weekend gauntlet of campaigning. It's a rat race to beat the pell-mell existence of ambitious New York lawyers, Chicago stock- brokers, or independent Texas oilmen, and about as sterile personally. Part of this is necessity. Part of it is the high-powered, super-achiever, Benjamin Franklin work ethic that drives the city: people proving their own importance.

"The problem with Washington is it's all an input town" was the shrewd comment of Chris Matthews, spokesman for former House Speaker Tip O'Neill. "You can't measure outputs. You measure input. This is a town where the GNP is government. And government is measured not by output but by how many hours you put in. Everybody says, 'I've been really busy this week. Are you busy? I've been busy. I must be busy.' And it's like busy-ness is a value in itself."[26]

"A lot of us have that as part of our makeup," Senator David Durenburger, a thoughtful, introspective Minnesota Republican, ac- knowledged over dinner. "A lot of us have that need to be driven. You don't find many laid-back people in politics. What you really love is that whether you get up at six or eight in the morning, there's always too much to do.

"You are important if you are in demand. You work hard to prove how valuable you are. It's a volume-oriented kind of operation: the more hands you shake, the more letters you write, the more times you appear on TV, the more hearings you hold, the more valuable you are. Somehow quality is subsumed by quantity."[27]

He quoted the advice of one senior senator at a prayer breakfast: "If you want to really keep on a fast track, always have more than two things to do for any space on your schedule. Have people telling you about all the other things you should do. Go into politics, because there's always too much to do. And in politics, you can justify workaholism. After all, it's important for the country."

The irony is that Ronald Reagan, with the most powerful, most demanding job of all, has made a mockery of workaholism. Quite deliberately, he worked a relatively short day, in his office from about nine to four, taking naps or going off horseback riding, and then attending some official dinner or tackling a bit of overnight reading, though sometimes it was left unread while he and Nancy watched television. Reagan really preferred oral briefings. National security advisers read him documents aloud, got his approval, and initialed them on his behalf. On Iran, for example, Reagan apparently never bothered to look at the critical decision paper of January 17, 1986, that formally authorized the arms-for-hostages deal.

When the press and other politicians nicked Reagan for being too hands-off and laid-back, Reagan poked fun at his lazy ways. At one press dinner, he joshed, "It's true that hard work never killed anybody, but I figure why take the chance at this late age." The audience roared at his admission.

Until the Iran-*contra* scandal broke, Reagan got away with his light routine partly because Jimmy Carter had slaved like an indentured servant and the public watched him sink in the morass of detail. Reagan's gentler pace made him look at ease with the presidency and with his power, and that was reassuring to the public. What's more, Reagan clearly has enjoyed the time-consuming ceremonial part of the job, and that enjoyment radiated self-confidence. For a long time, and during his first four years certainly, Reagan got away with going light on substance by delegating enormous authority to a superb staff.

What the public didn't notice, or didn't mind, was that Reagan did not have the driving curiosity that most presidents have about major issues or the way their administrations operate, both to educate themselves and to protect themselves from trouble. Reagan trusted others to keep him out of harm's way. But Reagan's second-term staff was not sharp enough, either in judgment or political skill, and Reagan's failure to control the staff got him into a mountain of trouble, climaxed by the Iran affair. Then his laid-back, hands-off style backfired badly.

For many other politicians and government officials, the intense type-A Washington life-style takes its toll in divorce and family tensions. Washington has one of the highest numbers of psychiatrists per capita in the country, about as many as New York, testimony that workaholism and the pressure-cooker atmosphere of Washington life are an occupational hazard.[28] Washington's monochrome life-style also makes for grayness. Occasionally, of course, poets emerge in Congress (Senator William Cohen of Maine who wrote *The Baker's Nickel* and also coauthored a spy novel, *Double Man,* with Gary Hart), journalists put on amateur theatrical skits (the Gridiron Club), and everyone admires the cherry blossoms in springtime. People do get away for weekends on Chesapeake Bay or in the Blue Ridge Mountains. But there are not many real time-outs.

A few years ago, Blythe Babyak, a television journalist from New York who had a commuting marriage with Richard Holbrooke, a State Department policymaker, complained about the dessicated existence.

"Washington is a fifties kind of place," she observed in *Newsweek,* "a town whose inhabitants are relieved of the uncertainty about life's goals, those that provoke a deeper examination of our own lives and those of others. Washingtonians know what counts: getting ahead in a clearly defined bureaucratic context—running the country, running the world. That's what they think they are doing, and, indeed, that is what they do. Day and night. Breakfast meeting, lunch, and dinner—to the exclusion of life's trifles and its mysteries."[29]

Weekday evenings bring no relief because political Washington treats social life as an extension of business. People are often booked three or four nights a week, sometimes to several events a night, and people relate to each other in terms of position and title. At dinners or other informal occasions, there are implicit quid pro quos. Journalists turn to officials and politicians for stories; the politicians trade for favorable mention. Lobbyists need politicians for legislation, and the politicians need the lobbyists for money and votes. Of course, there are times of levity and humor, but the underlying transactions of the political bazaar sap most occasions of serendipity.

"People will go to an embassy party if they think they might see someone they have missed during the day," wrote Sondra Gotlieb, the irreverent wife of the Canadian ambassador. "Powerful Jobs comes to parties to trade information with other Powerful Jobs they hadn't made contact with during the day."[30]

In her chatty fictionalized portrait of Powertown, entitled *Wife of ...*, Gotlieb captured the impersonalism of operational relationships. She gave her characters stereotyped names: White House Person, Important Job, Supremely Powerful, Gentleman-in-Waiting, Close-To, Used-to-Be-Close-To, World's Most Expensive Lobbyist, World Famous Columnist, and Media Star. In real life, she and her husband, Allan Gotlieb, an extremely able diplomat, often operated by this utilitarian code.

"We invite *jobs*, not people as individuals," Sondra Gotlieb admitted to Sandra McElwaine, a well-informed chronicler of Washington's ways. "Our purpose is to promote our country. We don't spend the taxpayers' money for the neighbors."[31]

For a time, the Gotliebs became the most glamorous entertainers in Washington, creating a name for themselves and giving Canada a high political profile by luring many of the movers and shakers of the Reagan entourage to their dinner table. Their star dipped when, perhaps because of the pressure of it all, Sondra Gotlieb publicly slapped her social secretary just as her dinner for the Canadian prime minister was getting under way. The shock reverberated in social Washington, and the Gotliebs took a lower profile for a while. But they are an intelligent, likable couple with a flair for entertaining, and their parties came back into fashion.

Something more fundamental than job stress and the hollow superficiality of the cocktail circuit often squeezes the juice out of politicians' private lives. They seem to fit David Reisman's image of *The Lonely Crowd*. Their public lives bring them hundreds, if not thousands, of contacts. What stands in the way of deeper friendships is the Darwinism, the struggle to get to become king of the hill. The competitiveness of the power game inhibits people from revealing the kind of personal vulnerability and doubts about life that are vital to forming close and sincere friendships.

To a politician, weakness can be fatal. So it is only natural that they cover up their frailties and uncertainties from rivals as well as from voters. For the risk of inner self-revelation, which genuine intimacy requires, is too dangerous for most politicians and public officials.

Consider recent history: In 1968, George Romney, the former governor of Michigan, was fatally wounded as a Republican presidential contender when he lamely told the press he had been "brainwashed" by the Pentagon on Vietnam. Former Senator Edmund Muskie was hurt politically in the 1972 presidential race when reporters saw him shedding tears at a New Hampshire press conference over mean sniping at his wife in the *Manchester Union-Leader*. That same year, Senator Tom Eagleton of Missouri was dropped from the Democratic ticket because he disclosed that years earlier he had gotten psychiatric help. In 1984, Senator Gary Hart was winged by constant questioning about why he had changed his name and why his official biographies understated his age by a year; and in 1987, he left the presidential race, hounded by questions of marital infidelity. Senator Joseph Biden also had to give up his presidential bid after revelations that he had plagiarized sections of his stump speeches and exaggerated his law school record.

Most politicians carefully keep their guard up to hide such human flaws. Steven Pieczenik, a Washington psychiatrist who once held a State Department post, makes the case that politicians, journalists, and others in the political community require a kind of "obligatory paranoia" to operate effectively in the political arena. "They have to question other people's intentions, motives, manipulations to do their job," he said. "The problem comes when they bring that back to their family life or their close personal relationships."[32]

Watching members of the House gather on the floor for a vote, I have seen a boyish camaraderie among them, born of serving in the trenches together. The Senate is less ostentatiously chummy than the House and less of a club than it used to be. Some members do form a few close relationships, but more commonly, politicians maintain a guarded distance beneath the Rotarian backslapping and gregarious arm squeezing that they display in public. Close staff aides reveal that some of those who appear the most congenial, including Ronald Reagan and Howard Baker, have a self-protective way of reserving their real feelings and preventing others from drawing too close.

"We all have our little power-packages here," Senator David Durenburger said, admitting to that self-protective instinct. "When you're trying to put together fifty-one votes, you have to make it appear that you're not a vulnerable person. And yet a loving relationship, a friendship, is in making yourself vulnerable. At times you have to take criticism. You have to hear things that you'd rather not hear. That kind of vulnerability doesn't go over well in a political situation."

Durenburger reflected on how the tragedy of his own marital separation had made him more willing to take risks. "Because of my own problems, I began opening up to a few guys, and I found them parched for such contact," he told me. "I found a few of the newer senators opening up personally—Slade Gorton, Dave Pryor, Bill Armstrong. All of them have gone over some kind of life hurdle in recent years, and they are less defensive about talking about it now. But that's not typical."[33]

More generally, Dr. Pieczenik suggested, the quest for power and the relentless pace derive from a deep, inner feeling of inadequacy and dissatisfaction that breeds loneliness.

"There is an addictive quality to all of this," he said. "You've always got to go one higher. As that goes on, the loneliness price is very high. . . . Real friendship is very tough to come by in this town. Friendship is a very fragile commodity. It doesn't have a basis in the profession of political life. The politician never really trusts as much as one would imagine. So much is bled out of them in constituency demands, in legislative demands, in family demands that they wind up after a number of years saying, 'What's left of me? Who am I?' They're always on stage. They're like the comedian who's always got to have a joke. Some of them wind up forgetting what their roots are as individuals."

Sad to say, the most corrosive thing to personal relationships is the Darwinian drive. "Politicians are different from you and me," Richard Reeves, the political commentator, observed. "The business of reaching for power does something to a man: It closes him off from other men until, day by day, he reaches the point where he instinctively calculates each new situation and each other man with the simplest question: What can this do for me?"[34]

More Women, but Still a Man's Town

Over the past fifteen years, the power and responsibility of women has grown in the power game, though the feminist push has not changed the way the game is played. Politics has been a man's sport, and women have learned to play hardball.

Starting with the 1972 presidential campaign of George McGovern, women have become far more numerous, active, and visible in Washington—whether as a vice-presidential nominee, cabinet member, or Supreme Court justice, or as members of Congress, staffers, lobbyists, or journalists. The McGovern campaign, with its strong antiwar plank and its domestic themes of equality and social justice, fueled an explosion of feminist political activity and drew hundreds of able women into politics at the state and national level. The reforms that broke up the old power baronies in Congress opened up further opportunities.

In 1972, there were two women senators and thirteen women members of the House. By 1987, the figures were two senators and twenty-two House members. The inertia of past habits and the inertia of incumbency slow change. It takes years for the pipeline of qualified women candidates to develop at the grass-roots level. But at the state level, the tide of women is rising. In 1974, Ella Grasso of Connecticut became the first woman elected governor in modern times; now there are three. The numbers of women in state legislatures has tripled since 1973, to the point where women held fifteen percent of the seats nationwide in 1987.[35]

The numbers tell only part of the story: On Capitol Hill, manners have changed dramatically since 1973, when Patricia Schroeder, as a freshman anti–Vietnam War Democrat from Colorado, had to endure unprintable sexist insults from F. Edward Hebert, the Armed Services Committee chairman. His high-handed tactics help cost him his chairmanship two years later. More recently, women have become sought after by party leaders. Both party caucuses in the House have women in at least one leadership position. The women who in 1977 formed a caucus on women's issues open to both men and women have become more assertive, but it took until 1985 for women members to get admitted to the House members' gym, which remained a male holdout.

"You have a different kind of women in Congress now than a couple of decades ago," observed Ann Lewis, former political director of the Democratic National Committee. "They are far less likely now to be widows carrying out the family legacy and far more likely to be pursuing careers of their own. Take someone like Barbara Mikulski, who has just won a Senate seat in Maryland. She is sought after by other Democrats as a fund-raiser for their campaigns."[36]

The growth of women's political activism has spread into other fields: Congressional liaison for executive agencies, lobbying, public relations, journalism. Women lobbyists set up their own association in 1975 and now claim eight hundred members, the most prominent of whom are Anne Wexler and Nancy Reynolds, drawn from the Carter and Reagan White Houses and now with one of the best-known lobbying firms in town. Women journalists, barred from the National Press Club, flocked, in the 1970s, to the rival Washington Press Club, which gained several hundred members; the National Press Club agreed to a merger in 1985. Public relations has become such a promising field for women that Sheila Tate, former press secretary to Nancy Reagan and now a top public relations executive, told me that she worries that it may be turning into a "pink-collar ghetto for women."

"Washington is still a male-dominated city," Tate said, "because power is at the White House and on Capitol Hill. Those are earned offices. But one half of the staffers on the Hill are women. That's created a need for more women lobbyists. Women are better communicators than men."[37]

Of course, the most dramatic symbolic changes have come at the peak of government. From a single token woman in earlier presidential cabinets, Jimmy Carter and Ronald Reagan have each had two or three women in their cabinet. Reagan's precedent-shattering step was naming Sandra Day O'Connor the first woman on the Supreme Court in 1981. But an even larger breakthrough for women was the selection of New York Congresswoman Geraldine Ferraro as the Democratic vice-presidential nominee in 1984. I remember standing on the floor of the convention hall in San Francisco when she first appeared as the nominee and feeling the throbbing excitement throughout the hall, especially among the women there.

"Ferraro's presence on that platform and in those campaign debates sent a message to a whole lot of women that they could do it," Ann Lewis declared. "She made the possibilities real. All of a sudden, we realized what we had been missing."

"Forgetting the outcome and the problems she had, it broke the ice," agreed Nancy Reynolds, a lobbyist and a strong campaign fundraiser for Republicans. "It showed that a woman vice-presidential candidate is viable, and it's an open field now. You hear women mentioned all the time now."[38]

But even though women are pressing into new areas and male politicians recognize that they have to include some women at high levels, the power game is still a male-dominated world. If women are no longer exceptions, some old arithmetic still applies: For example, Lynn Martin, vice chair of the House Republican conference, observed that while women comprised fifty-one percent of the committee staff aides in the House, "seventy-five percent of those making $40,000 or more are men, and seventy-four percent of those making $20,000 or less are women."[39] Women are edging into more of the top jobs on the personal staffs of senators but they still have trouble penetrating the inner core of the White House staff. Anne Wexler, who was the liaison with outside political groups in the Carter White House, was an exception.

What is more, there are still policy and political arenas where men prevail almost totally, or only grudgingly let in women—among them defense, intelligence, arms control, the senior White House staff, and political campaign strategy. That point was politely but firmly impressed on me by Katharine Graham. As one of the most powerful women in the country, Kay Graham is no upstart feminist at seventy, but like many a forceful woman, she expects men to accept women more fully as equals.

"It's true there are a lot of women in good jobs," she said. "We have Nancy Kassebaum in the Senate and Elizabeth Dole in the cabinet." Then she paused and went on, both an edge and a sadness in her voice: "But I want to tell you, it's still a very male-chauvinist town, this town. And this has no impact on me anymore, but I think it's very hard on spouses who come down here from places where they've had jobs and they've mattered on their own. And they get to dinner and they absolutely are treated like somebody's wife. I mean people say, 'What does your husband think?'

"I just came back from an arms-control seminar up at the Wye Plantation," she went on, "and the administration people there were kind of applauding themselves on their press relations. I looked around the room and there wasn't a single woman there. There was *no* woman. I thought, this arms control is still a very male area."[40]

Jeane Kirkpatrick, who stirred excitement in late 1984 by making an unsuccessful run at capturing one of the three top foreign-policy jobs, has bristled publicly at unequal treatment in the press. Her complaint is symptomatic: The press refers to Henry Kissinger as "Dr." Kissinger while she is "Mrs." Kirkpatrick, though both have doctorate degrees.

In the rough-and-tumble game of campaign politics, women have had a hard time penetrating into the inner sanctums. One major reason is that fund-raising is a difficult nut for them to crack. Men have both made more money and have the habit of dispensing it. Pamela Harriman, widow of the late New York Governor Averell Harriman, has been a major force in raising funds for Democratic Senate candidates, helping them capture a Senate majority in 1986, but she is exceptional.

Talking about the keys to greater political clout for women, Nancy Reynolds commented: "The big secret is getting people to give and raise money, and that's where women have always been weakest. Money is the mother's milk of politics. Fund-raising for politicians, which has been an age-old habit for men, has been distasteful for many women. Raising money for charities is one thing, but they don't like raising money for politics. They find it hard to ask for. It's easier for men to tap the money-giving networks."[41]

Equally tough to penetrate is the hard-boiled work of campaign strategy and consulting. There are only a few women political pollsters, Linda DiVall for Republicans and Dottie Lynch for Democrats, and only a handful of political consultants and strategists.

But the 1988 presidential campaign brought a few breakthroughs: Susan Estrich, a senior campaign aide in the presidential bids of Ted

Kennedy in 1980 and Walter Mondale in 1984, became national campaign manager for Governor Michael Dukakis—the first woman to
hold the top campaign job for a major national candidate. Robert Dole
used Linda DiVall for poling and Mari Maseng as his press secretary,
and George Bush tapped Barbara Pardue as press secretary.

"The presidential campaign remains the last locker room of American politics," commented Ann Lewis, a top political consultant who
gave advice to presidential contender Jesse Jackson. "But this is the
year when we have finally seen the locker room door begin to open. It's
still very tough. Barriers remain. Even candidates who have been right
on our issues, like George McGovern, have lagged in practice. There
are teams and coaches with not nearly enough women in the inner
circle."[42]

Ann Lewis's "locker-room" image fits the power game in Washington. She and Sheila Tate and Kay Graham are right: Washington is still
a male town, and football is its game. I have friends who like to compare
politics to poker, with its high-stakes betting, its bluffing and its uncertainty. Others think of it more as a horse race or a steeplechase.

More often, politicians turn for analogies to those quintessentially
American pastimes, baseball and football. Barry Carter, a former national security aide and now a law professor at Georgetown University,
sees baseball as the sports metaphor for politics: the confrontation of
pitchers and batting stars balanced by the intricate choreography of
fielding plays or hit-and-run situations. Perhaps, but any city that cannot
sustain a major-league baseball team is not a baseball city at heart. The
Washington Senators packed up in 1972 and moved to Minnesota.

Washington is a football city, and football is the right metaphor for
its politics. Washington Redskins games are sellouts every year, in
Super Bowl seasons or when the team is way down in the league. In
fact, one of the most coveted perks in Washington is a good season
ticket to the Redskins games or, better yet, an invitation to the private
box of Jack Kent Cook, the Redskins' owner. Football thrives as a link
between the two cities of Washington: the solidly middle class, over-
whelmingly black central city and the largely white, upper-middle-class
political city which resides mostly in the bedroom suburbs of Maryland
and Virginia. The Redskins provide the missing symbol for a community that sprawls from the District of Columbia into two states, lacking
a single mayor or governor or any other unifying institution.

What's more, football fits the rhythm and soul of the power game.
Political Washington is a city with a terribly short attention span, quick
to shift from one political melodrama to another, more given to the
game-of-the-week mentality than the quiet patience of a baseball sea-

son with 162 games. Moreover, the action of the power game more
nearly mirrors football. Both are contact sports.

Consider the action: Baseball offers a neat linear focus, pitcher versus
batter, the crack of the bat, a fielder nimbly gathering the small white
globe against a field of green, the race between his throw and the batter
streaking to first base. To be sure, a bases-loaded home run or the flying
spikes of a stolen base offer high drama. But generally, baseball presents
a more orderly test of skills than the jarring mêlée of line play on the
gridiron or the crunch of ballcarrier and tacklers that evokes the brawling confusion and partisan wrangling in Congress or the bruising
clashes between White House and Capitol Hill. In football, as in
politics, the pass patterns are tricky; action everywhere at once.

Consider, too, the very rhythm of play: In baseball, a rally can erupt
in any inning, a low-scoring tie game can stretch into extra innings with
no time limit, or a game can simply peter out in the ninth. But in
football, especially pro football, the length of the game is set and the
script is usually predictable. As millions of television viewers can testify,
you can skip a lot of the early action so long as you're glued to your
set just before halftime and late in the fourth quarter. Then, the offense
goes into its two-minute drill, with frantic time-outs, commercials,
worried consultations between coach and quarterback, and the inevitable injuries, all building the suspense. In those final seconds, everything
goes razzle-dazzle, and those moments determine whether the fans go
home in delirium or dragging in despair.

That mirrors the pace of the Congress, slogging through inconclusive months of tedium on the budget, some dull midfield maneuvering
on the MX missile, diverted by the distraction of a hostage crisis. With
the onset of the summer recess, the tempo quickens, commencing the
political razzle-dazzle. Both parties, both houses go into their two-
minute drills. New budget and tax formulas emerge. Compromise is in
the air. Then a slow period in August and early September, building
up to the political equivalent of a frantic fourth quarter. In the melo-
dramatic windup, the president threatens to shut down the government. From the sidelines comes the magic play. Somehow a deal is
struck in the final seconds. Congress and the White House play right
on the brink. Like football players, they gamble on winning in the final
crunch and time their best plays for the deadline.

Government, of course, is a serious game about policy, but as the
football metaphor suggests, a lot of it is for show, and the action is fairly
well established, year after year. The repetitive gambits and maneuvers
make it easier for us spectators to study the players and the playing
fields, in order to understand the action better.

7. Congress and the Constant Campaign: Survival Politics and the New Breed

> *The campaign is never over.*
> —Robert Squier, media consultant

Well before the five-hour hearing began one September morning in 1985, there were the telltale signs of a major media event. Unusually large crowds of young people lined the columned hallways of the old Russell Senate Office Building to wait for seats. Several television crews set up video monitors and sound equipment in the hallways. The hearing room quickly filled to overflowing.

Inside, it was almost impossible to move. The press tables were jammed. Capitol guards, in starched white shirts, manned the doors. The audience, which had come for a show, was in a boisterous mood at the prospect of the Senate Commerce Committee scrutinizing the seamy, sinful side of rock music. Senator Jack Danforth, the committee chairman, warned against applause and demonstrations. The hearing, he said, was not to consider legislation but merely "to provide a forum for airing the issue."

The opening shot was the protest of Susan Baker, the wife of Treasury Secretary James Baker, and Tipper Gore, wife of Senator Albert Gore, Jr., of Tennessee, among others, against "porn rock," an escalating trend of violent, brutal erotica in rock music (*heavy metal,* in the

argot of its fans). Sexually explicit songs, Mrs. Baker told the committee, were "glorifying rape, sadomasochism, incest, the occult, and suicide" with palpable and pernicious effects on the young. Mrs. Gore,
speaking for the Parents Music Resource Center, carefully stopped
short of advocating censorship. But she urged record companies voluntarily to label record albums, the way cigarette packages are labeled,
with warnings of "violent and sexually explicit lyrics."[1]

Later, there was a rustle at the appearance of Dee Snider, a heavy-
metal singer-composer who was a particular target of the mothers'
criticism. Snider wriggled through the packed crowd in a faded-jeans
outfit, a thick shower of stringy long blond curls tumbling well over his
shoulders. At the witness table, he jauntily peeled off his jeans jacket
to expose a tattoo on his left shoulder and a sleeveless black T-shirt
promoting Twisted Sister, his rock group. Bare-armed, he faced the
somber-suited senators.

"I don't know if it's morning or afternoon," he said, peering through
dark glasses at the dais. "I'll say both: Good morning and good afternoon." He flashed a toothy grin at the nearest television camera.

Snider defensively declared himself a husband, a father, and a Christian. Then, he proceeded to accuse Mrs. Gore of "character assassination," of distorting his lyrics, and of spreading an "outright lie" by
claiming that a T-shirt marketed by his group showed "a woman in
handcuffs sort of spread-eagled." His song "Under the Blade," he
contended, was not a parable of rape in bondage but a tale of fear on
the operating table, an interpretation that met skepticism from Senator
Gore.

Frank Zappa, a rock voice from an earlier, tamer rock era, arrived
in jacket and tie, and with lawyer at his side warned against censorship.
What the mothers wanted, he cautioned, would be like "treating
dandruff by decapitation."

On the network news that night, the star was none of the above. It
was Senator Paula Hawkins of Florida, a petite, politically canny and
assertive grandmother, who made drug abuse, child abuse, missing
children, and pornography her cornerstone issues in the Senate. Hawkins was not a member of the Senate Commerce Committee, but she
has a nose for media events and a knack for attracting publicity that
enabled her to upstage the committee. Through senatorial courtesy,
Senator Hawkins arranged to be invited and appeared, eye-catching
and camera-catching, in a fire-engine-red suit.

Several other senators made predictable statements of moral outrage,
but Hawkins had a shrewder gambit. She had her statement, too, but

knowing that words were no match for pictures, she came armed with some near-irresistible visuals crafted by the graphic-arts staff of the Senate Republican Conference. On her own television set, plopped on the dais, she played a couple of sizzling porn-rock videocassettes—one of them "Hot for Teacher" by Eddie van Halen—to demonstrate for one and all that the new raunchiness of rock made Elvis Presley seem as innocent as a choirboy. And she waved aloft the blowup of a lurid, blood-dripping male figure and crude four-letter slogans on the album cover of a heavy-metal group called W.A.S.P.

Hawkins's performance caught the play on two national networks. But she and her handlers were taking no chances; to be sure of solid coverage in her home state of Florida, where she was engaged in a tough battle for reelection, Senator Hawkins provided "video feeds"— electronic press releases, videotapes of her in action. They were fed to more than thirty Florida television stations on a satellite hookup arranged through the Senate Republican Conference.

Indeed, according to Susan Baker, Paula Hawkins had been the catalyst behind the hearing in the first place. "She contacted me before any talk of a hearing surfaced," Mrs. Baker recalled. "The idea came from her." Senator Hawkins's political instincts were sound. It was a hot topic with wide audience appeal, because one side of the argument was outraged and the other side was titillated.[2] The six and a half minutes of network news time given that evening to the Senate's porn-rock hearing was more coverage than the massive congressional efforts on the budget deficit crisis received in a full month. C-Span, the cable network that covers congressional proceedings, got more requests for copies of the porn-rock hearing than anything else it has covered since it began operating in 1979.

Making political hay out of a televised hearing on a newsy topic is hardly a revolutionary idea. Since Senator Estes Kefauver's investigations of organized crime in 1951 and the Watergate investigations of Richard Nixon more than two decades later, many leading politicians have used televised hearings to catapult themselves to national prominence. Kefauver made himself a presidential contender partly by his crime probe; the Watergate hearings made Howard Baker, a Tennesseean like Kefauver, a national political figure. Even tapping celebrity entertainers to excite more popular interest is not an original angle—it was one of the many techniques used by Senator Joseph McCarthy during his postwar Communist hunts.

The new wrinkle is that video politics has become a prime vehicle for virtually every incumbent, even a relatively unnoticed freshman

Republican such as Paula Hawkins. What used to be rare is now routine. What used to be the sporadic, often sensational province of a few political heavyweights dealing with major national concerns has now become the regular practice of the rank-and-file backbenchers to publicize their activities and specialized agendas.

Everyone is advertising, trying to establish a successful brand name with the voters. The new breed of television-oriented congressmen and senators use satellite feeds to send their own versions of hearings to home-state television stations. The porn-rock hearing was a juicy enough topic to hit the national networks. But for wider play, three Republicans (Hawkins, Danforth of Missouri and Paul Trible of Virginia) and one Democrat (Fritz Hollings of South Carolina) beamed home their own video feeds in time for the local nightly news. Indeed, the whole point of regular, daily satellite feeds is to bypass the networks and go directly to local stations, often hungry for a Washington angle.

The Five Pillars of Incumbency

Video feeds epitomize the technology of the constant campaign. Above all, what was driving Paula Hawkins at the porn-rock hearing was the politics of survival. Obviously, politicians come to Washington with more than one motive. Most have some particular particular programs or policy lines they want to push; others have policy peeves, injustices they want to correct. Some have ambition to become substantial policymakers and master legislators. Many more are driven by the pursuit of prestige and notoriety, by the chance to be seen on television back home or the hopes of winning celebrity status among a wider audience. But one universal and paramount motive is reelection. All but a few want to continue in office. Many make it a career, running almost constantly to keep themselves in office while they are there.

The campaign has become the perpetual-motion machine. More than ever in our history, elections are an unbroken succession, each following the last without interruption. The techniques, mentality, and mercenary consultants of the campaign follow the winners right into office.

The current power game has given incumbents, especially those in the House of Representatives, enormous advantages. Once they are in Congress, they have a high-technology arsenal that insures that all but a tiny handful will survive any challenge. The five pillars of incumbency are: 1. video feeds; 2. high-tech computerized mail; 3. elaborately staffed casework, involving myriad little favors for constituents; 4. personal presence back home, often ingeniously publicized; and 5. political money.

Some politicians, especially the new breed in the House, have become extremely skilled at modern survival techniques. The record shows that. Since the mid-1960s, ninety-one percent of the House incumbents who sought reelection were successful. That trend reached a peak of 97.7 percent in 1986. Turnover comes mainly when people retire or in rare years of shock upsets. The Senate has been less secure, with a seventy-eight-percent reelection rate in the 1980s. Overall, the congressional record of survival is far higher than in the 1940s and 1950s, let alone earlier in our history.

The built-in resources of congressional office are so great that they not only give incumbents a nearly unbeatable advantage, but they scare off potential challengers. The costs of campaigning have become so great that there is a declining number of serious challengers who can mount the necessary effort. The result is that the techniques of survival politics, mostly financed at *taxpayer expense,* allow many members in the House to insulate themselves from the swings of the political pendulum in presidential elections.

To a striking degree, recent congressional campaigns have been decoupled from presidential campaigns. Ronald Reagan, even with fifty-nine percent of the popular vote in his 1984 landslide, could not pull many new Republicans into office on his coattails. In the House, 192 Democrats held their seats in districts that went for Reagan. Something similar happened in the Nixon landslide of 1972, prompting one well-known academic specialist on Congress, David Mayhew of Yale University, to comment that the smart House member should ignore national trends and work his district like an old-fashioned ward boss, doing favors, making his presence felt, cutting a visible figure.[3]

That political catechism has taken on new force in the past decade— and not accidentally. Ohio Congressman Wayne Hays deliberately liberalized the administrative rules of the House from 1971 to 1975 to favor incumbents. Hays served as both head of the Democratic Congressional Campaign Committee (DCCC)—concerned with reelection of House Democrats—and chairman of the House Administration Committee—which writes the housekeeping rules. Hays wanted to make it easier for incumbents to keep getting elected, according to Marty Franks, the DCCC's executive director; Hays wanted to protect the large Democratic class of '74, many of whom had won normally Republican seats and were especially vulnerable in 1976.[4] So Hays granted House members larger allowances, enabling them to expand their staffs and do more casework, and he liberalized accounting rules so that House members could spend more money on travel home and mail to constituents. These changes were a boon to the constant campaign and the Democratic House majority.

"What they've done, starting in '74," protested Newt Gingrich, an outspoken Georgia Republican, "is they built this huge wall of incumbency advantage which makes it very hard to beat the incumbent."[5]

The traditional way that American politicians have kept in good favor with the home folks is to obtain slices of federal "pork" for their districts: money from the federal pork barrel for dams, sewage plants, mass transit, military bases, defense contracts. That works with local civic, business, and political leaders, but for many ordinary voters, "pork" is too impersonal. The fresh angle, which has mushroomed since the mid-1970s, is doing a huge volume of little personal favors for constituents. In Congress, they call it "casework." That means having your staff track down missing Social Security checks, inquire about sons and husbands in the armed services, help veterans get medical care, pursue applications for small-business loans. With this technique, some senators and House members become more valued by thousands of voters as ombudsmen than as legislators.

The constant campaign has other new twists. One is the modern adaptation of that old-fashioned congressional privilege: the postage frank, which permits officeholders to mail a letter or package by merely writing a signature where the rest of us put a stamp. The idea was to let members of Congress keep voters informed about the actions of government. But the frank has become a tool for modern mass merchandising at taxpayers expense. The cost soared over $111 million in 1984, reflecting not only rising volume, but new technology. In one decade, the technology of political mail has gone through several generations. Twenty years ago, congressional offices did not have copying machines or computers. Nowadays, a senator or House member uses high-speed laser printers, automated letter folders, and computerized mass-mailing systems. Technical sophistication enables incumbents to ferret out friendly or swing segments of voters for carefully targeted messages. They tell people what those people want to hear, without aggravating others who disagree.

The object is to use mass-marketing techniques and yet somehow provide a personalized touch. This reflects a core concept of John Naisbitt, the futurist. In his book *Megatrends*, Naisbitt argues that modern life requires a combination of what he calls "high tech" and "high touch." "Whenever new technology is introduced into society, there must be a counterbalancing human response—that is, *high touch*—or the technology is rejected," Naisbitt wrote.[6] In short, successful high tech must have a human message and create an intimate, personal feeling. Since television is the most powerful technological intrusion it must be balanced by more personal contacts. Hence the drive for casework and direct mail with a personal feel.

Even so, the real cutting edge of the constant campaign is the video feed. Not glitzy, big-buck advertising paid for by political donations, but the week-in-and-week-out generation of prepackaged electronic press releases: videotapes for television outlets and audiotapes, or actualities, for radio stations. They go on the air (sometimes edited but sometimes untouched by the local stations) as straight news reports, usually without any indication that congressional politicians originated them and that taxpayer dollars usually paid for them. Along with regular news reporting, these become part of what politicians call "free media": publicity and coverage which is not labeled for its political sponsorship, even though the cameraman worked for a political party, not a TV station.

For example, the camera crew that Paula Hawkins asked to cover the porn-rock hearing worked not for the networks or for independent Florida stations, but for the Senate Republican Conference. The conference is the official organ of all the Republican senators; it is financed by a hefty annual taxpayer's subsidy of $565,000 a year. (Senate Democrats got a similar subsidy but ran a modest media operation, spending their funds on other activities.) These funds are part of the $1.6 billion in annual appropriations that Congress votes for its own operations. The Republican Conference staff includes two full camera crews, three graphic artists, and ten film editors, producers, and other media technicians. In four years, its operation went from nothing to sending out 4,032 satellite feeds for senators in 1986.[7]

Tighter rules in the House of Representatives forbid taxpayer subsidies for video feeds. In the House, the cost of self-generated video is picked up mostly by the political parties or by the members themselves. But members of both houses and both parties can use two congressional recording studios to tape their own weekly cable network interview shows and radio broadcasts, with the help of a staff of forty producers, cameraman, sound engineers, and technicians all paid for by about $1.4 million a year in tax dollars. In addition, the Republican party is rich enough so that its congressional arm can send out forty thousand radio feeds a year for its House members on automated phone banks.

The constant campaign demands a relentlessly reassuring presence for the home folks: regular weekend trips for luncheon speeches to the Rotary Club or the chamber of commerce, endless drop-ins at homes for the elderly, defense plants, or new shopping malls, and campaign-style innovations such as the "walking town meetings" (ambulatory open houses) that Senator Bill Bradley conducts on New Jersey beaches. But no chore is more important than the grinding preoccupation of incumbents with raising enough money for the next campaign, sometimes four or five years ahead of time for senators, often to finance periodic public-opinion polling so that incumbents can keep tabs on the mood of their voters and their own vulnerabilities.

One symbol of the permanent campaign stands in a suburban district outside of Denver where Representative Tim Wirth has kept a campaign office open continuously for fourteen years, since his first election in 1974. His staff jokingly calls it the "campaign office that never closed down."

Rule 1: Visibility at All Costs

The cardinal rule of the incumbency game has become: Be visible, even if substance suffers. Paul Tsongas, a Massachusetts Democrat, told me how he had been damaged by forgetting that rule when he shifted from the House to the Senate. Always a serious legislator, Tsongas had plunged conscientiously into the substance of his job as a new senator, especially his role on the Foreign Relations Committee. For several months, he put his home-district chores and television appearances on the back burner.

"I used to represent a congressional district where there were only three newspapers, so staying in print was very easy," he told me. "Then all of a sudden I represented the entire state and people thought I had dropped off the face of the earth. I got a lot of letters back saying, 'Are you still there? I worked for you, and we don't hear anything about you.' At the end of my first year, we were just getting so tired of the criticism that I started to do town meetings more regularly. We went through the whole process of sending out newsletters, just to generate a sense of movement. And we found that after running around the state and being visible, my poll numbers just soared."

"Even though what you were doing and saying in Washington was no different?" I asked him.

"In fact," he nodded ruefully, "you can argue that the staff resources that I had to allocate to become visible had to be taken away from the substantive work that we were doing. So I was probably a lesser senator while my numbers were going up."

Sometimes, visibility—saying and doing something that sticks in voters' minds—is stunningly primitive. Tsongas, who quit the Senate because of health reasons, was willing to admit publicly what other politicians will say only off the record or in private—namely, that content mattered less than sheer exposure and the ease people felt about you as a person. In his 1978 Senate race, Tsongas started late, produced several political ads on his policy positions, and found he was running third largely because people did not know his name or how to pronounce it (song-gus).

"What we did was put an ad on television of people mispronouncing my name," he recalled with a smile. "The end of the ad is this boy who just obliterates my name and in frustration calls me 'tickets.' That's the best he could do. That ad became a classic. I'd be in a parade and people would call me 'tickets.' Literally scores of people said they would be in the kitchen, hear the ad come on, and run into the living room to see it. You could not listen to that ad without smiling. That was the only ad anybody ever remembered. People would say, 'I like that idea that you could laugh at yourself.' Here I think of myself as a very issue-oriented, very substantive person, and I know in my heart of hearts I got elected to the Senate because my name wasn't Smith."

With energetic courtship of the voters during six years in the Senate, Tsongas gained such substantial visibility that his polls showed no serious opposition to his reelection before he announced his voluntary retirement. Obviously, he was helped by a heavily Democratic electorate, but he achieved what all incumbents aspire to—beating the opposition before it appears—by playing the incumbency game effectively.

"I'm not the most charismatic person that ever came down the pike, but it was just sort of an identification, a comfortableness that I was the senator, and there wasn't any serious threat," Tsongas observed.

"I would hear the same thing over and over again after we would make a significant effort to go on television," he said. "People would come up to me and say, 'I saw you on television last week,' and I'd say, 'Oh, what was it about?' and they'd say, 'Well, I don't remember, but you looked tired,' or 'I liked your tie.' It was purely an impressionistic response. I would say only maybe twenty percent of the time people who saw me could tell me what I was talking about. I used to be absolutely dumfounded by that. . . . People come to think of you as a person more than they think of you as somebody identified with a particular set of issues. And if they're comfortable with you as a person—and TV for me was a very good medium—then they'll forgive some of your positions. Reagan is a classic example."[8]

Many politicians believe that sheer repetitive exposure on television

is the key to survival because it gives them reach and personal imprint.
They will grab any opportunity. That leads to the second rule of video
politics: Develop techniques of leapfrogging the TV networks to get
on local channels.

"There are an awful lot of members of Congress who have never seen
their faces on network TV and who never will," observed Marty
Franks, executive director of the Democratic Congressional Campaign
Committee. "Since the mid-seventies, they began to look for ways to
get on their local channels. First, make sure there is a visual component
to your visit home—instead of doing a meeting about senior citizens
in your office, go out and talk to people at the senior center [to attract
coverage]. Out of Washington, you have to find ways to bypass the
networks."9

One evening in February 1986, I watched some Democratic congressmen doing that, by piggybacking on President Reagan's State of
the Union address. They were angling for quick thirty-second bursts of
publicity back home with their reactions to Reagan. In the old days,
they could have put out press releases or done radio "beepers" (phone
interviews) the next day with local stations, but that would have lost
immediacy. Now, their parties have organized something better.

After Reagan's address, I found about forty rank-and-file Democrats
tucked away in H-137, one of the Capitol's catacombs. Like college
graduates lined up to receive diplomas, they formed a quiet, orderly file.
One or two sipped coffee or a soft drink. The room was hushed. Only
moments before they had all been part of the pageantry of an American
ritual, the president's annual address to Congress and the nation. They
had cheered Reagan's salute to the "valor of our seven *Challenger*
heroes" who perished when the space shuttle exploded, but many had
folded their hands when he gave his economic prescriptions.

Now the tumult and the backslapping in the well of the House of
Representatives were over. The president's motorcade had headed off
into the foggy night and turned down Pennsylvania Avenue toward the
White House. The cabinet, which sat front-row seats center stage, and
the foreign diplomatic corps, which had filled the "violin sections" to
the left of the dais, had dispersed. The press corps were up in the
galleries inserting fresh bits of color (about Mrs. Reagan's cranberry
suit or Democratic reaction to Reagan's tribute to Tip O'Neill's ten
years as speaker) into stories previously crafted from the advance text
of the president's speech. The audience had headed for the parking
lots.

These Democrats were still at work. Some combed their hair and straightened their ties. Most were quietly rehearsing little set pieces, like students before an exam, nervously teasing each other about performing on cue. Each had forty-five seconds to a minute—no time for fluffs or retakes. The entire operation had to be completed within ninety minutes, if they were going to hit the eleven o'clock local news in New Haven, Cleveland, or San Francisco. The easterners had to make a feed to *Spacenet 1* and the westerners to *West Star 4*, two satellites each rented for half an hour for nine hundred dollars by the Democratic Congressional Campaign Committee.

The room had the bare rudiments of a set: an American flag as backdrop and a television camera mounted on tripod and focused toward the flag at a spot where a "T" had been marked off on the carpet with gray masking tape. Each member would stand on the "T" facing the camera and a young woman holding a microphone who gave the cue line: "Congressman, your reaction?"

"I'm new," admitted James Traficant, a freshman Democrat and a burly former sheriff from Youngstown, Ohio. "I thought the first State of the Union address was a combination of Walt Disney and Cedric [sic] B. deMille, and I think this one is sort of Steven Spielberg. I honestly got to believe that with a $150 billion trade deficit and the president submitting a budget that supposedly is going to call for another $28 billion plus in defense spending, he's out of touch with reality."

Some applause in the room, and the assembly line moved forward. Charles Rangel, a dapper black from Harlem with sixteen years in the House, gave Reagan a more practiced jab. "I think it was a great ending of a good class-B movie," quipped Rangel, "but it doesn't really take into consideration the problems of the homeless, the jobless, and the hopeless that we have in this country." Sandor Levin of Michigan, older, thoughtful, more sorrowful, decried the "major gap between the rhetoric of the speech and the reality of the programs."

Timothy Wirth, a Democrat from a heavily Republican district in Colorado who was running for the Senate, cast himself as a middle-of-the-road ally of the president. "I think the president did just right in talking about the future," Wirth said. "Making government work is clearly something we all want to do. The Pentagon has to be made to work just like every other program. . . . I think the president focusing on trade is right, as well. One job in five in the United States is now dependent on trade directly or indirectly. That's an enormous change and we have to have free trade, open trade, fair trade."

As we walked away together, Wirth, a lanky, handsome six-foot-five political Gary Cooper, spoke confidently of getting good exposure in Colorado from his video feed that night and on the morning news shows. His press office had alerted television stations from Denver to Colorado Springs, Grand Junction, and Durango that they could "pull" in his piece from the West Star 4 satellite with their dish antennas. Wirth preached the gospel of video politics.

"You've just gotta go up there and do your number," he enthused. "You have to get over the embarrassment of doing it and feeling it's hokey. What you have to realize is that in thirty-five or forty seconds, you have tens of thousands of people see you." Then, with a widening grin, he chirped a new-breed epigram: "Having a press conference is a good thing. Having a press conference with a television camera is a better thing. Having a press conference with television cameras in double figures is absolute bliss."[10]

The Political Video Race

Senate Republicans, long stuck in the underdog Avis position and determined to try harder, were the ones who changed the congressional video game. They pioneered the rapid shift in 1982 from old-fashioned radio "beepers" for the "mom and pop" radio stations to slicker, pre-packaged, newsy satellite feeds. Their first attempt was clumsy and primitive (it all but missed the relay satellite)—but the sheer Republican chutzpa titillated the commercial TV networks.

The only portable television camera on Capitol Hill (owned by Senator Ted Stevens of Alaska) was a relatively cheap six-thousand-dollar Japanese camera which produced film that was red at the edges, not of professional quality. Nor was the cameraman, Bill Livingston, a press aide at the Senate Republican Conference, who had studied filmmaking at the University of Southern California. On thirty separate cassettes, Livingston shot each senator responding to Reagan's address in a Capitol hideaway. The film was bicycled over to the Russell Senate Office Building for editing, driven downtown to Pyramid Video for further processing, and finally relayed by microwave to a satellite dish farm in suburban Virginia for the "uplink" to the satellite. At every step, there were fumbles, delays and near-misses.[11]

As a precaution, the Republican camera team began filming hours in advance, working from Reagan's prepared text. They were filmed in the act by network camera crews. Phil Jones of CBS News caught the canned reaction of Rudy Boschwitz of Minnesota. "It's only five-thirty, hours before President Reagan delivers his State of the Union address, but here is Senator Rudy Boschwitz giving his reaction," was Phil

Jones's tongue-in-cheek report on the evening news—*ahead* of Reagan's speech.

It is amazing how rapidly the technology developed after that. Playing catch-up, the Democrats set up a makeshift media center in 1984 in the converted garage of a Capitol Hill townhouse bought for them by Pamela Harriman, an important Democratic angel. Now, both parties have multimillion-dollar media complexes and studios on Capitol Hill that are technological wonders. They are equipped with state-of-the-art videotape recorders, mixers, modulators, electronic switching and blending machines with massive keyboards to mix sight and sound, live interviews, and fancy graphics. Most proudly, they include the latest, $250,000 ADOs (Ampex digital optics machines), which can simulate 3-D, spin and flip pictures upside down or inside out, and project all the dazzling cut-ins that viewers have come to expect from modern TV. Both parties also have the capacity to do satellite relays from their own studios instead of clumsily carting film cassettes to a downtown studio.

The Republicans, richer by far, still have the edge, especially on the Senate side. In the Hart Office Building, a few feet or a few floors from many Senate offices, the Senate Republican Conference has studios and film-editing rooms and dishes on the roof to provide satellite uplinks and downlinks. This means that senators can do live two-way press conferences, town meetings, and call-in shows on a toll-free 800 number with cable listeners from Maine to Montana, or Alabama to Alaska.

"The technology gives us an enormous advantage," enthused Bob Vastine, a former legislative director and now, in effect, the TV executive producer for the Republican Conference. "A senator can come into our studio from his office, four minutes away, and talk to a TV station in his state. The technology is fabulous. It can provide a real-time, live-news situation. What we are is a public relations agency for the Republican senators with our own broadcast bureau."[12]

In theory, the shots of senators in action, their town meetings, and press conferences are reports to voters, and that is why they are paid for by tax money, just like the congressional frank. But often they typify the blatant electioneering of Capitol Hill: senators or House members introducing bills they know will go nowhere, making floor speeches or inserting documents into the *Congressional Record* to impress the home audience rather than to persuade colleagues, running hearings that attract publicity but have little practical impact. Moreover, the line between reporting official duties and campaign publicity gets fuzzy when the Republican Senatorial Campaign Committee picks up the tab for satellite time and when the most aggressive users of the Republican Conference video service in 1986 were the eighteen Republican senators up for reelection.

The 1986 battle royal for control of the Senate demonstrated that video politics are important, but not infallible. A large class of freshman Republicans, many fairly new to politics in 1980 when the Reagan wave carried them into office, were struggling desperately to hang on to their seats. Satellite feeds were one of their principal tools in more than a dozen close races. Despite the help of video politics, freshman Republicans lost in North and South Dakota, Alabama, Georgia, Washington, and Florida. But other freshman Republican senators survived in 1986, significantly helped by incumbent video politics: Charles Grassley of Iowa, Steven Symms of Idaho, Don Nickles of Oklahoma, Robert Kasten of Wisconsin, and Arlen Specter of Pennsylvania.

"Those were competent senators who did their job well, worked hard at their grass-roots campaigns, and did a good job of organizing," one Republican Senate strategist contended. "That wasn't true of some Republicans who lost. They tried to make up for their failings with video feeds. You can't take a mediocre operation and do a video feed a day and have it make up for a lackluster performance as a senator. But with a quality operation, good video politics can make the difference."

For the home audience, the critical question is, How many stations take the political bait of video feeds? Some television stations are skittish about being used by politicians, without labeling the true source of their video reports. In Florida, for example, only about half the state's seventy TV stations used Senator Paula Hawkins's satellite feeds—mainly medium-sized stations in Fort Myers, West Palm Beach, Pensacola, Jacksonville, and Orlando, and especially independent stations with no network affiliation. Big stations in Miami, and network affiliates in other cities, shied away. That fits a national pattern. Republican-produced feeds got cool reactions in urban California but went over well in rural Idaho and the Dakotas.

"What we do is very controversial," Bob Vastine admitted. "A lot of people say that it is practically immoral. The newspapers get very holier-than-thou. A lot of newspapers have attacked the use of our stuff by TV stations, saying, 'You guys are using stuff that you didn't film.' The TV stations ought to turn on the newspapers and say, 'You guys routinely use press releases you didn't write.' The TV stations are embarrassed about it, and often they won't admit it even when they do use our stuff. They've been made to feel guilty by the print press."

New Breed vs. Old Breed

Satellite feeds reflect a far broader pattern of change in the power game. For television has organically altered the face of American politics. It has changed the ways of Congress, produced a new breed of politician in Washington, and forced the old breed to change their ways or fade out. Boss Tube has both brought the techniques of the constant campaign into the operations of Congress and emphasized the generational cleavage between the yuppie politicians who grew up with television and the gray-haired, old-fashioned "pols" who have had to adapt to video politics late in life. Though there are exceptions, the generational divide between old and new breed occurred in the Democratic party in 1974 and probably four years later among House Republicans.

Right after that pivotal election of 1974, Tim Wirth, a ringleader among seventy-five newly elected Democrats, got a phone call from House Speaker Carl Albert. They were a mismatch right from the start. As Wirth recalled, Albert offered congratulations and told Wirth, " 'We'll be sending you some material in the mail that'll cover all your health-care benefits and retirement benefits and parking privileges and so on'—as if that was why I'd run for the United States Congress."[13]

Then Albert told Wirth, "Oh, by the way, we're having a little organizational meeting here in December and hope you can get back for it." No hint of important doings, but With smelled something. It turned out to be the House Democratic Caucus at which longtime liberal reformers such as Richard Bolling of Missouri were going to push their challenge of the seniority system, begun in 1971. Wirth and another Democratic freshman, Edward Pattison of Troy, New York, decided to visit Speaker Albert.

When they asked the speaker how to organize their class to make it a force in the House, Albert suggested they leave the organizing to *his* lieutenants. But Wirth and company did it themselves. They raised $15,000 and set up their own office and staff to push their agenda: congressional reform and opposition to the Vietnam War. Rather than silently waiting to be called upon by their elders, they did unprecedented, upstart things such as organizing a class dinner and inviting the House leadership or having the temerity to request that powerful, previously unchallenged committee chairmen come answer questions from the freshmen.

Their moves to curb the old barons made network news, although the freshmen were so new in town that Frank Reynolds of ABC misidentified Tim Wirth as Max Baucus of Montana, another trim, sandy-haired freshman from the West. Ultimately, the reformist putsch, led by Richard Bolling, Phillip Burton of California, and David Obey of Wisconsin and using the freshmen as shock troops, toppled three old-line chairmen, sending tremors through the House. All this happened before the freshmen Democrats had formally taken their oaths of office. At one gathering, Wirth was approached by Jamie Whitten of Mississippi, a Faulknerian figure first elected just before Pearl Harbor.

"Here you've been on national television for the last three days, and you haven't even been sworn in yet!" Whitten muttered with asperity. "And in all my thirty-three years in Congress, I've never been on national television once."

As so often happens, the political changes in the House mirrored changes in the country at large—especially the demographic movement to the South and West and into the suburbs. Many new-breed Democrats came from suburban districts and from western or border states. Politically, they cut different figures from old-breed Democrats representing traditional strongholds in the Old South or in big cities— veterans such as House Speaker Tip O'Neill, a classic Irish politician from just outside Boston; Danny Rostenkowski, a gravel-voiced Polish-American from North Chicago, raised in the machine politics of Mayor Richard Daley; or Charlie Rangel, a black from Harlem who won away Adam Clayton Powell's seat in 1970 and quietly worked his way up the power ladder within the House.

By capitalizing on the voters' anti-Watergate mood, many freshmen Democrats won seats in traditionally Republican districts. Having run middle-of-the-road campaigns, they had much looser ties to party than the old breed, and they disdained political machines. "This brand-new bunch weren't very much *Democratic* politicians," commented Richard Bolling, a Truman Democrat who had been in the House since 1948. "They were running on the Democratic ticket, but they were managing their own campaigns. They were good on media. They had great success because of the Watergate situation. They were not dependent on party and were probably only really interested in being against the Vietnam War and for reform of Congress. Those two things held them together."[14]

In time, the new-breed Democrats differed with the old breed on economic policy. As the country swung conservative, they adjusted more easily than veteran New Dealers did. But more than issues marked the new breed apart; their backgrounds, their educations, their whole political styles were different.

The new breed went for high-tech politics; they ran as independents rather than partisans. Once in Congress, they bypassed the old power ladder by playing the new game of video politics, and they advanced quickly. Half a dozen moved on to the Senate, and others took large public roles in the House. Even little differences were noticed: The old breed used to play gin together at the University Club in the evenings; the new breed, puckishly self-styled the Hardwood Caucus, played basketball in the House gym—afternoon, bipartisan games with Republicans. The generational divide reflected different habits and upbringings.

"The new-breed guys were born in the TV studio, and the old breed were born in the political clubhouse" was how Chris Matthews, Tip O'Neill's spokesman, put it. Mathhews, at forty-one, is a curious blend of new-breed glibness and old-Irish roots in North Philadelphia. "It's the difference between Atari Democrats, high-tech Democrats, and street-corner Democrats," he went on. "The old guys worked their way up through the chairs, as Tip puts it. They're very hierarchical. They keep their friendships. They keep their alliances. They dance with the girl they came with. They stick together. The new-breed guys play one-night stands. They're always forming new coalitions. They're always worrying about their image and how to position themselves. They decide what image they want to project, and they position themselves to project that image."[15]

Roots explain a lot: Old-breed politicians such as O'Neill and Rostenkowski grew up in strong Catholic, ethnic enclaves that shaped their outlook and their dialect, while many of the new breed hail from WASP, suburbanite districts.

"The new-breed guys have no imprint of their districts," Matthews suggested. "Wirth or Les Aspin [of Wisconsin] could come from a hundred different districts around the country. The new-breed guys went away to college. They became unrooted. They were very mobile, and they are very national in their perspective. They don't represent a neighborhood. The old-breed guys stayed home. Tip went to Boston College, and Danny went to Loyola. Tip O'Neill could only come from Cambridge. He fits the district. Danny Rostenkowski is a telephone-book candidate. You could open the phone book in his district, point to a name, and come up with someone like Danny. Not as smart, but with his attitudes and style. And I think that's one reason why the older members have a greater instinct for the neighborhood."

In a witty and intriguing book, *Tribes on the Hill*, anthropologist J. McIver Weatherford compares the two types of politicians and their quite separate power games to tribal figures—shamans and warlords. By his account, tribal shamans are medicine men, witch doctors who win followers by seeming to dispense magic to protect warriors, end droughts, arrange love matches. "Unlike the chiefs and war leaders in a tribe, the shaman's power derives not from the authority of his position or from the practical results which he produces, as much as from the confidence he displays and the emotions he can extract from his followers," Weatherford wrote. "They publicize, play upon, and eventually help to allay the worst fears of the common people. They make real the threat of unseen demons, which they then exorcise. In the political world of Washington, shamans do not invoke the dread of evil spirits as much as the dreaded forces of world communism, the Mafia, monopoly cabals, the moral majority, or immoral minority."[16]

By contrast, the tribal warlords of Capitol Hill play a different power game entirely. "They carefully choose one piece of organizational terrain, slowly dominate it, strengthen it, and gradually extend it outward, increasing the scope of that special area," said Weatherford, who watched the process as an aide to Ohio's Senator John Glenn. "Theirs is a patient game of slowly adding staff in one certain area year after year. . . . Theirs is also the game of the career legislator willing to spend the remainder of his life in Congress and to eschew the glitter and fame of the White House. Even though the Warlords may be the least-known Congressional powers to outsiders, they ultimately have the clans that stretch furthest from Congress and into the bowels of government, exercising an influence that far outweighs the more media-oriented politicians."[17]

The differences are not purely generational, but they do generally match the generational lines. For television is a natural medium for modern political shamans whose most potent magic is mood, image, and symbolism—whether they be John Kennedy, Ronald Reagan, or the political new breed in Congress. Jealously, the old-warlord breed deride them as mere "show horses." Rather disdainfully, Christopher Matthews quipped that "the new-breed guys will go to a seminar and talk issues, but the old-breed guys like Danny Rostenkowski would never go to a seminar—they want to know when you're going to pass a bill."

That's a bit overdrawn; some older politicians have learned the tricks of the new-breed game, and some younger politicians have proven their skills at old-breed inside politics. For example, House Democratic leaders, such as Tip O'Neill, Jim Wright, and Tom Foley, have learned to master the media, and Rostenkowski ran economic seminars to get his committee to pass the 1986 tax-reform bill. And the best of the new

breed have been extremely able legislators, politicians such as Dick
Gephardt of Missouri, Leon Panetta of California, and Bill Gray of
Pennsylvania on the House Budget Committee.

But unquestionably, television has helped the new breed get ahead
much faster than newcomers used to. Some of the best and the brightest of that class of '74—Tom Downey and Stephen Solarz of New
York, Henry Waxman of California, Tim Wirth of Colorado, Chris
Dodd of Connecticut—ignored Sam Rayburn's old rule that in Congress "to get along, you go along." The Rayburn rule dictated silent
apprenticeship for junior members and a slow climb up the ladder, but
the new-breed leaders were quick to carve out important issues and
become spokesmen—Downey on arms control, Solarz on South Africa
and the Philippines, Waxman on health, Wirth on the breakup of
American Telephone and Telegraph, Dodd on Central America. Indeed, the dispersal of power in Congress meant fast advancement,
because old congressmen were retiring, and the two shock elections of
1974 and 1980, with their unusual numbers of upsets, pushed out many
others. By Reagan's inauguration, a majority of House members had
served no more than four years, and fifty-five senators were still in their
first terms. The new breed were taking over.

More broadly, video politics of the constant campaign invaded the
very operations of Congress. In 1979, the House started televising its
floor proceedings; in 1986, the Senate followed suit. In both bodies,
tele-wise junior members have taken to making brief topical morning
speeches, hoping for a pickup by the networks. During debates, some
members show up with huge graphic blowups, mounted on easels, for
good video viewing.

Along with changing political styles came a fleet of consultants who
sailed into the inner councils of politicians—not just during campaigns
but during governing sessions as well. They, too, altered the Washington power game. These are the real political shamans: the media advisers, political strategists, pollsters, direct mail operatives. And they have
replaced the old political bosses.

It's no longer news that Carter and Reagan in the White House
rarely gave a major speech without consulting their pollsters (Patrick
Caddell for Carter and Richard Wirthlin for Reagan), sometimes down
to the most minute detail. But few people know that old-breed House
Speaker Tip O'Neill formed an inner sanctum of half a dozen political
consultants to give him advice on overall Democratic legislative strategy, to help figure out how to oppose Ronald Reagan without offending
the voter.

Also, I remember sitting in the office of Peter Hart, one of the best Democratic pollster-strategists, shortly after the 1981 elections in which his candidate, Charles Robb, had been elected governor of Virginia. The phone rang, and Peter talked for about ten minutes. It was Robb asking Hart for detailed advice on how to set out his agenda as governor and how to craft his inaugural address.

"Today, you don't use your brain or your gut, all you use is your pollster and your filmmaker," groused Senator Thomas Eagleton near the end of his third term. "They've replaced the party boss. In the campaign, they have taught you something and the play continues afterward. If you've had a good pollster and a good filmmaker, they have told you how to craft issues and then how to get them into the public media in thirty-second clips. You've learned what will get on the nightly news in St. Louis or Kansas City. You've learned what press release, properly captioned, will play on page three of the *St. Louis Post-Dispatch*. So they've taught you. So once you're here, you say, 'Well, I've got to continue to play the game.' "[18]

Indeed, when the Senate decided to televise its proceedings, the staff worried that the mustard color of the walls was too drab a background for video and proposed blue or some earth tone. Some senators, including Robert Dole, complained that the angle of the four cameras in the gallery was too steep and unflattering. Roger Ailes, a well-known Republican media consultant, was summoned; at least a third of the Republican senators met Ailes secretly to get his advice. Here was a media consultant telling senators, not how to craft a campaign commercial, but how to behave as senators, on the Senate floor!

I was told that Ailes lectured the senators like a parent talking to children. He minced no words, warning senators that they would have to change their habits. He chided them for their tendency to rush onto the floor from very busy schedules, often appearing ill-prepared and then doing their business hastily, with an air of boredom.

"Listen, you've got to be at your best on the Senate floor from now on," Ailes told them. "Treat a floor appearance the way you would a major speech. There are four cardinal rules: The public won't forgive you if you're not prepared, if you're not committed, if you're not comfortable, and if you're not interesting. If you want to be liked, you yourself are the message, not just your words—your message, your energy, your eyes, your clothes, your everything. If you want to project likability, project commitment. In general, the public likes commitment. That is a very winning trait."

The implication was that the lure of the live camera would draw senators away from dusty committee deliberations and put new zip into floor debates. This presented yet another set of pressures on career patterns of the Old Senate Club, accustomed to doing its main business in back rooms or in committee. Televised floor debates opened the door for good performers and independent operators to gain a leg-up with the voters and thus perhaps with their own colleagues. Even before the coming of TV, the Republican majority had picked Bob Dole as their leader in 1985; one clear reason was Dole's agility on camera. Dole combined old-breed skills as a legislator with new-breed skills as a communicator. Robert Byrd, the Democratic leader, faced a revolt in 1985 because he was too much of an inside player with well-honed parliamentary skills but a reputation as weak on TV. To protect himself, Byrd spruced up his camera style enough to survive.

Playing the Press and TV Gallery

Clearly the media politics of the constant campaign have become a staple, not only for the politics of survival, but for ambitions of higher leadership. Six of the class of '74 Democrats have been sharp enough to move to the Senate: Timothy Wirth, Christopher Dodd, Paul Simon, Tom Harkin, Paul Tsongas, and Max Baucus. The presidential field for 1988 is thick with new-breed candidates from several recent congressional classes: Dick Gephardt, Jack Kemp, Paul Simon, and Albert Gore, each of whom has fashioned a TV image.

Even those who have stayed in the House work the media game for career advancement; they play not only to the folks back home but to the galleries in Washington—the press and TV galleries.

One of the sharpest headline hunters is Stephen Solarz, a bright, articulate Brooklyn Democrat from the class of '74, who has specialized in foreign policy, especially on the Middle East. Solarz worked the press assiduously during the Philippine political crisis. In August, 1983, Solarz flew hastily to the Philippines after Benigno Aquino, the opposition leader, was assassinated and managed to get himself photographed looking into Aquino's open coffin. That made the cover of *Newsweek*'s international edition.[19] When Corazon Aquino was elected president of the Philippines, House Speaker Tip O'Neill wrote her a letter saying that *if* she were ever in Washington, he would be pleased to have her address a joint session of Congress; O'Neill gave Solarz, as chairman of the House Foreign Affairs Subcommittee on Pacific and East Asian Affairs, his letter to forward. Within hours, Solarz called a press conference and, stretching the point, said that O'Neill had invited Aquino to Washington and had dispatched Solarz to Manila to deliver the invitation. Off he went.

During the controversy over corruption in the 1986 Philippine election and over the hidden wealth of the family of Ferdinand Marcos, Solarz was ubiquitous. By his staff's count, he appeared on thirty-four radio and television shows and was quoted in eighty articles in *The New York Times, The Washington Post,* and *The Wall Street Journal* in a five-month period. Solarz has been accused by some colleagues of media hogging, but he does not fit the caricature of a handsome, blow-dried, airhead TV politician. He is a brainy legislator, quick to master important issues and to make a policy point. By now, he has gained some seniority; but for years smart P.R. has made him better known than most of his elders.

A different maestro of the media among House Democrats is Les Aspin, who in 1985 parlayed a largely media-built reputation into an uprising that made him chairman of the House Armed Services Committee over six senior Democrats. Aspin had worked in the Pentagon under Defense Secretary Robert McNamara before winning a House seat from Wisconsin in 1970. Like Solarz, he is genuinely knowledgeable. Moreover, with a constant stream of shrewdly timed press releases, Aspin has gotten enormous press attention over the years, becoming known as an informed, influential power on defense issues. Among many other things, he has exposed the army for conducting poison gas tests on beagle puppies, disclosed that the navy's Phalanx missile had locked on a friendly American ship during a simulated firing test, blasted the Pentagon for a bloated pension system, and challenged the claims of the Reagan military buildup.

Aspin's techniques tell a great deal about how to play the press game. The fundamental rule, he asserts, is to provide genuinely fresh information. What that involves, Aspin says, is "staying ahead of the curve," or anticipating where the news is heading and getting a step ahead of the story rather than chasing old news.[20] A second fundamental rule is to time your news release for a slack news day. A typical Aspin operation includes some juicy Pentagon revelation, embargoed for release in Monday morning newspapers when there is little breaking news. The release is sent out to newspaper offices by two P.M. Thursday so that reporters can write it up on Friday and have their weekends free, but the Monday embargo insures that it does not get swamped by the heavy Sunday news flow. Aspin's press agents send his material to reporters specializing in defense or arms control issues. I have known them to circulate copies of one release to five different *New York Times* reporters and editors, playing on competitive instincts to insure that *someone* gets their story into print. The tactic works.

Finally, Aspin is unusual in this era of video politics because he prefers written press releases over televised press conferences for two reasons: First, his issues are complicated, and only print reporters have space to explain them fully; if they get good play in print, TV will follow. Second, with a written release accompanied by a fairly detailed study, Aspin sees greater chance that the story will emerge the way he originally cast it. Press conferences can take unpredictable bounces.

"I don't think press conferences work worth a damn," Aspin told the *Washington Journalism Review.* "Somebody will ask a cockamamie question, and that will be the story. A well-lobbied study and press release are worth twenty press conferences."[21]

Among House Republicans, the new-breed guru with a knack for publicity, who has gotten attention far beyond his legislative power and station, is Newt Gingrich, a bullish, abrasive former history professor from West Georgia College with an original turn of mind and a zest for intellectual combat. Gingrich has his own special flair for video politics and his own slant on playing the game: be splashy; be original; be outrageous; be strident, even be inflammatory. He is a classic show horse, more interested in promoting confrontations and ideas than in passing legislation.

Gingrich is a boyish forty-five-year-old with boundless energy, a mop of bushy gray hair on a lion-sized head, and a machine-gun tongue. He is given to grandiose pronouncements: "We need to rethink government"; "We are creating a revolution"; "I have an enormous personal ambition: I want to shift the entire planet and I'm doing it." His vision, limned in a book, *Window of Opportunity,* is a curious mix of Adam Smith and high tech, of slashing government on earth but promoting a government-financed space program with manned moon factories and voyaging to the "Hiltons and Marriotts of the solar system."

Politically, Gingrich has not only savaged Jimmy Carter, Speaker O'Neill, and the "liberal welfare state," he has blasted Republicans, too. A purist Reaganite, Gingrich in 1978 scored Richard Nixon and Gerald Ford for "a terrible job, a pathetic job" and declared that in his lifetime the Republican party had "not had a competent leader," including Barry Goldwater. Later, Gingrich roasted Robert Dole, Senate Finance Committee chairman, as "the tax collector of the welfare state." (Dole fired back that Gingrich was "making a lot of noise, but I haven't seen any impact.") Many times, he has derided the House Republican leadership for being "eunuchs" with "a defeatist, minority mentality."

Gingrich arrived in the House in 1978 in a class of thirty-six Republican freshmen, the vanguard of a New Right swing toward Reaganite conservativism; their ranks were swelled by more young Republicans in the Reagan sweep of 1980. These were Reagan's shock troops in his triumphant 1981 year.

The political champion of these upstart Republicans is Jack Kemp, the handsome, ebullient apostle of tax cutting and the creed of economic growth and opportunity. Around the country, Kemp has led the new-breed attack on the traditional budget-balancing, austerity politics of old-breed Republicans. But in the House, Kemp's approach has been fairly tame; Gingrich took the lead in brawling with Speaker Tip O'Neill and seizing the limelight.

Gingrich stole a leaf from Aspin's book—pick a slack time to grab attention. He made his mark by capitalizing ingeniously on some dead hours in the House schedule. At about seven P.M., after the regular order of business ends, the House goes into "special orders," where individual members can give long speeches because the rest have gone home. Gingrich gathered a band of like-minded Republican right-wingers such as Vin Weber of Minnesota and Robert Walker of Pennsylvania, in the Conservative Opportunity Society. With the C-Span cable network still broadcasting House proceedings, they would preach their brand of Reaganism in these quiet evening hours. Cameras were focused on the lectern, leaving viewers unaware that the House chamber was empty. Gingrich claimed a C-Span audience of 250,000 plus daily.

Gingrich's tactic was to provoke a Democratic response and to get a fight going. In May 1984, Gingrich drew blood, causing a huge uproar and vaulting into public view. On May 8, Gingrich and Walker used special-order time to read a report by the conservative Republican Study Committee slamming the foreign-policy views of about fifty House Democrats, by name, accusing these Democrats of defeatism from the Vietnam War to Central America. Some were outraged and accused Gingrich and Company of innuendos reminiscent of Joseph McCarthy. Without warning, two days later, Speaker O'Neill ordered the House cameras to pan the chamber, showing the home audience that the Democrats were not present in the chamber to defend themselves against Gingrich's charges. O'Neill denounced the Republican speechmaking as "a sham . . . for home consumption."

On a point of personal privilege, Gingrich demanded the right of reply and got the showdown for which he had been angling. He was given an hour of time on the House floor on May 15. During that hour, Speaker O'Neill asked Gingrich to let him speak and Gingrich agreed.

But O'Neill got no more than two sentences out before Gingrich reclaimed his control of the floor, a slight to the speaker. In a few quick exchanges, O'Neill's rage rose and suddenly he burst out: "My personal opinion is this:"—and the massive, accusing arm went up, finger outstretched—"you deliberately stood in that well before an empty House and challenged these people, and you challenged their Americanism, and it's the lowest thing I've ever seen in my thirty-two years in Congress."

In a shot, Trent Lott, the Republican whip, was on his feet demanding that the clerk "take down" the words of the speaker. That is a procedure requiring that the words be repeated and the parliamentarian decide whether Speaker O'Neill's attack on Gingrich had violated House rules, which forbid personal attacks and insults. The parliamentarian ruled that O'Neill was out of order. Joe Moakley, a Massachusetts Democrat and a close ally of O'Neill, was in the chair; he was forced by the rules to issue a reproach against the speaker. It made headline and network news.

By his cool, calculating style of video politics, Gingrich had gotten the better of the speaker and also won a national audience. Brash video politics had put Gingrich on the political map.

It would be wrong to leave the impression that new-breed politicians are all talk and little legislative action. That might fit Gingrich, or Paula Hawkins and other one-term Republican senators who lost in 1986, and a goodly number of House members. But the best of the new breed have become effective legislators as well as communicators—none more influential and effective than Dick Gephardt of Missouri, a serious presidential contender in 1988.

By many estimates, Gephardt has a rare blend of the skills of both inside and outside politics, better than John F. Kennedy at a similar stage in his career. More than any other new-breed Democrat in the House, Gephardt has come to personify the generational divide—on substance as well as on tactics. He can not only play the outside game of video politics but also work the inside game of coalition politics that is vital to making Congress function. On television, he has been an articulate Democratic spokesman on national issues; in Congress, he has often been at the heart of prolonged negotiations over tough, intricate, technical legislation.

If Congress is like high school, then Dick Gephardt is a classic student-council president: all-American good looks, intelligent, thoughtful, committed to public service. Under his sandy, close-cropped hair is a straight, sincere, direct gaze of the eyes, a firm jaw, and an open, receptive face.

Gephardt has volumes of energy and patience. He is a born organizer, a born leader, who manages to be everywhere at once and yet seems to do it all with ease. He is so purposeful, so results oriented that it is hard to imagine him just whiling away the time. Yet one of his favorite pastimes is listening to St. Louis Cardinals baseball games on the radio. He is such a fanatic that he will often go out in the evening and sit in his darkened car in the driveway listening to a play-by-play account because the car radio gets better reception than the radios in the house. Once or twice, he has even gone in the announcer's box to try a bit of play-by-play announcing himself.

Like other new breeders—he is forty-seven and was first elected in 1978—Gephardt has been eager to see his generation take over leadership. He has pressed the generational divide against older leaders. In late 1984, for example, Gephardt and Tony Coelho of California organized meetings of younger House Democrats, which became gripe sessions against the House Democratic leadership. That angered Speaker O'Neill. Gephardt even let out word that he might challenge Jim Wright for the speakership after O'Neill retired; wisely, Gephardt decided against a confrontation. He made an easy peace with O'Neill, whose wrath fell on Coehlo, but Gephardt later clashed with Wright on tax and protectionist issues. Organizationally, Gephardt went after and got the number four leadership position, Democratic caucus chairman. That was typical of Gephardt, for he is an agent of gradual change rather than sharp revolt. He is a compromiser, a coalition builder who waits for the best openings.

A favorite complaint of the old breed is that the new breed lack finesse at one-to-one politicking, at melding clashing factions in order to pass legislation, at sensing where the winds are blowing, at counting votes accurately ahead of time. They make an exception of Gephardt. "He's the best vote counter and vote getter of that group" was the admiring appraisal of Kirk O'Donnell, a Tip O'Neill lieutenant. "He's someone who has an excellent sense of the House. I think he's a good vote counter because he's a good listener, and people respect his political instincts, his political judgment. He is not an ideologue who is going to allow an issue to get in the way of his personal relations with other members. But Gephardt is a lot tougher than people think."[22]

Gephardt is emphatic that the generational divide among Democrats is a matter of substance as well as technique. The two generations, he told me as we walked from his office to the Capitol one morning, are defined by economic experience: the older Democratic leaders shaped by the searing shock of the Depression and mass unemployment, the new breed forged by the high inflation and the stagnant growth of the 1970s.[23] That has left Gephardt and his peers wary of big deficits and renewed inflation, quick to combine with conservative southerners on economic issues and trimming programs. While Lyndon Johnson's Great Society programs were being passed, Gephardt reminded me he was an alderman in St. Louis, and he remembers the federal regulations being too intrusive and restrictive. That left him not opposed to federal programs, but inclined to go sparingly and give more leeway to local governments.

Typical of the new breed, Gephardt is a centrist, both by temperament and by geography. Coming from a border state like Missouri makes him a natural bridge between North and South. On the budget, he has pressed Snowbelt liberals to accept more cuts than they wanted, but he has also gotten Sunbelt conservatives to help protect safety net programs.

In 1981, when the Democrats were floundering before Reagan's onslaught, Gephardt combined with Timothy Wirth and others to develop a Democratic economic policy. They focused on ways to make American industry more competitive by funding research and education and promoting high-tech industries. More fruitfully, Gephardt joined Senator Bill Bradley as cosponsor of the plan to cut tax rates and close loopholes that was adopted by Reagan and passed by Congress in 1986.

In the spring of 1987, Gephardt made his trademark tough protectionist legislation—an amendment requiring tariff reprisals against countries, such as Japan, if they did not reduce excessive trade surpluses with the United States. He showed his mastery of the inside power game by rallying 201 House Democrats, despite the combined opposition of Speaker Jim Wright, Majority Leader Tom Foley, Ways and Means Committee Chairman Danny Rostenkowski, plus the Reagan White House and Republican leaders. Gephardt's amendment won 218–214, a testament to his pull among peers.

"If the amendment was not offered by Dick Gephardt, we would have beaten it," Rostenkowski told my *New York Times* colleague Jonathan Fuerbringer. "Dick Gephardt is a popular young man."[24]

Gephardt had mastered the technical details of his legislation, and he spoke with passion. His amendment was doomed in the Senate. But more costly to Gephardt, he was knocked, mainly by the Reagan White House and in the press, for what was seen as a blatant pitch for support from organized labor with a harsh protectionist formula that risked starting a disastrous trade war.

Generally, Gephardt's stand on issues and his tactics mark him as new breed—less ideological and diehard than the old breed. For example, in 1985, Gephardt, fearing some southern Democrats were getting ready to bolt the party after Reagan's landslide reelection, took the lead in forming the new Democratic Leadership Council, a group of rising politicians, mostly from the South and West, to help keep them in the party. With a core group of Gephardt, former Governor Charles Robb of Virginia, Senator Sam Nunn of Georgia, and former Governor Bruce Babbit of Arizona, this largely new-breed group deliberately set out to show independence from the old, established, northern-dominated party leadership. Its hallmark was new-breed-style television campaigning and organizing and new-breed issues.

The formation of this group and Gephardt's leadership role, moreover, underscored his turning increasingly from the work of governing and the inside game of Congress to the outside game of the constant campaign, this time at a higher level—for the presidency. By 1985, three years ahead of the 1988 election, the campaign pulled Gephardt away from his legislative duties in Washington sixty percent of the time, more in later years. He was gone so much in 1987 that his press secretary, Don Foley, remarked in mid-May, "Last week, Dick was in Washington three and a half days, and that was a major exception," because his trade amendment was up for a vote. Otherwise, he would have been on the road even more.[25]

"Narrowcasting" with Targeted Mail

Obviously, television is the glitzy, visible tip of the power game. High-profile new-breed politicians such as Dick Gephardt and Jack Kemp have parlayed their skills at video politics into presidential candidacies. But for most congressional politicians, the cornerstone of the politics of survival and the constant campaign is free congressional mail.

The mail frank is exploited to the hilt by the new political breed. In 1984, the flow of mail generated by Congress reached the staggering volume of 920 million pieces, much more than double its volume just four years earlier. That means an output of 3,836,142 pieces of free mail on an average working day—for the 240 days that Congress is in session each year.

One senator alone—identified by aides as Pete Wilson, a California Republican—racked up $3.8 million in mail subsidies in 1984, nearly ten percent of the Senate's entire mail budget. Getting elected to the

Senate in 1982, Wilson had spent about $7 million; as a freshman senator, he was spending more than half that on mail.

The free-mail frank was born in the first Congress and has been controversial nearly ever since. Congress abolished it for twenty years in 1873, but it came back; in 1973, Common Cause, the public-interest lobby, filed suit to abolish the practice on grounds that free-mail privileges for incumbents violated the constitutional rights of their challengers. But in 1983, the Supreme Court upheld the privilege. Politicians from opposite poles decry the practice. "An appalling amount of public money is spent sending out mailings that are nothing but political puff pieces," complained North Carolina's New Right Senator Jesse Helms. Morris Udall, the liberal Arizona Democrat, warned of "evil consequences" unless limits are put on congressional mail.

Technically, the intent of the frank is to let officeholders report on their "official business, activities and duties." The rules forbid soliciting political support. To curb the most obvious self-promotion, Congress has some rules: No mass mailings 60 days prior to an election; on mass newsletters, the word *I* can be used no more than eight times per page; and there can be no more than two personal photos per page. Even so, there's no disguising the real purpose of franked mail. It shows up in the roller-coaster patterns of usage volume—it rises in election years and falls in off years. In fiscal 1981, for example, the congressional mail cost just over $50 million, and it doubled in 1982. By 1983, it dropped to about $70 million, and then jumped to $110 million in the 1984 election year. In 1985, the figure was $80 million and in 1986, the target was $144 million. Only congressional embarrassment during the battle to reduce the deficit forced 1986 mail costs down to $96 million.

The role of mail in the permanent campaign is very different from the role of television. Television is broadcasting; it reaches the widest possible audience with a general message. Old-fashioned newsletters, sent to every voter in a state or district, do the same, but newer, more sophisticated types of direct mail employ what politicians call narrowcasting—segmenting voters for special messages. The ultimate narrowcast is the candidate meeting one voter, face-to-face. The next-best substitute, the experts say, is direct mail targeted at subgroups, after finding out what they think and how to reach them.

The secret is to tap the modern technology of mass marketing and yet convey a personal touch. "As with everything in politics, it's image that counts, and the objective is to convince as many people as possible that I, the officeholder, am aware of and concerned with the issues that are important to them," said David Himes, a small specialist for the National Republican Congressional Committee.[26]

"We used to hear that congressmen got in trouble for not answering the mail," observed Marty Franks, Executive Director of the Democratic Congressional Campaign Committee. "But nowadays, it's not so much answering mail; it's generating mail to impress people. You can tailor a letter. Say you've gotten a lot of mail on aid to the *contras* in Nicaragua, pro and con, or on a balanced-budget amendment. Say, then, there's a political development, a report about Nicaraguan guns showing up in Colombia, or you vote for the Gramm-Rudman bill to balance the budget. One of your aides drafts a letter to the people who wrote in: 'Knowing of your interest in a balanced budget, I thought you would like to know that today I voted for Gramm-Rudman.' Or, 'Knowing of your interest in the *contras*, I thought you would like to know about this development.' You use the mail to keep in touch. You use the mail to remind people that you agree with them."[27]

Targeted direct mail was pioneered by conservatives frustrated by what they saw as the liberal slant of major media outlets. One of the first was Marvin Liebman, a former Israeli terrorist and later a Communist who converted to Catholicism, became a friend of William F. Buckley, Jr., and organized the Committee of One Million to support Nationalist China. Liebman used that list of a million names for other issues in the 1950s and 1960s. Later, he shared the list with a protégé, Richard Viguerie, who developed mass-fund-raising potential for Senator Jesse Helms and for New Right causes. In the mid-1970s, Bill Brock, as chairman of the Republican National Committee, moved the party heavily into direct mail to raise money, with phenomenal success, rebuilding the Republican apparatus from the top down.

The techniques spread quickly into political campaigns, because candidates found they could send different messages to different sets of voters.

"With our ability to segment the market with computers, we can go after people who have single-issue goals and motivation," asserts Robert Hacker, president of the Delta Group, an Atlanta-based direct-response-marketing company. "You have the ability to target people by an interest, for example, the abortion and the gun lobbies. In the old days, you had to get up on a stump and try to reach everyone. Television has made that worse. Mass political speeches are less and less specific and issue oriented. Where the candidates handle the specifics is the one-to-one communication with direct mail. The nice thing about direct mail is I can hit you in your home and make the pitch directly to you and tell you exactly what you want to hear and that I don't want other people to know I said to you."[28]

For the constant campaign, mail targeting is crucial. The trump card is the list, or rather the lists, of voters, compartmenting them into target segments. Roger Stone said: "I always tell the congressional incumbents I advise: 'Build a list of senior citizens in your district. Take the computer tape of registered voters, take the tape of licensed drivers—age is on the driver's license—and cross the tapes on the computer.' You can find Jews, find Irish, and others. We have a little table of all Italian names or all Jewish names or all Korean names or all whatever it may be and cross it with the voter tape and select the names. You can get people's religion. You can get people who rent as opposed to people who live at the same address for a long time. The long timers tend to be voters; renters are less responsive to the property tax issue."

The point is to refine your list—not to waste time, money, and effort on hostile or inert groups. Some congressmen get membership lists from organizations that support them in elections—small-business federations, farmers' groups, the American Legion, Veterans of Foreign Wars, environmental groups, labor unions. They also put in their computers the names of every person who sends a letter or postcard, or who drops in at their offices. Good lists are essential, especially by members in marginal districts or swing states. Those members circulate mass questionnaires with the prime purpose of getting people to say what issues matter most and to state their point of view: People who reply go on targeted mailing lists.

Take Tim Wirth's operation: He won a House seat in 1974 with fifty-one percent of the vote and scraped by in 1976 with 50.1 percent. As a matter of sheer survival, Wirth has cultivated and farmed his mail lists assiduously. In eight years, his computerized lists jumped from a total of twenty thousand names to 150,000 names, broken down into one thousand different categories: for example, twenty thousand people in business; 6,817 interested in the environment; 2,683 keen on energy issues; 117 on women's issues, including eight on women in mining; 1,136 who had written in about the nuclear freeze; 1,948 on the deficit; more than three hundred concerned about communications issues, a Wirth specialty; plus eighteen thousand people whom he had met personally on "Tim's #3 list" (#1 being family and #2 personal friends).[29]

As a senator, Wirth can use the Senate Computer Center, manned by a staff of 180 and financed in 1986 by a $31.9 million taxpayer subsidy. Its laser-powered printers can roll out fifty thousand letters daily, predesigned paragraph by paragraph by staff aides to produce the desired mix for target audiences. The Senate's computers store the names, addresses, and interests of millions of voters broken down into more than thirty-three hundred categories that reach beyond typical breakdowns to such politically useful target groups as "fat cats," "Jewish groups and interests," "fiscal conservatives," and "top bureaucrats" who got appointments with the help of some senator.

To disguise the assembly-line production, politicians strive for a personal touch. According to Roger Stone, the Republican consultant, vital ingredients are a chatty, punchy, conversational tone; short paragraphs; what is known as "fill": personalized references in the body of the letter that repeat the voter's name, his hometown, his group, or what prompted the voter to write; and ink that disguises that the signature was done by a machine. The best, Stone explained, is "a blue signature that smudges when it's wet or when you run your finger across it. That's important—people check. Millions and millions of people actually believe that Ronald Reagan or some senator sat down and dictated this letter to them, and signed it. A special ink can be found that will smudge as if someone did in fact sign it."[30]

Tim Wirth personalizes his mail. Staff aides at his elbows jot down notes about individuals with whom he talks and feed that information into the computer. So when a letter goes out, there will be a reference to someone's Aunt Sarah or their last contact with Wirth. The theory on mail is that it is a political life-or-death matter. Paige Reffe, Wirth's administrative assistant, recalled the day that Wirth announced he was running for the Senate, a grueling marathon of hopping around Colorado, ending late at night after a fund-raiser in a Denver hotel. The hotel banquet room was empty save for Wirth, a couple of aides, and a hotel custodian.

Wirth went over and stuck out his hand to the custodian. "Hey, I'm Tim Wirth," he said.

"Congressman, I know who you are," the man replied. "I wrote you a letter in 1975. I wrote it to everybody in the Colorado delegation, and you're the only person who responded. I will always remember that. I may never write you again, but whatever you're running for, I'll vote for you because you care about me."[31]

Casework: See "Mayor" D'Amato

That personal touch typifies one old-fashioned ingredient of the newfangled incumbency politics: casework. Think of the "politician" in a big city like Philadelphia, Chicago, New York, or Boston, and what often comes to mind is the ward boss or block captain, the person to whom people went if they had an immigration problem, a traffic ticket, a sanitation notice, or a kid in trouble with the law. Going to the "politician" was like going to a tribal chief or an elected judge. This was the guy who went to City Hall and fixed your case, and he checked on election day to be sure you were there with your family and your grandmother supporting his candidates. What's new is that congressmen and some senators are deep into that game, handling people's grief with the federal government in exchange for their support. It is probably true, as some contend, that Congress has a stake in the *in*efficiency of federal bureaucrats: It lets members and their staffs become important fixers for the ordinary folk back home.

No one fits that bill more than Senator Alfonse D'Amato, a pushy, competitive New Yorker who turned his pork-barrel, do-a-favor-style politics into a remarkable success story. When D'Amato arrived in the Senate in 1981, after twenty years working his way up in the local Republican political machine of Nassau County, Long Island, his Senate colleagues marked him down as a sure loser the next time around. They saw him as a small-timer, too narrow and locally bred to measure up to the prominence and issue influence of New York senators such as Jacob Javits, his predecessor, or Daniel Patrick Moynihan, his Democratic colleague. But D'Amato played his own brand of constant campaigning. In the classic style of a machine politician, he began doing favors for the whole state and grabbing every conceivable scrap of publicity for anything that came New York's way.

Within a couple of years Democratic mayors such as Ed Koch in New York and James Griffin in Buffalo were singing his praises as a politician who understood and remembered the local folks. "You would go to D'Amato if you wanted to get your passport expedited, but if you want a discussion on policy toward the People's Republic of China, you'd go to Moynihan," Koch told my *New York Times* colleague Frank Lynn. "D'Amato is a hands-on person. Give him a problem, he goes right to it. Moynihan is a much more reflective person who will see the policy end, the theoretical end, which is very helpful, too."[32]

"When you're a town official, you fight for the people in the town on a regular basis," D'Amato's press secretary, Ed Martin, explained. "D'Amato adopted the whole state. Placement on committees, that was the key to an ability to basically watch over the interests of his constituents."[33] D'Amato got himself put on the Appropriations Committee, and on the Banking, Housing and Urban Affairs Committee; he picked subcommittees that dealt with New York interests such as transportation and consumer affairs. The appropriations assignment positioned him well to slip into one money bill funding defense research at Syracuse University; to press the Pentagon to put a light army division at Fort Drum in upstate New York and to base a battleship at Staten Island; to bargain with the Reagan administration for $140 million to hire more customs agents and Coast Guard personnel to fight drug smuggling through New York City ports and harbors.

D'Amato became notorious for haggling in private with the Reagan White House, pushing what one official called his New York "shopping lists" before he would agree to support the president on big items such as the MX missile. Kiddingly, some of his colleagues call him the "mayor" because of his unabashed parochialism and his reputation for vote trading.

"D'Amato came out of being a county executive, and he's a county executive in the Senate," said Senator Warren Rudman, a New Hampshire Republican.

Alan Simpson of Wyoming, the Republican whip, told me that at the Wednesday Club, a Republican luncheon group, he had disclaimed being a bagman—a money man—for western water projects and said, pointing with a grin at D'Amato: "Now, if you want to see a real bagman, go to Al D'Amato." The other senators all laughed.[34]

D'Amato has thrived on publicity about his constituency politics. He used it to build such an impregnable base of support that when 1986 rolled around, prominent Democrats were hesitant to take him on. Without cutting a big figure on issues, D'Amato, the sure loser, had become D'Amato, the sure winner, all from the tactics of the constant campaign.

In House districts, some political scientists believe that casework and the ombudsman role can pull as much as five percent of the vote, and that explains why House incumbents have so successfully cushioned themselves against big swings of voter sentiment on national issues. Sometimes, constituency politics beats a criminal rap. Former representatives Daniel J. Flood of Pennsylvania and Charles C. Diggs, Jr., of Michigan built such support from pork-barrel and little-favor politics that they got reelected in spite of a criminal indictment in Flood's case and actual conviction in Diggs's case.

"Our surveys have shown that constituency service— especially in the House—is more important than issues," David Himes of the National Republican Congressional Committee told me. "Voting at the congressional level does not turn on the issues. There is considerable evidence that people's image of a congressman is more important to their vote than his stand on the issues."[35]

Casework politics are aimed primarily at projecting the incumbent's presence to voters and conveying a sense of engagement and compassion. New Jersey's Senator Bill Bradley has developed ingenious variations on that tactic. As a Rhodes Scholar from Princeton and a New York Knicks basketball star, Bradley did not go after the limelight in Washington to create an image; he already had one. He chose to develop a reputation for sound, substantive inside politics, and he won high marks with his proposal in April 1982 for a sweeping reform of the tax code by closing loopholes and lowering rates.

At home, Bradley created a typical network of constituent services, but as a likable, loping, rangy guy in his mid-forties, he came up with his own twist: "the walking town meeting." It fits him, for Bradley is one of those elemental politicians who thrives on direct physical contact with voters. The most effective modern campaigners, whether Ronald Reagan, Lyndon Johnson, or John Kennedy, have this quality. They get enjoyment and strength from immersing themselves in crowds, pressing the flesh, literally bumping up against humanity. It recharges them.

"Every summer I walk the seashore, and somebody walks thirty yards in front of me with a sign, MEET SENATOR BRADLEY, ASK SENATOR BRADLEY A QUESTION," Bradley told me over a quick sandwich lunch at his desk. "And I walk the shore and visit with the people. In the regular town-meeting format, people come to ask you a question. If you really want to know what people think, you gotta go where people are, surprise them, and ask them what's on their minds. In four hours on a New Jersey shore on a Sunday afternoon in July or August, you're going to see fifty to sixty thousand people, and you're going to get an immediate reaction"—his fingers snapping in the air. "The best example of that: The KAL 007 shoot down—it happened on a Friday. A day and a half later I was walking the shore. I have never seen such outrage from the people about the Soviet action. It was just intense.[36]

"I also appear at commuter stops," he went on. "For example, if you stand in the Port Authority bus terminal in New York between four and six P.M., you see an incredible amount of people—a minimum of a hundred pass you per minute. They are rushing to get the bus, right? And if they immediately recognize you, they're going to give you a response. It's physical. You stand there and they'll hit you, or they'll say, 'Ah, you, I don't want to talk to you.' Or they'll say, 'Keep going on that home care,' or, 'I'm with you on tax reform,' or 'What's going to happen with Reagan?' It is physically exhausting, but it is a remarkable way to interact."

"Where'd you get this idea?" I asked. "From the campaign?"

"No, no, no, no, no," Bradley shook his head. "Harry Truman."

"You mean Truman's going for a walk in the morning?"

"Yeah, he went for a walk in the morning. So then, well, why don't I go for a walk where people are?"

"What made you ask yourself that question?"

"Because I have all my life been a listener, and so it's a natural impulse for me," he said. "We tried it a couple of times and it really was good. Now I'll be somewhere in the state and people will say, 'Hey, I saw you last year down at Manasquan,' or 'Hey, I saw you at Seaside.' The point is, they're associating me with being there. Presence, right?"

"You're using campaign techniques as part of a constant campaign in office," I suggested.

"Well, they're campaign techniques but see—what are you trying to do in a campaign?" he parried. "You're trying to tell people you care. Right? Then the traditional assumption is you disappear. Then you come back later and tell them you care. Well, I don't stop caring. And it helps me do my job. I mean, you know, it's flesh and blood. It's emotion. You get on the floor of the Senate with the amendment to the amendment and the unanimous consent request to proceed, blah, blah, blah. You've gotta remember why you're here. You're here because of those people. The more interaction with them, the better you are."

I asked Bradley whether, like Paul Tsongas, he worried that he became less good as a senator while he was working at becoming more visible at home.

"I don't see it at all," Bradley came back. "I mean, I think part of being a good senator is being accessible to your constituents. Let me give you an example: At one town meeting a couple of years ago, the question was the defense budget, and why don't we spend more money, or why don't we spend less. This had gone on an hour and a half. There were about three hundred people, jam-packed in a city hall council chamber. There was a woman over at the side, and she said:

" 'Senator, one more question.' Pause. 'Senator, I heard the question about the defense budget, and I just want to tell you two years ago my son was killed.'

"And, okay, the audience had been restless. They go *total silence.* She said:

" 'I was in the military twenty-seven years.' *She* was. 'And my son was working at McGuire Air Force Base, and he was supposed to be wearing flame-retardant clothes, something happened, and he burned up. When are we going to spend our money on our people?'

"And, you know, all this debate about conventional military versus strategic weapons just kind of dissolved down into an individual experience of a mother who lost her son because she felt the military was not caring enough. That anecdote, that experience, first of all, sears you. Second of all, it's a part of everything that you do after that. That comes only because you put yourself out there in a town-meeting format and take the blows."[37]

The Ins and Outs of Chasing Money

Of the five pillars of the constant campaign (video politics, targeted mail, casework, personal presence, and money), the one that most grinds members of Congress is the drudgery of raising money. Except for the exceptionally wealthy, raising political money has become a throbbing headache that drains vital time and energy from the job of governing. This chore leaves many members part-time legislators and full-time fund-raisers.

Certainly since the 1890s when Mark Hanna passed the hat to the wealthy trusts, money has been mother's milk to American politics. But it used to fall mainly to political parties and political bosses to raise it. Today, at the national level, the Republican party and its various arms seem to have found a forest of money trees which they harvest. They raised $210 million in the two-year cycle leading up to the 1986 mid-term elections, and the Democrats raised a comparatively paltry $50.6 million.

Were it not for Tony Coelho, the miracle money man for congressional Democrats, that party would be even farther behind. A staff aide for years to a California congressman, Coelho is an agile, wiry, constantly-on-the-go politician with a phenomenal record as a supersalesman for Democrats. He was elected to the House in 1978, and as a mere second-term member in early 1981, he took on a thankless task for House Democrats and made an incredible success of it. With the Republican party riding a wave of fund-raising, Coelho became head of the Democratic Congressional Campaign Committee. He stunned older Democrats by promising to raise $5 million in two years, more than triple what had been done before, and he actually raised $6 million. Then, he offended his colleagues by refusing to pour all this new money into campaigns; instead he invested in rebuilding the party's apparatus: a media center, direct-mail fund-raising lists, and a bigger staff. Ultimately, he laid the financial cornerstones for a brand-new party headquarters in Washington.

Coelho, an ultimate new-breed politician, won enormous clout inside the House with his outsider style of politics, and he has been amply rewarded. He has shot up the career ladder with astonishing speed, becoming Democratic whip, the number three Democrat in the House, in just eight short years (it took Tip O'Neill nineteen years).

But the money campaigns of the Republican and Democratic parties have not spared individual incumbents. They must still hustle after their own millions. One night Senator David Durenburger, a Minnesota Republican, regaled me with the travails of his 1982 reelection, when millionaire businessman Bruce Dayton spent $7 million against him (the Senate lists twenty-five millionaire members; Durenberger is not one of them). "I got $214,000 from all the various Republican party organizations," Durenburger said. "I got $1 million from political action committees. That still left me $3 million short. I had to raise that myself from individual contributions."[38]

Campaign costs, driven by pricey television ads, have skyrocketed. Before 1974, most of the big political money went into presidential campaigns. But the 1974 reforms set up public subsidies for the presidential campaign in general elections; since then the money rivalry has shifted to congressional races. In the dozen years between 1974 and 1986, the average cost of a House incumbent's campaign jumped from $56,539 to $334,222 and the average cost for an incumbent senator leapt from $555,714 to $3,303,518.[39] As a result, members of the House, with their short two-year terms, virtually never stop raising money. As soon as one election is over, they begin passing the hat for the next.

"In a contested district, literally a quarter of the member's time in Washington is spent fund-raising, organizing, thinking about it, making the calls," a veteran congressional aide told me. He worked for a Northwest Democrat known as a conscientious legislator. It was nine months before Election Day, and in frustration, the staff man shoved the member's daily schedule to me, showing four to eight P.M. blocked off for fund-raising and campaign strategizing. "I've been on eleven congressional payrolls and they're all doing that!" my staff friend said in disgust. "The taxpayers are not getting their money's worth. Even under the most rose-tinted construction of the thing, where I'm ruling out any issue corruption, it's a scandal. And we all know that there's some influence on the issues."

Incumbents hit big-moneyed constituencies in their areas—defense contractors, agricultural interests, labor unions, major manufacturers in their district, and their Washington lobbyists—to build an early financial base and to form the steering committees for Washington fund-raising receptions. Incumbents have enormous advantages over challengers—some incumbents more than others: Members of the appropriations committees which vote the funds for the entire government, the tax-writing Finance Committee in the Senate, and the Ways and Means Committee in the House. Also, in the House, John Dingell, as chairman, has made the Energy and Commerce Committee a choice spot by pushing its powers and jurisdiction into many areas that affect business. But being on an intelligence committee is not worth much financially.

"The going rate at a fund-raiser for a member of Ways and Means is much higher than for the average member of the House," David Cohen, head of the Advocacy Institute, a public-interest group, told me. "For a normal member, the tab is usually no more than $250. I get invitations to fund-raisers for Ways and Means members and they get $500 to $1,000 a head."[40]

In the Senate, fund-raising is serious business, years ahead of time. "In my time here in Washington, it has grown from awful to odious, from odious to obscene," Senator Tom Eagleton of Missouri declared with disgust. After eighteen years in the Senate, Eagleton still has the air of a country lawyer, walking around his cluttered office in rumpled striped shirt and black suspenders, his graying hair tousled. On a desk littered with books, files, leaves of yellow legal pads, and other miscellanea, he has posted a sign: IF A CLUTTERED DESK IS THE SIGN OF A CLUTTERED MIND, WHAT IS AN EMPTY DESK THE SIGN OF?

"When I first ran in 1968, we raised about five or six hundred thousand," Eagleton recalled. "Now it's estimated that you need a war chest of about $4 million in Missouri," Eagleton harangued. "Back when I came, fund-raising was basically a one-year process. Now, had I been running for reelection, I would have been fund-raising, at the very minimum, for a three-year period, maybe a four-year period. And I know some illustrations where it's six years, where senators have started fund-raising within a few months of their being sworn in."[41]

I later learned, for example, that John Kerry, a Democrat who won a Senate seat from Massachusetts in 1984, had started collecting money for his reelection virtually right away. By the first six months of 1986, with their next Senate election still four and a half years away, Bill Bradley raised $1.1 million, Phil Gramm of Texas $804,170, Joseph Biden of Delaware $614,160, and Kerry $471,195. But in mid-1986, the incumbent senator with the biggest war chest for the 1990 election was Bennett Johnston, a Louisiana Democrat, with $1.6 million.

They were all taking a lesson from Al D'Amato of New York. D'Amato, with his pork-barrel politics, built a massive war chest long before his 1986 reelection contest. The word that he had amassed $4 million by the fall of 1985 scared off potential Democratic opponents such as Geraldine Ferraro. That is now a standard ploy for incumbents—the money scare-off tactic.

"I met D'Amato one day in the summer of 1985," Eagleton recalled. "D'Amato said to me, 'What are you doing this summer?' This was just after I had announced that I wasn't running, and I said, 'Oh, I'm going to have a good summer.' Told him about a trip I was going to take. And he said, 'Oh, you're lucky. Do you know how many fund-raisers I've got this month? I've got twenty. I got 'em in New York; I got 'em in Chicago; I got 'em in Dallas; I got 'em in Los Angeles.' "

Eagleton grimaced. "I would say that an incumbent senator in a hotly contested reelection campaign would devote seventy to eighty percent of his personal time, effort, thought, and worrying to fund-raising for the last two years of a six-year term," he said. Eagleton was including time spent chasing publicity, doing favors, and pork-barrel work aimed at getting supporters to ante up for the campaign. "It becomes an all-consuming obsession. Others may not subscribe to my seventy to seventy-five percent. You know, you can still stagger over to vote while you've just finished a call trying to raise some money. Your staff gives you a little card and says, 'By the way, there's a roll call up on the Eagleton amendment to do such and such,' and you stumble over and vote aye and then get back on the phone again raising money."

Imminent retirement had increased Eagleton's candor. Publicly, most politicians are gun-shy about discussing their fund-raising. A decade ago, senators used to deride the House as the "Tuesday-to-Thursday Club" because its members hustled home for a long weekend from Friday morning through Monday. The Senate then prided itself on active sessions all week long. But Eagleton and others complain that the Senate now works a short week, usually four days, in order to get out with the voters and the givers. Like D'Amato, many senators raise money in far-flung states from groups whose interests they affect or promote in their legislative work. In D'Amato's case, a seat on the Appropriations Committee provided ideal entrée.

"If you've got fund-raisers in these faraway states, you can't just fly to Los Angeles in an instant," Eagleton pointed out. "Your people have to set up these things. A Friday night in Los Angeles, a Saturday night in San Francisco, and a Sunday night in San Diego, for example. To do this money sweep of the West Coast, Friday's a shot day, and Monday's virtually a shot day."

"Go over and look when roll-call votes were held," he advised me, "and you will find precious few were held on a Monday or a Friday. It's to accommodate the fund-raising and campaign schedules of one third of the brethren up for reelection. That means our work here is all telescoped into a three-day time frame."[42]

Senator Christopher Dodd of Connecticut told me in early 1986 that out of 260 weekends over the previous five years, he had worked 124 on the road, making appearances in his home district or hustling money elsewhere. That is largely self-defense, for nothing so offends the voters as the impression that their senator is stuck on Washington and has lost touch with the home district. That fearful charge exacts a high price on congressional effectiveness, for it requires constant home campaiging. What the public often demands is public relations, not public service.

The toll falls heaviest on those from the West Coast, Rocky Mountains, Texas, or the Plains States, or House members from districts far from a big-city airport. California Congressmen regularly hop the red-eye overnight planes on Thursday nights going out to the Coast and come back on the Monday overnight flight. After weeks of that, they drag around Congress on Tuesdays.

The short congressional week—dictated by the politics of the constant campaign—deeply troubles experienced members.

"We aren't on the job," Senator McC. Mathias of Maryland worried aloud one day before his retirement. "We're spending time running around for media attention. We're spending too much time with constituents. We're not spending enough time with the issues. We're not spending enough time with each other."[43]

An echo came from two House Democrats, Patricia Schroeder of Colorado, and Don Edwards, dean of the California delegation. "The marketing branch is running things, and the power branch is on vacation," said Schroeder.[44] Edwards was more blunt: "The jet age has become the enemy of good government," he said. "You can't govern well with part-time legislators."[45]

In sum, the survival politics of the constant campaign take a toll on government. New-breed politicians like to build their own independent political organizations. And those require vast efforts—both by the members and their staffs—for casework, mail operations, travel home, or fund-raising around the country. Inevitably, the constant campaign competes with the regular work of senators and House members—and the business of governing suffers.

8. Pentagon Games: The Politics of Pork and Turf

> *I am saddened that the services are unable to put the national interest above parochial interest.*
>
> —Senator Barry Goldwater

> *Everybody scratches everybody else's back. I'd say it's very similar to the congressional system of pork-barrel projects. . . . I think the last thing we want in the military is to handle the business like a pork-barrel bill.*
>
> —Senator Sam Nunn

In the darkness shortly before one A.M., Chris Schall, a plump, good-natured, grandmother of nine, rolls out of bed and begins preparing for an early-morning rendezvous with Defense Secretary Caspar Weinberger and the top Pentagon brass.

Mrs. Schall, a $32,000-a-year GS-12 Air Force career civilian, has been in bed only three or four hours. "I sleep fast," she says. To get moving, she downs a couple of cups of coffee, fills another mug for the road, fixes her husband's lunch, and then heads for the Pentagon—only a fifteen-minute drive from her split-level rambler in Springfield, Virginia. "I can get on the expressway, put it on cruise control, and drink my coffee," she says.

Her five-member team has a little less than four hours to put together one of Washington's best-read and most-influential daily newspapers.

It is a compact, sixteen-page digest formally called *Current News*, but known simply as the "Early Bird." In sixteen *Time* magazine–sized pages, it provides a cut-and-paste distillation of the hottest Pentagon-oriented news articles culled and photocopied from nine major daily newspapers plus an overnight take from two wire services and the three television networks.[1] Producing it is a high-pressure operation. "I drink a lot of coffee, and I smoke a lot of cigarettes," chirps Mrs. Schall, as she chain-smokes Pall Mall Golds.[2]

At six A.M., the Early Bird must go to the Air Force printers, but Cris Schall's rendezvous with Weinberger comes at 5:50 A.M. That's when his chauffeur, Matt Turner, shows up for an advance copy of the Early Bird plus several major newspapers. Weinberger reads them on the ride from home to work.

But the Early Bird reaches far beyond the Pentagon. Just after six, a White House driver arrives for more copies, followed by couriers from the State Department and the Central Intelligence Agency and the personal driver of Vice President George Bush. Then runners from the civilian secretaries of the Army, Navy, and Air Force, the Joint Chiefs of Staff, and the top military brass. In no time, eighty copies are gone.

That's just the top-level trickle. Before noon, a full print-run of six thousand copies is dispatched, five hundred to key congressional committees, seventy to the senior White House staff, sixty to the State Department, eighty for the Defense Intelligence Agency, fifty for the National Security Agency, thousands for the military hierarchy and scores more for the reporters who cover the Pentagon. The Early Bird is also transmitted around the world by Wirephoto daily to fourteen American military-theater commanders. It gets into the bloodstream of the national security community.

Because the Early Bird sees the news through the special lens of the Pentagon, its yellow front page and its contents have a special slant. Often, it gives top play to articles dug out from page twenty of *The Wall Street Journal*, page forty-one of *The Washington Post*, page twenty-five of the Baltimore *Sun*, or page seventeen of *The New York Times*. But politically, the Early Bird pulls no punches. Echoing the regular press, it naturally headlines Weinberger's speeches and major Pentagon pronouncements, but it also reprints coverage on Pentagon waste, military incidents abroad, leaks about weapons systems in trouble, congressional feuding over the defense budget, controversies over arms control, or Star Wars strategic defense. Longer supplements, printed daily, weekly, or monthly, tap more than sixty newspapers nationwide and three hundred magazines.

"We print everything—both sides of the issues," explained Harry

Zubkoff, founder and for thirty-six years the guiding spirit behind *Current News* until his retirement in 1986. Zubkoff is a five-foot-five look-alike for Menachem Begin, a voracious reader, a man with a curious mind, a wide grin, and a tough hide toward military services jealously fretting that their achievements are underplayed and their gaffs are overcriticized. Over the years, Zubkoff, a self-taught editor, developed an independent sense of what is news and what the Pentagon should be reading. Some high officials credit "Mr. Z," as they call him, with making the Pentagon more literate by the think pieces he circulates and more alert by the alarms that he sounds.

"We don't print the scurrilous stuff, name-calling and profanity," Zubkoff told me before his retirement. "But I've often been the bearer of bad tidings. I see our job as bringing the bad news to the right people."[3]

The impact is immediate. In the Reagan era, people at the pinnacle of the Pentagon learned it was perilous to show up at Weinberger's morning staff meeting without having scoured the Early Bird and prepared their rebuttals. Similarly, the Pentagon's internal critics and whistle-blowers found out that the best way to get Weinberger's attention was to leak some headache to the press and get the story into the Early Bird.

Weinberger told me that some people exaggerate the influence of Early Bird, but half a dozen other high Pentagon officials contended that Weinberger leaned on the press—especially Early Bird—to keep the Pentagon on its toes. "Weinberger tends to manage the department by reading the Early Bird and asking his staff about it," said one close aide. "He's an information junkie. He will come into the morning staff meeting, flip through the Early Bird, and if he has a policy question, he's got the experts right there to question." Another regular at Weinberger's staff sessions said outsiders would be surprised how much the agenda was dominated by items plucked by Early Bird from deep inside the major newspapers. "Cap's management control system was the newspaper," said a third high official.

Weinberger's trigger reactions to the Early Bird exasperated Richard DeLauer, for nearly five years undersecretary for Research and Engineering. "Cap himself believed everything that was said about the costs of those spare parts," DeLauer told me. "He felt they were a rip-off."[4]

When DeLauer would come under Weinberger's fire in staff meetings for some weapons snafu, he would scowl and urge Weinberger to sidestep. "Look, you're a lightning rod," DeLauer would whine, his raspy voice rising in frustration. "Just ignore 'em. Tell 'em, 'I'm running this whole Defense Department, I can't be bothered with one little piece of the action.' Tell 'em, 'It's DeLauer's job or somebody else's job.' And it gets defused. *We're* not news. If you can't take on Cap Weinberger for the six o'clock news, who the hell wants to take on an undersecretary or an assistant secretary? Christ, we do sixteen million procurement actions a year. If you're better than Ivory Snow, ninety-nine and one half percent pure, that's still one half percent of mistakes. Christ, that's eight thousand a year!"

The Dissident Triangle

From the standpoint of the Pentagon hierarchy, DeLauer was right, but Weinberger largely ignored him; the Early Bird plays into the hands of the rank-and-file against the top brass. It is a central element in the "dissident triangle"—the triangular power network formed among the Pentagon's internal critics, their allies in Congress, and the press, which harvests news leaks from both.

The way the power game is played, this triangle operates against the top Pentagon hierarchy, and the Early Bird acts as a proxy for the Washington press in the Pentagon's inner circle, magnifying press influence by prodding policymakers to react to what is in print. The Early Bird puts the Pentagon's woes into Weinberger's ride-to-work reading: the $640 toilet seat; the $2,043 nut; the $1,118 plastic cap for a stool leg; the $7,622 coffee maker; the $9,606 Allen wrench; the General Dynamics executive who kenneled his dog and charged it to his Pentagon expense account.

In effect, the Early Bird is an institutional channel for rebels and whistle-blowers within the military establishment, giving these dissenters a voice—albeit an anonymous one—in the supreme councils of the Pentagon. This in-house press digest enshrines Schattschneider's basic principle—that the outcome of the conflict depends on how the audience grows and how it reacts. Pentagon dissidents use the Early Bird to change the arena of their internal battles with the generals and admirals over how to spend taxpayer money; the arena shifts from inside the Pentagon to the open battleground of Congress. Critics get their word out to the press, and the Early Bird ricochets it back into the corridors of power. That's in line with Zubkoff's motto: Bringing the bad news to the right people.

If the press, embodied in Early Bird, and the Pentagon whistle-blowers are two legs of the Dissident Triangle, the third leg is in Congress—not Congress as a whole but individual members with special slants on the military. Both Democrats and Republicans, some well known, some not, these Pentagon thorns have a streak of political independence—people such as senators William Proxmire of Wisconsin, Charles Grassley of Iowa, David Pryor of Arkansas, Warren Rudman of New Hampshire. Or, in the House, John Dingell of Michigan, Les Aspin of Wisconsin, and Denny Smith of Oregon. They are counter-punchers, jabbing at the ingrained habits of the Pentagon.

Some Pentagon sparring mates fit the maverick mold; others don't. When I first met Denny Smith, a clean-cut Republican conservative from Oregon, he struck me as a very unlikely Pentagon gadfly. He greeted me one evening in his office, in shirt-sleeves and unbuttoned vest, looking like a hard-working FBI agent. He is an air force veteran of 180 combat missions in Vietnam in an F-4 Phantom jet. He conjures up images of *The Right Stuff*, a Republican John Glenn, a Boy Scout in politics. Denny Smith lacks Glenn's winning smile, but he projects earnestness and sincerity. He has the close-cropped good looks and coat-and-tie decorum of an airline pilot or a businessman, both of which he has been. He is not a typical Pentagon baiter.

His political credentials match the personal impression. Denny Smith arrived in Congress in 1982; he had no political experience, but his voting quickly established him on the Republican right. The American Conservative Union, an anti-big-government lobby, gave him a one-hundred-percent rating in his first two years in Congress. In short, Denny Smith appeared to be a regular, not a maverick. He was a perfect guy to play ball with the administration—only he was not picked for the team. Even as a veteran, he was not put on the main committees dealing with defense.

For those familiar with the Washington power game, two clues about Denny Smith—besides Boy Scout innocence and integrity—foreshadowed his maverick role. First, he came from one of those rare congressional districts which has *no* military base and *no* major defense contractor. "Oregon ranks forty-ninth out of fifty states in defense spending," he told me. Lacking vested Pentagon interests, Denny Smith had the luxury of being able to challenge the Pentagon without fear of serious retribution back home. This was the main reason Smith was left off the defense committees. He fit an old pattern; generally the Pentagon's most dogged critics have come from states with little Pentagon business: Proxmire and Aspin from Wisconsin; Grassley from Iowa; in the 1970s, Iowa's Democratic senators Dick Clark and John Culver.

Second, Denny Smith had unusually good entrée to the Pentagon;

he had a channel to the anchor leg of the dissident triangle: middle-level military officers and defense civilians dismayed and outraged at what they honestly saw as the waste, rigidity, and cover-ups of the Pentagon hierarchy and military contractors. No sooner had Denny Smith, then in his mid-forties, arrived in Washington than he contacted old military buddies, now well-connected colonels. "They became my kitchen cabinet," he said, fifteen or twenty strong, telling him about hidden failures of weapons systems on which billions were being spent. Over time, Smith built a network of moles in the Pentagon, who armed him with under-the-table documents.

"It's surprising how many people down in the ranks don't buy the line of the top brass of the Pentagon," Smith told me. "You wouldn't believe how many of them will come in here in civilian clothes on their day off and tell you that they don't want their names bandied about, but there's something wrong with such-and-such program."[5]

By now, the pattern is well established. Some whistle-blowers have come out of the closet and deal directly with the press and Congress. Notoriety protects them. The foremost figures in this "Pentagon underground" are:

• A. Ernest Fitzgerald, who nearly twenty years ago exposed $2 billion cost overruns on the C-5A transport plane, then was fired by the Air Force and went to court to be reinstated;
• Franklin C. Spinney, a systems analyst who made the cover of *Time* in 1983 with his criticism of the Pentagon's endemic underestimating of weapons costs;
• John Boyd, an Air Force colonel who has challenged the "gold-plating" of modern weapons with excessive costly gadgetry that constantly breaks down;
• Colonel Jim Burton, another Air Force colonel, forced into retirement in 1986 after he took a tough stance on tests of the Army's Bradley Fighting Vehicle; and
• Tom Amilie, former technical director of the Navy's Special Weapons Laboratory at China Lake, California, who joined Fitzgerald as a cost fighter.[6]

Most Pentagon dissidents, however, prefer anonymity. These people find a Denny Smith, or they pass their material to intermediaries such as Dina Rasor, a thirty-one-year-old former news assistant for ABC News who now runs the Project on Military Procurement. The project became a major channel for the dissident triangle, gathering and dis-

seminating inside information—usually documents—on Pentagon
weapons. It is passed along by as many as one hundred Pentagon
sources, Rasor said to me, "from the airman on the flight line who sees
a spare part he thinks is too much, clear up to people who are working
very closely with the secretary of Defense."[7]

Denny Smith's feuds with the army and navy over multibillion-dollar
weapons systems are case studies of how the dissident triangle works.
They offer insight into the inner politics of the Pentagon: the bunker
mentality at the top, the cover-ups of weapons failures, the stubborn
inertia, and the ingenious game of the middle echelons to expose, even
undercut, their own top brass. These examples are all the more striking
because Denny Smith was no Democrat out to score partisan points
against a Republican-run Pentagon; nor was he a liberal ideologically
opposed to big military budgets. He was largely reacting as a citizen-
politician, innocent about the ways of Washington, at first upset and
later angered.

His first tangle came with the Navy: In June 1983, he became
suspicious of Pentagon claims that the new super-high-tech, guided-
missile Aegis cruiser, the *Ticonderoga*, had hit thirteen out of thirteen
target planes in a simulated test attack.

From combat experience, Denny Smith was convinced that no defender could have such perfect results in realistic tests. He asked the
Navy to see the test report. He also asked his own mole network about
the tests. Denny Smith was embarking on a familiar path, for Congress
usually tackles the Pentagon's weapons policy with two major questions: 1. Does the weapon work? and 2. Does it cost too much? The
deeper questions of whether it is really needed and how it fits into an
overall strategy are rarely addressed in earnest. Few members of Congress have a sure enough grasp to handle those questions. What's more,
questions like that could open a Pandora's box, a free-for-all debate on
national strategy that most military commanders, congressmen, and
policymakers want to avoid.

The Pentagon moles provided shocking confirmation of the Oregon
congressman's suspicions about the cruiser's tests. Later, a press article
reported that the *Ticonderoga* had hit only five of twenty-one targets,
and Smith indicated that was pretty accurate. The Navy stonewalled
for five months on Smith's request to see the test report. It was a typical
bureaucratic reflex: Keep an iron grip on all information so that policy
cannot be effectively challenged.

"The reason the Pentagon doesn't like testing is that testing may
interrupt the money flow to its programs," an Air Force colonel ex-

plained to me. "That's the strategy in the Pentagon: Don't interrupt the money flow."

Denny Smith's bout with the Navy was a vintage example of the clashing political cultures of Congress and the bureaucracy, typical of their power games. The congressman was trying to open up the policy debate; the Navy was keeping it shut tight. If Smith had been on the Armed Services or Appropriations committees, his vote on military programs would have given him leverage with the Pentagon. But as a freshman who was not on those committees, Smith had no political clout with the Navy. He had to appeal for help from more senior congressmen.

Finally, in December 1983, the Navy sent a six-man delegation to appease and silence Smith by offering him a quick, temporary peek at the voluminous technical report on the *Ticonderoga*'s test results. But they had underestimated their man. Glancing through the report, Smith immediately spotted that page A-29 was missing. From his own secretly obtained copy, Smith knew that *that page* contained the test report.

"Where's page A-29?" the congressman demanded.

Naval faces blanched white as naval uniforms. "Oh, isn't it there?" a Navy captain said, simulating innocence.

"Well, I don't find it here," Smith insisted.

A civilian engineer with the Navy cadre offered Smith his copy. "Here it is, right here in mine," he said, and Smith took permanent possession of the damning test report.

"Gosh, it must have been the Xerox," one of the Navy men said. Later, Denny Smith told me he felt the vital page had been purposefully omitted "because the rest of the report is about as dull as toilet paper."

Armed with the damning data, Smith called on the Navy to hold more tests of the Aegis cruiser. Fellow Republicans suggested he was out to "get" the military. Trent Lott, the House Republican whip, asked Smith if he knew that killing the Navy's Aegis cruiser program could affect sixteen thousand jobs at Ingalls Shipyard in Lott's home state of Mississippi.

"Hey, listen Trent, we're not trying to cancel the program," Smith replied. "What we're trying to do is get the Navy to be honest, number one, and, number two, if there are flaws in that ship, let's fix them."[8]

The stakes were enormous because the Navy planned twenty-six Aegis guided-missile cruisers at $1.25 billion apiece, and sixty destroyers, with similar technology, costing $1 billion each.

"I decided to go after them to prove that the ship could survive," Smith explained. "If we were going to spend $90 billion on this huge armada of radar ships to go out there and try to protect the fleet, let's be sure they work. The MX missile program is known by everybody in the country; it's about a $20 billion program. It's peanuts alongside of this thing."

Grudgingly, the Navy called the *Ticonderoga* home from the Mediterranean for further testing, in April 1984. This time, the Navy reported ten out of eleven hits, but the mole network passed word that the tests were too easy because there had been no low-level attackers and no saturation attacks by several planes at one time. Once again, Smith asked the Navy for the test report but never got it. The moles shifted him to another target.

Divad: The Gun with Nine Lives

In the Aegis cruiser episode, Denny Smith had been a green congressman who did not know how to gain political leverage through the press and allies in Congress. But by the time he went after the Army's Divad antiaircraft gun, Smith had political allies. He had become one of four cochairmen of the Military Reform Caucus, a bipartisan group of more than fifty senators and House members, ranging from Senator Gary Hart on the Democratic left to Representative Newt Gingrich on the Republican right. This group was pressing questions about military strategy, not to oppose defense but to make it more efficient. Linked to the caucus, Denny Smith's voice had more weight.

Divad, moreover, was a more vulnerable target. By mid-1984, it was deep in trouble, plagued by technical snafus, facing some high-level opposition within the Pentagon, and wounded by news leaks of rigged tests and embarrassing failures. Still, the Army top brass clung to it, and Weinberger sided with the Army.

Divad (short for division air defense) had been conceived in the mid-1970s to provide antiaircraft protection for Army tank divisions against Soviet fighters and helicopters. By most estimates, more modern air protection was needed. But Denny Smith, as an old fighter pilot, thought an expensive high-tech gun such as Divad was unnecessary and ill conceived. Flyers, he told me, have greater fear of traditional antiaircraft batteries, which are harder to evade.

With all its gear and ammunition, Divad cost upward of $6.3 million per gun, more than three times the cost of the M-1 tank it was supposed to protect. The Army ultimately intended spending $4.5 billion for 618

Divads. To speed up Divad's development, the Army combined several proven components: the chassis of an M-48 tank, two Swedish forty-millimeter cannons, radar adapted from the F-16 jet fighter, plus a one-million-dollar computer and other fancy electronics. But the real speed-up, and one major cause of Divad's problems, was the Army's policy of building and producing Divad *while* it was being tested, rather than testing it first.

Some strange decisions were made along the way. In a shoot-off competition between Ford Aerospace and General Dynamics in November 1980, Ford Aerospace scored worse but got the contract. General Dynamics hit nineteen targets and Ford only nine. The Army later said that Ford had a lot of near-misses which were counted. High Pentagon civilians on Weinberger's staff such as David Chu, director of Program Analysis and Evaluation, and Lawrence Korb, assistant secretary of Defense for Manpower, Installations and Logistics, opposed Divad. They warned that future Soviet helicopters would be able to stand outside Divad's best theoretical range of four thousand meters and fire at American tanks. Chu's staff also pointed out that Divad's reaction time was too slow, and its odds of killing Soviet planes only one half to one third of what the Army claimed.[9] Nonetheless, Frank Carlucci, who was Weinberger's deputy at the time, signed a $1.5 billion contract in May 1982 to buy 276 Divads.

Any new weapon has kinks, but Divad's were comic omens: In one check-out test in February 1982, top American and British Army brass went to Fort Bliss, Texas, to see Divad perform. Suddenly, Divad's turret swerved away from a target drone back toward the reviewing stand. The brass all ducked for cover. The gun did not fire at them, but it spent the rest of the day missing targets and lobbing shells into the weeds. Then in January 1984, the first full-fledged production model that Ford was proudly preparing to turn over to the Army made an embarrassing test debut: The radar-guided, computer-operated fire-control system focused on a false target—a rotating latrine fan in a nearby building—which the computer singled out as the closest threatening target.

This produced guffaws within the Army. One hand-drawn Army cartoon showed two GIs, one pointing to the sky and saying, "The Soviets have come up with a new way to foil the Divad." It pictured a Soviet helicopter towing an airborne outhouse to distract Divad.

The incident showed that Divad's radar was still having great difficulty distinguishing the right targets from "ground clutter" (other objects on the terrain). Senator Warren Rudman of New Hampshire, another Divad critic, said this problem highlighted a defect in the gun's basic design. The designers had used a radar system built for jet fighters and for operating against the clutter-free background of the sky, not on the ground. From the outset, Rudman told me, the Army set unrealistic requirements for Divad, dooming it to failure. Nonetheless, the Army stubbornly pressed on, partly out of need, partly out of pride, mostly out of bureaucratic momentum.

"The Divad is a classic example of how the military system keeps alive a weapons program that doesn't make any sense," Denny Smith remarked. "Once the system buys onto the program, there's almost no way you can stop the program. If you try to, you're either unpatriotic, you don't understand the situation, or you're out for publicity. They try to go after you. You can almost tell when they have a bad system because they get so defensive and come after you."[10]

Even so, Congress was growing wary of Divad. More awkward disclosures got into the news. Divad flunked cold-weather tests in early 1984. It had to be heated for six hours with the field equivalent of a hair dryer before it was ready to fire. In another test, the Army had to attach four large metal reflectors to an old target helicopter to help Divad's radar find the target. By late 1984, Ford Aerospace was months behind its production schedule, and Congress had barred further purchase until Divad passed realistic operational field tests. Congressional pressures forced Weinberger to take a personal interest.

In the spring of 1985, the Army ran a massive monthlong mock battle in the California desert with tanks, Bradley fighting vehicles, and Divads opposing A-10 and F-4 fighter planes and AH-64 Apache helicopters. The finale was the "live fire" tests at White Sands, New Mexico, in May 1985.

Afterward, the Army brass jubilantly proclaimed that Divad had hit and destroyed its targets. Jack Krings, civilian head of the Pentagon's new Office of Operational Tests and Evaluation, telephoned Denny Smith. "Boy, really impressive," Krings said. "Blew those mothers right out of the air." Army Secretary John Marsh, Undersecretary James Ambrose, and General John A. Wickam, Jr., the Army chief of staff, all recommended that Weinberger move ahead with Divad. Ambrose, a former Ford Aerospace vice president who had helped launch the Divad program while still at Ford, told me he felt Divad was a big leap forward, a ten- to twenty-percent improvement on existing antiaircraft weapons.[11]

But the Dissident Triangle had a very different story: It informed Congressman Smith that the mock battle showed Divad's range was inadequate, and the live fire tests were unrealistic; the Army's claims of success were misleading. What Denny Smith learned, he told me later, was that the target fighter planes were patsies. They were flown right past the Divad guns "at a suicide elevation of four hundred to five hundred feet, flying straight and level at 420 knots with no jinking [pilot talk for no evasive maneuvers]. The helicopters were flown up to a higher elevation than any sane person would ever do in a combat zone. What they set up was a shooting gallery and, even then, there were *no* direct hits—*none!*"[12]

If so, I asked, how could the Army be claiming success?

Moles at the test site had tipped off Smith to shenanigans on the firing range. For proof, he went after videotapes. The Army happily supplied tapes showing Divad firing and target drones exploding. "You could see that they had been destroyed almost immediately, and you thought maybe the guns had done that," Smith told me later. "The picture would be on the airplane. It would show maybe a couple of sparks. And then almost immediately, they'd blow up, looking like they'd been hit. But we knew better. We'd been told. The range-safety officer destroyed every one of the drones from the ground. None of them were destroyed by hits from the guns."

Others were less categorical than Smith. Two Pentagon skeptics told me that gunbursts showed a few Divad kills but asserted that on the large majority, the range-safety officer had been unusually quick to detonate safety charges on the target planes. Safety measures are routine, but Denny Smith and Lieutenant Colonel Tom Carter, a top Pentagon test analyst and a Vietnam veteran with 408 air missions, told me the safety officer used a fast trigger to make it look as though Divad had scored hits.

"We felt they were certainly flawed tests if they destroyed the drones that quickly," Smith told me. "Why didn't they let them go on for twenty more seconds?" Smith fired off protest letters to top Pentagon officials. The Army brass fought back, defending its weapon.

Smith's blast that Divad had not made "a single direct hit" touched off a firestorm in the media. The Early Bird gave hot running coverage to the charges of the maverick network for Weinberger's ride-to-work reading. The Schattschneider dynamic was at work: Television networks and news weeklies became seized with Divad. The videotapes of the live fire tests, and Smith's charges about how the targets were destroyed, gave the whiff of scandal and rigged tests to Divad.

Inside the Pentagon, the final test evaluations were being drafted for Weinberger in mid-August. One of them, done in the Office of Developmental Testing and Evaluation by Colonel Tom Carter, was a blistering and fatal indictment of Divad. "My worst suspicions were confirmed," Carter later told me. "The Divad gun couldn't detect and track and engage and shoot down enemy aircraft, unless the enemy's aircraft were using unrealistic tactics which no pilot—Russian or American—in his right mind will fly. The weapon failed miserably to perform."[13]

What happened to Carter's official report was an amusing wrinkle of the Dissident Triangle operations—not leaking, but flooding. My sources told me that the original draft of the second report, prepared by Jack Krings, director of the Office of Operational (as opposed to "Developmental") Testing and Analysis, was nowhere near as harsh as Carter's. On August 22, nine copies of Carter's no-nonsense report were circulated to top Pentagon officials. The next day, the top Pentagon echelon tried to squelch it.[14] Orders were given to retrieve every copy, but it was too late. Instead of nine copies, thirteen copies came back.

"That's what we call the flood strategy," one Pentagon gadfly told me with a grin. "Never leak anything yourself, but make plenty of copies. Flood the building. God will take care of the rest. As soon as Krings's people saw those thirteen copies, they knew they had a P.R. disaster on their hands, because the test results had gotten out of the building."

It was Friday afternoon, and Weinberger had already headed for a weekend in Maine. Krings's office spent the weekend redrafting its report to toughen it, more in line with Carter's.

The "flooder" was right. On August 22, Denny Smith wrote Weinberger a letter to say that he had "obtained and reviewed" the test reports on the Divad which "verify the same criticisms of the weapons flaws leveled over and over again since the inception of the program." He urged Weinberger to cancel the program, and on Monday, from his home in Oregon, Smith telephoned Weinberger to underscore the fact that he had the damaging report in his possession. "I hope you've seen that report, Mr. Secretary, and I just urge you to read that before you make your decision," he said with an implicit threat to go public if Weinberger did not act on the negative report.

The next day, Weinberger announced that he was canceling Divad because "operational tests have demonstrated that the system's performance does not effectively meet the growing military threat." What Divad would offer over existing weapons, he said, was "not worth the additional cost." He identified its main problems as "the lack of range and the lack of reliability. . . . The system didn't work well enough."

At that point, the Pentagon had sunk $1.8 billion into the program. Weinberger's decision to kill Divad marked a rare victory for the dissident triangle—one case in hundreds. I have heard many tales of other weapons systems having serious flaws, but they roll on. A few get stopped in the research-and-testing phase. Senator Warren Rudman, a combat infantry captain in the Korean War, fought three years to block production funds for the Viper, a defective antitank weapon with skyrocketing costs. He finally won before production was started.

But it is almost unheard of for the Pentagon to kill a weapon, such as Divad, once it is in production. Only pressure from the Dissident Triangle did that, by forcing the issue into the open and then hawking Weinberger relentlessly.

The Iron Triangle at Work

Far more powerful than the Dissident Triangle is the Iron Triangle— the symbiotic partnership of military services, defense contractors, and members of Congress from states and districts where military spending is heavy and visible.[15]

President Eisenhower called it the military-industrial complex. Others have called it an incestuous family network, where political, economic, and bureaucratic interests mesh and where cozy relations are nurtured not only by mutual back scratching, but also by a flow of corporate executives crisscrossing between high Pentagon jobs and the defense industry and a steady stream of retiring colonels, admirals, and generals moving right into jobs with Pentagon contractors. In 1983, for example, 13,682 Pentagon civilians and officers cashed in on their Pentagon connections by taking jobs in the defense industry.

To those two legs of the Iron Triangle, add the congressional defense committees. For Pentagon procurement is driven by what Anthony Battista, for years an influential senior staffer for the House Armed Services Committee, calls the "unholy alliance between congressional pork barrel and Pentagon wish lists."[16]

In fairness, the Iron Triangle is not unique to the Defense Department. That paradigm operates for virtually every department in the executive branch, for every major interest group, for every major region of the country. The Iron Triangle is a powerful force in the nation's farm policy, forging links between the Agriculture Department, farm organizations and farm-state senators and congressmen, usually concentrated on the agriculture committees of Congress. Basically, they unite to protect farm interests against competing demands for urban development or industrial bailouts. Ditto for the Labor Department, the Department of Health and Human Services, and so on. Rocky Mountain politicians gravitate toward the interior committees to watch over water and land use. Coastal representatives, like salmon instinctively swimming upstream to spawn, head for the maritime and fisheries committees. All form their own iron triangles—iron, because the partners want an unbreakable lock on the policies most vital to them and they want to shut out outsiders. The object of the Iron Triangle is a closed power game, just as the object of the Dissident Triangle is to open up the power game.

What gives the Pentagon's Iron Triangle extraordinary importance is its great influence on national security policy and the enormous sums of money at stake. In the five-year period from late 1981 into 1986, military spending was close to *$1.3 trillion.* With domestic programs largely held in check, the Pentagon budget was the one whopping federal cornucopia left for private contractors, the best remaining source of patronage for Congress. A local chunk of some big defense contract dwarfs any other government grant a congressman can deliver. The Pentagon budget is the last really big barrel of pork; its sheer volume feeds economic appetites.

"The military services want more money than they can afford, and the Pentagon wants more money than the country can afford," a longtime prodefense Senate committee staffer observed to me. "The senator or House member wants more for his district than the budget can afford. Each party is motivated by greed. The interests of the service and the contractors is to start new programs and not to worry about efficiency. Contractors like to stretch out production of weapons because they can employ more people for more years. And congressmen like to stretch out programs in their districts for the same reason and because Congress hates to take the responsibility for killing any weapons system."

One reason Divad survived so long was the protection of its own iron triangle. In 1983, when a wildcat effort was made on the House floor to kill Divad, its five most vociferous defenders had political and economic links to Divad:

· Robert Badham, a California Republican and a member of the House Armed Services Committee from the district where Divad was assembled;
· Marjorie Holt, another Republican on the Armed Services Com-

mittee from a Maryland district where Westinghouse Electric built
Divad's radar;
• Bill Nichols, an Alabama Democrat from Anniston, where Divad's
chassis was made;
• Ronald Coleman, a Texas Democrat whose district held the Army
base where Divad was conceived, fostered and tested; and
• Samuel Stratton, a New York Democrat and chairman of the
Armed Services Subcommittee on Procurement, who had a working
relationship with the Army and saw his political role as buying
weapons systems.

"The way the game is played now is one word: *jobs,*" asserted New
Hampshire Senator Warren Rudman, an evangelical skinflint. By jobs,
Rudman meant jobs for the contractor and jobs back home for which
senators and congressmen could claim credit—but also the careers of
the third leg of the Iron Triangle: the layers of Army brass from the
Divad program officers up to General John Wickham, then Army chief
of staff, who felt their careers were riding on its success.

"The Army's strategy is to keep you going and keep you going and
delay you, until they are so far into you in terms of money that you can't
afford to abandon the weapons program," Rudman complained.
"They'll admit to you that the weapon may not work as well as it was
supposed to, but they'll say it works pretty well. I don't think people
in the Army thought the Divad was such a good weapon; it's just that
too many careers were involved. The Army was committed to it because the top brass felt naked without a new air defense gun."[17]

"Somebody's career is made by keeping a program alive—in the
contractors, in the military and in Congress, too," was the way Denny
Smith put it. "It's not just the Army. The Navy designs a weapon and
if it doesn't work, their attitude is get the ship hull in the water and
then we'll fix it later."[18] A three-star Army general agreed. "Divad
survived so long because it remained at the level of program managers
and staff officers overseeing the program," the general told me. "These
majors and lieutenant colonels thought only of their program, and they
drove the generals over the brink." Actually, it is a vicious circle: The
generals ordered weapons built, and the lieutenant colonels felt compelled to deliver weapons, *not* bad news. Their optimistic reports kept
the generals locked into programs such as Divad, for the incentives of
the defense game are to build, spend, and appropriate, *not* to oppose,
question, or delay.

On the industrial side, the hierarchy at Ford Aerospace and its subcontractors fought tenaciously for jobs and profits from Divad. One Ford Aerospace vice president, James Ambrose, became undersecretary of the Army, and though he claimed to have stayed on the sidelines, several Pentagon officials told me Ambrose fought hard to save Divad.[19] Plenty of others had a personal stake in the program. Early in the competition for Divad, Ford Aerospace hired four recently retired three-star Army generals. Gregg Easterbrook of *The Atlantic*, who has written several detailed articles on Divad, asserted that having these revolving-door links helped Ford beat out General Dynamics. Ford denied any "improprieties or illegalities."[20]

But revolving-door connections do keep programs going and reduce critical questioning. They breed a coziness within the iron triangle that often costs taxpayers money, diminishes real competition, and sometimes perpetuates defective weapons.

In Congress, too, powerful members gain reputations as protectors of certain weapons and contractors. For years, Senator Henry Jackson was known as "the senator from Boeing" because he so openly pushed the interests of Boeing Aircraft, the biggest military contractor in his home state of Washington. Senator Barry Goldwater of Arizona, a retired major general in the Air Force Reserve who loved to fly jet fighters, watched over pet air force programs. Senator John Tower of Texas teamed up with another powerful Texan, George Mahon, to keep LTV's A-7 attack bomber in production at Fort Worth long after the Navy tired of the plane. The most legendary military pork barreler was L. Mendel Rivers; he landed so many bases and contracts for Charleston, South Carolina, during his thirty years in the House that Carl Vinson, another wily practitioner, once teased him: "Mendel, you put anything else down there in your district, and it's gonna sink."

Now, after the dispersal of power in Congress in the mid-1970s, such concentrated largesse in the district of a committee chairman is virtually impossible. More players have power, and all want their slices of Pentagon bacon. The Iron Triangle game has been expanded: The Navy, for example, has shipyards and bases on all coasts, insuring allies among senators intent on protecting thousands of jobs at home: John Warner of Virginia, John Stennis of Mississippi, William Cohen of Maine, Chris Dodd of Connecticut, John Chaffee of Rhode Island, Pete Wilson of California. Warner, a former Navy secretary, is perhaps the Navy's most ardent advocate. His state houses the Atlantic Fleet headquarters at Norfolk and the shipyard that builds aircraft carriers at Newport News.

Charles Bennett, a veteran Florida congressman and chairman of the

House Armed Services Seapower Subcommittee, minces no words about how his politics are influenced by the Navy base just outside Jacksonville. "The Navy brings $1 billion to my home district every year," he told me. "That's a big deal. It's the biggest thing we've got commercially. They've got some forty-odd ships there and they're going to get more. Anybody from Jacksonville would want to get onto the Armed Services Committee to protect that."[21]

The committee structure of Congress anchors the Iron Triangle. That is true as well for the Agriculture Department, Interior Department, Labor, and so on. For decades, the Armed Services committees in both houses, along with the appropriations subcommittees that oversee military spending, have been the Pentagon's staunchest partisans. These committees are more promilitary than Congress as a whole, though in recent years they have been infiltrated by a few Pentagon critics. But most members are there for logrolling. Generally, they approach the defense budget, not as a whole but piecemeal, weapon system by weapon system. The committee chairman often operates like a ward politician, parceling out goodies to the members. After the big money is doled out, a defense appropriations subcommittee aide told me: "If you've got something you want in your district, you can say, 'Put this in,' and no one will argue. Most of them are below $10 million, but sometimes more. If you get over $100 million, people will raise questions."

Political doves join the scramble, too. Senator Alan Cranston, a big advocate of arms control and the nuclear freeze, supports the B-1 bomber whose prime contractor is based in California. Senator Carl Levin of Michigan, another Pentagon critic, has added money to Army requests for the M-1 tank which is manufactured in Michigan. Senator Edward Kennedy and House Speaker Tip O'Neill have backed the F-18 fighter and other projects because Massachusetts gets large subcontracts. Mervyn Dymally, a liberal Democratic member of the Black Caucus, normally given to low-cost housing and programs for the poor, has voted for the MX missile because defense plants around his Los Angeles district mean jobs to his constituents. Dick Bolling of Missouri told me of Harry Truman's warning to him: "Dick, the one thing I'll tell you, never try to get a military installation in your district. It'll ruin you."[22]

In sum, the first law of the Pentagon's Iron Triangle is that "the district commands over ideology," says Gordon Adams, director for the Center on Budget and Policy Priorities, a private group that opposes high defense spending. In Speaker O'Neill's memorable aphorism, All politics is local—most emphatically in military procurement. "If your congressional district has dominant economic interests, you go with the people who work at those companies," Adams asserts. "People forget these guys in Congress are elected from a very small piece of geography every two years, and they can't afford to buck all the economic interests of their district."[23]

Few members of Congress epitomized this basic job protecting role more dramatically than the late Joseph Addabbo, a shrewd veteran with a little brush mustache and a wispy tuft on his bald pate. From 1960 until his death in 1986, Addabbo represented an Archie Bunker district in Queens, New York. As chairman of the House Appropriations Defense Subcommittee, Addabbo was a maverick in the Iron Triangle—a liberal Democrat, an advocate of arms control, and a tough-minded Pentagon critic. He led the 1982 fight against the MX missile; earlier he had opposed the B-1 bomber. As subcommittee chairman, he helped whack $50 billion off President Reagan's Pentagon budgets. Nonetheless, he fought and finagled for two military contractors within commuting distance of his Long Island district, Grumman and Fairchild Industries. He badgered the Navy to homeport a battleship on Staten Island to help New York City. And he used his leverage to get other military deals for New York State.

As Grumman's protector, Addabbo was a motive force in getting the Navy to increase its buy of F-14 fighters from 425 to 700. When the Navy wanted to stop production of Grumman's A-6 attack bomber in 1978, Addabbo just kept pushing funds into the appropriations bills. He went to his deathbed opposing Air Force efforts to kill Fairchild's T-46 trainer.

But Addabbo's battle for Fairchild's A-10 was a case study in protecting pork for the home folks. The A-10 is a slow two-engine fighter used for close air support of ground troops, a mission that bores Air Force jet fighter jockeys. In 1983, the Air Force stopped asking for money for the A-10, but Addabbo put money in. In 1984, John Tower, then Senate Armed Services Committee chairman, did the Pentagon's bidding and cut all funds for the A-10—violating a logrolling taboo. For a second rule of the Iron Triangle is that members of key committees do not shoot down each others' favorite projects. Addabbo retaliated by squeezing one of Tower's homestate projects: production of the Harm missile by Texas Instruments. Because the missile was needed, Addabbo did not kill it; he put in a requirement that the Pentagon buy it from two sources, taking some business away from Texas Instruments. So Tower backed off.

When I asked Addabbo about the inconsistency between his general anti-Pentagon stance and his protection of Long Island defense plants, he shrugged. "I fought for the A-10 and the A-6 because there was nothing around like them, and you needed them," he asserted. "So why not build them in your own area, the same as everyone else does."[24]

Contract Spreading Gets Weapons Built

The third basic rule of the Iron Triangle is for defense contractors and military services to make sure that enough regions get a piece of the pie so that a weapons program develops wide political support. All the services need new technology, and so they have a constant flow of projects at various stages of development. The standard technique is to get a project started by having the prime contractor give a low initial cost estimate to make it seem affordable and wait to add fancy electronics and other gadgets much later through engineering "change orders," which jack up the price and the profits. Anyone who has been through building or remodeling a house knows the problem.

"This is called the buy-in game," an experienced Senate defense staff specialist confided. "In conjunction with the contractors, the services give very rosy estimates of what the weapon will cost *per copy*, so Congress will buy in. Their estimates are based on the largest buy and the most efficient production rate—which never materializes." Once the Pentagon leaders and Congress are on board, costs rise, creating the "bow-wave" effect. Like waves on the bow of the ship, the costs start small, grow gradually as the project picks up speed, then swell for several years during the peak production phase, reach a crest, and subside. That initial commitment—first to research and then to development of a new system—is vital. It rarely bears much relationship to the ultimate cost. The key is to get the program going and keep it alive. Then if the subcontracts are well spread out politically, the weapon system has a secure future in the politics of procurement.

No case better illustrates the politics of contract spreading than Rockwell International's formidable campaign for the B-1 bomber. Joseph Addabbo told me that at Nellis Air Force Base in Nevada in 1983, he had seen a Rockwell display that illustrated the political strings Rockwell had tied to the B-1. It was a blown-up photo of the needle-nosed bomber with colored strings coming out of various components—the fuselage, wings, engine, tail section, cockpit, landing gear, and so on—to the states and districts where the parts were made.

"The whole country was covered with these strings," Addabbo said.

"Other contractors had done this thing, spreading the subcontracts, but the B-1 was the first time we really saw it in large numbers. This was the biggest of that type of operation by far. People would come to me and say, 'Joe, I'm not for it, but it's one of the biggest employers in my district. I've got to go with them.' "[25]

Thomas Downey, a Long Island Democrat, told me that when he arrived in Congress in 1975 and landed on the Armed Services Committee, Rockwell International was lobbying aggressively to keep the program going. "Rockwell would show you the B-1 program and bring out that it had forty-eight states of the Union covered—to prevent what they called [political] 'turbulence'—that was their great term. Translated, *turbulence* meant canceling the contract," Downey told me.

"They thought I was crazy the first few times Rockwell briefed me," he went on. "I was one of the leading advocates to kill the B-1. One guy from Airborne Instruments Labs in my district, which makes the electronic countermeasures for the B-1, said to me: 'This is the third biggest contract we have, congressman. Except for the engine and the airframe, it's the third biggest. It's $2 billion just in the first few years.' I said, 'I know. I just think the plane's a bad idea.' Rockwell had it all worked up in a briefing kit. Defense had a map, showing where the subcontracts were. They said forty-eight states. Conscious decision on their part from day one."[26]

Air Force and Rockwell officials claim the contract spreading happened naturally—that the B-1 is such a complex, modern system of weaponry and electronics that it naturally tapped a vast and diverse network of parts suppliers all over the country. Practically no one in Congress takes that claim at face value; virtually everyone regards B-1 contract spreading as deliberate. In the mid-1970s Rockwell paid Chase Econometrics $110,000 for a study to help show each senator and representative the impact of the project in his area. Over seven years, Rockwell figured the $30 billion B-1 program meant 192,000 jobs for a total of 5,200 subcontractors and nearby businesses "due to the economic cascade effect." Its lobbyists worked hundreds of members of Congress, one by one, with specific information about the subcontractors, jobs, and money involved in their districts.

Bill Gray, the House Budget Committee chairman, told me one computer printout showed subcontractors in more than 400 of the 435 congressional districts, a phenomenal political spread.[27] This big a project activates industrial unions as well as corporate management, especially in key states such as California, Ohio, and Massachusetts.

Rockwell also had stockholders and employes writing members of Congress—on company time, which meant at least partly at taxpayers' expense.

"That is one of the ways they sell these things to Congress," protested Representative John Seiberling, an Ohio Democrat. "That is another scandal—that we are allowing this engine of spending taxpayers' money for defense programs to be used to propagandize and manipulate the Congress."[28]

Seiberling showed me a letter from J. W. Rane, Jr., of Rockwell's B-1 Division in June 1973 asserting that Seiberling's fourteenth district of Ohio had "a potential of approximately $60 million new business" from development of the B-1 prototype, mainly to Goodyear Aerospace, for brakes and wheels. But Seiberling was skeptical. His staff calculated that the subcontracts were so small that his district would pay out more in taxes to underwrite the B-1 than it would earn from the B-1. Seiberling argued that was typical for most congressional districts, but he was no match for Rockwell.

The company's enormous lobbying effort was so potent that Congress nearly overrode President Carter's decision in 1977 against B-1 production. Strong congressional support did keep alive research and development for testing four prototype bombers. Rockwell did an uncanny job of keeping together its skilled work force for a quick start-up of B-1 production, banking on a Republican president in 1981. Reagan aides told me of financial contributions to Reagan's campaign by Rockwell company executives, and the company's lobbying of the Reagan forces during the 1980 campaign, gaining entrée through Michael Deaver, Reagan's public relations adviser. When Reagan entered the White House, the B-1 was one of the first military projects revived, a hallmark of Reagan defense policy—and of Rockwell's success at the Iron Triangle game.

The B-1 has become a model for other contractors. It has been imitated by the Reagan administration itself with the rapid spread of contracts for its strategic defense initiative (SDI), not only in this country but in Western Europe and possibly Japan and Israel. By 1986, Reagan's strategic defense program had research contracts in forty-two of the fifty states, covering seventeen of the nineteen states represented on the Senate Armed Services Committee and twenty of the twenty-six on the Appropriations Committee. Paul Warnke, a former Carter administration arms control adviser, suggested that Reagan's Star Wars proposal was being converted "from stardust and moonbeams to that great pork barrel in the sky." Moreover, the initial alarm of West

European governments about the SDI program abated as Weinberger worked out agreements for the British, Germans, Japanese, and Israelis, among others, to bid for the project's research contracts.

"This is the internationalization of the military-industrial complex that Eisenhower talked about," Gary Hart commented ruefully. "What you've got with Star Wars is a unique phenomenon where they're building not just a national constituency, but an international constituency."[29]

What left the program's long-term future in doubt was congressional resistance to going beyond the research phase. For the critical point in building political support for any big weapons system, Gordon Adams observed, comes with moving from research into development and production and with the selection of a prime contractor, which, like Rockwell, leads the political campaign. Research involves relatively small teams of white-collar scientists and engineers, but production involves tens of thousands of blue-collar workers. That massive job constituency gives a weapon system almost irresistible momentum.

In *The Defense Game,* a book drawing on his nineteen years experience as a defense specialist for the Office of Management and Budget through six presidential administrations, Richard Stubbings bluntly summarized the workings of the Iron Triangle:

> At stake in our defense program is not only our national security, but also large opportunities for personal and economic success. Congressmen favor programs and facilities in their states and districts regardless of efficiency. Industry officials seek to boost their sales and profits, ofttimes at the expense of the government and the taxpayer. Military officers seek promotion and advancement under accepted standards of performance which often conflict with hard-nosed business practices. And the service hierarchies see close working relations with the other services as not in their interest. Thus, not only is the defense budget the vehicle by which our nation plans how to fight the battles of tomorrow, but it is also a battleground itself, where politicians, corporations, and military officers seek to serve their personal and parochial interests.[30]

Army Lobby: Tropical Troops for Alaska

The military services have their own gambits in the Iron Triangle game. They not only spread subcontractors; they spread military bases. Generally, the Army is considered less crafty at politics than the Navy and the Air Force, but from time to time it shows creativity. Take, for example, its decision in late 1983 to form three new light-infantry divisions, an idea that Weinberger snapped up despite advice from his own staff that American divisions in Europe were still undermanned and filling them should take first priority. In the 1970s, the Army had "heavied up" its divisions for war in Europe with tanks and armor. But with the rising threat in the third world in the early 1980s, Army generals decided to "go light," that is, to have divisions without heavy armor that could hop easily to world trouble spots. The Army plan was to pare down two existing divisions and to create one new light division.

"Primarily, they wanted to get in on the action," I was told by Larry Korb, who was an assistant secretary of Defense at the time. "In other words, the hot spots in Central America and Africa were certainly not susceptible to M-1 tanks. The light division was an attempt to create a marine corps within the Army. The Army was anxious to add a new division because the internal pressures within the Army were furious. The Air Force was adding wings; the Navy was adding ships—what the hell's the Army doing? You know, why are these other guys growing and the Army has the smallest share of the budget?"[31]

Creating a new division, of course, meant finding a home for it. The Army put out the word on Capitol Hill and set up a political auction for this nice little military-patronage plum. Six states showed interest; four already had Army posts: California, Georgia, Kentucky, and Washington; two did not: New York and Alaska. The lure was obvious. The Army reckoned that building facilities for a division of ten thousand soldiers would involve from $500 million to $1 billion in construction costs, fifteen hundred permanent jobs for civilians, and $4.5 million in annual purchasing power pumped into the local economy. New York made a heavy pitch. Governor Mario Cuomo, senators Pat Moynihan and Al D'Amato, congressmen Joe Addabbo, Sam Stratton, and Dave Martin all lobbied for Fort Drum, an old and largely unused military reservation about seventy-five miles north of Syracuse in a severely depressed part of the state.

Not that Fort Drum was ideal from a military standpoint. For one thing, the temperature averages about twenty-four degrees in January, with snowfall from late October to April; hardly the right environment to train troops for combat in the Persian Gulf, Central America, or Southeast Asia. Moreover, Fort Drum's existing airstrips could not accommodate a fully loaded C-141 transport, meaning that until a new airfield was completed, troops would have to be trucked to air bases at Rome or Syracuse, a minimum of fifty-five miles, a considerable nuisance in wintertime. Nonetheless, the Army settled on Fort Drum.

"The Army did a smart thing," said Larry Korb, sizing up the Army's political game. "At Fort Benning and Fort Bragg, they already had stuff. I mean they already had support in that part of the country to the extent they needed it. They didn't have it in New York."

But the Army did not reckon properly on Ted Stevens, then chairman of the Senate Defense Appropriations Subcommittee and, as a Pentagon power-game player, probably the Senate's single most influential voice on military spending. Repeatedly, he has worked billions cut by others back into the defense budget. Stevens wanted the light division for Alaska. When he heard it was going to New York, he was outraged; he pressed Alaska's case with Weinberger. Stevens sent the Defense secretary a chart showing how little defense money was being spent in Alaska and attached a handwritten note, obtained by Michael Gordon, then a reporter for the *National Journal*, which read:

> Dear Cap,
>   When you examine the enclosed and realize that Alaska's votes in Congress have been consistently pro-defense, the request for consideration of Alaska as the place to deploy the light division just doesn't seem unreasonable.
>   Hope to see you soon.
>
> Regards,
> Ted.[32]

Within no time, the Army brass was talking about the need to provide for "theater defense," or regional protection, of Alaska and the Aleutian Island chain. Somehow the Alaskan trouble spot had been omitted from the Army's original rationale for its light divisions. It had never been mentioned in testimony to Congress. But Weinberger obviously felt Stevens had to be appeased, and the Army saw the chance for yet another light division with such attendant goodies as a juicy two-star billet for some Army general. So, timed for maximum political impact a few weeks before the 1984 elections, the Army announced in mid-September that it was forming not one but two new light divisions, one for New York *and* one for Alaska. Oddly, one third of each division was to be drawn from existing reserve units located in other states; this would save money though it would slow deployment.

Assistant Defense Secretary Larry Korb could not contain his laughter. "The whole light division thing is hilarious," Korb clucked to me. "Training for hot-weather action at cold-weather bases. Taking buses from Fort Drum to the airfields in winter." As for Alaska, Korb said,

"It's a political thing, pure and simple. Ted Stevens made no bones about it's being pure politics. Cap and the Army realized they couldn't tell Stevens, 'Well, you lost.' So they gave the other division to him. People had been giving lip service for years to defending the Aleutians. Once it was decided to give Stevens his division, people said, 'Aha, there's our rationale. We'll defend the Aleutians.' Never mind that the proposed light division is supposed to be mobile."[33]

The Alaska division underscores another rule of military lobbying in the Iron Triangle game: Take care of friends; play hard ball with critics. The military flatters members of Congress with courtesies and perquisites, courting them with guided tours of military bases or rides on aircraft carriers, arranging foreign trips, assigning escort officers, providing the aircraft.

"It's slightly incestuous," said Senator Warren Rudman. "I'm three months in office, and I get invited to the Pentagon. An Army car picks me up. I arrive, and I'm taken to a nice office and order my breakfast. Well-dressed stewards, a four-star general on my right, the secretary of the Army to my left, one- and two-star generals around the table. I told General Wickam, the Army chief of staff, 'If my battalion commander in Korea could see me now, he'd never believe it.' Wickam laughed. He told me, 'There is a kind of awe, and I hope you'll get over it. But there is a close relationship between Congress and the military.' "[34]

If angered, the military can turn off the faucet. John Dingell, the powerful, prying chairman of the House Energy and Commerce Committee who called General Dynamics Corporation and the Navy on the carpet for month after month of embarrassing exposures about cost overruns and contract shenanigans, was told in July 1985 that the Defense Department could not provide the normal courtesy plane for his committee's proposed trip to Eastern Europe. Later, in early 1986, the Pentagon rapped other critics on the knuckles. In a tried-and-true political gambit, it announced plans to close some domestic military installations. Just three were selected, all in the backyards of Pentagon critics: a large section of Lowry Air Force Base in Denver, home turf of then-Senator Gary Hart and Representative Patricia Schroeder; the Army Materials Technology Laboratory in Watertown, Massachusetts, not far from the home of House Speaker Tip O'Neill; and the naval hospital in Philadelphia, home of House Budget Committee Chairman Bill Gray, a key figure in trimming Pentagon budgets.

Unabashedly, the military services lobby senators and House members, occasionally creating an uproar when the arm-twisting goes too far. In July 1982, for example, the Navy got caught red-handed compiling and circulating political box scores on members of the Military Reform Caucus, whose views on defense strategy and priorities differ from the Pentagon. Caucus members contend they are not antidefense; they simply have their own ideas. But the Navy regarded them as intrusive. Its box score on selected votes, compiled by its legislative liaison staff under Rear Admiral A. K. Knoizen, gave each senator or congressman a "national security index." Knoizen's June 16 memo to Navy Secretary John Lehman, the chief of Naval Operations, the Marine commandant, and twenty other high Navy officials, was leaked to *Defense Week* and touched off an uproar in Congress.[35]

Senator Ted Stevens, then the Republican whip, was furious. He got a fifty-seven-percent Navy rating, though he was not even a member of the Military Reform Caucus. Despite his ardent prodefense record, Stevens had been graded down, in part, for opposing Secretary Lehman's plans to take battleships out of mothballs. "Some admirals just wanted a battleship under their feet again," the blunt-spoken Stevens groused. He was so irate that he warned the Navy to stop wasting tax money on such "misguided" and "unethical" activities. Other senators were also outraged at the blatant political ratings, which they considered a reversal of the doctrine of civilian control of the military.

"Congress is getting tired of the Defense Department winking at the law forbidding the use of public funds to lobby Congress," Stevens declared in a Senate speech.[36] "I think Congress is tired of the Department viewing Congressional relations as a license to maneuver and manipulate those of us who are elected to oversee the use of taxpayer support of the Government." Lehman and his top brass took cover by blaming it on an overzealous legislative team. Admiral Knoizen became the fall guy. Within a month, he was retired from active duty.

But the practice did not stop. In 1983, Senator David Pryor of Arkansas found himself being scolded face-to-face by an Air Force general for his voting record on military issues.

Pryor, a longtime foe of chemical weapons, had irked the Pentagon and defied the pork-barrel norms by offering to cut funds for making nerve gas at a small factory in his home state. In addition, he was a target of Air Force pressure on the C-17 transport plane. An Air Force general and a colonel, trying to swing Pryor into line, suggested that if the C-17 were built, it might be based in Little Rock. Pryor was not immediately persuaded, and the general shifted from soft sell to hard sell. In his gentle, curling Arkansas drawl, barely containing his anger at the memory of crass political pressure from a uniformed officer, Pryor recounted the event as I sat across from his desk:

"That general looks me in the eye and says, 'You know, Senator, you're not considered very pro-defense.' And I say, 'Let's go into that a little bit.' He turns to this colonel and says, 'Let's see Senator Pryor's sheet.' And literally, I thought the colonel was going to choke. He pulls it out and hands it to the general, sitting in that rocking chair right there where you are. The general opens it up and starts readin' it. Every vote that I passed up: aid to the *contras*, aid to this, statements on Reagan, statements on defense, votes on nerve gas."

Pryor fell silent, visualizing the scene. Then I asked him, "Do you want to say who that general was?"

"I'd rather not," he said. "And you know why?"

"Why?"

"Because right now he has been promoted," Pryor answered. "He's very high in the Strategic Air Command, and what that general does really has life-or-death over our SAC base in Blytheville, Arkansas. Then you say, 'Well, are you cowed by this?' I don't want to say cowed. But you know, why would I go out and whip up a fight knowin' what the detrimental effect might be to my own constituents? The fact is they have denied that they keep sheets on people, but they do. I saw mine. In fact, I asked him for it. They sent it to me the next day."

We were talking more than two years after the incident, but it still roiled Pryor. "The idea that some defense policy might be based on whether or not a senator or congressman supports the Pentagon position or not," he simmered, "that's dangerous."[37]

John Lehman, Cocky Operator

If any single Pentagon figure personifies the Iron Triangle game, it is John Lehman, for six years Reagan's secretary of the Navy. No one in the Pentagon in recent years has played the Iron Triangle game more successfully than Lehman. He is a slick, cocky, rough-and-tumble operator, a self-proclaimed naval strategist and a showboater who enjoys making waves, thrives on controversy, knows his stuff, and has few peers as a bureaucratic infighter. Normally, a military service secretary is a figurehead position. It is generally an honorific bestowed on a campaign benefactor or some political ally of the president who becomes the easy captive of his own military brass or is overrun by the tiers of civilian staff of the secretary of Defense. But Lehman's combination of brilliance, brazenness, and guile gave him real power and won him more of what he was after than any other major figure in the Pentagon, including Weinberger.

Bill Cohen, a Maine Republican, one of the Senate's most thought-ful prodefense moderates, called Lehman the "most effective individ-ual in the administration on defense policy. . . . He's probably the most effective service chief that I have seen, or anyone has seen, in a long, long time."[38]

"Tough, able, and mean" was the blunt rundown given me by a bureaucratic ally of Lehman. I heard similar assessments often. Leh-man dared to clash openly with his superiors, and when they tried to put him down, he covertly ran to allies in the White House or in Congress and got his superiors overturned. When he was exposed for alley-fighting tactics in Weinberger's staff meetings, he argued down critics and grinned at Weinberger. He got the Navy admirals a fleetful of new ships but annoyed them by invading their prized turf: their promotion boards and the internal management of the uniformed Navy. He infuriated defense contractors such as General Dynamics by bargaining down their prices or ostentatiously suspending them from bidding on new business, and then infuriated military reformers by letting the contractors back into competition before excommunication had cost them seriously. But even detractors credit Lehman with bring-ing down prices on certain Navy weapons, such as the F-18 fighter, and introducing more competition into Navy procurement. In short, Leh-man is the master of bureaucratic ploys: the fast opening, the legislative blitz, the head-on clash, the bureaucratic end run, and bargaining to gain networks of support.

In Congress, he sometimes rankled his backers by browbeating them for not doing more and then cutting deals with adversaries to win them over. Senators say he could charm them with camaraderie at cozy little breakfasts, but high Pentagon officials describe him as ruthless toward his foes. For example, when Lawrence Korb moved into private indus-try after five years as an assistant secretary of Defense, and then, in 1986, as a private citizen, endorsed a group statement opposing further Pentagon budget increases, two of Lehman's close lieutenants pro-tested to Korb's new employer, the Raytheon Company. Those pres-sure calls cost Korb his high-salaried job as Raytheon's vice president for corporate operations. He was forced out of the defense business entirely, eventually becoming dean of the Graduate School of Public and International Affairs at the University of Pittsburgh.

"Phillip Phalon, Raytheon's senior vice president for marketing, told me that the Navy said, 'We never want to see Korb again,' and that, of course, jeopardized Raytheon's ability to get contracts," Korb told me. "I think people who use methods like that should not be entrusted with public positions. . . . I was outraged, because my feeling was that people ought to be free to express their opinions. I couldn't imagine a great company like Raytheon caving in to that kind of pressure. It was the Iron Triangle [at work]."[39]

In person, Lehman, a compact, five-nine, 170-pounder who once stroked the crew for Caius College, Cambridge, cuts a jaunty, swash-buckling figure, given to wide-shouldered, double-breasted blazers. Now in his early forties, he keeps qualified as a Naval Reserve helicopter pilot and a navigator-bombardier on a Navy A-6E Intruder; he gets in flying hours while inspecting the far-flung fleet. He has a politician's zest for debate, a love of politicking among a friendly crowd, and a politician's monumental ego. In his Navy public relations officer's room, I found myself surrounded by four walls of framed magazine covers and newspaper layouts of John Lehman in flight suit, John Lehman in aviator's helmut, John Lehman in dramatic debating pose. Another Navy official, showing the room to visitors, gestured to the walls: "This is the secretary's I-love-me room. Every once in a while he comes in here. It's an ego trip for him." His admirers, and even some detractors, say that in a future Republican administration, he could be a Defense secretary or national security adviser, or perhaps senator or even president.

Lehman's operation as Navy secretary was an object lesson in the power game. What gave immediate thrust to Lehman when the Reagan administration took office in 1981 were four things: powerful political allies, his own clear sense of direction, a head start on rival officials, and his savvy for the politics of the Iron Triangle.

Lehman entered the administration as the darling of the hawks, the personal symbol to right-wing conservatives of Reagan's military buildup. He was pushed for his job by political patrons such as senators John Tower of Texas and John Warner of Virginia, powerful figures on the Armed Services Committee, and Richard V. Allen, Reagan's first National Security adviser. Back in 1969, as an aide to National Security Adviser Henry Kissinger, Lehman developed his rationale for a six-hundred-ship Navy and a forward naval strategy of attacking the Soviet Navy in its home waters and ports. Afterward, as a consultant on naval affairs, he helped Tower and others battle Jimmy Carter for more carriers. Then in 1980, Lehman helped draft the national security plank of the Republican platform and got his naval notions formally endorsed.

In short, Lehman arrived in the Pentagon with a ready blueprint while other officials were feeling their way. Weinberger had to lean heavily on Lehman when Reagan tapped him as secretary of Defense. In a great rush, Lehman and William Howard Taft IV, a longtime Weinberger lieutenant, had to prep Weinberger for his confirmation hearings.

Even supporters of Lehman have questioned his "forward strategy" against the Russians, his emphasis on building large carriers, and investing so heavily in the surface fleet. But in the critical months of the new administration, Lehman was equipped with a rationale and a slogan: "the six-hundred-ship Navy"—expanding from 479 to 600 ships. (Fifty of those ships were started by Carter.) It was a shrewd tactic politically. Just how shrewd became clear when Lehman persuaded Weinberger to buy not one, but two new aircraft carriers, with the argument that buying two at once was more efficient. Indeed, Lehman was able to claim savings of $750 million from the Newport News shipyard by ordering two carriers, at a total cost of $7.3 billion. As Lehman described it to me, he went to Weinberger and said, "Give me a big jump this year [fiscal year 1983] and I'll give it back to you next year." In Pentagon lingo, that's "front loading" the budget, getting money and a commitment up front now, and taking less later.

It was a supremely canny stroke. It meant "bending a lot of metal," in Navy lingo, getting construction going so the program would be impossible to stop. Lehman had the advantage of pushing this huge package early in the Reagan years while Congress was still enamored of defense. For deploying carrier battle groups meant building scores of cruisers, destroyers, frigates, and submarines, not to mention hundreds of aircraft, along with the two carriers. The $7.3 billion for the two carriers was just the tip of a forty- to fifty-billion-dollar iceberg. It was a classic "buy-in." Lehman's scheme also followed Rockwell's model on the B-1; it spread subcontracts all over the country and engineered wide political support. Lehman told me proudly that the flow of dollars from one carrier alone would go to all fifty states and would cover three hundred to four hundred congressional districts.

"And the Congressional Budget Office did a study, which we distributed to everybody during that debate, that showed that every billion dollars in the ship-building account created twenty-seven thousand direct jobs for a year and fifteen thousand indirect jobs," he said. "That's just one billion. And a carrier uses every kind of equipment, and it's produced all over the country—basic heavy equipment and electronics and pumps and valves and beds and mattresses and toilets and, you know, every kind of conceivable thing that you'd put in a city is in a carrier."[40]

As if that were not enough, Lehman and his Navy admirals dreamed up another scheme for broadening their political base geographically. Their idea was far more ambitious than the Army's light divisions. Lehman called it home-porting; critics quickly nicknamed it *home-porking*. Lehman's plan was to spread patronage from his expanded Navy to ports and states along the Atlantic, Pacific, and Gulf coasts beyond existing navy bases. With legendary bluntness, Senator Barry Goldwater, who became Armed Services Committee chairman in 1985, scoffed to Weinberger that this was "pure unadulterated politics" and a waste of money. Lehman claimed that "strategic dispersal" of the fleet would make it less vulnerable to nuclear attack and complicate Soviet targeting. Nonsense, cried critics in Congress and the Pentagon. Adding ten or a dozen more naval ports—soft or easily destroyable targets for nuclear weapons—would make no significant difference in a barrage by thousands of warheads.

But Lehman had politicians all over the country eating out of his hand, angling for new naval bases, construction, and jobs. Just before the 1982 election, he dangled the hint that San Francisco would become a new home port and Mayor Diane Feinstein became an enthusiast. Another leak that Everett, Washington, was on the tentative list made political converts up there. When Lehman floated the notion of putting the battleship *Wisconsin* somewhere on the Gulf Coast, the competition was so intense that the Navy split up its battleship group in seven chunks spread across five states from Texas to Florida.

New York's senators and congressmen were in a lather to have the battleship *Iowa* based at Staten Island. They fought rival bids from Boston and Newport. New York's Senator Alfonse D'Amato cornered Lawrence Korb, a New Yorker who was Weinberger's assistant secretary for Manpower, Installations and Logistics, in a restaurant during a summer thunderstorm in 1983. "Listen, you don't want to go to Boston," D'Amato insisted. "You buy nothing up there [politically]. It's all Democrats. Who gives a damn about Rhode Island? Hempstead, New York, where I come from, is bigger than that whole state. You gotta go to New York. It just makes good political sense."[41] D'Amato made the same pitch to Weinberger at a Pentagon lunch. Other New Yorkers reminded Lehman that New York's delegation voted more prodefense than the Massachusetts delegation did.

Inside the Pentagon, the home-porting scheme was opposed by top officials such as Paul Thayer, number two to Weinberger, and Richard DeLauer, undersecretary for Research, Development and Engineering.

They shared Goldwater's dim view that this was a cynical political ploy. In late July 1983, Weinberger had still not yet given a firm go-ahead.

Lehman went directly to Weinberger around his higher-ranking adversaries. According to one high official, Lehman phoned Weinberger, who was traveling in Hartford, to say that New York had been selected for the *Iowa*. Weinberger agreed on the phone without going through the normal staff review. Instructions were given for Lehman to talk to Paul Thayer, but that evening Weinberger's military aide was unable to reach Thayer. The next morning Lehman was in New York for a gala breakfast aboard the *Intrepid*, a retired aircraft carrier now a museum docked in the city. With great fanfare before a gathering of six hundred invited guests, Lehman announced the Navy's plans to base the battleship *Iowa*, one cruiser, three destroyers and two frigates between piers 8 and 18 on the eastern shore of Staten Island. "It's like bringing the Brooklyn Dodgers back home," gushed Mayor Ed Koch. "It means jobs, jobs, jobs," cheered D'Amato.[42] In Washington, Thayer was furious at being outflanked, but the genie was out of the bottle.

Thayer was no patsy; like Lehman, he was a pilot and a tough fighter. He was also an experienced executive who brought notions of his own into the Pentagon, from experience in the defense industry. His most fundamental brawl with Lehman, over the six-hundred-ship Navy, reached a climax in August 1983.

Thayer had been forced upon Weinberger by the White House in late 1982, and was never close to the secretary personally. Thayer was also immediately skeptical of the six-hundred-ship Navy. Warned by other high officials that Congress would squeeze future defense budgets, he figured the full naval buildup would never be financed. Moreover, Thayer felt that Lehman's power grab had left the Army with short shrift, and he wanted to right the balance. Lehman told me that Thayer wanted to cut forty to fifty ships from his buildup. Others said Thayer planned to cut $18 billion from Navy procurement over the five years and to transfer more than half of it to the Army. Lehman told congressional allies he was sick of "senior officials"—meaning Thayer—waging "guerrilla warfare" against him, and Thayer exploded to Weinberger: "The place isn't big enough for the both of us."

The showdown came on August 11, 1983. Under Weinberger's system, the deputy secretary runs the Pentagon inside, while Weinberger takes its case to the president and Congress. Thayer had been putting pressure on the services to tighten their budgets and had summoned the Defense Resources Board, which he headed, to go over the figures. He was furious at Lehman's bookkeeping. He had intended for Lehman to cut ships to meet the budget targets; instead, Lehman merely lowered his estimates of what each ship would cost, a paper exercise.

"I don't believe those cost figures any more than I believe in the tooth fairy," Thayer boomed at Lehman, according to one participant of the meeting. Then Weinberger walked in and engaged Thayer in a discussion about military contracts.

When Lehman tried to interject, Thayer shouted, "Shut up."

"Mercy," muttered Lehman, playing the victim.

The meeting ended in a standoff, with Thayer warning Weinberger that if he protected Lehman's six hundred ships, "then the other services are going to be in trouble."

In his no-bull way, Thayer then gave Lehman a written instruction to cut back to one carrier from two, but he did not reckon on Lehman's guile, his power network, and his speed. That very day, Lehman did an end run. He went to allies in the White House—Robert McFarlane, an ex-Marine who was then deputy national security adviser, and John Poindexter, an active duty Navy rear admiral who was then number three on the national security staff. Through them, he got President Reagan's approval on *names* for the two new aircraft carriers. The White House, uninformed on the latest fracas inside the Pentagon, issued an innocuous-sounding three-paragraph press release saying that the president had decided to name the two new carriers *George Washington* and *Abraham Lincoln.* That release also contained a routine-sounding statement from President Reagan endorsing the "six-hundred-ship Navy." Thus armed, Lehman got Weinberger to overrule Thayer. His carriers and his six hundred ships were enshrined anew.

Lehman was occasionally hoist by his own petard: In 1986, the Navy pulled an end run on him, when he tried to name a personal protégé, Vice Admiral Frank Kelso, the Sixth Fleet commander, as the new chief of Naval Operations. Lehman won the acquiescence of Weinberger, who dislikes overruling individual services. But the Navy brass resented Lehman's move; they felt that Kelso, only a vice admiral, was too junior for the top job. The "old Navy," I was told, got its message to John Poindexter, by then Reagan's national security adviser. Poindexter blocked Kelso's appointment, and got Reagan to demand another choice. With Lehman threatening to resign, Weinberger nominated Admiral Carlisle Trost, the Atlantic Fleet commander and a more senior figure. Trost got the nod and later declared that Lehman, with his brashness and his playing favorites, was "not a balanced human being."[43]

For all his rumblings, Lehman remained for several more months but he resigned shrewdly in early 1987, as Congress grew more resistant to the Navy's funding requests. Ever the smart politician, Lehman quit while ahead of the game.

The Military Turf Cartel

John Lehman epitomizes a vital truth about the Pentagon power game: that it is driven by the parochialism of the individual military services. From a distance, people treat the Defense Department as one great hulking whole, but it is far from monolithic. It is a confederation of bureaucratic tribes with celebrated rivalries and long established but less well-known patterns of communal collusion. The iron law of bureaucracies is to grow and to control their own fiefdoms, and the military services—being bureaucracies—follow that law.

Turf is the prize they protect: Turf, meaning their roles and missions. Turf, meaning their market shares of the budget. Turf, meaning their autonomy, their power to develop their own strategies, their own weapons systems. The military services have been extraordinarily successful, especially in the Reagan era when money was plentiful and when the Defense secretary believed in letting them have their heads.

Almost everyone knows that in the Pentagon turf game, the Army, Navy, Air Force, and Marine Corps each jealously guards and nourishes its own special identity. But they do not engage in unbridled competition. They have reached an accommodation, a pact not to intrude upon each other's turf or to challenge each other's missions.

By operating as a cartel, they foil attempts at ruling them, made by outsiders—including the secretary of Defense and his sprawling staff of 1,765 civilians. The service turf cartel does not decide paramount issues of war and peace or determine American policy toward the Soviet Union. But the cartel enables the services to define their own strategies and budgets and pick their own weapons systems. The service military chiefs have a habit of withdrawing into the "tank"—their top-secret meeting area, generally off-limits to civilian officials—to broker their differences before civilian leaders intervene. Then each service uses its own iron triangle to protect its turf and interests.

The rivalry of the military services has caught the public eye. Think of the drama of the annual Army-Navy football game, or the stirring fife-and-drum traditions of the Marines. Take a public tour of the

Pentagon, and service rivalries are imprinted on you. Each tribe owns a pie-shaped wedge of the Pentagon and marks off its territory with symbols and tokens. On the elite E-wing overlooking the Potomac River, each has its own power center, the office of its civilian secretary, and nearby, the quarters of its chief of staff. Its corridors are lined with oil portraits of former secretaries, former chiefs of staff in uniform, and photographs of the special heroes of that service.

In the Air Force wedge, the tour guides point out a portrait of Chappie James, who flew 101 combat missions in Korea and became the first black to achieve four-star rank. Nearby, in glass display cases, are models of Air Force weaponry: models the black SR-71 spy plane, a silver B-1B bomber, white Minuteman II and III missiles, a big KC-135 tanker. The main Navy corridor is marked off by plush nautical paneling and refurbished ship-captain's doors complete with brass numbers and eagle door knocks. Navy bells chime the hours as on shipboard. Mingled with likenesses of former Navy Secretary Teddy Roosevelt and Assistant Navy Secretary Franklin Roosevelt are oils of famous naval escapades such as the Battle at Coral Sea. The models range from the CSS *Virginia,* commissioned in 1862, to the huge honeycombed facsimile of the aircraft carrier USS *Carl Vinson,* which in real life is twenty-four stories tall and three and a half football fields long. Down another hall are historic recruiting posters including one— of Americans in colonial dress—proclaiming, MARINES—SINCE 1775. But the Marine commandant is off in another building, the Navy Annex.

In the Army section, you pass models of the Stinger missile, the Pershing II, the M-1 tank, and the AH-1 Cobra Tow helicopter. On my tour, the guide, Army Private, First Class, Lee Edwards, showed off the medals and the famous braided visor cap of General Douglas MacArthur and mementos of MacArthur's father, who was a colonel in the civil war at nineteen. Edwards stopped by a flag with 168 battle streamers. "This is the Army flag," Edwards announced. "I'm in the Army so this is my favorite flag. Since you're in my tour group, it's your favorite flag, too."

The services have their own personalities. An Army general told me that the Navy represented old wealth and old aristocracy, the Air Force represented new wealth, and the Army was the populist service representing ordinary people. Defense expert William Kaufman compared the Navy, which has its own air force, fleet, and army (the Marines) to a diversified, integrated modern corporation which competes well for resources under any conditions. He compared the Air Force to a high-tech electronics firm, which flies high when its weapons and strategy are in fashion. Both the Navy and the Air Force are better at competing for money than the Army, which Kaufman likened to an old, labor-intensive smokestack industry that rises and falls with the business cycle, or in this case, with war and peace. He meant the Army's share of the Pentagon budget is smaller in peacetime than in wartime. The Navy is the most independent minded, the most prone to separateness, and the most resistant to joint operations and unified, central control.[44]

In the Reagan years, service parochialism offend and alarm powerful prodefense members of Congress. "You will be shocked at the serious deficiencies in the organization and procedures of the Department of Defense and the Congress," Barry Goldwater thundered to the Senate in late 1985. "If we have to fight tomorrow, these problems will cause Americans to die unnecessarily. Even more, they may cause us to lose. . . . I am saddened that *the services are unable to put the national interest above parochial interest* [emphasis added]. The problem is twofold: first, there is a lack of true unity of command, and second, there is inadequate cooperation among U.S. military services when called upon to perform joint operations. Without true unity, we remain vulnerable to military disasters. . . . When the rope from the individual services pulls in one direction and the rope from the Joint Chiefs pulls in the other direction, *the individual services invariably win the tug-of-war* [emphasis added]. The individual services win, but the country loses."[45]

It was a harsh condemnation, coming from a conservative and an old friend of the military finishing thirty-four years in the Senate as chairman of the Armed Services Committee. Goldwater's House counterpart, Les Aspin of Wisconsin, also damned "servicitis," giving it the ring of pathology. Other knowledgeable voices added critiques, not just about the peacetime business of buying weapons but about performance in combat.

In *The Pentagon and the Art of War*, Edward Luttwak asserts that in Vietnam, American forces suffered from the "institutional self-indulgence" of various services and their subdivisions, because all wanted a piece of the action to fatten their budgets, get promotions, push careers, and protect their turf. "Even a Napoleon would have been paralyzed by the system," he contends.

Luttwak, a conservative prodefense academic and consultant to Reagan's national security staff, argues that rampant parochialism left the services waging five largely separate air wars in Vietnam: a long-range, high altitude B-52 bombing run by the Strategic Air Command from the Philippines; a naval air war from carriers offshore; a Marine air war around Marine ground units; an Army helicopter war supporting Army units; and Air Force close tactical support run by the Tactical Air Command. According to Luttwak, that left no single commander clearly in charge and no coherent strategy. "The petty politics of interservice rivalry," he contends, "was in fact the only medium of decision."[46]

The ill-fated mission to rescue American hostages in Iran in 1980 was damned with similar charges. Zbigniew Brzezinski, President Carter's national security adviser, said that one basic lesson from the mission's failure was that "interservice interests dictated" how the operation was run and "that did not enhance cohesion and integration." Others pointed to faulty coordination in training and execution. A special Pentagon panel, led by a retired Navy admiral, suggested that Air Force helicopters and Air Force crews would have been better suited to the long-range mission than Marine crews trained in short-range attack missions. But interservice politics blocked that: The Navy wanted Marine helicopters, not Air Force helicopters, operating from the carriers which launched the mission.

Even in the 1983 operation against Grenada, trumpeted by the Reagan administration as an unalloyed triumph, experts pointed to major deficiencies caused by servicitis. According to one Army general, bickering broke out between Army Ranger units, who landed in the south, and a Marine amphibious unit, who landed in the north, because there was no common ground commander. The services lacked a common radio network, forcing Army officers to fly helicopters to the naval vessels offshore to arrange for naval fire support. The most ludicrous incident, mentioned in the Pentagon's own assessment, cited an Army officer so frustrated by difficulties in communicating with Navy ships that he used his AT&T Calling Card on an ordinary pay telephone to his office at Fort Bragg, North Carolina, to relay his plea for fire support to higher headquarters and finally down to the Navy ships a few miles away from him. Because Grenada was so lightly defended, these and many other interservice problems did not cause defeat. But they were so embarrassing that they fueled congressional pressures for better joint operations.

One former chairman of the Joint Chiefs of Staff, General David C. Jones, told me these problems were merely the latest evidence of a "great cultural gap" deeply imbedded within the military establishment since the Spanish-American War, when the Army would not invite the Navy to the surrender ceremony. The War and Navy Departments, representing the two main services, have a long separate history, with the Air Force an outgrowth of the Army and the Marines an off-shoot of the Navy. Despite formation of the Defense Department after World War II, Jones contended that two rival "cultures" persisted—Army and Navy; he could have added a third, his own Air Force. Talking with me in early 1986 before Congress enacted some reforms, General Jones asserted that the military services were "terrible at handling crises and initial actions" because they clung steadfastly to separate chains of command.[47] With minor variations, he said, most naval forces around the world are under the Navy chain of command except in the European theater, and Army forces are generally under the Army chain of command except in Korea. Jointness, he said, is a facade.

Others contend that the members of the Joint Chiefs of Staff operated primarily as heads of their individual services rather than as a joint body with overriding national concerns. Significantly, they keep their main offices in their service areas; only those of the chairman and his deputy are in the Joint Chiefs' area. The Joint Staff "really doesn't perform the joint function well," Jones asserted. It rotates so rapidly that officers lack proper experience in joint planning; moreover, its officers are loyal first to their own services because that is where careers are made and promotions awarded.

Senior Pentagon civilians complain frequently that parochial impulses make the military services averse to joint functions and inclined to slough off common tasks. The list of relative neglect is disturbing: crucial functions of command, control, and joint communications; the Defense Intelligence Agency; large-scale airlift and sealift transportation capacity for Army troops; common operation of special forces to combat terrorism, an area treated so poorly that Congress moved in 1986 to set up a joint agency under the command of a civilian, in a direct slap at the generals and admirals.

The Carter White House used to have to fight to get funds into the Pentagon budget for the vital airborne command and communications planes that maintain contact with the Navy's nuclear-missile-firing submarines. "We'd get the money put into the budget and then come back on Monday morning and find out that over the weekend someone in the Pentagon had taken the money out," one former Carter White House official groused to me. A Reagan administration official confirmed six years later that the Navy was "still trying to kill" funding these planes. "The service chiefs don't like strategic programs because they take money away from them to play with," another high Reagan Pentagon official told me.

One favorite gambit of John Lehman was to omit funding in his budget for Trident submarines, the undersea arm of the American nuclear deterrent. He did that in 1982, 1983, and 1985. When I asked why, Lehman said he had proposed skipping a few years, stretching the life of old Poseidon submarines and "using that billion and a half dollars for other conventional combatants" such as destroyers or attack submarines that the admirals see as serving the Navy's prime missions. To others, this was a calculated Lehman ploy, to get more of what the Navy really wanted, knowing that Reagan and Weinberger would insist on adding Trident submarines. One senior Pentagon planner told me: "The Tridents, they're the gold watch"—meaning the most prized systems—"John knew the president, or the secretary, had his gold watch and they'd always put it back in the budget."

Lehman, exercising the Navy's independence, also blocked several joint efficiencies. Transportation is a perennial headache to the Pentagon's top civilians because each service has a partial network—the Army on land, the Navy at sea—and they do not mesh well. In 1981, Frank Carlucci, then deputy Defense secretary, proposed to set up a joint command to manage the interservice network and reduce bottlenecks. It got approved by the Joint Chiefs of Staff. But before it was fully instituted, Lehman sabotaged it by getting one of the Navy's friends in Congress, Representative Charles Bennett of Jacksonville, to amend the defense-funding bill to forbid such a command. By the time others woke up, it was too late.

Probably the most egregious example of Air Force reluctance toward joint functions is its long resistance toward the A-10 fighter used for close support of Army troops. The A-10 is a slow-flying, two-engine ugly duckling, well armed and well protected for low-flying ground support. Its mission lacks glamour for would-be jet aces, and it is given short shrift by Air Force generals. The Army would be happy to provide its own air cover, but back in 1948 when the military chiefs met at Key West to carve up their missions, the Air Force—then part of the Army—won all rights to the land-based air mission. By what amounted to a treaty among the services, the Army was denied the right to fly any fixed-wing aircraft weighing over five thousand pounds. Of necessity, the Army has developed massive fleets of helicopters, even though defense planners regard helicopters as more vulnerable to ground fire than fixed-wing fighters.

Duplication is another price of service parochialism. In the early 1960s former Defense Secretary Robert McNamara tried to get the Navy and Air Force to develop a common fighter plane, the TFX, and failed. The Air Force eventually took it as the F-111, but the Navy took another plane. More recently, the F-16 was originally designed to be used by both services, but the Navy chose a competitor, the F-18. In the missile field, planners have suggested the Air Force adapt the Navy's Trident missile but the Air Force preferred to develop its own MX missile.

In the Pentagon, this is known as the N-I-H syndrome, for "not invented here." No service wants to take a weapon developed by another service. Anthony Battista, influential staff aide to the House Armed Services Committee, told me of his having developed a laser-guided artillery shell, a smart bullet, for Navy guns while he was working fifteen years ago at the Naval Weapons Laboratory in Virginia. For years, Battista tried to get the Army to adapt the same shell to save money. Once he invited Army officers to a demonstration test, firing the shell out of Army howitzers to prove the feasibility of a joint program.

"You've got to be joking," one green-uniformed Army officer told Battista. "You've got the wrong color uniform."

"Hey, I'm a civilian," Battista protested.

"But you work for a Navy lab," the Army man objected.

"But I pay my taxes on April fifteenth like everybody else," Battista insisted. "Why don't we just save a lot of money?"

The Army refused.[48]

More recently, the Navy and Air Force launched separate programs—to cost $3 billion—to develop elaborate radio communications for their jet fighters. These were high-tech systems that would resist enemy electronic jamming and even produce blips on a pilot's radar screen showing other aircraft.

It was Grenada all over again, each service wanting its own system. The Air Force, starting first, wanted voice communications, and the Navy had a different system for date exchange. The two systems were not compatible; Navy and Air Force pilots could not communicate with each other. The Navy's allies on the Senate Armed Services Committee wanted to fund its system. Air Force friends on the House Armed Services Committee funded its system. The standard Pentagon approach was to do both, but some House members balked, demanding that Weinberger stop the duplication and pick one system. Instead, he delayed. Finally, in 1985, the House committee blocked all funds for both systems to force a choice. Eventually, because its contractors were in financial trouble, the Navy backed down—a rare event—and the Air Force system was developed for both services.

The Façade of Jointness

To many in Congress and the Pentagon, this story typifies Wein-berger's style of management. Compared with other Defense secretar-ies, Weinberger did not exercise strong discipline over the military services—unless Congress put heavy pressures on him. His permissive management played into the hands of the turf cartel. For without a tough, critical eye at the top, each branch of service knew there was no one else to challenge it seriously—least of all the other services.

Clearly, the services know the flaws and problems in each other's strategies and weapons. If rivalry were their guiding principle, interser-vice critiques would rise constantly. But they do not, because the name of the game for years has been logrolling and mutual accomodation. The way General David Jones and others describe the inner workings of the Joint Chiefs of Staff, it sounds like the heads of big corporations carving up the market, rather than the nation's military leaders ham-mering out the most impartial, argument-tested advice for the presi-dent. The operating assumption is that the nation will be properly defended if each service presses its own needs. Obviously that works up to a point. But if one service is pursuing a foolhardy strategy or buying ridiculously costly weapons, the other services do not challenge it. Nor for that matter do they get into a serious clash of ideas about the fundamentals of national strategy.

"It's a gentleman's club," griped Senator Warren Rudman. "You never hear them knock another service's proposal, even if they don't think it's a good idea. One of the chiefs told me, 'I have all I can do fighting my own bureaucracy, fighting the top Pentagon bureaucracy, and fighting you guys on the Hill. I'm not taking on another fight with someone else in the other services.' "[49] Similarly, a four-star Air Force general told me that the Air Force and the Army adamantly disap-proved of John Lehman's naval strategy and his six-hundred-ship Navy, but they never seriously challenged Lehman for fear of inviting the Navy to take pot shots at their own pet projects.

"The services did not want to debate whether or not there was a better alternative than buying two aircraft carriers or bringing ships out of mothballs," General Jones told me.

"Basically it's hands-off," said Senator Sam Nunn. "Everybody scratches everybody else's back. I'd say it's very similar to the congres-sional system of pork-barrel projects in the appropriations committee: 'You let my project alone and I'll let yours alone. You start callin' mine

a dog, and here we go.' But there's a difference. I think the last thing
we want in the military is to handle the business like a pork barrel
bill."[50] Richard Boiling, recalling warnings from Harry Truman, asserted that the military services have "made deals with each other to
control the budget and a president has a limited amount of power to
control them unless he's got friends on the Hill. It's like antitrust. You
can't ever catch 'em doing it, but obviously they work it out."[51]

The roots of brokered politics among the services lie in painful
history. "In 1948, there was a very bitter fight between the Air Force
and the Navy over the B-36 strategic bomber versus aircraft carriers,"
General Jones recalled. "The Air Force was saying the carriers are very
vulnerable and they weren't needed and they cost too much money,
and the Navy was saying the B-36's were vulnerable and they couldn't
do the mission. There was a very bitter fight. People resigned, and it
made it very tough to work, service to service. And so now, we don't
have the Navy saying there's a better way to spend $25 billion than
buying one hundred B-1 bombers or the Air Force saying, rather than
pulling the battleships out of mothballs, that money would be better
spent on airlift or on munitions. The real tough issues—roles and
missions, unified command plan, distribution of forces—I call the
'too-hard box.' "[52]

In other words, the military services simply find it too hard to take
on the toughest, most crucial choices of national strategy: Just how
large should the Navy be? What's the best strategy for defending
Europe? Which missiles and bombers fit the future threat best? Which
divisions, Army or Marine, are better suited for a Persian Gulf crisis?
That is what brings cries of protest from the Military Reform Caucus
in Congress. One expert, James Woolsey, a former undersecretary of
the Navy who served on two major Reagan commissions on defense
issues, asserts there is too little service rivalry, not too much. "I would
far more favor having a good deal more competition and more overlap
even between the services' roles and mission to get new and different
approaches to things," Woolsey told me.[53] But the services want to
avoid upsetting well-established arrangements.

The political nonaggression pact among the services was embodied
in the Key West Agreement of 1948, a thirty-three-page top-secret
document with fine print and subsequent codicils that settled the
B-36-versus-carrier fight. The Air Force got the strategic-bombing role,
though the Navy later got some strategic targets for its carrier bombers.
Another bruising brawl occurred in the 1950s between the Air Force
and the Army over control of land-based missile systems; again the Air

Force won. Those rare and painful donnybrooks left the services wary of further battles.

For self-preservation, their operating principle for years has been a de facto veto allowing each service to protect its turf. That produced a standoff in the Joint Chiefs of Staff. Each service chief represented his own service. The chairman, the fifth member, was a token "façade of jointness," in General Jones's phrase. As one Pentagon civilian put it: "There isn't any Joint Chiefs of Staff. It's a holding company for the services." A three-star Army general agreed: "That committee is the basis of paralysis in the Pentagon. Any position by the military leadership has to be agreed upon by five people, and they won't agree unless their service interest is taken care of."

Joint military budget documents and procurement plans emerge as intricately balanced bureaucratic mosaics which allocate shares of money not only to each service tribe but to all the subtribes. The Navy has its carrier admirals, its surface fleet, its submariners, and its aviators to satisfy, all wanting new weapons, new units, new symbols of modernization and expansion. The Army has the infantry, armor, artillery, airborne units, and helicopter units. The Air Force has bomber wings, tactical air wings, missile commands, and so on. Inevitably, a Pentagon budget is a negotiated treaty to satisfy all these constituencies, like a politically balanced ticket in Los Angeles or Chicago. The list of "priority" weapons is terribly long because each weapon has its own constituency. So when Congress asks Weinberger for guidance on where to cut, his inclination is to resist rather than alienating some constituency. Congress is forced to make an overall cut and then have the services do what is least effective for national strategy: cut programs across the board from everyone, so that market shares are not disturbed. Hard choices are not made. Nothing is killed. Programs are stretched out. Costs rise because of inefficiency. The taxpayer gets less bang for the buck.

Service collusion has irked even such prodefense Republicans as Georgia's Representative Newt Gingrich. One evening, he groaned that despite the sudden infusion of spending pumped into the Pentagon budget by the Reagan administration in 1981 and 1982, the budget shares of the various services changed little: the Navy got just under thirty-three percent, the Air Force thirty percent, the Army twenty-four percent, and thirteen percent went to defensewide spending. A fresh look at national strategy should have produced some reordering of priorities and some shift in spending patterns, he declared. But the long-established service missions perpetuated the market cartel.

"Of course, if you haven't got any strategic rationale for dividing the money, you go to 'fairness,' " an Army general blurted out in frustration. "That means you stick with tradition. In other words, you go with what you got before."

Weinberger: Softball and Stonewall

For the turf cartel, Caspar Weinberger was an ideal chairman of the board. His basic notion—following Reagan—was: Spend more; buy more; build more. The assumption was that all the services had massively neglected needs and that the national security would be improved by taking care of them all. In Washington jargon, it was an input-oriented strategy, as if simply pouring in lots more money were the cure.

Like Reagan, moreover, Weinberger believed in delegating authority. He deliberately gave the services ample leeway. When his own staff tried to impose central discipline, Weinberger often stopped them. His handling of Lehman's six-hundred-ship Navy, and the Army's Divad and light-division programs, are cases in point. Early on, one senior official told me, he warned Weinberger that the "services are such powerful bureaucracies that any time you give them any more advantages, it's going to be almost impossible to control them." But Weinberger waved him off, saying that was how he had run the Department of Health, Education and Welfare in the Nixon and Ford administrations.

In the Pentagon, his laissez-faire management style let the turf cartel decide what it wanted and made him their salesman. Indeed, he acted less as the architect than as the advocate of the military buildup. He was a loyal servant of a big-defense-spending president and a tireless attorney for the military services. In short, Weinberger played softball inside the Pentagon and stonewall on the outside with Congress. Much of the top military brass were delighted. I have heard Navy officers, and others, applaud Weinberger's track record as the best among recent Defense secretaries; "a golden era of defense," one said to me—because Weinberger got the most weaponry and funding. To his credit, Weinberger worked hard to keep them out of war, again reflecting the views of his top military brass, who were still gun-shy from Vietnam.

In some ways, Weinberger followed a Republican pattern. Typically, Democratic Defense secretaries such as Robert S. McNamara in the Kennedy administration and Harold Brown in the Carter administration have ridden herd on the military services. They have empowered the massive staffs of the office of the secretary of Defense to assert centralized control and to challenge the weapons decisions of the services. Normally, Republican Defense secretaries apply looser reins on the services. Weinberger has been a more extreme decentralizer than other Republican Defense secretaries. He is at the opposite end from McNamara, the most ardent centralizer. In between, Melvin Laird in the Nixon administration used his deputy, industrialist David Packard, to press efficiencies and hard choices on the military. Weinberger and his deputies were considerably less demanding, especially in their early years, though under pressure from Congress, Weinberger began to tighten a bit in 1986 and 1987.

Weinberger's approach sprang largely from his lack of direct Pentagon experience. In California, he had been Governor Reagan's director of finance, and later he was budget director and a domestic cabinet secretary in the Nixon-Ford years. He entered the Pentagon considerably less prepared than James Schlesinger, who had been chairman of the Atomic Energy Commission and director of Central Intelligence; than Harold Brown, a former secretary of the Air Force and Pentagon research and development boss; than Melvin Laird, who had dealt with the Pentagon as a veteran congressman; or than Robert McNamara, who had been a captain of industry, as president of the Ford Motor Company. Weinberger's one connection was as budget director, where he had been known as Cap the Knife because he had used a scalpel on agency budgets for Nixon. Initially, that reputation scared Republican hawks who feared he would be tough on the Pentagon.

Weinberger's record justified their fears. During the Nixon years, he had publicly defended the sharp drop in military spending during the gradual pull out from Vietnam, and he had been a foe of the B-1 bomber. Even in 1980, when it looked as though he might be secretary of State, Weinberger seemed wary of excessive defense spending. Right after Reagan's victory, Mel Laird wrote an opinion piece in *The Washington Post* headlined NOT A BINGE, BUT A BUILDUP.[54] It urged an additional $10 billion a year for Defense appropriations, to build to a level of $240 billion in three years. I was told that privately Weinberger informed Laird he thought that was too much, too fast.

But once picked to head the Pentagon, Weinberger turned around. Within two months, he was proposing an immediate $33 billion jump on defense appropriations and, on top of that, a far steeper climb than Laird proposed. He had gotten Reagan's marching orders for a whopping buildup and was leaning on advice from ardent hawks such as John Lehman and William Schneider, who had written an ambitious defense blueprint for the right-wing Heritage Foundation. Weinberger's trademark became hoarding money for the Pentagon. Knowing that military spending goes through up and down cycles, he charged through the political window of opportunity to push military spending up to a much higher plateau. He got David Stockman, unknowing at that time about defense, to agree to a $1.5 billion, five-year spending program, and he clung tenaciously to his money.

But unlike Brown and Schlesinger who had thought about national security issues for years, Weinberger entered office without a clear strategy, except to build more of everything—which sounded all right at first, but which created problems when, predictably, the money ran short. Concepts like the six-hundred-ship Navy, reviving the B-1 bomber, and scrapping Carter's plan for mobile basing of the MX missile were handed to Weinberger from the Reagan 1980 campaign. Reagan's point was to strike a difference with Carter. In 1981, Weinberger had no alternative plan for basing the MX missile that would satisfy even pro-MX hawks such as senators John Tower of Texas and Scoop Jackson of Washington; six years later, he was still struggling to devise one. Reluctantly he reversed his old opposition to the B-1 bomber and got a hundred of them, but only fifty MX missiles (instead of Carter's two hundred), leaving the American strategic nuclear arsenal with about the same strength that Carter had planned.

Other important strategic weapons, like the Trident D-5 submarine missile and the Stealth bomber, were put on track by previous administrations. In the Reagan years, the initiative for the mobile Midgetman missile came from Congress, not from Weinberger's Pentagon, and the Strategic Defense Initiative, while floated by Admiral James Watkins, chief of Naval Operations, was really the creature of President Reagan and was mainly developed in the White House, with the Pentagon surprised by Reagan's announcement.

What came to frustrate many key members of Congress, including strongly prodefense Republicans and Democrats, is that Weinberger steadfastly refused their pleas to set priorities among service requests and to help them cut budgets intelligently. Instead, they saw him trying to satisfy all the Pentagon constituencies rather than showing firm leadership. Indeed, by the start of Reagan's second term, congressional frustration with Weinberger's management of the Pentagon boiled over in the drive to force more centralized leadership on the military hierarchy, despite Weinberger's open resistance.

"This secretary of Defense sets no priorities," complained Dave McCurdy, an Oklahoma Democrat who has become a respected spokesman on defense issues. "He plays a budget game with us and it gives more power to the bureaucratic forces [in the Pentagon]. So you get more logrolling, more bureaucratic input. He doesn't instill any discipline in the Department of Defense itself to make the choices between the Navy and the Air Force and the Army, or even within the branches of one service. So the bureaucrats have their field day. He's elevated each of these bureaucracies to the level of individual fiefdoms. And there's no king!"[55]

I have heard Army and Air Force generals and Republican Senators echo McCurdy's judgment. "There's nobody involved in centralized planning," was the curt complaint of Sam Nunn, who became Senate Armed Services Committee chairman in 1987.[56] In the Pentagon, Weinberger was seen by his civilian lieutenants as a weak manager who pressured the services only when Congress or public controversy forced his hand, as on the Divad or the MX. Several of Weinberger's top subordinates complained to me that he was no executive. Richard DeLauer, the undersecretary for research, complained to me: "We'd tell Cap, 'You know, we're gonna have a destroyer that's gonna cost a billion dollars,' and Cap says, 'Oh, we can't have that.' But then nothing else would happen. He didn't apply the damn leadership. That's the problem."[57]

Weinberger bristled at such talk. In several sessions with me, he insisted the criticism was unfair and inaccurate. He pointed out— accurately—that he presided over the greatest spending in Defense Department history. And he claimed—properly—that sometimes the services, especially the Navy, got contractors to trim their prices. He had no apologies for tackling everything at once rather than picking priorities.

"We needed to do a great deal to regain military strength very quickly," he asserted, recalling 1981. "We didn't have much time, and we had to do a lot in a lot of different areas at once. When we came, there were huge backlogs, a lot of maintenance backlogs, a lot of repair, a lot of ammunition shortages, and then we needed modernization of the strategic systems and the strategic triad. We needed to improve our conventional strength. We needed to do a great deal about manpower and morale. . . . This point [about letting the services have their way] goes along with the criticism that we didn't have any priorities, that we just got a lot of money and threw it at the problems, and I don't think either of those is correct."[58]

As yardsticks of successes, Weinberger and his supporters point to the skyrocketing growth of the military budget. In the first two years, it jumped twenty-five percent above inflation. That set in motion the doubling of the Pentagon budget in five years. Even when Congress tried to apply restraint, actual defense outlays kept rolling upward, for two reasons: One was that the inflation assumptions in Pentagon budgets were excessive. In 1986, the General Accounting Office reported that over five years inflationary cost increases were $44 billion less than the Pentagon had predicted. Weinberger simply pocketed the inflation savings, using them to offset congressional cuts, which robbed those cuts of real impact. The other cause is the delay between congressional authorization of funds and the actual spending on weapons systems. For example, the $7.3 billion set aside in 1983 for two aircraft carriers will not be entirely spent until 1991. In effect, Congress gives the Pentagon a huge line of credit every year to spend over several years. That backlog had reached the enormous sum of $270 billion in early 1987, assuring that no downturn in actual spending would occur until the 1990s—because the system was awash with money.

Weinberger entered office with real power, and he kept it with Reagan because he was loyally doing Reagan's bidding on defense. But over time he lost influence with Congress because he exercised his early power too rashly. As former Senate Majority Leader Robert Dole quipped, "Cap Weinberger is the first person in history to overdraw a blank check."[59]

In his first eighteen months as Defense secretary, Weinberger enjoyed a honeymoon because Congress was so prodefense that, except for the MX missile, it did not look closely at the particulars of the military buildup. But Weinberger's very success with mammoth early funding, coupled with the huge deficits created by the 1981 Reagan tax cuts, set in train the public's—and Congress's—urge to moderate the military buildup. Weinberger was too rigid to bend in 1983 and thereby missed an opportunity to solidify support for the long haul. With Congress, he was a lonesome end, not a team player. He played a stonewalling game, without the subtlety and guile of John Lehman, and it cost him dearly over the years.

In an odd way, Weinberger was like McNamara. Although they were opposites as managers of the Pentagon, they were similar in disdaining partnership with Congress or even a few key leaders. McNamara was infuriated by the protective alliances forged by the military services with friendly members of Congress. Weinberger resented the seemingly endless wickets of the congressional budget process. Both were messianic. They treated their own budgets and prescriptions for defense as inviolate gospel. It was a matter of style. McNamara became a defense intellectual and argued his doctrine passionately. Weinberger took his brief from Reagan and the military brass and never wavered. Both were unsuccessful as Iron Triangle players. Either they failed to understand that running the Pentagon requires alliances with Congress, or they could not crack the code of the Iron Triangle game. For it is axiomatic that no president and no secretary of Defense can control the military services, build durable support for his budget, or contain his critics without powerful alliances on Capitol Hill.

Weinberger's problems were especially ironic. Like Melvin Laird, he cast himself as the public defender of the Pentagon. But Laird, as a veteran member of Congress, arrived at the Pentagon with important networks on Capitol Hill. Schlesinger and Donald Rumsfeld, another Republican Defense secretary, also had ties in Congress. Yet Weinberger, who is amiable in manner, never really built the essential political networks. He was tireless in testifying and in after-hours socializing, forever arguing his case. But his geniality could not overcome his rigidity.

In the first two years, Weinberger leaned on his deputy, Frank Carlucci, who had political savvy, and on Senator John Tower of Texas. But Carlucci resigned in 1982, and Tower left the Senate in 1984. Weinberger's later deputies could not woo Congress effectively, and Barry Goldwater, Tower's replacement as chairman of the Armed Services Committee, took an independent course and finally became the spearhead for reforms reacting against Weinberger's Pentagon. In short, Weinberger lacked allies to fight reform and the backlash against the Pentagon budget.

Les Aspin, Democratic chairman of the House Armed Services Committee, told me that in a private conversation he had once burst out at Weinberger, "Jesus, Cap, negotiating with you is like negotiating with the Russians. All you do is keep repeating your position."[60] Sam Nunn was offended that Weinberger was so partisan, so quick to condemn all that went before Reagan. "Some of his statements are just preposterous," Senator Nunn told me with some heat. "In an open hearing, he said that all the strategic modernization programs started in 1981, and I went back and named the systems that started under either Ford or Carter or Nixon. He never did back off of it. I think that's hurt Weinberger up here with an awful lot of prodefense Democrats and with some Republicans, too."[61]

Indeed, Republicans echoed Democratic impatience with Weinberger. "Cap does not have . . . a willingness to accommodate, soothe, work with senatorial, congressional egos," Maine's Bill Cohen asserted.

"I don't think Cap particularly has the time, the patience, the inclination to want to sit down and try to take into account congressional concerns or proposals. There is almost an automatic knee-jerk reaction to us [in his] saying, 'We've looked at it, and it's out of the question. We don't need it.' Period. He has a mind-set which precludes, for the most part, taking into account diversity of opinion or at least recognizing the legitimacy of a diverse opinion. That may be unfair, but that's the perception. And so as a result, he doesn't have anybody who can carry the water for him."[62]

Weinberger's Waterloo—Losing More than Money

After Weinberger's early defense-budget increases, his Waterloo with Congress came in the spring of 1983. His insistence on ten-percent real growth in the Pentagon budget created an uproar among conservative Republicans worried about the deficit. Pete Domenici, the chain-smoking, tough-talking Senate Budget Committee chairman, protested Weinberger's tendency to "highball" and "stonewall" the budget and his Chicken Little rhetoric about the dangers of cutting defense. "His sky's-falling-in theory was no more than a theory," Domenici told me, "and so it cemented the mood into an absolute majority who had become extremely skeptical" toward the Pentagon.[63]

The showdown came on April 7, 1983. All spring, Domenici and Senate Majority Leader Howard Baker had been urging Weinberger and William Clark, then national security adviser, to get President Reagan to compromise and accept a 7.5 percent defense increase. For weeks, the White House stalled. Two days before the crucial Senate Budget Committee vote, Weinberger insisted that anything less than a ten-percent rise would jeopardize the nation's security. The budget committee, angry and frustrated, was moving the other way; Domenici sensed that with domestic programs being cut, his committee would grant the Pentagon no more than five percent. On the critical day, Senate Majority Leader Howard Baker called the White House to push for 7.5 percent and Chief of Staff Jim Baker phoned Weinberger, urging him to accept it. Weinberger promised an answer and then disappeared for a few hours. White House officials suspected he was ducking them.

Then, unexpectedly, Weinberger showed up in the White House West Wing. In the hallway outside the Oval Office, two of Jim Baker's top aides, his deputy Dick Darman and Ken Duberstein, the chief White House legislative lobbyist, made one last pitch for compromise

to Weinberger and William Clark. Finally, Weinberger said "7.9 percent is the lowest I can go." It was too little, too late, in Duberstein's
mind; Weinberger had not read the mood of the committee. Howard
Baker cautioned Duberstein, in a voice filled with futility, "Kenny, I'll
run it up the flagpole, but I wouldn't have the president call
Domenici." Baker knew it would be rejected and did not want Reagan
to be rebuffed in person.

Weinberger and Clark disregarded the warning. In the Oval Office,
they urged Reagan to call Domenici and tell him to "get the Republican troops in line" on the Pentagon budget.

"Order him!" Clark said. "You're the commander in chief."

Ken Duberstein threw in a warning. "I just spoke with Senator
Baker," he said. "The committee is going forward. There's no way to
stop Senator Domenici. It's too late."

The president phoned anyway, catching Domenici on the verge of
the committee's vote. As Domenici remembered the conversation, it
was tense and hard. One White House official told me it ended in a
shouting match.[64]

"Pete, I understand you're about to finish the budget," the president
began.

"Yes, Mr. President, we are," Domenici replied, perspiring in a small
hallway phone booth and bracing for the pressure.

"I understand you're going to give us five percent," the president
said, voice hardening. "You can't do that."

"That's the best I can do," Domenici countered gruffly.

"You can't," the president insisted, his voice rising. "You have to
wait. Come and see us. Let's talk."

The president's aides recall his raising the possibility of compromise
at 7.9 percent and Duberstein's scribbling the figures 7.5 and 7.9 on
a paper, holding it up to the president with his fingers measuring off
a tiny distance. But Domenici does not recall 7.9 percent being mentioned. Anyway, it would not have satisfied him. Two months earlier,
it might have worked; but coming so late, it reflected Reagan's reliance
on Weinberger and Weinberger's poor timing and his failure to understand Congress.

"I can't wait," Domenici declared. He was reflecting his committee's
impatience with delays and vagueness. "I have all the respect in the
world for you, but I've been waiting for weeks. There is no give on your
side. Cap Weinberger won't give an inch. I have a responsibility, too.
I have twenty-two senators on this committee. It's an important part
of the United States Senate and I have a job. It wouldn't do any good

to talk. What for? We could talk again. We can sit down, but there isn't any room. You've had all the time you can get. There's just no more time. I'm sorry."

The president was growing angry. His voice hard and rising, he was barely able to control his temper.

"You can't finish today," he ordered Domenici. "You have to put it off."

"No, I will not," Domenici boomed back, sweating from the tension. "I'm sorry, Mr. President."

Reagan hung up abruptly. Furious, he slammed down the phone so hard that it bounced out of the cradle. That angry burst was like a hand grenade tossed into a small knot of people. It broke up the Oval Office session. Clark, Weinberger, Darman, and Duberstein left almost without a word.

Domenici, shaking, went back to vote. His committee rejected Weinberger's ten-percent increase 19–2 and passed a five-percent increase 17–4. Eight Republican senators broke sharply with Reagan-Weinberger that day. Eventually, the Senate passed the five-percent increase; the House passed three percent, and the ultimate compromise was under four percent. Had Weinberger shown flexibility sooner, Domenici contended, "We could maybe have come out with six percent."

That episode was a watershed for Weinberger, for it galled Senate Republicans to have him insist that cutting so much as a dime from his Pentagon budget would put the nation's defense in dire peril, and then to see him adjust to much less. It took them several years to decipher his game. They did not notice the enormous inflation assumptions built into Weinberger's five-year buildup, which ran up the costs of weapons systems; nor did they catch on that when inflation came down, Weinberger just kept the old figures, always "discovering" billions of dollars in "savings" from the exaggerated inflation estimates to offset congressional budget cuts. When Congress caught on, even his Republican backers were furious at having been duped.

Weinberger lost more than money. He lost credibility—the White House staff knew that—and he lost control of the defense debate. Reagan and Weinberger tried to make the issue simply "more" or "less." But the public mood had shifted dramatically. (In January 1981, sixty-one percent of the public felt defense spending should be increased, and only thirty-five percent felt it should be cut or kept about the same, according to a *New York Times*/CBS News poll. Five years later, only seventeen percent favored an increase and seventy-nine percent favored cuts or keeping it level.) The deficit had become an overriding concern. Moreover, the furor about scandalously priced coffeepots and wrenches reached a crescendo in 1985, eroding the pro-defense coalition that Reagan inherited from the Carter presidency. The political agenda changed. No longer was defense debate fueled by fear of the Soviet threat—which had not significantly changed since 1981—but by Pentagon waste and bad management.

Five years into the $1.5 trillion Reagan-Weinberger buildup, pro-defense Democrats such as Nunn and Aspin were boldly declaring that the nation had not gotten its money's worth. Nunn assailed the terrible inefficiency of building too many things at once and then stretching out production. Other Democratic defense experts charged that Weinberger's "bloated and unbalanced" Pentagon budget had lavished money on nuclear weapons and the Navy "at the expense of everything else," particularily conventional preparedness in Europe and for crisis trouble spots.

Republican Senator Charles Grassley of Iowa complained that defense contractors were less efficient than the Japanese and than other sectors of American industry but were reaping much higher profits and often paying no taxes. Even Navy Secretary John Lehman admitted that weapons systems were gold plated, contractor costs were excessive, and defense-industry profits had, for two decades, "averaged nearly four times the norm of nongovernment profit." He blamed Congress. New Hampshire's Warren Rudman shot back that the military bureaucracy was so fat that it contained more clerks than combat personnel, more generals and admirals than during World War II, with only one sixth as many troops to command.

The underlying premise of the criticism was that defense was too important to leave the military turf cartel to its own devices, as Weinberger had done. That suspicion lay behind repeated congressional requirements for more competition in Pentagon procurement contracts, independent testing for faulty weapons systems, more detailed reporting on cost overruns. Moreover, that was the central message of bipartisan reforms pushed by Goldwater and Nunn in the Senate and by Aspin in the House. It was a message echoed by President Reagan's own Pentagon management commission. Despite Weinberger's protests and the howling of the Joint Chiefs of Staff, congressional leaders slapped Weinberger down. In mid-1986, both houses voted to centralize more power in the Pentagon, and Reagan went along. Several architects of reform told me privately they could not force Weinberger's ouster so they changed the structure around him, stripping the service chiefs of some power and giving more authority to the chairman of the Joint Chiefs of Staff to override the turf cartel, and granting more power to regional commanders in Europe, the Pacific, and elsewhere, to impose more discipline on the individual services.

A parallel, though less drastic approach was taken by the President's Blue-Ribbon Commission on Defense Management, headed by David Packard, a former deputy Defense secretary. Weinberger opposed naming this commission, but Reagan went ahead, key senators were told, because he had grown impatient with Pentagon inefficiency and with the homogenized advice of the service chiefs. At one point, I was told, Vice President Bush brought Reagan thirty yards of diagrams showing communications circuits in the Pentagon. "Eisenhower waged World War II with a staff of three hundred," Bush told the president, according to one high official. "We can't wage the peace with a Joint Staff of three thousand."

Reagan's Blue-Ribbon Commission rendered a harsh judgment. "Today, there is *no rational system* [emphasis added] whereby the Executive Branch and the Congress reach coherent and enduring agreement on national military strategy, the forces to carry it out, and the funding that should be provided—in light of the overall economy and competing claims on national resources," the Packard commission asserted. "The absence of such a system contributes substantially to the instability and uncertainty that plague our defense program. These cause imbalances in our military forces and capabilities, and increase the costs of procuring military equipment."[65]

Echoing congressional critics of Weinberger but without naming him, the commission proposed more centralized control by strengthening the chairman of the Joint Chiefs and by appointing a new undersecretary for acquisition to ride herd on weapons procurement.

But the turf cartel and its iron triangles are so entrenched that by mid-1987, reformers were complaining that Weinberger had watered down the congressional reforms of 1986 and, the military had blunted the policy impact of the Packard Commission report, especially the independent procurement czar. Les Aspin protested that the new post lacked real power. "A czar without authority is a eunuch," he declared. The czar, Undersecretary of Defense for Acquisition Richard Godwin, was so frustrated at being hamstrung that he quit in frustration in September 1987. Although he was supposed to have centralized authority, Godwin declared that he "couldn't make anything stick" against the labyrinthine Pentagon bureaucracy and the ingrained parochialism of the services.

From two former four-star generals, as well as top former Pentagon civilians, I heard dark estimates of the costs of service parochialism in actual battle. General David Jones, who retired in 1982 after serving as chairman of the Joint Chiefs, told me he was fearful the military branches could not fight well together in crises.[66] General E. C. Meyer, who retired in 1985 after serving as Army chief of staff, warned that this problem was so grave it could lead to nuclear war.

"The biggest danger would be that as a result of our current capability, you would have to use nuclear weapons far more rapidly than you might otherwise have to do," he told me. "And it may even mean that you have to use nuclear weapons, where if you had a better capability, you wouldn't have to use nuclear weapons."[67]

Fundamentally, the reforms underscored the dramatic change of mood on defense by the mid-1980s. The push for reform represented a setback for the Iron Triangle at the hands of the Dissident Triangle— as well as reflecting historic rhythms. Since World War II, the public has supported no more than three years in a row of increasing military appropriations. The Reagan-Weinberger team beat that record. Jimmy Carter had begun the buildup in 1980, and the Reagan-Weinberger combination carried it forward until 1985, though the backlog of billions kept actual spending on the rise.

There was a deeper lesson in the backlash against the Reagan-Weinberger political strategy. For all their alarm about the Soviet threat, Weinberger and Reagan had gone for a big, fast buildup, only to have conventional forces in Europe still in need, the Navy complaining in 1987 that it was short of seamen to man its fleet, and Air Force units so short of spare parts that flight mechanics were cannibalizing some aircraft to keep others flying. In short, the Reagan team had gone long on procurement and short on operations and maintenance. Boom was in danger of being followed by bust. What was needed was steadiness in policy to win long-term political support for defense. Reagan and Weinberger had squandered the opportunity in the early 1980s to build a durable bipartisan consensus in Congress and the country for moderate, steady, long-term growth of defense budgets to replace the roller-coaster record of feast or famine.

9. The New Lobbying Game: Grass Roots Pressure and PAC Money

Democracy is not a spectator sport. God damn, it's a hands-on sport to help those that help us.
—Tom Korologos, lobbyist

When I came to Washington as a reporter in the early 1960s, one of the most powerful influences on Congress was the pro-Israeli lobby. Those were years when Egypt's Gamal Abdel Nasser kept threatening Israel, and the Arab cause was unpopular on Capitol Hill. But in the late 1970s, the political situation changed, first with the dramatic journey to Jerusalem in November 1977 of Anwar Sadat and the 1978 Camp David accords that led to a peace treaty between Sadat and Israeli Prime Minister Menachem Begin. Second, things changed with the skyrocketing prices of oil and the Western impulse to secure a flow of oil from the Persian Gulf through better relations with Saudi Arabia and other Arab states. Third, they changed dramatically with the fall of the Shah of Iran and the Soviet invasion of Afghanistan in late 1979.

Sadat projected a friendly, peaceful Arab face to Americans, and his willingness to make peace with Israel gave Egypt what seemed a moral claim, almost on a par with Israel's for huge volumes of American aid. The steady production of oil for the West by Kuwait and Saudi Arabia persuaded President Carter in 1978 to promise the Saudis F-15 jet fighters as a sign of gratitude and friendship. That sent shivers through the pro-Israeli lobby which claimed the jets could be used against Israel. Then in 1981, the new Reagan administration decided to sell the Saudis several enormously expensive and valuable airborne radar command posts, known as AWACS for Air Warning and Control System. The pro-Israeli lobby fought that sale bitterly, and lost—a loss which suggested to many that the political balance on Arab-Israeli issues had tipped.

But that is not the end of the story; it is actually the beginning. In the next four years, the American Israel Public Affairs Committee (AIPAC), leading edge of the pro-Israeli lobby working Congress, literally transformed itself and gained greater power than ever before. The loss on AWACS jolted AIPAC into a new political strategy, and it became a superlobby. Its budget shot up eightfold in nine years, its membership multiplied from nine thousand households in 1978 to fifty-five thousand in 1987, its staff grew from twenty-five to eighty-five. By the mid-eighties, its leadership was steering roughly $4 million in campaign contributions to friendly candidates and punishing political foes, and AIPAC's lobbying became more bipartisan.

One policy payoff was that American aid to Israel rocketed from $93.4 million in 1962, to nearly $3.8 billion in 1986. Most importantly, AIPAC gained so much political muscle that by 1985, AIPAC and its allies could force President Reagan to renege on an arms deal he had promised King Hussein. By 1986, the pro-Israeli lobby could stop Reagan from making another jet-fighter deal with Saudi Arabia; and Secretary of State George Shultz had to sit down with AIPAC's executive director—not congressional leaders—to find out what level of arms sales to the Saudis AIPAC would tolerate. In 1987, AIPAC's lobbying blocked the sale of sixteen hundred Maverick missiles to Saudi Arabia.

The story of how AIPAC reversed its fortunes in the mid-1980s is not only an insight into this one lobby, but a revealing case study of how all lobbying has changed in the new Washington power game. AIPAC's evolution is a microcosm of a larger phenomenon. Its leaders were sharp enough to respond to the dispersal of power triggered by the political earthquake of 1974, breaking up the old power structure. The new lobbying game patterned itself after the new politics of Congress and the new breed; the old inside game of lobbying was upstaged by the new outside game of lobbying. Intensive private lobbying was often less potent than extensive mass lobbying.

Shrewd lobbyists understood that they could no longer focus on a few committee barons to push their issues, but they had to chase virtually every member of the House and Senate, certainly every member of key committees. Lobby groups could no longer bank on some pricey Washington superlawyer to make their pitch in private; they had to generate grass-roots movements to pressure scores of legislators. That meant turning increasingly to the techniques of political campaigns and campaign organizers, pollsters and direct mail specialists to tap and manipulate public opinion.

By now, it is a cliché that lobbies have more power than two decades ago, but not everyone understands why. The fragmented power game, fostered by the 1974 power earthquake, played into the hands of lobbies. It not only helped AIPAC block President Reagan on Arab arms deals, but the more open power game enabled the bank lobby to resist a tax law backed by the president and leaders of both houses of Congress, by stimulating such a popular groundswell that congressional members turned against their political leaders. Those episodes reflect the new politics and the new lobbying game.

For the fact is that lobbies have increasingly filled a vacuum left by the loose structure of political parties. The parties used to provide the most essential organization, money, and endorsement that politicians needed. Parties and their leaders weighed the competing demands of interest groups, sorted out priorities, struck compromises and then provided what politicians call "cover" for the votes of individual Congress members: taking the political heat for unpopular votes and delivering bad news to groups that were not satisfied. Oddly, national political parties now contribute larger sums of money than ever to political campaigns, but overall they have not recovered their old power.

For survival, members of Congress rely primarily on personal organizations and their ties with well-organized constituencies—which they are loath to antagonize. That means incumbents, relying heavily on special interest groups for political support and campaign funds, are dependent on these groups and more susceptible to their pressures. Clever lobby groups understand the symbiotic relationship and exploit it, careful to hedge their political bets by spreading favors and support with far more officeholders than was necessary in the old power game.

This sprawling new lobbying game has raised the price of playing. Campaigns targeted on one single legislative issue and costing in the millions are common. AIPAC's budget, for example, shot up from $750,000 in 1978 to $6.1 million in 1987 just to cover pro-Israeli issues. Business and right-to-work groups spent $5 million in 1978 killing what organized labor called "labor law reform," and the unions spent $2.5

million to try to win better organizing rights. The insurance industry spent $5 million in 1985 to protect billions of dollars in tax exemptions. Blue Cross–Blue Shield spent another $4 million just to protect its tax-exempt nonprofit status. The trucking industry spent $3 million in 1979 trying to stave off deregulation. Lobbying changed from an insiders' game to an industry.

AIPAC: Before and After

The AIPAC case is a before-and-after story. The first episode begins on September 28, 1980, less than a year after the Soviet invasion of Afghanistan and six days after the border skirmishes between Iran and Iraq exploded into full-scale war. On that day, General David Jones, chairman of the Joint Chiefs of Staff, flew into Saudi Arabia. The outbreak of war at the head of the Persian Gulf had set off alarms in Washington and had given the royal house of Saud an extreme case of jitters.

When Jones landed, he was grabbed by Prince Fahd bin Abdullah, director of operations for the Saudi Air Force, and Prince Bandar bin Sultan, an American-trained Saudi Air Force major and son of the defense minister. "We want AWACS immediately," they told him. "We want AWACS for twenty-four-hour surveillance of the gulf. We need it. We can't protect the kingdom without it. Can you get it for us?"[1]

AWACS, an Airborne Warning and Control System, the epitome of modern weaponry, is a large Boeing 707 with a dish radar on its fuselage, chock-full of high-tech electronics to monitor an entire battle region. It is a symbol of modern air might and sophistication. The Saudi monarchy wanted temporary loan of American AWACS planes with American crews as a signal to Ayatollah Khomeini's warlike Iran that Saudi Arabia enjoyed American protection.

For years, the U.S. Air Force had been encouraging the Saudis to buy AWACS, partly to provide rationale for American-built air bases in Saudi Arabia that American planes could use in a Middle East crisis. Jones, an AWACS zealot, sensed an opening; he immediately messaged Washington and pushed the Pentagon and Carter White House to send AWACS planes. Carter's advisers, near the climax of the 1980 campaign, feared voter backlash. They balked, but Jones nursed Carter into agreement. Within two days, four American AWACS landed in Saudi Arabia on a "temporary training mission" that would operate around the clock 365 days a year. (They were still there seven years later when an Iraqi warplane hit the American frigate *Stark* in the Persian Gulf in May 1987.) In gratitude, the Saudi monarchy told Jones it was stepping up Saudi oil production.

Very soon, the Saudi government asked the explosive question: Would the Carter administration conclude a whopping $8.4 billion arms sale—five AWACS planes plus seven huge KC-135 tankers, some F-15 jet fighters, and other equipment? That request was political dynamite: Israel feared a modern Saudi Air Force, and Congress had been promised in 1978 that the Saudis would not be allowed to buy AWACS. Even so, Defense Secretary Harold Brown informed the Saudis that Carter was "favorably disposed" to sell AWACS. After Reagan won the 1980 election, Carter urged him to carry out the deal, and Reagan entered the White House "believing we should do it," according to Jim Baker, his Chief of Staff.[2] Saudi expectations had been raised and the Air Force wanted to sell the AWACS planes, as General Jones told me, "to keep the production line open"—meaning that Boeing, AWACS's maker, needed a big customer. The Saudis would share the plane's heavy development costs.

When formal announcement of the deal came on April 21, 1981, the Israelis and their allies in Congress erupted, bent on persuading Congress to prevent the AWACS sale. It became a pitched battle of powerful lobbies, a test of Israeli and Arab influence. Prime Minister Menachem Begin, who had previously written Reagan privately condemning the deal, now openly denounced it, in apocalyptic terms, as a threat to Israel.

In Congress, the opposition got an early jump. By late June, Senator Bob Packwood, the Oregon Republican, had teamed up with Tom Dine, AIPAC's Executive Director, to line up fifty-four senators and 224 House members to write President Reagan opposing the arms sale. In July, AIPAC declared its goal "to keep the package from ever being submitted" to Congress for a required vote of approval (majorities in both houses could block the deal). Indeed, fearing a political disaster that would derail the Reagan economic program, Senate Majority Leader Howard Baker got the White House to put off the AWACS vote from April to October. And when President Reagan sent formal notice to Congress on October 1, Baker warned the president that the outlook was bad. "We've got twelve votes, and that's counting me," Baker told Reagan, "and I don't want to vote for it."[3]

But Reagan, riding the crest of his budget and tax victories, pressed ahead. In the House, the AWACS sale was voted down 301–11. Administration efforts focussed on the Senate. It was a classic inside-the-beltway battle.

First, the old Iron Triangle went to work. Powerful corporations, some with links to the Air Force and to Saudi arms sales, got behind the deal. The American Businessmen's Group of Riyadh, including some top Fortune 500 companies such as Citibank, American Express, A&P, Merrill Lynch International, Mobil, Northrop, and Boeing, called on its members (heavy campaign contributors in 1980) to tell Congress "how important your business in Saudi Arabia is to your company." The oil industry, huge grain companies and rice millers, and construction firms such as the Bechtel Corporation went after western and southwestern senators and congressmen. Omaha Banks and the Union Pacific Railroad put pressure on Democratic senators James Exon and Edward Zorinsky of Nebraska.

The Israeli government hurt its own cause. While the Saudi leadership promulgated a Middle East peace plan and provided more oil, Prime Minister Begin clashed with the Reagan administration, first over Israel's air raid against an Iraqi nuclear reactor and then over bombing missions that caused heavy civilian casualties around Beirut. In September, Begin infuriated the White House by lobbying personally on Capitol Hill against the AWACS deal, challenging the president on his home court. Fred Dutton, a former Kennedy White House official and a Saudi lobbyist, cleverly framed the choice: "Reagan or Begin."

The pro-Israeli coalition, a narrow majority of fifty-four, was wobbly. One by one, senators were stolen away; the coalition lacked strong popular underpinnings in many states. Utah's Orrin Hatch used the assassination of Anwar Sadat to assert the need for helping other moderate Arab states. Other senators, especially freshmen Republicans, were cleverly peeled away by White House strategists Jim Baker and his deputy, Richard Darman. They crafted a letter offering Reagan's assurances that AWACS planes would be used only by American and Saudi personnel—not by other Arabs; that AWACS intelligence could not be shared with any other nation unless Washington approved; and that AWACS would be protected against falling into hostile hands. For wavering senators, said Jim Baker, "the letter gave 'em a legitimate out, an excuse" to go along with the deal.

Reagan personally talked with forty-four senators; quite a few succumbed, among them Iowa Republican Roger Jepsen. His loss was a hard blow to AIPAC because Jepsen had been in the core of original AWACS foes. Jepsen, racked by conflicting pressures, literally broke down crying as he told other Republicans that "highly classified" White House information and his desire not to hurt Reagan's prestige had switched his vote. That broke loose others. Reagan ultimately prevailed 52–48, and the AWACS sale to Saudi Arabia went through.

The underlying message to AIPAC and the pro-Israel lobby was that its ties to many senators were too weak.

And so begins the "after" half of the story: modernization and reshaping of AIPAC. As if there were some Newtonian law of politics, the AWACS triumph triggered a powerful reaction that came back to haunt Reagan four years later.

AIPAC had suffered a severe jolt. It had nearly stopped the president, but ultimately it had failed. And failure galvanized it into a more national strategy, targeted at the grass roots. For years AIPAC had ridden on an outspoken, committed, activist constituency based mainly in the big cities of the Northeast and Midwest. That constituency had always given it commanding strength in the House. But AIPAC was now compelled to go after the more conservative Senate in new ways, in order to marshal unassailable majorities in Reagan's second term.

In 1985, for example, after President Reagan had personally promised modern arms to King Hussein as inducement to negotiate with Israel, AIPAC and its allies lined up seventy-four senators to cosponsor a resolution to block a $1.5 billion arms package to Jordan. The number of Senators was critical: a jump of twenty senators above the high point against AWACS in 1981. The White House could not peel off a few wavering senators and win. By early 1986, Reagan had to renege on his promise to Hussein; he withdrew the Jordanian arms package without a vote, demonstrating AIPAC's power to deter presidential initiatives. "The best vote is a vote avoided," Doug Bloomfield, AIPAC's legislative director, commented to me. "If you can win and avoid a confrontation, everyone is better off. In a political community, you have to live for another day, so it doesn't pay to rub anybody's nose in defeat."[4]

Again in 1985, after the Saudis had submitted a new $3 billion arms request, President Reagan promised King Fahd more F-15 fighter aircraft. The congressional climate was so hostile that Reagan had to withdraw the offer; instead, the Saudis spent their billions on British jets. Gradually, the administration whittled down the Saudi shopping list, dropping M-1 tanks and Black Hawk helicopters, looking for a package that Congress—and AIPAC—would accept.

Finally, on February 28, 1986, Secretary of State George Shultz called in Tom Dine, AIPAC's executive director, to find out what the administration could get through Congress. Normally, in the Jewish community's lobbying, AIPAC lobbies Congress, while the executive branch is handled by the Conference of Presidents of Major American Jewish Organizations. Shultz's meeting with Dine was a measure of AIPAC's increased clout.

Over the years, AIPAC had developed from a pro-Israel public affairs forum in the 1950s to a fifty-five-thousand-member lobby to which scores of senators and congressmen turn for authoritative guidance. AIPAC is an American lobby, not a registered foreign agent, but it has close ties with the Israeli government. Its political tally sheets and strategy reports wind up in the Israeli prime minister's office, I was told. Some Israeli journalists jokingly refer to AIPAC as "our embassy." And Tom Dine, a Kennedy Democrat with ten years of staff experience in Congress, is not above pulling a card from his wallet to show that he carries the Israeli prime minister's twenty-four-hour phone number. Other American Jewish lobbyists, such as Dave Brody of B'nai B'rith and Hyman Bookbinder of the American Jewish Committee, have proclaimed their independence from AIPAC. But many Jewish political activists get their cues from AIPAC.

In October 1985, for example, Senator Howard Metzenbaum, an Ohio Democrat and spokesman for a pro-Israel coalition, was negotiating with Majority Leader Robert Dole on terms of a legislative compromise postponing the Jordan arms sale. At times, Metzenbaum would shuttle down the hall to a Capitol hideaway to talk to Tom Dine. Republican Senate staffers intimately involved told me AIPAC was literally writing the resolution for Metzenbaum. AIPAC officials confirmed that Metzenbaum wanted their "sign-off" before striking a deal with Dole. Then, the AIPAC-approved bargain was circulated to other key senators.

So in February 1986, Shultz was acknowledging AIPAC's central role when he invited Dine to discuss the Saudi arms deal, which AIPAC was then vigorously opposing. For a couple of hours the two men sat by a roaring fire in Shultz's spacious office on the seventh floor of the State Department.

As Shultz talked, his own change of heart became clear to Dine. When Shultz had entered the administration in 1982, the Israelis feared he would be pro-Arab because he had been president of the Bechtel Corporation, a firm with big construction projects in Saudi Arabia. Indeed, Shultz drafted a framework for Middle East peace in September 1982 that angered Prime Minister Begin because it called for Palestinian autonomy and West Bank affiliation with Jordan. But

Shultz had become disillusioned with the Arabs after seeing Lebanon—under Syrian pressure—wriggle out of the Lebanon-Israel agreement that Shultz had mediated in May 1983. Since then, Shultz had
worked to increase aid to Israel, and he had come to bank on the Israeli
relationship—so much so that he told Dine he wanted to insulate
American-Israeli relations from political ups and downs.

But on that February afternoon, Shultz also wanted to protect
American influence with moderate Arabs. He argued that the Saudi
arms deal was necessary. He wanted to send a message that would
"reverberate" in Tehran. Moreover, Shultz reasoned, President Reagan
had been snubbed by Congress on the Jordanian arms package and
badly needed some show of support to bolster his standing in the
Middle East. Shultz proposed to sell the Saudis a modest $354 million
package of Sidewinder air-to-air missiles, Harpoon naval missiles, and
Stinger antiaircraft missiles. Although Dine told me that Shultz did not
offer any direct quid pro quo, a deal seemed implicit. Shultz said that
if this package passed, there would not be any more important arms
sales to the Saudis in 1986.[5]

Dine was interested, but he cautioned Shultz that to get it through
Congress, "You're going to have to eliminate the Stingers." They were
an explosive item because of Israeli and American congressional fears
that Saudi Stingers would get into the hands of Arab terrorists and be
used against American airlines. Shultz did not heed the advice.

Dine went off to consult important senators and Jewish leaders such
as Bob Asher, the Chicago businessman who is AIPAC's president, and
Kenneth Bialkin, then president of the Conference of Presidents of
Major Jewish Organizations. A senior AIPAC official told me that
Shimon Peres, the Israeli Prime Minister, signaled through private
channels that he did not oppose a modest Saudi arms package. This
gave AIPAC a chance to have things both ways. Its opposition to the
Saudi arms package was already on record; AIPAC could now afford
to accommodate Shultz. On March 20, Dine called on Shultz. "I've
got good news for you," he said. "We won't fight the Saudi missile
deal."

But momentum against the deal had developed beyond AIPAC's
control. Prominent pro-Israel politicians such as Senator Alan Cranston
and Representative Mel Levine, both California Democrats, kept Congress whipped up against the deal. The House trounced the missile
package, and the Senate voted 73–22 against it. Both votes occurred
while President Reagan was away in Tokyo. When Reagan came home,
he vetoed the resolution of disapproval. It took his all-out effort to get

his veto sustained in the Senate—*but only after* he dropped the eight hundred Stinger missiles. The final package was worth about $250 million, less than one tenth of the original Saudi request.

This outcome was a measure of how dramatically the climate had shifted since the 1981 AWACS deal. It pointed up stunning changes in the Middle East. In the intervening five years, Congress had become deeply disillusioned with the peace process. With the TWA airliner hijacking, the *Achille Lauro* hijacking, and European airport bombings, Congress and the country were obsessed with Arab terrorism. Some Senators and House members put blame on Saudi Arabia, for they suspected the Saudis of bankrolling Palestinian and Syrian-backed terrorism. Moreover, the Saudi "oil weapon" had lost its sting with the steep drop in oil prices from thirty-six dollars a barrel in 1981 to fifteen dollars a barrel in 1986. Finally, Prime Minister Shimon Peres was a much smoother salesman for Israel than Menachem Begin had been.

AIPAC Organizing the Sunbelt

But AIPAC was not merely riding a favorable tide; it had undergone a transformation. It was not only capable of blocking major Arab arms deals, but it had promoted a quantum jump in aid to the ailing Israeli economy, from $2.1 billion in 1980, mostly loans, to $3.8 billion in 1986, all outright grants.

AIPAC was not omnipotent, of course. In early 1986, for example, its leaders contemplated trying to block actual delivery of the AWACS planes approved in 1981; they found that politically impossible. But AIPAC's increased political leverage was undeniable. It had adapted to the new power game: to the dispersal of power in Congress, to the increasing importance of grass-roots lobbying, to the conservative mood of the country, and to six years of Republican control of the Senate. Those changes, coupled with migration of voters from the Snowbelt to the Sunbelt, dictated a new, nationally oriented AIPAC strategy. The old cozy relationships no longer sufficed.

"In the old days," Tom Dine recalled, "Sy Kenen [who founded AIPAC] used to work with a couple of recognized leaders—Hubert Humphrey on the Democratic side and Hugh Scott of Pennsylvania on the Republican side. At the outbreak of the Yom Kippur War [in 1967], we drafted a resolution for Sy to take to Humphrey and Scott, and that's all he had to do. You couldn't do that today. You initiate an idea. You go to somebody to hopefully persuade them of it. I don't care if he's got a title, chairman of the Senate Foreign Relations

Committee, minority leader, majority leader, he has to sell it to everybody else. There are now 535 potential secretaries of State."[6]

That power dispersion has forced AIPAC to spread its power base.
For two decades, it banked on the political and financial muscle of large
Jewish communities in the big states: New York, California, Pennsylvania, Illinois, Michigan, Florida, New Jersey, Massachusetts. What
the 1981 AWACS vote drove home was the weakness of the pro-Israel
lobby in twenty-five states of the Southeast, Southwest, Prairie, and
Rocky Mountain regions, especially among conservative Republicans.

"Where were we outlobbied by the administration in '81, and why?"
Dine asked aloud, his brown eyes intent. "We were thin. You can't win
with just the big-state senators. We have worked on the premise that
votes are won or lost at the grass roots. We have to go not where the
Jews are, but where the *votes* are."

At first glance, Dine seems an odd choice to revamp a traditionally
Democratic lobby in a conservative Republican era. He is a tall foreign-
policy intellectual in his mid-forties who would be at home teaching
political science. All his political mentors were liberal Democrats. As
a scared twenty-six-year-old, he was the congressional liaison for the
Peace Corps in the Johnson administration, then went to India as
special assistant to Ambassador Chester Bowles. He returned in 1969
to work five years for Senator Frank Church, then under Senator
Edmund Muskie on the budget committee, and finally as a defense
issues specialist for Ted Kennedy's abortive 1980 presidential campaign. After the 1981 AWACS defeat, some conservative Senate
Republicans urged AIPAC board members to put a Republican supe-
rior over Dine and more Republicans on AIPAC's board. The board
was broadened, but Dine was kept in charge.

What fit Dine for the task of reorienting AIPAC's strategy was his
new creed of lobbying and his instinct for grass-roots work. Two years
as a Peace Corps volunteer in the Philippines had given Dine a zest
for community action. That was his prescription for the pro-Israel
lobby: Spread the power base. Go to the grass roots. Get involved in
the political process.

Some Jewish migration to the Sunbelt helped. As Doug Bloomfield,
AIPAC's legislative director, put it, Jewish leaders feared that "as Jews
go from the Rust Belt to the Sunbelt, they would leave their Jewishness
in New York because it was easy to be a Jew there." Instead, Bloomfield
said AIPAC found that under-forty "jumpies" (Jewish upwardly mobile
professionals) "are taking their political activism with them into the
Sunbelt. I found in Sarasota, Florida, there were two Jewish communi-

ties. There's one over fifty, and they have a synagogue there and a Jewish community. Along comes the under-forty generation. They're not intimidated. They're a much more self-confident generation. They start Jewish PACs and community-relations councils and day schools and country clubs. There's no fear that, Gosh, if people know I'm Jewish, it's going to hurt business, or I won't get a job."[7]

Dine and Bloomfield followed the migration to the Southwest. In 1983, AIPAC opened its first regional office in Austin, Texas; later it opened three others. From Austin—the cornerstone of Dine's strategy—AIPAC covered six states: Texas, Arkansas, Louisiana, Oklahoma, New Mexico, and Arizona (where AIPAC had always done poorly). In 1981, only four of the twelve senators from these six states opposed the AWACS sale and only about one third of the region's fifty-three House members had a record of voting for aid to Israel. AIPAC's objective was to change this record by activating grass-roots organizing in local Jewish communities, running political workshops, and getting local leaders to make personal contact with senators and congressmen.

In Seminole, Oklahoma, Dine located six Jews who had grown up with Senator David Boren. Dine flew to Seminole and had lunch with them, urging all six, now successful businessmen, to get back in touch with Boren. Exposed to a pro-Israel message, Boren moved from opposing AIPAC in 1981 to voting with it four years later. In rural northeast Texas, AIPAC found three local Jews who knew Congressman Sam Hall. At AIPAC's urging, they met with him and asked why he had always opposed foreign aid, including aid to Israel. "You never asked me to vote for it," Hall replied. "If we ask you, will you vote for it?" they inquired. "If it's important to you, sure," Hall said. He voted for foreign aid for the first time in 1984.

These patient, piecemeal efforts by AIPAC, Dine said, produced a "sea change" in that six-state region. By 1985, nine of its twelve senators lined up with AIPAC against the Jordan arms sale and seven against the new Saudi sale. Support for aid to Israel in the House doubled.

AIPAC has not done as well in the Rocky Mountain and Prairie regions, or in the Southeast, but it is making headway in selected states, such as Virginia. It has even courted old foes such as Senator Jesse Helms of North Carolina. In 1984, it tried to defeat Helms and then, having failed, helped arrange for him to visit Jerusalem. Later, AIPAC officials claimed Helms had been "sensitized" by his travels, showing more understanding of Israel and occasionally voting with AIPAC.

AIPAC's political tactics have changed in other important ways. During six years of Senate domination by Republicans, AIPAC has become more bipartisan, helping incumbent Republicans. It has also backed non-Jewish incumbents against Jewish challengers. Both the bipartisan approach and the proincumbent bias reflect the new style of lobbying and have raised hackles among AIPAC's traditional allies. Some Democratic politicians, accustomed to AIPAC's previous pro-Democratic traditions, bristled at seeing increased support and campaign money from pro-Israel lobbies going to Republican incumbents. In 1982, for example, Missouri State Senator Harriet Woods, a liberal Democrat and a Jew, was challenging incumbent Republican Senator Jack Danforth. AIPAC advised the Jewish community to back Danforth, who had stood with AIPAC on the AWACS vote. "Years ago, you would automatically support one of the *meshpucha*, the family, meaning a Jew," an AIPAC activist told me. "But just because Harriet Woods is Jewish and Jack Danforth is not, doesn't mean you support Harriet. This was an important test of the sophistication of the community. You stick with your friends, and it pays off."

In 1986, Dine discouraged Ron Wyden, a Jewish Democratic congressman with an excellent pro-Israeli voting record, from running against Republican Bob Packwood in Oregon. Dine argued that Packwood had a strong record as a friend of Israel, the Jewish community was already backing him to the hilt, and Wyden stood little chance of getting Jewish financial backing. Dine and Bob Asher, AIPAC's president, who is a Republican, also discouraged Dan Glickman of Kansas, another Democratic congressman who is Jewish, from running against Senate Majority Leader Bob Dole. AIPAC officials told me Glickman was angered, in part because Dole's voting record was not as strongly pro-Israel as Glickman's. But AIPAC's reasoning was that Dole had been as friendly as he could be, in his leadership position, and AIPAC did not want to antagonize him when Glickman had little chance of winning. Some Democratic senators, bent on regaining control of the Senate in 1986, were also upset over AIPAC's warm political endorsements of the pro-Israel records of Republican conservatives such as Alfonse D'Amato in New York and Robert Kasten in Wisconsin. AIPAC discouraged more than one prominent New York Democrat from opposing D'Amato. As Bob Asher explained, AIPAC's position is to "stick with friends who have been up-front and out-front for Israel." With more incumbent Republican senators running in 1986 than in twenty-five years, AIPAC was inevitably more in the Republican column than before, Asher said.[8]

AIPAC also reflects the new lobbying trends in the way it plays the
political money game. Its officers make a point that AIPAC is not a
political action committee but a public-affairs committee that does not
make campaign contributions. But many leaders in the "Jewish community" as politically active American Jews refer to themselves, talk
freely of the political guidance AIPAC provides to more than eighty
pro-Israel PACs set up by Jewish organizations or community groups
to raise and funnel campaign funds to friendly candidates. Most pro-
Israeli PACs have innocuous names like National PAC, Joint Action
Committee, Florida Congressional Committee, Hudson Valley PAC
or St. Louisans for Better Government. Those pro-Israel PACs donated
roughly $4 million to candidates in 1986, according to Federal Election
Commission Records.[9]

AIPAC keeps close tally on every congressional vote and provides the
pro-Israeli PACs with thumbs-up or thumbs-down on Senators or
House members. AIPAC follows one determining issue—American
policy toward Israel and issues that affect Israel's interest—and it cares
little about other issues of concern to Jews. But on that one touchstone,
AIPAC rewards friends and goes after adversaries. AIPAC's guidance
is reinforced by interlocking leadership in the pro-Israel groups; many
of its leaders and activists are founders and leaders of the pro-Israel
PACs. For example, Morris Amitay, who was AIPAC's executive director from 1974 to 1980 and who still sits on AIPAC's executive committee, is treasurer of the second largest pro-Israel PAC, the Washington
Political Action Committee, and puts out a newsletter describing various senators as "down-the-line supporters" of Israel and others, such as
Daniel J. Evans of Washington as "the most negative member of the
Foreign Relations Committee."

One sign of AIPAC's increased leverage has been its ability to punish
adversaries. In 1982, its prime candidate for reprisal was Representative
Paul Findlay, a ten-term Republican from Illinois. AIPAC attacked
Findlay as a friend of Palestine Liberation Organization leader Yasir
Arafat. According to Dine, Jews donated ninety percent of the cam-
paign funds raised by Richard Durbin, the Democrat who beat Findlay.
In 1984, more than forty percent of the $3.2 million contributed by
Jewish PACs to Senate races went to Democratic opponents of five
Republicans who voted for the AWACS sale. One of its top targets was
Senator Roger Jepsen of Iowa—"J for Judas," one AIPAC official
sneered.

AIPAC officials make no secret that AIPAC's prime target in 1984
was Charles Percy of Illinois, chairman of the Senate Foreign Relations

Committee, whom AIPAC had tabbed as the most influential pro-Arab member of Congress. Jewish PAC's gave $274,144 to Paul Simon, Percy's ultimately victorious Democratic opponent. In addition, Michael Goland, a Jewish businessman from California, spent more than $1 million in negative advertising against Percy. In a lawsuit, Percy charged that Goland was operating with guidance from former AIPAC executive director Morris Amitay. But Goland, AIPAC, Amitay, and Simon's campaign all contended that Goland was operating independently.

Even so, Tom Dine claimed after the election that Jewish efforts and money had beaten Percy and helped tip other races. "Like an Indian elephant, we don't forget," Dine boasted to a Jewish audience in Toronto. Both Percy and Jepsen lost close races that were affected by many factors; but unquestionably strong Jewish opposition hurt them. In 1986, another AIPAC executive told me that the "Percy factor" and the "Jepsen factor"—that is, memories of AIPAC's opposition to them in 1984—had swayed senators against the Jordan and Saudi arms sales, especially among Republicans facing reelection in 1986. Speaking to the Council of Jewish Federations in Chicago in November, 1986, Tom Dine rated the newly elected Senate as more supportive than the former Senate (he said eight of thirteen newly elected senators were more friendly to Israel than their predecessors). More to the point, Dine urged the Jewish community to remember the "friends" of Israel running for reelection in 1988—and he mentioned eighteen of them by name.

Sometimes, the political arm-twisting goes too far and backfires. When the Saudi arms sale came to a Senate vote on May 6, 1986, Senator Rudy Boschwitz, one of AIPAC's leading allies, called two Republicans, Phil Gramm of Texas and Daniel Evans of Washington, off the Senate floor during the vote to meet Michael Goland, who had put $1 million into defeating Percy. In that vote, the Saudi arms package still included Stinger antiaircraft missiles, and Goland suggested to Evans that the Saudis might let these get to Palestinian terrorists.

As Evans recalled their encounter, Goland asked, "What would you think about someone using an ad that would start—" Goland described the ad very vividly: the senator raising his hand, voting aye on this arms sale, and then a picture of an Arab in a kaffiyeh headdress, assembling a Stinger, an airplane taking off, an explosion, crosses in a graveyard, and reading off a list of names. "So he had it well thought out," Evans said, "or at least he had a picture of what might be done. And when he asked me, 'Well, what do you think?' I said, 'Well, I think that it would be an inappropriate and outrageous way to campaign.' But I said that I think that in my state, people are too smart to be taken in by something like that."[10]

Both Evans and Gramm voted for the Saudi sale despite Goland's threat. Tom Dine told me that the incident had been a grave embarrassment because "it fits the stereotype of how the pro-Israel lobby really works." Dine insisted that it had been done by Boschwitz on his own. "It's a disaster," Dine said. "The whole thing hurts. It's everything that I disagree with. In no way were we involved with Goland. He was a lone ranger."

Whatever the case, plenty of senators and House members regard AIPAC's political clout as awesome. Overall, AIPAC has gathered strength and gained muscle by adapting to the New Washington politics: the spread of power in Congress, the potency of grass-roots lobbying, the need to be bipartisan, and the importance of throwing financial support to friends and against enemies, and then advertising the results. That is the way the new lobbying game is played.

Old-Breed Lobbying

In the abstract, lobbying kindles an image of wickedness only barely less disreputable than the skullduggery of the Mafia. It conjures up Upton Sinclair's exposés of the beef and sugar trusts or Thomas Nast's oils of robber barons closeted in back rooms, their corpulent figures framed in thick black strokes against a backdrop in red. It has the illicit aroma of cigar smoke, booze, and money delivered in brown envelopes. Or it smacks of big labor muscling congressional minions. But that is a caricature, for lobbying has changed immensely with the rise of mass citizen protests in the 1960s over civil rights and the Vietnam War. It changed further with the breakup of the old power baronies, the arrival of new-breed politicians, and the intrusion of campaign techniques.

Of course, plenty of lobbyists still practice old-fashioned lobbying. At heart, the old-breed game is inside politics. That is why so many lobbyists are former members of Congress, former White House officials, former legislative staff aides, former cabinet officers. Their game thrives on the clubbiness of the old-boy network. It turns on the camaraderie of personal friendships, on expertise born of experience. It taps old loyalties and well-practiced access. It draws on the common bond of old battles and the certain knowledge that you may lose on this year's tax bill, but you'll be back to revise it next year, and that yesterday's foe may be tomorrow's ally. It depends on relationships for the long haul.

The superlobbyists of the old-breed game are people such as Clark Clifford, a courtly, genteel former White House counsel to Harry Truman and secretary of Defense to Lyndon Johnson; Robert Strauss, the wisecracking former Democratic party chairman and Mr. Everything for Jimmy Carter; and Howard Baker, between stints as Senate majority leader and White House chief of staff. Close behind are Tommy Boggs, the able, likable, paunchy son of Representative Lindy Boggs and the late House Democratic Majority Leader Hale Boggs; Charls Walker, an astute, drawling Texas-born tax attorney with high Treasury experience in the Nixon years; and Robert Gray, secretary to the Eisenhower cabinet, who got to know the Reagans in California. These inside fixers cannot do what was possible a generation ago. Yet in a game where access and reputation are the coin of the marketplace, king rainmakers still have influence.

For the essence of the old-breed game is *retail* lobbying: the one-on-one pitch. It is Bob Strauss's note to Treasury Secretary Jim Baker to help a friend seek appointment to the World Bank. It is Howard Baker's contact with an old Senate colleague to see that some client gets a break on the "transition rules" of a tax bill. It is Bob Gray's phone call to the White House to ask the president to address some convention or to wangle an invitation to a state dinner for an industrial big shot. It is breakfast with a committee staff director who is drafting intricate legislation. It is little favors such as tickets to a Washington Redskins football game or helping Ed Meese's wife get a job. It is knowing which buttons to push.

"The best lobbyists' work is basically just socializing," former Speaker O'Neill's spokesman, Chris Matthews, advised me. "They know members of Congress are here three nights a week, alone, without their families. So they say, 'Let's have dinner. Let's go see a ballgame.' Shmooze with them. Make friends. And they don't lean on it all the time. Every once in a while, they call up—maybe once or twice a year—ask a few questions. Call you up and say, 'Say, what's Danny going to do on this tax-reform bill?' Anne Wexler [a former Carter White House official, now a lobbyist] will call up and spend half an hour talking about left-wing politics, and suddenly she'll pop a question, pick up something. They want that little bit of access. That's what does it. You can hear it. It clicks home. They'll call their chief executive officer, and they've delivered. That's how it works. It's not illegal. They work on a personal basis."[11]

An inside tip can be gold. Right after Reagan's inauguration in 1981, John Gunther, executive director of the U.S. Conference of Mayors, got a tip from a cabinet staff aide that the Reagan administration was planning to kill the revenue-sharing program which funneled billions to states, counties, and cities. The timing was serendipitous. The next day a mayor's delegation was scheduled to lunch with the president. Over lunch, the mayors of Peoria, Indianapolis, Denver, and Columbus, lobbied Reagan and top aides. The program escaped the guillotine for several years, though it was ultimately reduced.

In another case, a former Reagan White House official turned lobbyist told me that a Washington lawyer telephoned him on behalf of a businessman who had a $497,000 cost overrun on a contract with the Department of Housing and Urban Development. In one telephone call, my lobbyist source learned that HUD had already decided to pay the contractor $350,000 and would tell him in about two weeks. My friend phoned the lawyer back, but before he could speak, the lawyer said his client was willing to pay the lobbyist ten percent of whatever he got. My source stopped in mid-sentence and replied, "Well, let me see what I can do." With some misgivings, but rationalizing that the contractor or the lawyer could have made the same phone call, my source waited a couple of days and then called back to report that the contractor would get $350,000. He never claimed to have fixed the deal, but he got a check for $35,000—for simply knowing whom to ask.

"A lot of it is direct contact," Christopher Matthews commented. "You see Tip, he'll be out at a country club playing golf [usually Burning Tree Country Club], and some lobbyist will walk up to him just as he's about ready to tee up his ball and say, 'Tip, you know, I got to tell you one thing. Do me one favor. Just don't push that state-and-local tax thing through on the tax bill.' You don't think that has an impression? Of course it does. They know what they're doing. Tip's mood can be affected by who the heck he's seen over the weekend. And these guys do their homework. They know right where these members socialize. You think it's an accident some guy walks up and talks to Tip on the golf tee? No. It's smart. It's natural. It's easy."

That is classic old-breed lobbying, and as an old-breed politician, Tip O'Neill was particularly susceptible. Indeed, practically no politician is immune to the flattery and personal attention that are the essence of old-breed lobbying. I remember an article in 1978 about Tongsun Park, a Korean lobbyist who had been close to O'Neill and who wound up getting several other congressmen indicted for taking illegal campaign contributions from a foreigner. But the article, by William Grieder in

The Washington Post, was emphasizing something else: Park's simple but shrewd understanding that politicians need to feel loved.

"Park exploited this weakness with his Georgetown parties and gifts, but that hardly makes him unique," Greider wrote.

> The most effective lobbies on Capitol Hill, whether it is the Pentagon or the Farm Bureau, have always been the ones that played most skillfully to the Congressmen's egos. The military treats them like generals, flies them around in big airplanes and fires off rocket shows to entertain them. The Farm Bureau awards them plaques and holds banquets in their honor. Politicians are not different in this respect from the rest of us, except that many of them have a stronger personal need for ego gratification. It's what drew them into politics in the first place, the roar of the crowd and all that.
>
> Now, picture a scrambling politician who works his way up the local ladder, who finally wins a coveted seat in Congress and comes to Washington to collect his glory. The first thing he discovers is that glory gets spread pretty thin in this town. . . . He hardly ever sees his name in the daily newspaper unless he gets into trouble or creates an outrageous media stunt which the press can't resist. When he opens the mail from home, it is a hot blast of complaints, demands, threats. In the last decade, his status has declined considerably, displaced by the new celebrities who dominate Washington's glitter: movie stars, cause advocates, rock musicians, even members of the news media. In this environment, politicians, some of them anyway, will behave like the rest of us—they will devote their attention to people who appreciate them. Lobbyists appreciate Congressmen. They thank them constantly for their hard work. They provide them with the trappings, however phony, of exalted status. They protect a Congressman, with small favors, while the rest of the world beats up on him.[12]

Old-breed lobbying also thrives on an aura of influence, a promise of the inside track, the hint of priceless contacts. A certain amount of this promise of influence is hokum. There is no year-in, year-out box-score, but even the big-name lobbyist "rainmakers" lose major battles or settle for much less than they had hoped for. "One of the great myths around is that wheelers and dealers can come in there and write policy and have their way in whatever they want—it's simply not the case," asserts Norm Ornstein, one of the best-known scholars on Congress, who is at the American Enterprise Institute for Public Policy Research. "You pick any big shot, and you're dealing with *some* wins and losses. Any sophisticated person is going to know that you hire a Tommy Boggs, and that doesn't mean you buy victory. What you buy with a Tommy Boggs is access. Very few people are gonna say they won't see him. You buy acumen. This is somebody who understands how the process works."[13]

Ornstein's skepticism is well taken, for lobbyists are prone to oversell their influence; but his assertion that lobbyists do not write policy is too sweeping. Their effectiveness, suggested David Cohen, codirector of the Advocacy Institute, depends largely on the public visibility of issues. Large issues like the MX missile, environmental legislation, the Voting Rights Act, or broad provisions of tax law are "less susceptible to the superlobbyists because they are highly visible," Cohen argues—correctly, I think. "But when you're dealing with invisible issues and the narrower details of legislation, you can still use the superlawyers and the superlobbyists."[14]

Access is the first arrow in any lobbyist's quiver, especially lobbyists of the old breed. Scores of times I have been told that votes are won simply by gaining an audience with a time-harassed congressman, so he could hear your case. In this access game, the lobbyist's first rule is to make his own services so reliable and indispensable that officeholders become dependent on him—for his information, his contacts, his policy advice, not to mention his money. "A good lobbyist is simply an extension of a congressional member's staff," I was told by Terry Lierman, an energetic health lobbyist and former staff aide for the Senate Appropriations Committee. "If you're a good lobbyist and you're working something, all the members know where you're coming from," Lierman said. "So if they want information and they trust you, they'll call *you* for that information."[15]

That takes expertise. For instance, Representative Tony Coelho, a California Democrat, pointed out how lobbyists work hand in glove with the members and staffs of the highly specialized subcommittees of the House Agriculture Committee. They help craft legislation that covers their own sector. "There are lobbyists who are extremely influential in the subcommittees," Coelho asserted. "They know more about the subject than the staff or the committee members. The Cotton Council will be writing legislation for the cotton industry in the cotton subcommittee."[16]

A top real estate lobbyist explained the premium value of expertise in the final stages of writing a tax bill and why lobbyists gather by the score outside the committee room. "There are very arcane, very turgid, complicated sections of the tax code, and members and their staffs often are not as familiar with how they apply to the industry as we are," explained Wayne Thevnot, president of the National Realty Committee. "So if you've got entrée there and you understand the process and

you're present, you can influence the specific drafting of these proposals. Staff and others will come out and seek you out in the halls and
say, 'We're on the passive-loss provision, and this is the material-
participation test that the staff is proposing. Does that work? Does that
solve your problem? And, if not, how can we correct it?' "[17]

AIPAC has institutionalized its influence through this technique.
Tom Dine and other staffers draft speeches and legislation for many
members of both House and Senate, offering detailed rundowns on the
Arab-Israeli military balance, or doing spot checks on Middle Eastern
visitors. "We'll get a call from a congressional staffer, say at nine in the
morning, and they want a speech on an issue," one midlevel AIPAC
legislative assistant disclosed. "By ten-thirty, they'll have a speech."
AIPAC has a research staff of fifteen people, well-stocked with papers
on many topical issues. Practically every senator or House member
known as a spokesman on Israeli issues and scores of lesser lights have
leaned on this service or gotten AIPAC's staff to ghostwrite or edit
op-ed articles on Middle East issues.

Charles Peters, in his slim and knowing handbook on Washington,
How Washington Really Works, argues that the name of the game for
politicians and administration officials is survival, and lobbyists work to
become an integral part of the survival networks of people in power.
"The smart lobbyist knows he must build networks not only for himself, but for those officials he tries to influence," Peters wrote. "Each
time the lobbyist meets an official whose help he needs, he tries to let
that official know—in the most subtle ways possible—that he can be
an important part of that official's survival network."[18]

Ultimately, that urge to prove a vital part of an officeholder's network gets into campaign money and demonstrating clout with the
voters. And that begins to bridge from the old inside game of lobbying
to the new outside game.

New-Breed Lobbying

The new-breed game reflects the organic changes in American politics
and the institutional changes in Congress. Its medium is mass marketing; its style is packaging issues; its hallmark is wholesale lobbying.
New-breed lobbying borrows heavily from the techniques of political
campaigns, with their slick P.R., television advertising, orchestrated
coalitions, targeted mass mailings, and their crowds of activists. It is the
National Rifle Association generating three million telegrams in sev-
enty-two hours and blanketing Capitol Hill with so many phone calls

that members cannot make outgoing calls. It is the "gray lobby" dumping up to fifteen million postcards and letters on Jim Wright in one day to warn Congress not to tamper with Social Security cost-of-living adjustments. It is legions of insurance or real estate lobby agents swarming Capitol Hill as a tax markup nears a climax. It is political consultants and campaign strategists elbowing superlawyers aside, to generate grass-roots support for their lobbying clients or to do public-relations campaigns.

For example, when Jonas Savimbi, the Angolan rebel leader, wanted to push his cause in Washington in late 1985 and to bring pressure on Congress and the administration to supply him with missiles to combat Soviet tanks and jets, he paid a fancy $600,000 fee to Black, Manafort, Stone, and Kelly, a hot-shot lobbying firm set up by a group of young political campaign managers and consultants. The firm, whose campaign work gave it ties to the Reagan White House and influential Republican senators, not only arranged entrée at the highest levels of the administration and Congress, but it orchestrated a massive public-relations blitz for Savimbi. In his two-week visit, the jaunty, bearded anti-Communist rebel had scores of press interviews and television appearances. Suddenly Savimbi became a cause célèbre, which helped him get the weapons.

There are literally hundreds of deals like these, tapping the ranks of political campaign specialists for lobbying. That is an important shift away from reliance on lawyers and former government officials for lobbying—a shift symptomatic of how the new politics have altered the Washington power game.

The essence of the new-breed game is grass-roots lobbying. It developed in the 1960s with the advent of citizen protest. The civil rights movement, mass marches against the Vietnam War, and then Ralph Nader and public-interest groups such as Common Cause opened up mass lobbying. Those movements spawned a new generation, a new cadre of players trained in grass-roots activism, many of whom settled into the Washington power game. Business was initially slow to react, but it arrived with a vengeance to play on the new terrain in the late 1970s and gained the upper hand in the 1980s. Now old-breed and new-breed lobbyists jostle, borrowing techniques from each other.

The new game has made lobbying a boom industry. It takes a lot more money and manpower than it did in the old days to touch all the power bases in Congress, and the campaign techniques of working the grass roots shoot costs up exponentially. The swarm of lobbyists in Washington seems to reach new highs every year: from 5,662 regis-

tered with the secretary of the Senate in 1981 to 23,011 in mid-1987
(registration is required to work the halls of Congress legally), plus
another fifty or sixty thousand more lobbyists and workers in law firms
and trade association offices. In the new Washington, practically no big
client will settle these days for a single lobbying firm. The style now
is "team lobbying" to make all the necessary contacts and to handle
all aspects of the influence game: a law firm, a public-relations outfit,
a lobbying firm, plus grass-roots political specialists.

One hallmark of new-breed lobbying is its strange political bedfel-
lows. With Congress split for six of the past eight years between a
Democratic-controlled House and a Republican-dominated Senate,
bipartisan lobbying coalitions became a necessity. Even in 1978, when
the Chrysler Corporation was looking for a government bailout loan,
it pulled together a big Democratic law firm (Patton, Boggs and Blow)
and a big Republican lobbying firm (Timmons and Company). The
latest pattern is for each firm to have its own in-house bipartisan
coalition. For example, Bill Timmons—who regularly runs Republican
national conventions—hired Democratic lobbyists such as Bill Cable
from the Carter White House staff and Howard Paster, formerly with
the United Auto Workers union.

It is not unusual for lobbying partners to wind up on opposite sides
of political campaigns. One striking example is the highly respected
firm of Wexler, Reynolds, Harrison & Schule, which principally pairs
Anne Wexler, a liberal Democrat from the Carter White House, and
Nancy Reynolds, a close confidante and White House aide to Nancy
Reagan. In the hot 1986 Senate campaign, their rivalries stretched
across the country; Wexler and Reynolds ran fund-raisers for rival
candidates in Senate races from Florida and Maryland to Idaho and
Nevada. "We don't think anything of it," Anne Wexler told me. "Our
having contacts on both sides benefits our clients."[19]

The swarm of lobbyists is so great that members of Congress have
grown jaded—quick to challenge Washington lobbyists for evidence
that their case has real pull among the voters. Danny Rostenkowski,
chairman of the House Ways and Means Committee, told me that
while his committee was drafting the 1986 tax bill, he refused to see
Washington lobbyists—though he would grant time to constituents
from home. And Tom Korologos, an old-breed lobbyist who learned the
power game in the 1960s under Utah Senator Wallace Bennett and as
congressional liaison in the Nixon White House, concedes: "We have
a different breed of congressman who is more active, more publicity
prone, more responsive to his district. . . .

"On the Senate side in the old days you could go talk to two or three committee chairmen," Korologos recalled, "you could talk to John Stennis and Russell Long and Allen Ellender and Warren Magnuson, and you had a policy. You had a defense bill. You had an oil policy. Now, you've got to talk to fifty-one guys. So you fly in the Utah plant manager to see Orrin Hatch and Jake Garn [Utah's two senators], and the Utah plant manager gets in to see 'em. If he doesn't get in, he goes back home and goes to church on Sunday and bowling on Monday and to coffee on Tuesday and says, 'I was in Washington, and the son of a bitch wouldn't see me.' And let that spread around for a while. Political graveyards are filled with statesmen who forgot the folks back home."[20]

"The logistics of trying to persuade Congress have changed enormously," agreed Jim Mooney, for years a top House Democratic staff aide and now chief lobbyist for the cable-television industry. "What's changed is there are so many more groups now and simultaneously a diminution of power in the power centers of Congress. You've got to persuade members one by one."[21]

In the new game, another maxim is that lobbyists must demonstrate that the home folks are with them to prove their political legitimacy. "There's a suspicion on the part of elected officials toward paid lobbyists," acknowledged David Cohen, the public-interest lobbyist. "They often sense a gap between leaders and the rank and file, whether labor unions or other organizations like church groups. I don't think you're a player unless you have a constituency to mobilize."

In an earlier era, labor unions had a near monopoly on lobbying with a mass base. Disgruntled farmers also rolled their tractors onto the Capitol Mall to demonstrate mass anger. Business has now entered that game. Mass-marketing techniques are being used even by people like Charls Walker, a traditional Washington insider whose normal style is lobbying at intimate dinners for selected members of Congress. After serving as an inside tax adviser to the 1980 Reagan campaign, Walker got important tax write-offs for business written into the 1981 tax bill. But more recently he has enlisted help from new-breed lobbyists.

"When a member says to you, 'Go convince my constituents,' then you are thrown into those arenas," Walker explained to me. "You get into targeted mail and all that sort of stuff. The lobbying business is moving toward a full service which will include not just your legislative experts and administration experts, but your public-relations experts, experts in grass-roots communications, targeted communications, cluster-group approaches, grass-roots coalition building." Charls Walker was talking the lingo of the modern political campaign, and in fact, the old-breed lobbyists are turning increasingly to campaign consultants.

Campaign-Style Lobbying

For organizations like AIPAC, the National Rifle Association, and the American Association of Retired People, a natural constituency is out there, ready to be activated. The Jewish community, the gun lobby, and the gray lobby all have a long history of political activism. Their issues are emotional flash points that engender powerful, visceral reactions. Antiabortion conservatives or New Right advocates of school prayer are armed with similar grass-roots dynamite. But the modern, high-tech part of the lobbying industry has learned how to tickle other free-floating "hot buttons" in the public consciousness. Washington lobbyists or trade associations can now go out and "buy" their own grass-roots movement. Rather than wait for emotions to gestate spontaneously, new-breed lobbyists engage in artificial insemination. Campaign-style, they plant, nurture and orchestrate coalitions.

When the American Trucking Association was trying in 1980 to stave off deregulation of truck routes and rates, they paid $3 million to Hill & Knowlton, Washington's biggest P.R. firm, not just to publicize their case with speeches and press conferences—but to inject deregulation into the presidential campaign. It was an ingenious gambit, the brainchild of Bob Gray, head of Hill & Knowlton's Washington office. Gray's idea was to use the six months before the February 26, 1980 primary to persuade the New Hampshire press that trucking deregulation would grievously damage the state's economy. He reckoned that if the New Hampshire press produced a slew of editorials, presidential candidates would feel pressure to take a stand while the national political spotlight was on New Hampshire—and that would magnify the appearance of public opposition.[22]

In October 1979, Gray sent Betsy Weltner, a twenty-seven-year-old P.R. specialist, daughter of a former congressman from Georgia, to New Hampshire to preach the dire effects of deregulation. To a region hard hit by the loss of textile mills, Weltner made the pitch "that if there were deregulation of trucking, the small towns would be deserted because those aren't profitable truck runs." The Manchester, New Hampshire, *Union Leader,* which hated the two main backers of deregulation, President Carter and Senator Edward Kennedy, was happy to find a new issue for savaging them. Other papers in Berlin, Claremont, Keane, and Concord ran editorials picking up Weltner's line. Weltner ghostwrote op-ed articles for local truckers. She got other truckers on radio call-in shows. A few civic organizations passed resolutions. In four months, Weltner manufactured enough clippings to pressure the presidential campaigns.

John Connally, the former governor of Texas, was the first to come out against deregulation. "Connally really helped us. He was desperate" for an issue with local appeal, Weltner recalled. California's Democratic Governor Jerry Brown followed suit. But the big moment came when Weltner cornered George Bush at a truck stop near Manchester. A truck driver, coached by Weltner, bearded him on deregulation and Bush came out against it. The Manchester *Union-Leader* made the encounter a front-page photo. Hill & Knowlton flashed Bush's comments across the country. One national news agency suggested that trucking deregulation might be a "sleeper issue" in the presidential race.[23] On her solo political campaign, Weltner got a lot of visibility for the truckers; but there was not much genuine public interest. Deregulation was too popular to prevent, but this unusual lobbying technique did water down the change.

Another new-breed lobbying technique is to activate the state-level political networks that most senators and members of Congress depend on for their reelection campaigns. Roger Stone, a brash thirty-three-year-old, $450,000-a-year Republican political consultant turned lobbyist, put it bluntly: "Political power in Washington emanates from outside Washington—the gun behind the door, as Woodrow Wilson used to say. All politicians are preoccupied by reelection. They respond to the power brokers back home, especially those who might want their seats. So you mobilize those guys, and Congress pays attention."[24]

Ironically, Stone, a razor-sharp Republican partisan who ran Reagan's 1984 presidential campaign in the Northeast, teamed up with Robert Beckel, Walter Mondale's national campaign manager. Only a few months after warring across the campaign trenches, they joined forces on behalf of the Public Securities Association (PSA), a group of big banks and investment houses on Wall Street which wanted to keep Congress from taking away the tax exemptions of the municipal bond industry. Beckel, who was the linchpin of the PSA lobbying operation, hired Stone; Jim Johnson, Mondale's former campaign chairman; and Jim Lake, who was Reagan's campaign press secretary in 1976, 1980, and 1984.[25] The PSA paid more than $1 million for their campaign-style lobbying effort.

Beckel personifies the new lobbying game. By his own account, at thirty-nine, he is "a battered, beat-up" veteran of 150 campaigns who

felt it was time to come in from the cold and turn his political skills
into earning a six-figure salary. When I saw him in the zany atmosphere
of Mondale's 1984 campaign headquarters, Beckel was a rumpled,
frazzled figure in jeans and a worn polo shirt. Beckel was the aide who
urged Mondale to challenge Gary Hart with the Wendy's Hamburger
ad slogan, "Where's the beef?" When Mondale said he had never seen
the ad, Beckel got down on his knees and imitated the little old lady
who spouted the colorful punch line. The new Beckel turns out in a
dignified dark suit and vest.

His background and Democratic network made him an ideal middleman for the Public Securities Association. The bankers, hardly blessed
with a populist image, could not do their own grass-roots organizing.
"Nobody likes investment bankers," Beckel smiled wryly. "If we'd said
we need to protect the investment-banking community in New York,
we'd have gotten a big yawn." But after years of working the vineyard
of mayors, legislators, and local power brokers all over the country,
Beckel quickly discovered that his old political network was a natural
constituency to support tax breaks for those bonds. The bonds are used
to finance hospitals, stadiums, airports, university dormitories, mul-
tifamily housing, convention centers, sewage plants, and industrial
development parks. Their natural proponents range from city finance
officers to local industry, trade unions, college presidents, and charities.

Beckel laid out the basic theory of new-breed lobbying. "What we
do is take campaign techniques and go out to the districts of these guys
in Congress and organize the districts like a campaign," he explained.
"What we can do is get some real honest-to-goodness back-home pressure. We do a lot of subcontract work for lobby firms who say, 'We
got a real problem with Congressman X on this issue.' And so we'll go
into his district, and because we invariably know a lot of people in every
district in the country, we'll find somebody who in a sense becomes a
campaign manager for us. And we go to work on the congressman."[26]

Roger Stone tapped his network on the Republican side. In Houston,
Beckel told me, "We had people from the Sisters of Mercy to labor
guys to businessmen from downtown. The labor guys and the businessmen hadn't talked to each other in fifteen years. They didn't like each
other, but they had one reason to be in the room together. They both
had an economic interest in these bonds. They didn't talk much, except
they all agreed to contact their congressman and say this is important."

That kind of back-home coalition has built-in clout with Congress.

Beckel's lobbying target was the House Ways and Means Committee, which was working on the tax bill. The committee has thirty-six

members; Beckel and Stone set up campaign-style coalitions in nineteen of their districts. Initially, tax-free bonds faced opposition from Chairman Dan Rostenkowski and other ranking Democrats. But when committee members went home for weekend visits, the local coalitions lobbied them and began lining up support—from Charlie Rangel of New York, Robert Matsui of California, Jack Murtha and William Coyne of Pennsylvania, Ronnie Flippo of Alabama, Henson Moore of Louisiana, Wyche Fowler of Georgia, Bill Frenzel of Minnesota, Bill Archer of Texas. These members bargained to protect their pet local tax-free bonds.

The changing mood of the committee meant billions of dollars to the bond industry and the localities. The Treasury Department reckoned on $13 billion in tax revenues over five years by killing tax exemptions for the $200 billion-a-year private-purpose, municipal bond business. When the tax bill left the House Ways and Means Committee, exemptions had been restored for fifty-five to sixty percent of the bonds, and the tax burden had been cut to $6 billion. In the Senate, the Beckel-Stone operation restored more exemptions and cut the tax burden to about $3 billion—an enormous gain for the Public Securities Association, impossible to achieve through old-breed lobbying.

In short, campaign-style lobbying paid off handsomely for the bond industry. It worked so well that Beckel's firm, National Strategies, became known as the "Kelly Girls" of lobbying because they could quickly form and rent out lobbying operations in virtually every congressional district in the country. They could focus heavy pressure for corporate clients on two or three swing members on pivotal committees on any issue.

The Beckel-Stone operation was successful because it followed the first commandment of the new lobbying game: *The most influential voices with Congress are power brokers back home.*

Finding "Hot Spots" to Turn on Voters

Arousing voters themselves can be even more effective. The banking industry did that in 1983, by borrowing yet another campaign technique to score a stunning lobbying triumph—after traditional, old-breed lobbying had failed.

The banks were outraged by an amendment to the 1982 tax law which required them to withhold ten percent of their customers' income from interest and dividends, just as employers must withhold taxes on workers' earnings. The law, backed by President Reagan,

Senator Bob Dole, and other congressional leaders, sought to collect an estimated $7.5 billion a year in tax revenues that people owed but were not paying.

To the nation's fourteen thousand banks, the role of tax collector was anathema. They feared untold grief from customers. But the regular lobbying arm of the American Bankers Association had tried to block the law, and failed. The ABA's communications division proposed an experiment—they asked a Chicago advertising agency, the Leo Burnett Company, to find out if there were any hot buttons in public attitudes to exploit.

Just as campaign pollsters do, Burnett's people gathered two "focus groups" of ordinary middle-class Chicagoans. Focus groups are small clusters of people that pollsters, sociologists, and advertisers assemble when they want to probe the public glands in depth on some matter. In political campaigns, they are often used to explore hidden feelings about candidates. Commercially, advertisers use them to find out what hook will sell their product. Trained interviewers probe for sharp emotional reflexes, known as hot buttons in the advertising world. "We knew if we didn't find some hot button, it would be impossible to build a grass-roots movement," I was told by Fritz Elmendorf, the ABA's assistant manager for public relations.[27]

ABA's two focus groups were led through a ninety-minute discussion of their feelings about government regulation. Elmendorf and other ABA officials, watching through one-way mirrors, were surprised by the outrage expressed. Some people were hostile toward banks and other big business; a few even blamed the banks for letting the tax law pass, suspecting the banks of profiting somehow.

The focus groups also revealed powerful resentment at the idea that the government did not trust people to pay own taxes and that Uncle Sam was about to invade their private savings accounts. Still, Burnett advised the ABA to generate a mass campaign because the public did not seem to see the law as "enough of a threat or enough of an issue to generate *sufficient spontaneous* and independent protest [emphasis added]." In short, needling was needed.

"We knew we had an emotional issue, but we'd never done anything like this before," Elmendorf told me. "We weren't sure what it would take to transmit this emotion into communication to Congress." By late 1982, the ABA had produced fifteen thousand "repeal kits" for member banks. Not all banks were enthusiastic. Big banks were fearful of a backlash in Congress to blatant mass pressure; banks in small and middle-sized towns took the lead.

In the lobbying kits were prefabricated press statements that bank officers could issue, warning that the withholding law was a "consumer volcano that's about to erupt"; there were drafts of letters to congressmen from senior citizens protesting "an invasion of my privacy"; and prepackaged op-ed articles, which bankers were advised to retype on their bank's stationery with a personal note to local editors. Banks also got vestibule posters trumpeting: CONGRESS WANTS A PIECE OF YOUR SAVINGS. WHAT THEY NEED IS A PIECE OF YOUR MIND! But the coup de grace came from millions of preprinted, preaddressed postcard protests, stuffed in monthly bank statements for customers to mail to Congress. Savings and loan associations and credit unions ran newspaper ads and a postcard pullout in Reader's Digest. Together, this produced an avalanche of twenty-two million pieces of mail.

President Reagan could not stem the tide. When the banks first challenged the law, Reagan lashed them as a "selfish special-interest group," and said he was "fed up to my keister" with banks. He called for lower interest rates to help speed economic recovery. But his message wilted before the public heat. Senator Durenburger of Minnesota, originally a backer of the law, told me he was inundated with 250,000 postcards. He demanded the lobbyists give him their computer tape of addresses to help him answer his mail. Senator Dole, the law's sponsor, was so swamped he had to hire thirteen extra temporary mail workers. By June 16, 1983, just two weeks before the original law was to take effect, the Senate reversed itself, voting 86–4 against tax withholding. The law was killed soon thereafter.

The banks' mass mailings touched off a prairie fire. "When congressmen went home, they got peppered with questions," Elmendorf asserted. "We didn't manipulate the public attitude. We inflamed it. But we didn't use deception to create an issue that wasn't there. It was genuine. We've never done anything like it before or since. We tried several focus groups on the budget deficit, and you just couldn't find the hot buttons on that one."

In short, the bankers had a natural pocketbook issue. Their campaign followed the second commandment of grass-roots lobbying: Be sure the public is genuinely behind you.

Grass Roots or Astroturf?

As the campaign techniques of lobbying get increasingly sophisticated, the drive to demonstrate grass-roots support runs the risk of creating a synthetic popular movement. "Astroturf"—the artificial grass of modern sports stadiums—is what my *New York Times* colleague William Keller once called it. Often the commercial hand that plants Astroturf and tries to make it look green and genuine is deliberately kept hidden.

One of the most sophisticated lobbying efforts—based on a fascinating new system of pigeonholing and labeling voters by their psychological-sociological "neighborhoods"—was attempted by the Natural Gas Supply Association in 1983. The NGSA, an industry group, was trying to mobilize popular support for ending price controls on natural gas. It was a tricky issue, appealing to free-market enthusiasts but upsetting to many middle-class consumers. So the NGSA hired campaign consultants to slice off those segments of voters most likely to respond to its message. Unlike the bankers, the gas companies did not want to go broadside, for fear of stirring up opposition. They invested about $2 million in what some see as the wave of the future in grass-roots manipulation.

The gas producers hired Matt Reese, a white-haired guru to other political consultants. Reese is a mountain of a man, a legendary veteran of 450 political campaigns who won acclaim in 1960 for helping John Kennedy win the crucial West Virginia primary. In recent years, Reese has formed companies specializing in targeted mail, tapping the latest marketing-style sociological analysis—a system called Claritas. It was developed in the mid-1970s by geodemographer Jonathan Robbins. Reese has used the system for corporations such as AT&T, which wanted to generate pressures on Congress to preserve its right to bill telephone users a two-dollar monthly access charge. That was an item worth several billion dollars to Ma Bell over the years, and Reese helped keep it alive with his sophisticated mail techniques.

"We work on the theory that birds of a feather flock together—in neighborhoods," explained Mike McAdams, a Reese lieutenant. "People may change throughout their lifetimes and move from one place to another, but neighborhoods rarely change."[28] In short, the neighborhood embodies people's values, attitudes, and life-styles, provided you can narrow it down small enough. The average ZIP code won't do; it generally includes an average of 2,320 households, embracing several neighborhoods. The sophisticated target mailers work from a "census-block group" of 340 households, far more likely to be homogenous than a ZIP code. When Robbins analyzed the nation's 250,000 census blocks, he computerized scores of traits that tell what kind of homes, cars, magazines, clothes, records, and gadgetry people buy.

Robbins divided America into forty prototype neighborhoods, cover-

ing eighty-seven percent of the population. For example, McAdams
said, there was a ritzy, artsy, fashionable residential section such as
Georgetown not only in Washington but in New York, Boston, San
Francisco, Phoenix, or Seattle; and the inhabitants of all these "neighborhoods" were similar to each other and yet different from folks who
lived very nearby, in more leafy residential Cleveland Park or suburban
Chevy Chase. In fact, within Georgetown were different subsections.
Nationwide, there were similar "neighborhoods" for urban ghettos,
country-club suburbs, blue-collar districts, and small towns, each producing a freckled map across the nation.

This system of voter labeling is more detailed and more value oriented than traditional breakdowns.

Robbins gave his "neighborhoods" pop names: At or near the top
of the economic and social scale are groups such as Blue Blood Estates
(inherited wealth and corporate CEOs—concerned with status and
prestige), Money and Brains (the technocratic elite, who run corporations and institutions but do not hit the very top, or who own their own
businesses—much motivated by rational arguments), and Urban Gold
Coast (successful professionals, usually liberal, often Jewish, living in
high-rise apartments and more attuned to social causes than fairly
similar suburban upper-middle-class types in Furs and Station Wagons). In the old days, age, money, and education might stamp these
groups as similar, but the new political prism segments them for specialized targeting. The hot buttons, the messages that move these groups
are different.

Similarly, the old blue-collar strata is divided by Robbins into ten
categories. These range across a spectrum: Blue-Chip Blues (the elite
of the industrial workers, the aristocrats of the union movement, often
younger technicians in high-tech industries with bright futures); the
redneck workers of Norma Rae-ville" (a prototype southern textile
town); the seasonal farm laborers and garage mechanics of the Shot-
guns and Pickups crowd that people the crossroads towns from New
England to the Far West. What Reese calls Mid-America Blues are
older workers in middling cities, who are a few notches below the best
blue-collar jobs, are going nowhere, and are mostly non-union, or if they
are in a union, they hate organized labor. They have very different
attitudes from Mines and Mills, the traditional, ethnic, often Catholic
workers concentrated near big cities.

This system of labeling is invaluable, Reese and his colleagues contend, because it cuts the electorate into manageable slices whose political reactions are fairly predictable, who can easily be reached by mail

and then targeted for a political pitch. "If you just send out mass mailings to the public, you're throwing craps," insists Lynn Pounian, president of Targeting Systems, a Reese subsidiary. "We're saying that we can really increase the odds of your sending the right message to the right people."[29] Mass-market advertising and political campaigns were quick to latch on to these concepts. Corporate lobbyists began tapping this expertise in the 1980s.

NGSA, for example, was particularly keen on Reese because of his record in recruiting door-to-door volunteers for political campaigns. Nicholas Bush, the NGSA president, wanted to put his own citizen army in the field because a Citizen/Labor Energy Coalition was generating pressures to restore price control, which had been partially lifted in 1978. Reese worked out a two-pronged strategy: one to generate a mass flow of Mailgrams to the Senate and another to recruit door-to-door volunteers in sixteen House districts. On the House side, Reese's mailings were followed up with telephone banks, campaign-style, to generate postcards to Congress. "The crazy thing," Mike McAdams told me, "is that we recruited more people for this thing than we normally do in a political campaign." One reason is that political campaigns try to swing undecided voters, but issue lobbyists, as McAdams pointed out, "go after the clusters we think are with us." Most people are left alone.

Political common sense and opinion polling showed that conservative executives in the Money and Brains crowd, prosperous farmers in the Agribusiness category and what Claritas calls the "Small-Town Middle" Rotary Club types would fight for free enterprise. The real surprise, the tricky target, was Mid-America Blues. The Reese analysts saw them as solidly middle-class folks who had made a down payment on the American dream but were now struggling with the mortgage payments—people of volatile moods and perennial anger, easy to incite to action.

"The good news is they hate the federal government," a Reese company memo said. "The bad news is they hate the gas companies about as much. The trick will be to point out the failing of the former without raising consciousness on the latter." The angle with these people was: "Let Congress have their way and things will only get worse." The tactic: "Give the blues a 'them,' then play demagogue; play off their obsessive 'buy America' spirit. *Blame government.*" Final advice: "Don't even hint at a connection to the gas companies if you can avoid it."[30]

In practice, the Money and Brains crowd got the high-toned pitch pegged to groups and newspapers they respect, all of which had endorsed decontrol: the National Audobon Society, the U.S. Chamber of Commerce, the American Farm Bureau, The *Chicago Tribune* and *The New York Times*. Mid-America Blues got a more earthy belt to the gut: a Herblock cartoon showing an OPEC Oil sheikh with a huge stack of poker chips playing blackjack with a sucker who had already lost his shirt and pants. The sucker was labeled "U.S. Energy Non-Policy." The caption read: "Hit me again." The brochure played to the patriotic *kvetch* in the souls of Mid-America Blues. It demanded: "Why do we go to *foreign countries* for something we've got in Texas, and California, and Oklahoma and Kansas, and New Mexico, and Ohio, and Alabama and Wyoming, and Colorado, and Pennsylvania, and Michigan and North Dakota and West Virginia?" Those states just happened to include home districts of House Energy and Commerce Committee members, who were considering the legislation.

The pitch was clever, but it ran afoul of the third commandment of grass-roots lobbying: *Make sure that your grass-roots movement is authentic and looks authentic.* The natural gas companies got into trouble on two counts. Senator Charles Percy of Illinois protested that one of his aides had spot-checked the Mailgrams and found twenty people who claimed they had not given permission to use their names.[31] Fearing charges of running a bogus campaign, NGSA's President Nicholas Bush quickly ran an outside audit: seventy percent of the sample (373 people) remembered giving permission, *but* eight percent said flatly that they had not consented and another twenty-two percent did not clearly recollect being called. To me, Bush conceded some "glitches" in Reese's phone banks, but insisted there was "no wholesale misrepresentation."[32]

Secondly, the NGSA tried to broaden its political appeal by setting up an innocuously named coalition, the Alliance for Energy Security, but reporters could not find its home office—except at NGSA headquarters. Although the coalition listed thirty-five business groups and natural gas users, its operations were funded by $1 million from NGSA. This change-the-name ploy boomeranged in Congress. Representative Philip Sharp, an Indiana Democrat, accused NGSA of a "deliberate attempt to mislead citizens about the sponsors of this effort and a lack of integrity about defining clearly the funding and interests of the sponsors." Bush replied that NGSA had put out a press release announcing the coalition and its funding, but the damage had been done, and the gas producers failed to win decontrol. Bush contended, however, that the other side did not get full *re*control of natural gas prices.

"We moderated the hysteria against us, and we laid seeds for the future," Bush claimed.

This case points up the risks of grass-roots lobbying by mail. Clearly, orchestrated mailings and prefabricated postcards are more likely to succeed, as they did for the banks, when they reflect genuine public opinion. If there is real emotion out in the country, the movement picks up popular momentum. When a lobby-by-mail effort is ill timed or too contrived, it can even anger its own supporters. For example, the gas producers angered some prodecontrol members of Congress, such as Mike Synar of Oklahoma, who resented the heavy pressure.

More broadly, mass mail campaigns have become such an industry that they engender political cynicism. At least three Washington commercial firms sell computer tapes matching lists of members of Congress (broken down by subcommittees and issue specialties) with lists of voters (broken down by congressional districts, ZIP codes, and interest groups)—all for easy targeting. Some trade associations, poised for battle, collect advance proxies from their members and have their names computerized, ready for generating instant mass mail. The National Education Association, a teachers group with 1.8 million members, has about 250,000 authorized proxies on issues such as defending Social Security or federal aid to education. NEA officials say they adopted this technique because otherwise their "turnaround time" on mail was not fast enough to match the computer-generated mail of right-wing groups.

Senators and House members rail against "synthetic" mail, asserting that they pay no attention to mass mail campaigns where the same text crops up over thousands of different signatures. "It's ridiculous to have our computers answering their computers," Senator David Durenburger complained to me. But of course, members of Congress take care with individual letters, especially handwritten ones. Their problem is that mail technology is getting so sophisticated that sometimes it's hard to tell the personalized letter from the mass-produced. Case in point: Life insurance industry lobbying kits used in 1985 included pretyped letters addressed from their supporters to individual members of Congress, using varied texts, with laser-printed personalized letterheads, on different colors of stationery—all to avoid the appearance of mass production.

No one expects members of Congress to read all their mail. The conventional wisdom is they weigh it, put the names in their computer banks, and disregard it. But that is too cavalier. Even when members of Congress suspect that their mail is a synthetic, computer-generated groundswell, many will cite mail figures—if the mail favors their side of an issue. Or if it is running against them, they sometimes generate a counter campaign. Victor Kamber, a lobbyist with ties to organized labor, recalled the battle in 1978 over the labor-law reform bill. According to Kamber, Senator Harrison Williams, a New Jersey Democrat who sponsored the bill, publicly scoffed at the huge mail generated against the bill by the U.S. Chamber of Commerce and National Association of Manufacturers. But he ordered Kamber to "match it."

"We literally matched the opposition tactic for tactic." Kamber recalled. "They had an economic study showing the damage the bill would do. We had an economic study on our side. They did an opinion poll. We did a poll. They had a list of editorials backing them. We had a list of editorials backing us. They had a mass mailing. We had our mass mailing. We did it not to change their positions but to neutralize the opposition's efforts." Overall, he ruefully noted, the two sides together generated about 8.5 million pieces of mail on an issue that "less than one half of one percent of the public had ever heard of."[33]

Even when mail lobbying fails to swing votes, it has deterrent force. As Kamber observed, a lobby group or trade association risks losing out—unless it gets into the grass-roots-lobbying game. Some members of Congress, especially those from marginal districts or junior members, are afraid to risk alienating large constituencies. They dare not ignore any major pressure group, even if its pressure looks contrived. For mass mail usually shows organizational force, and that threatens to touch the politician's lifeline of survival and reelection. Any group that can mobilize masses of people to sign letters—or get their proxies—can mobilize those people to vote, or so the logic goes. Hence, the veiled connection between mass mail and Roger Stone's "gun behind the door."

PAC-Man: Raising Big Money

The big gun of lobbying, the political weapon of choice, is money. It looms over the political landscape like the Matterhorn. It is the principal common denominator between the old lobbying game and the new lobbying game, except that the dimensions of the game—the staggering sums involved, and the sheer constant crazy circus of fund-raising—have made money a more visible force than ever before. Legislators are not so readily bought nowadays as during the Yazoo land frauds of the 1790s; nor are they owned outright by a single patron, as in the time of Ulysses S. Grant. Nor does any legislator act quite so openly as agent for a company, as Senator Lyndon Johnson did, for Brown & Root. But organized money oils the machinery of many a congressional subcommittee.

Our political system is literally awash with money, rising to new levels every presidential election. In 1984, a total of $595 million was spent on the presidential race and congressional races. In 1986, even without a presidential race, $450 million was spent on congressional elections. The Republicans have steadily been outstripping the Democrats. In 1986, for example, the Republican National Committee and its two congressional arms spent $254.2 million, compared to $62.7 million for the Democratic National Committee and its congressional arms.[34]

Paradoxically, the campaign finance reforms of 1974 granted legitimacy to organized fund-raising and gave a rocket thrust to the new giant of American politics—PAC-Man, the inside-the-beltway nickname of the ubiquitous political action committees. Nowadays, it is routine for a corporation, union, trade association, or interest group to have a PAC to raise funds from its members and then funnel cash to political candidates, in order to push the political agenda of its parent organization.

The reforms of 1974 were aimed at stopping individual fat cats and secret corporate slush funds from bankrolling pet legislators and covertly buying influence. To reduce risk of corruption, the reformers established contribution limits for individuals ($1,000), for political action committees ($5,000 per candidate per election), and for political parties (varied limits and formulas based the office and the size of the electorate). All candidates were forced to report funding sources. But that reform, like many others, had unintended consequences. Court decisions, interpreting the law, legalized PACs formed by government contractors; that opened the floodgates and made PACs more attractive to business. Suddenly, PACs became the major new money channel. In 1985–86, for example, the top political spenders were the National Congressional Club (Jesse Helms's PAC): $15.8 million; the National Conservative PAC: $9.3 million; the National Committee to Preserve Social Security PAC: $6.2 million; the Realtors PAC: $6 million; the American Medical Association PAC: $5.4 million; and the National Rifle Association Political Victory Fund: $4.7 million.[35]

PACs had their origin in the 1940s with the CIO, but really sprang to life in the 1970s. Their number shot up from 608 in 1974 to 4,157 in 1986; their contributions to congressional campaigns skyrocketed even more sharply, from $8.5 million in 1974 to $132.2 million in 1986.[36] By far the steepest growth came among corporate PACs:

eighty-nine in 1974 up to 1,902 in 1986 (compared to 418 for organized labor). More important, the legal limits on PAC giving are full of loopholes. PACs have learned how to "bundle" and "target" their bankrolls to gain a tremendous wallop, making a mockery of the ceilings.

"PAC money is destroying the electoral process," Barry Goldwater protested in a public hearing. "It feeds the growth of special interest groups created solely to channel money into political campaigns. It creates an impression that every candidate is bought and owned by the biggest givers."[37]

"Money has changed the character of this town," lamented Kenneth Schlossberg, a former congressional aide turned lobbyist. In a *New York Times* opinion piece, he wrote what many echo:

> The proliferation of PACs ignited a fund-raising explosion that has led to an unhealthy relationship between those who seek office and those who seek influence. The most common defense is that because everybody is buying influence, nobody is buying influence. That's true when major interests are evenly matched against each other. But usually one side has more money than the other, and that side wins. The truth is that money has replaced brains and hard work as the way for a lobbyist to get something done for his client. Washington's atmosphere is reminiscent of what city halls must have been like in the days of Boss Tweed—only now the bagmen have fancy college degrees, $500 suits, big cars, and the best tables.[38]

"The change has been monumental," fumed Fred Wertheimer, the head of Common Cause. "You look at the amount of money spent to hire lobbyists, the amount of money spent on campaign contributions, the amount of money spent on speaking fees to members of Congress, the amount of money spent to stimulate direct mail and grass-roots lobbying campaigns, the amount of money spent on institutional advertising, the amount of money spent to influence the process here on television—no one has any idea what that adds up to. It's a very subtle system. There are no smoking guns. It's designed so there are no smoking guns. There's a $5,000 limit on PAC campaign donations, but the players in the game do not see that as a limit. They see that as a license."[39]

Lloyd Cutler, former White House counsel for President Carter, was more direct. "It's one step away from bribery. PACs contribute because they count on you to vote with them. You've got to take the money from PACs to survive, and then you're under obligation to them."[40]

This view is prevalent, but not every one agrees. Such academic experts as Michael Malbin of the American Enterprise Institute contend that it is hard to prove that PAC money buys votes, or that the situation is worse than before the 1974 reforms. In an excellent book on campaign funding, Malbin wrote, "What emerges from the sordid record of the 1972 campaign is a picture of semi-coercive fund raising, under-the-table cash contributions, and financial dominance by a handful of large givers most of whom had an interest ax to grind. . . . It takes a large set of blinders to miss the fact that the emergence of PACs represents an improvement over what went before."[41]

Lobbyists such as Charls Walker, an ardently probusiness tax lawyer, and Tom Korologos, another Republican veteran with large corporate clients, contend that PACs are being made scapegoats unfairly. They argue that the system is far better now than in the "old days," because there are thousands of competing PACs raising money, with the entire process subject to public scrutiny. Walker reminded me that in 1956, the late Senator Francis P. Case of South Dakota revealed indignantly to the Senate that an anonymous donor interested in decontrol of natural gas had left an envelope containing $2,500 in cash with his receptionist. The decontrol bill passed but President Eisenhower vetoed the bill because of the taint of corruption. "We've got rid of the little black bags filled with cash," Walker emphasized. "We have a dispersal of power. That's why I say things are a hell of a lot better from an ethics standpoint than they were twenty-five years ago."[42]

But the view is widely disputed. As Mark Green, Democratic candidate for Senate in New York in 1986, pointed out, only well-heeled political forces have PACs—not the poor, the unemployed, the minorities, or even most consumers.[43] Moreover, a $2,500 payoff is small potatoes these days. In recent years members of Congress have legally raised campaign money from PACs or private individuals and kept what was left over for personal use. Year in and year out, strong incumbents who faced no opposition, or only token opposition, accumulated hundreds of thousands of dollars in cash. After the 1986 elections, for example, twenty House members had net cash on hand of $400,000 or more, and all but three had either no opposition or only token opposition. With such safe seats, they had built up huge personal treasuries; at the top of the list, David Dreiler, a California Republican, with $943,371 in the bank left over from campaigns; Steven Solarz, a Brooklyn Democrat, with $793,864; and Ronnie Flippo, an Alabama Democrat, with $594,680[44]; the practice was so dubious that Congress passed a law in 1979 forbidding new members from building up personal funds this way; but those already in Congress were allowed to keep piling up personal fortunes.

Many lobbyists who decry the current system take part in it. Anne Wexler, a former Carter White House official turned lobbyist, feels the spiraling money game has gotten out of control. "But you have to give," she told me. "It's part of how you do business here. And you want to help out the people you like and respect in Congress."[45] In 1986, Wexler gave about $25,000 of her personal money to candidates, a tiny fraction of what she was asked for. Invitations to political fund-raisers come to her by the bushel—probably two thousand in one campaign year, seeking a total of several hundred thousand dollars. "Our firm gets as many as ten a day," Wexler said. "We could go to literally two or three every night."

Actually, the way political poker is now played, having a PAC or buying a ticket to a $250 or $1,000-a-head fund-raiser, is just the price of admission for a lobbyist—the ante for the first deal. A hustling lobbyist must sweeten the kitty by joining the "steering committee" for a candidate, which means sponsoring and pushing that candidate, selling tickets to his fund-raisers to others. Veteran lobbyists help each other out by trading tickets to fund-raisers. Tommy Boggs, the well-known lawyer, holds something of a record—serving on more than fifty steering committees. But for big stakes, a lobbyist must play host to fund-raising dinners at home, personally raising cash donations.

"The small dinner is a big deal now—thirty to forty people, mostly Washington types," explained a lobbyist with long congressional experience. "Some people call it 'face time' because they get to meet face to face with political big names. You see, it's not just our PACs that the senators and congressmen want; we are expected to go out and raise money ourselves."

Then he paused and burst out: "I *hate* fund-raising. I do not go to dinners or cocktail parties. But our trade association will probably do $400,000 in contributions this election cycle, through our PAC and through other activities. I will raise probably ten to fifteen thousand dollars personally for people who don't take PAC contributions. It's like a stoop labor. It's arduous and unpleasant."

"In effect," he explained, "the large firms and trade associations are the *investment bankers of the campaign world* [emphasis added]. You can't separate that from the business of lobbying. Except that unlike a banker, you can't get a signed note for your money. It's a more negative thing. The incumbents tell you, 'If you don't do this, you'd better look out.' It's particularly bad in the Senate. They are strongarming contributors. 'You'd better cough up or the next time your item comes up before our committee, we won't be for it.' So you've got to go out and beat the drum for them. Beat the drum or you've had it. You can't make your case. You can't get support. A big-state Republican senator from the Northeast sent us word through an intermediary, 'Your guys in Washington don't participate.' That's the euphemism of choice, *participate.* A Democratic senator from the Far West put it to me himself. I went to talk to him about a very important bill and he said, 'But you haven't participated.' That's what's getting scary."

Other lobbyists complain of virtual shakedowns by politicians. One lobbyist told me that a business partner telephoned for an appointment with a Republican congressman, but the congressman's administrative assistant replied: "We're sorry, we're not going to have a meeting with you. We looked at our contribution list and you haven't given to any of our campaigns." And a Democratic staffer told me of a close and heated debate in the Defense Appropriations Subcommittee in 1985 over whether to shift some funding from F-16 fighters made by General Dynamics to F-20 fighters made by Northrop. The shift of one vote would tip the balance. According to this staff aide, one committee Democrat proposed: "Let's set this aside for a day. I'm going to take bids from both contractors tonight."

What Does PAC Money Buy?

Most lobbyists and legislators are smart enough to use language vague enough to deny illegal vote buying. "There are still conventions observed," I was told by an experienced lobbyist. "You never talk about political money in the same conversation as you discuss a legislative issue. I will not do that, because I remember Senator Brewster. Remember the case?* There was nothing explicit," my lobbyist friend went on. "It was implicit. But the legal point was that the nature of the exchange was such that there was a relationship between the campaign contribution and Brewster's actions."

Bob Strauss, Tommy Boggs, Charls Walker, Anne Wexler, and other lobbyists contend that political donations merely get access: the return phone call, an office drop-in, or a quiet dinner with a client, the chance to make your case. That can be crucial, especially if the other side lacks equal access. "Access is important precisely because *there is*

---

*Former Senator Daniel Brewster of Maryland, a member of the Post Office and Civil Service Committee, was convicted in 1971 of accepting an unlawful gratuity—$24,500—to influence his action on postal-rate legislation.

no equal access," emphasized David Cohen, former head of Common Cause. "It's unequal access because there's a limited amount of time for members to consider anything. Access is important because it's what comes up on a legislator's screen that influences him."[46]

Strauss voiced the conventional wisdom when he insisted to me that helping raise $10,000 for a senator's primary and general election campaigns "won't buy his vote and shouldn't." But like many others, he is worried that "we will have a major financial scandal growing out of fund-raising in this town—not a Watergate but one level below it. I'm talking about—yes, some guy saying that, well, congressman or senator so-and-so told me that if we go out and raise $100,000 for him, that he'd vote for us."[47]

Most politicians handle the entire question with kid gloves. Very few will discuss it candidly for direct quotation, unless they are retired or about to retire. But a lot allude to the obvious. Senator Robert Dole once remarked that "when these political action committees give money, they expect something in return other than good government." Representative Barney Frank of Massachusetts, pokes fun at the pretense that big donations do not have political strings. "We are the only human beings in the world," teased Frank, "who are expected to take thousands of dollars from perfect strangers on important matters and not be affected by it." Dick Bolling, a liberal reformer who spent seventeen terms in the House, confessed to me that "even a guy like me will be conscious of the fellow that gives him $5,000—all you have to be is *conscious.*"

Senator Tom Eagleton, another Missouri Democrat, was more honest, talking shortly before his retirement in 1987. With the very process of cultivating special interest lobbies, he said, "you begin to lose your sense of independence." When I suggested that officeholders probably felt psychologically beholden, he replied: "The nicest word is *predisposed.*" The money clearly works on a politician's innards. It creates a sense of obligation that canny lobbyists know how to activate. Here's how Eagleton, deeply troubled, described it:

"I've never had—and perhaps other senators have—a guy come into this office or over the phone say, 'Tom, such-and-such vote's coming up next week. You remember I gave X in your last campaign, and I'm certainly expecting you to vote that way.' I've never had anything that direct, blunt, or obscene. However, let's change the phraseology to this: 'Tom, this is so-and-so. You know next week an important vote's coming up on such-and-such. I just want to remind you, Tom, I feel

very strongly about that issue. Okay, my friend, good to hear from you.'
Now, a senator receives 'gentle' calls of that sort."

In Eagleton's view, an unspoken bargain is implicit when the contribution is made, because both politician and lobbyist know the lobbyist's
legislative interests, and by taking the contribution the politician tacitly
agrees to give support.

Eagleton was backed for eighteen years by organized labor and
always had a strong prolabor voting record. But he admitted having
trouble sometimes meshing his conscience with labor's priorities. "If
one receives, as I did in my last election in 1980, over $100,000 from
labor PACs, and then if one were contemplating running for reelection
in 1986—which I did not—then when a labor vote is coming up, I'd
have to weigh the legitimacy and the merits of that particular vote
versus a funding source that I might be looking forward to in the future.
It so happens that my philosophical views tie in very closely with the
AFL-CIO on a whole range of domestic social issues. But nonetheless,
a vote or two or three might come along and I'd say, 'I can't make up
my mind on this issue,' and my staff would tell me, 'Well, let us remind
you that labor's keenly interested in this issue and we're looking forward
to labor's support next time.' "[48]

In 1978, for example, organized labor was pushing a law to make
union organizing easier. Eagleton thought one provision—allowing
union officials to do organizing on the work floor of plants—was "dead
wrong." The law was blocked by a filibuster, but Eagleton was prepared
to vote against that provision. "I wonder," he added honestly, "if I were
heavily dependent for my next reelection on huge amounts of labor
money, would that maybe have tilted my judgment?"

Moreover, Eagleton made the point that some lobbies allow leeway
and others do not. Organized labor has perhaps twenty votes on their
hit list every year, and voting against them two or three times is
tolerated. "Suppose you are heavily financed by the tobacco lobby," he
suggested. "There's only one tobacco vote a year. That's on price
supports for tobacco: Yes or no. Now if you're running for the Senate,
say the first time, you almost have to make up your mind right then
and there where you are on the tobacco issue. If you're from a tobacco
state like North Carolina or Kentucky, you're for tobacco. But suppose
you're from Missouri. We have one county that has about eight tobacco farms. So I'm running for the Senate, and someone says, 'Would
you like a contribution from the American Tobacco Growers Association, from their PAC?' Right then and there, if I take $1,000, I have
to make up my mind, and I am committed one way or the other. It's

not cricket to say I'm going to take the financial support of the tobacco association and not vote with them."

Obviously, as Eagleton implied, interest groups keep report cards and use them in making campaign contributions. But also, as Eagleton indicated in his remarks about his philosophical affinity for organized labor, PACs usually reinforce political ties rather than creating them. Labor PACs gravitate to prolabor members, corporate PACs to probusiness types, farm associations to their allies, and so on. In effect, most votes do not have to be bought; mutual interest is already there. PAC donations reinforce original attitudes, though as Eagleton said, there are always votes at the margin where a PAC relationship impinges on a member's independence. Finally, it is not the splashy-headline votes on the budget or the MX missile, where PAC leverage occurs. It is on special interest laws, such as a tobacco subsidy, a cargo-preference bill, or a tax break to a special industry, of little interest to most voters, that the PAC connection has its payoff.

Eagleton took issue with those who say a senator cannot be swung by $5,000 from one PAC because there are so many competing PACs. High costs make every $5,000 even more important. "If it costs $500,000 to run, and you lose a major contributor, or a major group of contributors, then there are ways of filling that void," he said. "But if it costs $4 million to run, and you lose some major contributors, then it's tougher to fill that void and get up to that $4 million level."

Eagleton makes the additional point—confirmed by ample experience—that PACs run in herds, not singly. They "target" and "bundle" their money, giving it a multiplier effect. "Instead of just indiscriminately putting $1,000 here and $2,000 there," Eagleton explained, "the corporate PACs get together, go over the races, and decide which ones are certain winners that don't need any money, which ones are certain losers where it would be a poor investment. And then decide which races are the ones that they should bomb, like a bombing raid on Dresden."

The guidance comes primarily from John Perkins, the Director of COPE, the AFL-CIO's Committee on Political Education, working with other top labor political strategists to swing big labor's money one way or another. On the corporate side, the guidance comes mainly from Bernadette Budde, vice president of the Business-Industry PAC; she has a similar network of big corporate PAC strategists pooling advice. In effect, there are PAC conglomerates or confederations. Some are industry by industry: oil-and-gas-industry PACs get political guidance from the American Petroleum Institute; pro-Israel PACs from AIPAC;

the same with the insurance industry, the real estate industry, and so on.

Overall corporate PAC guidance used to come from the U.S. Chamber of Commerce, but the Chamber lost credibility after endorsing one hundred candidates—all Republicans—in the 1982 election.[49] The corporate PAC tilt was so pro-Republican in the 1978, 1980, and 1982 elections that Tony Coelho, then head of the Democratic Congressional Campaign Committee, made a brass-knuckled pitch to the business PACs in 1981. He told them bluntly: "Look, if your shot was to beat us in '80 and you didn't, you're not going to beat us in '82, and we're going to stay in the majority. And it doesn't make any sense that you people treat us as the enemy. If you want to explain your problems to us, let's have an open dialogue."[50] In short, don't be blindly partisan and then expect good treatment afterward. Coelho's message struck home. In the 1984 and 1986 campaigns, corporate PACs were less partisan, supporting incumbents from both parties.

Bundling, as it is called by power-game insiders is another way through which organized campaign financing gains influence. Bundling is the practice by which a central PAC in some industry will appeal to individual executives in its field for contributions to individual senators or congressmen. The PAC acts as the collection point for private checks, but since those funds are not its own, these contributions do not count against its $5,000 legal limit. The PAC puts these checks together in a "bundle," delivers them to the politician, and reaps the political credit for raising the money.

In 1985, AlignPAC, the central PAC of the insurance industry, bundled $215,000 in individual contributions for Senator Bob Packwood of Oregon, chairman of the tax-writing Finance Committee. This was on top of $129,326 contributed directly to Packwood by PACs of individual insurance companies in 1985. There was good reason, for Packwood was a champion of retaining the tax-exempt status of important fringe benefits such as health insurance, life insurance, and pensions. In fairness, Packwood's views did not need to be bought. He was a firm believer in this approach—as opposed to government health insurance. The insurance was going all-out to protect Packwood well before his 1986 reelection. The strategy worked; as one of the best-funded incumbents, Packwood was not seriously threatened in 1986. The PAC tactic was a political insurance policy.

Bundling allowed the Republican party's senatorial campaign to get around campaign spending limits in 1986. In ten close races, all crucial to control of the Senate, the federal spending limits allowed each national party to funnel about $12 million to its candidates, but the

National Republican Senatorial Campaign Committee managed to funnel another $6.6 million into those races by stimulating and then bundling campaign contributions from individual donors. Even so, nine of the ten Republicans lost.[51] Although the Federal Election Commission has winked at bundling, this practice clearly makes a mockery of campaign funding limits. Some critics like Fred Wertheimer of Common Cause have called for revisions of federal election laws to forbid bundling if the courts do not outlaw it first.

Special Interest PACs Work Incumbents

By now, the basic tactics of the PAC game are fairly clear. First, PACs look for winners. They want entrée after election day. That means that their donations go first to incumbents. PAC money does not yet equal individual contributions in volume, but it is getting close. In 1986 House incumbents got forty-five percent of their campaign money from PACs, well up from twenty-one percent in 1974.[52] Second priority are "open seats," those up for grabs because some incumbent has retired. Last come challengers, and only those given a strong chance of upset victory.

As Senator Joseph Biden said, PAC money underwrites the "tyranny of the incumbency." Early funding—well before the election—goes heavily to incumbents. For example, in 1985, PACs gave $10.5 million to twenty-seven senators seeking reelection and only $1.1 million to their challengers. The safe money sticks with sure winners who will be on important committees when the real business gets going.

So well established is that pattern that Philip Stern, a Washington writer, filed suit in 1986 attacking PAC donations as a political charade. Stern's suit charged that PAC contributions violate the Federal Election Campaign Act, which restricts them to "political purposes," not lobbying. Stern's argument is that campaign contributions are made not to elect legislators but to "buy influence and build goodwill for legislative purposes," often with lawmakers who have little risk of losing. In short, it's lobbying money, not campaign money.

As a sizable stockholder in General Electric Company, Stern singled out GE and its Non-Partisan Political Support Committee as examples of the general pattern. In the 1983–84 period, he pointed out that GE's PAC had made contributions to 27 House incumbents who had no opponents in the general election; to 103 who had no serious opposition (that is, they won by seventy percent or more of the vote); and to only three challengers out of 210 races.

He contended that the GE PAC's payments went to incumbent

House members "without regard for their voting records or public positions on business issues," citing the low probusiness ratings of eighty-six incumbents. In the Senate, Stern pointed out that the GE PAC contributed to every single senator seeking reelection and to three challengers working both sides of tight elections in Illinois, North Carolina, and Iowa. GE was getting smart; two of those challengers won, and the third nearly did. Moreover, donations were made to eighteen other senators who were not even up for reelection in the 1983–84 cycle.[53]

Stern's exposure of the bogus rationale for the PAC game was underscored by the actions of 150 PACs *after* the 1986 senatorial election. Together, these PACs had supported seven incumbent Republican senators who lost, and right after the election, they donated $268,700 to the Democratic challengers who won, according to Common Cause.[54] In short, being on the right side of the winner was the critical motive for giving funds. PACs commonly help winning candidates liquidate campaign debts after elections—a particularly effective way of making the officeholder feel beholden.

In short, PAC funding and lobbying go hand in hand. Most organizations, whether labor, corporate, consumer, or other interest groups, had lobbying divisions before they had PACs. Now, PACs have become the money arm of lobbying.

Stern's suit, tossed by the courts to the Federal Election Commission in 1987, pointed to the serious danger that PAC financing poses to our political system. Even those such as political scientist Michael Malbin who contend that PACs cannot buy votes worry about the heavy "proincumbent bias" of PACs. Individual donors also lean toward incumbents, but it is early PAC money that scares off would-be challengers, reducing the number of genuinely competitive elections, especially in the House of Representatives, where there is a genuine challenge to sitting incumbents in less than one in seven races.

The political money system operating since 1974 has sharpened that negative trend. In 1986, for example, PACs gave six times as much money to House incumbents as to their challengers. But challengers who cannot raise enough money are never really in the race. The challengers' friends and ideological allies may support their cause, regardless of the uphill odds; but PACs see no value in helping a relatively unknown challenger. Without the help of PACs, the challenger has little chance—the PAC game is a catch-22 for challengers.

Another charge against PAC politics, pressed by Common Cause and some members of Congress, is that PAC money and PAC interests tear down cohesive influences and unifying concerns in our national politics and make Congress less workable—by pressing members to narrow their focus. Their argument is that PAC donations and lecture fees paid by trade associations, corporations, and other groups generally follow the congressional committee structure. The investment and commercial banking industries concentrate on members of the banking committee. The tobacco, cotton, dairy, cattle, and grain industries concentrate on members of key agriculture subcommittees. Labor money goes for its key committee members. The television networks, cable systems, and broadcasting industry concentrate on the communications subcommittees of the Commerce Committees. And so on.

Fred Wertheimer, president of Common Cause contends that the narrow focus of PACs distorts the perspective of Congress by pressing each member to think parochially. "PACs think differently from voters," he argues. "Voters are complex. They think about a number of issues. They have some things they care very much about, but they balance a whole variety of things. PACs balance far less."

"PAC money is like a laser beam," he asserts. "It helps a particular interest group play out very powerful influences on the issue that it cares about, while the general public is kind of diluted and left out of it. And you don't have the classic notion of interest groups competing with each other. They're worrying about their own thing here. This is not a question of, 'Well, we'll let the interest groups compete, and the public interest will prevail.' The banks are worrying about the banks. They're not over paying attention to what the dairy groups are doing in the agriculture committee or what the defense contractors are doing in terms of defense policy. In the case of the insurance industry, there may be two items. Period. A member of Congress can do everything else under the sun, it's not going to matter to them."

"So when you define representation in terms of one or two things for the insurance industry, three or four things for labor, and so on, you're just fragmented," Wertheimer concluded. "The question then becomes, What are the balance wheels? The issue is one of weighing. That whole balancing process is done by representatives. That's their job. If they are not free to balance, then our system's not working."[55]

In *Governing America*, Joseph Califano, former White House aide to Lyndon Johnson and a cabinet secretary in the Carter administration, writes that the PAC game is undermining representative government. "The members become more responsive to the special interests that are interested in what their subcommittee is doing than they are to their own constituents, because these interests are financing them,"

Califano complained to me. "I bet if you did a survey or a computer run, you'd find out that there's far more money coming to people from out of their state and out of their district than ever before."[56]

The risk, of course, is that out-of-state interests distort a member's ability to represent his own state or district. Ed Roeder of Sunshine News Service, which specializes in following political money, says the statistics support Califano. "Many states have become America's third world," Roeder remarked. "Politics is largely controlled by people who don't live there. Most of the Great Plains and sparsely populated poor states can't afford to compete with national special interests."[57] Heavy out-of-state funding has indeed become important to many members of Congress, especially those on House and Senate tax and appropriating committees. For example, Senator Dave Durenburger of Minnesota told me that he received more than $900,000 in out-of-state PAC contributions for his 1982 reelection campaign compared to home-state PAC giving of $90,792.

Durenburger claimed that his out-of-state money came from roughly the same groups as his in-state money, and therefore did not distort his priorities. However, Durenberger's records showed something different. His most generous home-state PAC contributions came from farming, food processing, manufacturing, and local power systems. His out-of-state PAC giving included some of those interests; but it was also heavy from health-related industries and the insurance industry—obviously motivated by interest in his role on the Senate Finance Committee (which handles taxes) and as chairman of its Health Subcommittee (which oversees Medicare and Medicaid).

Indeed, the Finance Committee is a mirror of special interest influence—its first version of the 1986 tax bill epitomized special interest politics. With or without PACs, there would have been intense lobbying on a bill worth so much money to so many people; PAC donations highlighted the lobbying. Nothing galvanizes special interests like a major tax bill.

In 1985, Common Cause released studies showing how the Finance Committee and its House counterpart, the Ways and Means Committee, were plastered by donations from groups with major interest in tax legislation. In 1985, for example, the twenty senators and thirty-six House members collected $6.7 million in PAC money, nearly two and a half times what they got in 1983, when they had no major tax bill to work on—indicating clear efforts to buy influence.[58] Another Common Cause report in February 1986 showed the 1985 PAC contributions of the most generous lobbies: labor PACs, $1,153,857; insurance industry PACs, $969,213; and energy PACs, $956,742—and that excludes bundling. Those are all powerful constituencies with strong influence among Finance Committee members in any circumstance. PAC contributions reinforced existing political linkage.

As Senator Eagleton suggested, it is hard to demonstrate the quid pro quo of vote buying because the expectation is often implicit. The oil-and-gas PACs were out to protect the oil depletion allowance and tax write-offs for intangible drilling costs and to avoid about $5 billion in new taxes over five years included in the original Reagan plan. Labor and the insurance industry were fighting to keep the tax-free status of fringe benefits (life insurance, health insurance, and pensions) for tens of millions of workers, which the Reagan plan would have stripped away. In addition, the life insurance industry was fighting the administration plan to start taxing the interest buildup on the cash value of insurance policies. Overall, the original administration plan would have put more than a $50 billion tax bite on the insurance industry, the unions, and their clientele over five years, according to congressional estimates. In a new-breed lobbying campaign par excellence, the life insurance industry combined a high-powered, five-million-dollar lobbying-and-media blitz with PAC giving. Under that pressure, the Reagan administration dropped its tax bite in this area to $25 billion, and Congress cut the bite to $12 billion.[59]

In fairness, the administration and the congressional tax-writing committees did shift more than $100 billion in taxes from private individuals to business, mainly by stripping away the 1981 investment tax credit. That big move hit business hard; it was an across-the-board shift that appealed to ordinary voters and gave the legislation a reform image. But in hundreds of pages of fine print, the politicians also took care of many special interests; the initial Senate Finance Committee tax bill was the most egregious. In fact, Bob Packwood, the committee chairman, made no bones about having tried to corral votes by deliberately catering to the "parochial interests" of his members.[60]

Now, as always, the Finance Committee has heavy membership from big natural-resource states: Texas, Louisiana, Oklahoma, Kansas, Idaho, Wyoming, Oregon, and Maine; and the committee has a history of protecting the important interests of those states. So the committee's bill naturally contained favorable provisions for the oil, gas, and timber interests from those states. Hard-hit smokestack industries championed by John Heinz of Pennsylvania got the right to sell back to the federal government $500 million in unused investment tax credits, at seventy cents on the dollar. Missouri's Jack Danforth, a

protector of McDonnell Douglas, the aircraft manufacturer, won restoration of a favorable method of tax accounting, worth $5 billion to
defense contractors over five years. Iowa's Charles Grassley inserted a
deduction for health-insurance costs for self-employed people, such as
farmers. New York's Pat Moynihan helped save deductions for symphony orchestras, universities, and charities. Packwood, personal patron of labor and the insurance and timber industries, smiled on small
business, too, by inserting a deduction for small-business investments
worth $20 billion in tax savings over five years. And so it went.

Back in Oregon, Packwood was attacked as "Mr. Special Interest,"
a man who topped the Senate with more than $5 million in campaign
donations in 1985. As the committee debated granting more lenient
tax write-offs to the tuxedo-rental business, Packwood was getting a bad
press in Washington. *The New Republic* headlined an article SENATOR
HACKWOOD. John Chaffee, a moderate Rhode Island Republican,
warned that if the committee continued to "loosen, loosen, loosen [the
tax code] all the way, it's going to be a disaster." The last straw for
Moynihan was a committee vote in mid-April 1986 that decided that,
for tax purposes, the depreciable life of an oil refinery should be five
years, obviously far short of its real life.

"What on earth are we doing?" Moynihan bellowed to his colleagues. "This system is collapsing. We're showing we're here representing quite narrow economic interests. That's the notion of
Madison—contending factions. It's my steel company against your
ranches. But we're not reforming the tax law. We're making it worse.
And we're putting in jeopardy the trust of the American people."[61]

Packwood, a master of the tax code but still unproven as a strong
committee leader, was embarrassed. Worried about the committee's
image, he stopped its work on April 18, fearing the loss of another $100
billion in giveaways that would have sunk the tax bill financially and
left his committee standing nakedly as the captive of special interests.
"Clearly we were voting egregious exceptions [to the tax law] that were
not justifiable economically, substantively, or politically," Packwood
conceded to me.

The White House was getting embarrassed, too. "We were thinking
we were going to have to jettison the whole idea," Chief of Staff
Donald Regan told me.[62] "because the bill was getting to be just
nothing but logrolling and a bill for special interests."

Within a week, Packwood dramatically shifted course, slamming the
door on $50 billion worth of tax loopholes for wealthy individuals and
imposing a stiff minimum tax on business and individuals. This pro-

vided the money for a dramatic cut in the top personal tax rate from fifty percent to twenty-seven percent. When the bill finally passed by a 26–0 vote in May, committee members applauded Packwood, but an overflow of lobbyists, listening on an audio system in a basement room, broke out in hisses.

The press and other senators gave Packwood credit for a 180-degree turn against the special interests. Unquestionably, Packwood rescued not only the possibility of a tax bill but the notion of reforming the individual side of the tax code. He was creative and daring beyond anyone's expectations, snatching a brilliant personal victory from the jaws of disaster. But he did not turn sharply against special interests.

With the major exception of the real estate industry, the package developed by Packwood and his core group of senators—Bill Bradley, John Chaffee, Jack Danforth, Pat Moynihan, Malcolm Wallop, and George Mitchell—did not revoke the industry privileges adopted earlier. The real estate industry, which had pumped nearly $1.3 million in PAC contributions to Finance Committee and Ways and Means Committee members, felt furious and betrayed. "It's kind of like the mating habits of the black widow spider," Wayne Thevenot, president of the National Realty Committee, protested to reporters. "The female has her fun, then she kills the male and devours him."

But other industries came off pretty well. The special nuggets treasured by the oil and timber industries, the insurance industry, small businesses, the smokestack industries, and others remained in the bill. Packwood also kept favorable depreciation rules, important to many corporations. Later, House Democrats forced some corporate concessions: depreciation write-offs were stretched out, and defense contractors lost the special accounting rules that Danforth had won for them (causing Danforth to turn against the bill). What revived the tax bill was the general impression that Packwood had held the special interests at bay—though actually he was not as hard on them as on the loopholes of the wealthy. Unquestionably, the tax bill was an improvement on the existing system, but it still had plenty of nuggets for special interests—testimony to effective lobbying.

Nouveau Riche Lobbying

The lionizing of Packwood by his Senate colleagues in 1986 signaled not only admiration at his legislative craftiness, but relief among other politicians that Packwood had kept them all from going over the brink of greed. As Moynihan suggested, political Washington was troubled about its appearance of venality.

Jitters about the potential for scandal explain much of the derision that rival lobbyists and politicians heaped on Michael K. Deaver, who made the cover of *Time* magazine on March 3, 1986, as Washington's newest high-flying influence peddler. Deaver was pictured, suggestively, phoning some high-level contact (the president?) from the back seat of his chauffer-driven Jaguar XJ6 limousine. In less than a year after resigning as President Reagan's White House deputy chief of staff, Deaver had lined up six-figure contracts representing Canada, Mexico, Singapore, Korea, Puerto Rico, CBS, TWA, Phillip Morris, and Rockwell International. Deaver later landed a $500,000 contract with Saudi Arabia. A British company was dickering to buy his firm for $18 million.

In the White House, Deaver was a public-relations wizard. He was also the closest confidant of both the president and Mrs. Reagan. I remember watching Nancy Reagan break down in uncontrollable tears at a small Rose Garden ceremony on the day that Deaver formally left the White House staff. It was as if she were losing a son.

The closeness of that relationship was widely known. Nearly a year after he left the president's staff, Deaver still played tennis on the White House court, kept his White House security pass, and received the president's daily schedule. Those were extraordinary privileges that made him attractive, especially to foreign clients, and also made him a mark for jealous rivals. His angling for a splashy *Time* cover photo with the boast "There's no question I've got as good access as anybody" only intensified criticism. By taking a high profile, Deaver made himself a target. When his publicity turned sour, Deaver lost his White House privileges as well as contracts with Canada, Mexico, and Singapore. The British firm backed away from buying him out.

In an official investigation, Deaver faced accusations that he had violated laws against lobbying former government officials within a year of leaving office and against dealing with officials on matters in which Deaver had had substantial involvement while he was in government. In one incident, Deaver, as Reagan's right-hand man, was accused of having taken part in a dozen government meetings about problems with Canada over acid rain, and having helped arrange the appointment of a special presidential envoy to Canada and then stepping into a $105,000 lobbying contract with Canada. A second accusation was that within that first forbidden year, Deaver had lobbied National Security Adviser Robert McFarlane about Puerto Rico's interests in

American tax laws. A third contention was that he had contacted another national security official on behalf of the Korean Broadcasting Corporation, and helped set up a meeting with President Reagan for a South Korean trade envoy. A fourth was that he had lobbied Budget Director James Miller on behalf of Rockwell International, builder of the B-1 bomber, again within the forbidden year and that he improperly used high-level government contacts in behalf of Trans World Airlines. The affair led to formal charges that Deaver had lied to a grand jury and a congressional committee investigating his activities and his conviction in mid-December 1987 on three charges of perjury involving the Korean, Puerto Rican, and TWA incidents.

Deaver's initial response was that he knew the law and had not violated it. His argument was that he had been on the White House staff, and that McFarlane, Miller, and NSC staffers—while part of the Executive Office of the President—were technically with other agencies, not part of the White House proper. Deaver lashed out at innuendos that he was trading on his long relationship with the Reagans. "I do not believe that my friendship with them is either a commodity to be exploited by me or a legitimate basis for my being hounded in the press or anywhere else," he declared. "In my view, the suggestion that after twenty years of selfless service I would suddenly begin to use that relationship for personal gain is not only mean-spirited but is also an implicit attack on the integrity of the president." But later Deaver told a grand jury that he did not remember several of the specific contacts of which he was accused; that became the basis of the perjury charges against him.

The thrust of Deaver's political defense in public was that he was not doing anything different from what a lot of other people were doing, except with higher visibility and a bigger payoff. In large measure, he was right. What *The Washington Post* headlined as the "Deaver syndrome" became inside-the-beltway shorthand for a wider phenomenon of high officials rapidly cashing in on high government posts. In the Reagan years, the revolving door between government service and private profit turned ever more richly. David Stockman sold a book for $2 million; Donald Regan and Jeane Kirkpatrick for about half that figure; David Fischer, Reagan's appointments secretary, left the White House and picked up a $20,000-a-month retainer merely for helping wealthy contributors to the *contra* cause get in to see the president. Plenty of officials left the administration or Congress, where they were making between sixty and seventy thousand dollars a year, and became consultants or lobbyists making a quarter of a million, half a million or even a million dollars a year.

Foreign governments and businesses, angling for an inside track, became the biggest clients of nouveau riche lobbying. The Justice Department reported 7,650 foreign agent registrations in 1985, including plenty of former government officials. In one year, Justice disclosed, Japanese firms and agencies spent $23.5 million on close to a hundred American lobbyists. In recent years, they have included former Reagan National Security Adviser Richard Allen; former Carter Transportation Secretary—now Senator—Brock Adams; former Director of Central Intelligence William Colby; former U.S. Trade Representative William Eberle; Robert Gray, former inaugural cochairman for Reagan in 1981, and retired Admiral Daniel Murphy, chief of staff to Vice President Bush. Plenty of other nations paid big money. The going fee structure broke through $300,000 a year in the late 1970s and just kept climbing.[63]

The gold-plated lobbying, high-priced foreign contracts, and big PAC war chests all underscore the blatant influence of money in the new power game. At neither end of Pennsylvania Avenue was a strong code of ethics set by the city's two prime political leaders, President Reagan or Speaker O'Neill. Each tolerated laxity. Both were old-fashioned politicians whose style was rewarding allies and turning a blind eye to their darker sides. Reagan's easy tolerance was legendary. While presidential counselor Ed Meese was not formally prosecuted, many in Congress felt Meese lacked a sense of propriety in accepting loans from people whom he rewarded with government jobs. The close Senate Judiciary Committee vote on his nomination as attorney general in 1985 was a sign of disapproval. Meese was back in trouble again in 1987 for failure to make the full financial disclosures required by law. Lyn Nofziger, another Reagan intimate and former White House official, was indicted on July 23, 1987 on six charges of illegally lobbying former White House colleagues on behalf of Wedtech Corporation and Fairchild Industries, two military contractors. Echoes of Deaver: Nofziger, who wound up with Wedtech stock worth $750,000, was charged with violating the 1978 Ethics in Government Act, forbidding a former government official from lobbying his former agency within one year of leaving government.

Without a strongly voiced public philosophy from the top, the ethics of public service suffered from a general climate of laxity. Reagan's lusty advocacy of free-enterprise individualism and go-for-the-gold sloganeering was read by many as a barely disguised doctrine of greed for politicians as well as ordinary people. To be sure, some politicians put a premium on virtue and self-restraint; many others had spasms of conscience. I have heard senators, congressmen, and lobbyists privately echo the sentiments of Ken Schlossberg, a former congressional staffer turned lobbyist, worried that excess was corrupting the game.

"I don't mean to suggest there is something fundamentally foul about the familiar relationship between politics, campaign fund-raising, and lobbying," he said, admitting his own part in the money game. "Like anything else, within acceptable limits the relationship can be ethical and legitimate. Unfortunately, in today's Washington, those limits are long gone."[64]

Enough senators were similarly troubled for forty-seven to cosponsor a bill to reform the campaign financing system in 1987. The bill called for limits on PAC contributions to each candidate and offered modest government subsidies to senators and their challengers, as inducement to accept voluntary ceilings on campaign spending. Its sponsor, Democrat Dave Boren of Oklahoma, said that it was needed "to protect the integrity of our election process." By June, a fifty-three-vote majority was lined up to support the bill, but a Republican filibuster stalled action for weeks, and the Democrats had to set the reform aside.

Certainly, there have been other periods of American history when graft and corruption were more rampant than today. A mental flashback to the Nixon campaign and its sordid record of under-the-table cash payoffs and millions of dollars in illegal slush funds is a reminder that fifteen years ago things were much worse. But as Barry Goldwater asserted, the sheer volume of PAC money has made the appearance of venality seem pervasive. Without some reforms, many politicians and lobbyists are fearful that some scandal of blatant vote buying will bring a voter backlash and blow the lid off the PAC-man game and big-bucks lobbying. For the most astute Washington players clearly fear that deep-pockets, me-first politics has gotten out of hand.

10. Shadow Government: The Power of Staff

> You skate along on the surface of things. More and more you
> are dependent on your staff. There is so much competition
> among staffs, fighting over issues . . .
> —Senator William Cohen

At the most vulnerable and uncertain period in the saga of the monumental 1986 tax bill, Senator Bob Packwood of Oregon called an extraordinary press conference. What made it so unusual was that Packwood, chairman of the powerful Senate Finance Committee, a politician who clearly basks in the limelight, summoned the press but *not* to hear him speak. Packwood turned center stage over to a Senate staff aide, a man far more accustomed to working in the shadows, as so many thousands of government bureaucrats do.

Packwood was deliberately violating one of the unwritten tribal codes of Congress—that every significant action should appear to be taken by senators and congressmen, and that staff can have strong influence on the substance of policy only if it remains unseen and unheard. Like priests entering a holy order, staffers must take an oath of anonymity: not to be seen, not to be quoted, always to push the Big Man in front of reporters and cameras. Yet here, at a moment of great importance for the tax bill, Packwood was intentionally walking away from microphones and TV cameras, turning them over to David Brockway, tacitly acknowledging Brockway's power and importance in a way that members of Congress rarely do.

Brockway is a bright, straight-shooting, fast-talking, chubby-faced congressional civil servant in his early forties from an Ivy League milieu: history at Cornell and tax law at Harvard. His title is chief of staff of the Joint Committee on Taxation—Joint Tax in congressional lingo. With a touch of whimsy, someone tacked on Brockway's door in the dismal Dickensian basement of the Longworth House Office Building, a sign: CHIEF TAX DRONE.

Brockway, who can be playful as well as serious, kept the sign, but he is much more than a green-eye-shade drone. In ten years, with Joint Tax, he has earned the trust of both houses and both parties; he is recognized not only for knowing tax law cold, but for his diplomatic touch with prideful politicians. As boss of forty highly regarded economic forecasters and tax lawyers, Brockway makes $73,600 a year. He could be earning four times that much with a private tax law firm. He tried that for five years in New York, but gave it up for public service. He also rejected academic life, fearing it would be too narrow.

"I didn't want to wake up at fifty-five and find myself in East Podunk having written a monograph on hoe-handle production in Bratislava," he explained. "If I could come up with some conceptual breakthrough and make a contribution, I might have done it. But I didn't want to be an also-ran. I wanted to be on the first team. You want to be somebody, do something. This is a very hands-on thing. You're here because it's what's going on. What you're dealing with every day is interesting. The problems are important. You sort of like the excitement. What you can do in jobs like this is infinitely more than you could ever hope to do in the private sector. You have a lot of influence, even if it's at the margin. Some of us are a little more crazy about it than others are. I mean, power—the exercise of power."[1]

Normally, Dave Brockway talks so fast that he trips over his own syntax. His tongue cannot keep up with his racing brain. He rattles off figures and arcane legislative provisions at breakneck speed, then twists them this way and that, looking for new patterns like a ten-year-old playing with a kaleidoscope. The volume of material that he and his staff must master is staggering. Senators and House members cannot hope to learn it; they have to depend on staff experts. Brockway's desk is covered with ocean swells of paper, great waves of computer printouts—tides of fat folders rolling in from subordinates while Brockway juggles phone calls from conservative Republicans or moderate Democrats.

Joint Tax is a nonpartisan committee staff which serves both House and Senate. In 1986, Brockway was flanked by wall photographs of his two rival bosses: Packwood, the Republican Senate Finance Committee chairman, and Democrat Dan Rostenkowski, chairman of the House Ways and Means Committee. Each man had has his own committee staff, more political, more partisan, closer to its single boss, than Joint Tax, which serves both houses, both parties. But Brockway's staff has the top technical expertise. For example, it was Joint Tax that put flesh and blood on the skeleton Democratic ideas for tax reform proposed by Senator Bill Bradley of New Jersey and Congressman Dick Gephardt of Missouri in 1982. Later, Joint Tax did the spadework for Republicans—the rival package of Representative Jack Kemp and Senator Robert Kasten of Wisconsin. In fact, when the outline of Reagan's tax plan was sent to Congress in 1985, Joint Tax did weeks of work converting it from general proposals into actual legislation.

Nonetheless, Brockway's public appearance on April 25, the day that Packwood called him before the cameras, was a rare, dramatic, even amusing event. Dramatic because just eight days before, Packwood had ordered a halt in the Senate Finance Committee's handling of Packwood's first doomed tax package. So many special interest provisions had been written into that bill and so much government tax revenue lost, that it was way out of balance. Packwood had shut down business for a week and huddled with his top political adviser, Bill Diefenderfer, Finance Committee chief of staff. With Diefenderfer's encouragement, Packwood had decided to attempt a radically new approach. He wanted to slash individual tax rates from 50 percent to 25 percent and close lots of tax loopholes. But neither Packwood nor Diefenderfer knew whether this approach would work—either financially or politically. First, they had to ask Brockway to devise an actual plan and run his computers to see if the tax books would balance. Brockway's answers and options made him more important as an author of the ultimate tax bill than most senators. On April 24, he had spelled out some ideas to the Finance Committee in a secret session, creating a great stir. But Packwood was not yet ready to embrace the new approach. That was what made the next day's press conference so amusing.

For close to half an hour, Packwood and Brockway did a political ritual, a Kabuki dance, in front of TV cameras. Packwood warmed up the press with preliminary remarks and then invited Brockway to the microphone for the main event: an explanation of the radical new approach to tax reform. Reporters kept trying to question Packwood, but he ducked. "Dave, where are you?" he called out. Then he admitted Brockway's expertise to reporters: "I think it's easier for Dave to answer your questions, and I'll answer a few if I can. But he knows the subject better." Brockway moved toward the lectern as Packwood danced away. The reporters called Packwood back and Brockway, who at five eleven is a shade taller than Packwood, deferentially gave up center stage. But Packwood bobbed away.

Their little seesaw game went on for about five minutes until Packwood firmly established Brockway as ringmaster. It was a deliciously ironic little byplay, a total role reversal. Normally, it is the staff aide who comes out to introduce the committee chairman and then quickly retires to the wings. This time, Packwood spent the press conference on the sidelines, leaning against a fireplace mantel, watching Brockway's performance, and wearing a lopsided, wistful grin. Even when Packwood was drawn back, he reminded the press that "these are the options that *Dave brought us*" and "this is *what Dave came up with* on his chart [emphasis added]."

Indeed, Brockway was the star that day. He handed out a three-page memo, showing what tax deductions would have to be canceled to bring the top individual income tax rates down to twenty-five, twenty-six, or twenty-seven percent. His memo contained political dynamite, for among other things it proposed eliminating tax deductions for interest on home mortgages, charitable contributions, state and local taxes, individual retirement accounts, the passive-loss loophole, and killing the special low tax rate for capital gains. It was a tough package for wealthy and upscale voters who use tax loopholes heavily.

In front of the cameras, Brockway came across as accomplished, cool, and easy to follow. He was as smooth as a performer as he was with the arithmetic of the tax code. The new plan, Brockway said, had the same thrust as the administration's proposal, as Bradley-Gephardt, and the House bill, "but it goes more completely to a simplified tax system with lower rates." On business taxes, Brockway had left the Packwood bill as it was. On personal taxes Brockway had made big changes, emphasizing that his chart "was simply trying to illustrate how you might accomplish" low tax rates. When reporters asked Packwood whether there would be a higher rate for the rich, the senator parried: "Don't know. Dave is working on that now, and he'll come back with an answer on Tuesday."

By so openly and dramatically acknowledging how much he was leaning on his staff, Packwood was letting the public in on the secret of staff power which is well known in Washington. Although Packwood was actually very knowledgeable about tax legislation, he was admitting for all to see that Brockway and the Joint Tax staff were his brain trust.

Months before, on the House side, Danny Rostenkowski had also leaned heavily on Brockway and on Rob Leonard, chief tax counsel of the House Ways and Means Committee, to produce a draft tax package which he candidly called the "staff option."

Although leaning on staff for substance is hardly a new phenomenon, it is more prevalent today than it was a decade or two ago. As issues have become more intricate, complex and technical, and as members of Congress have grown busier, their staffs have become more indispensable. That is especially true of tax bills, budget bills, and high-tech aspects of defense.

Actually, Packwood was playing up Brockway's role for his own political purposes. He was using Brockway for another classic staff function: political buffer. This is an ancient ploy in the Washington power game. A president will have a staff aide leak an idea to the press as a trial balloon and then disavow the idea if it gets a negative reaction. A senator or congressman will send staff aides to take the political heat from lobbyists or unhappy constituents. A committee chairman will use his staff director to deliver bad news to members or to do some early bargaining. In this case, Packwood was using Brockway as a public fall guy, in case this tentative shift in tax strategy backfired. By having Brockway float the idea, first to Packwood's own committee members and then to a wider public, Packwood left himself more room to walk away from it if it flopped. For those first couple of days, Packwood wanted the scheme labeled "Brockway's options" rather than "Packwood's plan." His gambit worked. As the new package took off politically, Packwood came back out front, leading the charge and harvesting acclaim for his gutsy strategy.

Even so, Brockway's rare day in the sun exposed the reality of the "shadow government" that stands behind senators and congressmen. Other staffers, vicariously enjoying Brockway's prominence, kiddingly called him "Senator Brockway." Schooled in the ethic of staff anonymity, Brockway was suitably shy in public but privately admitted the kick of having his picture in the newspapers and seeing the Joint Tax staff get public credit.

This episode illustrates one vital facet of power in Congress—namely, that the power of a committee and its chairman quite frequently rests on the quality of its staff. Packwood had been in a terrible political jam; he could not have produced a radical new tax package without the talent of Brockway's Joint Tax staff.

Back on April 17, Packwood had known that his original tax plan was doomed, and that it would be fatal to his committee chairmanship for tax reform to die on his doorstep. He was desperate. Packwood and his aide, Bill Diefenderfer, told me they had toyed months earlier with trying to lower tax rates dramatically, but that package had seemed unattainable because they could not figure out how to raise tax revenues to compensate for revenues lost by cutting tax rates. Suddenly they saw little to lose in gambling on such an effect.[2]

Packwood needed concrete alternatives and in a great hurry. Diefenderfer's Finance Committee staff lacked the technical expertise to produce a package fast enough. Joint Tax, and Brockway especially, was more capable and politically freer to dream up the options and do rapid computer runs. Without Joint Tax, Packwood would have been dead in the water. With it, he could regain political momentum.

Packwood kept control of the ultimate decisions, but delegated substantial authority to Brockway. To Brockway, who had studied tax law under Stanley Surrey—a former assistant secretary of the Treasury whose name is synonymous with knocking loopholes out of the tax code—this sudden opportunity was like a dream come true. While Brockway is politically neutral, he is not without an ideology: the ideology of reform. His professional bent is to eliminate tax credits, incentives, preferences, shelters, and loopholes and to use the tax code to collect revenues "on a level playing field"—the same for all—not to use the tax code as an instrument of social and economic engineering or to favor certain interest groups or to promote various policy goals. Indeed, the "nonpolitical" ethic of Joint Tax makes it an inevitable adversary to many special interests.[3]

Most senators and congressmen praise Brockway as a talented, honest staff chief who does not push his own agenda. But once Packwood offered him an opening, Brockway pulled his own pet ideas off the shelf. Like a halfback given a key block, he suddenly had running room in a broken field.

"You have a situation you can play," Brockway remarked later. "You try to get the most you can get, but you've got to read the field right to see what will go. You've got to make decisions that make sense to your bosses, the committee members."

When Brockway came back to Packwood with new options, he knew some were only theoretical because they would not fly politically. But two Brockway features were terribly important in cleaning up the tax code, and neither had been boldly pushed so far by the Reagan administration or by the tax-writing committees.

One key Brockway proposal was eliminating the special low rate for capital gains, which was worth about $150 billion in taxes to the government over five years. This idea, borrowed from the Democratic Bradley-Gephardt bill, had never really gotten a chance in either the House or Senate committee deliberations. But now, with the prospect of dramatically lower personal income tax rates, it commanded new attention when Brockway raised it.

A second Brockway idea became a cornerstone of the Packwood plan: closing the passive-loss loophole in the existing tax law. Passive loss was the gimmick by which promoters sold tax shelters to the rich, to generate passive or paper losses (often at several times the cost of their investment) in real estate deals, cattle herds, timberlands, art investments, and oil-and-gas programs. Wealthy investors would then write off these paper losses against actual cash income from other business, thereby drastically reducing their taxes or escaping the IRS entirely. Joint Tax estimated that killing this loophole would generate about $52 billion in tax revenues over five years.

To his credit, Packwood grabbed Brockway's idea and made it a vital point in selling the new tax package as serious reform. With a "reform" image, the tax bill got new life. Packwood and a reformist core of his committee adopted and modified the Brockway options to pass a surprising new tax package. Both the "passive-loss and capital-gains features made it into law—testimony to the power of an influential staff chief.

Moreover, in August 1986, when Packwood and Rostenkowski finally struck a broad compromise between the differing House and Senate versions of the tax bill, they turned over considerable discretionary power to their staff chiefs: Brockway, William Diefenderfer of the Senate Finance Committee, and Rob Leonard, Rostenkowski's top tax expert on the House Ways and Means Committee staff. It had been done before—in 1982, Brockway and staff drafted a compromise for rolling back $8 billion worth of tax breaks granted in 1981 to major corporations; and in 1984, the tax staffs produced the $50 billion in tax revenues that congressional leaders wanted.

Now in 1986, once again, huge items worth hundreds of millions of dollars to specific industries were crafted by the staff team. One important provision, affecting virtually every business, involved writing the legal rules for calculating business profits for tax purposes. Normally, corporations report bigger profits to stockholders than to the IRS, bragging to one audience, poor-mouthing to the other. This time the tax-writing staff insisted that the claims that companies were making to Wall Street had to be used on tax reports. That would bring in bigger tax revenues.

Moral: Never underestimate the power of writing the fine print. "The actual drafting of the legislation, the fine points, the statement of managers, the explanations, the things that can make millions and millions of dollars of difference have to be done by Joint Tax because of the complexity and technicality of the tax code," observed Stuart Eizenstat, former domestic policy chief in the Carter White House and now a lawyer-lobbyist. "They're the only ones who can deal with it. And every tax conference [between House and Senate] of necessity leaves significant areas for the Joint Committee to fill in. Significant areas, involving tens of millions of dollars in decision. So it's a tremendously important institution."[4]

Still, Brockway is sensitive to practical limits on his leeway. "You try to go for consensus with the other staffs involved, House and Senate, Treasury, the IRS," he said. Moreover, he senses what will sit right with his political chiefs. "If you start thinking you're a free agent, that you have independent power yourself, you're setting yourself up for a fall," Brockway cautioned. "Your power really is derivative. If you abuse it, they can take it away from you in an instant."

Moynihan's Iron Law of Emulation

Certainly, powerful staff is not new to Congress. When Lyndon Johnson was Senate majority leader in the 1950s, his aide Bobby Baker was known as the ninety-ninth senator (when there were ninety-eight elected Senate members) because Baker so visibly helped manage the Senate, dispensing space, patronage, and other favors, manipulating members, and gathering votes. From the mid-fifties to the mid-seventies, Dick Sullivan, a tough New Yorker, was the powerhouse staff director of the House Public Works Committee, a man who made a difference on where money got spent, for whom, and on what. Another important staff man who wielded money power in the late 1960s and 1970s was Harley Dirks of the Senate Appropriations Subcommittee on Labor, Health, Education and Welfare. A vigorous policy entrepreneur was Michael Pertschuk of the Senate Commerce Committee. An aggressive staff aide with close links to Ralph Nader and his consumer network, Pertschuk steered the committee chairman, Senator Warren Magnuson of Washington, into consumer activism.[5] Individual staff chiefs were sometimes more powerful in the old game than they are in the new game.

In fact, despite Brockway's considerable influence, he personally is less powerful than Lawrence Woodworth, the veteran tax expert who worked for the Joint Tax staff for thirty-two years and ran that staff from 1962 to 1976. The difference between the power of Woodworth and the power of Brockway reflects the "sunshine" laws forcing Congress to operate more in the open, as well as the dispersal of power in Congress. In the old-breed staff game, the process was more private, both houses were in control of Democrats, and the staffs of the Senate Finance Committee and House Ways and Means Committee were weaker. That allowed Woodworth to shape entire tax bills and negotiate deals between powerful committee chairmen such as Wilbur Mills in the House and Russell Long in the Senate. Typical of the old breed, Woodworth was a private power broker in a small club of congressional barons. When he died in 1977, Al Ullman, then chairman of the Ways and Means Committee, eulogized him as someone with "as much influence in shaping tax policy in this country as any committee chairman or treasury secretary or president in recent memory."

The climate has changed since Woodworth's heyday. During the half-dozen years when the Senate was controlled by Republicans and the House was under Democratic rule, Brockway had to toe a more careful nonpartisan line than Woodworth did. Moreover, in Woodworth's early years, Joint Tax did virtually all the tax work for both houses of Congress; in recent years, the staffs of the tax-writing committees in the two houses have taken over some of that load. "Larry had much more power than I do," Brockway readily conceded. "There are so many players now, so many other staffs, so many power centers involved." In sum, just as Congress stripped its power barons of some power, it also spread around staff power too. But while individual figures may not be as powerful as they used to be, overall staff power has grown. It has proliferated, multiplied, expanded, and spread so that now, in sheer numbers and talent, the new-breed staff are more important and pervasive than ever before.

Nowadays, staffers are a ubiquitous presence, riding elevators and congressional subways beside senators and House members rushing to a vote; at their elbows, giving advice; behind them at hearings, whispering questions; prepping their bosses for press interviews or shoving speeches into their hands; giving them political and substantive guidance; handling constituents; screening lobbyists; setting the agenda for committees; briefing members on the budget or haggling over its provisions; formulating proposals; making decisions; mastering procedure; managing hearings; cross-examining generals; probing the Central Intelligence Agency; negotiating with the White House.

"They are like millipedes crawling up the walls, coming out of every drawer—damnedest thing you ever saw," Bryce Harlow impatiently wheezed. His congressional staff work began in 1938, and he went on to become Eisenhower's chief congressional liaison.[6]

"If the image for the Senate in the 1950s was a few powerful whales and a lot of minnows, then the image now for congressional staff is field mice running all over the place," added Michael Malbin, a political scientist at the American Enterprise Institute and author of *Unelected Representatives*, an excellent book on Capitol Hill staff.

In short, the old game was played on a smaller board. Now there are many more active players in both houses, and far more staffers egging them on, angling for issues that will look good in the press and with constituents back home, fighting for turf against other committees, creating agendas that will put their senator or congressman on the map. The explosion of staff activity and numbers on Capitol Hill is an important hallmark of the new Washington.

This trend was set off by the congressional reforms of the early and mid-seventies, sparked by the bitter congressional distrust for the executive branch after the Vietnam War and the Watergate scandal. Intent on informing and arming itself for confrontations with the executive branch, the newly assertive Congress set up its own Congressional Budget Office and an Office of Technology Assessment to reinforce its investigative arm, the General Accounting Office. It expanded the Congressional Research Service. And it hired literally thousands of new people for the personal staffs of members and the committee staffs handling policy and legislation. From 1973 to 1985, the number of congressional staff leapt from about 11,500 to more than 24,000. If all the printers, administrators, cooks, barbers, security guards, and gym employees are thrown in, close to 32,000 people were working for the legislative branch by the mid-1980s.[7]

Historically, what happened was that Congress, looking at the burgeoning executive branch, saw staff as an instrument of power—a source of information and troops for battle. As time wore on, staff became not only an instrument of power but a measure of power. The larger a senator's or a House committee chairman's staff, the more power it was assumed he had. Small staff was a sign of weakness. Large and able staffs gravitated to powerful legislators. The political syllogism moved through phases—from staff buttresses power, to staff follows power, to staff symbolizes power.

With a wry Irish twist, Senator David Patrick Moynihan of New York suggested that Congress was driven by "the iron law of emulation."[8] It was copying the executive branch, building a bureaucracy to fight a bureaucracy. "Whenever any branch of government acquires a new technique which enhances its power in relation to the other branches, that technique will soon be adopted by those other branches as well," Moynihan argued. Opposing sides of the Washington power game borrow techniques from each other. Congress set up its own budget office to match the president's Office of Management and Budget and his Council of Economic Advisers. It formed new intelligence committees to cope with the Central Intelligence Agency and other intelligence arms. It set up its own technology office to offset the one in the White House. Its committee staffs grew to cope with the increasing complexity of executive departments.

Internally, there have been two important institutional engines of staff growth in Congress. One is the dispersal of power; in the old days, the power barons, the committee chairmen, ruled with a firm hand through small but powerful staffs. As power spread to subcommittees, everyone wanted more staff. First, subcommittee chairmen and ranking minority members, then individual committee members demanded *their own committee staffers* on each of their committees to protect their interests. The second institutional engine was the dramatic increase in constituent casework and the rising tide of mail that swamped Congress. Those needs made senators and congressmen demand a buildup in their *personal staffs*. In a typical House member's office, fourteen of eighteen staff aides are engaged in casework, travel, and administration; only a handful follow the substance of legislation. Most policy work is done by committee staffs.

The staff explosion was forced by the limits of time and rising demands. Senators and congressmen had to ease their own workloads, for they were stretched too thin, dealing with floor debates, subcommittee work, campaign fund-raising, and travel home every weekend. What's more, no single person can keep up with the sprawling substance of policy. On a normal day, a senator or congressman has two and sometimes three simultaneous committee hearings, floor votes, issues caucuses, meetings with other congressmen from his state or region, plus lobbyists, constituents, and press to handle. He will dart into one hearing, get a quick fill-in from his staffer, inject his ten minutes' worth and rush on to the next event, often told by an aide how to vote as he rushes onto the floor. Only the staff specialist has any continuity with substance. The member is constantly hopscotching.

"It's just a crazy life," remarked David Aylward, former staff director for the House Subcommittee on Telecommunications, Consumer Protection, and Finance under Timothy Wirth of Colorado. "What Wirth's administrative assistant did was manage chaos all day." Aylward told me, shaking his head at the thought. "You see, a really good politician becomes a spokesman rather than a hands-on expert. He can't afford to become a hands-on expert. Jimmy Carter was a classic example of somebody who tried to be a hands-on expert, and it just doesn't work."

"If you've ever seen an active member of Congress's daily schedule it's just scary," Aylward said. "When I got to the point in our subcommittee where we had an expert on securities, an expert on banking, an expert on telephone, an expert on television, an expert on motor-vehicle safety, and international trade and so on, I would get bounced through meetings where I would be brought in because Wirth had to do something else. So I was kind of half playing congressman. I started to get some feel for what his life was like. I'd get briefed for three minutes beforehand about what I was supposed to say in some meeting. I didn't understand it. I would just do what I was told to say. That got frightening. I didn't feel comfortable with that. But that's what a member's life is like. There's no way Wirth could be an expert on all of those things, much less the budget committee, which he was on, much less arms control that he cared about, much less clean air and other kinds of health issues. So the staff had become more and more important."[9]

Aylward voiced a typical staffer's view when he declared, "You wouldn't catch me dead running for office." Seeing the chaotic life, most staff aides pass up elective office. More frequently, they take highly paid jobs as Washington lawyers and lobbyists, as did Aylward. While in government, many enjoy exercising power anonymously. They care more about results than publicity. They prefer the mastery of substance and process to the glory and hassle of elective office. Some even come to feel that as staff, they have more power than senators or congressmen do.

Take Norman Dicks, who spent eight years as an aide to Senator Warren Magnuson of Washington and then won election to the House in 1976. A year later, he remarked to my *New York Times* colleague Martin Tolchin: "People asked me how I felt about being elected to Congress, and I told them I never thought I'd give up *that much power* voluntarily [emphasis added]."[10]

"Stafflation" in Congress

From an elective politician's point of view, staff is an extension of himself, a series of ever-widening circles starting with the close political family of his initial campaign staff. Then as an elected House member or senator gains power and builds his positions on committees, the staff family expands and becomes his or her network, clan, tribe, penetrating the federal bureaucracy for constituents, monitoring the actions of the congressional committees, pushing his policies, promoting his interests, dreaming up ideas for him.[11] The staff acts as his surrogate, his alter ego, like a battery of attorneys serving a client. Staff members extend the reach, impact, visibility, and output of the officeholder. But the more they do, the more power he must surrender to them. And ironically, the more staff that Congress hires to ease its workload, the more work staff generates and throws back on the senators and congressmen, often clogging the system!

"You skate along the surface of things," Bill Cohen of Maine, a well-versed, substantive senator, candidly conceded to me. "More and more you are dependent on your staff. There is so much competition among staffs, fighting over issues, that sometimes you'll call a senator and ask, 'Why are you opposing me on this?' and he'll say, 'I didn't know I was.' And you'll say, 'Well, check with your staff and see.' "[12]

An echo of Cohen's story came from Tony Coelho, a supercharged House member from California, now the Democratic whip. "What worries me is that I've lost control," Coelho said, looking at a daily "dance card" with seventeen appointments written on it.

"When I leave a meeting, I don't have time to do the follow-up," he admitted. "The staff controls that meeting, that issue. I don't have time to make phone calls, to listen to the lobbyists. What is power? Information. Follow-through. Drafting an op-ed article."[13]

As he was talking to me, an aide, Mark Johnson, handed Coelho his draft of an article to be printed over Coelho's name. Coelho read it rapidly and nodded his approval without any changes. "I've got to trust him," Coelho said to me. "What I've done now is put things in the hands of lobbyists and staff. I'm going to go home tonight with two or three [large manila] envelopes of memos to read, and I'm going to say yes or no. Who wrote the memos? My staff. I'm going to respond to their interpretation of the issues."

Many lobbyists consider it hopeless to approach a senator or congressman unless they have first laid out their position to the staff.

Without staff support, they reckon their chances are slim with the Big Man himself. After Howard Baker retired as Senate majority leader and joined a Washington law firm, he was astonished to learn how much effort lobbyists spend on congressional staff. "I was struck by the fact that they had list after list after list of people on the staff they'd gone to see," he told me. "That's a side of Washington I hadn't clearly seen while I was in the Senate. I was surprised that it was almost the total focus of this little group. They were bandying about names that I'd barely heard of. I thought, 'My God, I remember him. He's a kid whom senator so-and-so hired. What's he got to do with it?' Then I found out he is the deputy assistant staff director of such-and-such committee.

"I think part of it is an illusion," Baker cautioned. "Because, you know, when I met with most committee chairmen every Tuesday morning around the conference table in my office, I saw how it worked. They would really go at it hammer and tongs on particular items within their jurisdiction. So I think the impact of staff is overrated. But God knows, there's enough of them, they generate enough memos, and I know they attract lobbyists and lawyers like flies."[14]

Reporters know that usually the best place for accurate insight into substantive developments is staff aides. In private, staffers often talk more freely and with less political slant than members do. What's more, they usually know the substance better. Occasionally, members get embarrassed in public by looking like Charlie McCarthies to their staff Edgar Bergens.

Several years ago, during a committee markup of legislation on the Department of Energy, for example, Senator Jim Sasser of Tennessee lost a page from an amendment he was offering and had to turn to a staff aide and ask in an anguished whisper, "What comes next?" With a packed hearing room listening, the aide slowly told him what to say and he repeated what she said, word for word.[15] On another occasion, Delaware's Senator Joe Biden provided a laugh for the Judiciary Committee when he got tangled up over an amendment to the criminal code, which he called a two-for-one proposal to provide convicts time off for good behavior. "In other words for every day of good behavior in prison—excuse me, I am being corrected here," Bidden said, as his staff aides hastily shoved his own proposal in front of him. After some confusion, Biden—who is known for frankness—candidly confessed: "Obviously, I don't know what the hell I'm talking about. I thought I had a two-for-one provision there. The staff, in its wisdom, rewrote it so I guess I did not want that after all."[16]

Occasionally, dependence on staff becomes obvious even on the

Senate or House floor. It so offended former Senator James Allen of Alabama that he once proposed a rule barring Senate staffers from appearing on the floor and banning Senators themselves from reading staff-prepared speeches rather than debating in their own words. Allen knew the rule had no chance of passing; to this day, staff aides continue to sit by senators on the floor, passing notes and helping them debate.

Quite often, staff aides understand Senate rules and procedures better than their bosses do. In December 1982, for example, Quentin Crommelin, a staff aide to the late Senator John East of North Carolina, was masterminding East's filibuster against a gasoline tax bill favored by the Reagan administration and Senate leadership. It was close to Christmas and past midnight. Tempers were frayed. At one point, East mistakenly mentioned the lack of a Senate quorum, a vital tactical error because it enabled the presiding officer to break the filibuster and take control of the floor in order to call the attendance roll. At Crommelin's coaching, East protested that he was merely making a point of order, which would have let him keep the floor. Majority Leader Howard Baker and other Republicans got into a heated argument with Crommelin because Crommelin, knowing the rules better than East, was giving East instructions. Baker and others were furious at having to deal with a staff aide as an equal; they were especially angry that Crommelin had made it so obvious that he, not East, was running things.[17]

Staff as Policy Entrepreneurs

As the East-Crommelin episode showed, staff sometimes leads officeholders, not vice versa. For among the modern congressional staff, there is a culture of activism, a spirit of entrepreneurship, a highly charged sense of competition. Most legislative staffers are bright, young, aggressive, ambitious, full of ideas, and canny enough to know that their own ambitions are best served by expanding the power and turf of their bosses. Their relentless energy and initiative cause some members to complain of "stafflation."

Michael Malbin, the scholar, contends that the 1970s were the heyday of staff activism because many new government programs were being generated, whereas more recent budget cutbacks have curbed legislative entrepreneurship. But I believe that social issues, foreign policy, defense, tax legislation, and congressional oversight have left ample room for aggressive staffers, even without new programs. In my experience, staff rivalries are rampant in Congress, as in the executive branch. Staffers often generate battles for visibility, turf, agenda, and political credit on Capitol Hill.

For example, when the nuclear accident occurred at Three-Mile Island, Pennsylvania, in March 1979, a dozen congressional committees and subcommittees scurried to claim jurisdiction over that hot item, angling to hold hearings, write reports, draft legislation. But Senator Edward Kennedy, who then deployed the largest staff network on Capitol Hill—120 strong, working for him on three different committees—got the jump. His legions scored a publicity coup by being the first to organize a hearing on the accident.

In the mid-eighties, John Dingell of Michigan, chairman of the House Energy and Commerce Committee, exerted great power not only because of his personal force and position, but also because of his aggressive staff. Pete Stockton, a bird-dog congressional investigator, repeatedly helped Dingell get the press limelight for hearings on the questionable practices of defense contractors such as General Dynamics or lobbyists such as Michael Deaver. Not only did Stockton cross oceans to smoke out boondoggles and scandals but he pump-primed media coverage by leaking juicy tidbits to selected reporters just before scheduled hearings, generating extra publicity for his boss.

Stockton's activism and Dingell's own bulldog style gave the Michigan Democrat visibility and added to his political turf. It enabled him to rampage into the military-affairs terrain of the Armed Services Committee. For protecting and expanding turf is a vital function of legislative staffs. They know that gaining jurisdiction over the most controversial and important issues is central to the power game in Congress, for despite the established committee structure, jurisdictions overlap, and lines of authority are often unclear. So staffers elbow, scrap, and scramble to extend the political empires of their bosses and to build up their own importance.

One of the most stunning and crucial turf maneuvers in the Reagan presidency was engineered by Steve Bell, staff director of the Senate Budget Committee. It enabled Senator Pete Domenici, the Budget Committee chairman, to gain long-term control over congressional handling of the Reagan economic program, against rival efforts by Mark Hatfield, Senate Appropriations Committee chairman, and Bob Dole, Finance Committee chairman. The decisive gambit was an idea for which David Stockman, Reagan's budget director, was widely credited with devising; Stockman told me that it was actually Bell's brainchild.[18]

Bell, a brash, intense, hard-charging former reporter for the El Paso

Times and an English-literature major who learned budget economics from legislative economists, epitomizes the modern staff chief. He came out of New Mexico as part of Domenici's inner political family, a strategist in all of Domenici's campaigns, starting in 1972. Domenici and Bell are think-alike Republican conservatives with a passion for budget balancing and the same blunt-spoken drive to confront deficit spenders, whether liberal Democrats or the Reagan Pentagon. Bell, a muscular blond in his early forties, can enthrall or intimidate other staffers with theatrical outbursts and profanity, but shift quickly to "yessir" for senators. He possesses the crucial talents of the best staffers: technical mastery of legislation, political savvy, and a close, personal relationship with his boss.

"No one ever thought he would become a numbers man because he's a journalist, but he's as bright as could be," Domenici told me. "He's also a great writer, a great user of words. And to say he's politically astute is an understatement. Obviously, he has an instant fix on my state, but he understands the politics of the U.S. Senate, the politics of the Senate versus the presidency. We shared the leadership role there. . . . He and I together just pushed stuff down their [other senators'] throats and rolled them over and did a lot of partisan stuff where they had to go along."[19]

In late 1980, Bell, as Budget Committee staff chief, came up with a parliamentary technique that helped pass Reagan's economic program; it also gave Domenici's Budget Committee preeminent legislative control of the Reagan program. Bell's notion—quickly bought by Majority Leader Howard Baker and by Budget Director Stockman—was to employ a rarely used maneuver known as budget reconciliation. It was ideal for ramming Reagan's budget cuts through Congress in one package.

Normally, Congress passes thirteen separate appropriations bills without a central blueprint. A reconciliation bill would provide the blueprint; it would require a single up-or-down vote on the whole Reagan budget, and then its provisions would dictate that other committees bring the cost of their programs in line. It was written into law in 1974, and rarely used because established committee chairmen disliked the budget committee butting into their business. Reconciliation was designed to come at the end of the budget process, after the competing committees failed to agree. But Bell proposed using it at the start of the budget process to discipline all committees at once. Democrats howled that this was railroading the budget. But it pleased Republicans, in their early pro-Reagan enthusiasm. This strategy made

Domenici a preeminent figure. And it was crucial to Reagan's first-year success—a dramatic illustration of how a staff man's understanding of procedure critically affected major national policy. On his wall, Bell has letters of thanks from both President Reagan and Howard Baker.

In this case, Bell was implementing Reagan's and Domenici's agenda. But in other cases, staff aides have initiated policy agendas for their bosses. In 1977, staff aides, for example, were the catalysts for the Republican Kemp-Roth proposal to cut marginal tax rates by thirty percent, which later became the nucleus of President Reagan's 1981 tax bill. The initial sponsors were Representative Jack Kemp and Senator William Roth of Delaware, both of whom favored sharp cuts in tax rates. Kemp became the plan's prime public salesman, but its real architects were Paul Craig Roberts, a supply-side economist close to Kemp and then serving on the House Budget Committee staff; Bruce Bartlett, a Kemp staffer; and Bruce Thompson, an aide to Roth.[20]

In a different field—Soviet violations of arms agreements—David Sullivan, a burly, crewcut ex-Marine and former Central Intelligence Agency analyst, was the force behind a relentless campaign by Idaho's two conservative Republican senators, Jim McClure and Steven Symms, for whom Sullivan served as a staffer. Often working with highly classified information slipped to him by friends inside the government or planted in friendly newspapers, Sullivan ghostwrote speeches and letters of protest urging Reagan to revoke the 1972 and 1979 Strategic Arms Limitation Treaties. Senate pressures, stimulated by Sullivan, helped push Reagan to adopt this policy. On the other side, Leon Fuerth, a quiet, pipe-smoking, high-powered specialist on arms control, spent a year teaching then–Democratic Congressman, now-Senator Albert Gore the intracies of the nuclear-arms race. Then he helped Gore formulate the rationale for a new single-warhead missile to reduce the doomsday threat of multiwarhead missiles. Gore and others sold that idea to Reagan in 1983.

In none of these cases were the senators or congressmen unwitting dupes. They wanted to move in the direction the staff was pushing. But sometimes staffers steal the ball on policy, and members complain of being at the mercy of staffs, often forced to fight fires started by overly aggressive staff aides.

"There are many senators who feel that all they were doing is running around and responding to the staff: my staff fighting your staff, your staff competing with mine," Senator Fritz Hollings, a South Carolina Democrat, bleated in protest.[21] "It is sad. I heard a senator the other day tell me another senator hadn't been in his office for three years; it is just staff. Everybody is working for the staff, staff, staff, driving you nutty, in fact. It has gotten to the point where the senators never actually sit down and exchange ideas and learn from the experience of others and listen. Now it is how many nutty whiz kids you get on the staff, to get you magazine articles and get you headlines and get all of these other things done."

Bird-dogging the Executive Branch

Yet whatever the complaints, no one in Congress is prepared to give up any staff. All too clearly, members of Congress understand that staff is essential for competing with each other and especially for confronting the executive branch. Normally, when this confrontation occurs, staff and members work hand in hand with the congressional member leading the way—but not always. Some exceptional staffers are outchallenging the executive branch, bird-dogging it more aggressively than members. In other cases, congressional staff agencies operate almost as a third force, as referees between Congress and the White House.

For example, the Congressional Budget Office (CBO), set up in 1974, technically has no power; it passes no legislation. Unlike committee staffs, it cannot actually supervise the promoting, revising, or funding of programs. Its power derives purely from the intangible elements of information and credibility. Yet the CBO represents the most important institutional shift of power on domestic issues between the executive branch and Congress in several decades.

Before the CBO was created, the president's budget was, as scholar Hugh Heclo put it, "the only game in town for taking a comprehensive look" at government. The presidency, through the Council of Economic Advisers and the Office of Management and Budget (OMB), had a monopoly on the government's economic forecasting. Congress, like the president, used CEA and OMB forecasts of economic growth, inflation, and budget deficits.

Now, CBO gives Congress an independent perspective on those crucial matters, setting the framework of policy debate. CBO's deficit forecasts can differ from the administration's by $30 billion to $40 billion and that influence has a major impact on a whole session of Congress, because Congress is forced to cut more or mat cut less than the president proposed. In the Reagan years, CBO's capabilities enabled Congress largely to ignore Reagan budgets after 1981 and to develop its own budgets—something inconceivable without CBO.

By December 1985, when Congress passed the six-year deficit-reduction plan (the Gramm-Rudman bill) CBO was put on the political hot seat. To protect itself from politically tilted administration estimates, Congress gave CBO joint responsibility with the administration's OMB to set deficit estimates that would trigger automatic cutting of government programs, if the deficit targets were not met. Having that much political responsibility troubled Rudolph Penner, a Republican economist who was then head of CBO.

"It's hard to think of other instances where unelected officials have such power to do good or evil," said Penner, a bland, balding technocrat. He warned Congress that "substantial errors are possible" in economic forecasting and alerted it to the "disadvantages of conveying so much power to mere technicians."[22] But Congress had more faith in CBO than in OMB and put Penner in the middle.

In early 1986, Rudy Penner got caught in political crossfire. Pete Domenici, the Budget Committee chairman, was angry at Penner for making relatively optimistic forecasts on the economy and the deficit. House Democrats were happy with Penner's optimism because that meant less pressure to cut programs. Domenici likes to use gloomy forecasts to impose discipline on Congress to cut programs, and he felt Penner's estimates were undermining his strategy. As it turned out, the economy worsened, and the deficit estimates rose naturally, pleasing Domenici without forcing Penner to give in.

Penner had even sharper clashes with the Reagan administration on defense spending in the 1987 budget. Penner said the administration had understated the Pentagon's actual spending by $14.7 billion. (Administration figures, I was reliably told, were dictated by Weinberger rather than being economically calculated by Budget Director Miller.) Realizing that Penner's numbers would incite Congress to cut more from defense, the administration attacked Penner, and so did Senator Ted Stevens of Alaska, the hawkish chairman of the Defense Appropriations Subcommittee. At a hearing in July, Stevens raged at Penner, threatening to cut CBO's own budget if Penner did not change his estimate on the Pentagon. "That really rocks this defense bill," Stevens bellowed at Penner. "I am going to cut your money. You cannot put me in this position."[23] But Penner stood his ground. Later, the administration had to change its numbers, tacitly acknowledging that CBO had been right.

The CBO is a special example of congressional staff power. Its estimates are required by law, and that forces its opinions into full view. CBO cannot escape a high profile. But normally, success in the staff power game against the executive branch dictates a low profile. If information is power, anonymity is protection. The basic technique for staffers is to develop substantive mastery, to work contracts inside the administration, to feed critical information to key legislators, and then let them take the heat and get the publicity for battling the White House or the Pentagon. Only a few staffers voluntarily go against the grain and play risky, high-visibility tactics.

One of the most powerful in recent years is a blunt-talking weapons expert named Tony Battista, who struck me initially as a white-collar Fonzie (the TV sitcom character), with his jaunty, high-wave hairstyle and the accent of a Staten Island tough. A youthful-looking fifty, Battista looks as if he belongs in a garage, with his head popping out from under a car hood or wiping grease off his hands. That is where he would usually rather be, for Battista is an antique car buff who spends his weekends restoring such prestige models as a Bentley, a Lotus, and several, old Cadillacs, when he is not working overtime for the Research and Development (R and D) Subcommittee of the House Armed Services Committee. His engineering skills are definitely hands on. One of his frequent reactions to outrageous military parts prices is to tell the Pentagon, "I could make it for a fraction of that in my own garage." More than once, he has actually done so. Battista was trained as an engineer, worked a couple of years for the space agency and nine more at the Naval Surface Weapons Center before becoming a congressional staffer in 1974.

Battista may be unknown to the public, but he is respected and feared by Pentagon officials and defense contractors. "Tony's got a lot of power and he uses it," said Dave McCurdy, a rising Democratic star on defense issues.[24] Defense lobbyists say he is as powerful as a subcommittee chairman because his technical expertise, hard work, and tenacity carry the day nine times out of ten with committee members. "If Tony wants a certain program to succeed in his committee, chances are it will, and if he wants it not to succeed, chances are it won't," one defense lobbyist told me. Another bluntly told Richard Halloran of *The New York Times:* "If he's against you, you're in trouble. He'll fight a bear with a buggy whip."[25] Having Battista on your side, added Tom Downey, a liberal New York Democrat, "is like the old days when you got into a fight—you took the toughest guy in town with you."

Knowing Battista's clout but attacking his effort to cut spending on Star Wars space defense in 1985, a *Wall Street Journal* editorial blasted Battista as "an antidefense staffer" with "a line-item veto." (Pentagon budgets, like all others, come with each program or weapons procurement item as an entry on a single line, hence the term *line item*. The

Pentagon's research and development budget is broken down into some eight hundred line items, embracing 3,400 projects. A real "line-item veto" would give Battista the ability to kill some of those individual items. It is a significant power, one that Congress has refused to give to Reagan. The *Journal* meant that Battista had that kind of power in practice, not in law.)

To call Battista antidefense is inaccurate. Congressional hawks on defense such as Samuel Stratton, a New York Democrat, or Bob Dornan, a hard right California Republican, praise Battista's commitment to defense. Battista has backed the MX missile and favored research on space-based defenses, though he is sharply critical of portions of Reagan's program, which he insists were junked as unworkable or ridiculously expensive before Reagan enshrined SDI in 1983. During the Carter years, Battista quietly helped save research-and-development funding for the B-1 bomber. "Members trust him, both sides of the aisle," Dornan told me. "When he sinks his teeth into something, you know you're going to get a fair bipartisan assessment. He's got an excellent scientific grasp of all the R and D stuff. Tony alone, I believe, prevented the junking of the B-1 R and D program. I think SAC ought to name one plane *The Battista*."[26] Significantly, one defense contractor whose firm has large business with all three military services told me: "Battista's not in anyone's pocket. If you disagree with him, you'd better reexamine your position, because he's very smart and he does not take his position without good reasons."

In person, Battista is friendly, outgoing, almost casual, not pugnacious—but sure of himself in all things technical. He is good at reading the mood of Congress, and for a Congress that has grown skeptical of Pentagon procurement practices, he is ideal. He believes in both strong defense and efficient spending of tax dollars. At hearings, he grills generals mercilessly, more like a senior member of Congress than a staff aide. He will challenge an administration weapons system and get his subcommittee chairman to invite a bevy of top Pentagon brass to come debate him. In one hearing during the Carter years, Battista went toe-to-toe with Deputy Defense Secretary Graham Claytor, Defense Undersecretary William Perry, General P. X. Kelley, then chief of the Readiness Command, and two other generals, and he carried the day. The subcommittee bought his recommendation to kill funding for research on a new cargo plane. In the Reagan years, he challenged Donald Hicks, once Pentagon research-and-development chief, on three issues: the Star Wars space defense program, a new single-warhead mobile missile, and research into hardening concrete silos around

American ICBMs. Hicks went away bristling; Battista was unperturbed, and the committee took his advice on all three issues. Later, with committee support, Battista forced the Navy to drop a duplicate radio communications system and use a similar system being developed by the Air Force, a move that saved taxpayers several hundred million dollars.

"I'll debate anybody at the witness table," Battista told me. "I could be wrong. I have been wrong because I didn't have all the data and the facts on a few occasions. If I'd never been wrong, I haven't been doing my job. I'm not so pompous and cavalier to sit there and say I've never been wrong."

What grates the Pentagon, some contractors, and quite a few House members is that Battista presses his favorites quite openly, such as fiber-optics guided missiles and other high technology. He is a tireless foe of duplication and wasteful rivalry among the services. He insists that new weapons be run through combat-realistic tests. Experience makes him especially valuable to Congress. He has been around long enough to know which contractors are good during the research phase but inefficient on production. He has a keen sense of smell when things are going wrong. He is a bird dog. With the help of longtime contacts inside the Pentagon, he sniffs out weapons systems headed for trouble and huge cost overruns. And he barks very publicly.

Another thing that makes Battista so effective is thorough homework: ferreting out phony Pentagon reports and faulty weapons. Several years ago, for example, the Air Force had contracted with Hughes Aircraft for an air-to-surface missile called the Maverick. It was supposed to be a long-range tank killer using an infrared heat seeker to find the tanks. When an Air Force colonel told Battista that it could lock onto tanks at nearly thirteen miles (65,000 feet slant range, in technical jargon), Battista became suspicious. When the colonel threw technical jargon at Battista, he threw it right back. Their conversation, he recalled, went this way:

" 'Hold on, hold on,' I said. 'What's the minimum resolution of that seeker?' And he told me. And I said, 'What's the minimum resolvable temperature?' And I went through a list of parameters with him and I said, 'Well, I'll tell you what. I don't have a computer here, but I just did a rough calculation in my head and, Colonel, that's pure bullshit.' And he said, 'Oh, no, no, no. I've got it here on tape.' And I said, 'I don't care what you've got on that tape.' So he proceeded to show me this tape, and I said I didn't believe it. So the Air Force said, 'What will it take to make you a believer?' And I said, 'Let's go fly.'

"I hate to fly," Battista confessed to me. "I'm a white-knuckle flyer. So they stuck me in the back seat of an F-4 with a [Maverick] seeker on it. We went out looking for tanks. Only I did something that I didn't give them any advance warning of. I set up a bunch of little charcoal fires out there to simulate thermal clutter."[27]

Translated, that means that Battista took steps to make sure that the Maverick test was realistic. A normal battlefield has many things that generate heat, in addition to tanks; that is known as thermal clutter. Battista figured—quite correctly—that the Air Force had a clear, sandy test range with only one or two tanks, easy conditions for the Maverick heat seeker to find its target—no clutter. So Battista had a colleague, Tom Hahn, set charcoal fires out around the test range to simulate the normal thermal clutter of a battlefield.

"We had a lot of hot spots out there," Battista recalled with a grin. "So I said to the pilot, 'Okay, point me to the tank.' And when we came buzzing in, he found the tank. But at a very small fraction of sixty-five thousand feet slant range. He found the tank when he was practically inside the gun barrel." In short, the heat seeker had been confused by decoy fires and had to get so close to find the tank that the tank would have destroyed the fighter plane before it could have fired its Maverick-guided missile. When Battista reported that to his subcommittee, it slowed approval of the Maverick program.

About a year later, some Air Force brass brought in videotapes of planes using the Maverick system. The film seemed pretty impressive until Battista, tipped off by a Pentagon mole, told Representative Tom Downey, "Make 'em play the sound track." When Downey made the request, the Air Force generals got flustered. "They're hiding something," Downey charged. Finally the sound track was played.

"The reason they didn't want to play the sound was because it was hard to make out what was being destroyed," Downey recalled. "In a couple of instances they were blowing up burning bushes and trucks instead of tanks. You could tell from the sound track because you had the pilots talking to one another, saying such things as, 'Holy shit, you just blew up a truck!' One guy was very clever. In the tape he was talking about blowing up burning bushes, and he was glad he wasn't there in Moses' time, because he would have been responsible for killing God."[28]

Again, Battista's bird-dogging slowed the Maverick program and forced improvements. Battista later lamented, however, that the program was eventually pushed through by heavy lobbying on the Senate side. Battista had bird-dogged a wounded bird, but the political hunters did not choose to kill the program.

"Big constituency," Battista explained. "Program worth several billion dollars. It's a production item now."

Battista defies other axioms of the staff game. One such axiom claims that staff directors gain clout from powerful committee chairmen. Battista is an exception. He has been powerful for years, but never more powerful than when the R and D Subcommittee was chaired by Mel Price, a feeble, almost absentee boss in his late seventies. Battista stepped into the vacuum. "Tony runs that subcommittee; there's no question about that," veteran New York Democrat Samuel Stratton declared with gruff respect.[29]

Battista also leads with his chin, colliding with senior congressmen such as Stratton. Once he stormed into a hearing of the R and D Subcommittee to protest that Battista was invading the turf of Stratton's Procurement Subcommittee by investigating the Army's Bradley Fighting Vehicle. Since the Bradley was already being bought (procured, in Pentagon jargon), Stratton considered it his worry, not Battista's. But Battista was not intimidated; he insisted the R and D Subcommittee was investigating how the Bradley was tested. Stratton furiously stalked out.

More broadly, Battista has for years virtually set the R and D Subcommittee's agenda with his personal report to the subcommittee on the Pentagon's R and D budget. Normally, the weapons that he says are in trouble get close scrutiny, ones he says are okay pass easily. In 1985, Battista recommended killing twenty-two proposed weapons systems, and the House Armed Services Committee went along on every item, though in conference with the Senate, it backed down on most— but not before imposing restrictions urged by Battista.

Pentagon officials bristle over what they consider Battista's micromanagement of their programs. "What I object to is that Battista runs his own empire," one thirty-year Pentagon official turned lobbyist angrily told me. "He's like his own Department of Defense without accountability. Thousands of people put the defense budget together, generals and civilians. It's a consensus opinion. So it's sent up there, and here's one guy, Tony Battista, who hasn't been elected, who doesn't have anyone to answer to except the members, and he sits down and says, 'I don't like the way they're doing it.' In a few months, this one guy changes hundreds of things that thousands of people have worked on for a year. Mind you, he may be right on some items. He's intelligent. He's able. But it's not the right way to run a railroad."

But in Congress, some members compare Battista to Ken Dryden, the legendary ice hockey goal tender of the Montreal Canadiens; Battista does not let the Pentagon get things past him. "Day in and day out, Battista's the most honest, most knowledgeable staff guy around, and he's not afraid to jam some general," commented Thomas Downey, a Long Island Democrat.[30] "In the Pentagon, officers get rotated in and out of these jobs as often as the Yankees change relief pitchers. That always gave Battista an enormous competitive advantage. I mean, he's a hawk on defense. No two ways about it. But, he doesn't play favorites. He goes after people who he knows are notoriously ripping off the government."

Reagan's "Staff Presidency"

Just as the power of congressional staff has grown overall in the 1970s and 1980s, so has the force and authority of the White House staff—rising even more steeply. But there is an important difference: In Congress, staff power has sprawled and spread into many more hands; the opposite trend has taken place at the White House. The human apparatus of the Executive Office of the President has gained size and muscle since the 1960s, a symbol of more centralized power within the executive branch. And staff power has become more concentrated near the apex: the chief of staff, national security adviser, budget director, and one or two other aides, depending on the style of each president.

The common thread between the White House and Capitol Hill is that the shadow government of staff has gained power at the expense of those formally and publicly assumed to exercise power: Congress and the cabinet.

Never was White House staff power more dramatically demonstrated than in Ronald Reagan's disastrous Iranian hostage operation. That policy was devised, promoted, and protected by successive national security advisers Robert McFarlane and Rear Admiral John Poindexter and run by their staff aide, Lieutenant Colonel Oliver North—despite the objections of the senior cabinet figures, Secretary of State George Shultz, and Defense Secretary Caspar Weinberger. In particular, Poindexter and North skirted chains of command in other agencies, keeping the very top level officials in the dark. Poindexter even usurped the president's power by deciding to divert profits from the Iranian arms sales to the Nicaraguan *contras*. He carried staff power to excess, but Reagan's style of delegating power and his lack of interest in all but the broad sweep of policy invited bold action by his staff.

One of the hollow rituals of American political life is the periodic extolling of cabinet government by presidential candidates and presidents-elect. They love to proclaim their intention to restore collegial rule at the cabinet table. The myth is that cabinet secretaries run the government with the White House staff in the shadows. That is far from reality, but somehow new presidents, especially those who come from state governments, are innocents about this.

In August 1976, I visited Jimmy Carter at his home in Plains, Georgia, just after he had won the Democratic presidential nomination. Quite deliberately, Carter wanted to strike a contrast with the arrogant "palace guard" of Nixon's White House staff. He told me over mint-flavored iced tea that he would have no chief of staff, would institute genuine cabinet government, and that he was even considering a parliamentary "question time," where his Cabinet members would appear before the houses of Congress to answer questions.[31] Those ideas all fell victim to reality, without much serious attempt to apply them.

Four years later, during a campaign flight from St. Petersburg, Florida, to Columbia, South Carolina, I squeezed into an airline seat beside candidate Ronald Reagan, who explained how his administration would achieve true cabinet government, modeled after his governorship of California.[32] Indeed, Edmond Meese, who had run Governor Reagan's California staff and became presidential counselor in Reagan's White House, did set up an intricate structure of cabinet councils. But more significantly, Reagan quickly established one of the most powerful and effective White House staffs of the modern presidency under Meese and Chief of Staff James Baker III. Reagan delegated enormous authority to that staff.

In his first year as President, Reagan used the cabinet councils to "roundtable" issues, in one of Meese's pet phrases (shorthand for discussing it around the table). But pretty soon it was apparent that those councils were more a vehicle for White House control of the cabinet than a forum where the president hammered out policy decisions. As former Secretary of State Alexander Haig complained to me, White House staff members managed the council agendas. Ultimately, Reagan got a reputation for taking little snoozes in cabinet meetings. When the press found out, Reagan turned it into a joke. I remember his quipping at one press banquet that he did not have to worry about his place in history because it was already secure. "I can see it now," he said. "A plaque behind my chair in the Cabinet Room: RONALD REAGAN SLEPT HERE."

Reagan's practice, his intimates reported, was to thrash out his key decisions during small skull sessions with his first-term White House troika: Baker, Meese, and Reagan's close confidant, Michael Deaver, who was deputy chief of staff. One or two other key officials might be there, too—people such as David Stockman, director of the Office of Management and Budget; two less well known but very important aides, Richard Darman (Baker's deputy), and Craig Fuller (Meese's deputy). On foreign policy matters, National Security Adviser William P. Clark and his successor, Robert McFarlane, were often participants. Oval Office sessions were usually grouped around the president's desk or with Reagan sitting in a high-backed wing chair near the fireplace and the others in two facing couches. To me, Darman's version of those sessions was very revealing.

"It was a seven-vote presidency, with the president having four votes and Meese, Baker, and Deaver each having one vote," Darman told me. "Reagan was very reluctant to make a decision when Baker and Meese were divided. He didn't like casting the deciding vote between the two of them. To help them resolve the conflict, they'd call in the others. The rest of us did not have a vote. We were there as friends of the court, to provide information."[33]

In the first formative months in 1981, the headlines went to the president, Secretary Haig, and Stockman. But Meese, Baker, and Deaver—who became known as Reagan's troika—were the nerve center of the administration, orchestrating the Reagan presidency. They guided the new cabinet and the entire Reagan entourage, sifting all key appointments, setting the agenda and the priorities, formulating strategy and establishing links with Congress, helping the president set the tone for his stewardship. Baker and Meese took the substantive lead, and in that sphere Deaver was not their equal. But Deaver was the best at reading Reagan's moods, delivering bad news, staging him in public, or privately coaxing him into or out of some action the others thought wise or unwise.

The staff's power was clearly illustrated on March 30, 1981, the day Reagan was shot. The troika set up a command post at George Washington University Hospital. Deaver, who was emotionally closer to Reagan than anyone else, was at his side, catching the president's jokes, watching him scrawl wobbly notes, including one that asked murkily: "Am I dead?" Baker and Meese (with advice from Deaver) were the ones who decided—not the cabinet or the vice president—that Reagan's bullet wound and two hours of surgery did not require invoking the Twenty-fifth Amendment to the Constitution, which would have permitted naming Bush acting president until Reagan regained consciousness and strength. When documents for invoking the amendment appeared at a rump cabinet session in the White House Situation Room, another high staffer, Richard Darman, hustled them off the table and into a safe.[34]

In Reagan's second term, the main levers of White House power were largely taken over by one figure, Chief of Staff Donald T. Regan. Not only did Regan control the White House machinery, but he was also invariably a participant in the tight little meetings where key decisions were set, and which usually included Vice President Bush, sometimes the most important cabinet secretaries, or National Security Adviser Robert McFarlane and his successor, Vice Admiral John Poindexter.

When the president had surgery in 1985 for a cancerous polyp, Donald Regan (at the urging of Nancy Reagan, who did not want her bedridden husband disturbed) told Bush he could not see the president for several days and advised him to stay away in Maine on vacation—advice that Bush ignored. This pattern of staff supremacy was so pronounced that Lee Iacocca, the outspoken Chrysler chairman, protested that "Don Regan is the most powerful man in this country, and none of us ever had a chance to vote on it." That was an exaggeration, but Iacocca caught the drift.

The Reagan presidency has probably been simultaneously the most centralized and staff-dominated presidency in history. The broad vision was limned by Reagan; and the second-term Cabinet had more power than the first. But overall, the Reagan presidency could be called a staff presidency because Reagan gave so much authority and latitude to his senior staff aides. Budget strategy was the province of Baker and David Stockman in the first term, taken over by Donald Regan in the second term. To get around Congress and sidestep dissent in the cabinet, the national security staff became Reagan's agents for the Iranian arms caper and for funding and arming the Nicaraguan *contras*. Where there were political obstacles, Reagan bypassed them by using his staff and then claimed they were immune from the laws of Congress, as he claimed he was. That massive assumption of staff power, not accountable to Congress, provoked an uproar on Capitol Hill. Congress saw the president using his staff to avoid the checks and balances of the Constitution.

The stunning power of the White House staff, quite obviously, was not all of Reagan's making. It reflects a long-term trend, though Reagan carried it further than his predecessors. Sherman Adams, chief of staff to Dwight Eisenhower, was widely regarded as deputy president after Ike's heart attack in September 1955. Richard Nixon was largely isolated behind his "palace guard" (John Haldeman, John Ehrlichman) on whom he depended heavily.

Back in the 1920s, presidents had little more than executive assistants and personal service aides, and they looked to cabinet officers for policy advice. Then Franklin Roosevelt used the budget bureau to put a presidential stamp on the sprawling federal establishment—and the modern, centralized apparatus of the White House began to take shape.

Since FDR's death, "the presidency has been bureaucratized," as Stephen Hess of the Brookings Institution observed.[35] Over time, the presidential superstructure came to embrace the Council of Economic Advisers, the National Security Council, the President's Special Trade Representative, the Council on Environmental Quality, the Office of Science and Technology Policy, and other offices, all with sizable staffs. By 1987, the Executive Office of the President ran a budget of more than $114 million and a staff of more than sixteen hundred: 620 in the budget bureau alone and 325 in the White House proper.

But more significant than the prodigious growth of the apparatus is the way in which power relationships within the executive branch have changed. The more the public came to want an activist presidency, the more powers and functions the White House staff assumed. As modern presidents mistrusted the permanent civil service to carry out their policies, they added staff to develop the reach and expertise to impose presidential will on the parochial interests of the departments. In short, to fight the power of the permanent bureaucracy, presidents developed their own bureaucracy. As the lawyers expanded and the White House staff gained policy influence, the clout of the cabinet generally declined.

As far back as Roosevelt and Harry Truman, the policy lines between staff and cabinet began to blur. Later presidents have quite openly treated their staffs as policy advisers. In developing domestic policy, for example, Johnson, Nixon, and Carter looked to their chief White House domestic aides—Joseph Califano, John Ehrlichman, and Stuart Eizenstat, respectively. On foreign policy, national security advisers—such as Henry Kissinger under Nixon, Zbigniew Brzezinski under Carter, and William Clark and Robert McFarlane under Reagan—have rivaled (and Kissinger overshadowed) the influence of principal cabinet secretaries.

Under Reagan, the budget bureau became the main instrument for bringing cabinet members to heel. With the budget-driving policy, Stockman was clearly more at the cutting edge of most policy decisions than any cabinet secretary except Caspar Weinberger at the Pentagon. The other cabinet members had to come to Stockman, Meese, and Baker, three staff aides acting as a court of appeals on budget disputes.

More broadly, the White House political and propaganda apparatus gained in size and importance under Reagan. Prior to the Eisenhower years, most presidents left legislative relations to the Cabinet departments. But Eisenhower began to draw that function into the White House, setting up a three-man congressional-liaison team. Kennedy and Johnson expanded that operation, and the Reagan team carried centralized control of congressional relations to new heights through a legislative strategy group run by Chief of Staff Baker.

In communications, Nixon was the first president to go beyond the traditional press-secretary operation, to set up a White House Office of Communications. In his second term, Nixon was moving to reach over the heads of the Washington press corps to the regional press, and to tighten White House control over press operations throughout the executive branch. But Watergate stopped that. The Reagan team, which tapped both David Gergen and Pat Buchanan from the old Nixon White House, picked up where Nixon's operation left off, adding to the central machinery.

But it was in the realm of political appointments that the Reagan White House penetrated most deeply into the province of cabinet secretaries. Presidents such as Nixon, Ford, and Carter had a process for reviewing high-level political appointments, but in practice left much discretion to cabinet secretaries in filling subcabinet positions. The Reagan White House aggressively centralized the appointment process. It insisted on the litmus of Reaganite conservative ideology, pushed names from Reagan's conservative movement onto cabinet secretaries, and required White House political screening of all appointees. Out of roughly three thousand high-level presidential appointments, earlier administrations were content to review about one tenth; the Reagan team reviewed and approved the full slate, often causing long delays that left agencies decapitated and thus even more susceptible to White House control. In the first couple of years, the Meese-Baker-Deaver trio and Pendleton James, Meese's personnel deputy, spent thousands of hours handpicking undersecretaries and assistant secretaries. In the process they provided the White House with a political network for monitoring and managing the executive branch.

"They appointed people (to cabinet departments) who would cut their boss's throat to please the president," commented Paul Light, a political scientist at the National Academy of Public Administration. "They are an entirely different breed of appointee than in the Carter, Nixon, Ford administrations. They are ideologically committed. There is no allegiance to the department, but to the Oval Office or the conservative cause. No administration has penetrated so deeply."[36]

The Staff's Power of Proximity

In any administration, the power of the White House staff stems from personal links to the president: trust, proximity, and seeing the world from his personal perspective. Trust usually develops from long, loyal association, especially in the victorious campaign, and well before most cabinet officers get to know the president. The proximity of close day-in, day-out contact with the president reinforces the political intimacy of staff with president. The White House staff's leverage derives from control of the most rudimentary elements of the president's life: whom he sees, what he reads, what business and what events are worth his time, when he will give speeches and what he will say, what will be said in his name by his press spokesman, and what messages conveyed by his staff to his cabinet and congressional allies.

As former Secretary of State Haig observed somewhat ruefully in his memoir, *Caveat*, "There are three main levers of power in the White House, the flow of paper, the President's schedule, and the press."[37] Those vital elements are controlled by the people who are physically closest to him, who sit outside his door or beside him at meetings, who hand him papers and who can pop into his office at any time. So preoccupied were Meese, Baker, and Deaver with being close to Reagan in their early months that one other senior White House aide said "they went wherever the president went. They weren't in their offices. They trailed around with the president." With a president as dependent on others for the substance of policy as Reagan has been, proximity gives these people enormous power. A cabinet secretary needs their help just to get into the Oval Office. Essentially, no memo, no policy recommendation, no political appeal could reach Reagan, or any president, without staff approval.

In short, a president's immediate entourage sets his agenda—obviously subject to his disapproval. In Reagan's first term, Baker and his deputy, Richard Darman, kept deflecting action on proposals for abolishing the Energy and Education departments, despite Reagan's campaign promises to do that. They steered Reagan to focus on the economy. In those early months, Baker and Meese also relegated to the back burners the social agenda of the New Right and Haig's thrusts toward Central America. For Baker and Deaver, this approach suited both political priorities and their personal philosophies; Meese accepted the economic priority, though he did not share the others' moderate views. By the 1984 election year, Baker and Deaver encouraged Reagan to visit China and to drop his "evil empire" rhetoric toward Moscow.

In Reagan's second term, Donald Regan kept off Reagan's desk a cabinet dispute over whether to do away with the government's affirmative-action guidelines, as advocated by Edmund Meese, who was now in the cabinet as attorney general. Without Reagan's talking seriously with Shultz or Weinberger, Donald Regan persuaded the president in 1985 to support the Gramm-Rudman deficit-reduction law, although it had major impact on the Pentagon and foreign aid. A year later, at the urging of Senate Majority Leader Robert Dole, Donald Regan got the president to endorse new subsidies for foreign wheat sales, even though cheaper wheat for Moscow was vigorously opposed by Shultz, Weinberger, and William Casey, the CIA director. Regan, McFarlane, and Poindexter, this time with support from Casey, sold the president on making arms sales to Iran over the objections of Shultz and Weinberger. Repeatedly, the influence of top staff prevailed.

This is not to say that Ronald Reagan has simply been a puppet of his staff or that his staff has had a power monopoly. Time and again, Reagan demonstrated that on a handful of fundamental issues he has deep-seated beliefs and he calls his own tune—such as not raising taxes, going for a Star Wars defense, attending a summit meeting, pushing aid for Nicaraguan *contras,* or selling arms to Iran to free American hostages. A classic case was his stubborn refusal in 1982 and 1983 to trim back his Pentagon budget requests, despite intense urging from Stockman, Baker, and other staff aides—even Meese. In 1983 and afterward, Reagan suffered the consequences: Congress, frustrated by Reagan's and Weinberger's refusal to compromise, slashed his defense budgets.

Or for example, the night after he was shot in March 1981, Reagan sat in his hospital bed and wrote out by hand on a yellow legal pad an eight-page personal letter to then–Soviet leader Leonid Brezhnev. It was the heartfelt appeal of a man who had just escaped death. A few days later he shared it with his top staff, National Security Adviser Richard Allen and Secretary of State Haig. They met on the second floor of the White House mansion, Reagan in his pajamas. "Fellas, I wrote this, and I'd like you to look at it," he said. After another few days, Reagan's advisers offered a revised draft of the letter prepared by Haig and his State Department. It was watered down, much less personal, and written in bureacratic language.

"Wait a minute," objected Deaver, who was among the group talking with Reagan. "Nobody elected the experts. You're the president. The experts have been messing it up for years. If that's the way *you* want it to go, let it go."

Reagan thought a moment and, obviously pleased at Deaver's encouragement, decided to stick with his original letter. "Mike's right," he told Haig. "Let it go the way I wrote it."[38]

But aside from his own very broad ideas and within the framework that they set, Reagan has been legendary for bending to the advice of whichever person or group among his trusted advisers was the last to see him. This made it look as if Reagan was being tugged first this way and that way, as if no one was in charge. In his book *Caveat,* Haig angrily raised the telling complaint that while Reagan set the administration's general course, "the White House was as mysterious as a ghost ship; you heard the creak of the rigging and the groan of the timbers and sometimes even glimpsed the crew on deck. But which of the crew had the helm? Was it Meese, was it Baker, was it someone else? It was impossible to know for sure."[39] Such ghostly rule at the top puts a high premium on proximity and frequent access.

John Sears, Reagan's campaign manager in 1976 and for the start of the 1980 campaign, suggested to me that Reagan's willingness to place himself in the hands of his staff is the result of Reagan's training as an actor. He is used to having directors tell him what to do, choreograph his scenes, write his lines. To me, it is as if Reagan has two roles: One, as overall producer who announces his broad goals on budget, taxes, or Star Wars; and two, a role where he steps into his own production and becomes an actor taking cues from his staff.

Reagan has long understood his dependency on his staff and counted on his closest lieutenants to rein in some of his natural instincts to sound off on pet ideas even when they clash with policy. Right after signing the 1982 billion tax bill which increased taxes (mainly corporate taxes) by $100 billion over three years, the president darted off in the opposite direction. Like a mischievous boy, he knew his staff would chide him. "I know I'm going to kick myself for saying this," Reagan told a Boston audience, "but I'd really like to get rid of the corporate income tax."

Dick Darman, a member of Reagan's first-term inner circle, compared the president to a frisky colt. "The horse will kick, but he also wants somebody reining him in," Darman observed. "He knows his own tendencies, and he is in fact a more complicated person than people give him credit for. He still likes to be the boy, the adolescent, the rebel, the guy pressing the outer limits. But he also likes to get things done and recognizes the need to move in the main stream" even when that means having a pragmatic staff to check his ideological impulses.[40]

Periodically, however, Reagan would kick over the traces just to show that he was in charge. Michael Deaver, a constant companion during Reagan's two successful election campaigns and his first term, recalled an incident during the 1980 campaign when Reagan was being hammered by the press for rhetorical gaffes and inaccurate statements. Deaver pulled Reagan aside. "You've got to stay away from the press," he advised Reagan. "All they're going to do is jump on you for the stupid things you said yesterday or what they think are the stupid things you said yesterday." Reagan said nothing. But as they were walking back to his motorcade, Reagan suddenly jumped up on the running board of his car and for ten minutes answered questions from reporters. Then he got into his car.

Deaver piled in after Reagan and demanded rather hotly: "What was that all about? I thought we just discussed that and decided you were going to stay away from the press."

In a rare burst of temper, Reagan shot back: "If you're so damned smart, why aren't you the one running for president?"

Half an hour later back at their hotel, Reagan, who has trouble dealing with close personal emotions, tried to make amends by wordlessly offering Deaver a gold pen set someone had given him.[41]

Staff Rolling the Cabinet

What is astonishing is that people with long experience in the Washington power game somehow forget that the president's staff generally can overpower cabinet members, regardless of protocol or formal rank. There are exceptions, especially when a powerful staff aide moves into a cabinet post, thereby combining rank with close presidential ties: both Baker and Meese did this during Reagan's second term, and Caspar Weinberger did it throughout the Reagan presidency. But generally, confusion arises because cabinet members are given public prominence, treated as symbols of the president's delegated authority. They must go through the process of Senate confirmation, whereas

White House staff aides do not (perhaps they should). Cabinet members are the public spokesmen for policies, even when the main outlines were formulated largely in the White House. Cabinet rank connotes prestige and influence—and occasionally the power to match.[42] But the smartest Cabinet officers know that they cross the White House staff at their peril. For when it comes to infighting, the inner circle has clear advantage over the outer circle.

Nothing more graphically illustrates the relative power of cabinet and staff than who "rolls" whom. To roll someone is Washington tough talk for overturning them, toppling them, bringing them down, as a wrestler or a street mugger might.

When Jimmy Carter's presidency was going through a siege of instability in late 1979, Carter took the advice of his chief of staff, Hamilton Jordan, and other personal advisers including his pollster, Pat Caddell, and fired four cabinet secretaries: Michael Blumenthal at Treasury, Joseph Califano at Health, Education and Welfare, James Schlesinger at Energy, and Brock Adams at Transportation. It was an open secret that White House staff aides wanted to settle scores with all four, especially Califano and Blumenthal, who had crossed swords with them.

Personally, Ronald Reagan was exceedingly reluctant to fire a cabinet officer, and yet his staff prompted him to ease out a string of cabinet members or near-cabinet-level officers: James Watt, Anne Burford, Margaret Heckler, John Block, Raymond Donovan, Alexander Haig—usually to rid his presidency of political boils, but not always. In Reagan's second term, for example, there was no evidence that the president was personally dissatisfied with Margaret Heckler as secretary of Health and Human Services. Her undoing is a case study in the political power of the White House staff. Chief of Staff Donald Regan set out to fire her, and he succeeded because he had the power to move the president and to have his staff aides undercut her with derogatory leaks.

Since Heckler was not a first-rank cabinet secretary and not a hard-line Reaganite, I suppose it can be argued that her ouster does not prove the preeminence of the White House staff. But that disclaimer cannot be used with former Secretary of State Alexander Haig, whose crisp military bearing, toughness toward Moscow, and experience as the four-star American NATO commander and deputy to Henry Kissinger deeply impressed Reagan. If there was anyone who should have understood the power of the White House palace guard, it was Haig. He had not only worked for Kissinger in the White House, but had been chief of staff when the Nixon presidency was crumbling. From experience, he knew how those at the center could hold those in the wings at bay. He understood that the machinery of policy-making gave important leverage, and he got himself in trouble on day one of the Reagan presidency by reaching too brashly to master that machinery.

Haig had reason to assume that Reagan wanted him to be the "vicar" of foreign policy. Because of constant feuds in the Carter administration between Secretary of State Cyrus R. Vance and National Security Adviser Zbigniew Brzezinski, the Reaganites decided to downgrade the NSC position. Reagan had promised Haig there would be no repeat of the Carter problems. On foreign policy, he had said, "I'll look to you, Al," and Haig had read that as his mandate.[43] Beyond that, Haig—though not a first-rank geopolitical strategist—regarded himself as a worldly veteran, a sophisticate among neophytes. He had respect for Reagan's political instincts but felt the president needed tutoring on foreign policy. "The President is the ultimate university," he wrote in his memoir *Caveat*. But his lecturing the president and his aides on global diplomacy grated on the White House staff.

What set off alarm bells was Haig's attempted "power grab" on Inauguration Day 1981. While the president and his closest subordinates were still in the formal inaugural attire, Haig handed Meese—then the dominant White House aide—a twenty-page memorandum setting out Haig's charter for the State Department to dominate foreign policy-making. State was to chair the old interdepartmental groups (IGs) that develop foreign policy, with Haig at the apex and other agencies in subordinate positions. Haig had learned from Kissinger that "he who controls the key IGs, controls the flow of options to the President and, therefore, to a degree, controls policy."[44]

Moreover, Haig wanted to move control of crisis management—the handling of foreign emergencies—from the National Security Council staff to the State Department. To embody his mandate, Haig wanted Reagan's quick signature on his draft of National Security Decision Directive Number 1—NSDD-1.

One White House official protested to me that Haig was in such a hurry, "he didn't even give the president a chance to change his clothes." But the White House staff blocked him.

Both sides immediately sensed what Haig called a "struggle for primacy." Much later, Haig told me that he believed that Baker, Deaver, and perhaps Meese "had designs from day one on establishing White House staff supremacy over the cabinet." And the senior White House staff were stunned by Haig's boldness. "Have you ever seen such a power play?" Baker said incredulously to the others. "Haig wants everything beyond the water's edge."

In some alarm, another top aide told me, "Haig thinks he's president." Recalling Haig's brief presidential candidacy in 1980 and sensing Haig's long-term ambitions for the White House, the Reagan inner circle decided to check him at once. Baker advised Meese that no secretary of State had ever had as broad a mandate as Haig sought. Although Haig had worked out his memo with Richard Allen, the national security adviser, Meese told him it would have to be reviewed by other cabinet officers. Weeks passed. The proposal was watered down and not signed by Reagan for more than a year. An interim decision gave Haig some of what he wanted but also awarded Defense Secretary Caspar Weinberger and CIA Director William Casey interagency groups to chair.

The fuse of confrontation between Haig and Reagan's staff was lit when Meese and Baker persuaded Reagan to turn over crisis management to Vice President Bush—the only other senior official with extensive foreign policy experience. It had been Meese's idea, so as not to offend Haig by leaving crisis management with Richard Allen. But Haig hit the ceiling. When word of this plan broke in the morning press, Haig openly challenged the White House by declaring his dissatisfaction at a congressional hearing. The troika, meeting with the president, were infuriated at Haig for having "gone public." Meese pushed his own plan. Baker, alarmed by exposure of an open rift, urged Reagan: "Before this thing goes further, it's got to be nipped in the bud." Reagan, heeding their advice, called to tell Haig he was naming Bush. That night, March 24, 1981, barely two months into the term, Haig was at the brink of resigning. But he was dissuaded by Reagan's old friend, William Clark, then Haig's deputy.[45]

Barely a week later, Haig stirred another controversy after the assassination attempt against President Reagan. With Vice President Bush flying back to Washington from Texas, Haig rushed to the White House Press Room, where he went on live television and tried to reassure the nation by asserting that "as of now, I am in control here, in the White House, pending the return of the vice president." Haig's intention was to calm the public. But he misquoted the Constitution on his place in the political line of succession, and his tense, quavery delivery caused more criticism. This time, Baker and Meese came to his political rescue: They went on television and praised Haig, in a show of unity during the administration's hour of trial.

Haig remained in the Reagan cabinet for another fifteen months, contributing to foreign policy decisions, but also to acrimony and tension between cabinet and the White House. With some justice, Haig felt that Weinberger repeatedly poached on his diplomatic turf. He subsequently complained that Clark, who became national security adviser in early 1982, and Jeane Kirkpatrick, chief delegate to the United Nations, had outflanked his efforts to mediate the Falklands Islands War by making their own contacts with Argentina. Accompanying Reagan to Europe in mid-1982, Haig accused the White House staff of denying him proper protocol; he feuded repeatedly with Clark over what instructions to send to Kirkpatrick and how Washington should deal with Israel's invasion of Lebanon. He later accused Clark of picking a day when Haig was out of town to schedule a National Security Council meeting on sanctions against a Soviet natural gas pipeline in Europe. The pot boiled over. Clark could have saved Haig then, as he had before, but he privately remarked that he had "begun to wonder about the man's mental balance." And he joined the White House troika in advising President Reagan to replace Haig with the steadier, more solid George Shultz.

Haig's own account, in *Caveat*, makes the White House staff the villains of his downfall, and admits his surprising naïveté at how he was constantly damaged by press leaks. Underlining the most rudimentary element of White House staff power, Haig complained to me that the inner circle denied him sufficient access to the president, which had "mortally handicapped" him in advising Reagan. "During the transition from the election to the inauguration, I saw the president alone once!" he protested. "That's all. That began to worry me very, very much, early on."[46] It never got better he said; it was hard for him even to reach the president by telephone. But it was the campaign of press leaks, turned on when the White House staff was irked with him, that provoked Haig's greatest resentment.

"In the Reagan Administration, they [leaks] were not merely a problem, they were a way of life, and in the end I concluded that they were a way of governing," Haig wrote. "Leaks constituted policy; they were the authentic voice of government. It is not surprising that this should have been so. The President's closest aides were essentially public relations men. They were consummate professionals—*wizards* is not too strong a word. In my view they were the most skillful handlers of the press since the New Deal."[47]

Haig speaks with some justice. Richard Allen used to talk to reporters privately about Haig's "megalomania" and to suggest that Haig's triple bypass surgery had made his behavior "weird." Several White House officials spoke to reporters about his "mercurial, pugnacious, power-grabbing behavior" in ways bound to undercut him in print or on television. Haig's protests—that the White House was waging a "guerrilla campaign" against him—did no good with Reagan. For that made Haig seem more the odd man out, the truculent complainer who could not be a team player, and team play was valued by Reagan above all else. Haig's tormentors surely knew that by taunting him, by keeping the pot of controversy boiling, they were arranging Haig's undoing—a classic lesson in the power of the White House staff to roll the most senior member of the cabinet.

Five Keys to White House Power

The power struggles within the White House staff are fully as fierce, if not fiercer, than those against cabinet members. In the Reagan years, I think it is revealing that in this power game at the pinnacle, Jim Baker emerged as the master of the first-term troika. Baker's success provides insight both into how the inside game of staff power is played and into how government can be made to operate effectively. It offers lessons for those who sit in these same chairs in the years to come.

The chief of staff's post is arguably the most testing job in any administration—next to the president's. Cabinet secretaries have specific responsibilities, a fixed agenda, particular constituencies, certain committees in Congress to work with. The agenda of the chief of staff, like the president's stretches from wall to wall. He must deal with every faction, consider every major issue, and most important scan the horizon for trouble and protect the president, opposing other top officials in the president's interest, and yet not alienate them, shut them off, or intimidate them so that their views are not heard by the president.

"You have to be smart but you mustn't be intellectual because most areas where you make decisions have to be politically possible, not intellectually perfect," commented Michael Blumenthal, Carter's treasury secretary and a White House appointee in the Kennedy-Johnson years. "You must have enormous energy, work very hard, and jump around between twenty topics a day. You must be a very good pleader in small meetings—you're always in meetings with two to ten other people, all of whom are strong-willed and persuasive. You must know when to speak and when to shut up. You must have a sense of power and a sense of deviousness, a gut feel for when there is an opening and where do I get things done. You must be able to judge the personality of the President and to figure out what appeals to him. You have to have good political judgment and a strong sense of priority. You have to be very hard. There has to be a steely quality. You have to know how to use your elbows and be prepared to do the dirty work."[48]

Baker's success is a textbook case: He had many of those qualities and a commitment to making government work. Understanding how Baker came out on top is important because so many natural advantages lay with Meese: He was a Californian, a longtime Reagan lieutenant, a man of proven loyalty, with a network of Reaganite allies and a sure grasp of Reagan's political views. Meese was bright, hard-working, dedicated. He had joined Governor Reagan's staff in 1967 as legal affairs adviser, and then for six years had served as the governor's chief of staff. In Sacramento, he had been Reagan's right arm in helping keep order on the University of California campuses and Reagan's chief negotiator with the state Assembly in working out a welfare plan. Moreover, Meese and Reagan were kindred ideological spirits; he knew Reagan's themes so well that he could finish the new president's sentences without fear of misstatement. Though Meese was in his late forties and Reagan in his early seventies, they were temperamentally similar. "Each was an amiable loner, compulsively spreading good cheer, friendly to all but friend to very, very few," Laurence Barrett of *Time* magazine shrewdly observed.[49]

As the Reagan crowd took over Washington, Meese was Mr. Everything: campaign chief of staff, director of the transition, architect of the new cabinet-council system, administration spokesman, and interpreter of Reagan to the new cabinet and the Washington political community. Those with California experience, like Lou Cannon of *The Washington Post*, who had covered Reagan in Sacramento, identified Meese as the man to watch. Meese was the authoritative voice. In the early cabinet meetings, it was Meese who synthesized the arguments, prodded the discussion, or shelved matters for another day. Others in the Reagan entourage privately called him "deputy president" or "the prime minister."

Had Meese been shrewd in the ways of Washington, he would have sensed those titles were setting him up for a fall. But he did not. He let his aides play up his role and power. One of them advised me that "the way Reagan operates, you've got a lot of running room for Ed." Meese, with his good-natured, breathy chortle and his conservative Adam Smith ties, insisted he was not making policy, only implementing Reagan's desires. "I'm not an assistant president like Sherman Adams," he assured me. "It's that I know Ronald Reagan and where he wants to go."[50]

Jim Baker, on the other hand, was an interloper. Not only was he an Ivy League Texan (educated at Princeton and the Hill School), but he had been the nemesis of the Reaganites in 1976, when he managed President Ford's campaign for reelection and blunted the Reagan rebellion. Again in 1980, Baker had fought against Reagan's cause as the mastermind of George Bush's campaign. Baker was regarded with suspicion by movement conservatives who knew he did not share their ideological agenda. Baker, scion of a patrician Houston family, was a pragmatic millionaire Republican in the corporate mold. Personally, he was not as hellbent for defense as the Reagan diehards, for he was no cold warrior. And he had no urge to carry the New Right banner on abortion, busing, or school prayer. Worse, he had close personal links to a sitting vice president, a figure of mistrust in the inner circle of any new president, especially if the vice president is a former rival. Baker had been Bush's manager when Bush blasted Reagan for preaching "voodoo economics."

Tall, trim, thin-lipped, handsome, always impeccably dressed and shined, and cool as a Texas gunslinger, Baker enjoyed politics the way some men enjoy the hunt. Indeed, Baker loves to hunt wild turkeys in Texas, a pastime that requires careful plotting, setting an ambush, endless patience, constant attention, exquisite timing, and fast, sure reaction at the critical moment. All of these attributes are typical of Jim Baker, in politics as in a turkey shoot.[51] For Baker is smart, cautious, patient, and decisive. He is savvy; he sees the interrelationships of issues, people, money, and votes, and he marshals his own forces extremely well. As I interviewed Baker or watched him in action, the one word that kept coming to mind was *control:* self-control, control of the situation, control of others. Baker keeps his intentions to himself or shares them with only a couple of trusted aides; he plots his moves with care and strikes when confident of a kill. He stalks his political prey with his pale-blue eyes set in a squint, gauging the political terrain and counting votes the way he would watch the skies or listen for the telltale rustle of a gobbler. He thrives on challenge. And he exults in the sport of politics and, most of all, in winning.

Baker was a prosperous and successful lawyer but "caught the bug" of politics rather late in life. In 1970, when he was forty, he gave up law; since then he has run an unsuccessful race for attorney general in Texas, managed two presidential campaigns, served as undersecretary of Commerce under President Ford, and spent seven years in the Reagan administration. And he seems far from done. He won his spurs with Reagan, not only as a masterful adversary, but by later urging

Reagan to enter the 1980 campaign debates against John Anderson and Carter when Reagan's other advisers counseled against debating. By staging live debate rehearsals to prepare Reagan, Baker made the gamble pay off; his stock rose with both the president-elect and Nancy Reagan.

The Meese-Baker staff "war," as one Reagan intimate called it, was not unique to the Reagan White House. It had the classic elements of any new presidency: the new boys against the old crowd; the pragmatists against the ideologues; the technocrats against the Reagan loyalists; the political strategists against the true believers. An ideological president like Reagan is prone to parenting such divisions within his staff, but they are common to many administrations. Had George McGovern been elected in 1972, he would surely have had to preside over a schism between the New Left ideologicals and centrist Democrats. Jimmy Carter had to bridge differences between substantive aides such as Stuart Eizenstat, with their connections to congressional liberals, and his more conservative home-state crowd of Hamilton Jordan and Jody Powell. The next president, whatever his party or philosophical stripe, will have to cope with similar divisions.

The White House war between Baker and Meese was foreshadowed in the 1980 campaign. As Baker's stock rose, he and Michael Deaver, Reagan's public relations specialist, urged that Reagan's ads attack Carter more vigorously, whereas Meese and Richard Wirthlin, Reagan's poll taker, wanted the ads focused on building Reagan's positive image. Old California Reaganites sensed Baker overreaching. Meese prevailed.

What eventually gave Baker his opening with Reagan was Meese's reputation as a mediocre manager in contrast to Baker's crisp, decisive style. Meese has a tendency to delay, to study problems to death. Baker's nature is to plunge quickly to the heart of problems. Deaver, who had long worked as a lieutenant to Meese but now wanted to be an equal, and Stuart K. Spencer, who was Reagan's oldest, most trusted California political strategist, urged Reagan to choose Baker not Meese as chief of staff. Spencer had been impressed with Baker during the 1976 Ford campaign when Spencer had briefly left the Reagan camp. Deaver and Spencer suggested that Meese, freed of administration, could be Reagan's chief policy adviser.

Toward the end of the 1980 campaign, the two of them arranged for Baker to fly on Reagan's campaign plane to let the two men get to know each other better and "see if the chemistry worked." Both Reagan and Nancy took to Baker. Mrs. Reagan, who has great influence with the president in personnel matters, championed Baker. Reagan, to his credit, sensed his need for a man with Baker's skills and Washington experience, despite their past differences.

When Reagan told Meese on Election Day that he had picked Baker as chief of staff, Meese was shocked and deeply hurt because he had "wanted the chief of staff position in the worst way," according to one Meese ally. Another Meese associate told me that Reagan's choice had "completely shattered" Meese. "I don't think the president himself understood how much he'd undermined Ed in his own mind by picking Baker," this friend said. But Meese masked his feelings to almost everyone, including Reagan. He adjusted loyally, picked for himself the title of "Presidential Counselor," and won domination over both domestic and national security policy-making staffs. Baker was given what sounded like the administrative task of "making the trains run on time"—that is, managing the White House.

To see how this game played out is to understand truly how power operates at the center of our government. Baker came out on top because he understood the five keys to power in the White House.

The first key is the division of duties: Like many people who are unsure of each other, Baker and Meese actually had a written compact, a one-page memo listing their responsibilities in two columns. One column gave Meese cabinet rank, which Baker did not have. This was intended to allow Meese, in the absence of president and vice president, to preside over the cabinet (and even a "supercabinet," which was then being bruited about). Under Meese fell "coordination and supervision" of the National Security and Domestic Council staffs—the policy operation inside the White House. Baker was to manage the staff that dealt with the outside world: press office, political office, speechwriters, congressional liaison, the president's scheduling, appointments, plus the paper flow to Reagan. Beyond that, Baker got the power to hire and fire all elements of the White House staff. And he got possession of the prized West Wing corner office normally used by the chief of staff. The office, a small point, was nevertheless important not only as a symbol to political Washington of Baker's eventual preeminence but also because, as the largest staff office, it could most easily accommodate the troika's daily breakfasts and larger strategy meetings. Baker, as host, always sat at the head of the table.[52]

The Meese group, as one of them put it to me, felt then that "Ed is taking over the whole government." But Baker knew what he was doing. He understood Alexander Haig's "three main levers of power" in the White House: the flow of paper, the president's schedule, and the press. As Baker later explained during a joint appearance with Meese "ultimately, everything goes *through one central point in my office* [emphasis added]. The staff secretary will see all paper that goes in [to the president], and he will finally pass on appointments."[53] Meese, not realizing how much vaster, more intricate, and fast-paced Washington was than Sacramento, did not understand the importance of managing the president's most immediate environment: his movements, his utterances, his sources of information.

Rule One: Do what Baker did: make sure that you and your people have the last crack at everything going to and from the president.

The second and perhaps more important key was Baker's alliance with Deaver, who enabled Baker to develop the president's trust. Deaver had begun in Sacramento as a man Friday to Reagan. He had worked his way up as scheduler and advance man, eventually becoming expert in public relations and choreographing Governor Reagan's schedule and then President Reagan's schedule. As a constant companion of the Reagan, Deaver had become closer to them emotionally— especially to Mrs. Reagan—than anyone else on the staff. In his early forties then, Deaver was like a son to them. He knew their moods, read the president's hidden tension in the grinding of his jaw, swapped jokes with him. Other people used Deaver to carry bad news to Reagan because Deaver knew best how to couch it.

Every political campaign, and virtually every top-rank politician, has a Deaver around him. In the crude lingo of politics, while Meese managed the broad world of policy and Baker did political strategy, Deaver's realm was the "body"—that is, Reagan personally. Deaver rarely got into substance, which made him less than a full equal to Baker and Meese. But having always worked under Meese in the past, Deaver wanted a new power relationship in Washington. He engineered the triangular power game because it suited his purposes. He brought in Baker to neutralize Meese's influence. Baker likewise needed Deaver to open the way to the president and to buttress his standing until he established his own relationship of trust with Reagan. Officially, Deaver became deputy chief of staff; Baker, chief of staff. The two forged an axis which lasted through Reagan's first term and enabled them to best Meese, although it cost Deaver his ties with the old California circle, who came to regard him as a renegade.

Rule Two: If you do not begin with the president's trust, find an ally close to the president who will pave the way; and especially in a troika, be sure the middleman is with you.

Baker's third key was to assemble an extraordinarily capable staff. Meese's staff, on the other hand, was largely mediocre. Some Meese aides, such as Martin Anderson, an economist in charge of domestic planning, were knowledgeable but too academic for the rough-and-tumble of government. The job of the national security adviser, put under Meese, had been downgraded from previous administrations and its occupant, Richard Allen, was substantively weaker than predecessors like Henry Kissinger or Zbigniew Brzezinski. Craig Fuller, the cabinet secretary under Meese, was very able but had been in Deaver's public relations firm before the election and wound up working closely with what became known as the "Baker side of the house."

Baker went after top talent and, remarkably, Reagan let him bring in other Republican moderates, some from other campaigns: David Gergen, the director of communications, who had Bush-Ford connections: James Brady, the press secretary, from the campaign of John Connally; Max Friedersdorf, chief legislative liaison, from the Ford administration; and Richard Darman, a former aide to Baker in the Commerce Department and longtime lieutenant of former Defense Secretary and Attorney General Elliott Richardson, an eastern-establishment Republican liberal.

Darman was the most astonishing choice politically and the most important of the Baker group. For he not only sat at the control point as staff secretary sifting the great flow of papers, deciding which papers Reagan should sign and which should be debated further, but he was superb at strategy. Darman is brilliant, if arrogant. A former professor of government, he simply knew more, studied more than the others. Moreover, he had an intellectual's fascination with power and process, with puzzling out the conundrums of government, with plotting, planning, drafting, scheming, making the pieces fall into place. Like Baker, he was deeply committed to making government work effectively and able to form alliances with mainstream Democrats as well as supply-side Republicans to achieve Reagan's broad ends.

Darman was bright and brash enough to have spotted holes in Reagan's economic program early on; to warn that the Reagan defense buildup would not match the administration's ambitious rhetoric but would still be more than Congress would buy; to tip off Baker on how to control the White House machinery and to beware of being cast as a compromiser while conservative purists attacked him from behind. Darman's job seemed focused on process, but Darman knew there is no dividing substance and politics from process. In charge of process, he provided the substantive understanding of policy that Baker needed.

Rule Three: Always go for the best talent that will work loyally for you. In this case, that was not merely Baker's doing but a sign of Reagan's strength as a leader, and of his personal self-confidence, that he could be surrounded by aides like Baker, Darman, and Gergen, despite past differences. Unlike Jimmy Carter, who had circled his wagons with young Georgians inexperienced in Washington and who suffered the consequences, Reagan knew he needed "outside" talents—people drawn from outside his California circle. That exasperated his right-wing but it served Reagan well.

Fourth, what made Baker personally so valuable to Reagan was his political sixth sense, his knowledge of Washington's power networks, his instinctive sense of how issues will play, where the votes will fall, what the pitfalls are. (Significantly, many in Washington said he would have saved Reagan from the Iran disaster had he remained at chief of staff in Reagan's second term.) From the outset, Baker understood the multidimensional Washington power game and began immediately preparing for it, building networks in the political community while Meese basked in the limelight. Meese assumed Washington was merely a bigger Sacramento and that he could operate there in the same way. But he knew only part of the arena—the Reagan entourage—where he was initially top dog. Baker played a waiting game, saying little in the early transition meetings, downgrading himself as the "new kid on the block" and letting Meese make pronouncements. Eventually, Meese got stretched too thin, with his cabinet councils, his elaborate planning groups, and all the paper he generated. No item seemed too small for his attention. His own partisans complained that he had a hard time setting priorities and making decisions. The common joke in the White House was that "once something gets into Ed Meese's briefcase, it's lost forever."

By contrast, Baker's expertise was strategy, leverage, and priorities. He was constantly working to narrow the focus, pick the action sequence, get rid of problems, forge pivotal alliances. While Meese was busy ideologically tutoring the new cabinet in Reaganism, Baker was moving in the vital political arena, forming the essential political partnership with Senate Majority Leader Howard Baker and drawing close to House Republican Leader Robert Michel. Within the administration, Baker spotted Stockman, the budget director, as the driving force behind the largest, most immediate policy issues and quickly made him an ally. Stockman had brains, speed, and practical experience enough to run circles around Meese's policy shop. What is more, Baker, sensitive that congressional right-wingers were skeptical of him, quickly established a reputation for accessibility to all sides. He paid special attention to Lyn Nofziger, a pet channel of Reaganite conservatives, and he returned congressional phone calls fast. That built support.

Moreover, the Baker side of the House—Baker, Deaver, Darman,

Gergen—understood the vital role of the press in the power game. They assiduously cultivated television and print reporters and columnists, publicized their case, explained their strategies, undercut their rivals. Meese, whose real love is law-and-order issues, police work, and criminology, had a district attorney's wariness of the press. His style was to make announcements and brush problems under the rug. He was accessible but less candid than other White House officials, and his press relations withered. Deaver was the master press agent. Knowing that perception is often reality, Deaver deftly built up Baker and himself as Meese's equals, furnishing detail for pieces on the Reagan troika. He used photographs to convey the message—not only to the public but to Congress and the bureaucracy. It was Deaver, for instance, who arranged photo sessions for my *New York Times Magazine* cover story on the troika in April 1981, photos showing all three together, with Baker—not Meese—in the center.

Rule Four: Develop political networks in Congress and the press and work them constantly.

Finally and most tellingly, Baker understood that in the chaotic, hothouse world of Washington, there was no such thing as separating strategy from tactics, long-term policy planning from short-term actions, policy from politics. He knew they had to be integrated and that often tactics can drive strategy and the immediate can overcome the long-term. He was action and result oriented. Meese, on the other hand, had great faith in organizational charts and long-term planning and little operational skill in Washington. His Office of Planning and Evaluation was supposed to set the administration's policy agenda, but it did not work out that way.

"Meese had a textbook notion of how government should be organized, and he assumed people behaved the way that organization charts suggested," observed one of Baker's allies. "That is utterly naïve."

While Meese busied himself with the architecture of the supercabinet (which never came into being), Baker quietly created the Legislative Strategy Group (LSG), an informal forum for battling out policies and strategies for getting the Reagan program through Congress. The LSG was Darman's idea; it became the vehicle to Baker's ascendancy over domestic policy in the first term. Its members included the Baker crew—Deaver, Darman, David Gergen, Max Friedersdorf and his congressional-liaison aide Kenneth Duberstein, plus David Stockman, and sometimes Dick Wirthlin, and as appropriate, cabinet secretaries such as Donald Regan at Treasury or Drew Lewis at Transportation. Baker never openly challenged Meese—for that risked losing the fight. Meese was invited to LSG meetings and often came. What gradually happened was that the tactics of how to deal with Congress or the press came to dominate White House decision-making, and Meese's more elaborate structure simply fell behind.

Rule Five: Once the ball game starts, move onto the field. There's no time to build imposing new grandstands.

By the peak of Reagan's legislative blitz in mid-1981, Baker was controlling the important levers of power and speaking out with authority rivaling Meese. He masterminded the passage of Reagan's economic program, still the overarching political achievement of Reagan's presidency. (On the domestic side, the only comparable achievement, in 1985–86, was the passage of the tax-reform bill, also managed by Baker, as Treasury secretary.) The triumphant passage of the 1981 budget and tax bills both marked Baker's ascendancy and assured his future influence with Reagan. By the end of 1981, even Meese partisans worried that their man was being eclipsed as a power broker, although his advice still carried strong personal influence with the president.

The sharpest public blow to Meese came in January 1982, when Dick Allen was replaced as national security adviser by William Clark, a tall, low-key, soft-spoken, boyish-looking Reagan crony for fifteen years. Clark, who had been on the California Supreme Court, was given to riding horses, ranching, and wearing western boots with his gray flannel suits. His only experience in foreign affairs was one year at the State Department as Haig's deputy. Yet Clark, who had preceded Meese in California as Governor Reagan's chief of staff, would report only to the president. (Allen had reported to Meese.) When Clark took the national security portfolio, he took half of Meese's empire out from under him. The troika became a foursome. The whole power situation became less stable. For actually, the cooperation among Meese, Baker and Deaver had been unusual in the first year. Baker's rise had come during a time of relative harmony. By early 1982, Meese was feeling bruised, one friend said, and deeper rifts lay ahead for the Reagan household. But the president seemed unknowing, and unprepared, when they struck.

The Staff Coup That Failed

The sixth key to White House power, and probably the most important axiom for power anywhere in the American system, is to tame your personal hunger for power. The inebriating atmosphere of the White House feeds that malady even among the wisest of power players, such as Jim Baker. Political overreaching is always damaging. Unbridled ambition set up Lyndon Johnson and Richard Nixon as targets for the press and other politicians; it led to Alexander Haig's downfall and contributed to the ouster of Donald Regan, as Reagan's second term chief of staff.

Steve Bell, a battle-scarred former congressional aide, is fond of warning politicians not to be too clever in hatching plots or laying traps for adversaries. "When you dig a grave for your enemy," says Bell, "dig two—one for yourself." It was a warning that Baker and Deaver should have heeded before their White House plot to expand their power.

Deaver, who had worked for Clark in Sacramento and teamed with him to smooth out problems with Haig, had looked to Clark as a potential ally as national security adviser. But Deaver misjudged Clark, who had a long personal relationship with Reagan and now commanded an independent apparatus and a direct channel to the president. Moreover, Clark felt that Baker, Deaver, and Stuart Spencer, Reagan's favorite campaign adviser, wanted to use him to ease Meese out as cabinet coordinator; he claimed they had sounded him out on taking over Meese's White House office as a first step. Clark threatened to go to the president to block them, for Clark had ties to Meese, both as a fellow California Reaganite and as a kindred conservative. Meese was a hard-liner on social and law-and-order issues, as Clark was on foreign policy.

Thus, Clark's arrival in the White House sharpened the internal power rift. Over time, Clark's secretive, independent power plays produced frequent and bitter clashes, between Clark and the Baker-Deaver axis.[54] Deaver was stunned to learn that Clark had given President Reagan a plan in early 1983 for reorganizing the White House staff, eliminating Baker's job as chief of staff, naming Meese the administration's spokesman, and making the foursome all coequals. When Reagan showed Clark's plan to Deaver during a flight on *Air Force One*, with Clark sitting nearby, Deaver objected strenuously. "It won't work," Deaver told the president. "If you do this, I'll have to leave." After that, Deaver and Clark were no longer on speaking terms.

Clark angered Deaver and Baker—and exasperated secretaries of State Alexander Haig and George Shultz—by keeping them in the dark on foreign-policy moves. He would work directly with the president on ideas such as launching a bid to meet Soviet President Leonid Brezhnev in mid-1982, or drafting an explosive executive order in October 1983, requiring top officials to undergo polygraphs to fight news leaks. Clark even toyed with opening a diplomatic back channel to Moscow through Soviet Ambassador Anatoly Dobrynin, without telling Shultz.

The climax came in October 1983, when Interior Secretary James Watt resigned. Clark, who told friends he was sick of the bitter White

House infighting and exhausted from the strain of a job for which he had little preparation, privately proposed to Reagan that he move to Interior, a job that appealed to Clark's western-rancher soul. Baker and Deaver, with support from Mrs. Reagan, also urged Reagan to move Clark to Interior, though they persuaded the president to delay for five days. They had faulted Clark to Reagan for bureaucratic end runs and for hard-line handling of Congress and had argued that he was substantively "over his head" on arms control. I was told that Secretary Shultz had also complained to Reagan that Clark's office was a bottleneck, slowing State Department papers for the president. But Shultz, like most of political Washington, was taken by surprise when late on Thursday afternoon, October 13, Reagan named Clark to be secretary of Interior.

It was a moment that Baker and Deaver had been awaiting; for they prepared the next step—Clark's replacement. They had proposed to Reagan that he install Baker as national security adviser and make Deaver White House chief of staff. These shifts would fulfill both their ambitions. Baker had long wanted a top foreign-policy post, secretary of State or Defense or CIA director—for a new challenge and prestige, said a colleague. For Deaver, this would fulfill a long personal climb to the top, though pro-Meese officials contended that Baker actually planned to run the whole White House apparatus.

Two Reagan intimates told me that Nancy Reagan had urged the president to adopt the Baker-Deaver plan. Stuart Spencer also helped sell Reagan. Other White House officials said that Vice President Bush had endorsed the plan and possibly Secretary Shultz, too. Darman, who was to be Baker's deputy national security adviser, drafted a press release for the president personally to announce these important shifts on Friday. White House reporters were alerted to wait for an important four P.M. announcement. But the announcement never came.

Reagan first had to attend a one-hour National Security Planning Group meeting with Clark, Shultz, Weinberger, Casey, Meese, and Jeane Kirkpatrick, chief U.S. delegate to the United Nations. Ordinarily, Baker would have attended and Deaver could have, too. Instead, they decided to wait in Baker's office, in what other officials later called a classic blunder: surrendering close control over the president. But Baker stayed away deliberately, to avoid putting the president in too obvious a squeeze. Deaver felt that by arming Reagan with the press announcement, they had presented their rivals with a fait accompli. It was a factional coup, the pragmatic faction of Baker, Deaver, and

Shultz besting the more hard-line faction of Clark, Weinberger, Casey, Meese, and Kirkpatrick.

According to the Clark faction's account, Reagan did not actually carry the press release with him. But walking down the hall to the national security meeting, Reagan pulled Clark aside and said, "I've got your successor already chosen."

"Who is it?" Clark asked.

"Jim Baker," Reagan replied, "and Mike will be chief of staff."

Clark was stunned. Later he told others that he thought the president was joking, but looking at his face, Clark could see the president was serious. The prospect horrified Clark.

"Have you talked to George Shultz or Cap Weinberger or Bill Casey about this?" he asked.

"No, and I'm not planning to," Reagan said. "I already have an announcement prepared."

They went into the meeting, Clark fearful that Reagan would announce his decision; but Reagan did nothing. Clark passed notes to Meese, Weinberger, and Casey about the president's intentions. After the session, Clark persuaded Reagan to come down to Clark's office in the White House basement. Weinberger, Casey, and Meese came along.

All four men strenuously argued against both Baker and Deaver. They contended that Deaver was not up to the job of chief of staff, not competent to handle the range of substantive issues. For Meese and Clark, for whom Deaver had served almost as a flunky in Reagan's California days, such elevation of Deaver was unthinkable. Weinberger and Casey were particularly outspoken against Baker. They argued that his appointment as national security adviser would shake the confidence of the international security community and would be viewed as a sign of weakness toward the Soviets, since Baker was known as a moderate. All four worked on Reagan, arguing that Baker be sent anywhere but to the NSC job.

"He can have my job even though I know he's the biggest leaker in town," Casey told Reagan. "He can't go to NSC!"

Clark had a different idea. With a chance to get Baker out of the White House, he was ready to reverse his own plans. He told the president: "Perhaps you should consider sending Jim to Interior, and I'll remain where I am."

The president replied quickly—to everyone's surprise—that Baker could not become secretary of Interior because of his ownership interests in oil and gas in Texas. He would be disqualified because of conflict of interest, unless he would be willing to dispossess himself.

For half an hour, the harangue went on. When Reagan did not make the press announcement or return to the Oval Office, Deaver called Clark's secretary, Jackie Hill, demanding, "Where is the president? Where is the president?"

Reagan felt opposing pulls within his official family. "He was torn inside in a hundred directions," said one Reagan intimate who was not directly involved. "He was being torn on both sides by old friends."

Finally, Reagan agreed to back off the appointments. He returned to the Oval Office to inform first Deaver and then Baker.

"I've had a lot of opposition to this from some of the boys," the president told them. "I want to think about it over the weekend."

By more than one account, Deaver was so deeply hurt personally that he yelled at Reagan. "You don't have enough confidence in me to make me chief of staff!" he shouted.

More calmly, Baker suggested dropping the whole scheme. "If it presents a problem for you, Mr. President, that's not what I want," he said. "The last thing I want to do is put you in a difficult position. Forget it."

"No, Jim, I'm not going to forget it," Reagan said. "I'm going to think about it over the weekend."

But when he came back on Monday, Reagan told them he was shelving the plan. Another battle immediately ensued over whether he should pick Kirkpatrick for the NSC job, as the Clark-Weinberger faction wanted, or pick Clark's more moderate deputy, Robert C. McFarlane, whom Baker, Deaver, and Shultz favored. Having disappointed Baker and Deaver on their own plans, the president took their advice on McFarlane.

But the tensions inside the White House remained for the rest of Reagan's first term. Throughout 1984 the White House was full of talk of an imminent shake-up, but Reagan did nothing to resolve the power conflicts. The entire episode left deep scars and ultimately contributed to the departure of Clark and Deaver from the administration and to the decisions of Meese and Baker to leave the White House at the start of Reagan's second term.

Back to the Republican Model

What is interesting about Reagan is that the competitive staff structure of his first term fits more with the pattern of Democratic presidents than the standard Republican model. Eisenhower, Nixon, and Ford liked to operate with a single strong chief of staff and a clear White House hierarchy. Historically, Eisenhower's Sherman Adams and Nixon's John Haldeman stand out as two of the strongest staff chiefs in modern presidential history. By contrast, Democratic presidents such as Franklin Roosevelt and Jack Kennedy preferred a more free-wheeling inner circle. They operated without a chief of staff, using several high-powered White House aides as spokes of a wheel with themselves at the hub. Lyndon Johnson, too, liked to play off his top aides against each other. Jimmy Carter's White House had a loose structure, leaving the lines of power unclear.

But as Reagan's second term began, he reverted to the Republican model—by accident. For in all this White House maneuvering, the president was strangely passive for a man with a reputation as a strong leader. It is a mark of his difficulty in dealing with personal matters that he was not the one to put his house in order. Ultimately, the independent urges of Reagan's subordinates solved the problem of staff rivalry: They left the White House. Jim Baker arranged a job swap with Don Regan (at Regan's initiative), with Baker becoming Treasury secretary and Regan becoming chief of staff. Deaver sold the idea to Reagan. It was a strange decision for a president who had understood in 1980 that he needed a chief of staff, such as Baker, with good political instincts and political antenna. Don Regan had none of these vital staff attributes, and both he and the president paid a heavy price. Throughout Donald Regan's two-year tenure, Reagan seemed constantly saddled with troubles, from the furor over his visit to the German cemetery in Bitburg in early 1985 to the crippling Iran-*contra* scandal in late 1986.

Inside the White House, Regan succeeded where Baker had not: in centralizing command and concentrating the troika's dividend powers in his own hands. As a scrappy, self-made Irishman, a poor boy from Boston who won a scholarship to Harvard and made it to the top as a millionaire chairman of Merrill Lynch, Regan ran the White House with the bullish, take-charge style he learned on Wall Street. Regan operated more like a corporate CEO or a Marine officer (he had been both) than a politician accustomed to the ways of sharing power. He personally held all the key levers in the White House power structure. His hand-picked aides controlled the president's paper flow and schedule but were so meek and dutiful that they were quickly nicknamed the "mice."

Given a free rein in the president's political household, Regan tolerated no competing power centers inside the White House. In 1985, Edward Rollins, the blunt-spoken political director who had managed Reagan's reelection campaign, clashed with Regan a few times and then resigned in frustration. Periodically, Pat Buchanan, the conservative columnist tapped as communications director, pushed for a confrontational strategy with Congress and the press. Under Buchanan, the strongly ideological speechwriting staff of Bentley Elliot, Peggy Noonan, and Tony Dolan produced sharper, more passionate Reaganite speeches than Regan wanted; Regan had his loyal lieutenants tone down the speeches. Eventually, Regan fired Ben Elliott, the chief speechwriter, and Buchanan went back to the freer life of the columnist. Gradually, the White House apparatus came to reflect more loyalty to Regan than to the president.

Robert McFarlane, the national security adviser, had the only internal channel direct to the president, and Regan moved to control it. Early on, the two men crossed swords when McFarlane awakened the president—*without first informing Regan*—on March 24, 1985 to advise him that an American major had been shot dead by a Soviet guard in East Germany. Regan, caught unawares during a morning staff session with the president, immediately called McFarlane on the carpet. People in nearby offices could hear Regan bellowing. He was in a shouting rage, and McFarlane, a fellow Marine, gradually responded in cold, rising anger.[55]

"I'm in charge and running this place, and I need to be kept informed," Regan blustered.

"You're right, you should have been informed," McFarlane conceded. "But I'm not going to stand here and put up with abuse of this kind."

"Well, I'll run the place the way I want, and you'll goddamn do it the way I say to do it," Regan shouted.

"No, I won't," McFarlane shot back.

McFarlane headed for the door, telling Regan that he was packing up for good. Within minutes Regan telephoned to apologize for losing his temper and to say he hoped McFarlane was not serious about leaving. A walkout by McFarlane would look bad so early in Regan's tenure. Their relations were strained, simmering until McFarlane resigned in December. Regan handpicked Rear Admiral John Poindexter as McFarlane's successor, but Poindexter was more secretive than McFarlane. Moreover, Regan knew little about foreign policy and left the substance to Poindexter, and Regan lacked the political horse sense to give the president independent judgment on the political risks in his foreign ventures.

Nonetheless, in domestic policy, Donald Regan enjoyed "the most extreme delegation [of presidential] authority to one person" in the

White House staff, since Sherman Adams after President Eisenhower's heart attack in 1955, according to presidential scholar Richard Neustadt of Harvard University.[56] It was an unfortunate, almost prophetic comparison, because Adams was forced from office by scandal, lacking defenders other than his president; Regan, too, was forced out in early 1987.

Actually, Regan's power was not as a great as it appeared. He had supremacy inside the White House but not a monopoly. The cabinet had more powerful figures than in the first term, evidence that power is often more in the person than in the job. With their ties to Reagan, Baker at Treasury and Meese as Attorney General were more powerful than their predecessors. With foreign policy more important in the second term, Shultz, Weinberger, McFarlane, Poindexter, and Casey had significant influence. And the NSC staff ran the funding and gunrunning to the Nicaraguan *contras* and the arms deals with Iran. The lesson was that even with control of the White House apparatus, the chief of staff could handle only so much.

Donald Regan tried to run a tidy ship. But alas, tidiness has never been a ringing virtue of American politics. What got lost in the corporate command were the political networking, the accessibility to outsiders, and the canny calculation of political gains and costs that had made Jim Baker so valuable to Reagan. The best staff people in Congress or the White House must protect their leaders by anticipating problems and sensing pitfalls, but Regan was full of political blindspots. He did not properly forsee the blow-up over the Bitburg visit, sanctions against South Africa, or the Iranian operation. He angered congressional Republicans by zigzags on the budget. For all of his talk about a millionaire's independence, he became known as a "yes man" to Reagan.

What is more, Regan ignored the staff man's axiom to take a low profile and let the spotlight fall on your boss. His attempt to make himself Ronald Reagan's strong man ultimately broke him, a lesson for future administrations, just as Sherman Adams's icy eminence had been. Regan's personal power lust marked him for a fall. Both Congress and the press react instinctively to power lust in politicians; ambition made Donald Regan a target and left him with few allies to protect him after the shattering news of the Iranian scandal broke. With his Marine stories, his Irish jokes, and his aura of corporate success, Regan appealed personally to the president. But he acted as if Reagan were his sole constituent, as if he did not need to cultivate networks in Congress and the political community to be summoned when he and his president were in trouble.

The deliberately cultivated impression that Regan was monopolizing power was his Achilles' heel as a top staff man. When the Iranian scandal broke, Regan put a sign on his desk, THE BUCK DOESN'T EVEN PAUSE HERE, but it was too late to duck responsibility, given how assiduously he had polished his power image. When the cry rose for scapegoats, staunch Republicans joined Nancy Reagan in calling for Donald Regan's head. Unwilling to fall on his sword to save the president, Regan was finally dumped unceremoniously.

The lesson, as one magazine article suggested, was that "in government, consensus is more important than command."[57] Significantly, the president replaced Don Regan with Howard Baker, a leader with friends and credibility throughout the political community and a reputation for patient persuasion and for building consensus. It was a reminder that a successful staff person needs as broad a view, and as sure and deft a political touch, as the president himself.

PART III

The Big Games of Power

The Big Games of Power

The great confrontations, the big power games which the public watches, are the culmination of the background games described in Part Two. In the titanic struggles, the background games all play a part: the working of power networks in Congress, the hidden leverage of staff and iron-triangle alliances, the video-driven independence of new-breed politicians, the divisive pressures of PAC money.

It is on this terrain—altered by the power earthquake of the early 1970s—that political leadership is tested.

Of the big games, the first for any president is the agenda game. No president can lead effectively without being able to fix an agenda, move it swiftly, and deflect the inevitable diversions—not only the moves of rivals but his own contrary impulses and the scattershot urgings of his supporters. With the magnifying power of television, the president has the advantage of commanding center stage. He is able to captivate the public with action or with image making, with substance or storytelling.

But the heart of governing is the solid carpentry of coalition building, the daunting task of not only passing legislation but of winning steady support to sustain policies and programs—especially in domestic affairs—long enough for them to take root. And for the opposition, there is the choice of whether to challenge the president, to bargain with him, or to make a show of collaboration and then—having drawn the president into dependency—how to reshape the content of his proposals.

Finally, on foreign policy, the test for the president is how to deal with the inescapable divisions within his official family. The president can either drag himself from one internal stalemate to the next or—as Reagan also did—simply bypass the internal wars by having his staff generate policies in secret.

II. *The Agenda Game: Speed, Focus, and Damage Control*

> *You've got to give it all you can, that first year. Doesn't matter what kind of majority you come in with. You've got just one year when they treat you right.*
>
> —Lyndon Johnson

In the grand scheme of American government, the paramount task and power of the president is to articulate the national purpose: to fix the nation's agenda. Of all the big games at the summit of American politics, the agenda game must be won first.

For the effectiveness of the presidency and the capacity of any president to lead depends on focusing the nation's political attention and its energies on two or three top priorities.

From the vantage point of history, the flow of events seems to have immutable logic, but political reality is inherently chaotic; it contains no automatic agenda. Order must be imposed. Events erupt: a nuclear accident at Three Mile Island, an American frigate shelled in the Persian Gulf, the emergence of a dynamic new Soviet leader, the quadrupling of oil prices, new shocks in trade competition with Japan. All these clamor for attention, and no question is more crucial to the exercise of power than determining which questions get top priority, what issues will be attacked first.

Our recent history shows that a president who cannot set and hold to a clear agenda loses the momentum of his election victory and fails to realize fully the potential of his presidency. For without vision, focus, and direction, government falls into disarray and the country falls adrift.

The Founding Fathers originally expected Congress to set the course of policy; the president, as the nation's chief magistrate, was supposed to implement congressional policy. But Congress is a teeming brawl of vying factions and competing committees, all feeling the insistent, divergent pressures of lobbies. Congress does initiate policies on occasion, but enormous natural advantages lie with the single voice in the White House—in historian Edwin Corwin's phrase, the "American people's one authentic trumpet."

As the head of the vast executive apparatus, the president has a unique opportunity to act as a unifying and purposeful force. A shrewd and forceful president can be the chief architect of policy and the catalyst of action. Television has magnified the president's unparalleled platform for leadership. "Only he, by attacking problems frontally and aggressively and by interpreting his power expansively, can slay the dragons of crisis and be the engine of change to move this nation forward," observed political scientist Thomas Cronin.[1]

The mere mantle of office, and even such personal popularity as John F. Kennedy enjoyed, do not guarantee political success, as the flawed presidencies of Kennedy, Carter, Gerald Ford, and Richard Nixon attest. Yet Ronald Reagan, in his remarkably successful first year, established his agenda and his personal dominance. As no president since Franklin Delano Roosevelt in 1933 and Lyndon Johnson in 1965, Reagan set the terms of debate and political action in 1981. And yet, strangely, Reagan failed badly at the agenda game in 1985, after his landslide reelection. The contrast between his record in 1981 and his record in 1985 demonstrates that Reagan did not have unbeatable magic and that electoral victory does not guarantee a president will dominate the action. In short, 1981 was a classic lesson in how to win—with a smooth, fast-opening game plan; and 1985 was a mirror-image lesson in the disasters of starting unprepared.

First impressions are critical. In the agenda game, a swift beginning is crucial for a new president to establish himself as leader—to show the nation that he will make a difference in people's lives. The first one hundred days are the vital test; in those weeks, the political community inside the beltway and the public measure a new president—to see whether he is active, dominant, sure, purposeful.

Franklin Roosevelt, with his famous New Deal legislative blitz in 1933, generated the modern presidency and created the model for focusing national initiative in the White House. FDR set the mark for subsequent presidents. The day after his inauguration, Roosevelt summoned Congress into extraordinary session to confront the nation's black despair over economic depression. To halt the run on the banks, Roosevelt got Congress to order them temporarily closed. There followed a slew of emergency measures to lay the foundations of the welfare state, with public-works jobs and new agencies, a score of press conferences, and the first couple of FDR's famous radio "fireside chats" to bolster the nation's spirits—all within Roosevelt's famous one hundred days. Although depression deepened, Roosevelt's reputation had been established, surviving setbacks and shortcomings later on.

Dwight Eisenhower struck a strong note even before his inauguration, by flying to Korea after his election to honor the central promise of his campaign: to end the bloody, inconclusive war in Korea and to restore peace and prosperity. Lyndon Johnson, in his early months as president, used the nation's grief and sympathy after Kennedy's assassination in November 1963 to push through the civil-rights bill and the tax-cut program that Kennedy could not get passed. Johnson, reelected in his own right, achieved a surge of Great Society legislation in 1985: a war on poverty, aid to education, and programs to revitalize cities and establish Medicaid and Medicare for the poor and elderly. With that outpouring of new programs, the greatest since the early New Deal, Johnson established his mark as the master of Congress.

Understanding the limits of presidential power, Johnson knew the need for a quick start while Congress was still in the thrall of a new president's election victory. "You've got to give it all you can, that first year," Johnson told Harry McPherson, a top aide. "Doesn't matter what kind of majority you come in with. You've got just one year when they treat you right, and before they start worrying about themselves. The third year, you lose votes. . . . The fourth's all politics. You can't put anything through when half the Congress is thinking how to beat you."[2]

What lay behind Johnson's words was an instinctive feel for the rhythm of the presidency, a rhythm as natural to politicians as the seasons are to migratory birds. The first honeymoon year gives way to a more trying second year, as members of Congress jockey for reelection. The third year, free of election worries, offers a new opening, but normally a president must compromise or must turn more to foreign policy because of his party's losses in Congress in the midterm elections. If a president does well in his third year (as Reagan did), he has a good shot at reelection, but if he does poorly (as Carter did), his chances are much slimmer. In domestic policy terms, the fourth year is largely lost to election politics. Reelection wins the president a new platform for action in his fifth year, and sometimes his sixth. But in the last two years, he is at his weakest; his time is running out, and usually his party loses ground in his sixth-year elections. (The Republicans lost the Senate in 1986, Reagan's sixth year. In 1966, the sixth year of the Kennedy-Johnson presidency, the Democrats lost forty-seven House seats and four Senate seats.)

In short, power ebbs and flows with the calendar. Even John F. Kennedy, glamorous and highly rated, was afflicted by the built-in rhythm of American government. He got the Peace Corps and Food for Peace established quickly in 1961, his first year, but his presidency was hurt that first spring by the disastrous failure of the CIA-backed exile invasion of Cuba at the Bay of Pigs. What is more, Kennedy retreated in March 1961 on his first big legislative initiative—aid to education—and he never mastered Congress after that early retreat.[3] He missed the 1981 honeymoon and got into a logjam when he mounted a legislative offensive in 1963, his third year. He failed to ride the natural rhythms of maximum presidential influence.

Kennedy has been so romanticized in memory that few people recall that the keystones of his legislative program (tax cut, civil-rights bill, aid to education) were passed by Lyndon Johnson after Kennedy's death. Indeed, one week before the assassination, James Reston wrote in *The New York Times* that "there is a vague feeling of doubt and disappointment in the country about President Kennedy's first term"—not because of any failure to capture the nation's heart or its media, but because Kennedy had not mastered "how to govern."[4]

Richard Nixon was forever embroiled in battles with Congress because he could not sell his agenda for cutting back government or for reform of the nation's welfare system. Like Kennedy, Nixon later recovered with foreign successes (his opening to China, his summit meetings and arms agreements with Soviet Leader Leonid Brezhnev), but Nixon's early clashes with Congress in 1969 on domestic affairs set a pattern of enmity and bogged down his domestic program. In 1974, Gerald Ford too was impaled politically by his early pardon of Nixon after the House had voted articles of impeachment against Nixon. The early storm was a prelude to Ford's two years of stalemate with Congress.

But it was Jimmy Carter, promising a political revival after the

Nixon-Ford years, who most tragically epitomized the failure of a president to forge a clear agenda and to lead a Congress dominated by his own party. Carter's failure set the stage for the stunning success of Ronald Reagan, whose politically brilliant opening revitalized the presidency and restored public confidence in the nation's highest office— until the Iran scandal broke, toward the end of his fateful sixth year.

Takeover: The Moment of Truth

The contrast between Carter and Reagan and their two political teams illustrates the crucial importance of the agenda game in fixing the image and power of a new president. Both leaders were intent on proclaiming national renewal after a time of turmoil. Each was eager to grasp the levers of power, and each was given to using symbolic politics to convey his fundamental political messages. Jimmy Carter strolled down Pennsylvania Avenue to stamp his presidency with a common touch and to show that he was doing away with the imperial presidency. Reagan staged his inaugural on the Capitol's West Front— a break with the tradition of holding it on the East Front—signaling a new, optimistic manifest destiny for the nation. Both had come as outsiders to seize the citadel of power in Washington, but the Reagan team understood what that entailed better than did the Carter crowd.

The contrast between these two beginnings, even in the very first hours in office, carries crucial lessons for future presidencies, vital clues as to what works and what does not work in governing America and in the Washington power game.

Carter's senior staff, fresh from the inaugural ceremonies and elated by their campaign conquest, gathered in the Roosevelt Room of the White House at around four o'clock. The mood was informal and casual, in keeping with Carter's deliberate effort to "depomp the presidency," as Press Secretary Jody Powell put it. But the nonchalance of Carter's staff also betrayed the lack of hierarchy and the absence of a clear Carter game plan.

In fact, divisive staff rivalries and Carter's distaste for hierarchy left him without a chief of staff. After conferring with presidential experts and past White House officials, Jack Watson developed a transition plan, only to be jealously blocked in its execution by Hamilton Jordan, Carter's senior political lieutenant. As the master campaign strategist, Jordan was brilliant, but he had thought little about the substance of governing and had little taste for Washington. Oddly, Jordan seemed to resent being in government. In seniority with Carter, he was the natural chief of staff, but he was neither ready to take charge nor to let anyone else do so, especially Watson. Carter did not resolve the problem. At this critical first moment, therefore, no one was clearly in command. It was a harbinger of troubles to come.

Carter's top staff chatted amiably that first afternoon, smiling and enjoying their collective rise to power—and yet, I was told, they shifted uneasily, too, fidgeting, not quite certain what to do or who would take the lead. After a few minutes—which seemed like hours—Robert Lipshutz, Carter's lawyer, spoke up. "I guess because I'm the oldest one here," he said, "I'll call this meeting to order." As he moved to the head of the table, there was an awkward silence because Lipshutz was really a secondary player. Others ignored him.

Frank Moore, another veteran from Carter's gubernatorial staff, turned to Hamilton Jordan and gave voice to the general uncertainty. "Ham, what do we do now?" Moore asked.

People laughed nervously. There was no order. No one giving instructions. No one taking notes. Moore's question got no answer, according to Mark Siegel, an experienced Democratic party worker who was relatively new to the Carter camp.[5] Someone else asked, "Should we have a staff meeting every day?"

"We'll have a meeting when there's something to meet about," Jordan replied offhandedly.

When Congress was mentioned, Frank Moore remarked naïvely, "It's just like in Georgia. Ham, you remember Senator . . ." mentioning some member of the Georgia legislature whom Jordan and Moore had outfoxed during Carter's term as governor, when they had handled his legislative liaison. Georgia's legislature was vastly more pliant than the proud, assertive, two-party Congress that now confronted the Georgians, but Moore and Jordan seemed oblivious. They fell into congenial reveries about Georgia legislators. The meeting dribbled on. After a while people left, without coming to any decisions or conclusions. "My God," thought Siegel, "what would the KGB think if they could see us now?"

Obviously, there was ultimately much more substance to the Carter presidency than emerged from that first staff meeting. President Carter, earnest and relentless as a law student cramming for bar exams, was determined to master every subject. He opened with a flurry of activity—in fact, too much, shooting off in too many directions. His campaign had raised high expectations for a fresh political beginning, and his early pronouncements piled those expectations even higher, too high to fulfill. Carter was an idealist, a good-government moralist, who had trouble connecting ends and means and converting his high-minded goals into politically salable programs.

With his Navy training, Carter had cultivated the image of a careful political planner, but in those early weeks in the White House his pace was pell-mell. "Restless and aggressive, he plunged ahead, sometimes heedless of the timetables established by his advisers, and even of his own political interests," commented Robert Shogan of the *Los Angeles Times*. [6]

Carter always had so many priorities that he seemed to have none. He suffered from what political scientist James MacGregor Burns of Williams College called "strategic myopia."[7] In the 1976 campaign, Carter had attacked the American tax system as "a disgrace to the human race" and promised reform, but it did not materialize. In his inaugural, he voiced the hope that "nuclear weapons could be eliminated from the face of the earth." That first spring, Carter advanced a dramatic new arms proposal, but dropped it when the Russians roared their disapproval. With technocratic enthusiasm, he asserted that "zero-based budgeting" would force every government program to be justified anew, as a means of controlling deficits and creating new efficiency, but deficits rose anyway. He repeatedly pledged a sweeping consolidation of many federal agencies but wound up adding the departments of Energy and Education.

Carter's administration seemed a series of economic programs, one nostrum following another. One early gambit was to offer a fifty-dollar tax rebate for every taxpayer; that plan was scrapped in less than three months. In that first year, Carter had a welfare-reform program which died stillborn. With ringing rhetoric, he promised to attack the nation's energy crisis with the "moral equivalent of war," but his program was so modest that Russell Baker, in a *New York Times* column, mocked Carter's pussycat program with the acronym MEOW. Whenever I would ask White House officials for Carter's top priorities, the list would run past a dozen items. The focus of the Carter presidency was not clear.

Of course, Carter later had major achievements: the Panama Canal treaties, the Camp David accords, his battles for human-rights policies. But before getting to the heart of what he wanted to do, Carter got entangled with Congress in an ill-considered fight over pork-barrel funding of public works and water projects, a perennial legislative favorite. However noble Carter's attack on such questionable largesse, it was a sure loser. That fight soured his relations with Congress right away and kept him from getting to his own pet items. Carter began the agenda game off-center and never fully gained command.

This was a lesson which the Reagan team took to heart. Its takeover was crisp.

Supreme power shifts abruptly. What the public observes is Ronald Reagan taking the oath of office and a twenty-one-gun salute confirming his ascendancy to the highest office in the land. In that same split second, the first wave of Reagan's political commandos captures the flag. They literally "seize the White House," claiming the inner citadel of power on Reagan's behalf.

Until that moment on January 20, 1981, the White House had been deserted, almost desolate.

Through the night, the Oval Office and the White House Situation Room in the basement had been throbbing. President Carter, Vice President Mondale, Hamilton Jordan, Jody Powell, and White House Counsel Lloyd Cutler had been working frantically to secure the release of the American hostages in Iran. Carter desperately wanted them freed on his watch. By late morning on Inauguration Day, the Oval Office was empty. A Carter rearguard had retreated to the Situation Room to pursue the hostage release.

A ghostly silence reigned over the West Wing—the honeycomb of high-powered offices for the president, vice president, and the top staff. In the Oval Office, the heavy, ornate desk first used by Rutherford B. Hayes stood idle, its top bare, its drawers vacant. In every office, tables were naked. The normal clutter of papers and phone banks connected to other power centers were gone. In-boxes were empty. Bookshelves were bereft. The throb of power had ebbed. The whole area was as lifeless as some eerie, abandoned place in a science-fiction movie, where everyone has died from radiation or suddenly vanished.[8]

As noon approached, cleanup crews and painters moved into the deserted offices. Eugene Eidenberg, secretary to Carter's cabinet, was saying farewell to White House guards, housekeepers, and the manager of the mess: the people who stay on from one president to the next. The guard at the basement entrance gave Eidenberg a friendly warning that his political lease was rapidly running out and he'd better not be late in leaving.

"Gene," the guard kidded, patting the gun on his hip, "you only got a couple of minutes. If you're not out of here by noon, I'll have to throw you out." Eidenberg took the hint and left. He was one of a handful of high officials who had a special red phone installed in his home, connecting him directly (without dialing) to the White House switchboard. His daughters, Danielle and Elizabeth, tried the red phone at quarter to twelve and it still worked. But precisely at noon, the line went dead.

At 12:01 P.M., John Rogers, a crisp, officious twenty-four-year-old, arrived at the Southwest Gate of the White House leading a seven-car caravan with files from Reagan transition headquarters.

Within moments, Rogers, chief administrator of the new Reagan White House staff, was efficiently rearranging furniture in the Oval Office, to set it up the way Reagan wanted it. The couches were placed facing each other instead of back to back. End tables were moved. New phone lines were installed to link Reagan directly to Jim Baker, Ed Meese, and Mike Deaver. While television sets broadcast Reagan's inaugural address, a carpenter screwed nameplates for the new president and his cabinet on the backs of chairs in the cabinet room.

Swiftly, the political symbols that adorn the White House were transformed. Portraits of Thomas Jefferson and Harry Truman came down in the cabinet room; they were immediately replaced by portraits of Calvin Coolidge and Dwight Eisenhower, two Republican symbols admired by Reagan. The portrait of Republican Abraham Lincoln was kept. In the Oval Office, the busts of George Washington and Benjamin Franklin stayed, but a bust of Harry Truman was carted off. Suddenly the walls of the West Wing blossomed with huge color photographs of the Reagan campaign, the Reagan staff, Reagan rallies, President and Mrs. Reagan.

"What we wanted," said John Rogers, "was a total change of image, to get the imprimatur of Ronald Reagan as president, by the time everyone came back from the inauguration."[9]

In an hour or two, a trickle of other Reaganites started settling in the White House offices. As the Reagan troops filtered into their new quarters, a phone rang in one office. Someone was asking for Hamilton Jordan, and Mike Deaver's secretary, Shirley Moore, answered that he was not there anymore. The caller then asked for Jack Watson. "I'm sorry," Moore said, "he doesn't work here anymore. In fact, they're all gone now. We're the new folks in town. We're the ones in charge now."

The Tactics of a Fast Start

From the stroke of noon, January 20, 1981, Ronald Reagan conveyed a confident new sense of direction, as Franklin Roosevelt had done in 1933. Reagan's ability to cast the nation's political debate in terms of his agenda, and thereby to achieve his central political objectives, has been one of the two singular achievements of his presidency. The other achievement was his restoration of the power of the presidency after a long period of deadlock and drift and amidst worries that special interests were rendering the country ungovernable. Reagan was able to achieve so much, especially in his first year, because of his skill, and that of his top team, at the agenda game.

Reagan himself has never been known as a good manager or strategist. His great political talent is as a visionary leader, painting themes and values broadbrush and in bold colors and thereby capturing the public imagination. Since 1964, when he made a celebrated television address for Barry Goldwater, Reagan had crisscrossed the country in three presidential bids of his own: 1968, 1976, and 1980. By the time he took office, his basic agenda was well known: less government, lower taxes, more defense, global anti-Communism. But in that 1980 campaign, other objectives clouded the old agenda: a balanced budget by 1983; early arms negotiations with Moscow; free trade, but help to Detroit's auto industry; eliminating the departments of Energy and Education; restoring prayer in schools and stopping abortions.

Reagan's vision needed focus and programmatic content. Reagan's men, having watched Carter's frayed beginning, understood full well that their president's game plan had to be clear, his priorities had to be winnowed. Clamoring factions among the conservative movement pushed rival objectives on Reagan, but his top strategists knew that their president could not succeed if he dissipated his energies chasing too many conservative goals. In the campaign, he had hit hardest on economic recovery, and that was a natural overriding priority, given skyrocketing interest rates and high unemployment. The framework had been set in the five-point economic program that Reagan outlined in a major economic policy speech in Chicago on September 9, 1980.[10] That meant pushing almost all other campaign promises to the back burner; some were let slip entirely. That was crucial—a narrowly focused agenda was one key to Reagan's stunning legislative blitzkreig in 1981 and to the aura of purpose and invincibility that buoyed him afterward.

"We recognized early on when we went for a simple agenda, we were staking Reagan's presidency on one issue," David Gergen, Reagan's director of communications, explained much later. "If it failed, we didn't have a big fallback. If it succeeded in terms of legislation, that would give us a second burst."[11]

Focus was the first priority; speed was the second. The Reaganites knew that time is short for a new president to make himself a winner and to convince the voters that he is a leader. In policy terms, the Reagan team wanted a transfer of power as clean and as swift as their physical takeover on Inauguration Day. Their catechism was to "hit the ground running," for they understood that vigor and purpose would draw a sharp contrast with Carter. They knew the political window for dramatic budget and tax cuts was preciously brief.

The reasons lie not only in the ongoing institutional power struggle between White House and Congress, but also in the administration's own human chemistry. The first flush of enthusiasm forges unity, before inevitable rivalries divide the White House into factions or set cabinet members at odds with each other and the White House.

"Everything depends on what you do in program formulation during the first six or seven months," a former Nixon adviser told scholar Thomas Cronin. "I have watched three presidencies, and I am increasingly convinced of that. Time goes by so fast. During the first six months or so, the White House staff is not hated by the cabinet, there is a period of friendship and cooperation and excitement. There is some animal energy going for you in those first six to eight months, especially if people perceive things in the same light. If that exists, and so long as that exists, you can get a lot done. You only have a year at the most for new initiatives, a time when you can establish some programs as your own, in contrast to what has gone on before."[12]

Understanding the time pressure, Reagan's strategists began laying plans even before Reagan won the election. In October 1980, Richard Wirthlin and Richard Beale, two of Reagan's strategists, started work on an "initial action plan," which urged Reagan immediately to claim a "mandate for change" and to go for bold actions in the first ninety days. "The window of opportunity opens and closes quickly," the study advised, "therefore, the President needs to take the initiative early and decisively."[13] For seven pages, the study charted week-by-week actions of presidents Roosevelt, Eisenhower, Kennedy, Nixon, and Carter from their election through their first hundred days in office. The charts showed legislative proposals, foreign trips, speeches, press conferences, meetings, television addresses, and unexpected developments such as the 1961 Bay of Pigs invasion.

"We drew three broad conclusions," David Gergen said. "One: In the first one hundred days, you have a chance to define your persona as president, to form anew in the public mind who you are and what your character is. Two: This is the critical time for setting the themes and agenda for your entire presidency. Remember, Ike went to Korea to begin to make peace during his transition [between election and inauguration]. Carter's agenda was diffuse. And three: The first one hundred days was a time when you were vulnerable to a grievous mistake that would haunt you, like Kennedy's Bay of Pigs. You have to avoid getting into mischief."[14]

Along with focus and speed, Reagan's game plan required staking an immediate claim to a sweeping popular mandate for his conservative program, for interpreting election results is a critical element in the Washington power game. Smart politicians know that one key to success in office is getting the press, rival politicians, and sometimes the public to accept your reading of what the vote meant.

But in 1980, could Reagan legitimately claim a big policy mandate? He was far from winning a landslide. Other presidents—Abraham Lincoln, Woodrow Wilson, and John Kennedy—had won with less than fifty percent of the popular vote. Reagan had won fifty-one percent, but only 26.8 percent of the nation's adult population had voted for him, fractionally fewer than had picked Carter in 1976 (26.9 percent). The reason was low voter turnout—fewer people voted; the 1980 turnout was the smallest since 1948. Only 52.4 percent of the eligible electorate voted. What is more, a good chunk of the Reagan vote was more anti-Carter than pro-Reagan. A *New York Times*/CBS News election-day poll found that three out of ten Reagan voters said their primary motivation was to get Carter out rather than to put Reagan in. But the Reagan team brushed aside the anti-Carter interpretation and simply claimed they had a public mandate for their man and their program.

What gave force and legitimacy to the Reagan claim was the dramatic Republican takeover of the Senate for the first time since 1954. A stunning Republican net gain of twelve seats in the Senate and thirty-three in the House filled the air with Republican talk of a grand political realignment: the Republican dream of replacing the Democrats as the nation's majority party. The Democrats, although still clinging to a fifty-one-vote majority in the House, were shattered and confused; they were in no frame of mind to dispute Reagan's claim of a political mandate.

Republican control of the Senate was vital, moreover, to Reagan's agenda game. Other recent Republican presidents had lacked that advantage. In the late 1950s, Eisenhower had to bargain with Democratic congressional leaders in order to get his proposals moving in Congress. In 1969, Nixon had trouble moving his congressional agenda largely because the Democrats controlled both Senate and House, and they opposed Nixon. Without the political anchor of a Republican Senate, the Reagan team could have organized the administration and then found itself at the mercy of a Democratic Congress. The president could have bills landing on his desk for signature or veto at the whim of the opposition and not according to his timing. Congress would dominate the agenda. The media would cover not a dominant president but a rebellious Congress, as it had under President Ford. With the Senate in Republican hands, the White House could develop timetables with Senate Majority Leader Howard Baker for its priorities and force the Democrats in the House to respond.

What is more, the political setting favored Reagan's boldness. The powers of the presidency seemed at low ebb, and the nation yearned for a strong leader. The wellsprings of public confidence in government had nearly run dry. Across the land, there was a palpable longing for America to regain control of its destiny. For a decade, the seemingly endless agony of Vietnam had sapped the nation's vitality and morale. Iran's seizure of fifty-two American hostages had sharpened the pain of national humiliation; the hostages became a concrete metaphor for the nation's sense of impotence.

Watergate had undermined public confidence in politics, and congressional assertiveness had thrown the presidency on the defensive. Some people were saying the government was in such trouble that the American political system had to be changed. Former Treasury Secretary John Connally proposed a six-year term to strengthen the president's hand. Lloyd Cutler, Carter's White House Counsel, urged that the president, vice president, and House members run on a "team ticket" in order to provide a more unified government. Some commentators worried that power had become so fragmented, and special interests so powerful, that the nation had become ungovernable. People wanted strong leadership.

Finally, Reagan was able to claim a mandate because the intellectual initiative had passed from the Democrats to the Republicans—and specifically to conservatives. Ideas *do* matter in politics. Commanding the intellectual initiative was a central source of political strength for Reagan. Conservative think tanks such as the American Enterprise Institute for Public Policy Research and the Heritage Foundation, both in Washington, and the Hoover Institution in Stanford, California, had been pouring out policy prescriptions and policymakers for the new administration. Young Turk Republicans, such as Representative Jack Kemp of Buffalo and David Stockman, were preaching a new economic gospel.

In short, Reaganism profited from an intellectual vaccuum in Washington. There was a general loss of faith in the old assumptions and the old political prescriptions. Deficit-spending Keynesian economics had been politically discredited; so had the big-government approach of Lyndon Johnson's Great Society programs. American politics seemed to have gone off track, its direction no longer clear. Three presidents had ventured forth to do battle with the twin-headed monster of inflation and stagnant growth—nicknamed stagflation—and had ultimately been devoured by that dragon. The nation sickly careened from one malaise to the other. America's aging industrial plants and stodgy managerial habits were losing out to foreign competitors.

The country and many politicians were ready to try new answers. The rumble of new thunder had come in 1978 with California's tax revolt. A popular referendum passed Proposition Thirteen, slashing state property taxes in half. A year or two before Reagan arrived in the White House, the power game in Washington began to shift. Even traditional Democrats such as House Speaker Tip O'Neill and Senate Majority Leader Robert Byrd had pressed multibillion-dollar budget cuts on President Carter in 1980, feeling Carter's budget cutting was inadequate. Shrinking government, or rather slowing its growth, was fashionable.

And on national-security issues, the relentless Soviet strategic buildup during the 1970s had created a strong prodefense mood; many politicians feared the Kremlin was aiming for nuclear superiority. With the Soviet invasion of Afghanistan in 1979, Carter began pushing his own strategic buildup. The political climate was receptive to Reagan's message.

For three decades, as a conservative crusader, Reagan had been preaching about less government and lower taxes. For years, he had been attacking Washington and the "puzzle palaces on the Potomac" as obstacles to the individual and the free market. He had romanticized the role of the business entrepreneur. As governor of California, he had actually taken some liberal actions—raising taxes, imposing tax withholding, giving cost-of-living increases to welfare recipients—but those had been lost in the contagion of his rhetorical blasts at big government.

Reagan's deep antitax instincts got intellectual underpinning from the new gospel of supply-side economics. Shrewdly, Reagan and the Republican New Right dressed up supply side as a radical innovation, but actually the idea was a throwback to classical economics, a nostalgic return to the laissez-faire probusiness politics of Calvin Coolidge.

As a theory, Reaganomics deliberately stood Keynesian economics on its head. Keynes had argued that demand, the purchasing power of consumers, was what drove the economy; when demand was insufficient, factories were idle, masses of workers were unemployed, and the government had to pump-prime the economy with deficit spending to create new jobs. The supply-side theology took the opposite tack. It reached back to one of the teachings of Jean-Baptiste Say, a nineteenth-century French economist and follower of Adam Smith: "Supply creates its own demand." In other words, production (supply) drives the economy, generating appetites among consumers. Hence the nickname supply-siders, coined by Herbert Stein, formerly chairman of Nixon's Council of Economic Advisers. The role of government, in the modern supply-side version of University of Southern California economist Arthur Laffer, is to free entrepreneurs from the burden of taxes and regulations, to let business innovate and produce.

This supply-side approach was an economic theology well suited to Reagan. It fit the classical, pre-Keynesian economics Reagan had studied at Eureka College in 1928–32, and it meshed with his sunny optimism. Supply-side economics explicitly rejected the pessimistic 1970s vogue of "limits to growth." With the magic of the marketplace free to operate, supply-siders said, growth would be unbounded.[15]

There were two other attractions for Reagan, important ingredients for his message and his agenda. One was known as the Laffer Curve. Arthur Laffer asserted that under certain conditions cutting tax *rates* could actually increase government tax *revenues* by giving people more incentive to work. With more work and more production to be taxed, there would be more taxes to collect. Laffer told Reagan that the natural expansion of the American economy was being constricted by the wasteful welfare state. It was music to Reagan's ears.

The other concept came from Columbia University economist Robert Mundell, who asserted that it was possible to have both tight money policies to check inflation and the fiscal stimulus of tax reduction to spur economic growth. Most economists and policymakers contended that monetary and fiscal policies have to be used together, against either inflation or unemployment. But Mundell said they could be used separately, one to slay inflation and the other to lick unemployment. Again, Mundell's argument was music to Reagan. A few advisers warned him that Mundell's approach would not work, could not work—indeed, Reagan's own experience would prove that in 1982–83. But Reagan bought Mundell's theory anyway, for it told Reagan what he wanted to believe: that you could cut taxes, cut inflation, have economic growth, and balance the budget all at the same time.

The main outlines of the supply-side gospel were infused into Reagan's political bloodstream during an all-day seminar at the swank Beverly Wilshire Hotel in Beverly Hills in January 1980. Reagan's economic tutors were an inner core of supply-siders: Jack Kemp, Arthur Laffer, and Jude Wanninski, a former editorial writer for *The Wall Street Journal.* [16] Banking on their theory, Reagan committed himself to Kemp's pet idea: a ten-percent-per-year cut in individual tax rates over three years, thirty percent in all. That was a critical step in setting Reagan's future presidential agenda. Other economic planks were added later.

During the 1980 campaign, Reagan's rivals cautioned the country not to buy the supply-side mirage. George Bush warned that the Kemp-Laffer-Mundell ideas were "voodoo economics." John Anderson, the independent third-party candidate, quipped prophetically that it would take "blue smoke and mirrors" for Reagan's economic policies to work, especially with a costly military buildup. But voters ignored such warnings, and Reagan nursed his impossible dream.

Reagan has a political genius for selling his message—like the genius of Franklin Roosevelt. His secret is his mastery of political shorthand. He knows how to make ideas accessible and popular. They became powerful political tools in Reagan's hands because of his ability to simplify, to project themes, to limn gossamer vistas of "a rising tide that will lift all boats" (a phrase borrowed from Kennedy). In an age of thirty-second television sound bites, politics lives by shorthand communication. Politicians and voters depend on labels, slogans, quick-stick, fast-fix clichés immediately recognizable to millions (though vaguely understood): Communists, welfare cheats, bureaucrats, New Right, New Deal, Star Wars, deficit spenders, supply-side, tax reform, evil empire. Reagan has a knack for coining phrases that tap into reservoirs of popular feeling—like his refrain to "get government off your back"—without having to explain what he means in policy terms, what his ideas will cost, or whom they will hurt. He is a master at using symbols that convey broad intention and leave him free later to interpret their meaning.

This political shorthand helped Reagan frame the political agenda, for when he entered the White House, people felt they knew what Reaganism meant. That gave Reagan a distinct advantage over Carter and Nixon, in the essential tasks of setting the battle plan and rallying the troops.

1981 Game Plan: Picking Priorities

The most important axiom of the agenda game is to keep the focus on your main priorities; don't get led astray. Any president is constantly buffeted by events and torn by conflicting advice. It is easy for him to lose his compass. For policy-making is a battle for a president's mind among rival factions, and Reagan's administration was faction ridden. Reagan had cast out the bait of many campaign pledges to lure his fifty-one-percent majority, and by the time he had won the White House, he had plenty of rival constituencies to satisfy—all with different agendas.

At the core, his movement embraced ideologues and pragmatists; an old-boy California network and new boys from the Bush and Ford camps; traditional Republicans and the New Right; the "Market Right," whose main agenda was laissez-faire economics; and the "Moralistic Right," whose priorities were outlawing abortion and restoring school prayer.[17] There were orthodox budget-balancing economists (Alan Greenspan and George Shultz), money-managing monetarists (Milton Friedman), and tax-cutting supply-siders (Paul Craig Roberts and Norman Ture). It was no easy trick to weld them together.

As Reagan's first term began, some supporters had to take a back seat if economic policy was to be given clear priority. The Moralistic Right, led by senators Jesse Helms of North Carolina and James McClure of Idaho, had to be told their social agenda of prayer in schools and battling abortion was going on the back burner. Then Reagan had to slough off his campaign pledges to eliminate the departments of Energy and Education. (Actually, he did ask Congress for authority to reorganize the executive branch but did not follow up.) Reagan also put off promised efforts to seek the power of line-item veto for himself and to pass a constitutional amendment requiring a balanced budget. Only one other priority stood on a par with his economic program: the defense buildup. That produced a conflict in priorities, a conflict that was ignored for several months.

In the critical early weeks, Secretary of State Alexander Haig nearly upset the Reagan applecart by taking attention away from economic policy and shifting it to foreign policy. Haig made Central America a dramatic, visible, and controversial issue. Taking his cue from Reagan's stridently anti-Communist campaign, Haig issued a State Department white paper on Soviet, Cuban, and Nicaraguan aid to leftist guerrillas in El Salvador and talked of escalating Central America into a global confrontation with Moscow.

By early March, Haig was getting almost daily front-page headlines, upstaging Reagan's desired focus on economic policy. Among a list of action options on Central America for Reagan, Haig proposed "going to the source"—meaning Cuba. State Department leaks indicated that Haig wanted to beef up American forces in the Caribbean and take some action against Cuba, possibly a naval quarantine. House Speaker Tip O'Neill quoted Haig as saying U.S. troops would have to be used in Nicaragua.[18] At a National Security Council meeting in March 1981, Haig pushed Reagan to be bold in El Salvador: "This is one you can win, Mr. President." After that session, one well-placed White House aide told me, Haig stunned Baker and Deaver with brash talk about bombing Cuba: "We can make that fucking place look like a parking lot!" On March 23, by Haig's account, he told Edwin Meese that action in the Caribbean had to get under way within ten days. But neither Defense Secretary Caspar Weinberger nor the Joint Chiefs of Staff favored military actions. Moreover, Haig's menacing talk had raised alarms in Congress and revived public worries about Reagan's warmonger image.

White House strategists were worried that events were getting out of control. According to their daily tabulation of television news coverage, Central America was getting more airtime than the Reagan economic program. Haig was trampling all over the White House agenda. Political advisers Meese, Baker, Deaver, and Darman feared Haig might draw Reagan into repeating Carter's ill-fated mistake in 1977 of fighting Congress prematurely on a secondary issue. Newspaper polls showed rising public anxiety about Central America. Baker, eager for ammunition that could persuade Reagan to call off Haig, secretly asked Reagan pollster Richard Wirthlin to do a rush poll of public reactions to Haig's talk against Cuba. "Dick," Baker told Wirthlin, "Al Haig is talking about throwing an embargo around Cuba. Let's get a study in the field so we can have something to present to the president."

"At the time, we were taking surveys week to week and we saw some slippage in Reagan's popularity," David Gergen recalled. "Our domestic stuff had dominated the news play in the first weeks, and Reagan's polls went up. Then we got the Salvadoran news, and Reagan's polls fell because it brought up the trigger-happy stuff [Democratic charges in 1980 that Reagan was trigger happy]. People got afraid of what Reagan would do. We were losing control of the agenda. We had a different game we wanted to play. Important as Central America was, it diverted attention from our top priority, which was economic recovery, which we wanted to be the only priority. Haig didn't understand that. We decided we had to cut off his story."[19]

Wirthlin's poll, conducted March 6–8, showed the public reacting negatively to Haig's bellicose talk and opposed to embargos and military action against Cuba. One Reagan intimate told me Baker took the poll results to the president to persuade him that Haig's tactics were hurting Reagan politically; the president got the message. According to one White House account, Baker telephoned Haig in late March and told him the president wanted him "to knock it off." Haig complied, only to kick up new troubles with the White House over who should manage foreign-policy crises. Control of Reagan's agenda continued to slip away, until the president was shot on March 30. The outpouring of public sympathy gave Reagan a boost in popularity. It also halted the drift in policy, for it gave Reagan a new platform to turn public attention back to his economic agenda. Reagan did that, after his hospital recovery, with a moving appearance before a joint session of Congress on April 28. Luck—bad luck turned to good fortune—as well as a superb political performance, rescued Reagan's wayward game plan.

Reagan's agenda was also kept on track—and given life—by David Stockman. No single figure, other than Reagan, was more important to Reagan's early success than Stockman, the cocky, zealous, young budget director whose oversized glasses gave him an owlish look. Without Stockman, the supply-side superachiever, Reagan would have been unable to fashion his first budget proposals and make his stunning start. Reagan had a vision; Stockman had a strategy.

Stockman's operation is a lesson in early game planning. No one else in the administration understood enough budget economics, enough of the operation of Congress, enough of the existing programs and policies to put a budget package together rapidly. None of the old Reagan crowd had the experience or the intellect to draft the Reagan blueprint, to convert Reagan's glowing visions into concrete proposals. It took enormous energy, knowledge, and intellect to impose order on the contending Reaganite factions and the sprawling complexities of the federal budget. The president had neither the driving intelligence nor the inclination to impose such order; nor did others in his inner circle. The intellectual leadership was turned over to Stockman, and even he, as he later admitted, was way over his head.

Stockman got a jump on everyone else because he had his own agenda and his own legislative blueprint already prepared, and he

understood the real levers of power. Two terms as a Michigan congressman plus a network of key Republican and Democratic connections
had taught Stockman how to play the power game. Through Jack
Kemp, Stockman gained entrée to the Reagan circle as one of the
drafters of the 1980 Republican economic platform. Because Stockman
had once worked for John Anderson, he was tapped as Reagan's sparring partner to rehearse for the presidential debates with Anderson, the
independent candidate, and President Carter. Stockman's impersona-
tions impressed Reagan, and when it came time to form the Reagan
cabinet, Kemp and Senator Paul Laxalt pushed Stockman for a top
post. Stockman was offered the job of Energy secretary, but he knew
enough about how power works in Washington to turn down a cabinet
post and ask for another job, theoretically more junior. Stockman
wanted to be budget director, or formally, director of the Office of
Management and Budget (OMB) because he understood how he could
make that more powerful than a cabinet position.

The Reagan Californians did not understand the importance of the
budget post. In those early, heady days, they were preoccupied with
settling prominent cabinet positions such as State, Defense, Treasury,
and Justice. Stockman had no real rivals for OMB, and he got the job
easily. Edwin Meese obviously expected to be making policy through
his cabinet councils and assumed that the budget would flow from his
policy outline. Like many others, he did not understand the power of
the technical expertise lodged in the budget bureau. "Meese had a
funny attitude," Stockman told me. "He thought that the Office of
Management and Budget was where they did the technical auditing
work to see if the motor pool had too many cars in it or something like
that. They didn't understand that *OMB is really the policy switchboard
of the executive branch* [emphasis added]."[20]

Stockman was enormously ambitious for real power. Political instinct
and knowledge of the power game told him that Reagan's plans for
sweeping changes in government and the tax system would inevitably
make budget economics the heart of the Reagan program. The budget
would drive policy, not vice versa. That would mean centralized authority for the budget director over cabinet members. Already, OMB had
become the choke point for most cabinet officers. It reviewed and cut
their budgets, approved their legislative proposals, the regulations they
wanted to issue, and all their major policy testimony to Congress. In
short, their policies had to clear through OMB. So long as Stockman
had backing at the White House—and he was quick to forge a working
alliance with Baker, Darman, and cabinet secretary Craig Fuller—he
had wide power.

Moreover, Stockman understood that to move rapidly in those first weeks would require a body of experts available only in OMB. For the apparatus of OMB is the second most powerful staff in Washington, almost rivaling the top White House staff. Inevitably, President Reagan and his entourage had to lean on OMB for the substance of the budget. Meese's White House domestic staff was far too small and too green in early 1981 to draft a budget or to keep pace with the trained civil servants at OMB. Its staff of six hundred included some of the very best career professionals in government, experts on every field.

"What Stockman did would not have been possible had OMB not had the kind of staff capability to turn out, within a thirty-day period, an enormous amount of collected historical wisdom on where you cut," Stuart Eizenstat, Carter's highly regarded domestic policy chief, remarked to me. "The fact is OMB enabled President Reagan to hit the ground running. It enabled him to get his package up to Congress very early, without delay, before opposition could form, both within the executive branch and in the Congress. That to me was the quintessential event in the entire administration—because had Reagan gotten off to a slow start on the budget cuts, had he permitted opposition to grow within the executive branch, and had opposition had a chance to form on Capitol Hill, you might have seen a very different situation with respect to the success of the budget cuts."[21]

Stockman's ace in the hole was the game plan he had developed and already market-tested in Congress. In March 1980, Stockman and Phil Gramm, then a radically conservative Democratic congressman from Texas, had drafted their own budget for fiscal year 1981, in what amounted to a dry run of the Reagan proposals.

The Gramm-Stockman budget gave Reagan's practical political agenda a head start. Their bill embraced both Kemp's ten-percent cut in individual income tax rates and a depreciation-based tax cut for business. The big budget cuts that Stockman would fashion for Reagan in 1981 were all there: multibillion-dollar cuts in the public service jobs program, food stamps, housing and energy subsidies to the poor, revenue sharing with state and local governments. The Gramm-Stockman bill also capped Medicaid reimbursement to the states, restricted longer term unemployment benefits, eliminated student and minimum benefits from Social Security, and cut mass transit subsidies. The Gramm-Stockman bill did not pass, but it got 170 votes—140 Republicans and thirty Democrats—a very solid core for Reagan's own budget coalition in 1981. That was a critical prelude for Reagan's agenda.[22]

Most importantly, Stockman's pretested budget gave Reagan a chance to move with incredible speed to impose retroactive cuts on

Carter's 1981 budget and to revamp Carter's 1982 budget. To Reagan's top advisers, speed was crucial, but it was an abstraction; to Stockman, speed meant concrete timetables and proposals. To feed the political stampede, Stockman and Kemp had written an alarmist memo warning that the nation, then in mild recession, faced an "economic Dunkirk." Once inside the Reagan team, Stockman spurred it on.

Stockman was named budget director on December 11, 1980, and impatiently dismissed Meese's preliminary budget work as inadequate. (Stockman confessed he was stunned by the "low level of fiscal literacy" of Reagan, Bush, Meese, and others.) Five days later, he told Baker that time was already running out because Reagan would have to put his stamp on the 1982 budget by the first week of February, two weeks after inauguration. "Let me game it out for you," Stockman advised. "By January 7, we need to have a rough idea what the plan looks like: budget, tax, and some other issues. . . . We've got to get Meese committed to it. We've got to get Reagan committed to it."[23]

Fixing the Action Sequence

Ideally, a president's legislative agenda must be plotted like a military campaign. For all the seeming unanimity in Reagan's top echelon, the commander and his key lieutenants could not agree on what to assault first: tax cuts or budget cuts. The action sequence was crucial to Reagan's political success. Reagan and his California advisers leaned toward starting with tax cuts. Stockman, appalled by the worsening economy, tried to stun them into starting with massive budget cuts. Since September, he told them at a meeting in early January, the likely deficit for Carter's departing 1981 budget had shot up from $20 billion to $58 billion, and by 1984, it would take $75 billion in cuts (later $130 billion) to produce the balanced budget Reagan had promised. Reagan missed Stockman's message; he suspected political sabotage.[24]

Baker and Wirthlin raised warning flags about the dangers of promising too much. They pushed for a combination of budget and tax cuts, with Baker arguing that it would be politically easier to take budget cuts ahead of tax cuts; Wirthlin, an economist by trade, worried that a tax cut first would widen the deficit. Both disputed, as impossibly optimistic, estimates by Stockman and Martin Anderson, Meese's aide, that Reagan policies would bring a five-percent economic growth rate.

Their warnings were on the mark but brushed aside by Reagan, who liked the sunny optimism of five-percent growth.

"All right, we've heard this argument," he said, looking around the table. "Does anyone else feel strongly about it?" No one else spoke up. "Well," the president-elect concluded, "we're going to go for tax cuts, first and foremost."[25]

As often happens with presidents, that decision did not stick. Pressures were building on Wall Street for postponing the tax cut for six months and for attacking the deficit first. Those sentiments were echoed by leading Senate Republicans such as Budget Committee Chairman Pete Domenici, Finance Committee Chairman Robert Dole, and Majority Leader Howard Baker. The legislative calendar, especially an early vote to increase the national debt, seemed to dictate budget cuts first. Because the White House needed the Senate leaders to put Reagan's proposals on the legislative calendar, their voices had weight at the White House. They reinforced Stockman's arguments and a consensus formed at the White House.

"A plan to permanently reduce the size of the federal budget must be launched within two or three weeks of the Inauguration and must be the *lead element* [emphasis added] in the total economic package," Wirthlin wrote in the initial action plan for Reagan. "Professional economic opinion and Wall Street sentiment could run against a major tax cut in the absence of real spending restraint." Moreover, Wirthlin told Reagan, opinion polling showed that the public "much preferred" cutting federal spending to cutting taxes. There is "strong" fear, he added, that tax cuts without "significant" budget cuts "will accelerate the rate of inflation."[26]

Ramming the Stockman budget cuts through the cabinet caused grumbling but was relatively easy because none of the new cabinet officers knew his department's programs well enough to defend them against Stockman, and only the Pentagon was exempt from Reagan's guillotine. The cabinet's period of innocence was an ideal moment for Stockman to strike, forcing cabinet secretaries to swallow $40 billion in cuts that Reagan sanctioned for his game plan.

Selling such a package to the nation and to the Washington community takes place on several levels. As a pair of supersalesmen, Reagan and Stockman were irresistible, working in tandem. On television and addressing joint sessions of Congress, Reagan gave the broad sweep and created an air of economic crisis that impelled fast action. Stockman, the wunderkind numbers cruncher, was the vital persuader of senators, congressmen, staff aides, and journalists who fancied themselves as budget specialists. He bedazzled both allies and adversaries with the razzle-dazzle of budget arithmetic. He gave rationales for Reagan's visions and protected Reagan and his agenda from the flak of technical arguments. Like a child prodigy chess champion playing fifty matches at once, Stockman answered every query, parried every countermove, checked every challenge. Congress was mesmerized. Even Speaker Tip O'Neill spoke in wonder of the economic whiz kid, a farm boy not yet nine years out of Michigan State University with a slide rule for a brain.

Stockman was a Washington phenomenon: an ambitious, politically canny operator with the cachet of factual knowledge as his armament. Most politicians deal in bromides, platitudes, and spongy generalities; they are drawn to—and often awed by—the precision of experts who deal in hard numbers and stick decimal points in the bottom line, even if the numbers can really be no more than rough guesstimates. Numbers smack of certitude to a world that lives on speculation; their appeal is that they sound concrete. Stockman on the budget was like Kennedy's defense secretary, Robert S. McNamara, with his reams of statistics showing how the Vietnam War was being won.

In early 1981, the Reagan economic agenda was aided by what the English poet Samuel Taylor Coleridge once called a "willing suspension of disbelief." Skepticism was way below normal. The novelty of Stockman's numbers helped to sell them. With the economy skidding around dangerously and inflation sky high, most Republicans and many Democrats wanted to believe that someone had the answers. They, like Reagan, were willing to invest Stockman with that authority. Stockman added a factual monopoly to the administration's intellectual initiative, at least temporarily. He spoke with such cocky self-assurance—arrogance, some said—rattling off his budget catechism, that he instilled a false confidence that the Reagan team knew exactly where it was going and how things would work out. Stockman's version of reality sold famously, while he himself was developing doubts.

"Even the appearance of being an expert is self-validating," Stockman confessed five years later. "I didn't know much about budgets but I knew more than the rest of them."[27]

The political game plan succeeded brilliantly for Ronald Reagan. It gave him the most stunning legislative victories that Congress had seen since the wizardry of Lyndon Johnson in the mid-1960s. The Reagan agenda prevailed: bigger budget cuts than anyone had previously imagined, the biggest cash flow into defense ever seen, and by far the largest tax cut in American history—a string of unbelievable legislative victories.

The fast, sure opening made it possible. Lyndon Johnson's political logic had been sound: Get all you can in the first year; later, it's impossible. Reagan's first budget was the only one that Congress passed virtually intact. In 1982, he had to backtrack and accept a whopping tax increase; after that, he had to compromise, or was simply ignored. But in the flush of Republican supply-side euphoria in 1981, Congress bowed to the Reagan-Stockman logic and bent to the swift-moving Reagan agenda. Reagan won his first budget victory in the House on May 7—just 108 days after his inauguration.

Damage Control: Protecting the Game Plan

Once the action is moving, the most important rule of the agenda game for any administration is not to step on its own parade or let secondary events derail the agenda. The keys to the opening phase of the agenda game are speed, a mandate, a game plan, and clear, focused priorities. In the next phase, the key to controlling the agenda is what White House strategists call effective damage control.

No presidency is free of accidents or events exploding unpredictably: terrorist attacks, shipjackings, unrest in South Africa or the Philippines, a *contra* plane shot down over Nicaragua, or political scandals over toxic waste, the price of Pentagon spare parts, or the actions of cabinet members. Like fire fighters, the president's inner circle battle the political blaze—first, to keep it from politically burning the president, and second, to keep it from consuming his game plan.

Often, the most disastrous political damage is caused not by some external explosion but by a self-inflicted wound. That happened to Reagan and the Republican party in 1981, the result of Reagan and Stockman's overconfidence and overreaching. It was a joint Reagan-Stockman disaster on Social Security, and they nearly did it a second time, but they were stopped by Jim Baker, Howard Baker, and House Republican Leader Robert Michel.

For years Reagan had urged that the Social Security system be made voluntary. Stockman knew that in order to curb runaway deficits, some adjustment had to be made in Social Security. Still, what Reagan and Stockman attempted was so inflammatory that they made Social Security the political "third rail" for Republicans—as fatal for them to touch as the middle rail of a subway line.

The Reagan-Stockman blunder was strange because it was unnecessary. Although it was known to very few, Reagan had actually been offered an attractive bipartisan package on Social Security by several Senate Democrats in March 1981. Senator Fritz Hollings of South Carolina, a ranking Democrat on the Budget Committee and cosponsor of Reagan's own budget package, had notified Committee Chairman Pete Domenici in early March that five of the committee's ten Democrats were ready to vote for a budget-saving cut in the annual cost-of-living adjustment (COLA) for Social Security. Hollings reckoned his plan would save the government $38 billion over three years; Domenici figured the savings were somewhat less, but he and other Republicans were very enthusiastic. A bipartisan initiative on this ticklish issue would give political cover to Reagan and the Republicans, sparing them from taking all the political blame.

When Reagan came to Capitol Hill on March 16 for a private session with Republican committee chairmen and budget committee members, Domenici made a pitch to freeze or modify the Social Security COLAs.

Reagan replied that he had promised in his campaign not to cut Social Security benefits.

"But you can keep your word and support a COLA freeze because a COLA is something which was never in the original law," Domenici insisted. "We could put the [Social Security] fund on a sound basis and set this budget on a sound basis by either freezing or modifying the COLA."[28]

Bill Armstrong of Colorado, Slade Gorton of Washington, and others supported Domenici, but no one pushed the new president hard. James Baker had already counseled Reagan against taking the political risk of touching Social Security. Stockman opposed Domenici's move because he had his own designs.

"I am not going to support that," Reagan told his Republicans, "and I really hope you don't either."

Reagan's reaction killed the idea.

That also made it all the more stunning when in May, just two months later—and with no offer of Democratic partnership—Reagan gave his blessing to a far more controversial slash in actual Social Security benefits. The plan had been developed by Stockman, Secretary of Health and Human Services Richard Schweiker, and Martin Anderson. It made structural changes in the program, among them a cut in disability benefits and a thirty-five-percent cut in benefits for early retirement at sixty-two. To the dismay of Jim Baker and Dick Darman, who opposed it, Reagan approved the plan on the spot during a briefing on May 11. Evidently deluded by the ease of his first big budget victory in the House just four days before, Reagan thought he could get just about anything through Congress, but he was violating all the basic rules of smart legislative politics, for he had not checked out the proposal with his Republican legislative leaders before giving the go-ahead. Baker and Darman, convinced this move was political suicide, tried to distance Reagan from it. Schweiker was left to announce it the next day.

The political cannonade was instantaneous. The main furor was over the cut in early-retirement benefits, to be effective the following January. Suddenly, people who had been counting on retiring at $470 a month would get only $311. "Despicable," boomed House Speaker Tip O'Neill. "Cruel and insidious," declaimed "Mr. Social Security"— septuagenarian Florida Democrat Claude Pepper. Republicans ran for cover. White House officials, seeking to dump blame elsewhere, anonymously derided it as Schweiker's Folly. New York Democratic Senator Daniel Patrick Moynihan offered a stinging resolution to condemn Reagan's "breach of faith" with millions of Americans approaching retirement; his resolution failed by one vote. In self-defense, Republican Robert Dole offered a milder substitute which sailed through, 96– 0. The bloom was off the Reagan rose.

Had it not been for Baker's damage-control tactics, the Social Security blunder could have derailed Reagan's economic package. But to keep the main agenda moving, Baker got Reagan and Stockman to get the issue out of the headlines by withdrawing the package.

Reagan and Stockman retreated but they did not give up. Their original budget eliminated the guaranteed minimum benefit and student benefits under Social Security. Each nursed hopes for more cuts. Come September, with Reaganism at high tide, Stockman was privately assembling a new package of budget cuts, plus a $50 billion tax increase and a slower defense buildup. Once again, he pushed Reagan to try restructuring the Social Security system, as they had tried in May—and Reagan agreed. Convinced that he could make a persuasive case to voters, he drafted a speech one September weekend at Camp David and told White House aides he wanted to address the nation.[29]

Sensing new political dynamite, Baker immediately began damage control. Needing powerful allies to dissuade Reagan, he alerted Howard Baker and Robert Michel, the two Republican leaders in Congress. Howard Baker told me he had called Michel.

"Bob," he asked, "can you pass that over in the House?"

"God no," Michel replied. "Can you pass it in the Senate?"

"Not a prayer," Baker replied.

"Who's going to tell the president?" Michel inquired.

"I guess we are," Baker said.[30]

In about an hour, Jim Baker had assembled the two congressional leaders, himself, and Richard Darman in the Oval Office with the president. Howard Baker tried to warn Reagan that his plan didn't stand a chance in Congress, but the president was very proud of his speech and wanted to read it to them—six or seven handwritten pages on a long yellow legal pad. Based on his mail and his sense of the country, he felt the public would accept his approach.

For about ten minutes, Reagan read aloud, explaining to the nation why it was necessary to reform Social Security, although it might not be popular. He said he was worried about the system's solvency. He thought younger people were angry at benefits being paid to older people and fearful they would not get their own. He laid out the rationale for the May package and defended canceling the minimum benefit (which Congress would later restore). Reagan argued that his reforms were fair and would save money. When he had finished reading, the president looked up and asked, "What do you think of that?"

"I think that's an awful good speech," Howard Baker replied tactfully. "But I don't think you'd better make it because we can't pass that thing."

"Well, what are we going to do about it?" the president pressed earnestly. "It has to be dealt with. The whole issue of Social Security has to be dealt with."

Howard Baker made a suggestion.

"I'll tell you what to do," he said. "I served on the National Water Quality Commission that Nelson Rockefeller chaired, and it worked awfully well. It was a noncongressional group, bipartisan, with staff. And what I recommend is that you emulate that example—that you, by executive order, create this commission and then invite me and Bob Byrd to appoint some members, and Tip [O'Neill] and Bob Michel to appoint some, and you appoint some and the chairman. And they may or may not work anything out. But that's going to at least put it over on another track, and I'm going to stop worrying about it for a while. And who knows? It might produce a result."

It was a classic damage-control maneuver. Presidential commissions have often been used to bury issues without resolving them. Plenty of political damage had already been done in May; Howard Baker's idea was a way out of more trouble, and Reagan bent with the prevailing wind. On September 24, he made a televised address deploring the "pure demagoguery" of Democrats on Social Security. Rather inconsistently, Reagan asked Congress to restore the minimum benefit that he had once wanted cut but also defended his May appeal for broader cuts. He finished by announcing that "to remove Social Security once and for all from politics," he was going to set up a bipartisan commission. Not until January 1983—after the next election—did it report. And it produced a modest, but successful bipartisan package.

The second major incident that stepped on the Reagan parade in 1981, and nearly derailed it, was another self-inflicted wound, and it produced one of the most sophisticated damage-control operations I have seen in Washington. By August 1981, Stockman had become an intellectual defector from Reaganomics—no longer convinced that the original budget and tax package would work. He had taken to heart Reagan's campaign pledge to balance the budget, and OMB's economic forecasts by August persuaded him that Reagan's deficits would soon double and triple those Reagan had inherited from Carter. Stockman also knew that his own budget calculations in early 1981 had been gravely inaccurate, that he had plastered together the superoptimism of the economic supply-siders (predicting five-percent real annual growth) and the high-inflation assumptions of other economists, to project artificially inflated estimates of government tax revenues in the coming years. Privately, Stockman later admitted to me that the success of Reaganomics had been based on a false "Rosy Scenario"—his own derisive term—which he had helped concoct.[31]

By mid-1981, Stockman understood that while the Reagan game plan was a stunning political success, its economics were heading the nation to ruinous deficits. So, almost literally on the morning after Reagan's big budget and tax victories, Stockman was privately trying to persuade President Reagan to raise taxes and cut back on his defense buildup, in order to try to restrain the burgeoning deficits. Baker, Darman, Gergen, Deaver, and eventually Meese joined this effort, but Reagan resisted.[32] His own pet agenda of tax cuts and a military buildup was on track, and he was sloughing off the promise of balancing the budget, though he was not yet ready to admit that to Congress and the voters. On the heels of his stunning 1981 legislative victories, Reagan did not want to change his agenda. When others told him his economic optimism was unfounded, he turned a deaf ear.

What nearly derailed the Reagan train was an exposé of Stockman's loss of faith in a stunning article by William Greider in the December 1981 *Atlantic Monthly*. The way the Reagan White House handled those damaging revelations is a classic lesson in snuffing out bad news before it damages the president.

The *Atlantic* article, based on Stockman's candid admissions to Greider, was political dynamite. Greider quoted Stockman as admitting he had jimmied the budget numbers when his computers produced appalling deficit projections from the Reagan package. Probably his most damaging admission was that the ten-percent-per-year tax cut "was always a Trojan horse to bring down the top [tax] rate" for the wealthy and to clothe old-fashioned Republican trickle-down economics in an attractive new package. "It's kind of hard to sell 'trickle down,'" Stockman told Greider. "So the supply-side formula was the only way to get a tax policy that was really 'trickle down.' Supply-side is 'trickle-down' theory."[33] That was a fuse to ignite the anger of the middle class and their protectors in Congress.

With an economy sliding into recession and Democrats already accusing Reagan of tax cuts that helped the rich and budget cuts that hurt the poor, those were explosive admissions. They certainly derailed Stockman's proposal for more budget cutting in late 1981, but clever damage limitation by the White House prevented far worse damage. Stockman's confessions were explosive enough to discredit Reaganomics permanently and to undermine the core of the president's agenda. The article made the shaky foundations of Reagan's economic program fit for national debate.

Instead, White House strategists—Stockman among them—ingeniously shifted the news focus. The substance of what Stockman had said got lost in a squabble over whether he should have said it. Very few people had time or interest to absorb the contents of the twenty-three-page article, which was devastating in the ignorance, cynicism, and hypocrisy it portrayed. Most people read no more than brief news summaries.

Thus, overnight, the issue became whether this Judas—Stockman—could survive on the Reagan team. Congressional Democrats were slow to pounce on Stockman's confessions, and the White House press corps focused on how Reagan would treat Stockman, so valuable and yet so sinful. Most of the top White House staff wanted Stockman's head on a platter; Jim Baker protected Stockman, though he gave Stockman a barracks-style cussing-out. Then Stockman, tail between his legs, was sent in to Reagan. The ingenious plot device was having Stockman describe his man-to-man talk with the president as a verbal thrashing "more in the nature of a trip to the woodshed after supper."

As Stockman later revealed, the "woodshed" metaphor had been his own invention. Reagan had actually listened sympathetically, eyes moist, to Stockman's apologies and had turned down Stockman's offer to resign. But, as Stockman put it, to "shut down" the *Atlantic* story, and to insure that its substance would be ignored, Stockman had to top it with an even juicier story: his own public self-humiliation. The woodshed line was irresistible. *Time* headlined its story of the whole episode "A Visit to the Woodshed." *Newsweek* had the young budget director as Brutus: "Et Tu, David Stockman?"

Partisan Democrats such as Christopher Matthews, Speaker Tip O'Neill's spokesman, marveled at White House cleverness.

"The most important thing, it shifted attention from the truth, the objective truth of what Stockman had said, to the subjective condition of his loyalty," groaned Matthews. "That served the interest of Reagan *and* Stockman. It gave Stockman expiation; [for] Reagan, it suggested the problem is not revelation but betrayal. The media fell for it in spades, the metaphor of the woodshed. Reagan never had to acknowledge the revelation being true. He was the father dealing with the wayward son, the Prodigal son. And it worked brilliantly."[34]

Nearly five years later, Reagan worked a similar gambit to wiggle away from even more damaging revelations in Stockman's book *The Triumph of Politics: Why the Reagan Revolution Failed*, about the gaping flaws in the Reagan economic program. Like an agile fighter deflecting a heavy punch without letting the crowd know how hard he has been hit, Reagan employed patronizing humor as if to say, There goes little David again. When someone asked whether he had read Stockman's shocking inside account of the deceptions and disasters of Reaganomics, the president quipped: "I don't have too much time for fiction." In the Washington power game, Reagan's soft-touch damage control worked wonders. Once again, Stockman's message was largely ignored.

1985 Game Plan: Broken Field

What is striking about the start of Reagan's second term is that this extremely popular president did not repeat the successful formula of his first year: have a clear game plan, claim a mandate, start fast, focus your agenda. Reagan's handling of Congress in 1981 and 1985 provides a contrast in dos and don'ts in the agenda game. His record in 1985 was more like Carter's in 1977 than his own in 1981: a demonstration that the size of an electoral victory is no guarantee that a president can control the political agenda.

By the arithmetic of election politics, Reagan should have done better in 1985 than in 1981; his reelection landslide was one of the most sweeping presidential victories in modern American politics. In 1980, he had gotten just fifty-one percent of the popular vote. In 1984, he won fifty-nine percent, carried forty-nine states, and got all but thirteen of the nation's 538 electoral votes.

Yet he did not capitalize on the window of opportunity he had created. From the start of his second term, Reagan was bogged down. Democrats were amazed at the openings they were able to seize, and Republicans were downcast at the opportunities lost. Reagan's budget was ignored. He got cut back from one hundred to fifty MX missiles. He wanted six-percent real growth for defense and got none; in fact, defense authorization was cut. He wanted military aid for the Nicaraguan *contras* and settled for nonlethal aid. He could not get arms for Jordan and had to welsh on a promise to provide new jets to Saudi Arabia. He was forced to impose economic sanctions on South Africa, which he had vowed not to do. All fall, he had to fight rearguard action to prevent protectionist trade legislation pushed by House Democrats.

For months, the president lost the political initiative. Others did his hard work in 1985. He was helped, up to a point, by the daring of Senate Republicans: Bob Dole on the budget, Phil Gramm and Warren Rudman on the deficit. Like many a second-term president, Reagan turned to foreign policy to project leadership. Near year's end, Reagan got a major boost from his Geneva summit meeting with Moscow's dynamic new leader, Mikhail Gorbachev, though the two men deadlocked on arms control and regional disputes. Reagan's one domestic triumph was his rescue of tax reform in the House in December—though it took Reagan nearly seven months after his reelection to make tax reform his domestic centerpiece. Overall, this was hardly the record of political invincibility that Reagan's landslide presaged.

Second terms are usually more difficult than first terms. Franklin Roosevelt, Woodrow Wilson, Lyndon Johnson, and Richard Nixon all fared worse during their second terms than in their first terms. The easier goals have been reached, the harder ones remain. Intellectual capital has been drawn down, the momentum of newness has been sapped, and fresh ideas are hard to come by. As Dennis Thomas, a senior second-term presidential aide observed: "Everyone talks about the honeymoon, but the honeymoon and the fifth anniversary are not the same."[35] Richard Neustadt, Harvard University's widely respected presidential scholar, points out that second-term presidents falter either because of fatigue or because of overconfidence. Reagan seemed to suffer from both. Obviously, he felt no political pressure from voters to undertake new initiatives.

In fact, the main cause of Reagan's poor second-term beginnings lay in the 1984 campaign. It was a feel-good campaign, wrapped around the glow of economic recovery, low inflation, the Olympic slogan "Go for the Gold," and the Reagan campaign ad "It's Morning Again in America." Riding far ahead of his Democratic rival, Walter Mondale,

Reagan was unwilling to take the risk of fighting for potentially un-popular policies, however responsible that might be.

On economic policy and the budget, Reagan promised more of the same, though exactly what he meant was unclear, since for three years running, Congress had set aside his budgets, and Reagan had signed tax increases. Trying to smoke out Reagan, Mondale took the supreme political risk of admitting he would propose a tax increase to help stanch the deficit. Mondale wanted an open, honest debate. Reagan, having promised to balance the budget by 1983, practiced the politics of evasion. House Republicans wanted him to attack Mondale by proving that Carter-Mondale programs would have led to bigger defi-cits than Reagan's. The problem was that impartial projections ob-tained by the Republicans showed projected Carter-Mondale deficits as having peaked in 1983 and heading down to $39 billion by 1987—compared to $248 billion in 1987 for projected Reagan deficits. So GOP strategists scrapped the idea of debating deficits.[36] Reagan was riding so far ahead politically that he could afford to be vague.

On taxes, Dick Darman sensibly crafted an ambiguous statement that a tax increase would be "only a last resort"—to convey Reagan's reluctance but also to avoid closing the door to what some Reagan aides deemed essential to taming $200 billion deficits. But Darman's ambi-guity did not accord with Reagan's gut instincts; Reagan closed the campaign declaring taxes would rise only "over my dead body."

On tax reform, Reagan was deliberately vague. In his 1984 State of the Union address, the president had put off the problem by ordering Treasury Secretary Don Regan to study the tax system—but not to report until after the election. Reform was an item Reagan could have taken to the voters, but he let the issue dangle. Dick Wirthlin's mid-summer polling found that many voters heard *tax reform* as code words for a tax increase, so Jim Baker, as top campaign strategist, advised Reagan to soft-pedal it. "We took a look at highlighting tax reform and concluded it would be a mistake," Baker later told me. "The polls showed us that tax reform was an absolute loser with the public. So we opted not to highlight it."[37] So, unlike Reagan's 1980 campaign, in which he outlined his main economic agenda, Reagan put down no clear marker in 1984. He cheered the country with his jaunty slogan "You ain't seen nothin' yet," but that was unrevealing in policy terms—great for politics, bad for governing. The voters got to choose a man and a mood, but not specific policies.

The play-it-safe campaign strategy caused two problems. First, in spite of Reagan's whopping popular vote, his vacuous campaign platform left him without a policy mandate from the voters to leverage Congress. In 1980, he had made budget cuts and tax cuts his main campaign planks, and he could claim to Congress that he had popular backing. Similarly, Lyndon Johnson had called in his 1964 campaign for a "war on poverty" and used that mandate to get Congress to pass his poverty legislation in 1965. By contrast, one of Jimmy Carter's problems in 1977 was trying to make energy proposals the centerpiece of his domestic program without having made that a major campaign issue.

Strangely, given how well Reagan had learned from Carter's mistakes in 1981, he suffered from Carter's problems in 1985. Like Carter in 1977, Reagan could not claim a mandate for tax reform because he had not made that a clear campaign issue.

Moreover, without a clear policy platform in the campaign, Reagan's advisers could not even agree on whether to claim any mandate—a symptom of disarray to come.

Richard Wirthlin, who had told Reagan on election morning that he would carry forty-nine states, and Ed Rollins, Reagan's feisty campaign manager, were both bullish. Favoring a quick second-term start, they wanted to play up the election as a broad legislative mandate. But Jim Baker stopped that.

"We're going to play down the mandate," Baker told Rollins, as Rollins was about to brief the White House press.[38]

Rollins was stunned. "Horseshit!" Rollins roared at Baker. "How're you going to play down forty-nine states?"

Baker insisted. He seemed not to want to inflate popular expectations. And Baker understood that Reagan lacked the congressional votes to revive his old 1981 conservative coalition in Congress. Reagan would need help from Speaker O'Neill for any major legislation. Baker did not want to cross swords with congressional Democrats on the morning after a partisan campaign.

"No," Baker declared. "We need to be gracious winners. We don't want to rub Tip the wrong way. The mandate will emerge from our results with Congress."

Baker himself told reporters: "It was a victory for his [Reagan's] philosophy and a victory for him personally. But I'm not sitting here claiming it's a big mandate."

That uncharacteristic caution reflected Baker's own intellectual fatigue and the policy emptiness of the campaign. In frustration, Wirthlin wrote a memorandum to Meese to push for an action agenda and a fast start, patterned after the first-term triumphs. "Meese was in agreement, but he had his own fish to fry"—namely, becoming attorney general, Wirthlin later lamented.[39]

A second problem arose from the 1984 Reagan campaign: Its themes were so vague that it provided no blueprint or clear legislative strategy. David Stockman favored another run at the Reagan deficits. By then, most thoughtful members of Congress, Democrats and Republicans, privately accepted Stockman's three-pronged formula: some tax increase, much slower growth in defense spending, and winching down cost-of-living adjustments in Social Security and big entitlement programs. But President Reagan rejected a tax increase, blocking Stockman's plan. So the budget initiative passed to Senate Majority Leader Bob Dole.

There were not many other political foundation stones for Reagan's domestic agenda; top Reagan aides privately admitted to me they were out of fresh ideas. Back in 1982, Reagan had tried New Federalism, a program to transfer major federal programs and revenues to the states, but it had flopped. Meese's domestic staff wanted to push welfare reform, Reagan's big achievement as governor of California, but it did not get off the ground. The Jack Kemp wing of House Republicans wanted tax reform, but given Wirthlin's polls showing lack of public enthusiasm, that was not a big favorite at the White House after the election.

Treasury Secretary Donald Regan wanted to bull ahead. On November 27, Regan put out the long-awaited Treasury Department proposal, later known as Treasury I, which called for significant cuts in individual tax rates and a bigger tax burden for business. It got a cool reception, both in Congress and from the president. Given Democratic strength in the House, Ken Duberstein, chief of congressional liaison, and Dick Darman, manager of the Legislative Strategy Group, advised negotiating privately with House Democratic leaders to insure bipartisan support before surfacing any presidential package.

"I'm not so sure the president himself was so enamored with tax reform," Ed Rollins, White House political director, told me. "I'm talking about December '84, January '85. My sense is that if Jim Baker hadn't gone over to Treasury [as secretary in January 1985], it may never have had all the weight it had.

"Treasury I became the first thing out of the box after the election," Rollins recalled. "Nobody was focusing on anything at that time. The bill was so disastrous from a political perspective, it created this tremendous wave of opposition. . . . It had never come to the White House for sign-off. It had never basically been discussed. You know, the two-month period after the election, everybody was just sort of in a letdown stage. And I think with Baker going over to Treasury, knowing that was his claim to fame for the year, they worked it, tried to make it more politically salable. [For] Don Regan going in the White House, clearly tax reform was the most important thing to him. . . . So that the two principal staff leaders certainly provided an impetus."[40]

President Reagan liked the idea of lowering rates but as he saw how tax reform would hit business, it took several months to sell him on the specifics. "I mean, he had to be convinced, day by day, of the merits of the whole thing [by] Baker and Regan," Rollins told me. "My sense is that the President thought it was a good idea, but as he started going through it piece by piece, and he started seeing whose ox got gored, you know, it had less appeal to it. . . . His friends were in the corporate world, and what you basically were doing was shifting your tax burden off of the individual taxpayers onto corporate America. Corporate America is who Ronald Reagan's friends were."

With Reagan lacking a game plan, Congress took the lead—a real oddity in the wake of a landslide presidential election. Congressional Democrats, and even some disgruntled Republicans, filled the vacuum left by the president. Overall, the spring of 1985 was a curious jumble of setbacks for the White House, a political minefield instead of a postelection springboard.

One reason is that while Reagan had soared to a personal victory in 1984, he had been unable to lift his party. The contrast with the big Republican gains of 1980 was dramatic—a portent of things to come. In the 1984 election, the Democrats gained two seats in the Senate, narrowing the Republican majority to 53–47. In the House, the Democrats held Republicans to a net gain of fourteen House seats. What was crucial—and everyone who understands the power game saw this at once—was that the Republican gain was not enough to restore the conservative coalition that had generated Reagan's legislative triumphs in 1981. Perhaps deliberately, the voters left a governmental deadlock, endorsing Reagan without buying all of his policies.

What is more, Congress was less cowed by Reagan than it had been in 1981, and so it cuffed him about. The Lilliputians began cutting up Gulliver. In one early vote, left over from an unsettled battle before the 1984 election, Congress cut in half Reagan's request on MX missiles, limiting him to fifty where he had wanted one hundred (and Carter had planned two hundred). Reagan was hog-tied over his long-delayed nomination of Edmund Meese for attorney general by farm-state senators, who were filibustering Meese's nomination in order to force an early vote on emergency farm credit. It was a no-win battle politically for the White House; either Reagan had to back down or, if he won, he offended farm state leaders and voters, while thousands of farmers faced foreclosure.

These were not good issues for Reagan. White House damage control should have disposed of them, but the second-term team was not that skilled. The smart move would have been to work out a private deal on farm credit before Meese's nomination got tangled in a public fight. However, the farm-credit bill passed, and Reagan, angered by the cost, vetoed it. The problem got worse, for the Senate wrote the same provision into an omnibus spending bill which Reagan signed. Eventually, he had to swallow a mammoth, budget-busting, five-year, $57.5 billion farm program. In 1986 alone, that program wound up costing $25.6 billion—five times its cost in the year before Reagan took office.

In sum, Reagan's hesitancy and his team's disarray threw away the golden moment of his reelection landslide. "The period of January to May of 1985 will be viewed as a time when we could have set in place an agenda which could have been driven by the mandate—and which really wasn't," lamented Richard Wirthlin. "We walked away from it, and I think we paid the piper."[41]

"Reagan had momentum and the high ground," agreed Kirk O'Donnell, Speaker O'Neill's political adviser. "He blew his opportunity to dominate the agenda by not going after the tax bill in February. Had he gone after it, he would have dominated the political horizon and the agenda the same way he did in 1981."[42]

Late Shake-Up, Slow Start

Reagan compounded these problems by reshuffling his top political team long after the elections—a contrast to the fast start of his first team. After his 1980 victory, Reagan installed Baker, Meese, and Deaver within a day or two of his election and added Stockman within a month. But in his second term, Reagan let things drift for a couple of months and then suddenly, on January 8, 1985, announced a major job swap: Chief of Staff Baker becoming treasury secretary and Treasury Secretary Regan taking over as chief of staff.

This signaled a complete—and belated—changing of the guard at the White House, throwing into turmoil efforts to formulate Reagan's agenda. Reagan made the mistake of letting the personal ambitions of his staff—Baker, Meese, and Deaver—take precedence over his own objectives. Meese wanted a policy domain all his own at the Justice

Department. Deaver, with financial problems, wanted to leave government and set up a public relations firm. Baker's departure was the most
costly to Reagan. Baker had been the linchpin for Reagan's first term,
facing down right-wing charges that his pragmatism had corrupted
Reagan and factional clashes with Meese, William Clark, and William
Casey.

Baker was bone-tired and wanted a top cabinet post. He had been
chief of staff for four years and two weeks. (Only two other men had
held the job longer: Sherman Adams, Eisenhower's chief of staff, who
had to resign because of the taint of graft; and Bob Haldeman, Nixon's
chief of staff, who went to jail for the Watergate cover-up.) A senior
cabinet post would let him show substance and gain prominence,
possibly to run for high office. For a couple of years, he had quietly
lobbied for a top cabinet job: secretary of State, Defense, Treasury, or
attorney general. Treasury was the only real possibility.

Treasury Secretary Donald Regan, knowing of Baker's ambition,
invited Baker over to lunch in his Treasury office on November 30,
close to a month after the election.

"I read in the paper where you sort of feel like you'd like to do
something different," Regan told Baker. "So would I. I'm going to
make you an offer you can't refuse: Let's switch jobs."[43]

"That's very interesting," Baker replied. "I'd like to think about it."

Baker and Regan talked again before Christmas, but not until early
January did Baker agree. Deaver sold the job swap to the president and
Mrs. Reagan. After one night's thought, Reagan agreed and announced
the shifts on January 8, 1985. What is stunning is how passive Reagan
was in all this, as if uncaring who was his chief lieutenant and unaware
that revamping his staff two months after his election would play havoc
with his game plan.

The president had just broken a cardinal rule of the Washington
power game: Time personnel changes *offensively*. The start of a second
term is a good time to make switches, provided the president acts
briskly and decisively right after the election. That conveys freshness
and purpose. But waiting two months and then reacting to a deal his
aides had concocted made Reagan look like a puppet manipulated by
lieutenants. The episode tarnished the gloss of his electoral success.
More important, it threw his administration into disarray for weeks
while Regan put together a new White House staff.

Regan's first seven or eight months were a period of very rough
on-the-job training. He lacked Jim Baker's well-developed political an-
tennae and established networks. His experience as Treasury secretary

and as a Wall Street corporate maverick were not adequate grooming for an inside job that is as much political as managerial. He was nowhere near as good as Baker at spotting troubles on the horizon or protecting Reagan from unnecessary confrontations. Moreover, Regan had a penchant for thrusting himself into the limelight that made him a target for criticism, especially in those early months.

"Don is not accustomed to being a staff man," one close associate remarked. "He likes to be out front, visible, in charge. He's the Al Haig of the second term." A lieutenant to Regan blurted out, "Don doesn't like to share power with anyone."

Regan, proud of his financial independence and not afraid of being fired, was fond of telling people, myself included, that he did not need to kowtow to anyone—meaning the president—because "I've got plenty of fuck-you money." Nonetheless, he became known as a yes-man to Reagan, unable or unwilling to press bad news on the president.

Accustomed to the power hierarchy of the corporate world, Regan lacked a natural feel for the interconnections of political issues and strategies. And he lacked the natural instinct for one central rule of the power game: Don't make enemies, because today's adversary may be tomorrow's ally. He was insensitive toward the easily bruised egos of other politicians. Even diehard Republican allies of the president bitched that Regan was inaccessible and treated their ideas with arrogant disdain. "He doesn't understand that elected officials are different from appointed officials," one Reagan intimate said. "They have their own interests, their own constituencies, their own agendas."

Regan's brash, Irish directness won him a reputation for take-charge toughness within the White House. But his real problem was that he was unsure of himself politically. Congressional leaders complained that Regan vacillated so much on issues and tactics that they could not count on him to set a presidential game plan and stick to it.

"Don Regan is a person of very considerable personal integrity," said a top administration official. "The problem, however, is that he hasn't thought through his own position in sufficient depth for the position to be stable. It's not because he is trying to be deceitful. . . . He has gotten himself into a fair amount of trouble by being unstable, for which you can read 'unreliable.' If one day of the week you're a *monetarist* and another day of the week, you're a *supply-sider;* if one day you say the problem *can't be solved* without Social Security, and another day you say it *can be,* that's really not duplicitous in its motive. He tends to be too quick to articulate. He's actually a victim of his own directness."

In 1985, the president paid the price for Regan's political inexperience. Regan talked initially of a confrontational strategy with Congress patterned after the President's 1981 blitz, not fully appreciating that the Democrats were too strong in 1985 to be rolled over. Regan zigzagged: In spring, he joined forces with budget-cutting Senate Republicans, encouraging them to take politically risky votes on Social Security; in midyear, he reversed tactics, cutting the ground from under them, which left them infuriated. Regan bowed to national security officials pressing for an early House vote on military aid to Nicaraguan contras, [44] but left too little time to prepare for the vote, setting up a defeat for Reagan. Much later, the president won more aid, but he had to settle for half a loaf: $27 million in nonlethal aid.

Regan was given to talking about "a scorched-earth veto strategy," slapping down Congress on every issue, without reckoning that would destroy the bipartisan partnership needed to pass the president's tax-reform bill. Some presidential intimates talked Regan out of that strategy before it boomeranged. But Regan's combative streak was reinforced by Pat Buchanan, the right-wing columnist and former Nixon aide, who became director of communications. Buchanan enjoyed savaging Democrats on Nicaragua. He encouraged Reagan to face down Congress over economic sanctions against South Africa. Buchanan's sallies left Regan putting out political bonfires.

Over time, Regan turned to more experienced hands to compensate for his own lapses. By mid-1985, he had brought in Dennis Thomas, an experienced Senate aide, and Mitchell Daniels, former Republican senatorial campaign director. And he got strategy advice in private sessions with a coterie of old Reagan hands outside of government: Stuart Spencer, Ken Duberstein, Lyn Nofziger, Bill Timmons, and others. But in the meantime, Reagan's agenda took a battering.

Bitburg: No Damage Control

No event more epitomized the disarray at the start of Reagan's second term—or played greater havoc with White House efforts to forge the 1985 agenda—than the president's visit to the German military cemetery at Bitburg in early May. It was a political nightmare—haunting, distracting, enervating the president and his staff with week upon week of searing controversy. It dominated the news. It threw the president off stride. It engulfed his staff in constant worry.

The White House inability to control the political fallout cost Reagan heavily. What began as an effort to bury past enmity and to emphasize modern Allied solidarity unintentionally raked up coals of anguish over Nazi atrocities because of the belated American discovery that there were graves of Waffen SS troops at the Bitburg cemetery.

Amidst the uproar over the president's including the hated SS, Hitler's storm troopers, in his tribute to the German war dead, Reagan and his aides kept up a brave front. Publicly, they stuck to Reagan's commitment to go to Bitburg, out of respect for West German Chancellor Helmut Kohl. But privately, everyone around the president—especially Nancy Reagan—urged him to back out. Michael Deaver tried to persuade the German government to alter the itinerary.

Just two days before leaving for Europe, the president himself, unknown to all but a handful, made a strong personal appeal to Kohl to drop the Bitburg visit. White House advance men had found a substitute, the memorial to the German war dead at Festung Ehrenbreitstein, a fortress on the Rhine. It had no graves and no links to the SS. In a long phone call, Reagan proposed Ehrenbreitstein in place of Bitburg, but Kohl stiffly refused.

The whole incredible episode came to have high stakes for both leaders: Kohl feeling his government was at stake and Reagan feeling his reputation and the glow of his reelection were at risk. The Bitburg controversy became impossible to unravel because the two leaders had struck a personal bargain from which their aides could not extricate them. Bitburg was a burning demonstration that even a skillful staff cannot protect a president's agenda or spare him from political damage if that president acts on impulse—even well-meant—and will not change until it is too late. Bitburg was Reagan's self-inflicted wound.

The Bitburg story was especially ironic because if Reagan, at seventy-three, should have had one advantage, it should have been his personal recollections of the Holocaust and the horrors kindled by the Nazi era. It would have been more understandable for a younger president not fully to have sensed the painful symbolism of an American leader visiting a German cemetery and including the Waffen SS. As the late Arthur Burns, then ambassador to Bonn, commented, "The original decision to go to Bitburg was ill conceived."[45] From that, the plot flowed with tragic ineluctability.

It began with a compact forged by Kohl and Reagan. Kohl personally was the architect and manager of Reagan's visit to Germany around the fortieth anniversary of the allied victory in Europe on May 8, 1985. The trip to Bitburg was Kohl's dream. It was to be the American analogue to Kohl's visit of reconciliation with French President François Mitterand to the graves of the French and German World War I dead at Verdun. Photographers had framed the moving symbolism of Kohl and Mitterand holding hands at the Verdun battlefield, with fields of white crosses as their backdrop. Kohl had also been deeply hurt by his exclusion from the Allied celebration of the fortieth anniversary of D day at Normandy on June 6, 1984. On November 30, soon after Reagan's reelection, Kohl pleaded in tears, top officials told me, for Reagan to agree to some gesture of German-American reconciliation to heal the wound of Normandy and to nourish the balm of Verdun.

"Anything you want," Reagan responded, not consulting the aides who sat by the two leaders in the Oval Office. According to American officials, Kohl proposed three things: a commemoration at Cologne Cathedral on V-E Day, a visit to a concentration camp, and a joint visit to a military cemetery. Evidently both he and Reagan were unaware that the gesture of Verdun could not be repeated because no American soldiers were buried in German cemeteries. Thus, in agreeing, Reagan committed himself to honor the German war dead alone.

The first hints of controversy came not over Bitburg, but over a story in the German magazine *Der Spiegel* on January 19, 1985, that Reagan was considering a visit to the Dachau concentration camp. Seeing the idea in print, Reagan recoiled. Mrs. Reagan found such a visit distasteful, one of her confidants told me. She was squeamish about visiting the death scenes and being shown the ovens and photographic displays of bodies being bulldozed into mass graves. Privately, she told aides, "I've talked to Ronnie, and that's not what we want to do." *Der Spiegel* implied that the Bonn government also did not want Reagan to visit Dachau. Within days, Reagan publicly indicated his desire not to go there, saying he wanted to stress "reconciliation" not "the hatred that went on at the time."

"The president was not hot to go to a camp," one official told Bernard Weinraub of *The New York Times*. "You know, he's a cheerful politician. He does not like to grovel in a grisly scene like Dachau. He was reluctant to go. I'm not saying opposed, but there was a coolness. And nobody pushed him on it."[46]

When Mike Deaver went to Germany in late February to develop the president's itinerary, Kohl had fixed on a visit to Bitburg. Deaver wanted a big European swing with stops in Germany, France, Spain, and Portugal, plus something unusual to add political spice: Hungary. The Budapest government was agreeable, but the White House backed off when Janoś Kádár, the Hungarian leader, wanted assurances that Reagan would not embarrass Kádár by baiting Moscow publicly on his European trip. Also, rather than celebrate V-E Day in Cologne, the

White House substituted an address to the European Parliament in Strasbourg, France. But Deaver was attracted to the Bitburg cemetery because it was conveniently located near an American Air Force base where Reagan could give a rousing speech to the troops.

It was a cold day, crystal clear, when Deaver and William Henkel, chief White House advance man, were driven out to the Kolmeshohe Military Cemetery at Bitburg by Werner von der Schulenberg, German chief of protocol, and William Woessner, deputy chief of the American Embassy in Bonn. The cemetery was a peaceful glen in a cloister of woods, with a large tower monument at the far end of a small field of gravestones.

"It was very picturesque," Deaver recalled. "A beautiful little spot. The graves were all covered with snow. I remember saying to our embassy people, 'I want them [the graves] checked out. Be sure there's nothing embarrassing here.' "[47]

Woessner remembered asking Schulenberg for assurances there were no war criminals and "that would have certainly included Waffen SS, as far as I was concerned." Schulenberg sent back assurance there was no problem.[48]

But there *was* a problem—a huge gulf between two nations, two memories, two attitudes. The American officials operated on the premise that Kohl's government, as a close ally, would not knowingly trip up the American president—specifically, that if the German government said there were no horrible embarrassments for Reagan, they could trust the Germans. They assumed that what would be embarrassing to Americans would be embarrassing to Germans. But as Jim Markham, bureau chief of *The New York Times* in Bonn, explained to me, Germans regard the Waffen SS troops as similar to regular military units, some of them press-ganged into service at early ages and not morally culpable, as the SS were, for the Holocaust atrocities. That is a distinction not made by Americans. Moreover, Markham said, the Germans felt that the reconciliation Kohl wanted from Reagan implied some pardon of the past and accepting the reality of the Waffen SS buried among other Germans. American officials felt bitterly misled.

Kohl's proposed itinerary included a stop at Munich, not far from Dachau. But the Americans got the distinct impression that Kohl really did not want Reagan going to a concentration camp. In their desire to move Reagan on to Spain, Portugal, and France, a stop in Munich seemed too cumbersome. So Deaver and Henkel scratched that stop— also dropping the concentration camp visit. It was a fatal error because they were setting up Reagan to pay homage to the German war dead, but not to bear witness to millions of victims of Nazism. "When we dropped Munich, none of us at that time thought about the fact that we still had the cemetery hanging out there and we did not have a compensating event," Henkel confessed. "That was a fatal fault."[49] Other American officials had qualms, and Jewish leaders were angry about dropping Dachau. Nonetheless, the itinerary was approved by Don Regan, National Security Adviser Robert McFarlane, and Secretary of State Shultz in early March; Reagan also accepted it.

By then, the Bitburg stop was fixed. A former American embassy official, Hans Tuck, was asked to draft remarks for Reagan to make at Bitburg cemetery. Tuck refused. "No," he said, "the president should not say a word."[50] When an American advance team went in late March 1985 to refine the travel plans, worry about Bitburg gnawed Henkel. Snow still covered the gravestones. Despite German assurances, Henkel asked embassy officials again to be sure there were no embarrassments lying beneath the snow. In frustration, a senior American diplomat burst out: "What do you think—Joseph Mengele [the hunted Nazi concentration camp doctor] is buried there?"

When Reagan's itinerary was announced on Thursday, April 11, Bitburg was finally mentioned in public. White House spokesman Larry Speakes was raked over the coals by reporters demanding whether American soldiers were buried at Bitburg and why the President was visiting a German military cemetery but not a concentration camp. That night, Regan and Speakes watched the television news, astonished that only CBS gave extensive coverage to Reagan's German trip. Regan felt they could ride out the situation. But Stuart Spencer warned Deaver, "Mike, you're going to see a firestorm on this one like you've never seen before."[51]

When the newspaper stories hit Friday morning, the blaze was lit. Jewish groups erupted in fury, their leaders demanding that Reagan not go to Bitburg. Editorials savaged the White House. Ed Rollins got angry calls from Republicans. "Paula Hawkins just raised all kinds of hell," he said. "Bob Dole left a message in my office about how outrageous this was, and how the veterans and everybody else would be outraged by it."[52] On that weekend came the first news of SS graves at Bitburg cemetery.

In just three days, the uproar was so strong that the White House decided it had to add a concentration camp—as damage control. The fiction was that Kohl had invited Reagan to a camp, but in fact, as one top American official said, "We told the Germans, 'We're coming.'" Deaver and Henkel flew to Germany on Monday, where they were dogged by TV cameras as they went to survey Dachau. They snuck away to look at Bergen-Belsen, which was less grisly, more solemnly mournful, with its mounds of mass graves. But already Elie Wiesel, a fifty-six-year-old camp survivor, world-reknowned writer, and chairman of the U.S. Holocaust Memorial Council, was declaring there could be no trade-off of a camp for Bitburg cemetery.

"This particular cemetery is to us unacceptable," Wiesel decreed. "This is not just a cemetery of soldiers. This is tombstones of the SS, which is beyond what we can imagine. These are and were criminals."

Privately, Deaver was trying to cut Reagan's political losses. In Germany, he asked Horst Teltschik, Kohl's national security adviser, to find a substitute for Bitburg, but Kohl did not budge. By now, the American Embassy had learned that *all* German military cemeteries included Waffen SS graves. Ambassador Burns cabled Washington that it would be a disaster for German-American relations if Bitburg were dropped. He argued that it would weaken Kohl by making him look like an American lackey.

At home, the White House was adding to its problems. Don Regan and Ed Rollins had hastily called a meeting with some Jewish Republican leaders—Max Fisher of Detroit, Gordon Zacks of Columbus, and Richard Fox of Philadelphia—ostensibly to get their advice. But before hearing them out, Regan caused offense by arriving late at the meeting and summarily announcing that the president had already decided to visit a concentration camp. The outrage of the Jewish leaders boiled over when they noticed that Pat Buchanan had written again and again in his notebook, "Succumbing to the pressure of the Jews."

Reagan himself fueled the emotional reactions two days later by equating the Nazi soldiers buried at Bitburg with Holocaust victims. Of the soldiers, he said, "They were victims, just as surely as the victims in the concentration camps." A few days later, Reagan got a letter from an American who said his life had been saved at Dachau no less than four times by Waffen SS troops. "So you see," Reagan told a large meeting of cabinet and staff aides, "as horrible as those places were, there were impulses of compassion." Deaver groaned a loud warning: "Oh, Christ, don't let this get out. I can see the headlines now: REAGAN SAYS CONCENTRATION CAMPS ARE HOTBEDS OF HUMANITY!"

By now, Bitburg was consuming the administration, pushing aside the rest of the agenda. Reagan was caught in a vise. Fifty-three senators wrote urging him to drop the cemetery visit. On April 19, Kohl telephoned, insisting on Bitburg, and wrung from Reagan a renewed pledge to stick to the itinerary that now included Bitburg and Bergen-

Belsen. The very same day, Elie Wiesel, invited to the White House long before to receive the Congressional Gold Medal for his writing on the Holocaust, implored Reagan at a nationally televised ceremony to cancel the cemetery visit. Reagan watched, pain etched across his face as Wiesel cried out: "That place, Mr. President, is not your place. Your place is with the victims of the SS."

The protests reached a crescendo in the second half of April. The president's popularity dropped several points. Deaver was trying to cushion the shock: shortening Reagan's time at Bitburg, arranging for retired Army General Matthew B. Ridgeway to lay the wreath instead of Reagan, preparing a moving speech at Bergen-Belsen to ease the anger of Jews. Still, almost everyone in the White House, including Mrs. Reagan, was badgering the president to call off the Bitburg stop. "Nancy felt very, very strongly—extremely strongly," one Reagan confidant told me. "She felt Kohl really bruised the president badly in the way Bitburg was handled." But Reagan resisted all entreaties, feeling he had no alternative. That is, until the morning of April 29, two days before his scheduled departure.

The American Embassy in Bonn, secretly scouring Germany for an alternative that did not include Waffen SS graves, had finally found the shrine to the five million German war dead from both world wars at Festung Ehrenbreitstein. It is an old fortress, with four-foot-thick stone walls, and located high on a bluff near Koblenz, overlooking the confluence of the Rhine and Moselle rivers. It has no graves (and hence no SS) and it had been used for memorial wreath layings in the past. After seeing it, White House advance man Frederick Ahearn excitedly telephoned Bill Henkel at the White House: "Bill, this is it!" He described its one twelve-foot granite casket with a German soldier lying prone, face up, shovel helmet down over his ears, and read memorial inscriptions with vows to peace.[53] The Americans saw it as a fitting equivalent to our tomb of the unknown soldier. It was, as Henkel later said, "the classic out."

Over breakfast in the White House mess on April 29, Henkel eagerly briefed Deaver, Regan, and McFarlane on Ehrenbreitstein. Deaver and Henkel made ready to fly to Germany at once to arrange for Reagan to go there. Hopefully, they took the plan to the president. About nine A.M., Reagan met with Bush, Shultz, Regan, McFarlane, Deaver, Henkel, and Assistant Secretary of State Rick Burt in the Oval Office. For the first time, the president was prepared to push Chancellor Kohl. Wearing his glasses and with some notes in hand, Reagan telephoned Kohl.

It was an unusually long call for two leaders—nineteen minutes. To others in the room, it felt like a test of wills.

"My people have told me that we can achieve the same purposes," Reagan said, mindful of Kohl's need for a symbol of reconciliation. "It's a memorial to your soldiers. It honors your four or five million war dead."

Kohl objected. He made impassioned pleas on personal terms, as if to say, one American said, "You can't do this to me."

"But, Helmut," Reagan countered, "you and I will be there together." Soothingly, Reagan tried to reassure Kohl that he was still committed to their joint objective of reconciliation. He read passages from the Ehrenbreitstein memorial with themes of "never again" and pointed out how fitting those themes were.

Kohl still objected. He had committed his prestige to Bitburg. He had faced down critics in the Bundestag. And always, there was the reminder, spoken or unspoken, that Kohl in 1983 had braved massive opposition to accept deployment of American Pershing II and cruise missiles, as Reagan had wanted. Kohl had stood by his friend, and now he needed Reagan to stand by him.

No, Kohl insisted, any change now could cause his government to fall. The Americans doubted that, but Reagan could hardly contest Kohl.

They talked on, Kohl fearful of the political backlash in his own country, and Reagan mindful of his own political firestorm and trying to persuade Kohl that Ehrenbreitstein had the symbolism without the political downside of Bitburg. But Kohl would not give ground, and Reagan would not force him.

Finally, Reagan put down the phone and told the others, "We have to do this. Helmut says his government would fall."[54]

Reagan, having failed, decided wisely that boldness now would make the ordeal pass faster. Crestfallen, Deaver and Henkel left for Germany on an overnight flight, Reagan emphasizing he would go through with the Bitburg visit.

"Don't you change anything!" he ordered Deaver. "What we're doing is right. History will prove it's right, and we're not going to back down."[55]

The day before Reagan himself left for Bonn, 390 members of the House urged him not to visit Bitburg. Mrs. Reagan, still deeply unhappy, was hesitant. Later she told one friend that the president knew how she dreaded the trip.

"Are you going with me?" he coaxed, a bit uncertain.

"I've been in this thing for thirty years," she replied, "and I'm not backing out now."

The actual visit was less of a trauma than the prolonged painful overture. Reagan's visit to Bergen-Belsen made some amends to angered Jews, though Reagan was personally wounded by the refusal of German-Jewish rabbis to join him there. Over American and international television, Reagan paid a quiet, eloquent tribute to the thousands who came to Bergen-Belsen: "Never to hope. Never to pray. Never to love. Never to heal. Never to laugh. Never to cry."

At Bitburg, I watched him silently tread the pathway around the graves, pause before the tall monument with Kohl at his side, but never touch the wreath, and then just as silently leave. Soon, at Bitburg Air Force Base, Reagan apologized. "Some old wounds have been reopened, and this I regret very much, because this should be a time of healing," he said. To the Germans, he offered reconciliation, and to Americans "worried that reconciliation means forgetting" he said, "I promise you, we will never forget."

The chorus of protest crested, and then it faded. Polling showed Americans equally divided over whether or not Reagan should have gone to Bitburg. But his dignified handling of that traumatic day lifted his popularity to pre-Bitburg levels, and even a bit above. It was fortunate because otherwise Kohl's intransigence could have severely damaged his personal relations with Reagan as well as German relations with this country. "Kohl was so absolutely unyielding that he was viewed as unreasonable" by many top American officials, Richard Wirthlin told me. "If Bitburg had not had that happy last chapter, I think that could have strained relations permanently."[56]

A Star-Crossed Game Plan

With Bitburg finally behind him, Reagan could proclaim his top agenda priority: tax reform. It was terribly late in coming—on May 28, nearly seven months after Reagan's election. The president unfurled it in a nationally televised address. His populist pitch not only promised lower tax rates for most Americans, but it tapped public bitterness toward the existing system, which he damned as "complicated, unfair, cluttered with gobbledygook and loopholes designed for those with the power and influence to hire high-priced legal and tax advisers."

The Reagan formula—to broaden the tax base by closing loopholes and to tax business more heavily to finance rate cuts for individuals—

borrowed heavily from the Democratic plan originated three years earlier by Senator Bill Bradley of New Jersey and Congressman Dick Gephardt of Missouri. In fact, Democrats were more receptive to it than were most House Republicans.

Once again, Reagan's 1985 game plan seemed star-crossed. Before he could build public support for his tax plan, he was distracted by the seizure of a TWA plane by Arab terrorists, then by his own cancer surgery, and *then* by the hijacking of the *Achille Lauro* passenger ship by Palestinian terrorists. From each diversion, Reagan got a political lift: The TWA passenger-hostages were freed, he came out of his surgery healthy, and the *Achille Lauro* hijackers were captured and tried in Italy.

In the fall, when Reagan had recovered enough personally to mount an offensive for his tax-reform bill, he lost control of the agenda again— this time on political issues that the White House should have deflected: sanctions on South Africa and the rising tide of protectionism in Congress. As in the spring, Democrats in Congress were riding high. These were their issues, their agenda—not Reagan's. The administration managed to shunt the trade controversy aside with Reagan's veto of a bill to protect the textile industry, with the promise of administrative action against unfair trade by other countries, and with Treasury Secretary Jim Baker's campaign to drive down the value of the dollar and check the skyrocketing trade deficit.

On South Africa, Reagan added to public outrage caused by weeks of racial violence after Pretoria imposed martial law. The president threw fat on the fire by defending the "reformist administration" of President Pieter Botha in a radio interview with WSB in Atlanta in August. "They have eliminated the segregation that we once had in our own country," Reagan declared, ignoring the apartheid pass laws, strict influx control, denial of citizenship and the right to vote. He had done the interview on vacation at his California ranch. His display of ignorance fired up the opposition and demonstrated that his second-term handlers had still not learned how to protect Reagan from himself.

"They should have protected him on South Africa," Michael Deaver commented, knowing Reagan's foibles intimately. "No one should have let him get on the phone to do that interview with the Atlanta radio station from his ranch. You never let Ronald Reagan do an interview from his ranch. He's so much the product of his environment. He's all alone out at his ranch, nobody with him. He's probably dreaming about riding his horse. Maybe the horse even went by at that moment. And he's on the phone, talking to one person and not thinking that hundreds of thousands will eventually be in the audience. He's relaxed.

"That's the wrong situation for him to be making policy pronouncements about South Africa. If he's going to be making policy pronouncements, it should be very carefully worked out in advance, and he should deliver it in a more formal setting. He should be standing up. You know, it's funny about Reagan. The way he thinks changes when he sits down. They had him sitting down for a press conference in the Oval Office the other day. I would never let him be sitting down. He's too relaxed when he's sitting. He's not careful. He's conversational, not presidential."[57]

The interview gaffe gave ammunition to Reagan's congressional critics and dealt another setback to his game plan. Reagan had vowed not to impose economic sanctions against Africa, but his position became politically untenable. Both houses passed legislation for limited sanctions, and if Reagan vetoed it, both houses had the votes to override his veto. Reagan had been deserted by House and Senate Republicans in overwhelming numbers. To avoid political humiliation, Reagan bowed to the inevitable and announced on September 9 that he was adopting some sanctions against South Africa. His own policy was in shambles.

On the budget, yet another congressional initiative intervened, this one to Reagan's liking: a six-year scheme to bring the $200 billion deficits down to zero. It was devised by Republican senators Phil Gramm and Warren Rudman and cosponsored by South Carolina Democrat Fritz Hollings. For Reagan it was a windfall. It saved him from naked exposure at an ignominious moment: the need to raise the national debt ceiling above $2 trillion, *more than double* what it was when he entered office.

While the Gramm-Rudman-Hollings scheme did not originate with the president, it gave new impetus to his long-term agenda of cutting government. The Reagan deficits had become so horrendous that there was wide consensus that Congress and the administration needed the discipline of an automatic cutting mechanism. Some politicians, such as New York Democratic Senator Daniel Patrick Moynihan, contended that big deficits were deliberate on Reagan's part—that he had cut tax rates deeply in 1981 knowing that this action would create massive deficits, which would force Congress to cut government programs for years to come. Indeed, Reagan's pet analogy was that of a daddy cutting his boy's allowance to stop his foolish spending. "Well, you know, we can lecture our children about extravagance until we run out of voice and breath," Reagan had said in February 1981. "Or we can cure their extravagance by simply reducing their allowance."

But Gramm-Rudman-Hollings cut against Reagan's agenda, for if Reagan intended to cut Congress's allowance, Congress was cutting his allowance, too. The new scheme envisioned a terrible bite on Reagan's prized defense buildup. Senate Republicans as well as House Democrats wanted to force him to raise taxes to pay for the defense program. But Reagan would not raise taxes; he preferred letting defense spending level off. Gramm-Rudman passed, with Reagan's support, and in 1985 the Pentagon budget was actually reduced for the first time in six years.

Literally at year's end, Reagan got to tax reform, a few weeks after his summit meeting with Mikhail Gorbachev. Just as bad luck with terrorist incidents had hurt Reagan earlier, now good luck—Gorbachev's drive for a summit—helped him late in the year. Because of Reagan's slow start in 1985, there was not time for the tax-reform bill to pass both houses that year, as Reagan had wanted. But the bill finally came to the fore, promoted by Jim Baker and Richard Darman, the Treasury Department's master strategists, as well as by House Democratic leaders: Speaker O'Neill and Ways and Means Committee Chairman Dan Rostenkowski. O'Neill and Rostenkowski favored the tax bill because it hit business and lowered rates for most middle-income taxpayers; their agenda protected Reagan's.

In most respects, 1985 had been a badly broken field for the president. He and his team were largely to blame. They had not played the agenda game well. Nonetheless, through it all, Reagan had personally pursued two priorities, both embraced belatedly: the summit with Gorbachev and the tax-reform bill. And in the end, he got to them both. The summit is less surprising because presidents can manage their agenda with foreigners better than with Congress, and Reagan had softened his conditions for a summit—dropping earlier demands for advance promise of agreements. But the tax bill's survival was testimony not only to the support of Democratic leaders but also to Reagan's tenacity. Reagan stubbornly clings to pet goals long after other politicians give up—a personal quality often underestimated by his critics, but essential to presidential success in the agenda game.

Fallacies of the Rosy Scenario

Reagan's 1985 game plan was bedeviled not only by misplayed political tactics and second-term overconfidence. Reagan's problems were also a matter of substance. His policies had generally lost credibility inside

Hedrick Smith

the beltway. In the 1984 campaign, the country bought Reagan's pitch for "more of the same," but the Washington political community was disbelieving. In 1981, other politicians, grasping for something new, had been willing to gamble on big Reagan tax cuts and a defense buildup; but by 1985 the political community had largely lost faith in Reaganomics. Big deficits had become an obsession. Senate Republicans, Reagan's most important allies, were frustrated with what they derided as Reagan's stand-pat, head-in-the-sand opposition to reducing deficits with a sizable tax increase, as well as his unwillingness to take the political risk of initiating changes in Social Security COLAs—even with his popularity at a peak and his last election behind him.

In sum, Reagan's game plan went astray in 1985 because it had gone astray—behind the scenes—in its initial conception, and that was starkly visible by 1985. The Reagan economic plan had not worked out as advertised because of massive mistakes made in 1981. Ironically, at the time in 1981 when Reagan and his budget genius, David Stockman, were most successful politically, the basic architecture of their economic plan was unsound. Stockman knew it then, but Reagan shied away from the bad news. The façade of Stockman's public certainty helped Reagan's agenda succeed in 1981. But Stockman had grave doubts, sensing even as he was selling the package to Congress that it was built on disastrously unsound economics. Privately, Stockman came to scoff at supply-side economics.

At the high-water mark in mid-1981, President Reagan told the nation that his massive tax cut would produce a new burst of economic growth and generate new tax revenues to help bring the budget into balance. On August 13, 1981, Reagan declared buoyantly: "Our tax proposals are based on the belief that a cut in tax rates would not mean a comparable cut in tax revenues, that the stimulant to the economy would be such that the government might find itself getting additional revenues as it did last year in the cut of the capital gains tax."

By 1985, most members of Congress regarded that as a colossal blunder; David Stockman had reached that conclusion back in 1981 when he created the "Rosy Scenario"—the nickname that economists and White House aides, with a jaunty combination of cynicism and self-mockery, had given their economic forecasts for Reagan's program. Stockman later admitted that the Rosy Scenario was so far off that if it had been used to project Jimmy Carter's budget, Carter would have had a *$365 billion budget surplus* over five years.[58] Reagan's promises of a balanced budget by 1984 were hollow because they were based on faulty economics.

For behind the unity and confident prescience of the administration, there had been massive wishful thinking in early 1981 and factions of economists who could not agree. So Stockman, assigned the task of drafting Reagan's program, plucked the assumptions from each faction most favorable to Reagan's desires and projected a far bigger economic boom and vastly larger tax revenues than actually occurred or could reasonably have been expected. He has since said so himself.

People outside the Reagan family had foreseen the danger. Economists such as Henry Kaufman of Salomon Brothers and Herbert Stein, formerly Nixon's chief economist and then at American Enterprise Institute in Washington, had warned that the Reagan economic numbers were too glossy. Echoes of George Bush's charge of voodoo economics and Howard Baker's wisecrack that Reaganomics was a "riverboat gamble." In fact, Stockman privately confessed to writer William Greider his fear that the Reagan edifice was built on sand.[59] The problem was not Reagan's general direction, but his vast overpromising, for Reagan was either not understanding or ignoring economic reality while Stockman and others were discovering gaping holes in the Reagan formula.

The problem lay not in the detailed cuts debated by Congress, but in the assumptions made before Congress ever got its hand on Reagan's program. For a president's estimates of balancing the budget or controlling deficits and how much of a tax cut or a defense buildup the nation can afford rest fundamentally on forecasts of how the economy will perform. Those forecasts often affect many more billions of dollars—plus or minus—than congressional votes or presidential actions.

There were three massive miscalculations in the 1981 budget planning that threw Reagan's economic game plan so far off track by 1985. The most fundamental error was that of supply-side economists: Stockman, Paul Craig Roberts, and Martin Anderson predicted that with Reagan's tax cut, the economy would grow at a rate of five percent per year—above and beyond inflation—from 1982 to 1986. Others, such as Dick Wirthlin, Jim Baker, and Murray Weidenbaum, chairman of Reagan's Council of Economic Advisers, warned Reagan that this was "promising too much." But Reagan blessed the supply-siders, and so Stockman used their rosy numbers. Stockman also expected a bull market on Wall Street after the Reagan economic program was unveiled.

In fact, the economy turned into a recession; in 1982, it showed not 5 percent real growth but a 1.5 percent decline, after discounting inflation. Supply-siders such as Jack Kemp blamed the tight money policies of Federal Reserve Chairman Paul Volcker. But Volcker was pursuing the Reagan line, the very anti-inflationary policies that Reagan had advocated in 1980.

The 1982 downturn meant many billions more spent on unemployment compensation and other antirecessionary programs plus $85 billion less in tax revenues than Reagan's program predicted—a whopping addition to the deficit in one year. Even after the economy recovered, real economic growth under Reagan was less than half what had been forecast and slower than in the Carter years—3.0 percent per year for Carter's four years, compared to 2.4 percent per year for Reagan's first four years.[60]

When I asked Stockman five years later how he and the others could have expected an immediate jump to 5 percent growth, he replied: "That was crazy. I admit that was an error."[61]

The second big error of Reagan's economists was disastrously overestimating inflation and the windfall in tax revenues it would bring. Tax revenues are based on the gross national product (GNP)—the money value of national output; "money GNP" rises both from real growth and from inflation. Inflation forecasts are crucial to figuring out how big this number will be and to reckoning tax revenues as a share of it. Murray Weidenbaum, Reagan's top economist, figured inflation would come down slowly from 10 percent under Carter to, say, 7.7 percent in 1982 and to 5 percent in 1985. Actually, it fell to 4.4 percent in 1982 and lower after that. Lower inflation meant the government lost a mountain of tax money that Reagan had counted on—"nearly $200 billion in phantom revenues" over five years, Stockman told me.[62]

Again, warnings were raised inside the White House—from Dick Darman, among others—that the numbers going into the Reagan plan were cockeyed. But Reagan and his top aides preferred Stockman's good-news estimates. Several officials, including Stockman, told me that the president's knowledge of economics was so shaky and so limited by the relatively simple one-year budgeting in California that Reagan had trouble handling Stockman's five-year federal budget projections. Stockman also said that Reagan did not grasp the huge difference between reckoning multiple-year budgets in "constant dollars" (factoring out inflation) and "current dollars" (including inflation). Finally, he said, Reagan had trouble understanding that Stockman's projections already included the best recovery Reagan could dream of; Reagan kept expecting more good news on top of the Rosy Scenario.

A third major reason the Reagan program was way out of whack was the haste with which Reagan's rapid defense buildup was projected, without Stockman or any other top White House official truly grasping it. Stockman told me, "Cap Weinberger and I did it [the long-term Pentagon budget] on a hand calculator one night in half an hour, and we made a big mistake."[63] The real architects were some defense hawks in the Madison Group, a tightly knit group of sharp, experienced, well-organized conservative congressional staff aides with links to senators Jesse Helms of North Carolina, John Tower of Texas, and Orrin Hatch of Utah. Some became the most canny and successful bureaucratic operators in the Reagan administration: John Lehman, secretary of the Navy; Richard Perle, the most influential Pentagon figure on arms control as assistant secretary of Defense for International Security Policy; and William Schneider, Jr., undersecretary of State for Security Assistance, Science and Technology.

At the outset Weinberger and Stockman had to rely heavily on their advice, for neither was expert in defense. At the decisive meeting on the Pentagon budget at seven P.M., Friday, January 30, 1981, Schneider was with Weinberger, Stockman, and Deputy Defense Secretary Frank Carlucci. Schneider, then a top deputy to Stockman and a former staff aide on the House Defense Appropriations Subcommittee, had been put in place by conservatives to see that the defense buildup got railroaded through the bureaucracy. In the defense chapter of the right-wing Heritage Foundation's *Agenda for Progress*, Schneider had provided a blueprint for the incoming Reagan team—an immediate jump in defense spending of $33.7 billion.[64] If accepted, this would shoot the Pentagon budget up to a new plateau, on top of which future increases would be added, for years to come. That plateau, that base level was crucial to long-term budget calculations.

When Reagan called in his 1980 campaign for five-percent real growth in defense spending over several years, Carter's defense budget level was $142 billion a year. But by the time Reagan took office, Carter's defense budget level had jumped to $176 billion in 1981; it was set for $200.3 billion in 1982 and projected to grow five percent a year on top of that into the mid-1980s. This was more than Reagan had promised. Piling Schneider's $33.7 billion on top of Carter's 1981 figure would shoot the Pentagon budget sky-high.

Career professionals at the Pentagon and OMB expected Weinberger to add something like $4 billion to $10 billion to Carter's departing budgets. But Weinberger went much bigger; he was under pressure from conservatives who feared he would not be hawkish enough, among them Senator John Tower, new chairman of the Armed Services Committee. Weinberger got Stockman's agreement to an immediate whopping $32.6 billion—essentially Schneider's figure. Weinberger told me that the Pentagon had specific spending items all laid out before his meeting with Stockman, but other officials insisted that very little had been done inside the Pentagon and that the Joint Chiefs of Staff were given the first two weeks in February to come up with requests to fill out the $32.6 billion.

"Weinberger's next action was to say, 'Okay, Army, Navy, Air Force, you go fill in the blanks. Fill it up. Tell me what programs you should have,'" according to Richard A. Stubbing, deputy chief of OMB's national security division. "There was no strategy, no priorities. It [the $32 billion] was just a number. Oddly, it was just about the same number they cut out of the domestic side of the budget. In one wink, Stockman gave away all he'd saved. We were stunned. As we heard it, the military services were stunned, too. Weinberger claims that he controlled the process, but no one did. There was almost no review. The services simply went to the shelf and took off everything that had been on their wish lists, even low-priority items. The staff in the office of the secretary of Defense were saying they were frozen out of the process. Same thing with Defense Systems Analysis. They had no real time to take a look at what the services had concocted. It blew us away. During my twenty years that request was the biggest thing ever put in, in peacetime."[65]

On top of that big bump, Stockman's long-term planning got a second jolt from the defense budget. Reagan and Weinberger felt compelled to do more than the five-percent annual increase, because Carter had gone for that. "The five percent now had a malodorous character to it," Schneider recalled. "The attitude was 'anything but five percent.'"[66] Weinberger wanted nine percent, according to Schneider; Stockman balked, but accepted seven-percent annual real growth, without grasping the enormity of the numbers. Moreover, Stockman agreed with Weinberger that the administration's big inflation forecasts would be added onto the seven-percent real growth. With that added, the Reagan defense budget would hit $386 billion in 1986, well over double Carter's 1981 budget.

Weinberger denied to me that he and Stockman had haggled over percentages,[67] but both Stockman and Schneider remembered discussing percentages.[68]

"They [defense budget figures] were not based on an assessment of national-defense needs," Stockman contended. "They were simply based on a rule of thumb that maybe seven-percent real growth was a good idea given how bad our defense establishment was. But I always assumed that was an interim number and that once we went through a three- or four-month exercise of taking stock of the deficiencies and what we really needed to spend, category by category—strategic, conventional, readiness, and so forth—we would then promulgate a revised five-year plan that would represent a balance between what we could afford and what we felt we needed. But that never happened. Instead what happened was the top line [seven-percent compounded growth], plus the inflation added to it, was parceled out to the military—$1.46 trillion over five years—and they in a matter of sixty days built a whole program down to the last six-hundred-dollar ashtray to spend it. Once that got wired into this massive bureaucracy and its correlates in Congress and the defense community, it was hard to ever do anything about it."[69]

For several years, Stockman, Jim Baker, Meese, Deaver, and growing numbers of Senate Republicans fought to correct what they saw as the original mistake of building excessive inflation into the Pentagon budget. But Reagan objected, because taking it out made his defense numbers look as low as or lower than Carter's.

Listening to Stockman describe this budgetary chicanery, I found him a strange figure. I remember my numbed shock as he was telling me how crazily and wrongfully the whole Reagan economic program had been put together. We were in the kitchen of his expensive home in Potomac, Maryland, then nearly stripped of furniture because he was moving to New York to a million-dollar-a-year job with Salomon Brothers investment house. Stockman was in a blue jogging outfit, smoking nervously, his slender fingers drumming the table as he awaited a call from the publisher of his then-forthcoming book, *The Triumph of Politics: Why the Reagan Revolution Failed.*

I was stunned both by what he said and by his cavalier candor about the hypocrisy of the private debate inside the administration and the obvious flimflam of its public façade. Stockman is a true believer, a political zealot, Jesuitical in his pursuit of whatever is his current truth, even if that means renunciation of what he believed a few months, or weeks, ago. Political loyalties do not bind him long. In his youth, he had gone from Goldwater Republicanism to anti-Vietnam campus radicalism at Michigan State University, then to Harvard Divinity School, and then he had proceeded to the liberal Republicanism of John Anderson, through supply-side fever into the Reagan camp, and now he was thoroughly disillusioned by what he had imagined as the Reagan revolution. He talked about past allies and enemies with caustic candor.

However helpful I found Stockman's frankness about "what happened" in putting together Reagan's economic agenda in 1981, I was deeply disturbed to hear him talk so offhandedly about fiddling with such huge numbers in private while selling the Reagan program in public. He was willing to admit his guilt and yet seemed to believe that his strange confessional would prove his good intentions and ultimately absolve him of responsibility. But the substance of what he said was damning for him as well as for the president.

Stockman scoffed that the Laffer curve, on which the Reagan-Kemp-Roth tax cut was based, was "miracle economics." In restrospect, he said the only way the country could afford a ten-percent annual cut in tax rates—without massive deficits—was through tax bracket creep caused by inflation. When inflation fell below five percent, Stockman said, a structural deficit was inevitable. It became permanently imbedded when Reagan agreed in 1981 to index the tax rates for inflation to stop bracket creep. In Stockman's view, both Reagan's program and the disastrous estimates of the Rosy Scenario made a mockery of Reagan's happy talk that lower tax rates would yield higher tax revenues and thus lead toward a balanced budget.

"On a five-year basis, our giant tax cut and big defense buildup cost nearly $900 billion," Stockman wrote in early 1986. "Our domestic spending cuts . . . came to only about half that. So how could you worsen a budget by $900 billion, cut it by $450 billion, and still come out with a balanced budget?"[70] Only by the Reagan Rosy Scenario, fat inflation forecasts, and superoptimism about economic growth. "We insisted that we had found the economic Rosetta stone," Stockman ruefully commented, but "our Rosetta stone was a fake."[71]

Not only did Stockman denounce what he called "the shameless, groundless fiscal fiction [that] steadily emanated from the White House," but he asserted that Reagan's presidency almost certainly would "record the lowest eight-year real GNP growth rate since World War II." Historians, he said, would be left with the riddle: "Why was this fiscal and financial mutation allowed to build and fester for seven years after it was evident that a stunning but correctable economic policy error had been made in the first six months of 1981?" Although Reagan always blamed Congress, Stockman blamed Reagan for mobilizing the nation's voters as "an overpowering bloc vote against necessary taxation."[72]

Without following all of Stockman's arithmetic or knowing how the Rosy Scenario had been put together inside the Reagan administration in 1981, most members of Congress had come to share Stockman's

conclusion about the false promise of Reaganomics by 1985. Disillusionment was rampant. Most leaders in both parties in both houses had
concluded that some tax increases were needed, and Reagan was simply
wrong and being stubborn about it. In short, Reagan and his team had
lost the intellectual initiative by 1985. That loss of faith was as important as the tactical blunders of Reagan and his lieutenants in stymieing
Reagan's agenda game in the second term.

12. The Image Game: Scripting the Video Presidency

> *That's what it comes down to: We are marketing; we are trying to mold public opinion by marketing strategies. That's what communications is all about.*
> —William Henkel, Reagan White House chief advance man

The annual spring dinner of the Gridiron Club, an elitist social club of sixty print journalists, is one of the high tribal rites of Washington insiders. It is a gathering of political celebrities that combines snob appeal with Hollywood glitter. The Gridiron dinner brings together six hundred of the most powerful, best-known people in America in an evening of poking fun. Every president since Benjamin Harrison has come to the Gridiron Club dinner at least once. To less exalted politicians, an invitation to the Gridiron banquet is coveted as a mark of making it. The occasion always draws a sidewalk crowd, as limousines deposit the high and mighty in white tie and tails and evening gowns at the Capitol Hilton hotel. Inside, the red-jacketed Marine band stirs a throb of patriotism with Sousa marches. Spotlights play over long tables, festooned with red roses, picking out Hollywood stars rubbing elbows with the captains of industry, the anchors of television, the publishers and other princes of the print press, the deans of the diplomatic corps, the elders of the Supreme Court, the movers and shakers of Congress, and the ranking echelons of the current administration.

For more than a century, the Gridiron has roasted the nation's leaders with vaudeville skits. By tradition, one politician from each party gets the right of reply: Geraldine Ferraro after the 1984 Democratic defeat, Bob Dole after the Republican loss in 1976. The president is always given the last word and receives a toast. Lyndon Johnson, who took heavy flak in his final years, once groused earthily that the Gridiron dinner was "about as much fun as throwing cowshit at the village idiot." More deftly, Ronald Reagan—who thrived on the by-play—called it "the most elegant lynching I have ever seen."

But Reagan got off his own sallies, year after year, especially at the 1984 dinner. Eyeing potential Democratic rivals, Reagan ruled out Gary Hart with the quip that "the country won't want a president who looks like a movie star." As for Alan Cranston, then a bald sixty-nine-year-old, he said: "Imagine running for president at his age! He won't have the problem I had—the press won't be bugging him, does he dye his hair?"

For some politicians, the Gridiron has been a priceless forum for reshaping their images and reputations by showing a human side, an ability to laugh at themselves, which is the principal formula of success at the dinner. After his "hatchet man" role as the vice-presidential nominee in 1976, Bob Dole turned a new leaf at the Gridiron by ruefully joking that the person wounded most by his razor tongue "was me." Senator Edward Kennedy, whose 1980 presidential hopes were badly damaged by his fumbling television interview with NBC's Roger Mudd, brought down the house in 1986 with his mock protest that Mudd, a Kennedy family intimate, "came up to *my* house on *my* Cape Cod and sat in one of *my* chairs on *my* front lawn and asked me trick questions, like 'Why do you want to be president?' "

Jimmy and Rosalynn Carter made a hit in 1978 by jitterbugging on stage. Richard Nixon and Vice President Spiro Agnew had a Gridiron audience roaring with a piano duet doing a parody on Nixon's "southern strategy" for the 1972 campaign. Whatever tune Nixon would start, Agnew would drown him out with "Dixie." Ronald Reagan scored with a soft-shoe routine in a black-and-silver sombrero as the surprise kicker in a Gridiron Club chorus line, doing a self-parody to the tune of "Mañana Is Soon Enough for Me."

But for a sheer turnaround—and a political facelift—no Gridiron guest in recent years has outdone Nancy Reagan.

By the end of 1981, the Reagans' first year in the White House, she had become a terrible political liability. The press was snapping at her as a frivolous clotheshorse who hobnobbed with the idle, partygoing rich. Her inaugural wardrobe—a red Adolfo dress, a black formal dress by Bill Blass, a white, beaded, off-the-shoulder gown by James Galanos, and a brand-new full-length Maximillian mink coat—was said to have cost twenty-five thousand dollars. She had three hairdressers at her beck and call.

Mrs. Reagan stirred up a hornet's nest by putting the arm on Republican fat cats for $800,000 in private donations to spruce up the White House mansion, inviting howls that the donors were buying influence. Another hullabaloo broke out when Mrs. Reagan purchased a 220-piece set of gilt-edged china, through similar private financing, for $209,508. When Mrs. Reagan went to London for the wedding of Prince Charles and Princess Diana, the British press knocked her for splashy fashions and cumbersome motorcades. Novelty shops sold postcards mocking her as "Queen Nancy" in ermine and a crown. In a 1981 poll by *Good Housekeeping*, Mrs. Reagan did not even make the ten top women in America.

Reagan strategists feared that Nancy Reagan's bad press could hurt the president's popularity; they held meeting after meeting to figure out how to fix her rich-girl image. They got her to donate her fancy designer dresses to the Smithsonian Institution. When an Air Florida passenger plane crashed into a Potomac River bridge in January 1982, Mrs. Reagan went to hospitals to comfort survivors. But unlike Lady Bird Johnson with her beautification projects, or Betty Ford with her antidrug work, Mrs. Reagan had no cause which touched a popular chord. Initially, the imagemakers had rejected the drug issue as too depressing, but now they agreed when Mrs. Reagan wanted to pursue that issue. Her staff developed a campaign that eventually had her making forays to drug rehabilitation centers, talking to teenagers, appearing on such popular television shows as *Diff'rent Strokes* and *Good Morning America*, and making a joint appeal to the nation with the president in 1986.

But the pivotal moment in her press coverage was the Gridiron dinner of March 27, 1982. The idea of having the first lady do a Gridiron appearance was the brainchild of Sheila Tate, Mrs. Reagan's Washington-wise press secretary. Tate figured (correctly) that Mrs. Reagan was bound to be a target of a press parody; her notion was to have Mrs. Reagan seize the moment by responding. "For an event that has no television coverage and almost no press coverage, the Gridiron dinner is the most influential three or four hours," Tate later explained. "The criticism of Nancy was coming mainly from the Washington political community. What better event for her to humanize herself?"[1]

Tate floated the idea with the first lady. "Would you sing?" Tate asked her. Nancy agreed. "Would you dance?" Another nod from the former movie starlet. Then Tate secretly tried out her notion with Helen Thomas, the veteran White House correspondent for United Press International who in 1975 had become the first woman elected to the Gridiron Club. Thomas, club President Ben Cole and club Vice President Charles McDowell, leaped at the offer to put Mrs. Reagan on stage. The club would parody Mrs. Reagan's lavish wardrobe; they wanted her to respond by making fun of the press. But wisely, Mrs. Reagan sidestepped a sparring match. "No," she told Tate and Deaver, "you have to be able to laugh at yourself. I think that's how we ought to do it."

Landon Parvin, a witty White House speechwriter, worked with Tate to put together a routine based on the old tune "Second Hand Rose" but restyled as "Secondhand Clothes." Secretly, Mrs. Reagan rehearsed it at the White House, without telling the president; she sneaked off for one tryout on the Gridiron stage. Her moment came when the Gridiron chorus did its version of "Secondhand Clothes," mocking her extravagance. Mrs. Reagan slipped away from the head table, her husband thinking she was headed for the ladies' room.

Tate, sitting between two newspaper publishers, recalled one telling the other, "Nancy Reagan has left the head table. I'll bet she's ticked"—presumably at the ribbing the Reagans had been taking. Tate pretended not to hear. "I felt that typified the feeling in the room," she said. "There was a delicious meanness toward Nancy. Her image was of a very brittle, uncaring, self-absorbed socialite." Then, moments later, Mrs. Reagan burst through a rack of clothes on stage. She was clad in an outlandish getup, an aqua skirt with red and yellow flowers held together by safety pins, a floppy feathered hat, and a feathered boa.

There was a moment of incredulous silence. "People were shocked," Tate recalled, which is how I remember it, too. No one thought that Mrs. Reagan had any slapstick, any self-mockery in her. "As it registered, people jumped to their feet and started to applaud. I felt the attitudes in that room change," Tate went on. "It was as if that was all she had to do. People were so surprised that she would do something that looked so foolish. It was very risky. She could have messed it up. The words were so self-deprecating. The point was that she cared what other people thought of her and she showed it."

Nancy Reagan, with a touch of soft-shoe and a steady voice, swung into her lyrics:

> Secondhand clothes,
> I'm wearing secondhand clothes.
> They're all the thing in spring fashion shows.
> Even my new trench coat with fur collar,
> Ronnie bought for ten cents on the dollar.
> . . . .
> The china is the only thing that's new.
> Even though they tell me that I'm no longer queen,
> Did Ronnie have to buy me that new sewing machine?
> Secondhand clothes, secondhand clothes.
> I sure hope Ed Meese sews.

For an exit, she was supposed to shatter a china plate on the stage. She slammed it down but it did not break. The audience did not care. She got a standing ovation and the cheering crowd brought her back for an encore. "It was a gutsy move on Nancy's part," observed Joseph Canzeri, then a presidential aide. "Nobody knows how anybody's going to react to that routine. It could have backfired. The factor of surprise was important. The fact that it couldn't be on TV helped make Nancy willing."[2]

Her success hinged on following one cardinal rule of politics: Hang a lantern on your problem; that is, play up a vulnerability and dispose of it by mocking your own foibles.[3] As Reagan himself proved many times, that technique can lance the boil of criticism. So often, criticism loses its edge if a politician simply admits his problem. Often the best way to disarm a hostile press is to embrace them; "love bombing," some call it. In this case, it was strictly an inside-the-beltway phenomenon. A story about Nancy Reagan at the Gridiron dinner appeared in Monday's *Washington Post,* but otherwise, according to Gridiron tradition, the affair remained unreported. Only the inner core of the Washington community had seen this side of Mrs. Reagan. But that community included most of the important journalists and politicians, and among this crucial audience, Mrs. Reagan's image had been remade in a few short minutes. Inside the beltway, people talked with amusement and warmth about her Gridiron appearance. She had won a new beginning—a new image—with the political press.

It would be many months before the country would realize that the stinging criticism of the first lady had become muted. Her public standing changed, with stories appearing about her antidrug campaign and her bringing home two deathly sick children from a trip to Korea. By Reagan's second inauguration, she rivaled the president in popularity. In fact, a *New York Times*/CBS News poll in January 1985 found her public approval rating was seventy-one percent compared to his sixty-two percent. *Time* magazine did a cover story on "Nancy Reagan's Growing Role" in policy and appointments. NBC followed up with an hour-long special on Mrs. Reagan "at the peak of her power and the peak of her popularity." Plenty of work and press agentry went into such flattering coverage, but the world beyond the beltway never knew what had propelled Nancy Reagan's image turnaround.

The Video Presidency

No presidency has been more image conscious or image driven than that of Ronald Reagan. During the Reagan era, Washington began calling itself "Hollywood East," exulting in celebrity politics. As the nation's first chief executive with a long show-business background, Reagan exploited his acting skills to the fullest. His choreographers played to those strengths as they staged his presidency. Reagan never seemed more at home as president than when performing: standing before an audience or landing on a former battlefield in Normandy or Korea to personify the nation's strength and determination. Reagan has loved the role of president, especially the ceremonial role, and he has played to the emotions of his countrymen in an almost-endless string of televised performances. For millions, the Reagan years became a political home movie.

Quite obviously, image making or political public relations was not invented by Reagan, though it reached new peaks of sophistication in the Reagan era. Theatrics are in the blood of most politicians. Fred Dutton, a well-known Washington lawyer and political strategist, told me of arriving at John F. Kennedy's home in Georgetown one morning to discuss a White House job, after Kennedy's election in 1960 but before his inauguration. From the hallway, Dutton could see Kennedy sitting alone in another room—wearing a bowler, smoking a cigar, holding a glass of brandy, and listening to recorded speeches by Winston Churchill—obviously imagining his own oratory.[4]

Probably the first President to grasp the power of modern public relations was Teddy Roosevelt, who originated regular press conferences and coined the memorable metaphor that the presidency is a "bully pulpit" for preaching to the nation. Roosevelt understood the hypnotic pull of the camera. During the Spanish-American War in 1898, he took along two movie cameramen who filmed his Rough Riders as they charged up Cuba's San Juan Hill. Actually, Roosevelt's biographer, Edmund Morris, recounts this "charge" was less a heroic dash to the ridge top than a bloody slaughter of the American troops, ambushed by Spanish riflemen while painfully seizing the terrain.[5] But the movie newsreels—turning news into entertainment—dramatized Roosevelt's heroics and launched a political legend.

Newsreels also helped make Franklin Roosevelt larger than life, but radio was his medium. FDR used radio vividly to evoke the miseries of the "little people" and to offer them hope amidst the economic holocaust of the Depression. His fireside chats deliberately eschewed silver oratory. They were compassionate conversations with a mass audience, FDR's easy, confident voice an immediate presence to millions of plain people. His folksy anecdotes invited listeners to conjure reality in the theater of the mind. Like Reagan, Franklin Roosevelt was a master at simplifying, at brushing aside the complexity of the nation's problems. He exulted in his own dramatic talents, once telling Orson Welles, "There are only two great actors in America—you are the other one."[6]

Television came of age politically in 1952. Political lieutenants of Dwight Eisenhower used it to wrest control of the Republican National Convention from Senator Robert A. Taft, the favorite of party regulars. They televised charges of convention chicanery by Taft's forces, helping Ike get nominated. That fall, Eisenhower became the first presidential candidate to use political ads on TV, to publicize not only his views but his famous grin and common touch. Ike's success set a pattern; television became the springboard for political outsiders to beat established politicans: Jack Kennedy in 1960, Jimmy Carter in 1976, Ronald Reagan in 1980. Experienced inside operators such as Lyndon Johnson, Richard Nixon, and Walter Mondale got to the top through orthodox organization politics. Image-game politics was the province of the upstarts.

Once in office, all modern presidents have enlisted the power of the tube to try to increase their bargaining leverage with Congress; they "go public" to sell their policies by demonstrating that public opinion is with them. Richard Nixon used prime-time television so often to promote his Vietnam policies that the Federal Communications Commission finally insisted that, under the "fairness doctrine," TV networks had to give Nixon's critics time to respond.[7] Jimmy Carter delivered four nationally televised addresses on the nation's energy crisis and was ready to do a fifth when his pollster, Patrick Caddell, persuaded him another TV pitch on energy would not work. But no president has used television more than Reagan to promote his personal popularity as well as his policies, and then to use his popularity as a club with Congress to pass his programs. In Reagan's hands, the presidency became the terrain of the permanent campaign.

Television is particularly well suited to presidents such as Reagan, Kennedy, and Eisenhower who sell mood, confidence, and image as much as the substance of policy. Television's compelling power is its immediacy. TV gives viewers a direct experience of political leaders and gives politicians direct access to the living rooms of the electorate. This immediacy fuels the politics of emotions, gut reactions, and impressions rather than the politics of logic, facts, and reason; it emphasizes personality rather than issues.

"Radio, and then television, drew our attention away from issues and caused us to focus on the more personal qualities of the politician, his ability to speak, and his style of presentation," wrote Tony Schwartz, a political consultant and disciple of the media scholar Marshall McLuhan. "Today, in judging [politicians], voters do not look for political labels. They look for what they consider to be good character: qualities such as conviction, compassion, steadiness, the willingness to work hard."[8]

On television, politics becomes seen and presented as cinema: a series of narrative episodes about political personalities, not an abstract running debate on policy. To the mass audience, issues are secondary. The mass audience focuses on the hero, with whom it identifies unless he does something so outrageous that it falls out of sympathy with him. Television feels driven to dramatize the news, to give it plot, theme, and continuity in order to make it comprehensible to a mass audience. Television needs action and drama. It needs to boil down complexities. It needs identifiable characters. Hence the focus on personality, preferably one personality.

In this simplified world, Congress is too brawling and diverse to follow easily, because it deals openly with the complexity of issues, whereas the White House deals with most complexities in private. The result is that comparatively speaking, Congress is undercovered and the president overcovered—and the imbalance has grown in the decade from the mid-seventies to the mid-eighties, when the actual power of Congress has grown. In an essay on "The Case of Our Disappearing Congress," two political scientists, Norman Ornstein and Michael Robinson of the American Enterprise Institute, found that network TV news gave Congress only half as much coverage in 1985 as it did in 1975.[9]

In what amounts to the running soap opera of politics, television needs a leading man, and the president fits the bill. As Austin Ranney, a political scientist at the University of California in Berkeley, observed, the public can follow the news only when the confusing tumble of daily developments becomes episodes in an ongoing story.[10] The presidency becomes a TV serial; the president, his family, his aides and cohorts become recognizable characters in the play—known and familiar, heroes and villains. Special episodes draw attention: "Ronald Reagan Goes to Peking," "Nancy Reagan Says No to Drugs," "Ollie North Sells Arms to Khomeini."

In the story line from day to day, the plot becomes binary: How is the hero faring: up or down, winning or losing? This is the John Wayne syndrome described earlier: politics treated as a western shoot-out, our sheriff versus the bad guys. The story becomes, Did Reagan's budget pass, or was he defeated; not, Did the deficit get solved? Was the summit a success or failure for Reagan; not, Are we closer to real security? American political reporting, preoccupied with winning and losing, also focuses on the fate of the main protagonist (the president, the challenger, the front-runner) and not on whether issues are being joined or problems resolved.

Reagan's approach is ideal for the television age. His political actions are cinematic. Both he and his political choreographers have played to the public's need for a clear plot line. The Reagan team recognized that the public and Congress can focus on only one major development or one major story at a time. In the presidential TV serial, each episode replaces the last one; most are almost instantly forgotten. Each sequence of events is treated like a minidrama, with beginning, middle, and end. When reporter Nicholas Daniloff was seized in Moscow, his drama became the central national concern, but when he was allowed to leave the Soviet Union, that show was over and forgotten, replaced first by the Iceland summit and then by the 1986 congressional election. When American Marines were shot at and bombed in Lebanon in late 1983, the nation shared their daily ordeal, but when the Marines were pulled out in February 1984, that show was over. Never mind the long-run policy consequences in the Middle East; never mind the wisdom of swapping a Soviet spy for Daniloff. The episodes were over; on to the next episode. For an incumbent president, this is a brilliant strategy. Problems do not accumulate, and that makes a president such as Reagan seem invincible: the Teflon image.

Television also breeds a box-office mentality in politics. The network evening news shows follow the ratings. Substance matters, but the bottom line is not how much information was imparted, but how big the audience was. In a world of audience ratings, "talking heads" discussing issues pose a risk that viewers will flip the button to another channel. Networks build audiences, and hence build coverage, around the strongest video coverage they can get. Live coverage is by far the most compelling, and the video managers of all presidents labor incessantly to create media events that the networks will find irresistible for live coverage. There is a symbiotic, as well as adversarial, relationship between network producers and White House video strategists, each side wanting a video drama that attracts and holds the largest audience.

With that mentality, White House political strategists are sometimes guided by what is good box office rather than by what is good long-run policy. Symbolism over substance.

That image game was played by Jimmy Carter's first team: Press Secretary Jody Powell, media adviser Gerald Rafshoon, and pollster Patrick Caddell. They saw Carter's inaugural walk down Pennsylvania Avenue was good box office. The Camp David summit with Egyptian President Anwar Sadat and Israeli Prime Minister Menachem Begin was both good policy and good box office. Carter's political problem was that it was extremely hard to sustain his Camp David peacemaking; it bogged down. Reagan, sensing bad box office in the tangled diplomacy of the Middle East, kept clear of personal involvement. For Carter, the Iranian hostage crisis was bad box office that he could not shake, for instead of playing it down publicly, he wrapped the fate of his presidency in the fate of the hostages and lost the gamble. Their freedom came too late to save him. Reagan did the opposite on Lebanon; after the terrible killings of the American Marines, he simply walked away from the episode. Eventually, Reagan got trapped by his own hostage crisis with Iran. His claims of ignorance, the attempted cover-ups, the official lying to Congress all fed that angry plot line. But until then, Reagan's politics escaped a destructive box-office image. Jody Powell, speaking before Reagan's Iranian debacle, rated the Reagan team as better than Carter's team in staging the president.

"The Reagan people had earlier White House experience and they had a much clearer strategy in terms of presidential image," Powell said one autumn afternoon, relaxing in his backyard. "Mike Deaver was better at it than I was, and Reagan is much more amenable to and more easily persuaded to public relations than Carter was. Carter would rather spend the next hour on the ifs, ands, or buts of the decision he had to make, than on the selling of the decision."[11]

What made Reagan's image-game politics distinctive were not only the president's formidable personal talents and salesman's instincts, but the conscious decision of his strategists *to make television the organizing framework* for the president, to an unprecedented degree. Their philosophy was reflected in a passage by Theodore White, reverently quoted to me by Pat Buchanan, the conservative columnist recruited for the second-term Reagan White House. White had declared that "power in America today is control of the means of communication."[12]

Substantive policymakers such as Budget Director David Stockman and former Secretary of State Alexander Haig, derided the public relations obsession of the Reagan White House. Haig repeatedly complained that the president's public relations managers ran policy. Knowing how much White House effort went into influencing ABC, CBS, and NBC, Stockman bitterly complained that "reality for the boys"— Reagan's monicker for his political strategists—"came at six o'clock" with the nightly news shows.

"I can't think of a single meeting I was at for more than an hour when someone didn't say, 'How will this play in the media?' " confessed Lee Atwater, a senior White House political strategist. "Cabinet officers got run out of office because the White House couldn't manage the story in the media. You got it all the time. Major decisions were influenced by the media."[13]

Reagan's highly skilled first-term team played the image game unabashedly. These political strategists saw a direct linkage between the president's image, his reputation, his standing in the polls, his seduction of the media—and his leverage with Congress and his success at governing. They had learned a lesson from seeing Jimmy Carter, sinking in the polls, paralyzed with Congress. They elevated the image game to primary importance, honing its rules and strategies. They demonstrated that the smoke-filled back rooms in modern American politics are not for cutting deals but for plotting image strategy for TV. They sold more than policies; they sold the presidency.

Media Jujitsu: Controlling the Stage

Quite obviously, the television networks (and the press in general) have power—however disorganized—to play havoc with the agenda games of presidents by crystallizing issues that the White House would rather ignore. As Reagan took office, many conservatives felt that the media had gained the upper hand. It does not require my rehearsing the battering given Lyndon Johnson over the Vietnam War and Richard Nixon over Watergate to make the point. And Jimmy Carter was bloodied by the networks' relentless count of "America Held Hostage" in Iran for 444 days. Lloyd Cutler, Carter's White House counsel, argued in *Foreign Policy* magazine that the deadline of "the TV doomsday clock" pressured Carter and his advisers into mishandling other issues: overreacting to the Soviet brigade in Cuba in 1979 and hastily instituting a grain embargo against Moscow after the Soviet invasion of Afghanistan. Cutler bemoaned the power of the media: "Whatever urgent but less televised problem may be on the White House agenda on any given morning, it is often put aside to consider and respond to the latest TV news bombshell in time for the next broadcast."[14]

Reagan too felt the pressure of events magnified in the press. Graphic television reporting of massacres in Palestinian refugee camps in Beirut in 1982 propelled Reagan to send in American Marines to help keep peace. Equally graphic portrayals of the bombings against the Marines later built political pressures on him to withdraw them in 1984. In 1985, the daily bombardment of televised reports from South Africa galvanized Congress and helped compel Reagan to agree to limited economic sanctions against South Africa. In early 1986, dramatic television reporting of vote fraud in the Philippines helped make Reagan abandon Ferdinand Marcos.

On a more personal plane, blunt coverage of Reagan's refusal on May 22, 1986, to take part in the "Hands Across America" demonstration shamed him into participating. NBC's report pointed out that this was an example of the private voluntary effort for the poor that the president had advocated and that its organizers had offered to run the line of outstretched arms through his front yard. The next day, Reagan told NBC's Chris Wallace that seeing NBC's broadcast had changed his mind.[15]

As the Reagan team took over the White House in 1981, it saw battling the press as political jujitsu. The trick in jujitsu is to take your adversary's force and turn it to your own advantage by clever maneuver. In media strategy, the goal is to use the power of television to enhance the president's power, not to let it break him. The most basic rule of the image game is to control the stage, according to David Gergen, Reagan's first White House communications director. Rather than let the press fix the news priorities and batter the president, Gergen said, the White House intended to set not only the political agenda for Congress but also the television agenda for the networks.

"We wanted to control what people saw, to the extent that we could," Gergen explained. "We wanted to shape it and not let television shape it. After all, in the minds of many people, what television did for the 1986 Democratic convention [showing police battling rioters] cost them the election. You had to figure out how to [control] it on your own. I mean, large aspects, the public aspects, of government have become staged, television-staged, and there is a real question who is going to control the stage. Is it going to be the networks or the people who work for the candidate or for the president?"[16]

Ironically, given the disaster of Watergate, the Nixon presidency provided the Reagan team with its textbook for managing the press and some of its top public relations experts: David Gergen, a former Nixon speechwriter; William Henkel, an advance man skilled in staging photogenic presidential trips; Ron Walker, a specialist in running political conventions; and Pat Buchanan, a communications expert. Reagan's California media handlers were the other stream of talent—Mike Deaver, Dick Wirthlin, and Stuart Spencer. Although Wirthlin never joined the White House staff, as Reagan's $1-million-a-year pollster-strategist (paid by the Republican party) he sat in weekly strategy meetings; his findings often guided the others. Spencer, a brilliant intuitive strategist close to Reagan, also gave advice from the outside. Deaver was the chief video manager inside the White House.

Two things are striking about this group: First, none was the press secretary, meaning all were freed from the consuming chore of press briefings to plot and manage image strategy, and second, almost all had a background in marketing: Henkel for Merrill Lynch, Deaver with his own public relations firm, Wirthlin and Spencer for rich corporate clients, Gergen as former editor of *Public Opinion* magazine.

The Nixonian gospel was brought into the Reagan camp by Gergen. Candid, compulsive, fast-talking, and a towering six foot five (at Yale, he had been nicknamed "The Giraffe"), Gergen was the author of Reagan's most telling line in his 1980 campaign debate with Carter: "Are you better off today than you were four years ago?" Gergen had watched the Democratic convention disaster of 1968 and seen George McGovern miss a national TV audience in 1972 by delivering his acceptance speech after midnight. And in 1972, Gergen had been put in charge of scripting the Republican convention to prevent such snafus. The technique is revealing:

"We had an advance script, even down to the applause lines worked into the script, so we could run it on a disciplined basis," Gergen recalled. "We figured that the importance of the convention was for show, for the people back home, and you had to run it like a TV production. So you were very conscious of the television values in scripting it. And we developed what we called the alternative script. We had a series of key figures we thought were good copy: good for television or interesting visually. And if you had somebody on the podium you thought was not terribly interesting, and we knew the networks would only carry for maybe three out of fifteen minutes [and then switch to their own reporting], we'd go to the networks in advance and say, 'We have John Connally, the Treasury secretary, in a holding room. He's going to be coming onto the floor in just a few minutes. Would you be interested in interviewing him?' The networks would love that. Or when Nixon moved somewhere [outside the hall], his movements were timed to coincide with events in the hall that were not very interesting. One night he went out to Sammy Davis, Jr., and there was a picture of him hugging Sammy Davis."[17]

In short, the game was to get television to follow the Nixon script and not to do its own slant on events. The Nixon people knew that reality to millions of viewers across the country was not what happened in the hall—but what happened on their television sets. What didn't happen on TV, even if it later appeared in print, was more dimly perceived.

In its image-game strategy, the Reagan White House operated by a similar P.R. script built around the "story line of the day." The imperative is to pick the main public relations message each day and frame it just the way White House strategists want it to appear in the short bites on the evening television news, in headlines, and in the lead paragraph of news-agency stories. The president does many things each day, and only a portion of his actions are made public. Getting the proper bit on TV requires organizing the public portions of the president's day—the portions that will be filmed or reported—to dramatize the story line or central message. Otherwise the press and TV apply their news judgment, their filter. The trick for White House video managers is to get their story line through the press filter in its purest form. Nothing is left to chance. The public may think it is witnessing spontaneous remarks or actions, but the Reagan White House rule was that no matter how spontaneous a presidential utterance might appear, it was to be scripted in advance. As an actor used to making things look ad-libbed, Reagan was ideal for "scripted spontaneity." But the basic tactic came from Nixon.

"We had a rule in the Nixon operation," Gergen explained, "that before any public event was put on his schedule, you had to know what the headline out of that event was going to be, what the picture was going to be, and what the lead paragraph would be. You had to think of it in those terms, and if you couldn't justify it, it didn't go on the [president's] schedule. So you learned to think that a president communicates through the media, through the press, and not directly. One of Nixon's rules about television was that it was very important that the White House determine what the line coming out from the president was and not let the networks determine that, not let New York edit you. You had to learn how to do the editing yourself.

"So that when Nixon went out to make a statement in the White House briefing room, he insisted that he be given one hundred words [a 'tight' TV news bite]. And we had to count 'em. We had to put up in the corner of the page how many words were on this paper. You couldn't go over one hundred. He would go out and deliver one hundred words, and he'd walk out. Because he knew that they had to use about one hundred words. They had to use what he wanted to say. And if you gave them five hundred words, they would select part of it and determine what the point of his statement was. It was a very rigorous system."

The Nixon method was quickly adopted by the Reagan White House. At their eight-fifteen morning strategy meeting, Jim Baker, Ed Meese, and Mike Deaver would decide on the day's story line; they would pass the word to Gergen and press spokesman Larry Speakes. The broad lines of the Reagan presidency are familiar: The president wants less government, more money for defense, military aid for Nicaraguan rebels; the president will veto the congressional budget (though he has rarely done so); the president will accept a tax increase only "as a last resort" (though he signed tax increases three years in a row).

Those are the big themes, but day in and day out, White House imagemakers fine-tune them, or they labor to deflect embarrassing stories. Often the official story line is directed at shaping how reporters cast White House stories. For example, when the White House was putting together the Reagan antidrug package in September 1986, Larry Speakes scolded reporters for highlighting mandatory drug testing for about one million federal employes. The mandatory tests had stirred up a hornet's nest. Speakes wanted testing played down as "just one part of a six-part package," to reduce public resistance to Reagan's plan.

Sometimes the story line surfaces almost casually, belying its careful plotting. My colleague, Steven Weisman of *The New York Times*, uncovered one such episode in September 1984, after Walter Mondale upstaged President Reagan by announcing that he would meet with then–Soviet Foreign Minister Andrei Gromyko. (In nearly four years,

Reagan had not yet met any top Soviet official.) Reagan's top White House staff considered the story-line options: Should the president suggest that Mondale was meddling in affairs of state? Should criticism be leaked by some official anonymously? They wanted to knock Mondale, without looking petty. They decided on the line that the president had "no problem" with the Gromyko-Mondale meeting. It was a two-edged tactic: to show that Reagan was above partisan pettiness, but to implant a kernel of doubt about the propriety of Mondale's move by injecting the notion of a "problem." When reporters asked the expected question, Speakes replied offhandedly, "We don't have any problems with it." Later, President Reagan himself was asked and replied: "I have no problem with that at all."[18] The echoes were hardly as casual as they were made to sound.

Putting Spin on the Story Line

Setting the story line is the easy part; selling it and protecting it are much harder, especially when the president is prone to trip over carefully crafted media strategies with a loose tongue, as Reagan often did. Three things can trash the White House story line: hotter, competitive news from elsewhere; independent-minded White House reporters who refuse to buy the White House slant on presidential news; and self-inflicted wounds—the administration's own snafus.

Far more than earlier administrations, the Reagan White House sought to impose tight discipline on other agencies. It did not want the Transportation Department taking a softer line on the air traffic controllers' strike than the president took; or the Commerce Department slashing at Japanese trade practices when Reagan was privately wooing Prime Minister Yasuhiro Nakasone. The sheer sprawling reach of the federal octopus makes controlling its tentacles hard. The aggressive, fragmented Washington press corps poses a challenge to centralized control.

Reporting in Washington is largely organized on a "beat system" (like a policeman's patrol beat), because reporters must specialize in specific policy fields, or individual agencies, to keep abreast of developments. Usually, networks, newspapers, or news agencies assign one or two reporters to each of the main beats: the White House, Pentagon, State Department, Congress, Labor Department, Federal Reserve Board, and so on. All agencies have policy axes to grind, often at White House expense, and they feed the word to their beat reporters. At budget time, for example, the Pentagon will leak word of some new

Soviet missile test or naval deployment, to justify a bigger budget. The Department of Health and Human Services will privately provide reporters a blueprint for a catastrophic health insurance plan to try to force President Reagan to endorse it.

To impose discipline, Reagan's White House press office instituted daily conference calls with press secretaries of other executive agencies—one conference on domestic issues, and one on foreign policy. Reagan's video managers grabbed good news for the president to announce and often made other agencies handle the bad news. White House spokesmen also one-upped other agencies by holding earlier daily briefings. Normally, major government agencies brief the press around noon, but at the Reagan White House, a dozen or so top reporters would gather in Larry Speakes's office around 9:15 A.M. for coffee and news tips. At first, these were "background" or "guidance" sessions—meaning that Speakes was not to be quoted, but he would give reporters the president's schedule, say which events would be open to press coverage, tell whether the president would make important remarks, and indicate where action might develop in other agencies or Congress. For the networks, this was valuable for deciding where to deploy their camera crews. Then, teams of cameramen, soundmen, reporters, and producers need warning to get to breaking news. With his tips, Speakes could steer the networks to items the White House wanted on the nightly news.

Eventually, Speakes made his 9:15 A.M. session an on-the-record briefing. By making the first comments on major overnight news and foreign developments, he could shape the Washington slant on the news before Congress or other agencies could react. "We jumped the gun on everyone," one White House press aide boasted. "We were stealing the thunder from State and Defense."

For TV coverage, the cards are stacked in favor of the White House. The beat system makes individual reporters vulnerable to government manipulation. It produces an institution-based press: cliques of reporters whose professional success depends greatly on the news generated by the beat or the institution they cover. Some reporters follow a news story such as aid to the Nicaraguan *contras* or the antidrug war wherever major developments lead. But more commonly, reporters work the angle that develops in their assigned agency, making them captives of the institution they cover and helping the White House to sell its story line, especially to TV networks.

"The president is the only nationally elected politician, and we're the national news media," explained Ed Fouhy, who has worked as a bureau chief or leading producer in Washington for ABC, CBS, and NBC. "On a slow news day at the White House, *The New York Times* can go [for big news] to the governor of New York and the mayor of New York City. But the networks have nowhere else to go. The president is our mayor. Congress is so tied up in its procedure that it's very hard to get access for the kind of pictures you need. And the Supreme Court doesn't allow anything [live TV coverage]. At the White House, you have your best correspondent, you've got all the logistical problems solved, and it's going to look like news, no matter what happens."[19]

The second rule of White House video merchants (after controlling the stage) is to minimize press editing of the White House story line. To get Reagan's message out to the country in pure form, Reagan's P.R. men sought to bypass the White House press corps. One technique was to play host periodically to regional broadcasters and editors, more awed by the presidential presence than White House regulars are and more inclined to take the spoon-fed story line. Another technique was to computerize the story line for mass marketing. In 1983, the Reagan team sent out ten thousand notices to newspapers, radio and television stations, and Republican organizations, telling them how to plug in electronically to prepackaged press statements and radio tapes—*unedited by the networks*. With Pat Buchanan as the driving force, the White House later beamed videotapes of uncut, unedited presidential appearances to nine hundred television stations via satellite uplinks owned by the U.S. Chamber of Commerce, the Republican party, or Conus, a private system. The goal was to have television anchors and producers in Dallas, Chicago, and Atlanta take the White House version rather than a network news package. "You can reach a huge audience with material which is shaped by the government rather than by the people in New York with the networks," David Gergen explained.

Moreover, for all its distaste for the controlled Soviet press, the Reagan White House toyed with setting up its own press agency. Evidently oblivious to parallels with Tass, the official Soviet news agency, Reagan backers proposed starting a government wire service to distribute government press releases. Gergen vetoed the idea. "I did not think it was appropriate to have a government wire service," Gergen said. "I think this is dangerous."[20]

But Gergen was famous for his "spin patrol"—a late effort by White House video managers to get a favorable slant in network news coverage. Normally, reporters spray out telephone calls to news sources during the day, probing for fresh angles, disagreements, difficulties, hidden costs, or covert actions. From such calls, Reagan's media men could sense when news was developing unfavorably, and they would telephone reporters on deadline to put the White House "spin" on the news.

"He'd [Gergen] always call me up about six o'clock, five-fifty—usually in response to a call from me," Sam Donaldson, ABC's senior White House correspondent told me. "He'd want to tell me the White House view of something, and I'd invariably have to say, 'David, I've already tracked my [news] piece. I mean, if I start tearing up the piece now, I'm probably not going to make air.' But he always knew that I would get in something of what he said. And also he knew that by making it so late, what I would have to do usually is get the White House version, to some extent, in my 'end piece.' He knew that the end pieces that sum up the story are the last impact that the viewer gets. You know, Reagan says something, and Tip O'Neill says something, and you [the viewer] see something, and then I come on and say, 'And so tonight it's clear, what the White House is attempting to do is . . .' Well, Gergen is pretty sharp. He knew that he would have an impact 'cause I'd feel constrained to sort of say, 'And so tonight, what seems clear is that the White House is going to do such and so, although a senior official said late today, "No, we're going to do it the other way." Thank you.' "[21]

"The reporters respond to that," Gergen said, defending his practice. "They like it. They need it. And you could get them to change their feed."[22]

The most lethal threat to the Reagan image game was loose talk in the White House, especially from the president. For getting the networks to do your bidding requires enormous internal discipline to hold the focus. The established story line was often upstaged by stories of internal feuding, or more likely, slips of the presidential tongue.

Reagan became famous for stepping on his own policy line with ad-libs. That is why his staff carefully plotted, coached, and rehearsed his statements and restricted his press conferences. In May 1986, for example, Reagan spoke to a visiting group about his budget priorities. But answering a question, he remarked that hunger in America was caused not by lack of money or food-distribution problems, but by a "lack of knowledge" among the poor about where to obtain help. His budget push got lost; his comments about the ignorance of hungry people became the headline, making Reagan look callous.

On other occasions, Reagan upset the image-game plan with serious misstatements. In early 1986, he tried to sway Congress on military aid for Nicaraguan rebels by claiming that Pope John Paul II was "urging us to continue our efforts in Central America." The Vatican immediately denied that the Pope backed Reagan's *contra* policy; Reagan's misleading gambit boomeranged. After the hijacking of the *Achille Lauro* luxury liner in October 1985, the president goofed badly by telling reporters that it would be "all right" to have the ship's hijackers turned over to the Palestine Liberation Organization so that "they can bring them to justice." Reagan was virtually granting the PLO the legitimacy of a government—something his administration had refused to do for nearly six years. Within hours, Reagan had to backtrack and call for a trial by an established Western government.

What is probably Reagan's most costly blooper came in August 1984, during a microphone test for one of his Saturday radio broadcasts. Instead of the standard 5-4-3-2-1, the president, intending a joke and thinking he was speaking in private, said: "My fellow Americans, I am pleased to tell you I just signed legislation which outlaws Russia forever. The bombing begins in five minutes." Network technical crews heard his remarks and the story quickly got into print. The Allies erupted, and it took an energetic diplomatic campaign to calm them. The episode also cost Reagan with American voters; his private polls showed a dip of several points, shrinking Reagan's lead over Mondale to its narrowest margin in the 1984 campaign.

One amusing story-line foul-up was caused by Caspar Weinberger's napping during a White House P.R. operation. In March 1986, White House strategists built a drumbeat of media pressure to win Congressional support for $100 million in aid to Nicaraguan *contras*. Every day they fabricated a new media event: Reagan made speeches, met with *contra* leaders, huddled with congressional allies. To demonstrate graphically that Nicaragua was funneling arms to Marxist rebels in El Salvador, Reagan's video managers decided to publicize an American M-16 rifle, lost in Vietnam and sent through Cuba to Nicaragua and then into El Salvador, where it was recaptured. To generate press interest, this M-16 was put on display at the State Department, and Reagan went there to speak. Moving Reagan even a few blocks helps attract TV coverage, because TV likes movement to convey the impression that something is happening.

"You can usually get greater credibility by taking certain events out of the White House," William Henkel explained. "Sometimes to elevate something, give it stature, just that little technique of taking the president five or ten minutes out of the White House creates an event."[23]

The Washington Times on Friday, March 14, produced what the White House wanted—a headline: REAGAN OFFERS CAPTURED ARMS AS PROOF. United Press International carried the guts of the White House story line; it had the president, "with a bristling display of the deadly tools of Central American conflict as his backdrop," warning Congress of the danger of "anti-American Communist dictatorships" in the region.

Television ran Reagan's show-and-tell session—except that Weinberger, in the audience, spoiled the show by nodding off while the president was speaking. As the cameras zoomed in on Weinberger's drooping head, NBC's Chris Wallace narrated: "While Mr. Reagan called the display an eye-opener, Secretary Weinberger fought a losing battle trying to do just that."

Weinberger killed Reagan's pitch with a yawn, for the picture of his catnap overrode Reagan's spoken message.

The Visual Beats the Verbal

In the image game, the essence is not words, but pictures. The Reagan imagemakers followed the rule framed by Bob Haldeman, the advertising man who was Nixon's chief of staff, the governing principle for politics in the television era: The visual wins over the verbal; the eye predominates over the ear; sight beats sound. As one Reagan official laughingly said to me, "What are you going to believe, the facts or your eyes?"

Reagan's video managers, like scores of other political strategists and media consultants, operate on the principle that pictures prevail over commentary—the "eyes" always win.

Lesley Stahl of CBS, a top network reporter proud of her critical independence, told me how this point was driven home to her after airing a very tough commentary on the 1984 campaign. It was a four-and-a-half-minute piece that ran on October 4, during the campaign homestretch, analyzing how Reagan strategists used video forays "to create amnesia" about Reagan's political record. Her piece was so blunt about Reagan's techniques, Stahl told me, that she braced for a violent reaction from Reagan's video managers.

"How does Ronald Reagan use television?" Stahl's script asked.

"Brilliantly. He's been criticized as the rich man's President, but the TV pictures say it isn't so. At 73, Mr. Reagan could have an age problem. But the TV pictures say it isn't so. Americans want to feel proud of their

country again, and of their President. And the TV pictures say you can. The
orchestration of television coverage absorbs the White House. Their goal?
To emphasize the President's greatest asset, which, his aides say, is his
personality. They provide pictures of him looking like a leader. Confident,
with his Marlboro man walk. A good family man.

"They also aim to erase the negatives. Mr. Reagan tried to counter the
memory of an unpopular issue with a carefully chosen backdrop that actually contradicts the President's policy. Look at the handicapped Olympics,
or the opening ceremony of an old-age home. No hint that he tried to cut
the budgets for the disabled and for federally subsidized housing for the
elderly. . . . Another technique for distancing the President from bad
news—have him disappear, as he did the day he pulled the Marines out of
Lebanon. He flew off to his California ranch, leaving others to hand out
the announcement. There are few visual reminders linking the President
to the tragic bombing of the Marine headquarters in Beirut. But two days
later, the invasion of Grenada succeeded, and the White House offered
television a variety of scenes associating the President with the joy and the
triumph. . . .

"President Reagan is accused of running a campaign in which he highlights the images and hides from the issues. But there's no evidence that
the charges will hurt him because when people see the President on television, he makes them feel good, about America, about themselves, and about
him."[24]

Stahl's producers created a montage of Reagan video vignettes to
illustrate her piece: Reagan cutting the ribbon at an old-folks home;
greeting handicapped athletes in wheelchairs; giving a hug to Olympic
gold-medal winner Mary Lou Retton; touring a cave saved by an environmental project; receiving a birthday cake and a kiss from Nancy;
pumping iron and tossing a football with his Secret Service guards;
mingling with black inner-city children and white kids in the suburbs;
relaxing on his ranch in faded jeans; talking with midwestern farmers
in an open field; paying tribute at Normandy to American G.I.'s who
had died in the World War II landing in Europe; bathing in a sea of
jubilant, flag-waving Reagan partisans while red-white-and-blue balloons floated toward the sky.

"I thought it was the single toughest piece I had ever done on
Reagan," Stahl said, recalling her apprehension about the White
House reaction. "The piece aired, and my phone rang. It was a senior
White House official and I thought, 'I keep telling people that they've
never yelled at me, but here it comes.'

"And the voice said, 'Great piece.'

"I said, 'What?'

"And he said, *'Great piece!'*

"I said, 'Did you listen to what I said?'

"He said, 'Lesley, when you're showing four and a half minutes of great pictures of Ronald Reagan, no one listens to what you say. Don't you know that the pictures are overriding your message because they conflict with your message? The public sees those pictures and they block your message. They didn't even hear what you said. So, in our minds, it was a four-and-a-half-minute free ad for the Ronald Reagan campaign for reelection.'

"I sat here numb. I began to feel dumb 'cause I'd covered him four years and I hadn't figured it out. Somebody had to explain it to me. Well, none of us had figured it out. I called the executive producer of the *Evening News* [Lane Venardos], and he went dead on the phone. And he said, 'Oh, my God.'

"None of us had figured that out. All of us were proud of that piece 'cause we thought we had done a good, tough job, and then"—She broke into laughter. *"They* loved it. They really did love it."[25]

The Vicar of Visuals

Mike Deaver, the self-styled "vicar of visuals," was the impresario of Reagan's visual choreography. A slim, creative, nervous, hands-in-the-pockets Californian who helped pay his way through college playing the piano, Deaver created Reagan's most memorable video images. Over the years Deaver had developed an unerring intuition for what event, what backdrop, what lighting would best convey Reagan and his message visually. He knew Reagan as a film director knows his leading man. His skills were inseparable from Reagan's political success.

Deaver was meticulous about the backdrops and settings for fashioning the proper Reagan image. He not only bathed Reagan in symbols of national pride and patriotism but set Reagan in flattering lights. Deaver disliked the plain beige curtains drawn behind Reagan's desk when he addressed the nation from the Oval Office. He felt Reagan's face faded into that backdrop. He decided to open the curtains, and he spent $20,000 on backlighting the window from the garden outside. "It made the president look ten years younger with nice, natural lighting and the green behind him or the snowstorm in the winter," Deaver said.[27]

In staging Reagan, Deaver spared no effort. At the 1984 Republican convention, I went to the podium several hours before the opening.

Carpenters were still hammering signs among an ocean of empty seats. On the podium, two men in suit jackets were crouching over a chair, one clicking close-ups of its arms, legs, and back with a thirty-five-millimeter camera. They were so absorbed that I startled them by asking why they were photographing a chair.

"Because we designed it," said the older man, David Clark, a designer for Imero Fiorentino Associates of New York and Hollywood. "We designed the entire podium."

"So why take pictures of the chair?"

"We're taking pictures of everything," Clark explained. "We've taken about four thousand pictures—the chair, the lectern, parts of the podium, the television camera platform. We know every piece of wood, and why it's here."

"What's special about the chair and the podium?" I asked.

"The whole effect." He gestured around. "Look, there are no square angles anywhere. Look at the chair: round top, curved legs. Look at edge of the podium: no sharp corners. They're all rounded. Look at the lectern: curves everywhere. Look at the colors: They're all earth tones—brown, beige, nothing jarring."

"What's the reason?" I asked.

"Those are the tones that [convention manager] Ron Walker and Mike Deaver wanted," Clark said. "It will help the president stand out."

"But I thought that to make somebody stand out, you did it with bright colors," I suggested. "At the Democratic convention, Gerry Ferraro wore an all-white suit—very dramatic against a blue background and all the red bunting. Red, white, and blue."

"We designed that podium, too," Clark said. "There are two ways to attract attention: either by making the podium the most lively point in the hall—the hottest, brightest spot, or by making it the most restful spot. In this hall, there'll be a lot of noise and activity, and so the calmest, most restful place will be the podium and at the center, the speaker. The eye comes to rest there. Earth tones and rounded shapes are peaceful."

The aura of calmness and confidence was the key. Deaver wanted Reagan to come across as a soothing, reassuring presence—to help lay to rest concerns about his troubled relations with Moscow and the mounting *contra* war in Central America. The podium backdrop conveyed a subliminal message of peaceableness.

To assure a stream of positive visual images emanating from Reagan, Deaver patented what he called the "visual press release." During the deep recession of 1982–83, when Reagan was accused of lacking compassion for the growing ranks of unemployed, Deaver had him photographed at events for unemployed dock workers or for people being retrained for new jobs. When the economy began to heal, Deaver would not let Reagan go into the pressroom to announce a statistical rise in new housing starts. Instead, Deaver flew Reagan—and the entire White House press corps—to a Fort Worth housing project to make that announcement against the backdrop of construction workers and a newly framed house. The idea, Deaver said, was to drive home the message to TV viewers that the economy was turning up.

Or, anticipating worries about Reagan's age in the 1984 campaign, Deaver and William Sitman arranged for Reagan to arm-wrestle weight lifter Dan Lurie, publisher of *Muscle Training Illustrated*. A White House photographer snapped a setup shot of Reagan pinning Lurie's biceps to his desk, and Deaver put it out to the press, counting on front-page play. David Gergen arranged a similar picture layout of Reagan pumping barbells for *Parade* magazine. Antidotes to fears about a seventy-four-year-old president.

Deep down, Deaver's goal was to become the de facto executive producer of the TV network news shows by crafting the administration's story for the networks. Because television producers like "news that wiggles" [news with action], Deaver developed the technique of theme campaigning—putting Reagan on the move. For two months in 1983, Deaver took Reagan on the road for a public relations blitz on education, an issue Reagan had largely ignored. Deaver scored a stunning success, changing the public's perception and attitudes toward Reagan's policy position, *without Reagan's changing his policy.*

The effort was a direct steal from election campaign tactics. It was triggered by *A Nation at Risk,* the report of an eighteen-member national commission that denounced the poor quality of American public education.[27] That report, issued in April 1983, was potentially devastating to Reagan politically because of his budget cutbacks in federal aid to primary and secondary schools. Dick Wirthlin had already flagged education as a danger issue for Reagan's reelection campaign. By tapping Wirthlin's poll analysis and using Deaver's theme campaigning, Reagan reversed the nation's negative assessment of him on education.

In mid-March, Wirthlin's polls had shown the public disapproved of Reagan's handling of education by 48–42 percent. The education report was going to make Reagan look worse—unless he rapidly put his spin on the report. "The commission was saying schools are in horrible shape," David Gergen recalled. "But it also said, here are some things that can be done that don't involve a lot of money. Our point was to let Reagan ride with the report, not have it ride over him. So Deaver whipped up a schedule of events."[28]

Deaver felt that so far the story-line strategy had been too "rifle shot," targeting one issue at a time and moving on quickly. Deaver knew it was impossible to shift public attitudes with a single-shot approach. "You've got to hammer and hammer and hammer and hammer on a theme, testing all the time [with polls] to see if you're getting movement on it," Deaver asserted to me. "If you're getting movement, stay with it."[29]

His image-game tactics leaned heavily on polling, used the way soap and cosmetic companies work mass marketing. In Reagan's presidency by polling, Wirthlin's firm, Decision Making Information, Inc., would "pretest" public attitudes before Reagan went barnstorming on issues; in this case, public attitudes on education. To keep from being overrun by the education report, the White House needed a quick fix on public attitudes. Wirthlin's firm (which has 250 telephone links for rapid polling) can do national polls on hot issues within twenty-four hours. Frequently, this speed put the Reagan operation far ahead of Congress, the television networks, or Democratic rivals in figuring out the best political line with the public.

On education, Wirthlin's pretesting told Reagan what buttons to push in the public psyche. It helped design positive points for Reagan to emphasize and negative points for him to avoid. Wirthlin found favorable public responses to some ideas in the report that fit Reagan's philosophy: tougher educational standards, more school discipline, emphasis on basic courses, and teacher accountability. By highlighting these proposals, Reagan could align himself with the report and sidetrack obvious pressures for more federal funding for education.

"We tested and found where the hot buttons were," Wirthlin told me. "We couldn't beat them [the critics] on the issue of money. *We had to change the terms of the debate.*"[30]

That was the essence of Deaver's theme campaigning and the key to changing Reagan's public image on education. Walter Mondale quickly called for an $11 billion program of federal aid to fund university research in math and the sciences, help for disadvantaged children, more student scholarships, loans, and grants. But Reagan, using his pretested line, blamed "misguided policymakers" in Washington for school problems and called on parents to push for tougher standards, better teachers, and local control. He made a whirlwind tour, attracting

TV coverage and newspaper headlines. Deaver's orchestration of events was intended to show that Reagan cared about education and was taking positions that people supported.

Reagan flew to South Orange, New Jersey, and called for merit pay for teachers. In Hopkins, Minnesota, he said the older generation bore responsibility for school problems. In Shawnee, Kansas, he blamed the disruptive effect of court-ordered desegregation. In Farragut, Tennessee, he lunched with home economics teachers, sat in a senior English class, and then declared that American schools have become "too easy" because of the "abandonment of compulsory courses." In Albuquerque, he had the temerity to warn that "education must never become a political football" and called for competency tests as well as merit pay for teachers. In Los Angeles, he accused a teachers' union, the National Education Association, of "brainwashing American schoolchildren."

Reagan never promised to change his education policy, and yet public attitudes changed in Reagan's favor. First, his high profile persuaded people he was concerned about education—a vital personal issue to millions of voters and one where Reagan had previously seemed uncaring. Second, his barnstorming surfaced some latent approval of conservative Republican views. A *Newsweek* poll in mid-June found that eighty percent of the public still favored more spending on public education, but ninety percent also wanted tougher curriculums and competency testing for teachers, and about eighty percent agreed with Reagan on merit pay.[31] Also, attitudes changed toward Reagan personally. The public disapproval he faced in March had switched by late June to 52–41 percent approval of his handling of education policy. The shift had occurred merely by his seizing the stage and shrewdly marketing his story line.

"That's what it comes down to—we are marketing," commented Bill Henkel, who staged Reagan's cross-country travels. "We are trying to mold public opinion by marketing strategies. That's what communications is all about. I've always had a fascination with trying to close a sale or make a sale, and that's what I'm doing with public opinion: creating events that convey a message. Many of our little playlets, or presidential events, have a relationship to the advertising business."[32]

When NBC's Chris Wallace told Deaver that reporters were contrasting Reagan's spoken concern about education with his cuts in the education budget, Deaver shrugged him off. "You can say whatever you want," Deaver retorted, "but the viewer sees Ronald Reagan out there in a classroom talking to teachers and kids, and what he takes from that is the impression that Ronald Reagan is concerned about education."[33]

The Storybook Presidency

Reagan's video managers created a storybook presidency, using the pageantry of presidential travel to hook the networks and captivate the popular imagination. They projected Reagan as the living symbol of nationhood. And there was a payoff for policy: The more Reagan wrapped himself in the flag, the harder it became for mere mortal politicians to challenge him, the more impossible he was to defeat come reelection, the more worthy he seemed of trust and latitude on policy.

Jimmy Carter had purposely deflated the pomp of the White House, but the Reagan team understood the prime value of the ceremonial presidency. Reagan has his common touch: his humor, his mistakes, and his quirks. But Reagan eschewed Carter's practice of carrying his own luggage. He reinstated "Hail to the Chief," which Carter had abolished. Reagan relished the royal side of the presidency. He is the master of the grand entry: the confident manly stride down the red-carpeted hallway for a press conference or helicopters moving him up the Mall in formation toward a floodlit Congress on triumphant return from a Geneva summit. He loves flapping flags, honor guards, anthems, ruffles and flourishes. He enjoys playing the role of commander in chief.

Reagan's video managers embellished the pageantry of the White House and lured the TV networks into partnership by staging irresistible visuals. Their goal was to imbed Reagan in public consciousness as the personification of the nation. They made dream productions impossible to edit by timing Reagan's most dramatic comings and goings for live coverage in prime time or for the morning news shows.

One rule of the image game is to attract viewers by taking them on trips. With Bill Henkel, the chief of advance (trip preparation), Deaver produced a Michener presidency which, like James Michener's immensely popular novels about Hawaii, Poland, Spain, or Texas, plunged a nation of viewers into new worlds and took them on glossy adventures that outdid *National Geographic*. Often the policy purpose seemed secondary to the travelogue. President Reagan not only went for business at economic summits in London, Tokyo, and Venice, but he took highly photogenic journeys to Versailles, Bali, Normandy's beaches, the Korean demilitarized zone, the Great Wall of China—all great box office staged by Deaver, Henkel, and Company.

Henkel, who came from the Nixon team, had a formula for "presidency-by-photo-op" (photo opportunity). He called it H-P-S, meaning headline, photo, story. This was the distillation of the story line, the intro of the television anchor, the single memorable snapshot event. As Deaver said: "You're always looking for a picture you don't ever have to explain. The picture tells the story regardless of what Ronald Reagan says."

Reagan's trip to the demilitarized zone in Korea in 1984 was a prime example. Deaver and Henkel wanted to place Reagan at the most exposed American bunker, Guardpost Collier, peering into North Korea—evoking John F. Kennedy's standing at the Berlin Wall in June 1963. But the Secret Service tried to veto that photogenic moment, fearing for the president's safety from North Korean sharpshooters or infiltrators. After days of haggling, Henkel got the Army to string thirty thousand yards of camouflage netting from specially erected telephone poles to protect Reagan. And to get the most dramatic camera shots, Henkel made the Army build camera platforms on the exposed hill just beyond Guardpost Collier, so photographers could snap Reagan surrounded by sandbags. Another camera platform was behind Reagan for the most celebrated video shot: looking over the president's shoulder as he raised binoculars toward North Korea. This was Reagan at the front—echoes of General Douglas MacArthur.

Again, to heighten the drama, Henkel wanted Guardpost Collier's sandbags low enough—waist-high—for a clear picture of Reagan in Army parka and flak jacket. The Secret Service wanted sandbags virtually up to Reagan's neck; Henkel compromised on four inches above Reagan's belly button. As if staging a play, Henkel's team put down red tapes showing Reagan precisely where to stand for the memorable picture. "This was it, the commander in chief on the front line against Communism," Henkel said. "It was a Ronald Reagan statement on American strength and resolve."[34] It was also textbook image game—one picture carried the message.

On another trip, to Normandy, Henkel battled the pride of French President François Mitterand in order to get Reagan the right to fly directly from Britain to Normandy's Pointe du Hoc—for stunning visual impact on television. Pointe du Hoc was an isolated cliff overlooking the beaches and the sea, chosen by Henkel as a vivid symbol of strongholds wrested from German troops on D day at cruel cost by American Ranger commandos.

Mitterand wanted all foreign leaders to follow normal protocol, flying first to a common welcoming point as they landed in France. For him, the climax of the fortieth anniversary of the June 6, 1944, D-day landing would be a joint ceremony at Utah Beach. But the White House wanted Reagan appearing alone first; the French plan did not fit the American TV schedule. Henkel timed Reagan's air landing at Pointe du Hoc for live coverage by the American morning TV shows— that was the jackpot, a riveting moment on camera with millions watching at home. Henkel got around Mitterand's protocol by the legal technicality that American battleground graves were American territory, and Reagan had a right to go there first before officially "entering" France. In public relations terms, the stakes were so high that Henkel risked offending the French with the threat that Reagan might not appear at Mitterand's ceremony on Utah Beach—unless Reagan got his separate early arrival at Pointe du Hoc.

In an even more moving moment, at Omaha Beach, Reagan read the letter of an American woman, Lisa Zanatta Henn, whose father, Private, First Class, Peter Zanatta, had been on the first wave landing at Omaha Beach in 1944. "He made me feel the fear of being on that boat waiting to land," she wrote the president. "I can smell the ocean and feel the seasickness. I can see the looks on his fellow soldiers' faces, the fear, the anguish, the uncertainty of what lay ahead. And when they landed, I can feel the strength and courage of the men who took those first steps through the tide to what must have surely looked like instant death. I don't know how or why I can feel this emptiness, this fear, or this determination, but I do. Maybe it's the bond I had with my father. . . . All I know is that it brings tears to my eyes to think about my father as a twenty-year-old boy having to face that beach."

When Reagan had received her letter months before, he wrote back offering to pay her way personally and fulfill her dream of going to Normandy for her father. As he read her moving words that day, she sat among graying Normandy veterans, television cameras tracing the glances between them. For part of Reagan's political genius is to make such moments personal for everyone by speaking to one person. The scene made a powerful visual symbol of Reagan the patriot-president, identifying him with the heroism of the common man, though Reagan himself had never seen combat.

At moments of supreme gravity, the Reagan team masterfully employed symbolism to give shape and meaning to events of uncertain outcome, such as Reagan's 1985 summit with Mikhail Gorbachev in Geneva. From policymakers and from their own intuition, Deaver and Henkel divined the proper symbolic message for the summit and then scouted months in advance to locate the right symbolic settings. Hen-

kel found an elegant old château, the Fleur d'Eau, as a site for Reagan
to host Gorbachev. But what caught Henkel's eye was a garden walk-
way leading to a pool house with a big fireplace—the symbolism of a
warm get-together.

"I knew Fleur d'Eau was the right place for the summit as soon as
I saw the pool house where you have the classic roaring fire," Henkel
recalled. "I know Mrs. Reagan was very keen on it. I think the president, at first, wasn't as receptive."[35] Both Mrs. Reagan and National
Security Adviser Robert McFarlane encouraged Reagan to use the pool
house for private, man-to-man talks by the fire. So the public relations
outcome was set before Reagan and Gorbachev met. It became the
"fireside summit."

Overall, the Geneva summit was an image-making triumph. As Ronald Reagan's first encounter with the top Soviet leader, it broke the
ice, and that was important. But otherwise there were no agreements,
no breakthroughs, no real progress.

Beforehand, the administration had shrewdly lowered public expectations, a critical image-game task—to protect the president from mass
disappointment. Virtually every advance briefing or press conference
predicted nothing would happen. The press and public were conditioned. A news blackout imposed during the summit was an imagemakers' delight, heightening the mystery and giving greater value to little
scraps about how the two leaders got along. The lack of substantive
information magnified symbolic details: Reagan, the ruddy seventy-
three-year-old going bareheaded in a bit of one-upmanship to meet the
young Soviet champ in a topcoat; the fireside chat itself. A postsummit
stop was inserted in Brussels—theoretically to brief NATO leaders, but
actually, Henkel told me, to retard Reagan's homecoming and to syn-
chronize it with the evening news shows. The live coverage, arranged
by Deaver and Henkel, created a magnetic effect: helicopters ferrying
the president from his encounter with the Kremlin boss on the final
leg home to report to Congress and the nation. It was a production to
inspire envy in Hollywood and to project an aura of success, however
modest the reality.

The President as Storyteller

Reagan obviously brought formidable talents to the image game. He
has the dramatic voice and the confident, jaunty air of Franklin Roosevelt, the warm optimism and aw-shucks smile of Dwight Eisenhower,
the easy masculinity and glamour of Jack Kennedy. Reagan is a leader

operating powerfully at the level of visions, dreams, and legends, the most magnetic ingredients of political imagery. He has the lure of a pied piper.

Especially at moments of triumph or despair, Reagan has sensed instinctively how to bond himself with the emotions of others and how to draw them into bonding with him. After the explosion of the *Challenger 7* and the bombing of the Marine barracks in Beirut, Reagan masterfully gave voice to the nation's grief and outrage. And as he identified with the nation's feelings, the public identified with him.

Reagan is so natural onstage that unlike most politicians, he creates the illusion of *not* being onstage. He is so practiced in using Tele-PrompTers that many viewers have mistakenly thought he knew his script by heart. And he has known so well how to create a sense of familiarity by tossing a smiling wave at an isolated camera crew that millions of folks back home felt he was sending them a personal greeting. Reagan's ideology is divisive, but he knows how to soften it with a mellow TV style. Years ago, other politicians mistakenly dismissed Reagan as "just an actor." But he has been so successful at the image game that acting experience is now reckoned an asset, not a handicap, in the new politics. Reagan has understood that politics for the millions—in the television age—is not rational, but emotional.

The storybook presidency is a form of political artistry for which Reagan was naturally suited as a born storyteller. Hence his reputation as the "great communicator." Some of his most compelling political speeches are masterpieces of narration: his report to the nation after the invasion of Grenada, his tragic story of the truck bombing in Beirut, his angry tale of the Soviet downing of the Korean airliner. The storyteller's skills were honed by Reagan during years of radio announcing, when he created the crack of the bat, the cheers of the crowd, the close plays at home plate from a skimpy wire-ticker report of baseball games. He created flesh-and-blood reality from a skeleton, drawing others into his special blend of fact and fiction. That same blend of wish and reality lies behind some of Reagan's most wayward policies, and that same storyteller's art lies at the heart of Reagan's power as a political leader.

Reagan loves to retell the story of how he landed his first radio job in 1932 as a sports announcer, at WOC in Davenport, Iowa. One afternoon in the Rose Garden, four of us gathered around as he recalled how the station manager, a crusty old Scotsman named Pete MacArthur, had asked whether he could make a game come alive. MacArthur led young Reagan into a studio and told him when the red light came on to broadcast a football game as if he were watching it. Reagan picked one of his college games, so that he could use familiar names and plays.

"I didn't want to start with the opening kickoff but with something else," he told us. "We won in the last few minutes of the game. Our star halfback, Bud Cole, had taken the ball near the end of the game and had come around my side. You see, I was a running guard then, and I was running interference for him. But I missed my block, and Bud had to reverse his field and zigzag his way through the secondary and then over to the opposite sidelines and went all the way for a touchdown." By this time, Reagan was tracing Bud Cole's run with his finger in the air. "So, that's the play I decided to broadcast, and when the light went on, I began. . . . " The president was rolling now, reliving the memory, his voice deepening, picking up tempo and excitement:

"Here we are late in the fourth quarter. The shadows are falling over the stadium. The Eureka Golden Tornadoes are deep in their own territory, trailing by six points. On the snap, the ball goes to Cole, who begins a sweep around right end. Ron Reagan, the running guard, pulls out of the line and leads the way into Western State's secondary and throws a key block on the opposing halfback." Interrupting his own replay, the president admitted, "And in that version, I made the block, and it was the best block you'd ever seen." Then he resumed his broadcast voice: *"And Bud Cole streaks down the sideline with the fans cheering wildly, and scores, to tie the game for Eureka."* The president smiled again. "And of course we made the extra point to go ahead and win the game. So that's how I got the job."[36]

Hugh Sidey of *Time* asked Reagan whether he had ever wanted to broadcast sports live, rather from the ticker. "Oh, no." Reagan shook his head. "You see, the thing about doing it from the wire was that you could create the scene on your own."

The moment was revealing, for it showed how Reagan relies on his imagination, to picture life in Nicaragua, in the Soviet Union, or how Star Wars will develop. Moreover, in the revisionism of his block as a running guard, Reagan displayed his politician's bent for varnishing the truth. Like others, Reagan has done that often, enthusiasm getting the better of his memory. One incident, tracked down by Lou Cannon of *The Washington Post*, stuck in my mind. According to Israeli Prime Minister Yitzhak Shamir, Reagan, expressing his sympathy for the Holocaust, told Shamir at the White House in late 1983, that near the end of World War II he had served as a photographer in an American Army unit assigned to film Nazi death camps. That contradicted what Reagan had told his staff. Reagan, who spent the war with an Army

Air Corps motion picture unit near Hollywood, had said that he never left the country during the war.[37]

The President as Salesman

As a political salesman, Reagan ranks with Franklin Roosevelt and Dwight Eisenhower, both of whom, like Reagan, sold mood and confidence as much as substance. Reagan hungered for his summit meetings with Gorbachev, aides told me, not for the negotiations, but because Reagan was convinced that he could talk Gorbachev into accepting his idea of a strategic defense. Reagan was that confident of his powers of persuasion, although it turned out he was wrong.

The contrast between Reagan and presidents such as Nixon, Ford, or Carter is stunning. Prior to Reagan, Nixon was the president most obsessed with "the selling of the president," in Joe McGinniss's memorable phrase; but Nixon lacked the ease and personal warmth that convey sincerity and come so readily to Reagan. Neither Ford nor Carter was as devoted as Reagan to making the sale. Both Ford and Nixon were clumsy onstage compared to Reagan. Carter was image conscious, flashing his famous toothy grin, but he was curiously ill at ease asking for votes. He saw the complexity of issues, agonized over decisions, and was too deeply torn by inner self-doubts to be a natural salesman. And Carter's inner conflicts came across on television, for all to see.

By contrast, Reagan has conveyed inner harmony. He has seemed at peace with himself, a man untroubled by insecurities, uncertainties, or the awful burdens of office. He has had dark moments, for example when Marines were dying in Lebanon, or when the nation anguished over Americans held hostage by terrorist groups. His closest aides admit he has been angered at the press or at congressional foes or by family spats with his son Michael or his daughter Patti. But the White House has kept his torment private.

By seeming at home in the presidency, Reagan helped build his political success, for with his easy manner, Reagan has dispelled the common perception of the misery and isolation of the presidency. Carter worked like an indentured servant; Reagan has enjoyed the presidency and let people see his enjoyment. He has worked relatively short hours, taken naps and joked about it, then turned his back on the White House, gone off to his ranch to ride horses and chop wood, and treated the presidency as a job, not as a ball and chain. Initially, his imagemakers were skittish about his light schedule—for fear it showed his superficiality—but as time wore on they made a point of having the public see Reagan's relaxed nine-to-five style. It made him seem less "Washington," less power hungry, and less menacing, say, than Johnson or Nixon. But Reagan's laid-back style came to haunt him in the imbroglio of his covert dealings with Iran; he looked gullible and foolish as well as duplicitous, his judgment a victim of his emotions and a conspiratorial staff.

Sheer likability, never to be underestimated in the image game, has been a great asset to Ronald Reagan. As Nancy Reagan's Gridiron Club venture showed, news coverage of a public figure can be affected by the personal feelings of the press corps. Popular, likable presidents such as Eisenhower and Reagan have fared better with the press than others, such as Johnson, whom White House reporters saw as too raw and manipulative; Nixon, whom many reporters distrusted and disliked; or Carter, who was ultimately regarded as meanspirited and holier-than-thou. Such feelings, which most reporters try to suppress in the interest of fair reporting, are more important than political ideology in affecting how the press treats political figures.

Obviously, Reagan's sense of humor in personal crises has endeared him not only to reporters but to millions who viewed him from afar. He was showered with public acclaim, admiration, and affection for his gallantry after being shot in 1981. To the doctors preparing to remove the bullet, he cracked, "Hope you guys are all Republicans." To his wife: "Honey, I forgot to duck." To a nurse: "Does Nancy know about us?" His one-liners made him an instant folk hero. They gave the country a reassuring glimpse of the president when his life was in danger; and that transformed his image. It was a turning point for Reagan: Overnight, he went from being a new president on trial to being the nation's heroic and sympathetic leader. That early impression of gallantry was reconfirmed four years later, when Reagan underwent surgery for a cancerous polyp and came out joking that he was going to send his surgeon to Congress to operate on the budget. As for the cancer, he said with the understated valor of a combat hero, "Well, I'm glad it's all out."

What came across was a personal model of courage and vigor; the sympathy he generated paid large political dividends. Even his flubs and misstatements, like Eisenhower's garbled syntax, added to his common touch. They made him human. They drove political opponents and the press wild, but ordinary people seemed unconcerned. The voters do not want their leaders to appear too much smarter than they are. To many people, Jimmy Carter was too smart for his own political good.

Other presidents have paid for inconsistencies and deceptions. Johnson was regarded as Machiavellian, Nixon as devious, Carter as wishy-washy. Reagan has been far from constant. He has flip-flopped on tax increases, on balancing the budget, on veto threats, on dealing with Moscow and Peking. But until he tripped up by secretly selling arms to Iran, Reagan got away with zigzags, backdowns, and compromises, by acting as if nothing had happened. Most voters seem not to regard it as hypocritical that he could preach the virtues of religion and prayer in school and not be a regular churchgoer; or that he could limn the old-time values of family, though Mrs. Reagan admitted to a three-year "estrangement" in the family; his adopted son, Michael, protested that Reagan had not seen his granddaughter until she was nearly two; his daughter Patti printed painful cameos of her parents in her novel, *Home Front.*

Such pretense might make other leaders feel a shade guilty, but Reagan always seems convinced of his own fundamental innocence—and that self-perception gives power to his salesmanship. Reagan is like a method actor: He feels whatever part he's playing—peace president, military-buildup president, tax-cutting president, tax-increasing president, foe of Ayatollah Khomeini's Iran, or secret bargainer with Iran. Reagan immerses himself in whatever he is saying at the moment, even if that contradicts his lifelong beliefs, and he always finds some way in his own mind to explain away the contradictions.

For decades, he denounced Red China but came home from his presidential visit there extolling the "so-called Communists" in Peking, as if their ideology had never been his bugaboo. He can demand a constitutional amendment to balance the budget and blithely submit budgets with $150 billion deficits. He can switch from economic sanctions against the Soviet Union to subsidizing cheap wheat exports to Moscow and talk—even within his inner circle—as if he had made no change in policy. Whatever Reagan is selling, he preaches like a true believer, and his appearance of sincerity makes him a powerful salesman.

Those around Reagan see a paradox. The popular myth about television is that it exposes character. Through the tube, the public feels it knows politicians such as Reagan, though some close associates and family members find him remote and hard to know. He shies away from intimacy, letting no one but Nancy Reagan get really close, his old political friends have told me. They say he cannot deal well with strong emotions, perhaps because of a painful childhood. In private, some Reagan intimates express their surprise and hurt at how readily Reagan has let some of his oldest, closest lieutenants leave him: Mike Deaver, Lyn Nofziger, Bill Clark. When Deaver, who was like a son to the Reagans, resigned in mid-1985, Mrs. Reagan wept openly at his small farewell party. The president had many kind words and expressed heartfelt appreciation for Deaver, but he showed no strong emotions. And yet, when Reagan tells and retells old war stories about total strangers to large political rallies, his voice is sure each time to thicken and choke at the punch line.

George Tames, a *New York Times* photographer who has covered every president since Franklin Roosevelt, called Reagan the hardest to know. "Reagan is onstage all the time," Tames remarked. "He looks immaculate, like he wears two suits a day. Reagan's the only one of them all [the presidents] who's been onstage constantly. You could always count on the others relaxing, one on one. He never took his coat off with me. He never calls me by my first name. All the others except Roosevelt did. I can't get to know him."[38]

That probably sounds odd coming from a White House regular, since Reagan makes a point of familiarity with the press at his news conferences, calling on Helen, Sam, Andrea, Bill, or Mike (Helen Thomas of UPI, Sam Donaldson of ABC, Andrea Mitchell of NBC, Bill Plante of CBS, Mike Putzel of Associated Press). He has made them characters in the presidential TV serial. The image of the press family helps project Reagan as a patient father figure dealing with unruly children—a very subtle but effective put-down. But few viewers realize that while Reagan genuinely knows a handful of reporters by name, he relies on a seating chart to recognize most others. If seats get mixed up, Reagan calls people by the wrong names—still affecting familiarity.

In personal contact, Reagan is unfailingly cheerful, gracious, polite; he makes people feel good. But to a reporter—and to senators and congressmen—he can sound wooden and staged at close quarters. I have interviewed him several times, all but once with frustration. His answers sounded like replays of a human cassette, his lines rehearsed, even the little jokes. He seemed to be reading a part. When I tried to probe Reagan's thinking behind the practiced formulations, I heard a script.

But once in 1985, by the roaring fire in the Oval Office, I felt a real Reagan. He was talking about his dream of strategic defense, and his tone of voice, his animation, his body language conveyed how deeply he felt. As he leaned into his answers, I gained a sense of his own passion and conviction in a way I would never forget.[39] After that interview, his refusal to compromise on strategic defense with Gorbachev at Geneva, Reykjavík, and Washington came as no surprise to me. Reality matched the image.

Arm's-Length Strategy vs. the Press

In 1980, as the Reagan team approached Washington, it was of two minds about the press. One approach was to charm and co-opt the press and make it a vehicle for spreading the Reagan line. But a second, mistrustful strain gained voice in a memorandum entitled "The Imperial Media," written by Robert Entman, a Duke University professor. It was part of a study produced for candidate Reagan by the Institute for Contemporary Studies in San Francisco, a think tank with links to Meese and Weinberger. Entman's advice was to hold the press at arm's length and make it accept the role of merely reporting the "what" of presidential policy and not probe for the "why" and "how." His memo cautioned against "personal mingling between press officers, other White House staff, and journalists." The White House press office, except for the top man, Entman said, should be kept "in the dark about the politics of White House decision-making" to reduce leaks on inside debates. The memo advocated taking several steps to "tame White House-beat reporting" by decreasing reporters' expectations of full access to officials.[40]

The Reagan team pursued both strategies: the charm offensive and arm's-length stonewalling. Reagan has been shielded from the press far more than other modern presidents. In his first term, Reagan held only twenty-six press conferences—fewer than any other modern four-year president and less than half Jimmy Carter's fifty-eight. His media managers cut the size, access, and rules for press pools—the small, rotating groups of photographers and reporters who cover the president on most events—with the result that White House regulars have had less daily access to Reagan than to his predecessors. Impromptu question-and-answer sessions were curtailed. When the White House was marketing its story line before critical votes in Congress or after foreign policy summits, Reagan video managers have flooded television shows with administration spokesmen but kept them under tight wraps when the news got rough. Reagan's P.R. men became experts at dumping bad news on Friday nights when few people notice. In the image game, these are all techniques for cutting your losses.

When it has come to making government officials available for television appearances, the Reagan team has applied the squeeze to protect its story line. I know TV correspondents who have scrapped stories because the White House barred senior officials from appearing, and the stories seemed unbalanced without government spokesmen. When top officials do appear, the White House imposes conditions. The networks will ask for one official: The White House, like a Hollywood studio doling out stars, will provide someone else, or demand *unequal* time. Connecticut's Senator Chris Dodd, a Democratic critic of Reagan's Central American policy, told me that when he appeared on ABC's *This Week with David Brinkley* in 1984, the White House price for producing a spokesman was to sandwich Dodd—with the smallest time segment—between its spokesman and former Secretary of State Henry Kissinger, who pushed the Reagan line. Major cabinet officers like Secretary Shultz set their own terms. Lesley Stahl said she could not get Shultz on CBS's *Face the Nation* unless she guaranteed Shultz two thirds of the airtime and promised that no unfriendly foreign spokesman would appear.

"In the beginning, the manipulation drove me crazy," Stahl admitted. "I've gotten a little used to it because if you really want to do a subject and they don't want you to do it, it becomes very, very difficult. More true on domestic issues than foreign issues, because you can always go to another country and, say, put on a Soviet spokesman."[41]

The administration's stonewall has forced networks to change topics. In late 1986, for example, Reagan officials had been privately encouraging stories that Libyan leader Muammar Qaddafi was planning a new spate of terrorism and was on a collision course with Washington. *Face the Nation,* Stahl told me, "wanted the administration to come on and talk about whether there was new evidence that Qaddafi was again instigating or reigniting his terrorist organization, whether there were or weren't plans to apply pressure on him, if we had evidence that his own power was deteriorating. They refused to play with us. Refused. Just shut down the government. So we did a show on nursing homes. Now, that's very infuriating."

The Reagan team was expert, moreover, at distancing the president from bad news. In any White House, the president announces good news and others—preferably other agencies—handle bad news. That's how the power game is played. Frequently, Reagan has appeared suddenly in the pressroom for "mini" briefings with bright economic news to announce and quickly ducked out, leaving aides to handle tough questions. In September 1986, Reagan personally announced the Soviet release of American reporter Nicholas Daniloff and left it to Shultz to break the bad news that in an undeclared swap, Gennady Zakharov, a Soviet accused of spying, had been let go by the United States.

But the most valuable defensive gambit for negative news is dumping it on Friday afternoon after four P.M. That gives the networks little time to work the story, and it relegates the news to Saturday newspapers, which are lightly read. It also increases chances the story will die over the weekend. Late release means that the first stories have an administration spin because reporters lack time to get balancing comment. Moreover, the main editorials and columns for the Sunday papers have usually been written by Friday afternoon. So odds are good that the bad news will not get heavy weekend comment and will look stale by Monday.

At times, the strategy has been extremely successful. In 1984, the White House picked March 30—after the president had flown off to his California ranch and the White House press plane was landing in Santa Barbara—to dump the news that American Marines were being pulled out of Lebanon. For all Reagan's grand declarations about the importance of the Marines to the entire American position in the Middle East, their withdrawal merited only a brief printed statement from the press office, handed to reporters late afternoon Pacific time. It was too late for Eastern prime-time network news; comment was light. By clever press agentry, Reagan limited the political scar.

It does not always work that way. In January 1982, the Reagan administration picked a Friday afternoon to disclose that it was filing a Supreme Court brief to stop denying tax-exempt status to private segregated schools and colleges. And in 1983, it picked a Friday in March to disclose a presidential executive order imposing lifetime secrecy agreements on more than 200,000 government officials. Burying these actions did not prevent such a hullabaloo that the administration had to reverse both actions. In 1986, the White House tried to bury the news of President Reagan's veto of sanctions against South Africa by releasing it at 7:58 P.M., Friday, September 26. The tactic backfired. Congressional Democrats anticipated the veto and staged demonstrations, and CBS anchor Dan Rather reported that Reagan was trying to duck news coverage of his veto.

Oddly for a politician who projects ease in public, Reagan's most defensive arena has been the press conference. Ever since Teddy Roosevelt first called in reporters, most presidents have welcomed the chance to put down criticism or convey some policy message at press conferences. Franklin Roosevelt was a master of the medium. Kennedy, with his wit and fluency, exulted in the intellectual sparring. Johnson loomed over the press like a titanic presence, reigning by force of personality. Nixon and Carter held reporters at bay by dogged command of the issues.

But for Reagan, who has trouble with details and even some essentials of policy, a press conference is an obstacle course, a minefield to be gingerly negotiated. His aides held their breath every time he met the press. They viewed each encounter as a bad gamble. "The problem is you're playing roulette at a press conference," one top Reagan lieutenant lamented to me. "With Reagan, he's either right on or he's off, way off. There's no middle ground."

Striding to the podium, Reagan projects vigor, poise, and command, but his strategy is one of avoidance. He promised press conferences once a month but never came close; he has lagged far behind other presidents except for Nixon. Franklin Roosevelt had an average of 6.9 news conferences a month, Harry Truman 3.4, Dwight Eisenhower 2, John Kennedy 1.9, Lyndon Johnson 2.2, Richard Nixon 0.5, Gerald Ford 1.3, Jimmy Carter 1.2, and Reagan 0.5, through 1987. Behind the scenes, Mike Deaver always had to break Reagan's tension by passing him some irreverent little note just before his entrance. Once, Deaver told me, he scribbled: "The answer to question No. 1 is no answer. The answer to question No. 2 is no answer. The answer to question No. 3 is no answer." It was meant as a joke, but it told a deeper truth: Reagan's tactic was to avoid direct answers.

To reduce the risks, Reagan's handlers ran him through major dress rehearsals for each press conference and interview. Nixon, Ford, and Carter used to get briefing books two or three days in advance, defining policy and anticipating questions, but Reagan's prepping was more rigorous. After boning up, Reagan would spend whole afternoons doing dry runs in the White House family theater with his staff. Two panels of aides would fire questions, one on domestic topics and the other on national security issues. Senior aides would critique Reagan's answers, suggesting where precision or vagueness would serve him better.

In his first term, Reagan was constantly coached to soften his rhetoric on Central America. In one early 1984 rehearsal, Reagan defended CIA Director William Casey for the Agency's mining of Nicaraguan harbors, but his staff talked him into fuzzing that answer in public. Because of controversy over Reagan's statements that Social Security did not affect the deficit, David Stockman would give Reagan a memo before every press conference reminding him that Social Security was part of the unified budget and therefore affected the deficit. "The president would listen—God, I heard it seven or eight times," one aide said. "Our concern was that it wasn't accurate and *The Washington Post* would write an editorial that the president didn't understand, in an accounting sense. But the president knew what was important to him politically. His answer was a political dodge, a hedge. No matter how they would prepare him, he'd give the same answer: that it didn't affect the deficit."

Sometimes, he would fool his staff. "Reagan treated the pre-briefs [rehearsals] as a chance for a stand-up comic routine, and then the staff was never quite sure whether he was going to use what he said in the real press conference," one official told me.

One such case—with real backlash—occurred in October 1983, during Senate debate of a national holiday for Martin Luther King, Jr. Senator Jesse Helms opposed it, arguing that King's associations "strongly suggest that King harbored a strong sympathy for the Communist Party and its goals." Helms called on the FBI to open its "raw files" on King, sealed until the year 2027. Civil rights leaders were furious and Senate Republican leaders wanted to get rid of the issue.

During a press conference rehearsal, one aide asked Reagan, "Do you think Martin Luther King was a Communist?"

"Well, we'll know in thirty-five years, won't we?" Reagan shot back.

Everyone laughed, assuming it was a gag. But when Reagan repeated the gag line at the press conference, his aides were stunned. The implication that Reagan shared Helms's suspicions caused Reagan such political embarrassment that he had to apologize to Coretta King.

Rehearsals did not stop blunders. Reagan would describe Syrian air-defense missiles as "offensive weapons" and mix up well-known United Nations resolutions on the Middle East. On occasion, he confused different Supreme Court decisions affecting major administration policies and freshly issued just a day or two before. He would respond to questions about conventional arms negotiations with answers on nuclear arms talks. In early 1982, he claimed there were a million more Americans at work than when he took office, when in fact there were 100,000 fewer. On other occasions, he has created doubts whether he was revoking the 1979 arms treaty (requiring clarifications by his spokesman) and asserted that he did not want his 1985 tax plan to increase the corporate tax burden (when that is precisely what it did). In June 1987, Reagan seemed out of touch with his own policy. He told reporters that there "could still be some lowering of the value" of the American dollar—touching off frantic denials from other top officials—because this was the opposite of what the administration wanted to happen.

Access Control and the Grenada Blackout

It is remarkable that Reagan's flow of bloopers has not been more costly politically. To limit the risk of his disrupting the story line, his political handlers imposed tight restrictions on press access to Reagan. For example, President Carter had made it a practice on Friday afternoons to take reporters' questions just before helicoptering to Camp David for the weekend. Reagan tried that initially, but after some flubs, his staff cut the time down and later had the helicopter pilot turn on the motors to drown out questions. That gave Reagan's imagemakers what they wanted: a television picture of the Reagans and a wave from the president, but no risky dialogue.

Within the White House, access to Reagan was cut. For years, a small pool of reporters would accompany cameramen into the Oval Office for "a photo opportunity," to see the president meet foreign leaders, congressional delegations, and various groups. That gave reporters a chance to ask about breaking news. In that setting, Reagan would talk off the cuff, often to the dismay of his handlers. In late 1981, Larry Speakes issued an edict: "Look, no more questions in the photo ops. If you feel you can't abide by it, you don't have to go in." According to Sam Donaldson of ABC, the TV correspondents replied: "Then no cameras. You don't want us in there, we're not going to send our cameras."[42] The White House, always angling for camera coverage, backed down; but in early 1982, Deaver laid down the law to network bureau chiefs, imposing what became known as the "Deaver rule": no questions in photo ops. The networks tried holding out their cameras, but after ten days, White House hardball prevailed.

Those strict guidelines marked a significant change. They created distance between regular White House reporters and the president. "I've covered city hall and the state house, I've covered Capitol Hill, and one of the things that's most useful, most important, and also most stimulating about the job is your engagement with the main player, not just the staff," remarked NBC's Chris Wallace. "In Boston, you'd sit around in the mayor's office with him late in the afternoon or go off to dinner and engage with him. You had a sense of who the man is, what he's thinking, what's his mood now. We don't have any of that with Ronald Reagan. There is no intellectual engagement at all."[43]

"I never see Reagan very much in relation to the times I saw Carter," echoed Donaldson. "I would see Jimmy Carter almost every working day of his presidency. With Reagan, cameras always get in. It's reporters they don't want there."[44]

The Reagan team's arm's-length strategy—shutting out reporters—reached a climax with the American invasion of Grenada on October 25, 1983. The administration barred print, radio, and television reporters during the early days of the operation, breaking military precedent and rejecting a long tradition of front-line press coverage dating back to the Civil War. Reporters had gone into combat with American troops in the Spanish-American War, World War I, World War II, Korea, Vietnam, Lebanon in 1956, and more than twenty Caribbean expeditions.

But what was fresh in mind to Reagan's imagemakers was the British handling of the Falklands Islands War in 1982. The Thatcher government had barred live broadcasting from the Royal Navy's task force. Still photographs of burning British warships were blocked by censors. Television films had to be shipped to London by boat or plane, a process that took weeks; the war was nearly over before the British people saw scenes of their warships being blown up or heard emotional interviews with survivors. The aim of the news blackout was quite clear: Prime Minister Thatcher and her cabinet colleagues asserted that it would have been hard to sustain popular support if the British public had been exposed to nightly TV coverage.[45]

On Grenada, the White House and Pentagon said they had refused to let American reporters on the beaches out of concern for their safety, though they let French and Latin American reporters cover the combat. When American newsmen tried to get to Grenada on commercial boats, American military planes threatened to fire on them. Four American reporters were held on a Navy ship for several days, forbidden to transmit stories, while the Pentagon set up its own news service, distributing reports with serious omissions and inaccuracies. The administration seemed to want a news monopoly until it could shape public attitudes.[46]

In the immediate aftermath of the invasion, the government's press muzzling played well in the country. Defense Secretary Weinberger defended the exclusion of reporters as a sound "operational order" by the military task force commander, to keep out all noncombatants to help assure the operation's success. Secretary of State Shultz declared that the press had been barred from Grenada because "reporters are always against us, and so they're always seeking to report something that's going to screw things up." It was an echo of former Secretary of State Dean Rusk's famous challenge to reporters during the Vietnam War: "Which side are you on?"[47] Early public reaction backed the news blackout.

But as more information emerged—disclosing the American dead and wounded, the difficulties the huge American force had in quelling a small force of Cuban defenders, the bombing of a hospital, communications foul-ups, and other military blunders—public attitudes shifted. By early December 1983, pollster Louis Harris found that a 65–32 percent majority felt the administration had been wrong not to let reporters accompany troops into Grenada. A similar majority said that excluding reporters might tempt the military to "cover up mistakes or lives lost."[48]

Even the administration's line shifted. Antagonism between the White House and the Washington press corps was white hot. The White House had compounded the initial blunder of excluding the American press by actual deception about the invasion—Larry Speakes had unwittingly lied to reporters the night before the invasion, denying an attack was imminent.

Late that afternoon, Bill Plante, a CBS White House reporter, received a tip from an old intelligence source that the Marines would launch an invasion the next morning. For more than twenty-four hours, Grenada's government radio had been warning its people that a "military invasion of our country is imminent." The Pentagon was confirming that a twenty-one-ship naval task force, originally bound for Lebanon with a Marine amphibious landing group, was now "on station" near Grenada. Plante put the question of an invasion to Speakes, who forwarded it to Rear Admiral John Poindexter, then deputy national security adviser. About twenty minutes later, Speakes came back: "Plante, no invasion of Grenada. Preposterous. Knock it down hard."[49]

The next morning, Speakes bore the brunt of reporters' anger over both the news blackout and the deception. An evasion or a "no comment" would have been understood, but not a flat denial of the truth. Later, Speakes told Plante he had answered in ignorance, repeating Poindexter's exact words. (After he left government in 1987, Speakes publicly chastised Poindexter for "misleading me as press spokesman."[50]) The White House press and editors across the nation, doubly infuriated, pushed to get reporters onto Grenada. The first small group went on a restricted basis—fifty-six hours after the initial assault.

In postmortems ten weeks later, the Reagan White House admitted second thoughts. Jim Baker acknowledged, "We took too long to get the press in there on an unrestricted basis" and "perhaps we should have given some consideration to press coverage" from the start.[51] Speakes endorsed sending a few reporters with the invasion force. "I think we could have preserved secrecy with a very small pool of reporters involved from the very first," he said.[52] The Pentagon, also somewhat chastened, set up a joint military-press commission, which took months to develop a mechanism for a small press pool to be secretly alerted in future surprise military operations.

Leaks and Lie Detectors

To the press, the Grenada affair epitomized the Reagan administration's zealotry in tightening secrecy. While Reagan and his top advisers maintained cordial personal relations with reporters, they engaged in the most sweeping efforts of any modern administration in peacetime to restrict the flow of information to the public. The Reagan team's dual track of cordiality and control is a model sure to be studied, and perhaps attempted, by Reagan's successors—though the final consequences of aggressive secrecy were fatal for Reagan's presidency.

Early on, the Reagan administration moved to limit the scope of the Freedom of Information Act by restricting both the type and amount of government material available to the public under this law. It also made the procedures more cumbersome, discouraging written requests. The Pentagon took steps to restrict publication of unclassified academic papers. More broadly, President Reagan issued an executive order in August 1982 giving agencies wide authority to classify information with no time limit—reversing the trend of the previous eighteen years. Reagan was expanding the amount of classified information, despite earlier presidential studies which found too much was already classified. Under Carter, the rule was *to release information* unless publication would cause "identifiable harm" to national security. The Reagan order leaned the opposite way—it allowed *withholding information* merely if it "relates" to national security; and it sanctioned *reclassifying information already in the public domain.* Reagan reversed another policy by allowing the CIA and FBI to monitor and infiltrate press and academic groups if the government saw a national security need.[53]

In 1985, the Reagan administration obtained the first espionage conviction against a government official, Samuel Loring Morrison, for passing classified photographs to the press—*Jane's Defence Weekly*— not to a foreign government (the former standard for espionage).[54] CIA Director William Casey pushed for prosecutions of the press for controversial disclosures, and he advocated surprise police raids on newsrooms, though this was barred by a 1980 law; the Reagan White House refused.

In several ways, the administration clamped down on government officials. In March 1983, President Reagan signed NSDD-84, a national security decision directive to require prepublication review— lifetime censorship—for 200,000 or more current and former government officials on any piece of writing or speech, and to make many thousands of officials subject to lie-detector tests. Critics in Congress raised such furor that Reagan suspended the order. But the administration found an alternative—Form 4193—which forced government officials to agree to prepublication review as a condition of being granted access to intelligence material. And by late 1986, 240,-000 officials had bowed to this "voluntary" requirement.[55] Moreover, in January 1985, the Pentagon announced it would use lie-detector tests for the first time on several thousand nonintelligence employees, not to investigate security breaches, but more generally—to determine their "trustworthiness, patriotism and integrity." (Such "screenings" jumped from forty-five in 1981 to 4,863 in 1985.)

Washington reporters have felt the squeeze. Walter Cronkite said he was "greatly worried" by the "pattern of restriction" by the Reagan administration. Bill Kovach, former Washington editor of *The New York Times*, said, "There is no area of government where information is not harder for us to get than it was when I was here in the Nixon and Ford years." Jack Landau, executive director of the Reporters' Committee for Freedom of the Press, contends the Reagan policies have imposed the "most significant media access restrictions on government information since the end of voluntary censorship in World War II." Jimmy Carter was even sharper. He called the Reagan restrictions "much more Draconian in nature, much more repressive in nature than anything I remember in the history of our country."[56]

In part, Reagan and his high command were reacting to a rash of serious spy cases in the mid-1980s, and their alarm at that threat was warranted. But often, they were trying to combat politically troublesome press leaks. What is surprising is how quickly leaks got under Reagan's skin. Only fifteen days after he took office in 1981, Reagan was "ticked off" about leaks of proposed cuts in the foreign aid budget. Within a year he was signing edicts to throttle leaks; a year after that, he declared, "I've had it up to my keister with these leaks."

It is an old gripe in the power game. Lyndon Johnson complained, "This goddamn town leaks like a worn-out boot." Gerald Ford squawked, "I'm damned sick and tired of a ship that has such leaky seams." Harry Truman yelped that "ninety-five percent of our secret information has been revealed in newspapers and slick magazines." Jimmy Carter served notice that "if there is another outbreak of misinformation, distortions, or self-serving leaks, I will direct the secretary of State to discharge the officials responsible . . . even if some innocent people might be punished." Richard Nixon's explosive orders were: "I don't give a damn how it is done, do whatever has to be done to stop these leaks and prevent further unauthorized disclosures."[57] And that figured in his impeachment.

Washingtonians define leaks in many ways, but generally leaks are inside government information passed *anonymously* to reporters by government officials. Aggrieved policymakers claim that leaks are "unauthorized" or "premature" disclosures, but often top policymakers do their own deliberate, authorized leaking, in which case the leak is technically a "plant"—information planted in the press to serve the established policy line. But in normal political argot, both types are "leaks" so long as the hand of the perpetrator is hidden. Most leaks play havoc with the White House story line—which, after all, is an effort to shape and limit policy debate.

Leaks are endemic to democracy—not an aberration, but the norm. In our Republic, they go back to George Washington. Aides to Treasury Secretary Alexander Hamilton leaked to allies of Thomas Jefferson that Hamilton was trying to make the United States a lackey of Britain. The practice has been going on ever since. It is a utopian notion that leaks can be stopped. In any community, gossip about people and policy is irrepressible unless strong ties of loyalty silence people from talking with outsiders. But government is unlike General Motors, the Catholic Church, *The Wall Street Journal,* or Harvard University, where long-term career interests and personal ties supposedly breed institutional loyalty. At high levels of government, diverse and highly ambitious people are suddenly thrown together in temporary alliances and learn quickly that they can push their pet ideas in the press, or cut down rivals, with hidden disclosures.

Moreover, some officials such as Dick Darman, a close first-term aide to Reagan and formerly an academic specialist in public policy at Harvard's graduate school of government, argue that leaks are not only inevitable, but healthy. "If you have homogeneity of ideas in an administration, you're probably going to be wrong—or right—for a short time and then sterile [of new ideas]," Darman observed. "It's probably unavoidable, humans being humans, that there'll be some diversity of views. In any case it's desirable. If you have diversity of views in the policy debate, you're going to have winners and losers. Winners leak out of pride in what they have won. Losers leak to try to change policies."[58]

Political scientist E. E. Schattschneider argued that the battle over policy always includes a conflict over the size of the political arena, and that leads to leaking. Within an administration, the officials who control policy want to keep the arena narrow. To them, leaks are anathema, especially if their policies are unpopular and would be rejected if widely known. So they often mask their intentions and clamp down on secrecy, as the Reagan White House did on its arms traffic with Iran. But officials who are losing the inside policy debate have incentive to broaden the fight, especially if they sense the public is with them. Leaking to the press is a primary tool of broadening the fight—a standard ploy in the power game.

But policy dissent covers only one motive for leaking. For leaking is a pervasive political art form practiced at all levels of government, by all ideological stripes, for all kinds of purposes. The motives of leakers, sometimes quite obvious and sometimes disguised, are often less sinister than outraged presidents make them sound.

In *The Government/Press Connection,* Stephen Hess of The Brookings Institution in Washington observed that among the common garden varieties are:

> • *the goodwill leak:* relaying juicy tidbits to reporters in order to earn IOUs in hopes of getting favorable press treatment;
> • *the ego leak:* a favorite of staff aides (though I have gotten them from cabinet members, too), who impart sensitive information for their own vanity to convey the impression, "I am an insider";
> • *the grudge leak:* a staple of bureaucratic infighting aimed at cutting down the influence or cutting short the career of some rival policymaker with stories about his temper, ineptitude, disloyalty, etc.;
> • *the trial-balloon leak:* often employed by presidential aides to test public reaction to some policy without political risk to the boss;
> • *the whistle-blower leak:* usually by career civil servants or military careerists outraged by waste, dishonesty, or a cover-up on defense contracts or scandalous pricing of Pentagon spare parts, and eager to expose the scandal;
> • *the policy leak:* done at all levels to promote or sabotage some policy line, especially when an administration is divided, which is always (each winter, it is as normal as snowfall for major departments to leak

word of intended White House cuts in their budgets, to rally support to save their programs. It became just as seasonal for David Stockman to leak gloomy estimates of the economic outlook and the deficit, to prime Reagan to make tough budget cuts).[59]

To Hess's list, I would add:

• *the brag leak:* usually a staff aide's leak of some brilliant inside maneuver that makes his boss look good; bosses also leak about themselves,
• *the inoculation leak:* a gambit, usually by presidential aides, to break forthcoming bad news early to cushion the public reaction (for example, Reagan aides predicting in the summer of 1984 that there would be a rise in interest rates that fall and a leftist guerrilla offensive in El Salvador in October);
• *the shortcut leak:* a quick way to force presidential attention to some problem or policy idea via the press (the late Henry Cabot Lodge, as U.S. ambassador in Saigon, leaked me his assessments and proposals, sensing they would hit *The New York Times* front page. "It's a damn sight easier," Lodge said, "to get it on the president's desk that way than to send another cable to the fudge factory"— meaning the State Department);
• *the preemptive leak:* settling an internal debate over whether to make information public by simply leaking it—as hard-liners did with delicate intelligence assessments about Soviet violations of arms agreements.

Some presidents—Lyndon Johnson was legendary—are notoriously indiscreet leakers themselves, with trial balloons, grudge leaks, or self-serving policy leaks that would look crass if made on the record. James Reston of *The New York Times* used to say that "government is the only known vessel that leaks from the top."[60] Reagan, who often feigned ignorance about anonymous sources, admitted in his sixth year that "we found that the White House is the leakiest place I've ever been in."[61]

Garden-variety leaks—even presidential ones—are a staple of every day's front page and a migraine to White House media managers. One reason leaks are so impossible to control is the well-worn practice of press "backgrounders" in government, a technique begun by Franklin Roosevelt in 1933. That game has been going on ever since: Government officials, from presidents down, briefing reporters or floating policy lines without being quoted by name and thereby avoiding direct accountability for the information. Background information can normally be attributed only to "senior administration officials," "White House officials," or "Pentagon officials," depending on who is speaking. For example, Larry Speakes would say no more than a rambling "no comment" to some news development during his regular briefing and then "go on background" to add details or comments or to introduce high officials, who would give full briefings on background. The same group of reporters was present; no one moved—only the rules for reporting changed. These backgrounders are not leaks, but they sanction ways of operating that encourage many officials to go on background to leak.

Most conversations between reporters and officials on national security issues are on background, so the amount of traffic is enormous, often making it hard for reporters to know for certain what is authorized backgrounding, a deliberate plant, or an unauthorized leak. Secrecy frays quickly because of factional disputes and rivalries. The game of leaks is so pervasive that it is hard to find a precise line between what Fred Iklé, undersecretary of Defense for policy, once called hard-core leaks—serious breaches of national security—and soft-core leaks—nuisance disclosures that cause political embarrassment or a negative reaction to policy but pose no real threat to the country. The border zone is large and vague, especially when the wisdom of policy is in dispute. Obviously some classified leaks can harm national security, but usually far fewer than most administrations claim. Generally, high officials bleat because their policy ox has been gored, but they see no principle violated when rivals are wounded.

Quite often, what really riles presidents and secrecy martinets is the presumed disloyalty of leakers. After one highly publicized Pentagon lie-detector hunt for the source of a leak about a high-level session on military budgeting, Pentagon spokesman Henry E. Catto, Jr., belatedly admitted that the brass were angered not so much by a revelation that would help the Russians but by the fact that information from the hush-hush meeting had leaked within two hours. "I certainly wouldn't for a minute say that the particular meeting dealing with budget is likely to endanger national defense," Catto said. "It's the principle of the thing that we strenuously object to, the expression of minority opinion via leaks to the news media designed to influence the course of events. We feel that things ought to be decided *in camera* and . . . policy supported by everyone who stays on the team."[62] In short, the lie detectors were enforcing team discipline and protecting the story line, not national security.

The Secrecy Obsession

Obsession with leaks and a compulsion for secrecy was ultimately the undoing of Reagan's carefully crafted image game. The political impulse to combat leaks is natural. Any administration prefers to keep its internal debates private until policy is set. But there is a large step from that impulse to believing that policy must be discussed and carried out only by a small band of true believers and that critics and opponents must be kept in the dark. Ironclad secrecy is a tool for a monopolistic control of policy. It becomes a consuming passion when an administration is not leveling with the public, especially about risks it is taking without a solid political consensus.

In Reagan's case, the unraveling of the image game—not to mention the Reagan presidency—came with the explosive disclosure of Reagan's duplicity on Iran in late 1986 and his ransoming American hostages in Lebanon through arms sales to Iran, despite his vows never to do business with terrorists and his castigation of Iran for "state-sponsored terrorism." Reagan's unmasking worsened in 1987 with week upon week of testimony that his aides had been financing and arming the Nicaraguan *contras*—despite a congressional ban on such actions—and then, as Oliver North admitted, lying to Congress.

There were advance tremors of that political shock, such as the mining of Nicaragua's harbors in 1984, expanded rules of military engagement in Lebanon in 1983, and the "disinformation" tactics against Libyan leader Muammar Qaddafi in 1986. In each case, the Reagan administration was playing at or beyond the fringes of what was acceptable to Congress and the public. In all, there was an assertion of unchecked executive authority, with secrecy imposed to foreclose dissent.

Not only did leaks about these episodes prompt confrontations with Congress and press, but there were violent strains among the Reagan inner circle over both policy issues and the tactics of secrecy. High-level factions were at loggerheads, top officials feeling betrayed by each other.

One important high-level clash came in September 1983, after the American Marines at Beirut airport had come under intensive shelling from Lebanese and Palestinian forces backed by Syria and Iran. Those forces, bent on toppling the American-backed government of President

Amin Gemayel, held the Suk al-Gharb ridge line, firing easily downhill at the American Embassy and the American ambassador's residence, where Reagan's special envoy, Robert McFarlane, was trying to arrange a cease-fire. McFarlane, Shultz, and National Security Adviser William P. Clark feared the Lebanese government was about to crumble. The Marines had gone to Lebanon as a peacekeeping force; now McFarlane and Shultz were pressing for them to become de facto protectors of the Gemayel government. Congressional Democrats—and the Pentagon high command—were worried about being sucked into another Vietnam. Over one weekend, President Reagan met secretly with his inner circle: Bush, Shultz, Clark, Weinberger, Casey, Meese, Jim Baker, and John W. Vessey, chairman of the Joint Chiefs of Staff.

Monday night, September 12, Chris Wallace of NBC disclosed that McFarlane and other top officials had proposed American air strikes from offshore aircraft carriers against Syrian positions in Lebanon "to stun the Syrians and get them to stop causing trouble." The next morning, my story in *The New York Times* said that President Reagan had authorized new, wider military engagement, which the White House was calling "aggressive self-defense." One high official told me the Marines could call in Navy planes and offshore bombardment "to make it more costly for Syria and their surrogates to attack U.S. personnel." Lou Cannon of *The Washington Post* reported that the decision to authorize air strikes was a signal to Syria that Washington was ready to escalate its firepower in Lebanon. Obviously, high-level leaks were intended to send Syria a message to cool down the fighting. But American escalation risked conflict with Syria, testing congressional tolerance. In fact, our news stories rekindled congressional calls for pulling back the Marines.

Bill Clark was livid. Since taking over as national security adviser, he had fumed about leaks, and he was outraged by this batch. With Casey and Meese, Clark went to the president, charging that these leaks had endangered McFarlane's life (which McFarlane later denied). Clark demanded an FBI investigation to find the culprits. Evidently, he saw a chance to discredit the Baker faction, whom he assumed to be the leakers. Going behind the backs of Bush, Shultz, Baker, and others, Clark drafted a letter, which he got Reagan to sign, instructing Attorney General William French Smith to have the FBI run lie-detector tests of all officials at the weekend meetings, and *to ask for the resignation of anyone who declined to take the lie-detector test.*[63] It was a stunning order. Neither the president nor Clark, a former California Supreme Court justice, nor Meese and Smith, both lawyers, stopped to realize that it violated the Constitution. For it empowered the attorney general to ask for the vice president's resignation if he refused a lie-detector test.

Baker learned of the plot accidentally. About noon on September 14, Deaver stumbled on Reagan closeted with Clark and Meese, who were urging him to sign the order. Within the hour, Deaver told Baker as they were riding to lunch at the nearby Madison Hotel. Baker turned the car around, went back to the White House, and barged in on the president, who was then lunching with Bush and Shultz. In some agitation, Baker told the president that his order meant that he was subjecting his closest associates, including the vice president, to polygraphs. Baker reminded Reagan that eighteen months earlier, Reagan had signed an order designating Baker as the official to decide when lie detectors should be used on high government officials. Baker had deliberately sought that power to curb the use of lie detectors and now pointed out that Clark had never checked with him. Reagan seemed taken aback.

Shultz immediately spoke up. "Nobody'd better polygraph me," he thundered. "I'll only be asked to take one polygraph"—a clear threat of resignation.

Baker volunteered the same.

Bush also criticized the lie-detector plan.

Reagan, irked by the predicament he'd gotten into, blurted out, "Bill shouldn't have done that." He reached for the phone and told Attorney General Smith: "I want that letter back. I want you over here this afternoon. I want to roundtable this thing."[64]

That afternoon, Reagan sat down with Smith, Clark, Meese, Baker, Deaver, and Fred Fielding, the White House counsel. It was a tense session. Clark and Meese wanted the instructions left as they were. Baker argued that would be a terrible mistake, a terrible reflection on the president to order the polygraphing of his top advisers. It was highly unlikely, he said, that any official in that meeting had leaked to the press, but they all had to brief their aides, who had probably been the news sources.

"Go ahead and have the investigation," Baker said, "but don't strap people up."

Shultz was not present, but his threat must have rung in Reagan's ears. Siding with Baker and Shultz, Reagan canceled the lie-detector tests. Clark stormed out of the Oval Office. "I've never seen Clark as mad in my life," said one high official. "He was about as red as that magazine cover."

The lie-detector issue did not die there. It continued to split the
Reagan high command. After a rash of major spy scandals, Reagan
secretly signed NSDD-196 on November 1, 1985, authorizing random
use of mandatory lie-detector tests on up to 182,000 federal employees
and defense contractors with access to especially sensitive information.[65] Donald Regan and Bud McFarlane, who had taken over as
White House chief of staff and national security adviser, persuaded
Reagan to sign the order over Shultz's objections but with backing from
Casey and Weinberger. Jim Baker, then Treasury secretary, was not
informed. Shultz, voicing grave reservations about polygraphs, had
given Reagan a paper asserting that lie detectors can be misleading—
sometimes trapping the innocent and being beaten by trained spies.
Moreover, he objected on grounds of principle.

The battle boiled on, internally, until December 11, when Robert
Toth of the *Los Angeles Times* broke the news of Reagan's NSDD-
196. Ten days later, Shultz, who had been abroad, issued a dramatic
open dissent. In an emotional outburst, he made the issue one of
personal integrity: "The minute in this government I am told that I'm
not trusted is the day that I leave," he declared. The next day Shultz
met with the president, and Reagan backed down again. Instead of
blanket and random use of lie detectors, a spokesman said, they would
be used as a "limited tool" in espionage investigations.

That repaired some damage, but Reagan's image had been hurt. His
willingness to order wide use of lie detectors raised grave concerns
about civil liberties, as well as fears that the White House was using
the espionage problem to throttle the flow of information and to slip
some covert operations past Congress. (In fact, both the secret arms
dealings with Iran and arms drops to the Nicaraguan *contras* were
under way by then.) Moreover, Reagan came across as neither understanding nor carefully reading what he was signing. His backing down
when challenged betrayed hasty initial approval—at the urging of some
aides, without consulting others. The fact that Shultz felt impelled to
dissent publicly foretold new dangers.

Death of a Salesman

The administration's success in manipulating the media in the first
term and the 1984 campaign bred an overconfidence in Reagan's
second-term inner circle that hastened its undoing. For Reagan's first-
term popularity and success had ridden in part on avoiding excessive
power plays or quickly repairing the damage when his administration

got caught off base. On Nicaragua, Casey at the CIA repeatedly over-reached and then banked on Shultz and others, who had credibility with Congress, to bail him out, and bail out Reagan, too. But under Don Regan, Bud McFarlane, and John Poindexter, the second-term White House team became more willful, and more secretive—a formula for political disaster.

One major storm warning came with the news leak in October 1986 that President Reagan had approved a strategy of disinformation and deliberate deception against Libyan leader Muammar Qaddafi.[66] Bob Woodward, writing in *The Washington Post*, quoted an August 14 memo to Reagan from then–Vice Admiral John Poindexter, who had become national security adviser. Poindexter advocated a plan that "combines real and illusionary events—through a disinformation program—with the basic goal of making Qaddafi *think* that there is a high degree of internal opposition to him within Libya, that his key trusted aides are disloyal, that the U.S. is about to move against him militarily." The goal was to topple Qaddafi. The Poindexter memo had a particularily bad ring because *disinformation* is the Soviet term for planting false information in the press.

In self-defense, the White House sought to draw a distinction between practicing deception toward Qaddafi and using the American press for disinformation. It admitted deception but denied disinformation. At one White House briefing that I attended in mid-November 1986, President Reagan acknowledged Poindexter's memo and said he wanted to keep Qaddafi off balance. Poindexter insisted, "We did not intend and did not plan or conspire to mislead the American press in any way." The problem was that many White House reporters felt—with good reason—that they had already been patsies for a planted story line about a phony crisis with Libya.

A high State Department official told me that some of Poindexter's national security aides fed false information to the American press about Libya, thinking (on the basis of an August 14 meeting with Reagan, Poindexter, and others) that a planted story "might be smiled upon" by Reagan. *The Wall Street Journal* ran a story on August 25, asserting that Qaddafi "has begun plotting new terrorist attacks" and "the U.S. and Libya are on a collision course again" (though Poindexter's mid-August memo had said there was no evidence of imminent terrorist attacks). For the record, Larry Speakes had "no comment" on the *Journal* story, but Speakes insured that its version would be widely repeated, by telling other reporters that the story was "authoritative." In short, the White House promoted its planted story but kept its hand hidden, leaving reporters furious when the bogus crisis was later exposed by Bob Woodward of *The Washington Post.*

Shultz added to Reagan's image problems by defending the principle of deception. "Frankly, I don't have any problems with a little psychological warfare against Qaddafi," Shultz declared. He recalled Winston Churchill's justifying deception against Hitler during World War II: "In time of war, the truth is so precious, it must be attended by a bodyguard of lies."

That story line not only sharpened Reagan's growing credibility problems, but it did not sell among Shultz's official family. Respected congressional figures in both parties castigated the operation. The hardest blow was the protest-resignation of Shultz's State Department spokesman—Bernard Kalb, a former CBS, NBC, and *New York Times* reporter. "Faith in the word of America is the pulsebeat of our democracy," Kalb said. "Anything that hurts America's credibility hurts America."

But the Libyan disinformation plot was an inside-the-beltway tempest. The devastating disclosure of Reagan's duplicity on his secret dealings with Iran was the coup de grace, echoing elements of the Watergate scandal, with some abuses of executive power, official attempts at cover-ups, shredding documents, and above all, the president's personal policy deception. Across the nation, this affair shattered Reagan's carefully crafted political image. His political magic melted.

Within the month after disclosure in early November 1986 of the Iranian operation, Reagan's extraordinary public standing plummeted—from sixty-seven-percent to forty-six-percent approval in *The New York Times*/CBS News poll. Sizable majorities who had taken Reagan's word on so many other things distrusted his disclaimer that he had not known about the diversion to the Nicaraguan *contras* of millions of dollars from profits made on the American arms sales to Iran. The political debacle was compounded by Chief of Staff Don Regan's crass boast that image-game manipulation could dispose of the Iranian affair, just as White House P.R. had sloughed off three earlier setbacks: the Libyan "disinformation" controversy, the collapse of the Reykjavík summit, and the Republican loss of the Senate in the 1986 elections.

"Some of us are like a shovel brigade that follow a parade down Main Street cleaning up," Don Regan told Bernie Weinraub, White House correspondent for *The New York Times.* "We took Reykjavík and turned what was really a sour situation into something that turned out pretty well. Who was it that took this disinformation thing and managed to turn it? Who was it took on this loss in the Senate and pointed out a few facts and managed to pull that? I don't say we'll be able to do it four times in a row. But here we go again and we're trying."[67]

Three months later, the president pushed Don Regan's shovel brigade out the White House door.

But the president had fabricated his own catastrophe. He had violated the cardinal rule of the image game: acting contrary to the image he had developed for himself. He was a victim of his own effective salesmanship. As president, Reagan had cast himself as a firm and unflinching foe of precisely what he was now caught doing—dealing with a terrorist state. Reagan had built the arguments against such double-dealing with Iran. He had castigated Carter harshly for pragmatism and patience in negotiating the release of earlier American Embassy hostages in Iran—a course Reagan derided as weakness.

Reagan's fall from grace was so swift and sharp precisely because so much of his popular appeal had ridden on image: his image of steadfastness, his image as a man of principle, his image of uncompromising refusal to deal with the devil. Suddenly he was none of those in reality. Public disapproval fell hard on Reagan when he was exposed as willing to traffic in arms with Ayatollah Khomeini's closest henchmen to buy freedom for three American hostages, because Reagan's actions did violence to the image he had created.

In *Death of a Salesman,* Arthur Miller has one character say about his protagonist, Willy Loman: "For a salesman, there is no rock bottom to the life. He don't put a bolt to a nut, he don't tell you the law or give you medicine. He's a man way out there in the blue, riding on a smile and a shoeshine. And when they start not smiling back—that's an earthquake."[68]

As Reagan demonstrated in late 1987, he still has a following and can strike arms agreements with Moscow. But in the Iranian quagmire, he lost credibility with millions of people. He had risked his most precious political asset for a single highly dubious strand of policy. For a long time, Reagan had stretched the truth on his Nicaraguan policy, officially pretending to Congress that his goals were limited and only belatedly admitting that his real objective was to force the Sandinistas to "say uncle" and give up power. And he had lived the fiction that his administration had not instigated the arming of the *contras* during the congressional ban on such action. But never before had Reagan been caught so baldly in a policy lie—saying one thing publicly about Iran and doing the opposite in private. Reagan violated a basic rule of the image game: The story line has to match reality, or come far closer than Reagan did, or the image game is mere gloss. After Iran, nothing else Reagan pushed would sell as well as it had before. What helped him hang on as well as he did was his personal popularity—his shoeshine and his smile.

Over the longer run, the unmasking of Reagan's secret Iranian policy—along with Gary Hart's political collapse over stories about his extramarital relations and Joe Biden's political plagiarism—may have fostered new public skepticism toward slick public relations and glitzy political image making. For in the 1988 election season, the pendulum was swinging back toward more emphasis on personal integrity and political competence—away from the strongly symbolic politics with which the Reagan era began.

13. The Coalition Game: The Heart of Governing

Putting a majority together is like a one-armed man wrapping cranberries: You can't get them all in the wrap.
—Senate Majority Leader Bob Dole

As Ronald Wilson Reagan was taking his oath of office as the fortieth president of the United States in 1981, Senator Howard Baker was sitting a few seats away, trying to make up his mind. Reagan had certainly not been Baker's first choice as president. In 1976, Baker had backed Gerald Ford against Reagan. In 1980, then in his third term as a senator, Baker had run against Reagan himself and would fashion the damning metaphor that Reagan's ambitious tax cuts were a "riverboat gamble" for the nation.

As Baker had hopped across Iowa and New Hampshire in 1980, seeking votes, he had asserted that Reagan might understand Sacramento after eight years as governor of California, but he lacked the experience for Washington. What is more, Baker was a mainstream Republican, one of those Washington insiders roundly denounced by Reagan.

Now, Reagan was taking the oath that Baker had wanted to take himself. As the leader of the new Republican Senate majority, Baker had a choice to make: He could either operate as an independent force, using the leverage of his position, judgment, and experience to challenge and modify Reagan's messianic conservatism, or he could become a loyal lieutenant to the new president.

In manner, Baker is as warming as the southern sunshine, as mellow as a Tennessee country waltz. But his mellowness can be misleading, for Baker has grit. The fires of presidential ambition still burned in him. There were, he reflected then, precedents for using his new post of majority leader as a springboard toward the presidency. Lyndon Johnson had done that in the late 1950s. Closer to Baker, as a Republican, was the example of William Knowland, an ambitious, old-guard California conservative and a prickly, jealous champion of congressional prerogatives as majority leader under President Eisenhower in the mid-1950s. Knowland had told Eisenhower repeatedly that the Senate should not merely be a rubber stamp. He struck an independent course, especially on foreign policy.

Glancing at the wintry skies and out over the inauguration throng toward the spire of the Washington Monument, Baker mused about another model, another Republican Senate leader, the late Everett McKinley Dirksen, his own father-in-law, whose gold watchband Baker was wearing. Dirksen had revered the presidency, even when the opposite party controlled it. Privately, Baker confessed a newfound respect for Reagan—he had beaten a field of Republican rivals and then vanquished a sitting president. But Baker still wondered how to deal with Reagan.

"I was listening to his speech, and I have to confess that it sounded a little like every other presidential Inaugural Address I'd ever heard," Baker later recalled. "He was making a lot of promises about this, that, and the other. But there was one difference, it seemed to me, and that is that he was promising to make fundamental changes—not incremental changes, but fundamental changes in policy. His reduction in the rate of growth of government, if not the size of government itself, reduction in taxes, vast increase in level of armaments, and the reduction of regulations. All the good things that he talked about in the campaign, he was saying those things. . . . I sort of toyed with the idea, sitting there, about whether I was going to stake out a different position on some things or not.

"But the striking difference to me between this and every other Inaugural Address I'd heard since I went to the Senate in 1966 was that we had a Republican majority in the Senate for the first time in twenty-six years. And that I was the majority leader and that man up there was making those promises for me, too. And I guess it was at that moment that I made sort of an unconscious decision that I'm going to carry his flag. That doesn't mean that you're forever going to stifle any concern or question about what he's doing. . . . [But] I decided that the Bill Knowland example was a disaster. He tried to be president in a way. He was always griping and scrapping with Eisenhower and finally went off to California and got beat. But he was never happy, never cooperative, and never really was sympathetic to the Eisenhower program. There are two roles for majority leader in the Senate: One is the president's spear-carrier, and the other is an independent force. And I chose to be a spear-carrier. And I have no apology for it."[1]

Howard Baker's private decision on Inaugural Day was critical to the success of Reagan's presidency, for Baker became one of the most effective Senate leaders in decades. His decision was symptomatic, too, of the Republican mood in the afterglow of their 1980 election victory. Multiply Baker by fifty-three Republicans in the Senate and 192 in the House, and you have the solid core of the Reagan coalition that voted time and again to produce Reagan's stunning 1981 budget and tax victories, shaking Democrats accustomed to running Congress for a quarter of a century.

The coalition game—building coalitions and making coalitions work—is the heart of our system of government. Although the coalition game is usually ignored during the passions of American election campaigns, no president can succeed unless he can build a governing coalition. For limited periods, presidents can act on their own: devaluing the dollar as Nixon did, negotiating an arms treaty with Moscow as Carter did, sending American Marines into Lebanon or working secret arms deals with Iran as Reagan did. But eventually a president must come to Congress to fund his programs, approve his treaties, finance his wars, or sanction his secret diplomacy. If he cannot bring Congress along—cannot form a governing coalition—his programs founder, his treaty must be shelved, the Marines must come home, his diplomacy must halt. Coalitions are the necessary engines for sustaining policies.

Triumphant coalition makers are rare: Franklin Roosevelt at the start of the New Deal, Lyndon Johnson in the mid-1960s, and Ronald Reagan in the early 1980s. Other presidents, such as Richard Nixon, Jimmy Carter, John F. Kennedy, and Gerald Ford did pass pieces of legislation or got particular treaties ratified, but they did not pass their major programs because they could not make coalition government work. Solid congressional majorities eluded them. Over the past half century, with Congress usually in Democratic hands, Democratic presidents have had an advantage. Roosevelt and Johnson, for example, built their legislative achievements on big partisan Democratic coalitions. But Kennedy never managed that, and Carter labored like Sisyphus with precious little to show for it because he could not pull the Democrats together. Republican presidents, normally faced with a Democratic Congress, usually have to take the bipartisan route to coalition government. Eisenhower did that fairly effectively, but Nixon and Ford were hamstrung by divided government—Congress in the hands of the political opposition.

Reagan, in his first, most triumphant year, chose to build his coalition with partisan hardball, not with Eisenhower-style bipartisan compromise. In 1981, Reagan did woo conservative southern Democrats and get some to vote with him against their own congressional party leadership. But Republican unity was Reagan's Gibraltar. That is the primary lesson of American politics—rule number one of the coalition game: *Secure your political base first.* Much was required for Reagan's first-year coalition: the President's wide popular appeal, his knack for lobbying Congress, some tough grass-roots politicking, and of course a winning idea to rally a coalition. But Republican unity was the anchor. With unity forged by Howard Baker and House Republican Leader Bob Michel of Illinois, Reagan made his legislative mark. Without that unity, he would have been destined to one-term mediocrity.

Republican solidarity was far from preordained, nor did it endure. In 1980, Reagan had run against Washington; he had been the populist candidate attacking the system, the radical western Republican overthrowing his party's mainstream eastern establishment, the citizen outsider mocking the inside political game. Now inside this den of power, he needed allies.

Historically, American presidents have turned to their political parties to rally support. But years of revolt and reform in the late 1960s and 1970s had weakened the cohesion of the American party system. Congress had been torn asunder, faction by faction, region by region, interest by interest. Congressional leaders had little patronage to bind followers to them. Many members ran almost independent of party. As Reagan came to power, few people prized the vital cohesion offered by parties, which for so long had served as crucibles of compromise and pulled together coalitions.

What is more, Republicans had been in the minority in both houses for so long that they had fallen into a "minority mentality." They were not trained or conditioned to govern. Instead, they had developed the habits of a permanent opposition. They were practiced in the arts of negative politics: how to stall, how to filibuster, how to resist, how to block. Newt Gingrich, a bright light among younger Reaganites, gloomily declared, "The House Republican party, as a culture, has a defeatist, minority mentality that either did nothing, or opposed for so long, that it has no internal habits of inventing a coherent strategy or following it through for any length of time."[2]

When Orrin Hatch, a staunch Utah conservative, took over from Ted Kennedy, the Massachussetts liberal, as chairman of the Labor and Human Resources Committee, his staff had to train him to work legislation through his committee. "His mind-set of what you do in the Labor Committee is oppose Ted Kennedy," a senior Republican aide said. "Suddenly he had a big chunk of the Reagan program thrust on him, and he didn't know what to do." Other Republicans were accustomed to cutting personal deals with Democratic chairmen, but not to passing bills. Newcomers such as Alfonse D'Amato of New York, Robert Kasten of Wisconsin, or Paula Hawkins of Florida were suddenly thrust into being subcommittee chairs without a single day's experience in the Senate.

"The first thought on my personal agenda was whether or not we can turn these folks into a real majority, a functioning majority, instead of a numerical majority," Howard Baker told me later. "No single person in the Republican branch had ever been a committee chairman or a subcommittee chairman before. Brand new. We were going to have to reinvent the role of the majority party in the Senate. We were going to have to figure out if we have a permanent minority mind-set or whether we can pull together. . . . I perceived the greatest responsibility I had [was] to make the place work, because it could quickly have devolved into chaos if we had two minority parties."[3]

That is rule number two in forming a functioning coalition: *Inculcate the mind-set of governing.* It is a subtle, intangible notion—one that comes naturally to parties long in power, but not to parties long out of power. Without that governing mind-set, little can be accomplished in our system; parties clash, factions stalemate each other, individual members of Congress push their agendas, selfish interests overwhelm the common interest, and the machinery of government is immobilized.

Fortunately, politics is like sports: There are electric moments which transform group psychology, dramatically altering the dynamics of the game. When the lead suddenly changes hands, emotions swing from one team to another. Elan soars; partisan juices flow; the other side is thrown off balance. A team or a party, once faltering, gains inspiration;

it is suddenly energized. Riding a collective high, individual players pick up tempo and confidence. Shrewd leaders keep the roll going. Winning generates its own momentum.

Early 1981 was one of those heady, pivotal moments for Republicans in Congress. Politically starved for a generation, they soared on an incredible crest of enthusiasm, emboldened as much by their own newfound muscle as by having a Republican president. After all, by 1984, Eisenhower, Nixon, and Reagan had won five presidential elections since 1952 (to just three for the Democrats). Now, the sudden net gain of twelve seats in the Senate, plus thirty-three in the House, created a surge of partisan optimism.

Some Republicans, sniffing a massive sea change in American politics, felt on the brink of a national political realignment. They believed American political history was crossing one of those major fault lines that come every generation or two. They sensed the end of the national hegemony of the Democratic party, begun half a century before, and they hungered for a new era—with Republicans as a majority party into the next century. Eisenhower and Nixon had won the White House, but Congress had eluded the GOP. Now full realignment finally seemed at hand. Partisan esprit was rampant among the Reaganite Young Turk Republicans elected in 1978 and 1980.

"The freshman and sophomore classes make up almost half of our 192 members," Max Friedersdorf, Reagan's chief congressional liaison, observed in 1981. "They are extremely aggressive to make their mark. They want to win and they are fully aware that they have power in unity. They have an influence on the more senior Republicans who have developed a minority complex over the years. They sense that they're getting close to having a majority in the House. This makes for an esprit that I've never seen before."[4]

King of the Hill

It takes more than enthusiasm to consolidate power. In the king of the hill game, rule number three is: *Strike quickly for a win, during the early rush of power.* That helps establish momentum and an aura of success. Lyndon Johnson had a colorful maxim for such moments. "Johnson operated under the philosophy with Congress—if you're not doing it to them, they're doing it to you. And frequently, he used a more vivid word than *doing,*" recalled Douglass Cater, one of Johnson's White House advisers.[5]

Winning is power, was the gut summation given me by Jim Baker.

"I've always felt that it is extremely important in terms of a president's power—power as opposed to popularity—that presidents succeed on the Hill with what they undertake up there," Baker asserted. "And I really believe that one reason that Ronald Reagan has been so successful is that he succeeded in the high-profile issues that he jumped on in the first term. The way presidents govern is to translate their philosophy into policy by working with Congress. That's why Carter failed in my view. Because he never learned that lesson."[6]

The image of success is crucial, as Dick Darman pointed out in a White House memo. On February 21, 1981, Darman told me that he had urged crafting a "plan for the preservation of the appearance of the president's continuing strength and effectiveness—the avoidance of association with 'losses,' the association with a planned string of 'successes.' "

Political gamesmanship required quickly tapping Republican optimism to translate electoral victory into legislative power and a governing majority. Otherwise, momentum could slip away.

But as Carter learned, there are no automatic legislative victories for a new president. Carter lost his first battles, on water projects, and Reagan was nearly upset by his own troops in the very first test—long before his celebrated victories.

In the Senate, Howard Baker faced a Republican revolt that threatened to shatter his narrow 53–47 majority before it would ever taste victory. That first test was critical, because Reagan had to make the Senate his coalition cornerstone. If he could not hold the Republican Senate majority in line, it would dash his hopes for a coalition with conservative House Democrats; if Reagan lost in the Senate, why should these House Democrats defy their own party leaders in the House to join forces with Reagan?

What forced Reagan's hand was the need to raise the legal ceiling on the national debt to $985 billion by February 6—so the government could borrow money to finance deficits and keep running. Democrats had long voted routinely to raise the debt ceiling because they believed in government programs, but conservative Republicans hated these votes. They opposed raising the debt ceiling because they opposed the government programs, and on principle they rejected deficit spending. Reagan too had felt that way, but now it was his responsibility to run the government. That meant getting conservative Republicans to bend their ideology to help him govern. In the House, Democrats and Republicans combined to pass the debt-ceiling bill.

But in the Senate, the Democrats played rougher. Initially, many

voted against the bill to force the distasteful chore on the Republican
majority. Very quickly, the debt-ceiling vote became a test of Reagan's
and Howard Baker's ability to secure their partisan base. There was
strong resistance.

Almost all thirteen Republican freshmen were opposed. Don Nickles
of Oklahoma, Mack Mattingly of Georgia, Slade Gorton of Washington, Steve Symms of Idaho, and Paula Hawkins of Florida protested
to Howard Baker. These Reaganites believed ardently in budget balancing. "We've told our constituents we're never going to vote to
increase the debt limit," they told Baker. "We're dead set against it.
It is an article of faith with us." Their rebellion left Baker shy of votes
to pass the measure.

Another obstacle was posed by William Armstrong of Colorado, one
of the brightest, most vigorous Senate conservatives on economic issues. In 1981, he vowed to vote against the debt bill unless it carried
an amendment giving the president power to cut spending unilaterally.
Armstrong saw the deadline pressure of the debt bill as a chance to
restore to Reagan and future presidents power taken away by Congress
in 1974. This was the power of "recision"—the power of a president
to notify Congress he will not spend certain funds. As the law stood
in 1981, a president's recision required congressional approval—winning majorities in both houses. But under Armstrong's amendment, the
president could act and his cuts would stick—unless Congress overrode
him within forty-five days. That put the burden of veto action on
Congress.

The day before the debt vote, Armstrong was summoned to Baker's
office to meet with Baker and Vice President Bush. Baker, fearing
filibusters from Democrats, wanted a clean debt bill with no amendments, to help get Reagan a quick victory.

"This is no time to rock the boat," Baker declared. "We've got a new
president. We ought not to buck him."

"But this is a once-in-a-lifetime opportunity," objected Armstrong.
"To dissipate it on making nickel-and-dime changes in the budget
instead of going for institutional reforms would be a terrible mistake."
He appealed to Bush: "The honeymoon lasts only so long. If the
president asks for it, think of the leverage he has. Don't you think this
is a golden opportunity?"

"It doesn't matter what I think," Bush replied. "The president
wants a clean debt-ceiling bill. So please back off."[7]

Armstrong relented, feeling it was ridiculous for a single senator to
try to force on Reagan a power he did not want.

But that still left the rebellious freshmen. Baker had played high cards—senior conservatives such as Barry Goldwater of Arizona and John Tower of Texas—to try to persuade them. The president had them to the White House in ones and twos. That softened them up, but it did not change their minds.

Howard Baker's ace in the hole was Strom Thurmond, the senior Senate Republican. Thurmond epitomized tight-fisted austerity and fierce independence. He had stood against the federal establishment as the segregationist governor of South Carolina and the Dixiecrat candidate for president in 1948. He had staged a one-man filibuster for twenty-four hours and eighteen minutes against the Civil Rights Act of 1957. In twenty-seven years as a senator, first as a Democrat and then as a Republican, Thurmond had *never* voted to raise the debt ceiling.

Baker ran into Thurmond on the Senate floor, found him willing to help, and quickly rounded up the Republican freshmen.

"I sat them down around the conference table, brought in Strom, and Strom started slow and low in that measured South Carolina cadence," Baker recalled. "He started working up, and at the end of three or four minutes—it wasn't very long—he said: 'Now some of you in this room say that you have promised never to vote for a debt-limit increase, and I understand that. And you ought to understand that I've never in my whole career voted to increase the debt limit before. But I've never had Ronald Reagan as president before either. And I'm going to vote for the debt-limit increase. And so are you.' And there was a deathly silence. Strom got up and left. And there was some grumbling and grousing and leaning back in the chairs, and they got up and wandered out."[8]

The Democrats, stung by Reagan's charges that they were big spenders, made the vote painful for the Republicans. One by one, they voted against the bill to force Republicans to swallow their ideology and their campaign promises, to show solidarity with the president. One by one, the Republicans voted aye. Henry "Scoop" Jackson, the veteran Democrat from Washington state was so tickled to see Republicans squirm that he danced a jig on the floor. Ultimately, all but three Republicans—Armstrong, Mattingly, and John East of North Carolina—supported Reagan. Baker let out a "whew" when he had fifty votes; then a score of Democrats switched sides to pass the measure, 73–18.

The public never grasped how narrowly Baker's control of the Senate had ridden in the balance. After the vote, Baker told Thurmond, "I never owed a greater debt of political gratitude to anybody than I do to you."

Because defeat that early, due to Republican defections, would have derailed the Reagan program. Had Republican ranks shattered just seventeen days after Reagan's inauguration, the initial momentum of Reagan's presidency would have been lost. Baker felt it vital to demonstrate command and to get Republicans to make sacrifices for the sake of unity behind Reagan. "Strom, more than just about anybody else, maybe except me, understood how important it was that we act like a majority," Baker said.

That debt-ceiling victory, seemingly minor, did three things: It forged Republican unity, it inculcated a governing mentality, and it established a winning momentum.

The President—Being Loved and Feared

Success in the coalition game depends enormously on presidential influence with the individual members of Congress; a president can pull enough reluctant votes his way if he has the right political touch. It is an old maxim of politics that an effective leader, mayor, governor, and above all, president, must be both loved and feared. That is how a president marshals support from his natural followers and deters attack from his natural enemies. Issues matter, of course, but so does human chemistry. A president has to make clear there are benefits for supporting him and consequences for opposing him.

No one understood this better than Lyndon Johnson, who was masterful at ferreting out the weak points and deepest hungers of other politicians. Yet Johnson was so blatantly Machiavellian that it hampered him. He made it hard for people to go along and still retain their dignity and independence. Carter had the opposite problem. Arm-twisting and deal-making were not his forte. When he tried to act strong, he often came across as mean and willful because exaggerated forcefulness was out of character.

At bottom, Carter seemed ill at ease with power, and ill at ease hobnobbing with other politicians. He immersed himself in substance but despised wheeling and dealing with Congress. Many a senator or House member told me that Carter was awkward or hesitant about asking directly for his or her vote. He frowned on horse-trading. Only from painful experience did he learn the value of doing little favors for other politicians. Both his intellect and his engineer's training at Annapolis made him impatient with that vital lubrication of the wheels of legislation: making other politicians feel important.

At intimate occasions—a small dinner at the White House or a

personal interview at his home in Plains, Georgia—I found Carter
engaging, but many members of Congress found him cool and brisk.
When he had groups for breakfast, he would arrive late because he had
been busy at work in his study. Then he would give a little speech on
whatever policy he was pushing. Carter once complained to Jack Nelson, Washington Bureau Chief of the *Los Angeles Times,* that some
members of Congress wasted his time because they were not well
prepared on substance. People who meet with me, Carter told Nelson,
"had better know the subject because I know it" and my time is
"extremely valuable."[9]

Carter did not sense what many members regard as the essence of
such sessions. "The problem was that the congressmen didn't come to
the White House to hear a logical argument from the president, which
they could have gotten just as well from his aides," observed Mark
Nimitz, a lawyer who served in Carter's State Department. "What
Carter didn't understand was that these guys came down to the White
House to swap stories and go back up to the Hill and brag to the others,
'I told the president . . . and he told me . . .' "[10]

"It doesn't take much in the White House to pick up the phone and
say, 'Is there anything we can do for you in the next two or three
months?' In the Carter White House that was regarded as treason,"
added Mark Siegel, a veteran Democratic party official who worked in
the Carter White House. "Congress was the enemy. The Democratic
party was the enemy. The Washington establishment was the enemy.
Tip O'Neill wanted to help a Democratic president enact a Democratic agenda, but the Carter people didn't understand Tip O'Neill.
They regarded him as a horse's ass, and if you call someone a horse's
ass in the White House, do you know how fast that gets back to that
someone?"[11]

Carter and his inner circle had been ill-trained for Washington. In
Georgia, a one-party state with a fairly docile legislature, Carter felt he
could afford aloofness. In time, Carter came to understand how that
cost him with Congress. In his third year, I heard him mock his own
ineptitude at a convention of southern state legislators. He said he used
to ask people how to deal with Congress. "Someone told me to treat
them like the Georgia legislature," Carter recounted. He paused to let
that sink in. "I tried it," he said. "And it didn't work."

As outsiders, Carter's team did not know the Washington power
game or its power networks. Their lack of understanding was almost
inevitable, given the type of presidential campaign Carter had waged.
Carter had won the 1976 nomination by running against Washington

and avoiding much contact with party leaders. After the election, Carter's Georgia political mafia arrived in Washington with a chip on their shoulders and then kept a cool distance. Initially, Jimmy and Rosalynn Carter made a point of not socializing with the Georgetown set and other Washington insiders. Carter not only disdained the trappings of the imperial presidency but the symbols of the Washington establishment. On his energy proposals, for example, Carter did not consult the Democratic legislative leaders, Tip O'Neill and Senator Robert Byrd. Hamilton Jordan was so remote that O'Neill complained months later that he had never met the president's right-hand man, whom he ridiculed as "Hannibal Jerkin."

Carter and his Georgians, having won an upstart, outsider's victory and enjoying partisan majorities in both houses, acted as if they did not need others to succeed. Carter seemed convinced that the sheer rationality of his proposals and his eminence as president would pass them. He was initially misled by enormous press attention, by his having beaten a slew of Washington politicians, and by his self-righteous self-confidence on the issues.

As Reagan roped together his first-year coalition, he profited greatly by striking contrasts with Jimmy Carter. It hardly requires much rehearsing of Reagan's Irish warmth and his love of personal banter to underscore the differences. Reagan is as comfortable shmoozing with other politicians as he is with power. He fitted the presidency easily, and that was reassuring to other politicians as well as to ordinary people.

Reagan was far from perfect. I have heard Republicans such as Bob Packwood, Pete Domenici, and Warren Rudman bridling after a session with President Reagan because he read from his cue cards or deflected serious discussion by repeating shopworn anecdotes about welfare queens supposedly defrauding taxpayers with high living. But in that first year, Reagan was in top form. He demonstrated rule number four in the coalition game: *Lavish attention on the Washington power structure.* Democrats were flattered to be courted. Republicans were tickled to walk away with a Reagan story to retell, or some Reagan cuff links, or tickets to the presidential box at the Kennedy Center.

For a man who, like Carter, had run his campaign against Washington, Reagan did a quick 180-degree turn in catering to the Washington establishment. He mounted a mellow social and political campaign that set a Dale Carnegie *(How to Win Friends and Influence People)* standard. Shelving his campaign rhetoric, Reagan played the gracious outsider eager to win acceptance inside the beltway.

That was in character: Despite his messianic rhetoric, Reagan was no dry ideologue of the right, but was ready to bend and bargain with mainstream Republicans. At the 1980 convention, Reagan had tried to enlist Gerald Ford as his vice president, shocking dyed-in-the-wool Reagan partisans, and then he picked his rival, George Bush, rather than his closest political ally, Senator Paul Laxalt. When right-wingers urged replacing Howard Baker as Senate Republican leader with Laxalt, Reagan—with Laxalt's encouragement—turned thumbs down. He reached beyond his California circle to tap former Ford and Nixon advisers for his White House staff.

On his first night in town as president-elect, Reagan wooed fifty local notables with a dinner at the F Street Club, an understated symbol of old money. Many of Washington's old names, snubbed by the Carters, were surprised and delighted to be invited: Harold Hughes, then Democratic governor of Maryland; Marion Barry, the outspokenly liberal Democratic mayor of Washington who had bashed Reagan in the campaign; James Cheek, president of Howard University; and attorney Edward Bennett Williams, a well-known Democrat and owner of the Baltimore Orioles. "When you come to town, there's a tendency as an officeholder to act as if you're a detached servant," Reagan explained to Elisabeth Bumiller of *The Washington Post.* "Well, I decided it was time to serve notice that we're residents."[12]

Eight years as governor of the nation's largest state, dealing with a Democratic majority in the California Assembly, had taught Reagan about seducing adversaries as well as allies. The next couple of nights, he was out first celebrating with Republican senators and then mingling with the Washington establishment—Katharine Graham, chairman of *The Washington Post;* Meg Greenfield, chief of the *Post's* editorial page; and Robert Strauss, Carter's former campaign chairman—at a small dinner given by George Will, the unabashedly pro-Reagan columnist who had helped coach Reagan for presidential debates. Later, Reagan met not only with friends but with such foes as Senator Ted Kennedy and paid a courtesy call on Speaker O'Neill, who purred afterward, "I liked him. He was very personable." As for Reagan's staff, O'Neill added, "I get along better with them than I did with Carter's staff."

Reagan's stroking of Washington's political egos was a brilliant gambit. Washington was captivated. It was ready for a shift from Georgia country to California gentry, and it was flattered by a president who paid court to the courtiers.

In sum, Reagan's confection of charm and deference seduced the citadels of power before the political battles began. He not only demonstrated that the presidency was now in the hands of an experienced politician, he also calmed the animal instincts of other politicians that his campaign had aroused. His charm treatment disarmed skeptics who had conjured him as a warmonger and a rabid ideologue.

Circumstance also gave Reagan one enormous advantage: After the failed presidencies of Johnson, Nixon, Ford, and Carter, the nation ached for a strong, effective leader. If another president failed, politicians were saying, it would show the presidency had been fatally crippled by Vietnam and Watergate. There was a widespread feeling that *some* president *has got to succeed.* That climate was a boon to Reagan. And his soft sell made other politicians want to help him. Case in point: the Republican moderates and liberals, a very important swing group in 1981. They disagreed with Reagan's philosophy, yet they responded to his appeals. James Leach, a thoughtful, sandy-haired, pro-Bush Iowan, described how the contrast between Reagan and Carter influenced him.

"I'll never forget the first time meeting with Carter," Leach said. "He walked in and he said two things. He said, 'You know, I want to tell you first of all that your constituents are my constituents. And secondly, I know that this is a really tough issue for you but . . . I hope you do what's best for the country and not what's politically expedient. That's what we're all here to do.' When he first expressed that, I was rather impressed. The ninth time I heard that, I wanted to fight. I mean there was something about Carter that brought out an instinct to do battle. And there is something about Reagan that has caused Republicans, even those that differ with him, to want to some extent to rally behind [him]. Particularly in '81 and '82, when the presidency itself was at risk. And secondly, the vulnerability of a president who came to Washington as an outsider . . . a very decent man who didn't know the insiders' game and therefore needed help. People genuinely liked helping Ronald Reagan."[13]

Events also helped Reagan. On his Inaugural Day, as he was taking his oath, the fifty-two American diplomats held hostage in Iran were freed. The shackles came off. America was no longer in chains. Carter deserves great credit for their release; that was his legacy to the nation and to Reagan. But their release helped feed the immediate notion that Reagan was "Lucky Dutch." And politicians, like athletes and gamblers, instinctively gravitate toward those who bring lady luck with them.

The second major event, of course, was one that Reagan turned magnificently to his own advantage: the attempt on his life on March

30, 1981. Before the shooting, Reagan's private polls showed his popularity slipping. Any crisis, let alone a presidential shooting, causes the nation to rally around its leader. That happened in 1981. And Reagan's personal gallantry created public sympathy and an aura of heroism around him.

"That [whole episode] was crucially important," Dick Darman asserted. "I think we would have been way out of the normal presidential honeymoon at the time of the crucial votes on the budget and tax cuts if there hadn't been a 'second life.' The shooting and Reagan's recovery was not only a second life for Reagan but a second life for Reagan's honeymoon. Sheer chance—and extraordinarily important. In fact, I think we would have had to compromise on the tax bill without it."[14]

Reagan and his team knew how to make the country's mood pay off in the inside power game. In lobbying Congress, they capitalized on his unusual popularity. There were precedents: Lyndon Johnson used to carry a card with polls showing his popularity and pull it out to show to other politicians—until his poll results began to slide in May 1966. But the wave of sympathy and approval that Reagan won after the shooting was unique—what Kennedy might have enjoyed had he survived. It gave Reagan more leverage than he had won in the 1980 election.

That personal popularity was an incomparable advantage in welding Reagan's coalition. It was an especially potent weapon against wavering Republicans and southern Democrats who came from congressional districts which Reagan had carried in 1980, with sixty or seventy percent of the vote, and could appeal directly to the voters. Strong, emotional public support gave Reagan the second half of that vital amalgam of a leader's leverage—love and fear. There were two dozen House Republicans who knew they had ridden Reagan's coattails into office in 1980, and half a dozen Republican senators for whom Reagan had added the final one or two percent for their paper-thin victories. These Republicans, indebted to Reagan, were reluctant to cross him. Southern Boll Weevil Democrats feared Reagan too—enough to extract a promise that he would not campaign against them in 1982 if they backed his program in 1981. "I couldn't look myself in the mirror in the morning if I campaigned against someone who helped me on this program," the president promised the Boll Weevils.

The fear factor helped lift Reagan to his 1981 victories.

The Steamroller Effect

In the making of a majority coalition, a new president has the great
advantage of casting his first major legislative proposal as a personal test
of confidence in his presidency. The key to this strategy is rule number
five of the coalition game: *Make the president himself the issue, as much
as the substance of his proposals.* That strategy immediately puts the
congressional opposition on the defensive. It makes voting against the
new president almost like repudiating the results of the election just
finished, which many politicians are loath to do.

Reagan was doubly armed for this strategy by his election victory and
by surging public sympathy after the attempt on his life. Communications Director David Gergen shrewdly proposed that Reagan capitalize
on the outpouring of public goodwill to make what amounted to a
second Inaugural Address in 1981, to a joint session of Congress on
April 28. It was a very powerful gambit. I remember Reagan that
evening, striding confidently into the House, the picture of manly vigor
and purpose, bathed in applause, acknowledging it with a frisky toss of
his head. Democrats as well as Republicans were cheered by his recovery, warmed by his ruddy good humor. The country was so pro-Reagan
then that it was easy for Reagan's lieutenants to frame virtually every
vote for another hundred days on Reagan personally: Are you with
Reagan or against him?

Republican control of the Senate in 1981 gave Reagan an excellent
arena to work that strategy and an important advantage over Nixon,
Ford, and Eisenhower, who had faced Democratic control of Congress—except in Eisenhower's first two years.

In the Senate, it fell to Majority Leader Howard Baker to translate
the "up-or-down strategy"—the strategy of a yes or no vote for Reagan—into tactics.

As a legislative leader, Howard Baker is a chess player, planning
moves far ahead, watching many pieces on the board. His method ws
to draw all fifteen Republican committee chairmen into what became
known as the "committee of dukes and earls," to let them feel a part
of his team. But he would personally work out Senate strategy, sharing
it only with close aides and surfacing it gradually, even to President
Reagan. "Baker is extremely logical, extremely firm-minded," said one
Senate staffer. "It is a mark of Baker's boldness—which most people
do not give him credit for—that he handled Reagan's budget the way
he did in 1981."

By 1981, Howard Baker had become impatient with the Senate, frustrated that it was no longer a great forum for debate and action but crippled by delaying tactics and filibusters. Not only were there filibusters on the issues, he blurted out to me, but filibusters on the leader's motion to start debate, filibusters on various amendments, and filibusters after a vote of cloture that theoretically cut off filibusters. Moreover, on most legislation, amendments were unlimited and often totally unrelated to the bill at hand. That meant bills could be strangled by endless amendments. Senators with one pet topic, especially a deadlocking issue such as abortion, could stalemate the Senate repeatedly.

In Baker's southern colloquialism, anybody could "sprague the wheel"—put a stick in the spokes. Getting the Senate to act, he groused, was like "pushing a wet noodle."¹⁵

That frustration welled up in Baker as he crafted a legislative strategy. Because Baker is so likable, so patient in stroking the egos of other politicians, many misjudged his grit in ramming through Reagan's economic program. The legislative instrument he adopted was a blunt weapon to impose discipline—"high-handed and draconian," he admitted.

Baker built his coalition around making all key votes a test of loyalty to the president, up or down. That was essential for pushing Reagan's ambitious budget cutting through Congress, for a budget is not just abstract figures—it is flesh-and-blood programs. A budget is a chart of national priorities, a menu of spending choices—missiles vs. Medicare, Star Wars vs. student loans, aircraft carriers vs. Amtrak, farm-price supports and food stamps vs. F-18 jet fighters. In theory, everyone in Congress is for cutting the budget and the deficit, but in practice, all resist cutting programs that help their states or districts. That was the political habit that Baker wanted to override.

Left to the normal procedures of Congress, a budget gets lost in a swamp of turf battles and rival committees' protecting pet programs. What Baker needed was a procedural club to crack legislative heads. He needed technical leverage—the technicalities of congressional procedure are an important form of power when shrewdly used—to force the Senate to place the common interest over special interests, the common interest of budget cutting over the special interests of budget protecting. He needed a legislative vehicle for forcing an up-or-down vote on Reagan's budget—in short, on Reagan.

At the urging of Budget Committee Chairman Pete Domenici and his staff director, Steve Bell, Howard Baker decided on a very strict procedure known as reconciliation. Without it, Reagan's dramatic

1981 budget victory would have been impossible. As it was, Reagan won the crucial test in the House by only four votes—and the issue on that vote was whether to apply a tight version of reconciliation. So the tactic of reconciliation became central to the whole Reagan legislative strategy.

The reconciliation procedure had been written into the 1974 budget act but never used as Baker intended to use it. For Baker, its attraction was this: Normally, budget committees in both houses draft a budget resolution which is a guideline for the tax-writing committees that raise revenue, the appropriating committees that vote funds, and the thirteen substantive committees that approve various programs: defense, agriculture, labor and human resources, interior, public works, and so on. But a normal budget resolution lacks the power of law, and those other committees, protective of their programs, are not tightly bound by its guidelines. The total of their individual budgets invariably adds up to more than the budget committee target. So there is a second budget resolution, and a third, as Congress tries again and again. If the totals are not in line by the third budget resolution, it can include reconciliation—that is, reconciling the different committee spending totals with the overall target. On this third round, reconciliation has the force of law—it imposes a specific target on each committee and can require that programs be cut to meet those targets.

In the Senate, which normally allows unlimited debate, reconciliation puts a flat lid of fifty hours on debate—that is, a debate on the full federal budget, a process which normally takes weeks upon weeks; reconciliation restricts filibusters. Finally, reconciliation forbids any amendment not germane to the budget—no wandering off into abortion, school prayer, or other issues that can paralyze the Senate; and it demands that whatever spending is added must be matched by tax increases or by spending cuts in other programs.

Howard Baker liked the idea of using the steamroller tactic of reconciliation right off the bat on Reagan's budget—on the *first* budget resolution—skipping months of maneuvering. Reagan's strategists embraced this tactic because it offered one big vote of confidence on Reagan and on joining his coalition. Democrats screamed that this tactic made David Stockman, as budget director, a legislative tyrant and turned Congress into a rubber stamp, shorn of institutional powers. Years later, Stockman agreed with them.

"We did not coronate Mr. Stockman as king," bellowed Jim Wright, then House majority leader. Privately, some Republicans, including House Republican Leader Robert Michel, worried about looking like

"Reagan robots." Bruce Vento, a militant Minnesota liberal Democrat, mocked the Republicans. "When Commander in Chief Stockman says jump, you do not ask why," Vento hooted. "You do not ask if it will be good for your district. You only ask *how high* and *how often!*"

Once the steamroller got going in the Senate, it was impossible to stop. Pete Domenici, the no-nonsense Budget Committee chairman, protested that in the headlong push for victory, the substance of the budget was getting lost. Domenici did not believe Reagan's Rosy Scenario, which promised huge tax cuts in 1981 and a balanced budget by 1984. Domenici, a laconic, plain-spoken father of eight from an Italian immigrant family, plays his politics the way he pitched minor league baseball in the West Texas–New Mexico league: straight and hard.

Using estimates of the Congressional Budget Office, Domenici disputed the economic claims of Reagan and Stockman. At a minimum, he warned, Reagan's tax cuts would leave a deficit of $44 billion in 1984 (actually, it would be $185.3 billion). Stockman promised to find another $44 billion of budget cuts for 1984—but later. "That's a pig in the poke!" Domenici protested. He led the Budget Committee to vote against Reagan's budget, on grounds that it broke faith with Republican pledges to balance the budget. But a few weeks later, at a White House strategy meeting, Howard Baker overruled Domenici—in one of the most critical decisions of 1981. As Reagan's loyal lieutenant, Baker accepted Stockman's promise to cut $44 billion and suggested that budget documents designate the cuts with a "magic asterisk." On paper that meant the Reagan program showed a balanced budget in 1984, making it more palatable to Senate Republicans. Domenici was conscience stricken, but he acquiesced.

"I knew the Rosy Scenario wasn't going to happen," Domenici told me much later. "It stuck in my craw."

When I asked Domenici why he had gone against his better judgment, his response showed how the bandwagon mentality swept Republicans along. "Here we have a new president, a new team, a new theory, a new set of committee chairmen," Domenici explained. "We just had to go along and say, 'We'll try to work with the president. Let's give the president and his team a chance.' We thought there would be a chance to correct the first resolution later, but there never was. It didn't take us too long before we started saying, 'The deficit is going to go haywire.' "[16]

Howard Baker swung Domenici in line—indeed, it is impossible to exaggerate the importance to Reagan's success of Howard Baker's personal influence with Senate Republicans or of his relationship to Jim Baker at the White House.

Rule number six: *Building a governing coalition hinges on a close working link between the president's top strategist and his party's congressional leaders.* The failures of Carter's aides, Hamilton Jordan and Frank Moore, demonstrated the cost of ignoring this link. In 1985, Reagan paid a high price for touchy relations between his new chief of staff, Don Regan, and Bob Dole, the new Senate majority leader. In his first term, Reagan had superb legislative liaisons led by Max Friedersdorf, a smooth diplomat from the Ford White House, and Ken Duberstein, an amiable, voluble political persuader, who worked the House. Reagan had a warm personal relationship with Howard Baker. But the crucial working alliance was between the two Bakers, Howard and Jim, who were constantly in touch.

"Jim Baker has a lot of great traits, but one is he can carry on a thirty-second conversation," Howard Baker said. "I place great value on the thirty-second conversation because my days were made up of hundreds of thirty-second conversations."[17]

Both Jim and Howard Baker—no relation to each other—are mainstream Republicans, temperamentally disposed to compromise and to making the legislative system work. Both Bakers have that vital sense of what was politically doable and what was not. They loyally carried Reagan's water in public, but they argued with him in private, trying to save him from lost causes. Their pragmatic cast of mind made them natural allies and natural coalition makers. Neither was a true Reaganite; both had worked for Gerald Ford against Reagan in 1976 and had initially opposed Reagan in 1980. They had ties with other Republicans and could widen the circle of Reagan's support. Indeed, if it had been left to hard-core Reaganite ideologues such as Edwin Meese, William Clark, Lyn Nofziger, or Pat Buchanan to pass the first Reagan program, it probably would have been defeated. For ideological rigidity can derail even a partisan coalition, and both Bakers were masterful at bending at the margins and helping Reagan corral the final few votes needed for victory.

Howard Baker gained national fame during the televised Watergate hearings as a symbol of Republican integrity. Actually, however, he lacks the charisma or phrase-making glibness of most media politicians. His natural terrain is legislative politics; three terms in the Senate made him a creature of Congress and its master. In 1981, he united Republicans who were as philosophically incompatible as arch-conservative Jesse Helms of North Carolina and outspokenly liberal Lowell Weicker of Connecticut. He got Helms to swallow a long delay before pushing against abortion and for school prayer, to allow Reagan's economic program first crack. When Republican committee chairmen got into a tug-of-war over who would handle the guts of the Reagan program, Baker massaged egos with charm and patience. Even Democrats liked him as leader.

"If you had a secret ballot for majority leader, I suspect Democrats would have picked him," observed Connecticut Democrat Christopher Dodd. "We wanted to see the place function."[18]

Unusual for a politician, Baker is a listener, attentive to his colleagues. "Baker led by a combination of intellect—being four steps ahead of everybody—and humanness and warmth," enthused Warren Rudman. "He had patience and compassion. When Howard Baker listened to you, you had the feeling that all that was going on for him was what you were saying at that moment."[19]

"He spent his whole day on the phone holding people's hands," added James Miller, one of Baker's aides. "He knew that if you beat someone, you might need him again. He knew the most important time to stroke some senator was right after you'd beaten him. Baker would roll [defeat] Jesse Helms on a cloture vote, and then he'd sit Helms down in the cloakroom and have a talk with him afterwards."[20]

In the Senate, declared Colorado's William Armstrong, "the success that Reagan had was sixty percent Reagan and forty percent Howard Baker. When you look at those first couple of years, you've got to admire the way Baker held the Republicans together, over and over. There was a selfless quality to his leadership. Everybody knew he was doing it to support the president and not to advance his own ideas. Baker is a beloved leader. He gets the break: People will vote with him because they love him. Not when they think he is dead wrong, but if there is reasonable room for maneuver or reasonable doubt, as so often there is, then they will support him."[21]

Hardball: Inside and Outside Politics

The Senate provided Reagan with the cornerstone for his 1981 coalition, but the real challenge lay in the House, where Democrats outnumbered Republicans 243–192. How the Reaganites forged a House majority is a lesson in modern coalition building. To the steamroller tactic of reconciliation, the Reagan team added another tactic: the grass-roots-lobbying blitz. Rule number seven of the coalition game is: *Use the muscle of the president's nationwide political apparatus to swing votes into line for his legislative coalition.* The Reagan operation in 1981 was a textbook case of how to use campaign and lobbying techniques to produce a functioning coalition in Congress.

The arithmetic of the Democratic majority in the House left Reagan with two options—both common to Republican presidents: He could either strike a deal with the House Democratic leadership to form a grand bipartisan coalition on budget cutting or go for a much narrower coalition by holding all the Republicans in line and chipping off a block of at least twenty-six Democratic votes, to reach a majority of 218. Although House Democratic leaders were willing to go along with some budget cuts, that would not satisfy Reagan. He disagreed philosophically with Speaker Tip O'Neill and he wanted a visible Republican victory. So Reagan played partisan hardball; in the argot of Congress, he decided to "roll Tip"—topple the speaker. That strategy required forging a conservative coalition—the kind of alliance between Republicans and conservative southern Democrats that had helped Eisenhower and Nixon.

In the House, the key to Reagan's victory lay with two groups. "Very seldom do you get one vote at a time in the House," explained Ken Duberstein, Reagan's likable, street-smart House lobbyist, who has the chutzpah and humor to deal with big-city Democrats as well as Republicans. "You usually get blocks of votes. You usually get state delegations, say, the Democrats from Tennessee or the Republicans from Oklahoma, or the oil-state boys, or you get the Cotton Clubbers, or you get the tobacco boys, or you get the textile guys or the timber folks or the Gypsy Moths [the Northeast-Midwest Republicans]. So you see wholesale merchandising in the House, even if you're meeting with them one by one or in small groups, whereas in the Senate it's really one by one."[22]

The first key group was the Boll Weevils—about fifty conservative Democrats from Virginia to Texas who had clashed for years with their national party leaders on defense spending and budget deficits. They styled themselves Boll Weevils because they were boring from within the Democratic party, just as insect weevils bore inside the cotton boll. Many won elections by running against their party and Speaker Tip O'Neill; they came largely from districts where Reagan solidly thumped Carter. These Democrats were lineal descendants of the former Democratic allies of Eisenhower and Nixon—with one big difference. In the old days, the Republican White House usually teamed up with the "barons"—conservative southern committee chairmen. But in 1981, most top committee posts were held by mainstream

Democrats and the southerners were mainly junior members relegated to the back benches. That left them in a renegade mood, ripe for recruitment by the Reagan forces.

The second key group was the Gypsy Moths, some fifteen to twenty liberal Republicans from the Northeast and Midwest. Their name was a parody on the Boll Weevils, making the point that they ate at the leaves of the Republican tree, just as real gypsy moths do. The Gypsy Moths were habitual defectors from Republican ranks, joining centrist and liberal Democrats in legislative coalitions. In 1981, Gypsy Moths, such as Manhattan liberal Bill Green or Iowa's progressive Republicans Jim Leach and Tom Tauke, were philosophically at odds with Reagan. They sympathized with some efficiencies in government, but not deep budget slashing. Reagan's coalition required every single Gypsy Moth vote.

That task fell mainly to Bob Michel, the hearty Republican leader from Peoria, a popular legislator given to *gol darn, geeminy Chrismus,* and barbershop harmonizing. "Look," Michel told his troops, "there's no way you can really convince some good votes on the other side [Boll Weevils] if we can't stick together on our own side. In unity, there is strength. We are still a minority party, but if we stick together and begin anew with a new president, we can accomplish great things."[23]

In 1980, the conservative coalition had a test run before Reagan won the presidency. The Republican–Boll Weevil alliance had produced 170 votes, thirty of them Democrats, for a Reagan-style program of deep budget cuts and supply-side, growth-oriented tax cuts. Moreover, smelling Reagan's victory and a chance to increase their leverage, the Boll Weevils formally organized as the Conservative Democratic Forum.

Reagan's basic approach delighted the Boll Weevils. In fact, some were more zealous for budget cuts than Reagan. After Reagan's State of the Union address, Ken Duberstein asked Charlie Stenholm, the Boll Weevil spokesman, "How'd we do? Did the president give you the cuts you were talking about?" Stenholm, a homey Texan from farm country near Abilene, wryly observed, "The president did fine, but I think he's a cheapskate—he could have gone with $10 billion or $15 billion more in cuts."

But House Democratic leaders were not prepared to give up Boll Weevil votes without a fight. Budget Committee Chairman James Jones of Oklahoma, put together a conservative Democratic budget that embraced nearly eighty percent of the Reagan budget cuts. (It had only a one-year tax cut; Reagan's had a three-year cut.) Jones probed

Stockman about chances for a broad bipartisan compromise, but Reagan flatly rejected any deal. "I'm convinced that the American people strongly support my program and don't want it watered down," he declared. In 1981, that strategy paid off, but it was unwise for the long run. By holding out for a total victory, Reagan sowed resentment among moderate Democrats such as House Democratic Whip Thomas Foley, and their resentments later tripped Reagan on other issues.

In 1981, the threat to Reagan's coalition strategy was that some Boll Weevils wanted to stick with their party if possible, and they were attracted to Jones's budget. In early May, the Boll Weevils had a showdown meeting, one after another praising Jones's package as a reasonable, workable compromise, consistent with Reagan's goals. But a rift opened: Phil Gramm, a firebrand free-market Texas conservative, insisted that Jones's budget "flunked" criteria the Boll Weevils had adopted earlier: no deficit bigger than Reagan's, no less savings on the big benefit-entitlement programs, and no less money for defense.

"It's time to draw the line in the sand," Gramm insisted. "I'm voting against this budget even if I have to stand alone, like the people at the Alamo."

Amidst the shouting that ensued, John Hightower reminded Gramm of Texas history: "Remember what happened to those people who crossed the line at the Alamo. They all got killed."

Marvin Leath, a third Texan, challenged Hightower. "The other people who didn't cross the line also got killed," Leath coldly countered. "Only no one remembers their names. By God, I'm going with Gramm. So there'll be two of us."[24]

The Boll Weevil revolt was launched, but it was unclear whether Reagan could capture enough defectors to win.

In the game of political persuasion, the Reagan White House took no chances. It played outside as well as inside politics, and it played hardball. Stockman lobbied his former allies in the Boll Weevil group. Reagan went public, stirring up popular support with nationally televised addresses. He sharpened the sense of economic crisis, focusing on the gloomy statistics of high inflation and economic stagnation. He bluntly reminded Congress on April 28 that it had been six months since his election and the people wanted action.

"The American people are slow to wrath but when their wrath is once kindled, it burns like a consuming flame," Reagan declared, quoting Theodore Roosevelt. "Well, perhaps that kind of wrath will be deserved," Reagan warned, if Congress resorted to "the old and comfortable way . . . to shave a little here and add a little there." His speech touched off an avalanche of mail to Congress.

For maximum leverage, the Reagan team mounted a massive political pressure operation against the Boll Weevils that must go down as one of the most effective grass-roots-lobbying campaigns of any modern presidency. It is an example to be studied by future presidents, for Jim Baker and Lyn Nofziger, Reagan's key political strategists, had properly fathomed the significance of the breakup of the old congressional power structure. No bargain could be struck with a few leaders; there were no barons in the House to deliver the southern Democratic votes. The defections of Gramm and Leath did not guarantee support of other Boll Weevils. That would take heat from back home, and the White House turned up the flame.

The concept was not new, but the Reaganites applied it with new sophistication. Under Lyndon Johnson in 1965, White House political chief Larry O'Brien had mobilized Democratic activists across the country to pressure Congress to pass Johnson's Great Society legislation. But the Reagan operation had new technology—computerized lists of campaign insiders and contributors to House members—so it knew precisely who could squeeze congressional waverers. In addition, Reagan had a better-organized national mass movement than any previous Republican president. In fifteen years of crisscrossing the country, he had built a network of conservative activists. His campaign volunteers were still in place, itching to show their muscle.

Reagan's political operation was masterminded by Lyn Nofziger, a rumpled California conservative with a black Charlie Chan mustache and goatee; and Lee Atwater, a bright, intense, young South Carolinian (later campaign manager for George Bush in 1988). Nofziger and Atwater ran a political blitz in fifty-four swing congressional districts, forty-five in the South. They used scare tactics on congressmen by getting their campaign contributors to threaten to oppose them in 1982 if they bucked the president now.

The Reagan team, working like a presidential campaign, generated direct mail, phone banks, radio and television ads, and sent out top speakers to put heat on targeted congressmen. They mobilized the Republican National Committee, Republican Congressional Campaign Committee, National Conservative Political Action Committee, Moral Majority, Fund for a Conservative Majority, and political action committees linked to the U.S. Chamber of Commerce, National Association of Manufacturers, Business Roundtable, American Medical

Association, and scores of groups interested in cutting federal spending and taxes.

"The premise of the whole operation is that political reforms and the impact of media have made it so that a congressman's behavior on legislation can be affected more by pressure from within his own district than by lobbying here in Washington," Atwater told me during the operation. "The way we operate, within forty-eight hours any congressman will know he has had a major strike in his district. All of a sudden, Vice President Bush is in your district; Congressman Jack Kemp is in your district. Ten of your top contributors are calling you, the head of the local AMA, the head of the local realtors' group, local officials. Twenty letters come in. Within forty-eight hours, you're hit by paid media, free media, mail, phone calls, all asking you to support the president."[25]

It was the nice-cop/tough-cop routine, with Reagan working the soft sell and his minions the hard sell. In the ten days leading up to the first House budget vote on May 7, Reagan met personally with a dozen Republicans and sixty Democrats, while the grass-roots blitz hit them from back home. A typical target was Butler Derrick, a South Carolina moderate Democrat.

"I've been here since 1974, and I've never seen an operation as well orchestrated as the way the Reagan administration has handled this budget battle," Derrick told Haynes Johnson of *The Washington Post.* "The president invited me down to the White House one morning with five other congressmen. It was very pleasant conversation. There wasn't any pushing. He was giving his views—kind of good-guy conversation."

Back home, Derrick said: "They have apparently gone back through my contributor files and pulled off prominent conservatives that have contributed to my campaign over the years and also probably have supported the national Republican ticket. They have gotten in touch with them. It's been very effective in the business community . . . probably sixty or seventy percent of the large-business people in my district have contacted me. And of course, I have had many small businessmen contact me. I don't recall that I've ever been lobbied quite as hard from the district."[26]

The Reagan hardballers jolted other congressional fence-sitters. Ronnie Flippo, an Alabama Boll Weevil, got hit with a call from then-Governor Forrest "Fob" James, a pro-Reagan Democrat. Dan Mica, another Democrat from Palm Beach, Florida, was pressured by his former campaign manager. "I had a call, too, from a local mayor, a

Democrat very active in the party and associated with liberal causes, and he asked me to vote with the president," Mica revealed. "That surprised me that they would get to him."

"Reagan had a big enough stick so that all we had to do is organize the support and no Boll Weevil would stand up to him," Atwater later boasted.[27] Indeed, Derrick, Mica, and Flippo were among sixty-three Democrats who voted on May 7 for the Reagan budget.

Similar lobbying tactics were used on liberal northern Gypsy Moth Republicans. "I got a call from Henry Kissinger," Manhattan's Bill Green told me, "and when I started arguing about the budget numbers, Kissinger said, 'I don't know anything about that. Let me just say that after four years where we have lost international leadership, it's important that we be seen as having someone who can lead the country. It's important from an international point of view that the president win this first key vote.' "[28]

That intense lobbying, behind Reagan's personal appeals, gave the new president a sweeping victory, 253–176. Every single Republican voted for his package. That was an extraordinary feat.

Johnson-Style Horsetrading

Forming the coalition is only the first step; sustaining it long enough to lock up final legislative victory is much harder. In the American system, victory rarely ends the fight—it marks the start of the next battle. This time, it was not Reagan's charm treatment or the grass-roots blitz that rescued the Reagan coalition. It was old-fashioned, Lyndon Johnson–style barter politics: buying votes by doling out favors—what some call "running the soup kitchen." Rule number eight of the coalition game is: *Bend at the margins and wheedle votes where you can; don't get hung up on ideological purity.* Horse-trading is the way the battle is fought in the final clinches.

Reagan's battle was not over because entrenched committees of Congress resorted to intricate, arcane maneuvers to undo the effects of that first budget vote. The reconciliation measure passed required implementing by regular committees, and they had a field day with the fine print of the legislation, molding it their way. The White House was shocked to see conservative Republicans and Boll Weevils engaging in legislative chicanery along with liberal Democrats, all protecting their favorite programs. Many of the "cuts" enacted were empty numbers that reduced spending only in theory.

"Sabotage!" shouted David Stockman, himself no slouch at fudging budget numbers and tilting estimates when it suited him. In June 1981, he accused the committees of shady bookkeeping, false arithmetic, and phony cutbacks. Pro-Reagan Republicans and the Congressional Budget Office estimated that House committees cut $55 billion for the year 1984, but Stockman reckoned only $25 billion was valid.[29]

In alarm, Stockman persuaded the president that he had to send another whole budget to Congress. "The committees have broken faith with the first budget resolution," Stockman told Reagan in mid-June. "It could jeopardize your entire economic program. We have to make a major fight to restore the provisions in your first budget. If you want to balance the budget in '84, you can't live with the cuts they've made."[30]

Stockman secretly prepared a massive new reconciliation measure, a line-by-line substitute for the congressional bill. It was a high-handed tactic, because Congress—not the budget bureau—is supposed to draft money bills. It meant rejecting the congressional bills and making a fresh effort. Reagan went along with the plan, still counting on one up-or-down vote and the pull of his own popularity to preserve his coalition.

But it was now summer and the Reagan coalition had begun to fray. Moral appeals were not enough to restore it. The White House was short of votes. Gypsy Moths were threatening to bolt unless some modest programs favored in the urban East and Midwest were restored. New York's Bill Green wanted $50 million more for the National Endowment for the Arts, a higher cap on Medicaid for the poor, and guaranteed student loans provided to more families; Jim Leach of Iowa sought $100 million in family planning; Carl Pursell of Michigan wanted $30 million for nurses' training. Others wanted $100 million more for Amtrak and Conrail, another $400 million in energy subsidies for the poor, restoration of economic development grants, and so on. The White House paid their price to get their votes for the final budget package.

The Boll Weevils were demanding sweeteners, too. Georgia Democrats got state-owned cotton warehouses exempted from a new user fee. Some $400 million in cuts of veterans' programs were restored to satisfy Mississippi's Sonny Montgomery, a powerhouse for veterans. Louisiana's John Breaux was lured aboard with a promise to revive sugar import quotas to protect his home state.

"I went for the best deal," Breaux crassly admitted afterward. He maintained his vote had not been bought but—he confessed—"I was rented."

The bargaining was like stock-market bidding, right to the wire. Ironically, to get votes, Stockman had to trade back to Congress things he had objected to in mid-June. The final budget was such a rush job that it reached the floor *after the debate began,* and it mistakenly listed the name and phone number of a congressional staffer—"Rita Seymour, 555-4844"—which someone had scribbled in the margin of a draft copy. Clearly, no one had proofread the retyped version.

The critical test vote came on procedure, not substance. House Democratic leaders tried to outmaneuver the power of Reagan's single up-or-down vote. They figured Reagan's budget would be tougher to pass if it were broken into five packages, forcing Gypsy Moth Republicans and Boll Weevil Democrats to be counted on separate votes—and some of those votes were bound to be unpopular back home. Hoping to break up the Reagan coalition that way, Democratic leaders fashioned a procedural rule which divided the budget into five separate packages.

It was an ingenious tactic, but it backfired, because members wanted to avoid the wrath of constituents who were telling them: Cut the budget, but save our programs. One big vote spared House members that dilemma; it was politically easier to handle. (Rule number nine of the coalition game: *Make votes politically easy.*) Once the big package of cuts was fixed, members could not both cut the budget and save local programs; they had only one choice: yes or no. Since budget cutting was generally popular, they could justify swallowing some distasteful cuts. The Democratic tactic would expose members to cross-pressures to both cut and save programs; so it rankled many House members. As a result, the Gypsy Moths backed Reagan and just enough Boll Weevils defected to beat the Democratic procedural rule by the perilous margin of 217–210. A shift of four votes would have beaten Reagan and radically altered the outcome.

That procedural vote on June 25 was little understood by the public, but it demonstrated the power of technicalities: The vote on the "rule" (for handling the budget bill) framed the ultimate vote on the substance of the budget (one vote or five separate packages).

Defeat of the Democratic rule, moreover, solidified Reagan's coalition and shattered the Democratic leadership's control of the House. It cleared the way for Reagan, on the very next day, to win a similarly close victory on the biggest budget cuts ever enacted at one time.

The pattern of coalition building for Reagan's big tax-cut bill in 1981 was similar—except that it was easier for the Reagan team. Cutting taxes is inherently more popular than cutting the budget, because in budget cutting some voters' favorite programs are going to be cut. Also, Reagan had developed such an image of invincibility from his budget victories that the main issue in the tax fight became not whether but how much to cut. Reagan once advocated a thirty-percent cut in individual tax rates over three years, later dropped to twenty-five percent. Business interests and orthodox Republicans insisted on big business tax cuts through an investment tax credit, generous depreciation write-offs, and favorable tax-leasing arrangements. Boll Weevils wanted cuts in estate and gift taxes; those from Texas, Louisiana, and Oklahoma also wanted to protect oil-depletion allowances.

Democratic leaders argued that a three-year tax cut was very dangerous because it was likely to produce huge deficits—and they were right, as many Republicans later admitted. But playing to win back the Boll Weevils, Dan Rostenkowski, House Ways and Means Committee chairman, tried to outbid Reagan. He never offered more than a two-year cut in individual tax rates, but in other areas, he was very generous. There were so many giveaways that at one point, David Obey, a liberal Wisconsin Democrat, wisecracked, "It would probably be cheaper [for the government] if we gave everybody in the country three wishes."

Stockman later reckoned the tax-cut package would cut tax revenues by $2 trillion over a decade, but substance got lost in the scramble to win. "The only real numbers being counted were the votes," Stockman later lamented. "Questions of tax policy and fiscal impact had long since been forgotten. When the final showdown came, it took the form of a raw struggle for political power and control of the House—and the nation's revenue base was the incidental loser."[31]

Once again, Reagan prevailed handsomely, leaving a political model for others on how to mold a majority coalition. Any coalition requires a single central idea with wide appeal, and Reagan's central core of convictions about less government and lower taxes provided a unifying force for Republicans. Reagan rallied the country and was masterful at courting Congress in twos and threes, while his lieutenants used reconciliation and the grass-roots blitz as instruments of persuasion. And for all his unyielding rhetoric, Reagan showed the tactical wisdom of horse-trading in the eleventh hour in order to paste his coalition together. Tip O'Neill paid him tribute by complaining that "every time you compromise [with Reagan], the president gets eighty percent of what he wants." And Reagan retorted: "I'll take eighty percent every time, and I'll go back the next year for the other twenty percent."

After a period of eroding party ties, Reagan held the Republicans in Congress together with remarkable unanimity. Only one of 192 House

Republicans had voted against him (James Jeffords of Vermont), and Senate Republicans had gone down the line several times. Democrats were awed. Gary Hymel, a top aide to O'Neill, told Ken Duberstein, Reagan's House liaison man: "What I admire most about you guys is not the Democratic votes. It's the fact that you got every single blessed Republican on a major substantive vote. That's almost unheard of."[32] It was true: Neither Eisenhower, nor Nixon, nor Ford had achieved that party discipline. Such solid Republican voting had not been equaled since the hardheaded rule of "Czar" Joe Cannon, Republican Speaker in 1910. Nor was Reagan ever again able to muster such Republican unity.

August 1981 was the high tide of Reaganism. In just eight months Reagan had pushed through Congress the most massive tax cut in American history and budget cuts far larger than anyone had imagined. Given the monumental deficits that ensued, it was a pyrrhic victory. But that August, political Washington was not heeding economics; it was stunned by Reagan's triumphant coalition making. His was a performance to match Woodrow Wilson's after his first election, FDR's at the start of the New Deal, and Lyndon Johnson's in 1965.

"The system works well at only one time—right after a landslide election," James Sundquist, a presidential scholar at the Brookings Institution, observed. "This is one of those brief periods in our history when a president comes riding a great tide of personal popularity."[33]

1985: The Lost Coalition

Sometimes even that great tide meets with heavy resistance. Nine days before Christmas 1985, President Reagan had to make a desperate pilgrimage to Capitol Hill. House Republicans had mutinied against his efforts to put together a coalition for tax reform, the domestic centerpiece of his second term. Five days earlier, they had stunned the Reagan White House by blocking a tax-reform bill from coming to the House floor for debate. Reagan's strategy was in tatters. Now, it required Reagan's personal plea, on bended knee, to revive the bill and to prevent his becoming a lame-duck president less than a year after his landslide reelection.

That personal journey was a mark of Reagan's tenacity and his personal pull with Republicans, because his appearance turned around just enough House Republicans at the last moment to extricate him from disaster. But the fact that Reagan had to go to Capitol Hill in such desperate straits underscored his troubles in playing the coalition game as his second term began. Instead of having a secure Republican base, Reagan spent most of the "honeymoon year" of his second term fighting—not with Democrats, but with Republicans. The summer in 1985 was consumed by angry clashes with Senate Republicans over the budget, and late in the year he faced the siege of House Republicans unhappy with tax reform. As the humorist Will Rogers once quipped, "Republicans have their splits right after the election and Democrats have theirs just before an election."

Other presidents, too, fought more with their own partisans than with the opposition—Lyndon Johnson, for example. After Johnson marshaled large Democratic majorities for his domestic program in 1964 and 1965, he faced an onslaught a few years later on the Vietnam War, clashing more with Democrats than Republicans. Senate Foreign Relations Committee Chairman William Fulbright of Arkansas was an unrelenting critic of the war. I remember the dramatic moment in 1967 when Robert Kennedy, then a New York senator, publicly broke with Johnson over Vietnam, deepening the Democratic rift. And of course, Senator Eugene McCarthy of Minnesota humiliated Johnson by nearly upsetting Johnson in the 1968 New Hampshire primary.

Reagan's Republican critics in 1985 were neither as brazen nor as hostile as Johnson's Democratic dissenters. But even with a forty-nine-state landslide, Reagan floundered in forming a governing coalition. That was a paradox, because Reagan's sweeping reelection victory in 1984 stirred expectations that his second term would start with legislative triumphs to match his first year in the White House. For three years he had actually been on the defensive, accepting tax increases in 1982, 1983, and 1984, seeing his budgets ignored, making compromises on Social Security, and suffering the cutoff of aid to Nicaraguan *contras* in 1984. A big reelection landslide was Reagan's chance to recoup, but his governing coalition was gone.

Reagan's experience tells a lot about second terms: They are notoriously hard, even on presidents who win landslide reelection. Woodrow Wilson, so triumphant in his first term, could not win Senate approval for his cherished League of Nations in his second term. Franklin Roosevelt, towering in his first term, was battered in his second term for his plan to pack the Supreme Court. He saw the New Deal slow down. Harry Truman, after reelection in 1948, became mired in Korea. Two decades later, the nation was so riven by the Vietnam War that Lyndon Johnson was politically crippled and dared not seek another term. Richard Nixon, who had made an opening to China and agreements with Moscow in his first term, was forced to resign in ignominy because of the Watergate scandal and other abuses of power. Eisenhower alone seemed to escape the painful rhythm.

Reagan's enormous personal popularity was not enough to protect him from the fateful pattern. He won individual issues as Jimmy Carter had, but the winning coalition formula of 1981 would not fall into place until the very end of 1985 with tax reform—and then just barely.

As president, Reagan was different from 1981. He was slow to engage forcefully with Congress, and he ignored some of his own lessons in coalition making, enshrined in 1981. A governing coalition needs a rallying idea, and in 1985 Reagan did not have one. His reelection victory was so personal that it did not build support for his program in Congress. Moreover, far from wooing other politicians assiduously, as he had in 1981, he spent much of his time attacking Congress. He waffled between proclaiming his role as captain of the ship of state and trashing its crew. That approach sometimes makes for good reelection strategy, as Harry Truman proved in 1948 by lambasting the Republican Congress. But blame-game tactics rarely make for sound coalition building after the election is over.

What is more, Reagan did not readjust quickly to the changed composition of Congress. In 1985, the political balance in the House did not permit Reagan's natural instincts for partisan hardball; he did not have enough Republican votes to revive his ideological majority of 1981. Circumstance dictated bipartisan coalition making, and that meant concessions on the budget, which Reagan resisted making. Belatedly, he tried bipartisanship on tax reform. But in the first hundred days, he was less effective, less focused, and less activist as a leader than in 1981, and that afflicted his whole second term.

As a result, the coalitions of 1985–86 emerged largely from below, from Congress, rather than from the president. As the new Senate majority leader, Bob Dole performed a near miracle in forging a Senate coalition for a courageous deficit-cutting budget in 1985, only to be cruelly cut down by Reagan and his new chief of staff, Don Regan. Two freshman Republican senators (Phil Gramm and Warren Rudman) produced a dramatic plan to balance the budget in six years. That forced a shotgun coalition: all sides pressed into an unwilling and unsustainable political marriage, less out of mutual interest than out of fear of being blamed for the mounting deficits (which nonetheless climbed higher in 1986). Reagan won a precarious House victory on tax reform, but on that too he was eventually rescued by Congress—by the brilliant coalition making of Oregon's Republican Senator Bob Packwood, in the spring of 1986.

It was an odd record for an immensely popular president. And the lessons of Reagan's failures at the start of his second term tell as much about the Washington power game as his first-term successes.

First, Reagan was still extremely popular, but his clout with other politicians—his presidential capacity to inspire love and fear—had diminished. In 1981, the Republican surge (Reagan's election, the Republican takeover of the Senate, and a gain of thirty-three House seats) had loomed like a political Matterhorn over Washington. Reagan had clout, in part, because other politicians believed his coattails pulled other Republicans into office. There was an X factor that magnified the numbers because Republicans were feasting on dreams of a larger political realignment. But in the elections of 1982 and 1984, Reagan had failed to translate his personal popularity into Republican dominance in Congress. In 1985, the X factor was working against Reagan; the Republican dream of realignment had faded. Republican numbers in the House had fallen back from the 1981 level. As voters gave Reagan his landslide, ticket splitting reached all-time highs in 1984. Either purposely or perversely, the voters denied Reagan a firm grip on Congress.

Some congressional Republicans blamed the president and his lieutenants for the Republican failure to make larger congressional gains in 1984. The Republicans had lost twenty-six House seats in the recession-dominated midterm elections of 1982, and they had looked to Reagan help to win back those twenty-six seats plus a few more for insurance, in order to lay the foundations for a new conservative coalition in Congress. They won only fourteen seats, and House Republican Leader Robert Michel accused the Reagan team of focusing on their own landslide, to the neglect of Congress.

"As good a communicator as the president is, he really never, in my opinion, joined the issue of what it really means to have [favorable Republican] numbers in the House," Michel complained the morning after the election. He was especially irked that while polls had shown Reagan far ahead of Walter Mondale, the president's strategists did not use more of Reagan's time to help Republicans win House seats. Reagan's aides contended that Reagan's appearances did help Republicans, but Michel argued that Reagan's campaign stops would have been chosen differently if the House races had been top priority. He was furious, for example, that Reagan's men were so bent on winning a fifty-state sweep that Reagan spent his final campaign day stumping in Mondale's home state of Minnesota, instead of boosting congressional Republicans elsewhere.

"Look at that last thing, going up to Minnesota—at the last minute, unannounced," Michel fumed to the Associated Press. "That had to be only an attempt to make it a clean sweep, fifty states. . . . Here the son of a buck ended up with fifty-nine percent and you bring in [only] fifteen [more Republican House] seats."[34] (Actually, it turned out to be only fourteen seats.)

Not only did these results irk Republicans, but they gave Democrats less reason to fear Reagan. Back in 1981, some of Reagan's coalition-building clout had come from the fear of Boll Weevil Democrats that Reagan would campaign against them unless they played ball with him. They were especially afraid when Reagan was on the ballot, pulling voters into the Republican camp. But in 1984, only a handful of House Democrats had lost; the far more salient fact was that 192 House Democrats had won reelection in congressional districts that Reagan had carried. In short, they had weathered Reagan's influence with the voters; the threat of a Reagan lobbying blitz was less intimidating in 1985 than four years earlier.

Reagan's second problem in forming a coalition in 1985 was even more his making: He wasted the political honeymoon period after his reelection landslide. Even without a Republican sweep, Reagan could have capitalized on his huge vote to create momentum—if he had quickly set firm priorities. But he moved slowly to frame his agenda and he allowed the belated shake-up of his White House staff. By late spring, he had lost his best chance to pressure Congress on the tide of popular goodwill. When he sent up his budget for 1986 in February 1985, Senate Republican leaders pronounced it "dead on arrival." In the House, it got only one vote (Jack Kemp's) out of 435.

Third, Reagan's credit and credibility were higher with the country than with politicians in Washington, for he was often out of step with most congressional leaders—Republican as well as Democratic. Congress and Reagan differed on priorities. In the campaign, Reagan had vaguely promised "more of the same," but virtually all factions on Capitol Hill, except the Young Turk Republicans in the House, were disillusioned with his budget formulas. Overall legislative support for Reagan's proposals had fallen from eighty-two percent in 1981 to sixty-six percent in 1984 and would fall further, to just under sixty percent in 1985.[35]

In part, this declining support reflects the passage of time. It is easier for a president to get support of his measures in the first term, before voters have seen their impact and voiced unhappiness with the consequences. But by the second term, members of Congress know public reactions and are loath to offend more voters. In Reagan's case, the tax cuts of 1981 and the explosion of military spending created a $212 billion deficit in 1985 that demanded fixing, and there was no popular solution. Reagan had been the pied piper in 1981, but in 1985, many in Congress found his tune far less seductive.

Senate Republican leaders as well as House Democratic leaders disagreed with the president on the deficit and taxes, on farm subsidies, protectionism, voting rights, the MX missile, and South Africa. By 1985, congressional leaders had reached a consensus that the deficit was the nation's most urgent issue, and the most sensible way to control it was to make everyone sacrifice: to slow defense spending, to freeze growth of the big social-entitlement programs, and to raise taxes. Reagan was the odd man out. He was against raising taxes, against slowing defense, and he waffled on freezing entitlements.

The fourth problem, largely of Reagan's making, was the weakening of the vital White House connection with Republican congressional leaders—a crucial ingredient of the 1981 coalition. The new link in 1985 was less reliable and less expert. The Bakers were gone: Jim Baker had become Treasury secretary and Howard Baker had retired. Howard Baker's successor was Bob Dole, a far more independent-minded, outspoken majority leader with presidential ambitions.

On the day of his election, November 24, 1984, Dole signaled his independence from the White House, making clear that his top priority was leading the Senate, not carrying the president's flag. His message, delivered in Kansas twang, was more cooperative than William Knowland's to Eisenhower, but not as loyal as Howard Baker's to Reagan. Dole would follow his own political instincts and call his own shots.

"We're going to retain the Republican majority in '86—that's our agenda—and at the same time support the president's program where we can," Dole told reporters in the Capitol. "We're members of the Senate. We have our own institution."

At the White House, a similar shift away took place. The president did not warm to Dole as he had to Howard Baker. They rarely met, except for congressional leadership meetings, and rarely talked on the phone. "We've had a couple of private meetings," Dole told me in 1986, "but my view is we're all adults and big boys, and we ought to be able to do our job and shouldn't have to bother the president with my problems, and they shouldn't have to bother me with theirs."[36]

But the president can set the tone of that relationship, and it was Reagan's mistake not to form a more personal tie with Dole. That cost him when it came to coalition making.

What is more astonishing is that Reagan let Jim Baker leave the pivot point for coalition making as chief of staff. Reagan seems not to have grasped how much that would affect his relations with Congress. Apparently he did not fathom how coolly Don Regan, his new chief of staff, was regarded on Capitol Hill or how Regan's limited political experience would hurt the presidency in this key spot. Regan was more confrontational than Jim Baker, and he had less feel for what would work with Congress and what would get the president into trouble.

"Don Regan is a financial genius," said Tip O'Neill, another blunt Irishman who, like Regan, had grown up in Cambridge, Massachusetts. "He thinks he knows everything about everything, and he has no political common sense whatsoever. No political knowledge, political talent, no political intuition."[37] A harsh view, but common on Capitol Hill.

As Regan took over, he did not properly reckon the power of the mainstream House Democratic leadership or the need for a consistent bipartisan strategy on major issues. Nor did he understand how to weave together rival Republican factions in one coalition. As a result, both Regan and the president swung like yo-yos between Republican factions, creating confusion and fury among Reagan's natural allies.

What saved the president in 1985 and 1986 was his own popularity and tenacity and the fact that his top domestic priority—tax reform—wound up in the hands of Jim Baker as Treasury secretary. For Baker, unlike Regan, had the good sense to see that the 1984 election results meant the president could pass major legislation only by forming a bipartisan coalition with mainstream Democrats. Baker held the president to that strategy—not without difficulty—and shepherded Reagan to his one major victory in 1985, on the tax bill.

The Republican Rift

The most serious obstacle to Reagan's second-term coalition making was the open political rift in Republican ranks, the shattering of the Republican unity that had been the cornerstone of his 1981 coalition. Any presidency, like any political party, is an umbrella for very different streams of partisans. Reagan's magic in 1981, typical of a popular leader at peak strength, was to hold these contending factions under one tent. But his success in 1981 had been a one-shot achievement. In 1982, House Republicans had split virtually down the middle when Reagan agreed to a major tax increase to check the rising deficit. Alliance with the Democrats carried that day, but the rift among Republicans had been opened.

After Reagan's reelection, there was little to check Republican rivalries. Republicans were looking to the future—beyond Reagan; the scramble to succeed him was under way. And that reality played havoc with Reagan's coalition making.

The two chief Republican protagonists, who personified competing camps in Congress, were Senator Bob Dole and Congressman Jack Kemp. The factional struggles between them had burst into the open at the Republican National Convention in Dallas, where their camps clashed over the party's platform. Kemp's well-organized Young Turk Republicans had won out. Factional warfare was suspended during the 1984 campaign, but once the campaign was over, it resumed.

"The post-Reagan era began the morning after his reelection," lamented Ed Rollins, then White House political director.

Dole and Kemp were natural rivals, both eyeing the presidential nomination in 1988. Their competition had all the electricity of a bristling personal feud. For years they had been taking swipes at each other. Talking about tax reform to college Republicans, Dole cracked that Kemp, known for his blow-dried-for-TV hair, wanted to take a business deduction for his hair spray. Kemp threw back a belittling zinger at Dole; he joked that in a recent fire, Dole's library had burned down and "both books" were lost—and that Dole had not finished coloring one of them.

"Kemp and Dole don't like each other," said a moderate Republican. "It's ad hominem, not just what they stand for."

Unquestionably, they grated on each other, but their political confrontation sprang less from personal frictions than from their bedrock disagreement over the proper economic philosophy, long-term strategy, and political priorities for the Republican party. They represented different philosophies, different interests, different regions.

And different political styles: Kemp is new breed, Dole is old breed; Kemp is preeminently an outside politician, Dole is preeminently an inside politician. Within the Republican party, Kemp represents the New Right and Dole the old guard. Theirs is a generational difference, though age is not the key—Dole is in his mid-sixties and Kemp is in his early fifties—the key is the different images they project.

Tall and handsome, Dole gracefully carries the scars of personal misfortune. During World War II, he was raked with machine-gun fire while leading an infantry charge on a German gun position. His right arm and shoulder were shattered, his neck was broken, and he lost a kidney. Some doctors feared he might not walk again or even survive, but he endured thirty-nine months in hospitals and a slew of operations. Even now, Dole plunges into crowds with his good left arm out shaking hands and his right arm held back, as if in a sling, and he has trouble buttoning shirts.

Kemp, by contrast, has the aura of a golden boy, born with a silver spoon. He exudes star quality, the electric energy of a former Super Bowl pro-football quarterback for the Buffalo Bills and the San Diego Chargers. His blow-dried, brush-backed sandy hair evokes the all-American good looks of Jack Kennedy, and Kemp happily nurtures that subliminal linkage—with refrains about American renaissance, an echo of Kennedy's 1960 campaign theme.

But the main difference between Dole and Kemp—the one that afflicted Reagan's coalition game in 1985—is ideological: Dole is an archetypical orthodox, budget-balancing Republican preoccupied with the deficit, and Kemp is the ardent apostle of the supply-side creed that derides traditional austerity and gives far higher priority to tax cutting and economic growth.

As the Senate Republican leader, who worked his way up the committee system, Dole is a supremely talented inside politician. Trim and witty, Dole also has a natural flair for television, the outside politician's medium. But he has taken seriously the less glamorous task of making government work and he has won respect from Democrats as well as Republicans. As Finance Committee chairman, charged with handling tax bills, he was taunted by Newt Gingrich, a firebrand Young Turk ally of Kemp, as the "tax collector for the welfare state." In rebuttal, Dole ridiculed Kemp's faction as a minority with the luxury of guerrilla tactics and airy theorizing but without the responsibility of governing. During a parade of prospective Republican candidates in Michigan in 1986, Dole took a jab at Kemp: "Some people deliver speeches. Some deliver votes. It's the votes that count."

As a traditional, farm-belt Republican from Kansas, Dole was deeply concerned by deficits and felt that tough antideficit policies were realistic and responsible. He protected his farm constituents, but he was gutsy enough to propose unpopular measures such as an oil-import fee, or freezing pensions, and then face the objections head-on. On a swing through his Kansas farm country in 1985, I heard him defend a controversial one-year freeze in Social Security cost-of-living adjustments that most other politicians did not dare to tackle so directly.

"It's not because we're out after senior citizens," Dole told an audience at Fort Hays. "We froze everything: veterans' pensions, civil service, the military, black lung, every federal pension program. It's pretty hard to freeze the others if you don't freeze them all. We also froze defense spending for a year. I understand Social Security is a very hot political issue. Some people in office won't even mention it. I think we have to mention everything. You have to reconcile everybody's problems."

Kemp is poles apart from Dole. What Dole proclaimed as realism on the deficits, Kemp attacked as wintry pessimism. He kept insisting that the old guard were "on the wrong side of the issue," trying to make Republicans the party of austerity and gloom. Deficit politics, Kemp boomed, are "root-canal politics"—painful political dentistry, sure to alienate the voters and destined to perpetuate Republicans as the minority party.

When Kemp first won his congressional seat from Buffalo in 1970, he ran as a traditional Republican, but to survive in a blue-collar, industrial, and largely Democratic district, he realized he had to change. "I realized there was no way I could get reelected as a balance-the-budget-at-all-costs Republican," he told me, flying to a campaign outing in Pennsylvania. "The old approach of the Republican party, which was associated in the public mind with the country clubs and big business, was not going to win in Buffalo. I was looking for change. I had to survive. It was very pragmatic. I had to be more jobs-oriented because my district was interested in jobs."[38]

Ever since his political conversion to growth-oriented, free-enterprise economic advocacy, Kemp's goal has been to broaden the reach of the Republican party with a new message. He does not fit political stereotypes. He is a self-proclaimed populist in the party of big business, a Republican partisan who deals with Democrats (Senator Bill Bradley of New Jersey and Congressman William Gray of Philadelphia), and an entrepreneur's son who urges his party to go for blacks and blue-collar voters.

In eighteen years in Congress, Kemp has become leader of the House Republican Conference, fourth in line. But he is no power broker, no legislator's legislator. Critics call him a show horse, not a workhorse. Actually, Kemp has worked in recent years at crafting legislation and developing alliances in Congress. But at heart, Kemp, like Reagan, is a political salesman: a marketer of ideas and themes, ricocheting his influence off the media and the voters back into Congress. Kemp is intense and evangelical, words gushing out like a waterfall as he preaches a gospel of growth, patriotism, and optimism. In 1981, he had an important influence on policy, pushing Reagan to go for a major tax cut.

In 1985, Kemp's formula was to beat the deficit by growing out of it, and that meant putting tax reform ahead of budget cutting and not squeezing too hard on popular programs. "Tax reform has the potential of a realigning issue," Kemp proclaimed, suggesting it could bring a tidal shift of blue-collar voters and others to the Republican party. Kemp urged Republicans to "stress the economics of growth rather than stability, the politics of hope rather than preservation." That put Kemp at odds with Dole—and left White House coalition makers caught in the crossfire.

Coalition in Search of a Leader

President Reagan was tantalizing and elusive in his handling of the budget coalition in 1985—and that is ultimately why that coalition fell so far short. Reagan preferred rhetorical leadership to active leadership. His constant theme was the need to make war on the deficit. But when his own budget was set aside by Congress as unrealistic, Reagan blamed congressional procedure for the lack of progress. His cures for the budget morass were a constitutional amendment to balance the budget and presidential power to veto individual "line items" (programs) in the budget. But the main obstacles were not institutional; they were political. A real attack on the budget deficit required a bipartisan approach. Reagan could not get either Democratic or Republican leaders in Congress to agree with his formula for curbing the deficit; and he would not agree to theirs.

For starters, Reagan left it to Bob Dole to forge a coalition—one that involved high political risks for Senate Republicans. Reagan gave Dole his blessing. But when Dole produced an impressive antideficit package, Reagan backtracked and sabotaged it, rather than using it as leverage for forging a grand coalition with Speaker Tip O'Neill.

Dole filled the leadership vaccuum left by Reagan because he saw political danger for Republicans in Reagan's economic program. He knew that while the public in 1985 credited Reagan and Republicans with producing economic recovery, Republicans would probably be saddled with blame for the deficits if the economy turned down—and there would be dire consequences for Republican control of the Senate in 1986. So Dole, who is a political gambler, a poker player who improvises as the cards are dealt, boldly staked his own fortunes on making deep cuts in the 1986 budget, hoping to reduce the risks of an economic downturn.

Dole's strategy was both courageous and risky. First, the task of taming the deficit was monumental, and he was going after $50 billion in budget cuts—more than Reagan had gotten from Congress in 1981. Second, his strategy meant getting the president to accept restraint on defense spending and probably some tax increases, both of which Reagan opposed. Third, Dole had to risk the ire of millions of voters for he was convinced that the deficit could be curbed only with a one-year freeze on COLAs for Social Security and various middle-class pension benefits. With Don Regan's help, Dole got the president to swallow his package, even the unpleasant medicine on the Pentagon budget and Social Security.

Dole's performance in the Senate was a tour de force in coalition building. Any coalition needs the cement of a driving idea, and in the Senate—especially among Republicans—it was passionate concern about the deficit. On that base, Dole built a coalition Lyndon Johnson-style, horse-trading with various groups and ultimately with individual members, vote by vote. Conservatives recoiled at pinching the Pentagon, but they liked Dole's entitlement freeze. Dole corralled moderates and farm-state senators by using big billions cut from the Pentagon to keep alive programs they wanted, such as Amtrak and the Small Business Administration, and by adding funds to other programs such as education, research, and programs for the handicapped. He wooed farm-state Republicans by plugging in modest funds for farm credits, farm exports, and rural electrification.

Like Howard Baker, Dole used Senate rules to give him control of the climactic debate, and Democrats again yelled "Steamroller." Dole's tactical weapon was an "amendment tree"—a structure of Republican amendments that effectively blocked Democrats from changing Dole's package. It granted wavering Republicans a chance—with Dole's advance approval—of offering amendments to go on record as protecting their pet programs. But when that show was done, Dole wiped out their amendments and restored his package with one final amendment—one up-or-down vote, as in 1981. Then Dole pressured Republicans to toe the line; he called Vice President Bush home from Phoenix to be ready to break a tie. And he lined up Pete Wilson of California to come from the hospital after an emergency appendectomy.

Dole's high-wire act reached a climax in the wee hours of May 10. He got forty-eight Republican votes, plus Democrat Edward Zorinsky. Pete Wilson was rolled through the Senate's double doors in a wheelchair, clad in hospital pajamas and a brown bathrobe. To standing cheers, he cast an aye vote. Bush broke the tie. At 1:48 A.M., the budget carried 50–49, including both a freeze on Pentagon spending and on Social Security COLAs.

Senate Republicans were euphoric; their coalition had cut the budget deficit by $56 billion. Coming back from Europe, President Reagan proclaimed it a "victory for spending restraint and no tax increase." Some might attack specific provisions of the Senate package, Reagan said, but he endorsed it—underlining "the importance of sending a signal, not only to the world but to our own business and financial communities, that we are determined to deal with [the] deficit problem."

But suddenly, the Republican coalition had a problem at its core: the President and Don Regan. A major White House push was needed to work the budget through the House, where neither Democrats nor Republicans liked Dole's tough budget. Instead of taking charge, or striking a grand compromise with O'Neill, Reagan became a reluctant, passive leader. On Regan's advice, he began zigzagging. They let go the partnership with Dole.

Dole and Regan were not natural allies. In the first term, Regan as Treasury secretary and Dole as Finance Committee chairman had worked on tax bills together. They respected each other's force and intelligence, but temperamentally, they mixed like oil and water. They were two strong-minded, outspoken personalities. During his sixteen years in the Senate, Dole had developed more of a sense of teamwork and of what was politically possible than Regan had. But neither one was disposed to take a back seat.

"I think there's a basic sense of distrust between Dole and Regan," one well-placed Republican commented to me at the time. "The personal chemistry is bad. The Jim Baker–Howard Baker relationship was two guys who could sit down and figure out a compromise and how to get there. The Dole-Regan relationship is two guys who are stubborn and neither one wants to bend. So they keep hitting head-on."

Privately, Regan spoke with Irish bluntness of Dole as brilliant: "One of the sharpest minds in Washington," he told me, "and one of the sharpest tongues. At times he can be acerbic. He can be impatient. At other times, he can be the most congenial person in the world. He gets mad—not mad, that's the wrong word—he gets upset if the president doesn't devote ninety percent of his time to the budget."[39]

Dole blew hot and cool publicly toward Regan. In private, some of his comments were unprintable. Dole became enraged by what he saw as Don Regan's double cross on the budget.

While the budget was bogged down in the House, Kemp moved to cut the White House away from Dole. Kemp and his faction had no enthusiasm for the Senate's deep budget cuts. Moreover, Kemp had no interest in seeing Dole's budget cutting succeed while his tax reform languished. Kemp hit Dole's formula at its most vulnerable point: the freeze on Social Security COLAs.

Secretly, Kemp and Trent Lott, the House Republican whip, met with Regan on June 27 to sink the Dole package. Their specific goal was to get Regan to have the president back off his support for a one-year freeze on Social Security COLAs and other entitlements. Without that freeze, the Dole budget package collapsed; about half its budget cuts were gone. Kemp and Lott told Regan that House Democrats would never accept the COLA freeze, and House Republicans were afraid to support it for fear of handing Democrats a 1986 campaign issue. It was an obvious point that Regan should have anticipated before backing the Senate Republican package. Now, belatedly, Regan flip-flopped. He agreed with Kemp and Lott—without telling Dole. The president took the same zigzag, secretly abandoning Dole and the Senate coalition.

Reagan still got a chance to create a bipartisan coalition, picking up where Dole had left off, by striking a deal with Tip O'Neill. The issue came to a head on July 9, a sweltering, sticky afternoon, when Reagan met under the oak tree on the South Lawn with bipartisan leaders from both houses. The group sat around in armchairs on the lawn—some in shirt-sleeves, Reagan kept on his jacket. White House stewards passed iced tea and Coke. Tip O'Neill sat next to Reagan, and Dole was a couple of chairs away. Their talk was drowned out from time to time by airliners making the final approach to National Airport.

The test issues at the oak-tree meeting were the Social Security freeze and whether to go for some kind of tax increase now being pushed by some Senate Republicans. O'Neill had recently made a gesture toward compromise, a willingness to increase taxes on Social Security benefits. But Reagan was haunted by the 1984 campaign, almost as if he had lost—not won—it. Democratic attacks had made him gun-shy on Social Security, and Kemp's prodding nudged him to move away from freezing COLAs. And obviously Mondale had gotten under Reagan's skin with his campaign declaration that he—Mondale—was honest enough to tell the country that beating the deficit required a tax increase and that Reagan would have to do it, too, but Reagan would not admit it. That hot July afternoon, Reagan lashed out at Mondale.

"I answered Mondale," Reagan declared. "When Mondale said what our country needs is a tax bill, I said, 'There'll never be a tax bill as long as I'm president of the United States.' "[40]

Then wheeling on O'Neill, he trumpeted: "Do you think I am ever going to have a tax bill? Never! Do you think I'm going to let Mondale say, 'Look, I told you I was right?' Never!"[41]

On Social Security, there was confusion about precisely what Reagan said because a plane droned over at the critical moment. Reagan said he did not want to touch Social Security. Dole thought he heard Reagan add "assuming" House Democrats could come up "with some offsetting savings" elsewhere in the budget.[42] But O'Neill, sitting next to Reagan, told me he had not heard any such qualifier and happily told reporters that the president "has taken Social Security off the table."

The president had dealt a severe blow to the Republican coalition and to chances for big reduction in the deficit, though both Reagan and O'Neill professed interest in a modest cut. Senate Republicans erupted in fury, feeling betrayed. Warren Rudman protested that they had taken the risk of "kamikaze pilots only to be shot down by our own leader." Dole remarked bitterly: "You know, we were left hanging out there. We marched up the hill and across the ravine, just right up to the cliff, and then they pushed us over."[43]

Still, so many senators were alarmed by the skyrocketing deficit that they gave Reagan another chance to form a bipartisan coalition. To make him feel less vulnerable to partisan attacks on taxes and Social Security, three Democrats joined three Republicans to devise a new Senate plan with major impact—to trim deficits over three years by $300 billion. It had everything—cuts in social programs, a one-year freeze on defense and Social Security, and $59 billion in new revenues. No taxes were specified, but the idea was to delay the tax-indexing plan adopted in 1981—putting off a tax reduction rather than raising tax rates, to meet Reagan's objections to a tax increase. But when they put their package to Reagan in late July, the president was so angered that he slammed his glasses on the table.[44]

Dole and Budget Chairman Domenici tried one final tack: a five-dollar-per-barrel fee on oil imports, thinking that was not literally a tax. Dole, Domenici, and Paul Laxalt were leaving Dole's office to seek a House-Senate compromise with Tip O'Neill on July 29, when the phone rang. It was President Reagan: thumbs down on the import tax. Dole went to see O'Neill anyway, thinking a bipartisan deal would be irresistible to Reagan. But he did not reckon on how far the White House would go in slapping him down.

As Dole, Domenici, and Laxalt were talking with O'Neill, White House spokesman Larry Speakes went before TV cameras at 9:28 A.M. to disclose Reagan's phone call to Dole. Reading a statement, Speakes emphasized that Reagan would "not support a tax increase in the form of an oil-import fee . . . a change in Social Security COLAs . . . [or] a change in tax indexing." Chris Matthews, the speaker's press aide, took a news bulletin to O'Neill. The speaker read it and handed the paper to Dole.

"He was absolutely stunned," O'Neill told reporters afterward. "His chin hit his chest."

Senate Republicans seethed. Reagan had torpedoed all hope of significant deficit reduction. Dole gave up. Three days later, a 1986 budget bill passed with Reagan's backing, and except for a freeze on defense appropriations, it was pretty tame. Reagan claimed a big win, but Senate Republicans mocked it as timid. (Officially, the White House claimed its package would lower the 1985 deficit by $40 billion in 1986; in fact, the deficit rose $8 billion to a new record of $220.7 billion.)

Back in January 1985, Dole had seen the storm signals for Republicans. "If we fall flat on the deficit, we're in deep trouble," he told me. "If we come up with some limp little package, we've lost the play." In short, a timid deficit package would weaken the economy and voters would penalize Republican Senate candidates in 1986. Dole's comments were prophetic: The economy sagged, and Republicans lost control of the Senate in 1986, with the economy a factor in pivotal states. Reagan's party paid a political price for his failure to forge an effective budget coalition.

The Pitfalls of Bipartisan Coalitions

On tax reform, President Reagan took the bipartisan approach dictated by the 1984 election results and which generally makes sense for paramount political issues. For the first time on his top-priority issue, Reagan began by reaching for a grand coalition with mainstream House Democrats instead of working from a partisan Republican base and chipping away Democratic defectors. He had entered earlier bipartisan coalitions in 1982 and 1983, during recession, when he had been on the political defensive. He had bowed to congressional pressure for a bipartisan three-year $98 billion tax increase and a plan to fund the MX missile; and he had used a bipartisan commission to fashion a modest plan to put the Social Security system on a sounder financial basis. Now once again, on tax reform, necessity dictated that Reagan strike a bargain with House Democratic leaders. Democrats had a whopping hundred-vote House majority and the Constitution requires tax bills to originate in the House. That meant working through the Ways and Means Committee, which was 2–1 Democrats and more liberal than the House as a whole.

This was a risky coalition game because it put Reagan's Republican base in jeopardy. The administration's partnership with Dan Rostenkowski, Democratic chairman of the House Ways and Means Committee, was bound to grate on House Republicans. Militant Young Turk Republicans regarded Rosty as the archetypal partisan foe. Rostenkowski, from the outset, counted on Reagan to get House Republicans to swallow a bill they were bound to dislike. He was fond of saying that Democrats could not pass a major tax-reform bill alone; it took alliance with a Republican president to get a majority coalition. Jim Baker, too, knew that success depended not only on Rostenkowski's corralling the Democrats but on Reagan's sway with a good chunk of Republicans.

Not only were there old partisan frictions to overcome, but very few Republicans in Congress had much enthusiasm for tax reform in principle. In 1981, Republicans had followed Reagan down the line on his tax bill, but there was a big difference this time. The 1981 tax bill was apple-pie politics; it was all tax cuts. Every individual and every interest group was a winner. But Reagan's 1985 tax-reform bill had losers as well as winners: regions, industries, and individuals who had to fork up more taxes to pay for the cuts of others. He wanted the new tax scheme kept "revenue neutral"—that is, no net gain or loss to the Treasury. The glue for the 1985 coalition was the lure of lowering personal income tax rates for the vast majority of Americans. Reagan tossed out that bait repeatedly, but he had trouble getting skeptical voters to bite. And the lack of popular trust and enthusiasm left Congress hard to convince.

Most congressional Republicans saw tax reform as antibusiness. To lower personal tax rates, the Reagan bill had to get more tax revenues from the corporate side. It rolled back advantages Reagan gave to business in 1981, most importantly the investment tax credit. The elimination of that tax write-off would cost business $100 billion over five years. Other big billions would have to come from changing depreciation schedules or tightening up tax breaks for real estate, insurance, banking, and other business. Picking up these tax revenues made possible a lower corporate tax rate overall, and that appealed to retail and high-tech industries. But the capital-intensive Snowbelt industries, such as steel, and the U.S. Chamber of Commerce were opposed. The Republican talk was that the bill would hurt the investment climate and push the economy toward recession. Jack Kemp, as a longtime advocate of tax reform, was a notable exception; in 1984, he had proposed a flat tax—a top rate of twenty-four percent—claiming tax reform would attract millions of new middle-class voters to the Republican party.

Reagan's constancy and strong engagement was the main difference between the failure of the 1985 budget coalition and the perilously narrow success of the tax-reform coalition in 1985. Reagan did not fight hard for the budget, but he put down his marker on the tax issue and he stuck to his position.

The success of the tax bill had other critical ingredients: Rostenkowski's shrewd bargaining to line up a sizable majority of Democrats; the patient legislative politics of Jim Baker and Deputy Treasury Secretary Dick Darman, whose stroking of Congress and the White House kept the coalition alive when it frayed from tension; and finally, the backing of Speaker O'Neill. In the Senate in 1986, Reagan's bill was literally saved by the ingenuity and astonishing legislative skill of Bob Packwood of Oregon, Senate Finance Committee chairman, who formed an even more genuine bipartisan coalition. In the House coalition, Reagan wheedled Republican votes, and Rostenkowski bargained for Democratic votes; but in the Senate, Packwood engineered support on both sides.

It was Reagan who put the ball in play and kept the game alive at the critical moment in December 1985. His goal was to bring down the top tax rates. In 1981, he had lowered them from seventy to fifty percent and now was pushing to thirty-five percent or below. That helped the rich the most. But Baker and Darman were smart enough to craft a bill with populist appeal—by removing six million poor people from the tax rolls, lowering most individual rates, and taxing corporations more. That made the Reagan bill as "populist a piece of legislation as Democrats could have written," John Sherman, Rostenkowski's press secretary, said admiringly.[45]

Stumping from Oklahoma City to Concord, New Hampshire, Reagan pushed his bill as a tax cut (though some people would pay more). But Reagan's main appeal was an attack on the existing tax code, for the engine that drove tax reform through Congress was tapping anger against the tax system. What made it hard for other politicians to let tax reform die was that killing reform became equated with protecting the despised status quo. As opinion polls showed, most voters did not trust promises of a tax cut. But they could identify with Reagan's savaging the rancid inequalities of the existing tax system as "complicated, unfair, cluttered with gobbledygook and loopholes designed for those with the power and influence to hire high-priced legal and tax advisers."

Reagan's pitch was more likely to move congressional Democrats than Republicans. *Reform* has a ring that appeals to Democrats traditionally; in this case, it had special appeal because *reform* was taken as a code word for shifting a bigger tax burden to business and closing tax loopholes. In fact, the model for Reagan's package had been conceived by Democrats Bill Bradley and Richard Gephardt, back in 1982; Tip O'Neill had urged Walter Mondale to adopt it for his 1984 campaign, but Mondale foolishly declined. But the Bradley-Gephardt bill opened the way to a bipartisan coalition and to Reagan's rough partnership with Rostenkowski, who got Reagan to promise not to interfere with his committee or to comment publicly until the work was done.

In short, the White House and Treasury Department harnessed themselves to Rostenkowski's wagon. They squirmed while Rostenkowski took Reagan's outline and revised it to give it Democratic flavor and to pick up Democratic votes. He raised the corporate tax rate from thirty-three to thirty-six percent and toughened depreciation rules on industry; he added a fourth personal tax bracket at thirty-eight percent (Reagan's top bracket was thirty-five percent) and upped the capital gains tax two points; and he imposed a tough minimum tax on individuals and corporations to prevent them from paying no taxes through deals allowed under Reagan's 1981 bill.

These changes sorely tried Republicans; they had not been happy with Reagan's original plan and they were more unhappy with Rostenkowski's. Moreover, Republicans felt shunted aside, excluded from helping write the tax bill because of Reagan's reliance on Rostenkowski's way of building support mainly among his own Democrats. This strained the coalition, and twice the administration nearly bailed out.

On October 24, the Treasury Department got wind that Rostenkowski had bartered away a $65 billion tax plum (over five years)—full federal tax deductions for state and local income taxes. With the tax bill dying, Rostenkowski used that concession to revive it—to corral New Yorkers and other big-state Democrats to construct a committee majority. Jim Baker had expected Rostenkowski to make only a partial concession, because Baker wanted some of that money to ease the tax burden on business and to appeal to moderate Republicans. Angered by Rostenkowski's secret maneuver, Baker phoned to protest. He chased down Rostenkowski, traveling in North Carolina, and they got into a shouting match. The coalition was in peril.[46]

The next afternoon, Reagan's top team—Jim Baker, Dick Darman, Don Regan, and his deputy, Dennis Thomas, and "B" Ogelsby, the top White House legislative liaison, met at Andrews Air Force Base to decide whether to stick with their bipartisan strategy or to pull out.

They picked the air base for secrecy and also because Regan, returning from the president's speech to the United Nations, was flying on to Augusta, Georgia, for a weekend golf game with Shultz, Bush, and Bush's friend, Nicholas Brady.

Despite their anger at Rostenkowski, Baker and Darman wanted to stick with him, but they warned the others that this was a turning point. "If we're going to pull the plug," Darman said, "we have to do it in the short term." Translated: If the president pulls out now, the blame for collapse of the tax bill can be put on Rostenkowski; but if Reagan waits, he too will bear the onus for failure—if Republicans revolt. After some talk, the Reagan team decided unanimously to swallow hard and keep on with Rostenkowski. "We'll stick with it," Don Regan said. "We're going all the way. We're not pulling the plug."[47]

To show displeasure, Baker and Darman boycotted Rostenkowski's committee sessions, which they had been attending. Even so, the administration kept bending. Reagan could not afford to abandon tax reform; he had made it the domestic centerpiece of his second term. Moreover, Baker argued internally that with all Reagan's other defeats in 1985—the budget, the MX missile, sanctions against South Africa, and trade legislation—Reagan needed a big win. Baker's strategy was to let Rostenkowski's bill pass in the House and then "fix it" in the Republican-controlled Senate. For Baker reasoned (correctly) that Rostenkowski's bill was more liberal than what Congress would ultimately pass.

The High Price of Hesitancy

The political base of any coalition needs careful tending, and Reagan's coalition was eroding at its base. Rebellion was festering in the Republican back benches. A Republican split had been inevitable, given the distaste of some Republicans for any tax reform. On the 1982 tax increase, only half the House Republicans had followed Reagan. This time, Baker and the White House hoped for respectable Republican support, but rebellion was spreading all across the spectrum, among Republican regulars, Young Turks, and even moderates. It was a far wider revolt than the administration expected, and it was fanned by the Treasury Department's closeness to Rostenkowski and by his largely partisan redrafting of Reagan's bill.

House Republicans had been a minority so long and were so frustrated with being ineffectual, that they were acutely touchy about being treated as bit players. They were not only vexed by the substance of Rostenkowski's bill, but they were also outraged at being neglected by their own Republican administration. They began sending letters to President Reagan, warning that tax reform had gone off track. Just as Rostenkowski's version was finally being passed by his committee through the night of November 22, Republican Whip Trent Lott and others pressed the White House not to endorse it. Earlier that afternoon, Reagan had given his approval, but once again he zigzagged with Regan and Dennis Thomas and withheld a public endorsement.

Reagan again paid a high price for hesitancy in backing a coalition partner. In 1981, he had been bold, clear, and constant. But in 1985, he had hamstrung Senate Republicans by welshing on his budget partnership with them. Now his position on the tax bill hung in the balance for several days—while Reagan ducked phone calls from Rostenkowski. Baker at Treasury argued that the president had to stick with his game plan to move the legislative process forward; otherwise tax reform would be killed in its crib. At the White House, Regan and Dennis Thomas equivocated, trying to find ways to placate angry Republicans.

The president's hesitancy merely fanned the Republican rebellion, undermining the coalition. Tax reform had lost momentum. Congress and antireform lobbyists read Reagan's delay as a signal that the president was going to reject Rostenkowski's bill. Young Turk Republicans got hold of a study by the president's Council of Economic Advisers, concluding that the long-run effects of the tax-reform bill were favorable but warning that in the short run, the bill would hasten a downturn. The study, leaked to conservative columnists Rowland Evans and Robert Novak, provided more ammunition for mutiny.

Full-scale insurrection was declared on December 4 at a two-hour House Republican Conference, presided over by Kemp, as conference chairman. The mutiny had more purpose and unity than the Reagan administration. That day, 112 House Republicans voted to instruct their leaders to go all out to defeat the tax-reform bill. All four top Republican leaders, Bob Michel, Trent Lott, Dick Cheney, and Jack Kemp, were against the bill. Cheney accused the administration of "selling out to Rostenkowski and cutting out our own guys" from writing the legislation.

Later that day, President Reagan finally took Jim Baker's advice and urged Republicans to back the process of tax reform. But his statement came too late, and it was lukewarm, obviously the product of conflicting advice and Reagan's personal uncertainty. He had misgivings about parts of Rostenkowski's bill, but it was his only practical vehicle.

One axiom of the coalition game is that in the clinch, the leader cannot flinch. Reagan did. He did not push firmly for Rostenkowski's bill; to keep the process moving, he urged the House to pass that bill or a Republican alternative. In fact, the Republican alternative had no chance. By hedging, Reagan undercut his own appeal and his only chance for a coalition. His appeal did not stanch the Republican mutiny. The next evening, House Republican Leader Bob Michel, a born loyalist, told me, "This is a personal trauma for me to be going against my president, but I just can't go for this bill."[48] It hurt industry in his Illinois district. For a congressional party leader to oppose a bill his president wants is fatal to the president.

As the message finally sank in at the White House, Reagan and his aides began warning House Republican leaders that the Republican party would suffer badly if they let down the president. Trent Lott, the torchbearer of revolt, was called to the White House and emerged to report defiantly, "I told him, 'Mr. President, if you're going to lie down with the dogs, you're going to get fleas.' "[49] So much for Reagan's cooperation with the Democrats. In the final two days before the House vote on December 11, 1985, Reagan personally telephoned Lott and Cheney to urge them not to lead the fight against the bill, even if they voted against it themselves. But both, vying to succeed Michel, wanted to be in the van of rebellion; neither would make Reagan the promise he sought.

That should have been ample warning; nonetheless, the president's men were ambushed. Somehow they expected Reagan's final appeals to prevail, but they had started to push too late and they were outsmarted. Lott and Cheney, two very clever legislative tacticians, saw the weak spot. Rather than attack the tax bill directly, they attacked the rule bringing the tax bill to the floor. In the House, every bill requires a rule to set terms of debate. No rule, no vote for the bill, the bill is dead. The White House did not expect an ambush on the rule.

Lott excluded White House lobbyists from the Republican whip meeting, leaving the White House in the dark. Attacking the rule got some extra votes because some House members like to play their votes both ways to appeal to opposing constituencies. They will vote *against* the rule to get credit with foes of the measure for having tried to stop it (but hoping that other members will pass the rule); then these same members will vote *for* the bill, to get credit with its supporters. The Lott-Cheney tactic worked brilliantly. The rule was beaten 223–202.

The jolt to Reagan was that 164 House Republicans had voted against him, and only fourteen for him. The process was dead unless Reagan could revive it.

Speaker O'Neill declared that Reagan would be a "lame-duck president" if he could not muster at least fifty Republican votes for a rule bringing the tax bill to a vote.

The endgame of this bipartisan coalition was striking because, unlike other Reagan coalition operations, the White House could not dole out goodies to buy support from alienated Republicans. Rostenkowski had already used the soup-kitchen approach; now the tax package was fixed. It took moral suasion and appeals to Republican self-interest to save the bill. For six days, the Reagan team—Baker, Darman, Ogelsby, Thomas, and Regan—begged for Republican votes, listening to House members vent their fury, appealing to them not to cripple their president and hurt their party and themselves in the process.

Baker and Darman used one well-tested power-game ploy to lure back some rebels: Lott and Cheney wanted no compromise, but Michel, like other Republicans, was stunned to see Reagan humiliated, and wanted to help him. So did Kemp, who needed tax reform kept alive as the banner for his presidential bid. But Kemp and Michel required some fig leaf to justify Republicans' switching back to Reagan's side. The ploy used by Baker and Darman had worked well on other tough votes, such as the AWACS sale to Saudi Arabia in 1981 and various *contra*-aid votes. With Kemp, they crafted a letter containing pledges from Reagan to placate House Republicans. If they would let Rostenkowski's plan pass, Reagan pledged to pressure the Senate for a better version. He promised to veto any bill with an individual tax rate over thirty-five percent and lacking a $2,000 personal exemption (a Kemp proviso), and he made some nice-sounding but spongy promises about protecting incentives for capital-intensive industries. In congressional lingo, that provided "cover" for vote switchers.

But the key to reviving the tax-reform coalition was to change the issue—from the contents of the tax bill to saving the president. Not only was Reagan immensely popular with Republicans, but they were counting on him to help them in the 1986 elections. It was stupid for them to mortally wound him now, and the White House played that theme hard.

Reagan himself was the trump card. In a week of relentless lobbying, the final move was Reagan's journey to Capitol Hill to plead for support. It was a big gamble. Failure to produce the fifty votes O'Neill demanded would have permanently disabled Reagan. But he had no choice; he was already wounded. Except for Kemp, the House leaders did not really want Reagan at their conference, because that trapped them between loyalties to their president and to their own troops. But the White House insisted, knowing Reagan's emotional pull on other Republicans. They also knew it was vital symbolically for the president to make a pilgrimage to his members. That gesture helped salve the wounds of neglect.

The fifty-minute session in the Rayburn Office Building crackled with tension. Reagan said little. He made no opening speech—to avoid any appearance of lecturing. Mostly, he listened as House members vented their spleen at Rostenkowski's bill and at being cut out of the bargaining, and he promised to "keep in better touch in the future than we have in the past." He admitted disliking parts of Rostenkowski's bill, but he pointed out that killing it would "doom our efforts." And if the Senate did not make improvements, he promised to use his veto.

On the spot, Kemp broke with the rebellion and announced he would "vote for the bill to keep the process going." After the session, a secret poll showed forty-seven votes with Reagan. By that night, Reagan's men had found their fifty votes.

Events unfolded with surprising swiftness the next day. Seventy Republicans voted for the rule to bring up the tax bill; defeated just six days before, the rule now passed by a large margin, 256–171. That cleared the logjam for consideration of the tax bill, and it passed *by voice vote without any debate* in a moment of total Republican confusion. After the routine voice vote, the normal procedure was for Republicans to demand a roll-call vote. But the Republican leadership was so disorganized after the rule vote, no one made a move. Before Republicans knew what happened, the action was all over. The next day, Republican backbenchers accused their leaders of conspiring to avoid a roll-call vote. Michel denied it, insisting he had voted for the rule to help the president but had wanted a chance to speak and vote against the tax bill because it hurt his district.

Kemp was the target of heavy fire. He had gotten caught in a squeeze—between his dream of using tax reform to bring about political realignment for the Republican party and his leadership position among House Republicans opposed to the Rostenkowski bill. Kemp got squeezed between the inside game of influence in Washington and the outside game of running for the presidency, with tax reform as his banner.

For days, Kemp's own Young Turks (Vin Weber and Newt Gingrich) charged him with betrayal, and with greater interest in his presidential ambitions than in his role as a House leader. They charged him with having violated the Republican Conference instructions ordering the party's leaders to do all in their power to defeat the bill. Kemp parried, saying he had met that obligation by voting against the first rule, and then by getting Reagan's promise to veto an unsatisfactory tax-reform bill.

"We have to decide whether we're going to be a business party or a people's party, whether we're going to be a party of tax breaks for corporate America or whether we're going to be a party that is aimed at all the people," Kemp replied to his Republican critics. Much later, he told me: "That was a key moment in the history of our party. Tax reform has never been popular in the Republican party and I see it as a big issue, a realignment issue."[50]

In fact, Reagan had barely won a patched-up victory in the House. This was not the stuff of realignment. The Republican rebellion and Reagan's obvious dependence on Democratic support, on Rostenkowski and O'Neill personally, had undercut claims that tax reform was a Republican-created boon to the middle class.

For coalition building, the long-term lesson was that the original base must be protected, in this case a bipartisan base. Knowing the risk of losing hard-line probusiness and supply-side Republicans, Reagan's team should have been doing more to stroke and satisfy Republican moderates earlier in the game. But Rostenkowski made it tough, because he insisted on Reagan's noninterference and because his idea of the coalition game was actually creating two separate partisan coalitions: his on the Democratic side and Reagan's on the Republican side. The problem was that Rostenkowski's way of winning Democrats made it harder for the White House and Treasury to hold many Republicans. Rosty did not appeal to some higher good to rally both sides; in only a few cases did he really draw Republicans into the process, and provisions used to gain Democratic support went down hardest with most Republicans, especially Reagan's partisans.

A Genuine Bipartisan Core

The real genius in forging a more genuine bipartisan coalition for tax reform turned out to be Bob Packwood, the maverick moderate Republican who became Finance Committee chairman in late 1984. More than any committee member except for Democrat Bill Bradley, Packwood mastered the substance of the tax bill. But for several weeks, he lost control of the bill in his committee, and neither President Reagan nor Jim Baker could rescue him. Various special business interests had gotten senators to add one provision after another to protect them; the bill had lost its reform flavor and its appeal. Don Regan told me that by mid-April 1986, the White House regarded the tax-reform bill as dead in the Finance Committee because special interests had overwhelmed Packwood.

Alarmed by his predicament, Packwood suddenly reversed field. Although business interests kept pretty much of what they had already gained, Packwood outflanked his committee by reaching for a more daring reform on individual tax rates than either Reagan or Rostenkowski had attempted. He chose one central concept to overcome special interests, excite popular support, and revive the notion of reform; it was precisely the kind of bold maneuver needed to pull together a coalition, for any successful coalition requires a single, fairly simple driving idea to attract support from a variety of factions: In 1981, Reagan's budget bill rode on the idea of cutting government; his 1981 tax bill rode on the idea of cutting taxes; Dole's 1985 budget bill rode on cutting the deficit; Reagan's tax bill, on cutting top individual tax rates and making business pay; and Rostenkowski's tax bill, on cutting middle-class tax rates and making the rich pay.

Packwood electrified Congress by going Reagan and Rostenkowski one better. He proposed to cut the top individual tax rate from fifty percent—not just to thirty-five percent as Reagan had proposed, but to twenty-five percent. He would finance that rate by raising $50 billion over five years through shutting down tax dodges for the rich and by raising another $150 billion over five years by ending the special capital gains tax rate, another boon to well-heeled investors. This was the stuff for a very broad coalition, for it appealed to both political extremes. The basic concept was so stunning that it attracted right-wing conservatives as well as liberals and moderates. The liberals had long wanted tax loopholes closed and conservatives liked driving the tax rates way down to twenty-five percent. After some initial press scoffing, Packwood's plan—borrowing heavily from the earlier Democratic bill of Bill Bradley and Dick Gephardt—had a magnetic effect on Congress.

In putting together his coalition, Packwood was ingenious enough to form a bipartisan core group with Democrats such as Bill Bradley, Daniel Patrick Moynihan of New York, and George Mitchell of Maine; moderate Republicans such as himself, John Chafee of Rhode Island, and Jack Danforth of Missouri; and a right-wing conservative such as Malcolm Wallop of Wyoming. As Moynihan told me, it was the millionaires—Chafee, Danforth, and Bradley—who were most fed up with the old tax loopholes. With a bipartisan core at the outset, Pack-wood avoided the kind of partisan revolt that took place in the House.

As it turned out, the tax books would not balance unless the top individual tax rate was taken up eventually to twenty-eight percent (with a hidden thirty-three-percent rate added later). Each rise caused some hesitation. But the sudden promise of bringing the top rate below thirty percent captured the popular imagination and generated unbeatable momentum in the Senate—the same coalition ingredients that had worked for Reagan in 1981. Packwood deftly worked the "soup kitchen" to dole out favors to gain more votes, one by one, and suddenly there was a bandwagon effect. His bill got unanimous approval from the Finance Committee; it sailed through the Senate. And after some long bargaining with Rostenkowski, a modified Packwood plan got passed by Congress.

In this final legislative round in 1986, President Reagan was not a central player—certainly not the coalition leader. He was mostly at the sidelines, encouraging Packwood and working near the end to make sure the House Republicans did not upset things. Actually, it is not surprising that a moderate Republican such as Packwood, rather than Reagan, had taken the lead. Grand coalition politics come more naturally to a moderate, centrist Republican such as Packwood than to Dole, a more partisan Republican, or to Reagan, an ideological conservative. A centrist such as Packwood lives by compromise, throwing his weight first to one flank and then the other. In this case, Packwood pulled the two flanks to the center. Reagan was very lucky, for his own strategists did not know how to rescue the tax bill. Packwood not only brought it back to life but redeemed Reagan's promises to the House Republicans.

What Packwood demonstrated, as Reagan himself had done in 1981 with his budget and tax cutting, was that the vision of a simple idea—in this case a dramatic cut in personal tax rates—was enough to overcome the opposition of special interests. To make the tax coalition work, it took that vision, some masterful committee bargaining by Rostenkowski as well as by Packwood, plus the tenacity and flexibility of Jim Baker and Dick Darman in improvising the politics of the bipartisan coalition, and Reagan's tenacity. Whatever the issue, any future president will need these same basic ingredients to pull together a governing coalition across party lines—as our system so often requires.

14. The Opposition Game: Fighting, Swapping, and Remodeling

I had to be tough. I had to be what they call bitterly partisan.

—Speaker Thomas P. O'Neill, Jr.

In the pantheon of twentieth-century Democratic politicians, Sam Rayburn stands for many as the model speaker of the House. Rayburn helped Franklin Delano Roosevelt in 1941 extend the prewar draft and enact many wartime measures. Rayburn helped Dwight Eisenhower in 1955 pass the Formosa Resolution, formally throwing American protection over the Chinese National Government on Formosa. Rayburn gave young Jack Kennedy a vital hand in 1961 in curbing the power of the House Rules Committee, the obstructionist bastion of conservatives. During forty-nine years in the House starting in 1913, Rayburn came to symbolize authority and cohesion. Rayburn, son of a Confederate cavalryman from Flag Springs, Texas, was physically intimidating: stocky and bull-like, with a strong, bald skull, penetrating eyes, and a barrel chest. He was known for a bristling temper, scolding younger members or punishing them like a schoolmaster. To his troops, he seemed stern, remote, imposing, powerful.

But the Rayburn legend is a bit misleading, for with presidents and other major power brokers, Rayburn was more accommodating than his wary scowl suggested. When Rayburn became speaker in 1938, Franklin Roosevelt was worried that Rayburn was too cautious by nature and delivered him a patronizing pep talk, lecturing Rayburn that "it is better to go down fighting than it is to accept defeat without fighting."[1] Over the years, senior committee chairmen sometimes defied Rayburn; he repeatedly shied away from dramatic confrontations with the Rules Committee, often acquiescing when it killed bills that he or the president wanted. And Rayburn worked at collaboration with the White House, no matter which party was in charge.

During the presidency of Dwight Eisenhower, Speaker Rayburn and his fellow Texan, Senate Majority Leader Lyndon Johnson, became renowned for cooperation with the Republican administration. They profited by the appearance of collaboration with the popular Eisenhower, who was a national hero and mostly a nonideological, nonpartisan president. As my colleague John Finney of *The New York Times* recalled, Johnson was fond of pulling from his pocket a card with a list of legislative achievements and bragging, "Look what I've gotten done for Ike."[2]

As leaders of the opposition, Rayburn and Johnson practiced bipartisanship—with a definite partisan twist. Unlike the Opposition leader in the British Parliament, who leads a minority, Rayburn and Johnson had real power; they led majorities in both houses. They knew Eisenhower needed them. They would go to the president's living quarters in the White House every few weeks and, in Johnson's homey image, "sip bourbon and branch water with Ike." The president told them what he wanted, and they would tell him the most he could expect from Congress. Basic deals were struck. Back on Capitol Hill, Rayburn and Johnson would shunt aside Democratic alternatives to Ike's pet legislation. Their tactic was to take White House bills (a massive highway act, a civil rights bill), leave the Republican label on them, and then remodel the contents to give them Democratic flavor. That was their way of playing the opposition game: cooperating and remodeling. Seen from the partisan 1980s, that was a halcyon period of bipartisanship.

Whenever a party loses the White House but controls one or both houses of Congress, its congressional leaders have a choice of opposition game. They can go for Rayburn-Johnson-style collaboration with the White House, or they can take on the president in head-on confrontation. After Richard Nixon's election in 1968, for example, House Democrats under Speaker John McCormack fought Nixon tooth and nail on domestic spending. Nixon's defiant stand that he did not have to spend all the funds that Congress voted for social programs left

McCormack and company little choice but to fight to protect the institutional powers of Congress. The showdowns over federal spending grew so heated that Congress finally passed the Budget and Impoundment Act of 1974 to force future presidents to abide by congressional appropriations.

Changing the Role of Speaker

When Ronald Reagan took over the presidency in 1981, Speaker Tip O'Neill had a choice of strategy, and his decision assumed even greater importance for the Democratic party than Rayburn's role under Eisenhower. For in Eisenhower's day, there had been Democratic leaders in both houses to share national party leadership. But in 1981, with the Republicans controlling the Senate, O'Neill stood alone as the nation's top-ranking Democrat, second in line of succession after the vice president.

O'Neill was suddenly thrust into performing as the voice of opposition, as spokesman as well as strategist for the Democratic party for six years—except during four months in 1984 when Walter Mondale was Reagan's official Democratic challenger. This high-profile role was not a function for which O'Neill, an old-fashioned, behind-the-scenes legislative tactician, had been trained. But circumstance demanded that O'Neill change, and he did; in the process, he altered the office of speaker, modernizing it for the media era. This Irish pol, long shy of cameras, became a far more visible national figure, better known to ordinary people than Rayburn and earlier speakers had been. His increased visibility and popularity gave him more leverage in the opposition game. At first, O'Neill was far outclassed by Reagan, but before he retired in 1987, O'Neill had fared surprisingly well.

In 1981, O'Neill had ambivalent feelings about how to play the opposition game; his strong partisan instincts were tempered by reverence for the presidency and the weakness of his political position. "I am the Opposition," O'Neill liked to thunder. But O'Neill had been tutored by Rayburn, who revered the nation's highest office; O'Neill picked up that reverence. Many times, I have heard O'Neill refer not merely to "The President" but more elaborately to "The President of the United States."

Nor is this mere verbal genuflection. For as speaker, Tip O'Neill believed it was his responsibility to make the process of government work. Despite the carping of liberal Democrats, he was determined to give Reagan's program a fair chance to stand or fall in 1981 and not to sabotage it by parliamentary obstruction. Early on, he gave Reagan his word that Reagan's main economic program would be voted on by the August recess in 1981. "I'll give you your right," he told Reagan— then adding with partisan exasperation, "but, Jesus, don't push me."[3] That commitment, kept by O'Neill, was a great boon to Reagan's presidency. Had the Democratic Congress given Jimmy Carter as firm a legislative schedule in 1977, Carter's record and reputation would have been far different. The Senate stalled Carter fatally.

Reagan's popularity and the national mood of economic crisis made it risky for O'Neill to obstruct the Reagan program; the 1982 recession could have been blamed on Democrats had they blocked the new president's first move. As a New Deal Democrat, O'Neill opposed many specifics of Reagan's program; but as speaker, he felt a parliamentary duty to give Reagan a fair shot.[4] For example, O'Neill was wary when Reagan phoned him in June 1981 to ask for a second try to toughen up the budget resolution (his first had passed but had been watered down). Nonetheless, O'Neill arranged the second chance. "Hey, I allowed the president of the United States to put it on the table," he declared to me one day. "My power is to stop things. I had all my ultraliberal friends saying, 'Jesus, you shouldn't let the son of a bitch get it on the floor.' But he'd just had an election that he'd won, and that isn't the way democracy works. You give him his opportunity to get his stuff on [for a vote]."[5]

Over the years, O'Neill occasionally joined forces with Reagan, especially when Reagan was in retreat and ready for genuine compromise. They pushed through a tax increase in 1982, agreed on modest changes in the Social Security program in 1983, and worked to pass the tax-reform bill of 1986. On another major issue, O'Neill also went far out on a limb to endorse Reagan's use of Marines in Lebanon in 1983— only to feel betrayed when Reagan pulled them out in 1984, one week after implying that O'Neill was cowardly for suggesting a pullout. In the second Reagan term, O'Neill's tactics became more canny. He let Senate Republicans battle Reagan on the budget and then rammed home Democratic victories on trade and South Africa.

In general, O'Neill's strategy, his way of playing the opposition game, was far different from Rayburn's. O'Neill's hallmark was the politics of confrontation. He fought Reagan on the war in Nicaragua, the budget, military spending, taxes, South Africa, trade. O'Neill is a partisan scrapper by nature and training. His political school had been the highly partisan Massachusetts legislature. In Congress, he stacked committee ratios heavily for Democrats, and he believed that the opposition's main function was to oppose on substance.

Moreover, Reagan left him little practical choice. Eisenhower had made collaboration easy for Rayburn and Johnson because he was *not* a very partisan president. But Reagan initially disdained cooperation; his sharp partisan hardball in 1981 provoked a partisan response from O'Neill. Their joint efforts amounted to temporary truces in running partisan warfare. For six years, the power game was largely animated by the rivalry of these two leaders, who stood at opposite philosophical poles and ruled at opposite ends of Pennsylvania Avenue.

Both had lived through Depression, war, and recovery, and both had reached opposite conclusions. Both came from humble beginnings, and Reagan had started life as a Democrat. But for Reagan, the New Deal was where the Democratic party took the wrong path into deficit spending. For O'Neill, the New Deal was what politics was all about, helping the underdog, lifting the country by its bootstraps. For Reagan, big government is the source of modern America's problems: intrusive, bloated, wasteful, and stifling to individual initiative. For O'Neill, big government had helped build America's strength as a society: succor to the needy, springboard for the aspiring. "I believe it is wrong for the people who have made it up the ladder to pull the ladder up behind them," he declared. "If the success stories of this country needed a helping hand up the ladder, why should we not give the same help to those young people trying to get ahead today?"[6]

Two radically different politicians, yet they sprang from similar humble roots: one from a blue-collar Boston suburb, the other from the small-town Midwest. Both about seventy, they were strong-willed, proud, stubborn in their convictions, and bent on rolling each other politically. And they exulted in the combat.

They cut enormously different figures. Here was Tip O'Neill, a self-proclaimed "old-hat FDR-liberal Democrat," like an aging heavyweight prizefighter, his shaggy thatch of white hair, his massive Hogarthian girth and jowls, big nose, and fat cigar (unsmoked), a walking cariacature of the inside politician. He was poised against Ronald Reagan, the antigovernment Republican crusader with his Hollywood glamour, agile as a middleweight, trim, far younger looking, the political outsider come to do battle with the bureaucracy. They seemed a mismatch: the plodding legislator and the dashing movie hero—the tortoise and the hare—matching halves of the American dream. Reagan limned the magic of opportunity; O'Neill preached the obligations of compassion.

The Reagan quickly crowd discounted O'Neill as an intellectual lightweight, an old-fashioned pol with a gift for gab, the prisoner of an outdated ideology who lacked the smarts and finesse for leadership.

And for liberal Democrats, the early "book"—the political tout sheet—on Ronald Reagan read much the same: another lightweight, a detached, hands-off president, ignorant of much in government, prone to delegate great authority to lieutenants, subject to their manipulations. There was truth in both assessments; they *were* similar. Both relied heavily on staffs; neither was strong on substance. But as political leaders, both were easy to underestimate. Reagan and O'Neill governed from the gut, with a sure sense of self that made each remarkably steadfast, when lesser leaders buckled. Both were enormously resilient, capable of absorbing defeat and rising from the canvas after a knock-down; both were tireless and tenacious. They were thematic leaders, not brilliant strategists or tacticians. Fighting rhetoric was their trumpet call.

For the television audience, the battle over Reagan's program became a heavyweight match of O'Neill vs. Reagan, man to man. Each relished that. Personalizing the clash fit the folksy style of an earthy Boston pol such as Tip O'Neill. To him, Reagan's Beverly Hills address and millionaire friends were as symbolic of Reagan's philosophy and as central to the president's political outlook as O'Neill's own immigrant upbringing and middle-class home were to his New Deal views.

Republicans welcomed using O'Neill as a target. In a 1980 campaign ad, the Republican party had parodied O'Neill as the stereotype of the overgrown federal government. They found a hefty, chortling, white-haired actor for O'Neill's stand-in and showed him getting stranded in a gas-guzzling American car on a highway to nowhere, while a passenger carped, "Congressman, we are running out of gas." O'Neill took the personal hit. But over time, he fought back well enough that Republicans stopped making him a butt of their ads. In the polls, he eventually became as popular a figure as Reagan.

Like Reagan, Tip O'Neill relished the macho battle. Despite sniping that he was over the hill, O'Neill adjusted rather rapidly to the new political game. O'Neill had been raised as an old-breed politician, son of a city councilman in Cambridge, Massachusetts. After arriving in Congress in 1953, he had learned from earlier speakers—Sam Rayburn, John McCormack, and Carl Albert—how to work the inner pathways of legislative politics. But Reagan's video presidency forced O'Neill to adapt; he had to pick up enough of the new-breed media game to compete. What's more, O'Neill pushed congressional Democrats, and the national Democratic party, into new fund-raising and media operations to do battle with the well-heeled, modernized Republican party. From a back-room operator, he became a media figure. He developed the apparatus of the speakership and brought new thrust to the opposition leader's game.

O'Neill's Opposition Predicament

Tip O'Neill began the Reagan era as a punching bag. The Democrats were the elected House majority—243 Democrats to 192 Republicans—but the numbers were misleading because congressional Democrats were demoralized. The 1980 election debacle had stunned them—not just Reagan's victory, but seeing Republican novices beat such prominent Senate liberals as Frank Church of Idaho, Birch Bayh of Indiana, John Culver of Iowa, and George McGovern of South Dakota. In the House, the Republican tide had swept off Democratic Whip John Brademas and Al Ullman, chairman of the Ways and Means Committee. "It was a total shock wave to the party," recalled Kirk O'Donnell, O'Neill's able political strategist.[7] "Like a hapless victim run over by a truck, the Democratic party knows what hit it last November but is uncertain of the extent of its injuries, how long it will take to recover and what shape it will be in once it gets out of intensive care," Dom Bonafede wrote in the *National Journal.*[8]

For the first time in fifty years, Democrats felt that not just their candidates but *their party* had lost an election. The long span of the New Deal had finally expired. Even before the 1980 campaign, many Democrats in Congress had stopped believing in Lyndon Johnson's Great Society programs, widely ridiculed as "throwing money at social problems." As Reagan took office, many Democrats wallowed in unhappy political self-analysis. The Democratic mainstream had lost its sense of direction.

The other side of the coin was Republican cockiness: the belief that a majority of voters were moving into the Republican camp for the long run. By mid-May 1981, Reagan's pollster, Richard Wirthlin, reported the stunning news that Republicans had pulled even with the Democrats—thirty-nine percent of voters polled by Wirthlin called themselves Republicans, forty percent Democrats, and twenty-one percent independents—a phenomenal change from longtime Democratic dominance. In Congress, Republican leaders predicted Democratic officeholders would defect; two did cross over in 1981, Bob Stump of Arizona and Eugene Atkinson of Pennsylvania. Later, Phil Gramm, the renegade Texas Democrat, switched parties, too.

Out in the country, the Democratic party had been hemorrhaging for years, losing the lifeblood of voter support, and the 1980 election displayed the trauma in living color. Since the 1950s, streams of southern white voters had defected to Republican candidates—Eisenhower, Nixon, Reagan—and had been choosing Democratic congressmen closer to the Republican mold than to the national Democratic mold. More recently, ethnic, Catholic, blue-collar voters from the urban Northeast and Midwest had become disillusioned by Carter's economic policies and moved to Reagan in 1980. The old New Deal coalition had finally been shattered after half a century. The Democratic party, as David Broder of *The Washington Post* observed, was "fragmented, frustrated, and politically frightened."[9]

Inside Congress, the power earthquake compounded O'Neill's problems as opposition Leader. Enviously, O'Neill lamented that he lacked the institutional power of Rayburn. In the Democratic disarray of the early 1980s, the legendary power of Rayburn was magnified; it was widely believed that "Mr. Sam" had held the House in the palm of his hand. Rocking back in his swivel chair, Tip O'Neill loved to tell stories about how Rayburn, during a tough vote, would line the front bench of the House chamber with junior Democrats awaiting Rayburn's command on how to vote. Their home-district politics dictated a vote against Rayburn, but they were in his debt for some favor: some committee assignment, some pork-barrel project, some tilt of the legislative process. To hear Tip tell it, Rayburn held them captive as he watched the vote tally, using their votes as he needed them or releasing them if his majority was ample. Richard Bolling, a Rayburn protégé and later Rules Committee chairman, said that O'Neill exaggerated Rayburn's powers.

Nonetheless, it was true that Congress had been transformed since the Rayburn era. The seniority system had been cracked, the committee chairmen had been weakened, subcommittee chairmen had proliferated—and new, independent attitudes had made House members more unruly. Bolling contended that the speaker had gained institutional power at the expense of the committee barons. He pointed out that Rayburn was all-powerful once a bill reached the House floor but Rayburn was often blocked or defied in committee by a coalition of Republicans and conservative Democrats. Speaker O'Neill, Bolling argued, had more power over the Rules Committee—which had often defied Rayburn; more control of the legislative schedule, even in committees; and more say on most committee appointments.[10]

But in Rayburn's day power had been more predictable. Power centers were fewer. Bargains could be struck by a handful of powerful barons, and Rayburn's great personal sway was bolstered by the seniority system that made junior members susceptible to his sticks and carrots. O'Neill had a more complicated task shepherding sprawling factions.

Above all, what made the process of House leadership so daunting was the ethic of political independence prevalent in the 1970s, eroding party discipline. In addition to regional and ideological splits, Democrats suffered a generational divide. The new breed, elected since 1974, were not awed by authority. They took their own importance for granted: They had run their own campaigns, raised their own money, put on their own TV ads, and felt little debt to the national Democratic party or to the speaker. In the old days, local party bosses such as Mayor Richard Daley of Chicago could give orders to the Democratic congressmen from the Chicago region and swing them in line for the speaker. But old-fashioned party machines no longer provided the glue to hold Democratic majorities together. After Vietnam, the political vogue was antiauthority politics.

On the issues, the new breed had a different slant from the old breed. To those in their thirties and forties, the Depression was dim history. Their bêtes noires were inflation, stagnation, and high interest rates. They talked less about unemployment than about deficits, swollen budgets, and waste. Old-breed leaders (Tip O'Neill, Richard Bolling, Danny Rostenkowski) called these newcomers "weak Democrats" who wore the party label but felt no deep loyalty. "There's no love for the party, there's no love for the leadership, there's no love for anybody out there," Tip O'Neill complained.[11]

Finally, O'Neill lacked a crucial element of Rayburn's power in opposition: a Senate under Democratic control. When both houses had been led by Democrats, a Republican president had to make deals with the Democratic leadership of Congress or suffer the consequences. Control of both houses meant the opposition's ability to set the legislative agenda and to rewrite legislation from the White House. Essentially, it put Congress on an equal footing with the president.

"If your party controlled all the committee and subcommittee chairmanships and scheduling on the floor, the president couldn't get very far without at least beginning to work with you," observed Norm Ornstein, congressional scholar at American Enterprise Institute. "Or if he did try to jam things through, he'd get awfully damn bloodied in the process, as we saw with Nixon long before Watergate."[12] Rayburn and Johnson worked Eisenhower as a pair. Democratic leaders had also outnumbered Nixon, two to one. But in 1981, Democrats were the Senate minority, and O'Neill did not get along well with Minority Leader Robert C. Byrd. Against Reagan, O'Neill stood alone.

1981: The Politics of Patience

Shorn of political leverage, O'Neill fell back on the politics of patience. His initial strategy was to retreat and regroup, nurse the party's wounds, give Reagan his chance, and try to pull the disparate strands of Democrats together. In policy terms, O'Neill was realistic enough to see that some retrenchment in social programs was inevitable. Congressional Democrats had begun that in 1979 and 1980, before Reagan's election, but O'Neill wanted to limit it. In political terms, his overriding priority was to protect the Democratic majority in the House and to prevent a national realignment in favor of Republicans. These were high stakes, and O'Neill's defensive reflex obeyed the first law of politics: *survival.*

That meant making a bid to disaffected Boll Weevils, the conservative southern Democrats enamored of Reagan. They had been neglected for years by House Democratic leaders. In 1980, many had run as "anti-Tip" Democrats. Belatedly, O'Neill and then–House Majority Leader Jim Wright tried to make amends in 1981 by putting Boll Weevil Phil Gramm on the House Budget Committee and Kent Hance, another conservative Texan, on the tax-writing Ways and Means Committee. The idea was to rope in Boll Weevils by letting them help draft Democratic legislation. But the move came too late; Gramm and Hance defected and became cosponsors of Reagan proposals. O'Neill felt betrayed, asserting that Gramm had promised to support the Democratic bill on the floor. "He broke his word—no question about it," O'Neill insisted bitterly.[13] And Boll Weevil defections were the speaker's downfall in 1981.

Moreover, O'Neill underestimated Reagan. O'Neill viewed the 1980 election not as a sweeping mandate for conservativism, but mainly as a rejection of Jimmy Carter. "I think there was a small minority, ten or fifteen percent, who voted for Reagan, who really wanted to deliver a mandate," O'Neill declared in May 1981. "But we know why we lost the election. We had an unpopular presidential candidate, inflation was too high, and so was unemployment."[14] He also blamed Carter's Iranian hostage crisis. But O'Neill failed to reckon on Reagan's skill at interpreting the election results as a policy mandate and selling that interpretation to the press and country. O'Neill made a classic opposition mistake: He did not argue vigorously for his interpretation of the election. By default, he left Reagan's claim largely unchallenged.

The speaker also underestimated Reagan's political mastery of Congress, his capacity to charm and intimidate the members and bend them to his will. Initially O'Neill, the veteran, patronized Reagan as another amateur newcomer, another hinterlander like Jimmy Carter, who would have to be taught the ways of Washington. When Reagan paid a courtesy call on the speaker after his election, O'Neill was condescending. "You were governor of a state, but a governor plays in the minor leagues," he told Reagan. "Now you're in the big leagues. Things might not move as quickly as you would like."

The speaker stressed the institutional pride of Congress, especially jealousy over powers regained since the Vietnam War and Watergate. "You know, you've run a state legislature, you've been governor, you can appreciate it," O'Neill opined. "The Congress will really fight for its rights. We want to cooperate. We want to do everything you want. [But] there was an eroding of the power of the Congress. We just got back our powers. They [the members] are feeling pretty good about that right now, and we want to be treated as equals."

"Oh, you know, no problem there," Reagan replied, no hint of his blitz to come.[15]

On Inauguration Day, Reagan was again in the speaker's office, two minutes after the inauguration ceremony. Ebulliently, Reagan gestured at a nameplate for President Grover Cleveland.

"I played him in the movies." Reagan grinned.

"No, you didn't," O'Neill corrected him. "You played Grover Cleveland Alexander, a baseball pitcher."

"Jeez," Reagan admitted. "That's right."[16]

Long afterward, the speaker told me that Reagan had not impressed him early on. Perhaps. And perhaps O'Neill believed that he could afford to let Reagan's economic program pass, confident that it would fail in practice. By Dan Rostenkowski's account, O'Neill promised Reagan in their first meeting "that he would give him all the rope he needed—to either herd the Congress or to hang himself."[17] To me, the opposite seems more likely, for O'Neill seemed cowed by Reagan's popularity, sensing that with Democrats split, he had no effective way to block the high-riding president. Retreat was realism.[18]

In any case, O'Neill did not gear up to fight Reagan in the early months of 1981. The old bulls, the Democratic Committee chairmen, urged him to obstruct the Reagan program; liberals wanted him to counterattack. But O'Neill reckoned that was both wrong and futile. He feared permanent defection by the Boll Weevils if he tackled Reagan hard. "It would have been a schism within my own party," he told me. "They'd have overrun me."[19]

I recall vividly one press breakfast, a vintage O'Neill performance defending the bygone liberal era. O'Neill talked of a program to help dwarfs grow taller. It made him sound hopelessly out of date. "I didn't become speaker to dismantle the programs I've fought for all my life," O'Neill boomed bravely, only to lapse into damaging admissions. "You know, I've been one of the big spenders of all time," he said. "It's true: I am a big spender. . . . Once a doctor came down here to talk to us. He said the average dwarf grows only forty-six inches high, and if we appropriated $45 million for research, maybe that could be increased to fifty-two inches. So I got the $45 million into the budget."

Around Washington, reporters and politicians told and retold the "dwarf story" at Tip's expense.

Nothing epitomized more vividly the contrast between Reagan's ebullient vigor and O'Neill's weary fatalism than the speaker's junket to Australia and New Zealand during the 1981 Easter recess with a delegation of Democrats. Reagan used the recess to lobby Democrats around the country by phone. One was Tom Bevill of Alabama, an important Appropriations Subcommittee chairman who was in O'Neill's traveling group. The president woke up Bevill half a world away, right under O'Neill's nose.

"This is President Reagan, what time is it, and where are you?" Reagan asked Bevill.

"It's three o'clock in the morning," Bevill replied sleepily, "and I'm in New Zealand."

Reagan apologized for awakening him. "Have a good trip and when you get back to Washington, I want you to come in and see me," he said. "I want to sit and talk to you about the budget."[20]

When O'Neill got home, preliminary Democratic nose counts showed Reagan would win the first budget battle of 1981 by fifty votes. Reagan's popularity had soared after his gallant response to the attempt on his life. He was inviting Democrats to breakfast by the carload. An enormous tide of support washed over Congress after Reagan appeared before a Joint Session. "The mail was running 300,000 against 6,000— in his favor—on the Gramm-Latta [budget] bill and the reconciliation," O'Neill recalled. "The papers were saying it was time for a fiscal change in the politics of America."[21]

O'Neill compounded his problems by predicting defeat. "I can read Congress," he told reporters on April 27. "They go with the will of the people, and the will of the people is to go along with the president. . . . I've been in politics a long time and I know when you fight and when you don't."

It was an honest, accurate prediction but it riled other Democrats who saw it as a colossal blunder, fueling revolt. Indeed, on May 7, Reagan swept to victory—gaining sixty-three Democratic defectors. House Democrats heaped opprobrium on O'Neill, like an angry, beaten football team out to lynch the coach. Les Aspin, a Democratic moderate from Wisconsin, delivered the most stinging, seditious commentary in a newsletter to constituents:

> Tip is reeling on the ropes. . . . Tip doesn't understand the explosions that have been going on since November. He's in a fog. Tip is smart enough to understand that there's been a seismic event, but he also realizes that he doesn't understand its nature. He's not part of what's happening and he has no idea where to go. . . . The Democratic Party needs some new leadership and it needs it badly.

Tip O'Neill's Turnaround

The lesson was clear: A passive strategy is fatal for the opposition. It not only produces losses but feeds political depression. Politics is like football: The team with forward motion gets the breaks and gains the extra yardage; the team on its heels loses and becomes dispirited. The moral was contained in Roosevelt's spur to Rayburn in 1938: "Better to go down fighting than to accept defeat without fighting."

Savaged by his own troops, O'Neill abruptly changed his game. To friends and aides, he admitted how badly he had been hurt by that first knockdown, and he switched from passive speaker to opposition point man against Reagan. "Tip took him on," Richard Bolling remembered. "Rostenkowski didn't take him on. The rest of them wouldn't take him on. Jim Wright was scared to death of Reagan in 1981. . . . Tip was getting *no support* from Democratic chairmen, except the black ones."[22]

Like an oak, the speaker bore the whiplash of defeat for his party and weathered the storm for months. The more partisan O'Neill became, the more visible were his defeats. Republican House Leader Robert Michel protested that O'Neill was breaking tradition by leaving the impartiality of the speaker's high-backed chair on the dais to enter the partisan fray down on the House floor. But even if activism meant more defeats, it staked out a Democratic position and built a record.

The first break for the Democrats—giving them an issue to exploit in 1982 and 1984—was a Reagan mistake. A bit too cocky, Reagan sent Stockman's package of Social Security cuts to Congress, only to have them whipped back by the Republican Senate, 96–0. Unsteadily,

Democrats regained their legs, and O'Neill launched his confrontation politics. "I had to be tough," O'Neill said. "I had to be what they call bitterly partisan."[23] Democratic pollster Peter Hart advised O'Neill to stop defending the poor and start attacking the rich as recipients of Reagan's largesse—a gambit that nettled Reagan personally.

Until then, O'Neill had almost never appeared on the Sunday television interview shows. But in early June 1981, as Reagan was moving toward the final budget showdown, O'Neill used a rare Sunday TV appearance to jab at the president. Picking up Peter Hart's cue, the speaker not only denounced Reagan's proposed tax cuts as a "windfall for the rich" but he taunted Reagan personally—saying Reagan did not understand working people because he was surrounded by rich, selfish advisers and probably did not know anyone earning less than $20,000.

It was unusual for a House speaker to throw such a personalized punch at a president—and O'Neill's haymaker bruised Reagan. For ten days the president stewed. Still stinging at his June 16 press conference, Reagan rose to the bait when ABC's Sam Donaldson shouted a reminder of O'Neill's barb, as Reagan was leaving the podium. The president spun around and came back. He recalled his humble beginnings in Tampico, Illinois, and seemed to cast an aspersion on the speaker, implying that O'Neill lived in a worse neighborhood than his family.

"We didn't live on the wrong side of the tracks, but we lived so close to them that we could hear the whistle real loud," he said. "And I know very much about the working group. I grew up in poverty and got what education I got all by myself and so forth, and I think it is sheer demagoguery to pretend that this economic program which we've submitted is not aimed at helping the great cross section of people in this country that have been burdened for too long by big government and high taxes."

Like spectators at a tennis match, reporters watched for the speaker's reaction. It was a turning point. O'Neill was getting divided advice; old-timers such as Leo Diehl, O'Neill's home-state patronage man and inside staffer for decades, thought it inappropriate to spar personally with the president.

"Leave it alone," he recommended.

But Chris Matthews, O'Neill's combative new media adviser, urged O'Neill to hit back. "You got to fight this thing," he insisted. Matthews operated by the maxim that any public accusation—especially one made on television—is assumed to be true unless it is answered. It was weakness to let the other guy get the last word.

"You got to go, Mr. Speaker," Matthews urged.

That warmed O'Neill's Irish blood. Talking that evening with reporters during a dinner for two hundred Democratic party bigwigs, O'Neill struck back. O'Neill invited invidious comparisons with Reagan's Hollywood riches by observing that he himself had neither *left* his own humble beginnings, nor *forgotten* them.

"I still live in the same neighborhood I did as a young boy," O'Neill snorted. Moreover, he insisted the issue was not Reagan's family roots, but his policies—"all geared to the wealthy of America."

As for the charge of demagoguery, O'Neill acted as though such tactics were beneath his high office. "I'm surprised that the president of the United States would make a statement about the speaker like that," he said, regally enshrining himself in the near-papal dignity of the third person singular. "I trust in the future he'll have more respect for the title of speakership."

When a reporter asked about O'Neill's future with Reagan, O'Neill advised: "Well, I'd have to say the honeymoon is over."[24]

It was their first sharp, toe-to-toe exchange.

Rather than hit back, the president phoned the speaker to say that he had not meant to give personal offense. O'Neill replied in kind: "Politics is politics. We may disagree during the day but come six P.M., we become friends."

The truce of manners was for show. Within twenty-four hours, O'Neill was blasting Reagan's "dictatorial" treatment of Congress, and Reagan was on the phone again—with a less friendly message.

Reagan had been persuaded by David Stockman that House Democratic Committee chairmen—"the Politburo of the Welfare State," as Stockman mocked them—had made a sham of cutting the budget. He persuaded Reagan to fire another thunderbolt.

"I want a chance to send some substitute language up there on the budget and have it voted on," the president told O'Neill on the phone. Oiling the machinery, Reagan added patronizingly, "The House has worked hard and done a good job, but it hasn't gone far enough and I . . ."

Irritation and frustration flashed across Reagan's face as the speaker burst in. O'Neill smelled a Reagan power play, and he wanted to head it off. The House committees had done their work, O'Neill insisted, and there was no need for a new resolution.

O'Neill went on to needle Reagan: "Did you ever hear of the separation of powers?"

Then in his booming baritone, O'Neill lectured Reagan on Civics

I: "The Congress of the United States will be responsible for spending. You're not supposed to be writing legislation."

"I know the Constitution," snapped the president.

O'Neill pressed Reagan to "be specific about what you're going to send up. You always talk to me in vague generalities. I don't want to see the Republicans trying to shove something through without full consideration."

"Oh, c'mon, you mean the Democrats," tweaked the president. "I was a Democrat myself, longer than I've been a Republican, and the Democrats have been known to make a few power plays."

The speaker backed off, rather than pursue partisan pinpricking. "Okay, we'll have a look," he said.

Reagan inserted belated congratulations on O'Neill's fortieth wedding anniversary, and the speaker closed by advising him, "Have your people talk to Jones and Bolling [the Democratic chairmen of the Budget and the Rules committees]."[25]

Despite this genial sign-off, the battle was on. In the forty-eight hours from Reagan's press conference to his second prickly phone call, the two leaders had indulged in the mutual needling, the posturing, and the punching that characterized their rivalry. That rapid sequence captures their Irish tempers and their Irish blarney, their little digs and their substantive clashes, their compulsion to combat and their lust for the power game.

O'Neill now wanted to win. The Democratic-controlled Budget Committee crafted a package designed to lure back the Boll Weevils. It cut less from domestic social programs than Reagan's package; it built up defense, but not as much; it cut taxes for one year, not three. It did not beat Reagan, but it lured home more than half of the Boll Weevil defectors. Reagan's victory margin dropped from seventy-seven votes in May to just seven votes in the second budget battle in June.

The speaker was making some headway—playing "me too" on substance and slugging Reagan rhetorically. In the final test of 1981, on cutting taxes, Reagan beat O'Neill again by outbidding the Democrats in passing out tax cuts. O'Neill and Rostenkowski, his tax strategist, warned (correctly) that Reagan's three-year tax cut risked big future deficits and refused to match Reagan. Also by then, the president was harvesting his image of invincibility from earlier victories. On July 29, O'Neill suffered his third major loss of the year, a 238–195 vote for Reagan's tax package. This time, forty-eight Democrats defected.

"Certainly, it was my worst time," Tip O'Neill confessed to me. "He had the votes. He had me licked. . . . I was about as low as anybody could be."

O'Neill would come home and share his pain with his wife.

"I'd come home, I'd be feeling so low. Millie used to say to me, 'Well, d'you think you're right?'

"I'd say, 'Of course, I'm right. I know I'm right in conscience. I know I'm right in philosophy. I know I'm right in my mind. I know I'm right for America.'

"Well, she used to say, 'Hey, put on a clean shirt and a new tie and press your suit, and go out and keep your chin up. Don't let 'em know you're down. That's all."

"And I did. I took that attitude and I kept fighting."

Teaching the Old Dog New Tricks

After that early pummeling, O'Neill learned the new power game. Everyone knew Tip O'Neill as an old shoe—a friendly, clubby backroom man. He liked card games and shmoozing with cronies at the University Club. His wife, Millie, had no taste for Washington and had remained in North Cambridge. So, O'Neill shared a bachelor pad with Congressman Edward Boland, another Massachusetts liberal. They were an odd couple: Boland, trim, quiet-spoken, and immaculate; O'Neill, gregarious, rumpled, and endlessly dieting to get below 250 pounds. Weekends, he would commute to Boston to play golf near his Cape Cod home, his score hovering near 100. And he loved visiting barbershops and factories or swapping small talk with little old ladies down the street. His favorite aphorism—All politics is local—epitomized the parochialism of the House and marked him as a classic old-breed politician.

But Tip O'Neill was surprisingly adaptable; he became a modern politician who changed the ways of the House. He moved the House into the media age by bringing in cameras for live coverage of floor debate in 1979. He developed his own public relations tactics for jousting with Reagan. Despite touting localism, he thought in national terms. He hired pollsters to help plot a national strategy for congressional Democrats. He saw the rising strength of younger-generation moderates and neoliberals (more pragmatic than old-style liberals) and drew them into the leadership. His own thundering liberal rhetoric made him an anchor of consistency for a party adrift; yet, simultaneously he accommodated on both tactics and substance—all to protect his party's precious bastion in the House.

Few people outside Washington are aware of how open O'Neill was in his final years to politicians half his age. That fit his record; he had been an agent of change a decade before. In the early 1970s, he had been a prime mover in changing the seniority system, in opening up House proceedings, and in setting House ethics standards. He had been among the first big-city Democrats to break with Lyndon Johnson over the Vietnam War and, later, to assert that Richard Nixon should be impeached.

As speaker, he readily tapped the talents of the new generation. After the 1980 election debacle, he gambled on Tony Coelho, a hard-driving Californian just starting his second term, to revitalize the Democratic Congressional Campaign Committee. Coelho was so phenomenally successful at fund-raising and modernizing the party apparatus that in six years he jumped way up to the number three job, Democratic whip. On economic issues, O'Neill would set up special task forces to leaven old committee chairmen with younger neoliberals (Richard Gephardt of Missouri, Tim Wirth of Colorado, and Leon Panetta of California). Open to new ideas, O'Neill quickly endorsed the tax-reform plan proposed in 1982 by Gephardt and Senator Bill Bradley of New Jersey, which became the model for Reagan's 1985 tax plan. O'Neill urged Walter Mondale to adopt it in 1984, but Mondale declined.

Institutionally, O'Neill copied the executive branch, building up the speaker's office. He delegated much authority to a talented young staff: Ari Weiss, a slender, bearded, serious-minded Orthodox Jew, who mastered the substance of legislation and the politics of the House; Kirk O'Donnell, a tall, lanky, straight-talking, Boston Irish protégé of Mayor Kevin White, who was O'Neill's sage and able national strategist; and Christopher Matthews, a witty, grinning, wisecracking phrasemaker with quick reflexes, canny media instincts, and a partisan lust for combat. O'Neill was in awe of Weiss, who finished college in three years and whom he treated like a son and a one-man brain trust. He leaned on O'Donnell for broad judgments and foreign policy advice, and he used Matthews to teach him the modern counterpunch. Together, all under forty, they moved O'Neill into the new era.

"In the old days, it was show horses versus workhorses in Congress," commented Thomas Mann, executive director of the American Political Science Association. "If you wanted to get something done, you had to work inside the legislature. And the show horses were just posturing to the public. That's changed. Now, it's seen that playing the media is an important resource in passing legislation. Serious members understand that they have to sell their story outside of the institution to have an impact inside it. They mobilize constituencies and communicate to each other through the media.

"The Democratic leadership thinks long and hard about how to mobilize public support. That is a change, and O'Neill as the point man ought to get credit. O'Neill in effect ushered the House into a much more public posture. The Republicans saw O'Neill as a perfect foil, a perfect stereotype to hit in the media. But in time they found out he could use it, too. He had a way of reaching outside the House, a certain sincerity and consistency in his beliefs that communicated to the public."[26]

O'Neill's most dramatic evolution came in the media game. He became the first media speaker. After his drubbings in 1981, he took on Tony Coelho's media coach—Chris Matthews. "He rolled up his sleeves, those huge arms of his, just sat there, and looked at me like I was a stranger, a guy from a new era," Matthews recalled. "He looked me in the eye and he said, 'Tell me what I'm doing wrong and what I'm doing right. Let's have a little conversation.' And he basically listened. But he said, 'You know, an old dog can learn new tricks.' It was an amazing meeting."[27]

The media game was hard because O'Neill had always been shy of cameras. "They used to say, you know O'Neill, you know he's big and fat and overweight, and he's got gray hair and a bulbous nose and cabbage ears—he's afraid of television," the speaker admitted. "I never was afraid of the television. I always figure—anytime that I'm on television—*I* set the agenda here [in Congress]. I know more about the Congress than anybody up here." But his defensive tone betrayed that old shyness.

As speaker, O'Neill mostly ducked the Sunday talk shows, wary of a half hour's steady exposure. Reporters liked him but knew he fractured grammar. In O'Neill argot, Reagan's talk of a voluntary Social Security program came out as "Social Security volunteer"; the Nicaraguan rebels were not always *contras* but sometimes *contadoras* (nickname of the Central American group of mediators). O'Neill rarely gave the Democratic response to Reagan's nationally televised addresses but tapped others.

But O'Neill's daily press conferences became his platform for attacking Reagan and setting out Democratic priorities. With Matthews crafting darts for O'Neill to toss at Reagan, O'Neill drew a good crowd of reporters. Television crews would catch him in the morning arriving at the Capitol. His jabs at "Beverly Hills budgets" and at other "lemons of Reaganomics" became political staples. By one count, he appeared on the nightly network news shows 120 times a year, three or four times as often his predecessors, Carl Albert and John McCormack.[28]

With greater visibility, O'Neill became a more formidable figure, influencing the House as much by his public line as by institutional powers. Tom Foley, from Spokane, Washington, then Democratic whip, was fond of saying, "Sam Rayburn could have walked down the streets of Spokane without anybody noticing him, but Tip O'Neill couldn't do that." In 1981, the number of Americans who recognized the speaker shot up from forty-five percent early in the year to eighty percent in the fall, according to opinion polls. That did not put him on a par with Reagan, but it gave him national clout to press the Democrats' case.

O'Neill also learned from Reagan's media game that a simple thematic message is vital. Normally, the opposition in Congress is a caterwauling babble. But by late 1981, O'Neill was framing a Democratic counterattack around the social and economic impact of Reagan's program. He was setting up issues for the 1982 election, to protect the Democratic majority and blunt Republican realignment. "Fairness" was the theme that emerged from O'Neill's skull sessions with staff and pollsters. The speaker pounced on Reagan as a foe of little people after Reagan's bid to cut Social Security benefits—an issue which the Democrats milked hard in 1982. In the final 1981 budget vote, two or three dozen Republicans had voted to eliminate the minimum Social Security benefit, and Democrats used those votes against those Republicans in the 1982 campaign. On tax cuts, O'Neill and Rostenkowski had worked to make the Democratic bill better than Reagan's bill for middle-income families with taxable incomes under $50,000. They called that the "$50,000 question," arguing that Reagan's tax bill tilted in favor of the rich. By fall 1982, the Democrats tied these issues together with national campaign ads declaring: "It's unfair. It's Republican."

At the high tide of Reaganism in August 1981, O'Neill's team was preparing to turn legislative losses into campaign advantages. That is a classic opposition-game tactic: Make the White House pay when its victories bring bad consequences. "A recession brought about by tight money is at hand," Kirk O'Donnell predicted in a strategy memo to O'Neill on August 4. "The economy is *no longer our burden* [emphasis added]," O'Donnell advised. "It is a Republican Economy. The economic program is uniquely Reagan's and his party's. By not choosing to compromise with House Democrats, Reagan has assumed total responsibility for economic recovery."²⁹ O'Donnell cited NBC polls indicating that American voters were already having second thoughts about Reagan's moves. The polls had shown fifty-eight-percent support for the Reagan program in May, but only thirty-eight-percent support in July. O'Donnell urged that Democratic-led committees hold hearings around the country to generate news coverage about ill effects of Reagan's budget cutbacks in housing and education. It was a new game: The media presidency had spawned a media-oriented opposition.

On the advice of pollsters such as Peter Hart, Pat Caddell, Bill Hamilton, and Dotty Lynch, the speaker began attacking Reagan as Herbert Hoover with a smile. That was an important tactical shift. O'Neill's strategists had concluded that the middle class was far more worried about recession than budget cuts. Hoover carried echoes of Depression. By late 1981, O'Neill was charging Reagan with pursuing the "same old trickle-down tax policies" of Hoover and Coolidge and turning "an economic recovery into an economic disaster for millions of American workers." O'Neill sharpened his class attack on Reagan's tax cut as a windfall for the rich while the poor were getting socked by budget cuts. Reagan, he allowed, "is warm and congenial and a genuinely attractive personality. Unfortunately for Americans there is nothing warm and congenial about his policies. His policies hurt people." With an economic downturn visible on the horizon, O'Neill accused Reagan of fighting inflation with a deliberate recession.

In the inside game, O'Neill sought to heal his party's rifts. In midsummer, mainstream Democrats had been demanding punishment of the Boll Weevils who had defected to Reagan's cause. By fall, fifty loyal Democrats petitioned the leadership to discipline fifty renegades. Instead, O'Neill and Majority Leader Jim Wright granted a political amnesty. Much later, Phil Gramm and Kent Hance, the two Texas Democrats who had connived with the Reagan White House, were deprived of their choice committee posts. But in general the defectors were invited back into the fold. Said Wright, "We welcome the sinners back."

1982: The Confrontation Game

O'Neill was now pursuing a second goal in his opposition game. The first was to protect his party's base; the second was to gain enough leverage to force Reagan to bargain with him or to retreat on policy—to dent Reagan's image of invincibility. Gradually, shrewdly, O'Neill was regaining strength. Each step was crucial—allowing Reagan's program a fast legislative track, pushing Democratic alternatives, moving to unify House Democrats, taking the president head-on in the media. Finally, rising recession and Wall Street's sinking confidence in what O'Neill derisively labeled "Reaganomics" had forced Reagan to recognize that he needed O'Neill politically and to try to bargain with the speaker. The politics of patience had paid off.

Early in 1982, the president approved three-cornered negotiations between the White House, the Senate Republican leadership, and the House Democratic leadership to seek a genuine bipartisan budget to curb runaway deficits and to calm Wall Street. Reagan and O'Neill stayed in the background while their lieutenants labored from January through April 1982. Always, the negotiations foundered on Social Security, taxes, and defense.

When all else had failed, the president and the speaker met face to face to try to break the deadlock. The public, its hopes fanned by the drama built in the press, puts great stock in "summit meetings," expecting leaders to break through deadlocks and strike agreements. It does happen that way—but rarely. There is a much better chance for success for top leaders when their aides have made headway and all that is needed is a final push for full agreement. Moreover, bipartisanship does not spring up instantly between two adversaries. It has to be patiently nurtured, as President Eisenhower had nurtured it with Sam Rayburn and Lyndon Johnson in their private talks.

Reagan had not laid that groundwork with O'Neill. Since the inauguration, they had had only a couple of private encounters. Once in 1981, the president and Nancy Reagan had a gracious private dinner for the speaker and Millie O'Neill. The second time was the speaker's sixty-ninth birthday on December 9, 1981; Reagan had him to lunch with only three aides, Jim Baker, Mike Deaver and Ken Duberstein. No politics or policies came up. They were just two Irishmen swapping stories until Reagan wistfully looked at his watch as if to say, "I don't want this to stop. Why do we have to go back and run the country?" They walked to the elevator, arms on each other's shoulders.[30]

But that personal warmth was gone when they met head to head on April 27, 1982, in the President's Room of the Capitol. The air was thick with distrust. Places had been set for them side by side, but the speaker—maintaining a posture of equality and the politics of confrontation—moved his chair on the other side of the table, opposite Reagan. Then the two men squabbled about what aides could be present. O'Neill, who was accompanied by Majority Leader Jim Wright and Rules Committee Chairman Richard Bolling, wanted to add his aide,

Ari Weiss. Reagan, who had come with Ed Meese and Jim Baker, added David Stockman and Treasury Secretary Don Regan. Majority Leader Howard Baker and Reagan's close friend, Paul Laxalt of Nevada, represented the Senate.

Each leader wanted compromise from the other. Reagan was looking for O'Neill's willingness to cut social programs and Social Security COLAs. O'Neill wanted Reagan to roll back some of his 1981 tax cuts and his proposed increases on defense. Both men entered the arena warily. Aides told me that neither had much desire for the meeting; both had to be coaxed into going to avoid the public appearance of blocking agreement. Their private exchange echoed their public confrontations.[31]

After a rambling review of the spring's negotiations, Reagan said he understood there were areas "where a little bit of give on everyone's part could resolve the issue."

But O'Neill, still burning from last year's defeats, was not going to let 1981 pass unmentioned. He wanted first "to evaluate the 1981 cuts and how they affect this year's spending." Last year's budget, he asserted, was unfair to many Americans.

Reagan, obviously nettled, parried firmly: "Our budget cuts have not done damage to America."

"Mr. President," O'Neill shot back, "the damage is that you have a rapid defense buildup and massive tax cuts."

Reagan, his voice rising in anger, tartly reminded O'Neill of Jack Kennedy, who had held O'Neill's congressional seat before him. Said Reagan: "Our defense spending as a percentage of the budget is much lower than in Kennedy's days."

O'Neill shifted to another pet line of attack, accusing Reagan of "just advocating trickle-down economics" and putting the nation in a "fiscal mess" and the economy into a downspin. "If we don't have agreement, there will be massive deficits," O'Neill declared. "If you're going to be in cement [unyielding], we are not going to get a budget."

Reagan's response was equally sharp. "I've heard all that crap," he burst out. "You have the first actual deflation in seventeen years. Interest rates are down." And he ticked off gains from his program.

For nearly two hours, they swung at each other—"big roundhouse exchanges," Stockman called them, "about who betrayed the Roosevelt revolution and what was the Roosevelt revolution. Tip would say what made America great was the New Deal and all of the things that we have brought to the American people: Now everybody has a retirement pension; now everybody can go to college; people can get day care; they have health insurance. And then the president would say that we've been going to hell in a handbasket since 1932 when we started deficit spending and got government in all kinds of things it shouldn't be in."[32]

The argument never got nasty, but it was frequently abrasive. It got hung up over who was responsible for the "going-in" paper setting out a possible compromise budget formula, including a controversial five-percent ceiling on Social Security COLAs. Stockman had prepared the paper, picking up something once suggested by Bolling. Had the mood been right, it could have been a joint proposal. But it was a political orphan—it carried no one's name, least of all Reagan's. The mutual mistrust made it the devil at the critical moment.

Bolling smelled a political trap. O'Neill felt Reagan was trying to avoid taking political responsibility, and he asked whether Reagan was offering a Social Security proposal.

Reagan, also fearful of being trapped, dodged the question. Instead of urging a joint approach, he protected himself. "I didn't put this proposal on the table," he said. "This is the proposal that came from Congress."

O'Neill stiffened. If anything was to be done on Social Security, he asserted, it had to be done by both sides. He paused and waited. When Reagan did not seize that opportunity, O'Neill pulled back. "If the president isn't putting this on the table, then I'm taking ours off the table," O'Neill asserted.

From then on, things went downhill. They all took a recess. The Democrats came back angry that reporters had been told by White House officials that the Democrats were proposing cuts in Social Security COLAs. Howard Baker, trying to salvage the bipartisan approach, came up with a complicated, staggered freeze in COLAs in exchange for a matching delay in Reagan's tax cuts. "It feels like passing a pineapple," said Reagan, who did not want to give an inch on his tax cuts, "but I'm willing to do it." But it was an uneven deal. Financially the Baker plan had much greater long-term impact on Social Security COLAs than on tax cuts, and the Democrats rejected it as unequal.

Jim Wright ventured another idea—leaving out Social Security entirely, but postponing Reagan's tax cut for a year in exchange for domestic spending cuts and other measures.

Reagan erupted. "You can get me to crap a pineapple"—he grimaced—"but you can't get me to crap a cactus."

Silence. It was over. Neither Reagan nor O'Neill wanted to to get up first and take the blame for ending the meeting. Jim Baker broke the deadlock: "Let's all get up at the same time."

The session had been ill fated. O'Neill complained that Reagan was never serious, and cited Donald Regan's handing the president a prepared press statement as they left the room—evidence of advance planning for failure. The Republicans were equally critical of O'Neill as aggressively partisan and unyielding. Obviously, neither side was ready yet for a grand compromise on terms that would satisfy the other.

"They were just two Irishmen going at each other," Howard Baker told his aides later. "There was no way they were going to agree. They were not even close all day."

Eventually, with recession worsening, O'Neill got his way. Reagan had to give ground to try to tame the deficit. Congress took the initiative, Tip O'Neill allying with Howard Baker and Senate Finance Committee Chairman Robert Dole, to produce a three-year $98 billion tax increase. It repealed important parts of Reagan's 1981 tax cut, especially on the business side, and made cuts of roughly $150 billion in domestic programs. Reagan mistakenly thought he was getting a three-for-one deal, three dollars in budget cuts for every one dollar in tax increases. Actually, Stockman's fancy arithmetic made it look that way to Reagan—a fateful problem because it blocked future attempts at a grand compromise.* Reagan complained for five years Congress gypped him in 1982. But Dole, O'Neill, and Howard Baker all insisted to me that Congress came up with the promised budget cuts. Stockman agreed. "It was totally a myth that we got gypped," he said, "Totally."[33]

As opposition leader, O'Neill got the satisfaction of substantive triumph in 1982: Reagan's swallowing a huge partial rollback of his 1981 tax cuts. That so enraged ardent Reaganites that half of the House Republicans voted against the big tax bill, despite Reagan's backing it. Instead of Democrats being badly split as in 1981, Republicans were now factionally divided. Quick with public relations gimmickry, the White House hailed the tax increase as a Reagan victory—though Reagan had resisted tax increases for months. Substantively this was O'Neill's triumph. His opposition game was working.

In the 1982 elections, with the country plunging into the deepest recession since the 1930s, Democrats regained twenty-six House seats.

---

*Stockman admitted to me that to get the three-to-one figure, he took $50 billion in "management savings" from Reagan's original budget (which did not materialize), another $50 billion from reduced Pentagon increases (which Weinberger resisted making), plus billions more from Stockman's optimistic assumptions about economic growth and interest savings on the national debt (which did not work out). Stockman added all that to the real cuts promised by Congress to achieve savings of nearly $300 billion, for nearly $100 billion in tax cuts.

They knocked off a batch of freshman Republicans who had voted loyally with Reagan in 1981. The Democratic comeback cooled Republican talk of realignment, for the time being. For Reagan, the 1982 election was a political low point; for O'Neill it was sweet vindication for his politics of confrontation.

1985: Democratic Damage Control

Two years later, after the drubbing that Reagan handed Walter Mondale in 1984, Tip O'Neill shifted to a cannier opposition game: selective confrontation. He did not fight Reagan head-on across the board as in 1981–82. He picked fights carefully and thereby raised his odds of winning, and he pulled many of the 1981 Democratic defectors back into the party fold. In early 1985, the speaker lay back in wait, but his tactics got more aggressive in the fall, when he zinged Reagan on South Africa, trade, the MX missile, and aid to the Nicaraguan *contras*.

The highly partisan 1984 campaign had snuffed out the brief period of bipartisan cooperation in 1983. The one issue where Reagan and O'Neill agreed in 1985 was tax reform. But in the aftermath of Reagan's landslide, O'Neill deflected White House assaults on the deficit issue, and protected his Democratic majority by letting Republicans feud among themselves. By Reagan's second term, Senate Republican leaders and House Democratic leaders had moved closer together on economic issues, and the gap had widened between Reagan and the entire Congress.

For congressional Democrats, the 1984 election had been a tactical and moral victory. Despite low inflation, economic recovery, and Reagan's enormous popularity, Democrats picked up two seats in the Senate and lost only fourteen in the House, much less than Republicans had been gunning for. As O'Neill pointed out, Reagan won the presidency by 16 million votes, but Democrats outpolled Republicans for the House by 5.7 million votes.

Nonetheless, after his painful beatings in 1981, Tip O'Neill was wary of President Reagan, riding high again after his landslide. Mondale's disaster had damaged the Democratic party's national image, and O'Neill had to adapt his strategy to that fact. Like Reagan, he was relying on pollsters to coach his opposition game. Right after the 1984 election, O'Neill had Bill Hamilton, a widely respected Democratic pollster, survey public attitudes toward the Democratic party. Years of Reagan's attacks, as well as Mondale's campaign, had taken their toll. Hamilton found that Democrats had the image of big taxers and big spenders who were soft on defense. Moreover, the speaker was hearing from little people in his home district.

"I went around to some places, walked a few mills," he told me, voice rising in surprise. "Jesus, this lady stops me and she's packing sausages, minimum wage: 'Tip, I love you. I voted for you for fifty years. I'm sorry you're gonna leave [retire].' She says, 'I love the president. Tip, don't be mean with him.' "[34]

That kind of talk, plus Hamilton's advice, persuaded O'Neill to change his tune. In 1981, he had tried to defend social programs and to limit retrenchment. After the 1982 election, he had pushed through a couple of modest jobs programs. Now, in early February 1985, he did an about-face. He publicly called for cutting government programs—programs for which he had never had great love, such as Nixon's federal revenue sharing with state and local governments, Small Business Administration, and Economic Development Administration, as well as Jimmy Carter's urban development grant program. Reagan wanted to go much further. His budget proposed killing more than twenty programs and slashing a score of others. O'Neill's tried damage control: Go with the flow, but channel it to protect your favorites.

Just as important, O'Neill was determined to keep Democrats from stepping on a political landmine by pushing a tax hike to lower the deficit. He wanted to erase that bogey from the Mondale campaign and to force Reagan to take the initiative. Majority Leader Jim Wright took the opposite tack. "We owe it to the future generations to start paying our way," Wright asserted, "and we ought to be responsible enough to go ahead and recommend . . . the minimum tax on the successful corporations, the most profitable businesses, and individuals of the country, and devote the proceeds of that tax to deficit reduction."[35] As speaker in 1987–88 and with the Senate back in Democratic hands, Wright played hardball against Reagan on taxes. But in 1985, O'Neill overruled Wright; he gave orders to kill all Democratic proposals to raise taxes. It was tactics, not conviction.

O'Neill felt Reagan had demagogued the tax issue in 1984 against Mondale (as Democrats had demagogued Social Security against Republicans), even though Reagan had signed tax increases in 1982, 1983, and 1984. In 1985 he was not going to give Reagan ammunition. "Do I personally think the nation needs taxes? Sure, I think the nation needs taxes," O'Neill told me in 1985. "I think we're on a temporary economic surge, that down the road eighteen months or two years from now we can be in one hell of a recession and ultimately a depression. We're living on borrowed funds. . . . We get investments from all over the world, and that's keeping our economy fluid at the present time. So our nation needs a tax bill, but we're not gonna give you a tax bill until the president of the United States says, 'Hey, the time has come. My policy has been wrong.' "[36]

O'Neill still sharply disagreed with Reagan's spending priorities, but by laying back he did not dramatize the confrontation. On defense and Social Security, he let the Senate Republicans touch the hot wires of controversy first. O'Neill insisted that Republicans take the responsibility for governing. Long clashes between Senate Republicans and Weinberger over the Senate demands to restrain military spending spared Democrats the political cost of looking soft on defense.

That was O'Neill's new game: opposition by damage control. In the spring, he let Senate Majority Leader Bob Dole take the flak for trying to push Reagan into a politically realistic policy on defense and for tackling Social Security COLAs. In the fall, when Senate Republicans came up with the Gramm-Rudman six-year scheme to balance the budget, O'Neill swallowed hard and went along—up to a point. He faced down Democratic liberals, blacks, and committee chairmen, who feared that their programs would be decimated. Then he empowered two leading centrists, Tom Foley and Dick Gephardt, to negotiate changes in the bill to protect the Democrats' most precious social programs. The Democratic maneuver cut the Pentagon hard and pressed Reagan to raise taxes. Thus, on what became a touchstone of responsible governing, the Democratic leadership matched the Republicans. As Kirk O'Donnell put it, the Speaker managed "to preserve the status quo without getting blamed for the status quo."[37]

So it went in 1985 and 1986. The speaker turned confrontational when he found openings for a Democratic agenda. It was easy to push through economic sanctions against South Africa, get the Senate to go along, and to force Reagan to turn around. On trade, the Democrats adopted protectionist legislation that was either blocked in the Senate or vetoed by the president, and thus scored political points in the Southeast and elsewhere, helping Democrats in the 1986 elections—especially in the Senate. Under O'Neill's pressure, Reagan had to adjust.

No issue was more emotional to O'Neill than aid to Nicaraguan contras. He feared another Vietnam. Over breakfast in February 1981, Secretary of State Alexander Haig had alarmed O'Neill by advocating forceful American action in Central America. This was before the contra operation. "What Tip heard, and this is not what Haig said, is that we'll go in and take Grenada and Nicaragua, even if it means using

American boys," recalled Tom Foley.[38] O'Neill never forgot Haig's bellicose blustering and remained convinced that Reagan's policy would lead to American troops in Nicaragua. "In my opinion," he would say, "the president of the United States will not be satisfied or happy until the United States troops are in there."

In 1984, O'Neill's House Democrats killed military aid to the *contras.* In 1985, O'Neill staved off Reagan for a while, then had to bow to $27 million in nonlethal aid. Finally in 1986, Reagan pushed through $100 million in aid, including military aid, by sheer doggedness. Long after the fact, O'Neill could savor some satisfaction when Reagan ran into stormy bipartisan criticism in 1987 for his efforts to circumvent the two-year congressional ban on military aid, with secret Saudi funding aid and Oliver North's private money-raising.

In sum, against an immensely popular president, O'Neill's tough, combative opposition paid off surprisingly well. Not only did the "fairness issue" set up Republican defeat in 1982, but it so embarrassed the White House that Reagan toned down his second inaugural from the mink-and-limousine first inaugural. On policy, Reagan did slow the growth of government, but O'Neill and company prevented the outright shutdown of many programs. Year by year, O'Neill's opposition game—in tandem with Senate Republicans—shifted the priorities of Reagan's budgets, so that Reagan's military buildup became the prime target of controversy.

O'Neill proved himself the most powerful speaker since Rayburn. As O'Neill approached retirement, his approval rating in opinion polls (67 percent approval, 23 percent disapproval on November 1, 1986) was on a par with Reagan's (66 percent approval, 33 percent disapproval).[39] The public had come to see them both as partisans, forceful leaders, sincere in their convictions—likable, recognizable, opposite political poles. Most important to O'Neill, his six years of standing toe to toe against Reagan had blunted the Republican drive for realignment and protected his party.

Ever aware of comparisons to Rayburn, O'Neill remarked to me that Rayburn had been speaker much longer than he had. But then O'Neill added proudly: "He lost the House twice [to Republicans]. I've never lost the House."[40]

The Swapping Game: Bridge, Not Poker

The polarized politics that Reagan and O'Neill played most of the time is what mathematicians call a zero-sum game: winner takes all. Like two stud-poker players facing each other across the table, both went for the jackpot. Usually, when Reagan won, O'Neill lost, and vice versa. In a zero-sum game no chips are left on the table. The wins cancel out the losses. The balance is zero.

The other basic game is the positive-sum game—in which there can be more than one winner. Players on opposite sides can form a partnership, as in bridge. By joining, they can both have a positive outcome. It is a different style of game.

That works in politics, too. Some very sharp Democrats played a positive-sum opposition game with Reagan during the titanic fights over the MX missile in 1983. This kind of game often emerges when a political stalemate has developed; that happened in the case of the MX. By shrewdly leveraging their political strength at a time of Reagan's weakness, a band of swing Democrats changed administration policy. Rather than trying to match Reagan blow for blow, Tip O'Neill style, these moderates bargained. Instead of poker, they played bridge. They traded with Reagan. Their votes helped Reagan get money for the MX, and in return, they injected their policy concepts into Reagan's military buildup and his arms proposals. Each side won something.

Both in style and substance, these moderate House Democrats played a brand of opposition game radically different from Tip O'Neill's. In their 1983 maneuver on MX and arms control, they had the conceptual initiative. They played an intellectual game. Reagan was not only politically stymied on MX, but at a loss for ideas on how to sell it. New-breed Democrats such as Albert Gore, Jr., and Les Aspin filled the intellectual vaccuum, operating as entrepreneurs of policy. They developed new policies and worked these ideas into the policy mainstream with media politics, speeches, op-ed articles, and press interviews. Their group was inchoate, bound together by outlook, but largely independent of the standard bases of power in Congress: the House leadership, regional groups, and the committee structure. But their game succeeded, even without a formal power base.

Their basic game plan was simple: Reagan badly wanted the MX (for Missile Experimental) as the centerpiece of his military buildup. It would be by far the biggest missile in the American inventory, with ten warheads and sharp enough accuracy to knock out Soviet ICBMs in their concrete silos. Normally, Congress goes along with a president on a big weapons system. But the MX, and especially its basing mode, had become so controversial that Congress resisted Reagan on MX. Deadlock enabled the House moderates to hold Reagan's pet missile hostage.

The story begins on December 7, 1982—the day Reagan and Defense Secretary Caspar Weinberger lost political control of the MX issue. A congressional mutiny of 195 Democrats and 50 Republicans voted 245–176 to block MX production. Reagan protested that this vote offered comfort to Moscow, but he had to retreat. On December 20, he bowed when Congress voted to appropriate $560 million for full development of MX—short of actual production *and* with the critical condition that the money could not be spent until Congress approved a basing mode for MX. In legislative lingo, the MX money was "fenced." This restriction gave leverage to the centrist Democrats for a trading game.

For nearly two years, Weinberger had wrestled with trying to devise an acceptable alternative to Jimmy Carter's mobile basing for the MX. In all, the Air Force and various Pentagon commissions conjured up thirty-four basing schemes: plans to cart the big missiles around in trucks, put them on trains, hang them from dirigibles, or base them in tunnels. Weinberger favored deep underground basing or flying the MX on huge C-5A cargo planes, but these were technically impractical. When he suggested putting the MX in existing American missile silos, even Senator John Tower, a pro-MX hawk from Texas, scoffed that MX would be a sitting duck to the Soviets. Another Weinberger scheme, called Dense Pack, was widely ridiculed. The idea was to jam a lot of MX missiles in small areas so that Soviet warheads would blow up in each other's way; theoretically MX would survive. Three of the five Joint Chiefs of Staff opposed Dense Pack.

The MX became the Pentagon's albatross. Defense planners could not devise a way to make it invulnerable and survivable. Moreover, the pressures of the nuclear-freeze movement and losses in the 1982 congressional elections had thrown Reagan on the political defensive by December 1982. Compromise was in the air.

Enter the Democratic moderates, about thirty strong and bent on compromise. They were mainly issue-oriented new-breed politicians, relatively young power brokers. Their pragmatism offended liberals who wanted to kill the MX missile, arguing that it was expensive, unworkable, and would appear as a menacing first-strike weapon. The moderates also disliked the MX but they saw a chance to bargain. Like the liberals, they were suspicious that Reagan was not serious about arms control—that he was making excessive negotiating demands to avoid real give-and-take with Moscow. They wanted him to be more flexible and realistic.

Their game succeeded for five key reasons: First, the MX deadlock was a lever for moving policy in their direction. Second, their political instinct was to find a way out of the impasse, rather than to score partisan points or to maintain ideological purity. Third, they had enough votes in the House to swing the balance of power on MX. Fourth, legislative procedure enabled them to force Reagan to ransom the MX with policy concessions, not just once but several times, because every year the MX faced at least two votes: one on authorizing each new step in the MX program and another on appropriating funds. Finally, their leaders had real mastery of the staggering intricacies of weapons and arms control. They could not only dicker politically, but they could match wits with administration experts.

The moderate ringleaders were Les Aspin, Al Gore, and Norman Dicks. Gore, a tall, telegenic political golden boy from Tennessee, and Dicks, a burly, curly-haired, chubby-cheeked football star from the University of Washington, had arrived in the class of '76. They became buddies playing basketball in the House gym. Gore, son of a well-known liberal Tennessee senator, had Ivy League credentials. Cerebral and serious, he had gone to Harvard, Vanderbilt University divinity school, and had served in Vietnam as a draftee. For five years, he had worked as a newspaper reporter before winning a House seat at age twenty-eight. Dicks, tutored in inside politics as an aide for eight years to Washington's powerful Senator Warren Magnuson, was a more rough-and-tumble politician than Gore. At forty-three, he was savvy and brimming with energy, and he sat on the House Defense Appropriations Subcommittee, which voted on funding the MX.

Aspin, elected from Wisconsin in 1970, was the trio's senior partner. His bland face, folksy style, and middle-age paunch belied a whiz-kid résumé—Yale, Oxford, MIT Ph.D. in economics, service in the Kennedy administration, first as an aide to Walter Heller, chairman of the Council of Economic Advisers, and then working on systems analysis in Robert McNamara's Pentagon. He had also been an economics professor at Marquette University. In Congress, Aspin quickly became known as a gadfly critic of the Pentagon, hot on exposing military waste.

By 1983, Aspin had emerged as a defense strategist and chairman of a House Armed Services subcommittee. He had voted against the MX in 1980 and 1982 and in favor of the nuclear freeze in 1982 and 1983, though he helped water down the 1983 freeze resolution so that it did not tie Reagan's hands. In short, Aspin was more hawkish than his liberal image. He knew how to work both sides of an issue, and he was ambitious. In 1981, he had called for overthrowing Tip O'Neill as speaker, and in 1985, he would stage a new-breed revolt to leap over six senior Democrats to become Armed Services Committee chairman.

Aspin's opposition game was pragmatic. He mocked the MX as the "homeless waif of weapons," asserting that it could not be fully deployed. But he also said it could not be wholly blocked; so it was time to strike a deal. What's more, Aspin felt it was a tactical mistake for Democrats to appear soft and negative on defense. What Democrats needed, Aspin said, was a credible defense strategy, instead of merely playing "Doctor No."

"For the Democrats to just blindly oppose Ronald Reagan and all defense was politically a losing game," Aspin told me in early 1986. "We had an antidefense image in '83–'84 and still do, to a certain extent. But that's not the way to play the game. The way to play the game is to agree with Reagan on some things and to oppose him and argue against him on some things. That meant, you know, arguing our point of view, which was that the vulnerability of [U.S.] land-based missiles was an important issue but what Reagan wanted to do [with MX] was crazy. You couldn't come up with a survivable MX. We tried thirty-four basing modes over the years and none of them worked. Either they were too expensive, they were still vulnerable, or you ran into opposition of farmers or somebody [who] didn't like where MX was [being put]. You couldn't find a solution to the problem. We think what we want to do is a better way to get there."[41]

Aspin and other Democratic moderates wanted a smaller, mobile ICBM with one warhead known as Midgetman because it was about one sixth the size of the MX. That notion had been advocated in the mid-1970s by Paul Nitze, a conservative Wall Street banker who had been Kennedy's deputy Defense secretary and then an arms negotiator for both Nixon and Reagan.

Among the Democratic moderates, Albert Gore revived the idea. Although not on defense or foreign-affairs committees, Gore boned up on strategic-arms issues with an intensive thirteen-month program of reading and consulting experts, especially his own arms specialist, Leon Fuerth. Gore gained influence on arms policy by sheer intellectual effort and a drive to find some path toward a safer, more stable nuclear balance. His game was a new breed tour de force, end-running the committee system.

The root of the problem, as many strategic analysts saw it, was the American decision in 1968, later copied by the Soviets, to put multiple warheads on strategic missiles. These were called MIRVs, for multiple independently targetable reentry vehicles. MIRVs were not merely like buckshot scattered out of a shotgun; each could be independently guided to its target. The American Minuteman 3 missile had three

MIRV warheads; the Soviet SS-17 had four, the SS-19 had six, and the SS-18 had ten. The Carter and Reagan administrations planned to put ten warheads on each MX and eight on the Navy's Trident D-5 submarine-launched missiles. Multiple warheads were what made a first strike theoretically advantageous and made the arms race so scary.

MIRVing had created serious instability in the nuclear balance. The critical yardstick was the *ratio* between warheads on one side and missile launchers on the other side, especially when the attacking warheads were extremely accurate and carried high destructive power. Such warheads were called "hard-target killers" or "silo busters" because they could knock out missiles based in fixed, hardened silos. As a rule of thumb, the nuclear-arms experts calculated that because of problems with reliability, accuracy, and blast power, it would take two hard-target warheads to knock out one missile in its silo.

To one committee, Gore illustrated the significance of the 2–1 ratio, and why MIRVs caused such fear and instability. He put six paper cups on a table, three for each side.

"If the USSR and the US have three missiles apiece and that's their total arsenal, and each missile has six warheads, then the nation launching a first strike can launch one missile and put two warheads there, two there, and two there," he said, hitting the other side's cups—smash, smash, smash. "In the aftermath, the aggressor has two thirds of its forces remaining, and the victim has none," he said. "If you have the same scenario with only one warhead on each missile, then the nation striking first has to use up two missiles to knock out one missile on the other side." The attacker winds up with one missile left while the victim has two—no incentive for surprise attack.

"So the key for me became the ratio of counterforce [hard-target] warheads on one side to targetable silos on the other side," Gore said. "If you get that ratio down to two for one, then it's impossible to gain an advantage from a first strike. If you get the ratio above that, then it becomes increasingly capable of generating fear and wild responses on the other side."[42]

What caused angst in the Pentagon was the estimate that the Soviets had more than three thousand hard-target warheads on their 308 SS-18 missiles, plus another fifteen hundred warheads (not all silo busters) on SS-17's and SS-19. That was more than enough to knock out America's 1,054 land-based ICBMs plus bomber bases, radars, and command headquarters. The fateful ratio of Soviet hard-target killers was *well over* 3–1, leaving the United States very vulnerable.

The ratio of American warheads to Soviet silos was *under* 2–1 because only part of America's two thousand ICBM warheads were silo busters, not enough to eliminate Moscow's 1,398 ICBM launchers. The United States also had 5,500 warheads on submarine-launched missiles, but they were not accurate and powerful enough to be silo busters. That's why Reagan and Carter wanted the MX and the Trident D-5 missiles: to get more hard-target warheads and make Soviet leaders feel the same threat that the White House felt. The danger was that mutual fear could accidentally trigger a holocaust.

Gore's idea, shared by others, was to go in the opposite direction, to "de-MIRV." In other words, to move away from multiple warheads and go back to single-warhead missiles so that the warhead-to-silo ratio would go *down*, not up. On the House floor on March 22, 1982, Gore argued for an immediate freeze on silo-busting weapons under the 1979 strategic arms agreement, the freeze to be followed by gradual dismantling of multiple-warhead weapons and new arms agreements requiring both sides to shift to single-warhead missiles. Gore proposed building one thousand single-warhead missiles, enough to disperse and protect the American force but not enough to menace Moscow seriously. His goal was nuclear "stability"—no advantage to either side in pursuing the arms race. In short, a safer balance.

Gore's position required changing President Reagan's military buildup and his arms proposals. For by Gore's logic, Reagan's 1982 arms proposals increased the dangers. They called for dramatic fifty-percent reductions in both sides' nuclear arsenals to five thousand warheads, but they also would cut land-based launchers to 850 for each side. Appealing as those reductions sounded, they failed to push the warhead-to-silo ratio below 2–1. Better to have more missile launchers and fewer warheads, Gore argued, so as to lower the fatal ratio. That would make each side's nuclear forces less vulnerable—removing the advantages of surprise attack and reducing the risk of nuclear catastrophe.

In April 1982, Soviet arms specialists told an American delegation in Moscow they found the Gore's approach "an interesting basis for negotiations."[43] In early 1983, former Secretary of State Henry Kissinger endorsed the same approach. It was a turnaround for Kissinger; he admitted that putting multiple warheads on missiles—which he had pushed in the 1970s—had eroded the arms agreements which he had negotiated.[44]

Dickering Through the Middlemen

Enter the middlemen: The opposition game played by Aspin, Gore, and Dicks usually requires mediators. Stymied by Congress, Reagan farmed out his MX problem to a presidential commission, a time-honored gambit. In years past, presidential commissions have often served as burial grounds for controversy. They are appointed to let the president unload a political hot potato and consign it to limbo, preferably to be forgotten. Their function is damage control, not problem solving.

But occasionally, presidents intend a commission to forge a solution. That was the case with Reagan's Social Security commission in 1982–83. It was also the case with the bipartisan MX commission appointed on January 3, 1983, led by Brent Scowcroft, a former three-star Air Force general and national security adviser under President Ford. The Scowcroft Commission became the broker for the White House and moderate House Democrats. It succeeded because both sides wanted it to. Also because its two chief operators were skilled in the power game: Brent Scowcroft, who is a trim, soft-spoken, thoughtful military intellectual, and James Woolsey, a bright, agile, imaginative Democratic thinker who had been Navy undersecretary in the Carter administration.

Scowcroft and Woolsey are classic Washington insiders: knowledgeable and well connected with power networks in Congress, the administration, and in both parties. Many administrations rely on retired generals like Scowcroft and policy-oriented attorneys like Woolsey to lubricate the political machinery and build consensus. Both are respected as fair-minded policymakers with a knack for working inside politics as well as the issues. Happily, Scowcroft was a mentor of Robert C. McFarlane, then Reagan's deputy national security adviser, and Woolsey was a crony and tennis partner of Les Aspin. What is more, serving on Reagan's Pentagon advisory panel in 1981, Woolsey and Scowcroft had favored a small, single-warhead missile, an idea that was shunted aside by the panel. So their thinking paralleled Gore's.

Moreover, they saw that Reagan's MX problem was more political than technical, for they understood a basic rule of the power game that Reagan and Weinberger sometimes ignored: No president's nuclear strategy can survive over time without a durable political consensus. Jimmy Carter had ignored that in 1979 in negotiating the SALT II Arms Treaty. Carter could never submit the treaty for Senate approval because he could not sell it politically. Reagan had that problem on MX.

"Politics is really part of strategy," Woolsey said, laying out the game. "For a democracy, the degree to which the country can unify behind a coherent strategic policy is a very important part of strategy. So we felt the solution had to be strategically sound in a military hardware sense. But it also had to be a deal between the Reagan White House and a Democratic House. Now there were other players: The Senate was important; the Pentagon was important. But basically, if Ronald Reagan and enough House Democrats got behind a common solution to the problem of ICBM survivability, then a lot of other things could be worked out."[45]

Woolsey's instincts led him straight to Aspin as an ally and sounding board. Before long, he, Scowcroft, and Aspin were huddling at Aspin's town house in fashionable Georgetown. Aspin bragged that the Democrats had "kicked the administration all over the block on the MX," but he added that "obviously this is a serious national problem and something has to be done."[46]

Aspin's willingness to seek a middle way got the trading game started. Gore and Dicks were brought in. The first session between Gore and Scowcroft was prickly. "*Confrontation* is probably too strong a word—but acerbic," Scowcroft told me later. "We had a long talk and some very sharp words. Gore said, 'Let's scrap the MX and go with a small missile that makes sense,' and I was arguing why a direct transition to a small missile was not the way to go."

Scowcroft found other Democrats chilly, too. "Part of the problem was the residue of the Defense Department's image up there in Congress," Scowcroft recalled. "People were mad at Defense, mad at Weinberger. You know, the notion that Defense didn't really want to hear what the Hill had to say."[47]

It took time to thaw the partisan iciness on MX. Significantly, Democratic Whip Tom Foley was willing to consider compromise. Foley played a crucial role; he persuaded Speaker O'Neill to keep the MX issue out of the Democratic Caucus, where liberals were likely to make it a partisan cause against Reagan. "I always thought it extremely unwise to take a Caucus position on national security issues or emotional issues like abortion," Foley told me. "That sort of thing is divisive. It'll tear the party apart."[48] It would also have nipped the budding moderate partnership with Scowcroft and Woolsey.

In three months of round-robin talks, the House Democrats dickered with the Reagan team through Scowcroft and Woolsey. In time, it became obvious that the final bargain had to include some MX missiles to satisfy Reagan, some Midgetman missiles to bring in Gore and others, and some changes in Reagan's arms proposals to placate moderates who felt his negotiating terms were too hard-line. Gore and Dicks argued "fifty was going to be the limit on MX."[49] (Carter had sought two hundred.) The issue was settled one Saturday afternoon in Aspin's living room by Scowcroft and Woolsey. "They decided fifty was too low, that Reagan wouldn't accept it, we'd better go for a hundred," Aspin recalled.[50]

The Scowcroft Commission issued its report April 11, 1983, echoing the Gore-Aspin logic and exposing the destabilizing threat of multiwarhead missiles. The report advocated long-run nuclear stability by developing single-warhead Midgetman missiles, but it gave Reagan one hundred MX missiles in fixed silos for the interim. And it gently nudged Reagan to shift his arms-control position. The Pentagon squawked, but Reagan endorsed the report.

The Gang of Six Rides High

One of the enduring lessons of the Washington power game is that agreement does not equal solution. It is merely a transition point to a new struggle, the winners trying to secure their gains, the losers trying to undo them. The Scowcroft report, backed by former Defense secretaries Harold Brown (under Carter) and James R. Schlesinger (under Ford), gave the politicians "cover" for compromise. But it left no one fully satisfied. It had something for everyone—but it was also something distasteful to everyone. In Aspin's apt metaphor, it was a "stapled-together job," and the stapling nearly came undone.

The House moderates felt Reagan's endorsement of the Midgetman missile and his promise to review his arms-control position were too vague and lukewarm; they feared he might sabotage their game. So the core group of Gore, Dicks, and Aspin, joined by six other Democrats and one Republican, wrote Reagan asking for more concrete assurances. After weeks of dickering, Reagan tried to swing them in line with a letter sent on May 11—just minutes before the scheduled House Defense Appropriations Subcommittee vote on the frozen MX funding. Gore and Dicks objected that the letter had a loophole, implying that Reagan need not change his arms-control package. "This is unacceptable," Dicks declared.[51] Bowing to the leverage of the moderates, the White House produced a reworded letter—in only twenty minutes. With that obstacle cleared, the subcommittee began the process of freeing up the MX money that had been fenced in December 1982.

On the eve of the first big MX vote by the full House, Reagan nearly upset the applecart. He invited about thirty House members to the White House for dinner, and afterward made a rambling speech that showed how poorly he grasped the issues and the package he was pushing. Previously, Reagan had admitted his ignorance to the House group. "You know, I didn't realize my original position required the Soviets to dismantle two thirds of their land-based missiles," he said. "No wonder they thought it was unfair."[52] Now, I was told, Reagan's effort to answer questions at the White House dinner were so embarrassing that Brent Scowcroft had to take over. Near the end, Tom Foley, as the ranking Democrat, thanked the president and put in a word for developing "bipartisan approaches to national security matters." Even that mild a pro-Reagan pitch angered some Democrats, and White House legislative strategist Ken Duberstein said Foley's prestige provided crucial support to Reagan.

Finally, on May 24, the House voted to release funds for MX development and flight testing—and forty-four House members who had opposed MX in 1982 swung over to join the 239–186 pro-MX majority. Reagan now had what he had wanted. The House moderates watched to see whether Reagan kept his part of the bargain by making his arms-control position more flexible.

On June 7, Reagan made some modest changes in his arms position, lifting his proposed cutbacks in missile launchers from 850 to 1,200. That was easier on the Soviets and more in keeping with Gore's notions of the right ratio. But there was a hitch—the Pentagon showed no enthusiasm for the Midgetman missile. Moreover, some House moderates said that the one hundred MX missiles recommended by the Scowcroft Commission were only "bargaining chips" to be traded with Moscow, but Weinberger insisted they had to be deployed. The bargain was fraying.

The trading game developed a pattern that went this way: The Democratic moderates made demands on Reagan, dickered for concessions, traded their votes, and monitored Reagan's actions.

The next round was quickly upon them. No sooner had Congress released funds for developing the MX than Reagan and Weinberger wanted more money to start building MX missiles in 1984. The moderates were still dissatisfied with Reagan's strategic-arms proposals, fearing that their pet—the single-warhead missile—was unlikely to get anywhere without an arms agreement. So they resumed demands for more flexibility from Reagan, in exchange for another round of votes for MX.

By late summer, Senate moderates had moved into the game, too. Senators William Cohen, a moderate Republican from Maine, and Sam Nunn, a Georgia conservative and the Senate's most influential Democrat on defense issues, were pushing Reagan to accept their idea of a "build-down": a scheme to decrease the size (and threat) of Soviet and American arsenals, even as the arsenals were being modernized. Like Gore, they wanted to push toward safer ratios. Both Nunn and Cohen were highly respected by their colleagues. Cohen had written an article for *The Washington Post* back on January 3, 1983, pushing the build-down concept, and Reagan had phoned Cohen to say he liked the idea. Cohen was trying to give a fresh twist to the nuclear freeze. Since both Moscow and Washington wanted to bring new weapons into their nuclear arsenals, Cohen argued they should accept some overall ceiling and then each pay a price for modernization that would help arms control.

"We could, for example, agree with the level of strategic weapons contained in the [1979] SALT II treaty and then insist that for every new weapon added to the force by either side, two older, less stabilizing weapons must be eliminated," Cohen had written. "This guaranteed build-down, while not offered as a panacea, would raise the nuclear threshold to a higher, safer level, improve the prospects for lessening world tensions, and reassure our citizens that we recognize the peril of arms escalation."[53]

To Cohen, Nunn, and forty-three Senate cosponsors of build-down, it fit with Reagan's call for arms reductions. By making the reductions gradual, the senators hoped this would appeal to Moscow, more than Reagan's drastic cuts did. But build-down could translate into very significant sacrifices in Reagan's program. For building one hundred MX missiles with one thousand new warheads would require throwing away two thousand warheads, old warheads—or dismantling the entire American force of Minuteman and Titan ICBMs.

The Pentagon balked at build-down even though Reagan and the Scowcroft Commission endorsed the idea. Cohen and Nunn, joined by Senator Charles Percy, the Foreign Relations Committee chairman, accused the administration of dragging its feet. They combined forces with Aspin, Gore, and Dicks to bargain with the White House as the "gang of six"—four Democrats and two Republicans who epitomized the leverage that centrists can achieve in the power game. Reagan could not win without the swing group in Congress that they represented.

Reinforced by the senators, the House moderates played hardball to get their way. In late July, they attached riders to Reagan's bill authorizing MX production. One Aspin amendment tied procurement of the MX to the pace of work on Midgetman. Another rider, by Gore and Dicks, cut back the administration from twenty-seven to twenty-one MX missiles in 1984. Support for MX was shrinking in the House, giving more leverage to the gang of six, who were pushing new arms proposals. By late September, the six were negotiating intensely with William Clark, Reagan's national security adviser, and his deputy, Bud McFarlane.

For one thing, they wanted Reagan's promise to pursue build-down vigorously. For another, they wanted assurances that American arms proposals would promote the safer single-warhead Midgetman and penalize multiwarhead missiles. Third, they wanted Reagan to make arms concessions in areas where the United States was ahead of Moscow: strategic bombers carrying nuclear-tipped cruise missiles. Chief arms negotiator Ed Rowny was talking about building up to eight thousand air-launched cruise missiles, nearly four times the level permitted by the 1979 SALT II treaty. To achieve progress in the arms talks, the gang of six argued, Reagan would have to trade off areas of American advantage for areas of Soviet advantage, and not just demand Soviet concessions.

The White House found it hard to accept trading American advantages in bombers and cruise missiles for Soviet advantages in ICBMs. Reagan always drew a distinction between "fast flyers"—meaning missile warheads that can cross oceans in thirty minutes—and "slow flyers"—meaning bombers and cruise missiles which take hours. Bill Clark tried a fuzzy-sounding proposal on the gang of six on September 30, but Cohen brushed it aside as "weasel worded."

"That isn't good enough, it's no commitment at all," he complained. "It's got to be made a lot firmer."[54]

When Clark tried coaxing, Cohen refused to be budged.

"We can't satisfy this guy," said Clark in some irritation.

"Not with crap like that," Cohen retorted.

Ron Lehman, an aide to Clark, suggested that the administration had gone the last mile; Cohen shot back: "You'd better not have, or you're not going to have me with you."

At another point, Nunn declared: "We're in a position to provide support now, but not if the administration doesn't keep its part of the bargain."

Three days later, Reagan himself met the gang of six. Again, they pressed him to pledge that his negotiators would "seek" trade-offs of American bomber cuts for Soviet missile cuts. A new White House memo said only that American negotiators would "explore" the subject. Cohen was still dissatisfied.

"I want the administration to actually go out and do this," he insisted. "I know what *explore* means in diplomatic language. It's like mercury on a mirror. Nothing gets resolved."

To bridge the gap, Ron Lehman suggested saying that the administration would "negotiate" a bomber-missile trade-off. Reagan bought it; so did the others. Once again, the moderates had shifted Reagan's stance—at least on paper.

The very next day, Reagan announced that he was incorporating a "series of build-down proposals" into his strategic-arms package and "we're also prepared to negotiate limits on bomber and air-launch cruise missile limits below SALT II levels." That meant about two thousand, a far cry from Ed Rowny's eight thousand. Also, Reagan said he recognized "there will have to be trade-offs" between areas of Soviet and American advantage. His public statement sending American negotiators back to Geneva was a paean to bipartisan consensus. Pleased by those shifts, the House moderates helped defeat an attempt by liberal Democrats to block initial MX production. On November 18, 1983, the House voted $2.1 billion for production of the first twenty-one MX missiles.

That was the high-water mark for the trading game of the House Democratic moderates, for partnership across party and philosophical lines is hard to sustain: The moderates felt their arms proposals never really got a fair hearing in Geneva. "They were dumped in the Atlantic on the way over to Geneva," Cohen groused. The Russians, frustrated by American deployment of intermediate-range missiles in Europe, walked out of the arms talks, not to return until 1985. By then, President Reagan's commitment to strategic defenses had become the central issue, overshadowing build-down and the single-warhead missile.

By 1984, the collaboration of House moderates and the White House collapsed under the partisan pressures of an election year. No issue exists in a vacuum. Several key participants, including Brent Scowcroft, felt the fragile partnership on MX was derailed by Reagan's zigzags on the use of American Marines in Lebanon and Speaker O'Neill's feeling that Reagan double-crossed him. In 1983, O'Neill had prevented the MX from becoming a highly flammable partisan issue. But in 1984 and 1985, O'Neill and his House Democrats beat Reagan on the MX, and there is reason to believe that happened because O'Neill felt burned on Lebanon.

In the fall of 1983, the speaker had taken the heat for Reagan by

getting the House to pass a resolution authorizing deployment of the
Marines for eighteen months. O'Neill faced down sharp criticism from
other Democrats, saying he had pledged Reagan his support. It was a
mark of O'Neill's traditionalism, his loyalty to the presidency on foreign policy, wherever possible. Reagan and McFarlane convinced him
the Marines were on a peacekeeping mission that would stabilize the
pro-Western Lebanese government and lead to withdrawal of Syrian
and Israeli armies from Lebanon.

"They hoodwinked me into going along with a bipartisan matter to
put the troops in," O'Neill recalled bitterly. "But they never told me
the Marines were there for guarding of the airport. They were there
as a symbol. Everything was supposed to have been put together and
peace was going to come, but it never happened."[55]

O'Neill's disillusionment deepened after the bombing of the Marine
barracks on October 23, 1983, that took 241 lives. For several weeks,
the White House denounced pressures for withdrawing the Marines as
cowardly "cut and run" tactics. At the White House on January 25,
1984, O'Neill and Reagan got into a shouting match over the situation.
Six days later, O'Neill and other Democratic leaders formally urged the
"prompt and orderly withdrawal" of the Marines. The speaker told me
he had protected Reagan as long as possible, and he went along with
a withdrawal resolution only after being tipped off by a high administration official that Reagan had already approved a phased pullout and
"the orders had been given and that it had been settled."[56] Reagan
reportedly signed the pullout order on February 1—the very same day
that White House spokesman Larry Speakes questioned the "patriotism" of Democrats calling for a pullout.

What enraged O'Neill was a personal slam at him by President
Reagan in *The Wall Street Journal* on February 2. Asked about
O'Neill's call for a pullout, Reagan snapped, "He may be ready to
surrender, but I'm not." Then he added: "If we get out, that means
the end of Lebanon. And if we get out, it also means the end of any
ability on our part to bring about an overall peace in the Middle East.
And I would have to say that it means a pretty disastrous result for us
worldwide."

Six days later, on February 8, the White House officially announced
that Reagan had ordered the fourteen hundred Marines in Beirut to
begin what was termed a phased redeployment—taking them out of
Lebanon. The incident deeply embittered O'Neill. He operated by the
old Irish school politics which say: Don't get mad, get even.

Politically, the MX was a good issue for O'Neill's settling the score with Reagan. Since mid-1983, the pro-MX majority had shrunk. In the election year, O'Neill could turn up the partisan heat. Swinging a handful of votes was enough to fence the funds for MX missiles in 1984. The centrist swing group was dwindling. Foley and Cohen were unhappy with Reagan's arms positions. Others, such as Nunn, Aspin, and Gore, felt gulled by the Pentagon's endless delays on Midgetman. It took until December 17, 1986, for the administration to move ahead on full engineering and development of Midgetman. By then, the positive-sum game had collapsed. Reacting to Reagan's failure to keep his part of the bargain, both Nunn and Aspin helped impose a ceiling of fifty MXs in 1985. Both sides, White House and moderates, accused the other of welshing on the deal.

Even so, the trading game had paid off enough for both sides to get half a loaf—Reagan, fifty MXs; and the moderates, both Midgetman and some flexibility in Reagan's arms positions.

Rostenkowski: "To Get Along, Go Along"

O'Neill's head-to-head fighting with Reagan was a classic opposition game. The swapping game of the House moderates on MX illustrates a contrary strategy. Danny Rostenkowski played a third style of opposition game on tax reform on 1985. Rostenkowski's game was a throwback to the opposition politics of Sam Rayburn and Lyndon Johnson with President Eisenhower. Rostenkowski found he could not force Reagan to retreat, as O'Neill had in 1982, and he could not afford to let Reagan overrun him or smother him in a Republican-run partnership that would hurt congressional Democrats with the voters.

With the oncoming recession in 1982, O'Neill had had an advantage against Reagan; in 1983, the House "MX moderates" had a similar built-in advantage. In both cases, President Reagan had to meet the terms of the opposition. He was on the defensive, at the low ebb of his first-term power.

But Reagan's tide had turned by the time of the power struggle over tax reform in 1985. Reagan's enormous landslide reelection in 1984 made him look invincible once again. Also, Rostenkowski had tried wrestling Reagan in 1981 and had been brutally rolled. As chairman of the House Ways and Means Committee, the big Chicago congressman had tried to bargain, but Reagan had rebuffed him. Then he tried to compete by offering an alternative tax-cut package, but Reagan had outbid him. The battle had bruised Rostenkowski.

In 1985, Rostenkowski was again on the defensive. The Reagan crowd, Pat Buchanan at the White House and Congressman Jack Kemp, were trumpeting tax reform as a "realigning issue," destined to lift Republicans to national dominance.

Tax reform, declared Republican National Chairman Frank Fahrenkopf, "will go a long way toward making the Republican Party the majority party. What we're reaching out for is the last bulwark of the Democratic party: working people, families—especially large families—and not only ethnics but blacks, Hispanics, Catholics. This is a reach by the conservative movement to bring these people into the Republican party."[57]

Rostenkowski's task was tricky. Tax reform appealed to him; he wanted a bill that would refurbish his image as a can-do leader who could pass big legislation. But his opposition game was aimed really at keeping Reagan from taking the lion's share of the credit. He had to blunt the Republican drive to use tax reform to build long-term Republican appeal with the voters.

By instinct and habit, Rostenkowski fell back on the strategy Rayburn and Johnson had used with Eisenhower. Rayburn's motto had been "To get along, go along," and Rostenkowski adapted it to his situation. For junior members, that meant supporting the elders and working your way up patiently through seniority. For an opposition leader facing a popular president, it meant aligning with him publicly and then quietly revamping his proposals—keeping the brand name and changing the product inside the box. Remodeling: That's what Rostenkowski did with Reagan's tax-reform plan. His variation of the positive-sum game was proclaiming alliance with Reagan, putting a Democratic stamp on the tax bill, and then boxing the president in to accepting policy changes.

Success required a clever balancing act. He had to fend off schemes of rival Democrats. Liberals wanted to sock a minimum tax to corporations and use it to cut the deficit. Second, Rostenkowski had to build a committee majority, playing on personal ties and team loyalties. Sheer doggedness paid off. Third, he and his staff had to maneuver the committee to rework Reagan's plan and give it a Democratic flavor. Fourth, he had to keep Reagan quiet, at bay, and in harness even while revolt was rumbling in the Republican ranks. And finally, when Reagan waffled and Republicans mutinied, he and Speaker O'Neill had to pressure Reagan to rescue Rostenkowski's bill.

As an old-breed politician with twenty-six years in Congress, Rostenkowski played a different game from the one the new-breed moderates played. His long suit is not drafting policy papers, doing TV interviews, or writing op-ed articles. Substance is not his forte. He is a vote counter, a bargainer, a tactical leader. He works the insider's skills in caucus and committee: horse-trading and bluffing, man-to-man talk, facing down recalcitrants, parceling out plums, protecting his turf, and playing to the peculiar pride and passions that remembers feel for their committees. He admitted he would rather have become House Democratic whip than chairman of the tax-writing Ways and Means Committee, but O'Neill pushed him to take the committee job.

"I like the floor action much more," he told me. "You know, the maneuvering around the floor, the counting heads, getting people lined up. And then the Ways and Means Chairmanship just isolated me because I'm sitting there studying, trying to understand what the hell I'm doing."[58]

Ways and Means, one of the premier committees in Congress, became the symbol of Rostenkowski's power and the key to his game. It was what forced Reagan and Treasury Secretary James Baker to deal with him. He commanded the gates through which any tax bill had to pass. But that committee can be hard to manage; its members run the ideological gamut. Since they write tax law, they are targeted by almost every lobbying group and are prone to protect state and regional interests. Despite a 23–13 Democratic majority, the unruly committee nearly trampled Rostenkowski but he managed to ride the tiger. "He played the committee like Yehudi Menuhin plays a Stradivarius," Henson Moore, a Louisiana Republican, remarked admiringly.[59]

Outside of Washington, people pay attention less to committees than to the televised debates on the House or Senate floor. But by the time legislation hits the floor, it has been shaped in committee. Usually, only a few choices remain: an up-or-down vote or a few big amendments.

For most members (and lobbyists), the committee is the prime arena, the focal point for influence and action. But a committee is much more: It is a political home for members of Congress, an anchor of personal definition. Committees have their own personalities and identities: Agriculture; Armed Services; Energy and Commerce; Judiciary; Interior and Insular Affairs. They are hubs of members' lives, the focus of work and ideas, the sources of power and advancement, cozy dens of camaraderie. Politicians gravitate to committees of interest to them personally or to their regions. Then, they spend ten years, fifteen years, their entire careers on one or two committees with the same colleagues. They virtually live together. Relations can be close or fractious. A chairman can be a boss, a team coach, a father figure, or his members can defy or ignore him.

Rostenkowski—everyone calls him Rosty or Danny—runs the Ways and Means Committee like an extension of Chicago ward politics. Rosty is not only the congressman from Illinois's 8th District, an ethnic (largely Polish) blue-collar enclave in Northwest Chicago. He is also the committeeman or boss of Chicago's 32nd ward. His dad, Joe Rostenkowski, was the ward boss, too. As a boy, Rosty used to help his dad deliver Christmas packages to the needy, and some folks would write *Joe Rostenkowski for President* on their ballots. Rosty still lives in the brick home built by his grandfather across from St. Stanislaus Kostka Church. His wife and four daughters never moved to Washington, and Rosty commuted home on weekends.

In an era of video politicians who rarely work the street or step inside a political clubhouse, Dan Rostenkowski is one of a declining breed: an organization politician. He was schooled in the machine politics of Chicago's big boss, the late Mayor Richard Daley, who tapped Danny for the Illinois legislature and then for Congress. Rosty follows the rules of organization politics: A handshake is a firm deal; a politician's word is his bond; play with your own team; never forget who crosses you.

Rosty is a likable pile driver: six foot two, over two hundred pounds, with the brawn and force of a Chicago Bears linebacker. He has a gravel voice and sometimes the syntax of a stevedore. But he dresses Ivy League, in a trench coat, charcoal gray suit, a rep tie and button-down shirt. Now in his late fifties, his rusty hair is thinning, and when he smiles, his face creases and his eyes become little slits squinting beside his ski-jump Bob Hope nose. You notice his hands: They are big, strong, and constantly in motion, rapping the table, gesturing, pointing, persuading, directing. He acts out scenes. In a restaurant, telling me how he handled one foe, he reached across the table to jab a large index finger into my chest, and declared, "I'm targeting tax reform." Or as he told how House Republicans opposed it, up went his big basketball hands, palms out, fingers spread, defying passage. He is such a natural ham that I asked whether he had done any acting.

"Yeah," he said, chuckling. He had at St. John's Military Academy in Wisconsin. "I was never good. I was a football player and a basketball player, and the drama coach, he thought it was good to have all the basketball players and the football players do some theater. So we did. We were called the Swagger Stick Club."[60]

After two years in the Army during World War II, Rosty got a shot at playing professional baseball with the Philadelphia Athletics. At

twenty-three, he was in the Florida Grapefruit League, and his dad
wanted him to come home.

"Are you gonna be Babe Ruth?" he needled Rosty. "Are you gonna
be Lou Gehrig? You're a late swinger. Forget it. You can't hit the
goddamn golf ball. Come on home and go to school. Your mother's
sick."

Rosty gave up baseball, went home, finished Loyola University, and
went into politics. His decades in the Daley machine made him a
staunch Democratic partisan. Ironically, they also made him receptive
to alliance with Reagan, for that experience imbedded not only partisanship but awe of authority, especially of the presidency. Rosty was
immensely flattered when, in 1981, Reagan shrewdly rescheduled his
first State of the Union address to accommodate Rostenkowski, who
had a long-standing speaking engagement in Chicago. Despite their
clashes in 1981, Rosty spoke proudly of working with the president on
trade legislation and aid to the Caribbean basin. As one pol sizing up
another, he found Reagan an awesome stump politician. "He makes all
the right moves," Rosty gushed. In his macho way, he bragged about
dealing with Reagan man to man on tax reform.

The irony is that Rostenkowski is not a reformer by nature. "That
really isn't my chemistry, reform," he confessed to me. "I'm a businessman. I've always been a businessman. I like deductions. . . . I enjoy
going to dinners. I enjoy walking in restaurants. I enjoy taking the
check. I enjoy meeting people and being with people. That's my whole
life-style."

The part about being a businessman isn't literally accurate. Also,
Rosty is more likely to be on a corporate junket collecting a fancy
lecture fee than picking up the dinner tab. But his comments suggest
how he views himself. He's climbed from Chicago ward leader to major
figure on the national scene, and he's proud of making it. His constituents may be blue-collar, but with Daley-style pragmatism, Rosty has
kept a protective eye out for Chicago business. He has written plenty
of business tax breaks into law, especially in 1981, and he likes hobnobbing with corporate CEOs. "What atmosphere do I ever expect to live
in when I leave Congress?" he asked rhetorically. "I want to mingle in
this community of business activities. Where has my life been? My life
has been in the business community."[61]

Nonetheless, by 1985 he was bitter at the "deceit of business" in
exploiting the enormous tax credits, depreciation write-offs, and other
corporate loopholes in Reagan's 1981 tax plan. Angrily, he recalled
having fought to ease the tax load of the steel industry and corporations

like General Electric as a stimulus to economic growth, only to see them plunge into mergers and paper deals rather than reinvesting. In 1985, he was eager to correct the damage, curb the excess, and see more fair play put into a tax system where his grown daughters on modest salaries were paying more taxes than multimillionaires with tax dodges. Moreover, Rosty wanted a trophy. He wanted a legacy attached to his name. He bucked the conventional wisdom that passing tax reform was impossible, feeling that success might give him an outside shot at being speaker when O'Neill retired in 1986. Alliance with Reagan held all that promise.

Rosty to Reagan: "Keep Your Powder Dry"

Getting into the ring on tax reform with the nation's undisputed political champ required fancy footwork. For a year, Rostenkowski had to bob and weave, jockeying between cooperation and independence from the president. His improvised opposition game went through five phases: touching gloves in alliance with Reagan; jabbing back at Democratic rivals and skeptics; putting the Democratic mark on the tax bill; getting Reagan to hold off his counterpunches; and finally, maneuvering Reagan into a corner where he had to get Republicans in line.

It was a tricky relationship that required Rosty's keeping some distance from Reagan. If the Democrats were to share the political credit, Rostenkowski's partnership with Reagan had to be loose. He could not agree to a precooked deal or he would get politically smothered. In early 1985, Treasury Secretary Jim Baker and his deputy, Richard Darman, tried to lure Rostenkowski into crafting a joint bipartisan tax proposal. They wanted him on board before the president's plan was unveiled. But Rosty refused. Burned by Reagan's backing away from a deal in 1981, he was leery of being fooled the second time around. Also, if Baker and Darman wrapped up Rosty, he would have no bargaining chips to bring his committee Democrats on board. Finally, he was jealous of institutional prerogatives.

"I'm the chairman of the committee," he told Reagan's men bluntly. "You get the ball off to me, and I'll handle the ball. We're [the committee] going to write the bill."[62]

Echoes of former congressional barons: Rosty could afford a bit of swagger because he knew House Republicans would balk at a reform bill hitting business with $125 billion in additional taxes over five years. Reagan's plan brought the maximum individual tax rate down from 50 percent to 35 percent, cut the capital gains rate from 20 percent to 17.5

percent, raised the personal exemption from $1,000 to $2,000, and took 6 million poor off the tax rolls. And it lowered the corporate tax rate from 46 percent to 33 percent. But it was not a Republican-style bill; it paid for those tax reductions by revoking the corporate investment tax credit and closing some corporate loopholes. To pass it, Reagan needed mainstream Democrats, meaning Rostenkowski.

In public, Rostenkowski wrapped himself in Reagan's banner but raised the Democratic flag, too—never more artfully than on May 28, after Reagan unveiled his plan on national television. Rosty's response was classic one-upmanship, an exercise in playing the opposition game sotto voce. Like O'Neill, Rostenkowski altered his style and tried video politicking.

Never a TV star and always reluctant to be paired on television opposite Reagan, Rosty surprised everyone with a polished performance. He had hired Joe Rothstein, a media consultant, who put him through rehearsals with a TelePrompTer. Rothstein made the square-faced Chicago ward boss swap his spectacles for contact lenses, primped his makeup, showed him a relaxed, folksy delivery style, and told him to smile. Rostenkowski's speechwriter, John Sherman, delivered a slick text which claimed tax reform as a Democratic issue since Harry Truman and welcomed Reagan as a maverick Republican. It was pitched deftly at the blue-collar Knights of Columbus crowd that Danny grew up with and that Reagan wanted to steal away from the Democratic party. Rosty identified with their bellyaches.

"Every year politicians get up and promise to make the tax code fairer and simpler—but every year we seem to slip further behind," he said. "Now most of us pay taxes with bitterness and frustration. Working families file their tax forms with the nagging feeling that they're the country's biggest chumps. Their taxes are withheld at work—while the elite have enormous freedom to move their money from one tax shelter to another. Their bitterness is about to boil over. And it's time it did. But this time there's a difference in the push for tax reform. This time it's a Republican president who's bucking his party's tradition as protector of big business and the wealthy. His words and feelings go back to Roosevelt and Truman and Kennedy. But the commitment comes from Ronald Reagan. And that's so important—and so welcome. . . . A Republican president has joined the Democrats in Congress to try to redeem this long-standing commitment to a tax system that's simple and fair."[63]

Rosty put Reagan on notice that Congress would not merely rubber-stamp his tax plan, but would make it fairer. Then he stole a leaf from

Reagan's book—he appealed for listeners to write in. WRITE ROSTY buttons blossomed on Democratic lapels and more than eighty thousand letters poured in. Reagan was so impressed that he phoned Rosty to thank him.

Round one: Rosty had put himself in contention with Reagan.

Before he began recrafting Reagan's bill, Rostenkowski arranged a nonaggression pact, extracting Reagan's promise not to try to influence Rosty's committee or take potshots at its bill until the committee had finally approved it.

"Mr. President, you know if you're gonna criticize me the first day we start, if you're gonna take shots at this thing as we're proceeding through it, this bill's going nowhere," Rostenkowski told Reagan.

"What is it that you want?" Reagan asked.

"I don't want you to make any comment on it," Rostenkowski said. "I want you to keep your powder dry."

"All right," Reagan replied, "I'll make a deal with you. I'll keep my powder dry. I won't say a word about the bill."[64]

Round two: An implicit swap—Rosty bought Reagan's outline, and he got Reagan's star hitched to his own wagon.

Rostenkowski wanted plenty of time to work on the bill—seven months in all—to drive home the point to the voters that the Democrats had a vital hand in producing the new law. His early problems were with Democrats, not Republicans. Back in May, Jim Wright, then House majority leader, and Democratic Study Group liberals were pushing for a minimum tax on corporations and wealthy individuals that would raise $35 billion to $40 billion a year—to lower the deficit. Rostenkowski fought this plan because it would take away a huge chunk of tax revenues that his reform bill needed to finance tax breaks to individual middle-income taxpayers. And he got backing from Speaker O'Neill, who was dead set against Democrats' sponsoring any tax increase.

In the fall, Rostenkowski's committee rebelled. His staff had made Reagan's bill tougher on corporations and the rich and more favorable to the middle class. But day by day through late September and early October, committee Republicans and some Democrats picked apart reform and restored special-interest provisions. The lobbyists were riding high. Loopholes were going back into the law. Members from oil-and-gas states were teaming up with timber interests, banking interests, and the big-state members, demanding full deductibility of state and local taxes. Rostenkowski, unable to muster a steady majority, was losing control. His press clippings were turning sour. Tax reform was dying. The nadir came on October 15: Instead of clamping down on loopholes, as Reagan and Rostenkowski had proposed, the committee voted to sweeten a favorite tax shelter of commercial banks—the reduction in taxes allowed for bad-debt reserves. Rostenkowski threw down his pencil in anger. Outside the committee chamber, bank lobbyists shouted for joy.

"The tax bill stinks like a dead fish," John Sherman, Rosty's press spokesman, groaned to me afterward.[65]

Rostenkowski was in despair. He went home alone to his apartment. "I wrote myself a letter when I was in the bottom of the valley," he admitted to me later. "I wrote myself how lonely and how miserable I was. You know, do people really want reform? I mean, are we all so phony?"[66]

Remodeling, Democratic Style

Shrewdly and patiently, Rostenkowski turned the game around and put a Democratic majority together. Some Democratic committee members were shocked at how far they had gone in catering to special interests. Rostenkowski shamed them into reversing the bank vote and tightening up on banks. He played on their loyalty to him and their pride in their team, the Ways and Means Committee, like a football coach at half time after a disgraceful first half. "The press was kickin' the crap out of the committee," he recalled. "So I had the committee get together and I said, 'Is this what we want? Is this the image the Ways and Means Committee is gonna have? We're liberalizing [loopholes] even from present law? I mean, is this reform? Are these Democrats? Is this the issue we're gonna develop?' "

Then, like a ward boss, he made the rounds, asking his members for their bottom line—what they absolutely had to have in the tax bill for their districts. On the problem areas, he set up bipartisan task forces, stacked 4–2 in favor of Democrats, and dictated just how much tax revenue could be given away in certain areas, and he let the task forces carve up that money. It gave Democratic members a sense of participation.

In his first big move away from Reagan, he gave away his major plum to the big-state members: continuation of existing federal tax deductions for state and local taxes. Reagan wanted to knock that off and pick up huge tax revenues. Governor Mario Cuomo of New York, accusing Reagan of anti–New York bias, had turned that issue into his crusade. Cuomo made splashy appearances in Washington and called home

New York's senators and congressmen to toe his line. (Charles Rangel, a Harlem Democrat, poking fun at Cuomo's heavy-handed tactics, had joked to Cuomo, "I don't mind being your puppet, just don't shine the light on the strings.")

Deductibility of state and local income taxes was worth $60 billion to $65 billion in tax revenues over five years. Rosty felt he had to trade it away to corral a committee majority. That concession was vital to gaining steady support from big-state members: Charlie Rangel, Tom Downey, and Raymond McGrath of New York; Robert Matsui and Pete Stark of California; his own protégé, Marty Russo from West Chicago; and others like Barbara Kennelly of Connecticut, Brian Donnelly of Massachusetts, and William Coyne of Pennsylvania. Downey and McGrath had told Rosty they would fight his whole bill—until he yielded on state and local taxes.

A week after the disastrous bank vote, Rosty made his deals, one member at a time, demanding their loyal support in return. "You've got it—$65 billion," he told Downey. "But you gotta be with me on everything else. I want you to be my ally. I need you to convince other people and to speak on the floor."[67]

Member by member, Rostenkowski built momentum for the tax bill. Later he would cement it with transition rules—favors to each of his allies: a special break to a stadium here, an airport there, a few businesses, some partnerships, all written in such fine print that only tax lawyers could decipher it. That was the essence of Rosty's Chicago ward politics, the goodies doled out to members for playing ball with the chairman.

Round three: Rosty had bought a guaranteed nineteen-vote majority on all but a handful of tough issues.

But he had crossed the administration on state and local taxes. On October 24, when Jim Baker learned of that concession, he chased Rostenkowski by phone to North Carolina, where Rosty was giving a speech. Baker had wanted to use some of that tax money for concessions to probusiness Republicans. Baker was mad.

"Goddamn, Danny, what did you do to me?" Baker demanded. "How can you do this?"

"Hey, I'm not gettin' any support from you!" Rosty shouted back, blaming Baker for the way committee Republicans were undercutting him. "What the hell do you think I am? You think I'm gonna run up against my Democrats?"

Baker scolded Rosty for making the move without warning.

"I'm gonna hang up on you, you son of a bitch," Rostenkowski threatened.

"No, no, no, don't hang up," Baker warned.[68]

Rostenkowski slammed the phone in Baker's ear. They resumed shouting face to face the next day in the Ways and Means Committee library. Others could hear them through the walls.

That same afternoon, the administration's top team considered pulling out of its partnership with Rostenkowski. But essentially he had them trapped, and they kept going. Still, Rosty had to play his game carefully—pulling Reagan along in his direction, while he put a Democratic stamp on the bill. He fretted that only four or five committee Republicans were being helpful, and he berated top administration officials for not bringing the Republicans along. Jim Baker and Dick Darman told Rosty that he himself should develop Republican support.

By early November, Reagan was chafing at Rostenkowski's tactics, especially Rosty's plans for a fourth tax bracket (above Reagan's three) to hit the rich. That violated one of Reagan's "lines in the sand"— guidelines that he insisted on. On November 6, Reagan complained publicly about the "watering down" of his package. Rostenkowski quickly phoned the president to remind him of his vows of silence. It was bravado, but it worked.

"What's going on here?" Rostenkowski complained.

"Sorry it happened," Reagan apologized. "Won't happen again."[69]

Round four: Rostenkowski had kept Reagan, Baker, Regan, and Darman in line as he altered Reagan's package.

In the next two weeks Rostenkowski reshaped the bill more to Democratic liking, which drove House Republicans wild and put Reagan in a difficult box. Rostenkowski was now playing his opposition game to the hilt and getting plenty of press play. The corporate tax rate went up from Reagan's 33 percent to 36 percent; a fourth personal tax bracket was added at 38 percent; the capital gains tax was hiked from 17.5 percent to 22 percent; and a tough, 25 percent minimum tax was imposed on individuals and corporations. Business lost handsome tax write-offs from accelerated depreciation. Rostenkowski's Democrats were tougher than Reagan on the oil-and-gas industry, on real estate shelters, on defense contractors, and on depletion allowances for coal, iron ore, and other minerals. And they gave better tax-rate schedules to the middle class, as well as deduction of mortgage interest on two homes.

For Rostenkowski, the climax came on the night of November 22. He was near physical and nervous exhaustion. That afternoon, Reagan had privately given his approval to passing Rostenkowski's bill, but the bill would change that night. Rostenkowski was under enormous pressure from Russo, Rangel, Downey, Frank Guarini, and others to yield to organized labor, which wanted to make all employee fringe benefits tax free. Reagan and Rostenkowski had proposed partial taxation.

As chairman, Rostenkowski felt every group should make sacrifices for tax reform. He did not want to tilt prolabor. But Rangel had pledged union lobbyists he would try that final night to make *all* fringe benefits tax free: health and life insurance, educational costs, prepaid legal fees. That would cost $11 billion to $12 billion in tax revenues over five years and throw Rostenkowski's revenue-neutral tax bill out of whack. Rosty refused.

During a recess, Marty Russo asked Rob Leonard, chief counsel and staff economic wizard, how much tax revenue would be raised over five years from a one-percent increase in the corporate tax rate. Leonard said $13 billion.

"That's it, the ballgame's solved," Russo shouted—meaning that a one-percent increase in the corporate rate would make up for the tax revenue lost by granting tax-free fringe benefits.[70]

Rostenkowski was adamant. Months before, lining up some corporate support for tax reform, he had pledged CEOs from IBM, General Motors, General Foods, Procter & Gamble, Dart & Kraft, Sara Lee, and others that he would hold the corporate tax rate at 35 percent. Now, his Democrats, his team were trying to push him to 36 percent and he would not break his word. He was caught in a vise. He walked away into a side room, leaned against the wall, and broke down crying. His chief of staff, Joe Dowley, walked in.

"Boss . . ." said Dowley, offering sympathy.

"Just leave me alone, Joe," Rosty croaked.[71]

Marty Russo, a big, lumbering, aggressive politician, a chip off Rostenkowski's block, wouldn't let go. When Rostenkowski came back, Russo argued that Rosty would need labor's support to pass the bill on the House floor. It was a politically smart trade-off to make, he said. He hunted down Jim Baker and Dick Darman, who had come to monitor the final votes. Baker conceded that at best, Rosty's bill would only get about forty Republican votes on the floor, out of 218 votes needed.

"Are you telling me that I have to get 178 Democrats to pass the bill?" asked Russo, one of Rosty's chief vote whips.

"Probably," Baker said.

Russo took that piece of intelligence back to the caucusing Democrats. "We can't get 178 Democrats if we don't take care of fringe benefits," he told Rosty.[72] That rekindled the revolt of the prolabor group. Rostenkowski tried to stop them, calling for loyalty, recalling his pledge to the business executives, pleading not to upset things when victory was so close. But they called for a show of hands. Rosty lost.

He tried another gambit of the old-breed power game. It was his bill, his fight, and they were his team. He asked for a chairman's prerogative. He proposed that when Rangel offered the amendment on fringe benefits, Rosty would call for a voice vote and declare Rangel's proposal beaten. But if a roll call were demanded, Rangel would win, and Rosty himself would propose raising the corporate tax rate. Team feeling was strong. The other Democrats agreed.

Formal committee sessions resumed, close to midnight. The Republicans were angry, demanding roll-call votes on everything. Rangel's fringe-benefit amendment came up. Roll call. It passed with an easy Democratic majority. Rostenkowski proposed upping the corporate rate; the Democrats passed it. They finished the bill close to three A.M. The Republicans were furious.

With House Republicans in open revolt, Reagan stalled on making any endorsement. Rostenkowski telephoned the president to appeal for Reagan's support, but Reagan dodged him for four days. Rosty wanted to fly with Reagan to the West Coast over the Thanksgiving break, but Jim Baker headed him off. Reagan finally called Rostenkowski back on November 30—angry that Rosty had bleated to the press about phoning Reagan and getting no answer.

"You asked me to keep my powder dry," the president reminded him. "You asked me not to make any comment. Now, I'm asking you to do the same thing. Don't you make any comment."

"Mr. President, I'm your biggest fan," Rosty replied. "I won't do a thing. But I think you're making a mistake by not having endorsed this bill that night."[73]

Reagan delayed several more days; by then it was impossible to quell the Republican mutiny. The shock came on December 11, when 188 Republicans bolted from Reagan and, joined by thirty-five Democrats, prevented the tax bill from coming up for a vote. Rostenkowski was crestfallen. He went into Tip O'Neill's office, his tail between his legs.

"You know, Danny, we're gonna get it through," O'Neill encouraged him.

"Jesus, I put too much time on this thing to have it die like this," Rosty moaned. "Jesus, if they kill it on us, what are we gonna do?"

"We're gonna put the challenge on the president," O'Neill retorted. "We're gonna make the president go out and get the votes."[74]

Actually, O'Neill could have taken the tack that the bill was dead, the war was over, and Republicans were to blame for killing their own

President's number one domestic priority. But the speaker thought that tax reform made good sense. And seeing a chance for Democrats to score some partisan points, he laid on Reagan the responsibility for rescuing Rostenkowski's bill.

"If the president really cares about tax reform, then he will deliver the votes," O'Neill declared. "Otherwise, December 11 will be remembered as the date that Ronald Reagan became a lame duck on the floor of the House."

To be worth another try, O'Neill said, the president would have to deliver fifty Republican votes. Tough but not impossible. If O'Neill had wanted to kill tax reform, he could have said seventy-five or even ninety votes, half the House Republicans. But he did not want to kill the bill; he wanted to make Reagan sweat.

For six days, the White House struggled desperately. As each day passed, Rostenkowski basked in credit and saw Republicans take a licking in the press. His opposition game was paying off: Democratic success and Republicans humiliating the president were there for all to see. Reagan had to plead for votes, endure the wrath of rebellious backbenchers, and play upon their loyalty. When Republican nose counts reached the magic number of fifty that evening, the White House had its switchboard operators chasing Tip O'Neill. But having taken plenty of beatings from Reagan, O'Neill wanted to savor the time that Reagan needed him so badly.

"He called me that night that he had the fifty votes, and I was down at the Phoenix Park Hotel eating supper, and I didn't return the call," the speaker told me. "Three times he called, and they tell me at the White House he was in a dither he was so upset." Tip mimicked a pouting Reagan. " 'You think he's [meaning Tip] gonna renege on me? I got the fifty votes. Do you think he's gonna come up and demand that we have seventy-five votes or a hundred votes?' And finally when I called him, and I said I'd put the thing on [for a vote], and that I'd trust that he'd have the fifty votes or more, they were completely relieved."[75]

On the next rule vote, Reagan had seventy Republicans. The bill finally passed on a voice vote in confusion. Once again, Reagan was the hero, arriving like the Cavalry to rescue the damsel.

But it was a positive-sum game. Rostenkowski had also won round five. He had provided the Democrats with a political win either way. He had outwitted the Cassandras by actually producing a tax-reform bill that got 188 Democratic votes. If his bill had died, Republicans would obviously have killed it. Since it passed, Rosty and the Democrats had earned a share of credit.

In the Senate, the bill was revamped again, much more to Republican liking, as Jim Baker and Dick Darman had predicted. With brilliant maneuvers, Bob Packwood, the Senate Finance Committee chairman, not only got rid of Rostenkowski's fourth bracket but restored a lot of tax breaks for business. The final result was a bipartisan hybrid.[76]

But Rostenkowski had stolen the Republican thunder long enough so that neither Reagan nor other Republicans could fly tax reform as their realignment banner in the 1986 election. Unlike the House moderates whose prime motivation on MX was the substance of the issues, Rosty's opposition game was a power struggle at heart, matching Reagan's appeal by shrewd legislative maneuver and some clever Democratic PR. In tandem with Reagan and Packwood, Rosty's game had worked well enough to pass the tax bill and to give the country a fairer tax law. And it had neutralized the issue politically. For an opposition chairman like Rostenkowski, that was a political ten strike.

All three opposition games—Tip O'Neill's confrontation politics, the trading game of the House moderates, and Rostenkowski's strategy of alliance and remodeling—have importance far beyond the 1980s. Those patterns will crop up again and again in the decade ahead, and beyond. Certainly the tactics, and even some of the very same moves, will be repeated, for these are the basic ways the game is played by opposition leaders and by ambitious upstarts eager to put their mark on policy.

15. The Foreign Policy Game: Bureaucratic Tribal Warfare

> *Nothing ever gets settled in this town. It's not like running a company or even a university. It's a seething debating society in which the debate never stops, in which people never give up, including me, and that's the atmosphere in which you administer.*
>
> —George Shultz, secretary of State

One enduring myth of American politics is that foreign policy is run— and is supposed to be run—by the secretary of State. It is also a ritual of our presidential campaigns for challengers to denounce the disarray of the existing foreign policy team and to promise reform that will bring unity and clarity. True to form, Ronald Reagan in 1980 lashed out at the Carter administration's inability "to speak with one voice in foreign policy." Reagan promised to restore order and structure and to halt the internal feuding that had hobbled President Carter. He solemnly pledged to make the secretary of State his "principal spokesman and adviser" on foreign affairs.[1]

In my early years of reporting in Washington, I used to take such statements seriously. But after following six administrations, it's one of the first campaign pledges I discount. It has been made by every American President since John F. Kennedy—made, and then broken, by all but one of them.

Kennedy's secretary of State was Dean Rusk, but on Vietnam and arms control, he more frequently took his cues from Defense Secretary Robert S. McNamara. Lyndon Johnson's pattern was similar. Richard Nixon installed William P. Rogers as secretary of State but Henry Kissinger, as national security adviser, ran policy on Nixon's behalf. After Kissinger shifted to the State Department, he reigned supreme under President Ford—the first strongman secretary of State since John Foster Dulles under Eisenhower (making Ford the one recent president to let State run foreign policy). Jimmy Carter vacillated between Secretary of State Cyrus Vance and National Security Adviser Zbigniew Brzezinski, Vance finally resigning after objecting in vain to Carter's ill-fated mission to rescue American hostages in Iran.

Reagan fits the historic pattern. Initially, Reagan picked Alexander M. Haig, Jr., as secretary of State—impressed with Haig's strong anti-Communist views, his military career, and his White House experience. In a comment that came to haunt Reagan—because Haig took it to heart—Reagan told Haig that on foreign policy, "I'll look to you, Al." Even so, Reagan probably did not anticipate Haig's pronouncing himself "vicar" and "general manager" of Reagan's foreign policy.[2] Reagan and his advisers did not want strong, one-man rule in foreign policy à la Kissinger. They had disliked both Kissinger's diplomatic style and the substance of his arms agreements with Moscow.

Haig never got to taste Kissinger's glories. Just before his Senate confirmation hearings in January 1981, Haig's policy turf and his role as the nation's number one diplomat were trampled on by Defense Secretary–designate Caspar Weinberger. Normally, arms control is the province of the secretary of State; Haig intended to move quickly. But Weinberger stole Haig's thunder. He declared in a press interview that new arms talks with Moscow should wait at least six months, in order to get Reagan's military buildup under way first. That was an ill omen; the White House and Weinberger frequently blocked Haig's initiatives. Fuming in frustration, Haig left the administration after seventeen months.

For all Haig's idiosyncrasies, the problem was not unique to Haig. George Shultz, the next secretary of State, spent years battling the same forces, trying to control his diplomatic bailiwick. Shultz was constantly reacting to inroads from Weinberger and from four successive national security advisers: Bill Clark, Bud McFarlane, John Poindexter, and Frank Carlucci. Reagan would consult others and blithely bypass his secretary of State and simply inform him at the eleventh hour of major decisions: huge American troop maneuvers in Central

America in 1983, which affected regional policy; withdrawal of American Marines from Lebanon in 1984, which drastically altered Shultz's diplomacy; adopting a new nuclear doctrine with his Strategic Defense Initiative in 1983, which altered arms control policy; plunging ahead with his secret arms deals with Iran. Each time, Shultz objected belatedly to the president—to no avail.

Indeed, as the Iranian arms scandal surfaced in November 1986, Shultz was forced to the ultimate indignity for a secretary of State—admitting on national television that he did not have "the authority to speak for the entire Administration" on its most acute policy issue. In short, he was out in the cold.

The bureaucratic warfare that beset Shultz was like a governmental migraine—a chronic symptom of problems in Reagan's foreign policy apparatus. Actually, such institutional battling is normal in most administrations. But Reagan's apparatus was especially divided, rent from start to finish by personal rivalries and institutional cleavages. Those rifts became ingrained because Reagan as president was so often detached, uncertain, indecisive. In foreign affairs, he had gut attitudes, but Reagan zigzagged. He did not project the sure sense of direction that he had in domestic affairs. His leadership style was laissez-faire, or else policy by impulse.

In managing foreign policy, a president has two main options: One model is to frame an overall strategy with one chief adviser and have this collaborator put policy into practice, forcing other senior officials to fall in line. Richard Nixon used this formula with Henry Kissinger in withdrawing American forces from Vietnam and in scoring breakthroughs with the Soviet Union and China. Both Nixon and Kissinger had a keen sense of global strategy and the interrelationship of issues. In the early 1970s, Nixon was prepared to sign arms treaties with Moscow that codified a rough nuclear parity. He fixed the bait for a deal with Moscow by his dramatic opening to Peking. As a president with a grand design, he provided a strong sense of direction in foreign policy.

The other presidential option is to follow an essentially reactive policy, responding to world events, improvising policy strands as opportunities arise or as the public mood—or the president's own mood—changes, because there is no grand design. Essentially this was Reagan's approach. His typical method for reaching major decisions—though there were crucial exceptions, among them the Iranian arms deals—was to have his principal policy advisers debate the options in front of him, groping for consensus. In Meese's image, this cast Reagan as "chairman of the board," listening and deciding.

That hunt for a collegial consensus sometimes left Reagan captive to stalemates and policy paralysis because his favorite advisers disagreed sharply—a problem that Carter also had. Any president is buffeted by strong-willed advisers, especially a president who, like Reagan, lacks foreign policy experience, is weak on substance, and has conflicting impulses (both to want arms agreements with Moscow and to mistrust the Soviets). And those failings showed in Reagan's policies.

Like Jimmy Carter, Reagan vacillated between policies and policy advisers. The Weinberger faction would prod him to institute an economic embargo against a Soviet natural gas pipeline to Western Europe, and Shultz would later get him to lift the embargo. Shultz and his policy allies would talk the President into sending American Marines into Lebanon, and Weinberger would persuade Reagan to pull them out. The Pentagon crowd pushed a brand new interpretation of the Anti-Ballistics Missile Treaty of 1972, and Shultz raced back from a trip to prevent Reagan from implementing the new interpretation. This endless tug-of-war within Reagan's inner circle made Reaganism less consistent in practice than Reagan's speeches sounded.

Tribal Rivalries

The factional strife that plagued the making of Reagan's foreign policy will outlive Reagan—just as it preceded his presidency—because it lies deeply imbedded in our governmental system. Most of the skirmishes of the Reagan period are microcosms of the foreign policy game. They fit a pattern of bureaucratic tribal warfare—institutional conflict fired by the pride, interests, loyalties, and jealousies of large bureaucratic clans, protecting their policy turf and using guile as well as argument to prevail in the battle over policy.

The clashes between cabinet secretaries such as Shultz and Weinberger are collisions at the tips of bureaucratic icebergs. Their disagreements are an echo of long, bitter feuds within previous administrations, a reminder of the institutional competition built into the structure of the executive branch—some of it healthy and necessary, some of it rancid and futile.

The patterns of conflict are well established in the national security triangle formed by the State Department, Defense Department, and the White House national security staff. It's like the old proverb, "Two's company, three's a crowd." Invariably there's an odd man out, dissenting, battling for the president's ear. Sometimes all three act like odd men out.

In some administrations, the running warfare is mainly between State and Defense. In the Ford administration, for example, Secretary of State Henry Kissinger and Defense Secretary James Schlesinger were scathing adversaries, Kissinger pushing détente and Schlesinger warning of its dangers. Late in Lyndon Johnson's White House years, Defense Secretary Robert McNamara clashed with Secretary of State Dean Rusk's loyal pursuit of the Vietnam War. But when the leaders of State and Defense get along reasonably, as they did in the Carter administration, then State is usually at swords' points with the White House. The running feud between Carter's Secretary of State Cyrus Vance and National Security Adviser Zbigniew Brzezinski was regular front-page news. By Reagan's second term, two successive security advisers ran the Iranian arms sales right around *both* State and Defense.

The truth is that presidential promises to put the secretary of State in charge of foreign policy are virtually impossible to deliver on. Presidents enjoy their own power of diplomatic initiative too much to let control of foreign policy pass to a secretary of State, and White House aides exploit presidential vanity to assert their power over policy.

What is more, the machinery of American foreign policy has become so sprawling and cumbersome that no one has exclusive domain over foreign and national security policy. In addition to the State and Defense Departments, the inner group on arms issues includes the national security adviser and other presidential aides, the Central Intelligence Agency, the Joint Chiefs of Staff, and the Arms Control and Disarmament Agency. More broadly, the foreign policy apparatus embraces the Agency for International Development, the United States Information Agency, and the Peace Corps. On economic policy, add the Treasury Department, Commerce Department, Agriculture Department, and the president's special trade representative. In the intelligence field, the CIA plus State's intelligence branch, the Defense Intelligence Agency, the National Security Agency (which breaks foreign codes by electronic eavesdropping), and the National Reconnaissance Organization (which runs spy satellites).

Twenty years ago, Stewart Alsop decried the "rich jungle growth of bureaucracy" and Nicholas deB. Katzenbach, then undersecretary of State, complained that only twenty percent of the people representing the United States overseas actually worked for the State Department.[3] The jungle is thicker now. George Shultz protested that "government action is crab-like" because "everybody wants to get into the act."[4]

Nor is it easy to carve up the action, as the military services carve up the Pentagon—with State handling diplomacy, Defense handling military matters, and the CIA doing covert operations, for policy issues intertwine. A military buildup affects arms control negotiations and vice versa. An embargo against Nicaragua affects diplomacy in Europe. The jurisdictions are so overlapping, the lines of responsibility so ambiguous, and the temptations to barge into each other's policy terrain so strong that only the most clear-headed, strong-willed president can impose order. Each cabinet department jealously fights for its views, its mission, its autonomy, its prerogatives.

Seeking some structure for the labyrinth, five successive presidents set up interagency groups to coordinate different policies. By Reagan's second term, there were twenty-five senior interagency groups (high-level), fifty-five interagency groups (mid-level), and more than one hundred other task forces, committees, and working groups. And all were riven by institutional rivalries.

While tribal warfare feeds off bad personal chemistry at the top, it is really driven by more basic organizational imperatives. Generally, cabinet officials become champions of the bureaucratic legions below, the advocates of their agencies—*localities*, in Washington lingo. Exceptions do occur, but usually policymakers identify national security with the programs, actions, budgets, roles, and functions—the very essence—of the agency they run. Their instinct is to influence presidential policy to foster the growth and importance of their own agencies. Typically, the policy options they promote are the ones which *they* will carry out if the president approves.[5]

As James Reston of *The New York Times* says: "Where you stand depends on where you sit." In short, an official's policy viewpoint flows from his or her job. The State Department has a vested interest in diplomacy, negotiations, stable relations with other countries, summit meetings, and making concessions to get concessions in return. The Pentagon has a vested interest in building up forces, buying and selling arms, making deployments, creating a show of force, getting the technological jump on the Russians, and persuading others of the worst-case danger if the Russians get a jump on us. The stock in trade of the Central Intelligence Agency is spying and covert operations. The White House, ever mindful of the president's political standing, wants bold-sounding initiatives—either tough talk or peace proposals, to make the president look good politically.

One seeming anomaly is that State presses harder to use American military force abroad than does the Pentagon. But that, too, reflects organizational interests. The top military brass, burned by defeat in Vietnam, has been gun-shy of new American military interventions abroad. The Joint Chiefs of Staff are wary of getting caught in battle without mass political support. For State, the use of force puts steel behind diplomacy and costs the State Department nothing, either in coin or blood. Historically, secretaries of State such as Dean Acheson under Truman and John Foster Dulles under Eisenhower were more eager to commit American troops in Korea or in Indochina than the military chiefs were. And George Shultz was true to that pattern under Reagan.

In general, Reagan's main foreign policy advisers—Weinberger, Casey, and Shultz—fitted the institutional molds almost to a T. Weinberger, a tough budget cutter under Nixon, became the Pentagon's most tireless, tenacious salesman; his theme song was more money, more weaponry. Shultz, reflecting State's interests, has been a proponent of patient diplomacy, of summitry with Moscow, of flexibility on tough issues, caution about strategic defenses. Casey, an old espionage fox from the World War II OSS (Office of Strategic Services, a forerunner of the CIA), was a passionate proponent of covert operations in Nicaragua, Afghanistan, Angola, and under-the-table deals with Iran.

The personal tendencies at the top are reinforced by the bureaucracies below; institutional loyalty is a powerful centrifugal force in the foreign policy game. Careerists feel strong tribal identity and loyalty, fueling policy conflicts higher up. Top-level policymakers feel pressure from their career bureaucracies not to compromise agency positions. Of course, agencies have internal differences, but they like to thrash them out within the family and present a solid front to outsiders. For one axiom of the foreign policy game is that career officials generally defend their agency's position and undercut proposals from other agencies. The shorthand is "N.I.H."—meaning an idea is "not invented here," and hence dubious. The competitive instincts thrive: Which agency's option does the president buy? Who wins? Who loses?

Throughout the executive branch, and especially in the foreign policy arena, people identify with the institution they work for and its building. State has its square-cut modern building in Foggy Bottom near Georgetown; Defense has the "five-sided funny factory" across the Potomac River in Virginia; CIA headquarters has a wooded campus setting at Langley, Virginia.

"Buildings are important," Michael Pillsbury, formerly a high Pentagon official, mused one night. "A building is territory. It has flags out front. It has symbols. It has its own security badge, a different color and design from all the others. People who belong to a building have tribal feelings.

"It's almost animal behavior. Animals band together when they have to protect common territory or seek food or face a common enemy. Animals mark off their territory. Wolves and dogs go around and urinate on different bushes to mark out their territory. Within the government bureaucracy, people do the same thing with memos. They write memos to say, 'This is my subject. This is my turf.'

"People are creatures of the organization and the physical building they belong to. Look at the shorthand terms they use to describe where they work. They say "State" or "Defense." That's like saying, 'I belong to the Zulu tribe.' At interagency meetings, people will ask, 'What's State's position on this?' or, 'What does Defense think?' Never mind that different parts of State have fought over it internally or the Pentagon has its own differences inside. When they go out to meet with the other tribes, they have a tribal position."[6]

That habit, of organizational identity, has roots far back in American history. Historian James Sterling Young described how Washington worked in the Jeffersonian era, executive-branch departments battling each other and lining up their support in Congress. "Each was an organizational empire unto itself, with its own field forces, its own independent system of communication with the outside world, its own sources of information, its own considerable resources and patronage," Young wrote. "Departmental segmentation locks conflict into the system of Executive Government. . . ."[7] The words fit today, 180 years later.

Other laws of political behavior and Washington sociology affect the foreign policy game, regardless of party or administration. We take it for granted that Congress will battle with the executive branch, usually over money but also over foreign policy, especially since the Vietnam War. But more is at work here than traditional clashes between institutions. People's differing functions and careers play affect how policy is made, as much as institutional boxes do.

What is involved is not just a conflict of two branches of government but a clash of two different cultures: the open brawling of Capitol Hill and the hidden processes of executive agencies. Basically, politicians and bureaucrats represent two different personality types, playing two different games. By nature and function, they are bound to clash.

Success for each group requires strikingly different behavior. For starters, the foreign policy bureaucrat has a passion for anonymity and the congressman a passion for publicity. The reasons are simple: The keys to survival and advancement for a bureaucrat are operating efficiently in private and staying out of trouble. The key to reelection for a congressman is making a name for himself, often by making a public fuss. The bureaucrat benefits by blending in; the congressman, by speaking out. The bureaucrat makes his way by developing professional expertise; the congressman by being a quick-study generalist who can jump from field to field, exploiting political openings. Most bureaucrats put a high premium on continuity in policies, careful to make slow, incremental changes so as not to jar the system. Plenty of congressman get their ride to Washington by denouncing the misguided policies of the past and by casting themselves as agents of change—the more dramatic, the better. According to Stanley Heginbotham of the Congressional Research Service, the normal tensions between politicians and bureaucrats are most acute in the foreign policy game.[8]

Officials inside the administration try to address other governments with one voice, one policy line. Career diplomats, and even Pentagon officials, want to conduct their negotiations with foreign governments in private. One of their most vital goals is to have stable, friendly relations with countries such as South Korea, the Philippines, Greece, and Turkey, and that means avoiding avoid noisy squabbles over human rights or military bases. Their tendency is to cast policy in terms of national interest, to avoid crises with other governments, to minimize the impact of crises when then arise, and to seek solutions through mutual accommodation.

Those characteristics invite clashes with Congress. In the Capitol Hill game, there is a political payoff for senators and House members who cultivate reputations for independence, by challenging the established foreign policy line. Quite often, they cast policy in terms of parochial rather than national interests, such as the economic impact of foreign imports on industries in their home state. Also, most elected officials have to deal with too many issues to follow closely foreign policy toward any one country or region. So they jump on hot crises to score P.R. points and to maximize personal influence.

Or again, the diplomatic game requires long, arduous negotiations and reassuring other governments that agreements will be ratified. But the congressional game exploits delay, surprise, and procedural maneuver to increase congressional leverage during ratification. In short, the two games don't mesh.

Dozens of examples come to mind: In the early 1970s, Henry Kiss-

inger's insisted on "quiet diplomacy" to arrange for large-scale emigra-
tion for Soviet Jews, but Senator Henry Jackson of Washington and
Congressman Charles Vanik of Ohio preferred the public club of
denying trade benefits to Moscow. Jackson and Vanik won, and emigra-
tion later dwindled. The Reagan team suffered gadflies, pouncing on
controversial disclosures about Nicaraguan *contras* or the perennial
ulcer of Pentagon cost overruns and spare-parts scandals. Clearly, Capitol Hill thrives on broken-field play, while the administration prefers
what sports writers call "ball control"—keeping policy in its hands.

Obviously, debate is healthy for winnowing out bad ideas and formulating sound, durable policy, but it can also be paralyzing when
divisions run rampant inside an administration. Then, it takes some
grand design to give shape to policy, and a powerful hand at the center
to control the clutter and cacapohony of government. Kennedy and
Nixon, both bright, intensely curious and assertive, reached out to
resolve internal controversy. Kennedy probed the bureaucracy. Nixon
and Kissinger labored above it. But President Reagan's normal slack
disengagement from foreign policy, except during the run up to a
summit meeting or in some crisis, fed conflict within his foreign-policy
apparatus.

What's more, Reagan's well-advertised preference for consensus
among his advisers rewarded obstinacy. A holdout knew the president
was reluctant to move without his assent. In his first term especially,
Reagan's urge for collegialism made it hard to formulate policy. It
increased the power of obstruction.

"It's almost impossible to move because the American position has
to be checked with so many people: State, Defense, Joint Chiefs, NSC,
White House, the Arms Control Agency," groaned a top Reagan aide,
exhausted by internal strife. "The biggest problem in government is
that there are too many overlapping functions. Too many people are
doing the same job. That creates turf problems and infighting, and you
can't get anything done."

Policy by Preemptive Strike

One case of prolonged paralysis was the epic bureaucratic battle fought
in the Reagan administration over the Strategic Arms Limitation
Treaty signed by President Carter in 1979. It took Ronald Reagan
nearly *six years* to decide what to do about that treaty, known in the
arms control fraternity as SALT II.

What makes that prolonged delay so amazing is that for Reagan,

SALT II was anathema. He and his partisans reacted to it viscerally, as did the Committee on the Present Danger, a bipartisan conservative group that supplied many top-drawer policymakers for Reagan. The SALT II treaty, never ratified, was nonetheless being observed by Washington and Moscow in 1980. It was the prime symbol of what Reagan and company felt had been wrong with arms control. They had even disliked the SALT I Treaty signed by Nixon in 1972.

In the 1980 campaign, Reagan condemned the Carter treaty as "fatally flawed." What galled Reagan and his hawkish advisers was SALT II's acceptance of the nuclear status quo. They felt the treaty legitimized Moscow's huge arsenal of heavy, multiwarhead missiles and created a "window of vulnerability" for American land-based ICBM's—years when the American force was vulnerable to Soviet attack. Reagan vilified SALT II as false arms control because it sought only arms *limitation*—limits on future buildups—but not actual *reduction* in existing nuclear arsenals. Late in the campaign, Reagan pledged to negotiate a new treaty. The implication was that he would quickly discard SALT II.

But paradoxically, once Reagan was in office, he got hooked into keeping Carter's treaty by failing to understand how the foreign policy game is played. He got trapped by a typical bureaucratic skirmish— because the White House did not grasp its significance. This was one of those quintessential behind-the-scenes Washington episodes that barely causes a ripple in the press and is often missed entirely by TV. Yet its outcome established an important policy line for nearly six years.

That first skirmish was a microcosm of the foreign policy game: ploy and counterploy between some of very sharp policy players. On March 3, 1981, just five weeks into Reagan's term, John Lehman, the outspoken Navy secretary, fired the first official Reaganite salvo against SALT II. Under President Ford, Lehman had been deputy director of the Arms Control and Disarmament Agency, under Fred Iklé; together they had helped block Kissinger, then secretary of State, from achieving a SALT II treaty before the 1976 elections. In 1980, Lehman had helped draft the anti–SALT II Republican party platform. Now, Lehman at Navy and Iklé, number three in Reagan's Pentagon as undersecretary of Defense for Policy, were bent on killing Carter's treaty.

Even though arms control was not his bailiwick, Lehman made the opening move. He told reporters that the United States should stop complying with both SALT I and SALT II. Technically, SALT I had expired in 1977, and Lehman contended that Carter had extended it illegally—without Senate approval. Since SALT II had never been ratified, Lehman said he would recommend that the Reagan administration stop adhering to it informally.

It was a bold opening gambit. Lehman was not high enough ranking to be on the National Security Council. But as a savvy power player, Lehman was short-circuiting the policy hierarchy by going public.

At State, the press agency report carrying Lehman's remarks rang alarm bells. State saw Lehman invading its policy turf and attempting unilaterally to force policy action—before there had been high-level discussion of arms policy.

Ranking State Department officials favored SALT II. They saw benefits in the limits it imposed on Soviet multiwarhead missile deployments and believed it helped the United States monitor and predict Soviet weapons development. Some State officials, having helped develop the SALT I and SALT II agreements, had a personal stake in them. As a former NATO commander, Secretary Haig knew that West European governments liked the SALT treaties because they set a climate of accommodation between East and West. Also, Haig reasoned that it was unwise to scrap an existing treaty without something to replace it.

Haig reacted swiftly to Lehman's encroachment on his turf; he decided to "countermand" Lehman's statement. Otherwise, Lehman's comments would gain legitimacy; they would be read in government circles and foreign embassies as the authoritative word on Reagan's policy. There was no time—and for that matter no inclination at State—to check with the Reagan White House, where both National Security Adviser Richard Allen and his boss, presidential counselor Edwin Meese, shared Lehman's antipathy to SALT II. Haig acted on his own, using newspapers to fix a policy line. Haig had his spokesman phone a statement to *The New York Times* and *The Washington Post,* just before their evening deadlines. That timing insured headline play for the State Department, repudiating Lehman and setting out Haig's policy.

The statement crafted by Haig and two high officials, Larry Eagleburger and Richard Burt, was a masterpiece of bureaucratic gamesmanship, for it was disarmingly simple but it had major policy impact. The statement said that arms-control policy was being reviewed and that "no decision has yet been taken on our adherence to existing SALT agreements." Then it added: "John Lehman's statements on SALT, as reported by the press, were not authorized, nor did they reflect administration policy. While we are reviewing our SALT policy, *we will take no action that would undercut existing agreements* so long as the Soviet Union exercises the same restraint [emphasis added]."

Technically, that did not commit the administration to abide by every detail of SALT I and SALT II, though it did promise not to take any action that would permanently abrogate the treaties.

Haig's statement, issued anonymously, landed on the inside pages, only a few paragraphs in the *Times* and the *Post.* It deserved more play, for Haig was unilaterally declaring that SALT I and SALT II remained in force for the foreseeable future—and, as it turned out, that policy stayed in force until mid-1986.

In the foreign policy game, Haig had two trump cards that Lehman lacked. First, Haig had enough rank to disown Lehman's statement; second, Haig had command of the State Department's worldwide network of communications. He could—and did—send cables to all American embassies, instructing them to brief foreign governments on his statement. Those briefings reinforced Haig's policy. Only the president could reverse Haig.

Indeed, the next morning, Reagan was perplexed by news reports of anonymous officials saying that the United States would not undercut SALT II. "Who in the world is saying that?" he demanded. No one had forewarned him. When Reagan learned Haig was the source, he let the matter drop, not sensing its importance. Reagan's White House aides, still relatively new to high-level infighting, felt powerless to overrule Haig at that point.

"There was nothing we could do," protested one anti-SALT official. "We would have had to get another cable countermanding Haig's cable. But we would have had to get Haig to sign it. No chance. We protested, but we found out what a weak link Dick Allen would be. Allen complained and groaned, but would do nothing. Ed Meese took a legalistic approach: There was no way to punish Haig."

It was a case study of how policy can be set by one official's preemptive action—so long as other policymakers remain passive. The episode also illustrates why experienced players such as Haig, Eagleburger, and Burt were so quick to react to Lehman, and why all agencies immediately fire back at bureaucratic rivals: to protect themselves from policy invasions.

That early skirmish was a critical moment for the Reagan presidency, though few people then recognized it as such. It showed that Reagan came into office lacking a master plan for foreign policy; he was preoccupied with his domestic economic program. So when SALT II came up quickly, neither he nor his White House aides had a policy framework for dealing with it.

Moreover, in his desire to avoid the foreign policy squabbles of the Carter presidency, Reagan had deliberately weakened and downgraded the role of national security adviser, any president's personal protector on foreign policy. He had picked Richard Allen, who was no match for Henry Kissinger, Carter's Zbigniew Brzezinski, or Alexander Haig as a strategist or bureaucratic infighter; so Reagan was underprotected. Nor was Reagan prepared, as an alternative, to anoint someone else— Haig, for example—as his foreign-policy czar. That left the field wide open for hit-and-run tactics. On this first big issue of SALT II, the White House let control of policy dribble away.

The Elephant vs. the Terrier

From my observation, there are four paths to dominance on national security policy for a secretary of State. Path number one is to be clearly designated by the president as the policy architect, the president's alter ego. This is what President Truman granted two secretaries of State, George Marshall and Dean Acheson; it is what Dwight Eisenhower did for John Foster Dulles. Truman and Eisenhower exercised supreme power occasionally, but on most issues they let their secretaries of State reign. Except for Henry Kissinger in the mid-1970s, more recent secretaries have lacked this clearcut mandate.

Path number two is to grab power by bureaucratic fiat and preemptive policy moves. That was Haig's tactic in 1981: seizing the initiative before his rivals had learned the power game. It won Haig some skirmishes. The risk, as Haig found out, is that this tactic makes a policymaker look power hungry to his president and to rival officials, who find ways of getting even.

Path number three to policy victories is to end-run cabinet rivals and privately sell the president on a policy action, without having to answer the counterarguments and crossfire of other officials. George Shultz did that on occasion and so did Caspar Weinberger, not to mention Reagan's national security advisers. In fact, the end run became a trademark of the foreign policy game under Reagan—on arms control, Central America, strategic defense, and most notably, on the Iranian arms deals.

But equally typical of the Reagan period, and other administrations, is path number four: marshaling bureaucratic alliances and waging a campaign to sway the president with support from cohorts in other agencies, in Congress, and among allies abroad.

The long-term policy jousting over the SALT II treaty was just such

a marathon tug-of-war between rival policy clans. It was classic bureaucratic tribal warfare, with Shultz and Weinberger deploying forces like
tribal chieftains.

For five years that pair clashed over almost every major policy line:
the use of American Marines in Lebanon, air reprisals against Arab
terrorists, the proper strategy on Central America, summitry with the
Soviet Union and American negotiating terms, and interpretations of
past arms treaties. Even lie detectors: Weinberger used them to battle
press leaks in the Pentagon. When Reagan ordered using them
throughout the government, Shultz trumpeted his opposition: "The
minute in this government I am told that I'm not trusted is the day
that I leave."

At least two of Reagan's national security advisers, Bill Clark and
Bud McFarlane, despaired of the collisions and machinations of Shultz
and Weinberger and their paralyzing deadlocks. I have heard Clark and
McFarlane complain about their inability to control the feuding cabinet barons; I know that the internecine combat was one reason why
both security advisers quit. The Shultz-Weinberger feud took on the
crusading passions of holy warfare. Sometimes, other officials said, one
or both would take more extreme positions to oppose the other. Shultz
privately expressed dismay to aides. "He told me that he was surprised
by the viciousness of arms-control politics in this administration," an
official close to Shultz revealed. "He said he'd been around this city a
lot, in government, but he'd never seen anything as intense and vicious
as that."

Reagan himself was upset by the testy wrangling between Shultz and
Weinberger. "He knows about their fighting," one presidential intimate told me. "It bothers him. But he doesn't want to do anything
about it. He doesn't like those kinds of personal confrontations."

The rivalry between Weinberger and Shultz had an unusually long
history, one in which Shultz usually had the upper hand. "George tends
to dominate everything and everyone around him," said a former
Shultz lieutenant. "He takes the reins of power and doesn't appreciate
sharing it." Twice, Weinberger was cast as Shultz's subordinate, and
playing second fiddle apparently left him determined to prove his parity
in the Reagan cabinet. White House officials detected that Weinberger was not only aggravated at Shultz for assuming that power was
rightly his, but also that Weinberger felt he was brighter than Shultz,
despite Shultz's academic pedigrees as an economist.

In 1970, Shultz became Nixon's budget director and the White
House installed Weinberger as his deputy. Shultz tried to make his own

favorite, Arnold Webber, the de facto number two. Weinberger was so frustrated that he finally wrote a memo for Shultz to sign, naming Weinberger as acting director whenever Shultz was away. After Shultz signed the memo, Weinberger secured his status by circulating the memo to other agency officials. Later when Shultz became Treasury secretary, word went out that Shultz would still conduct the annual budget briefing. Weinberger, the new budget director, was crushed because he expected to do it. But he was evidently too awed by Shultz to phone him directly. An intermediary worked out a joint press conference.

When they returned to private life, both wound up working for the Bechtel Corporation, a multibillion-dollar world-wide construction firm based in California. Weinberger became Bechtel's top legal executive, once again in the shadow of Shultz, the company president. After Reagan's election in 1980, Shultz was bruited about as a likely secretary of State, a post that Weinberger aspired to. When Weinberger learned that he would get Defense, Reagan political advisers told me, he subtly blocked Shultz from becoming secretary of State by privately suggesting that it would be inappropriate to have "two Bechtel men" in Reagan's cabinet. Instead, Haig got State.

Shultz and Weinberger cut radically different figures, physically and temperamentally. Shultz is a sturdy Buddha, a teddy bear, solid, and bland-looking. Shultz likes to be a comfortable old shoe—cooking steaks on his backyard grill for foreign leaders or conducting office interviews in a sweater by a roaring fire. For many years, he shunned publicity and became known for dull press conferences. Shultz's temper flares when he is crossed personally, and he erupts in indignation, as he did during congressional hearings on the Iran-*contra* operation. But normally he is even-tempered and reassuring. In Europe, he offset Reagan's cowboy image with his reassuring manner. He talks with the hedging, inbred caution of an economist. Generally, his style is conciliatory, compromising, pragmatic. He is a labor mediator by training, a blender and a fixer.

Weinberger by contrast is a feisty partisan who cannot resist producing fireworks. Angular, agile, and dapper, he tugs on his plastic cheeks, eyes rolling, mouth turned in a wry smile. His style is confrontational. A lawyer by training, Weinberger is a debater, an advocate, a Reagan ideologue, sharp and unyielding. He likes the Washington social circuit and the limelight. Inside the administration as well as in Congress, he has exasperated many officials by his rigidity. "Stubborn," "bull-headed," "arguing with him is like the Chinese water torture"—those are things other officials say about him. Shultz's world is painted in grays; Weinberger's, in blacks and whites.

"Shultz moves like an elephant," observed Joe Laitin, a longtime government press officer who has worked for both men. "Shultz moves that one big elephant foot forward cautiously and checks to see if the ground will hold it. And then he moves the next foot and gradually shifts his weight. Weinberger is like a fox terrier. He darts out here and there. He races into dangerous areas where angels fear to tread. He's a pretty feisty guy who gets himself in trouble because he talks without thinking and then he refuses to budge. But he has a personal charm."

Like cabinet secretaries in many administrations, both men proclaimed loyalty to the president even as they tugged him in different directions. The Iranian affair was a rare instance of agreement between Shultz and Weinberger; in that case, their rivalry may have reduced their influence because they were not in the habit of going to President Reagan with a combined position.

Normally they have been on opposite sides of the barricades. Weinberger has sent Reagan memos warning of the trap of negotiations and summits with the Russians. Before he resigned in late 1987, he relentlessly pressed Reagan to junk previous arms treaties and to deploy a partial strategic defense. Shultz has urged Reagan to negotiate with Gorbachev. He has promoted flexibility in American negotiating terms, tried to keep past treaties alive, and cautioned Reagan that strategic defense must be proven feasible, survivable, and cheaper than the Soviet offense.

One of their most telling conflicts arose over the use of American military force, where their roles were oddly reversed. Although Weinberger championed Reagan's costly military buildup, he resisted using those forces, whereas Shultz pushed Reagan to exercise the nation's military muscle. In January 1986, for example, Shultz called for swift reprisal against Libya for terrorist bombings. Weinberger cautioned against those who seek "instant gratification from some kind of bombing attack without being too worried about the details." Three months later, after more terrorism, he relented in the raid against Libya, but only one swift strike.

At virtually every step, Weinberger resisted sending American Marines into Lebanon and escalating American military action there, as advocated by Shultz, Bill Clark (then national security adviser), and Bud McFarlane (then Clark's deputy). "The hard reality is that diplomacy not backed by military strength is ineffectual," Shultz argued in one speech. "Leverage, as well as good will, is required. Power and diplomacy are not alternatives. They must go together, or we will accomplish very little in this world."

Later, Weinberger derided "theorists"—obviously meaning Shultz—who send troops into perilous situations for fuzzy diplomatic purposes. "Employing our forces almost indiscriminately and as a regular and customary part of our diplomatic efforts," he declared, "would surely plunge us headlong into the sort of domestic turmoil we experienced during the Vietnam War, without accomplishing the goal for which we committed our forces."

Even before the fateful truck bombing that took 241 Marine lives in October 1983, Weinberger was privately urging Reagan to pull those troops out of Lebanon. As fighting escalated, he argued that the United States was being sucked into taking sides in the Lebanese civil war. When Shultz, Clark and others wanted to step up American air actions, Weinberger warned against stumbling into a war with Syria. At times, Shultz needled Weinberger, once suggesting sarcastically that if Weinberger was not willing to use force, "maybe we should cut your budget."

The most stunning episode occurred after Shultz and McFarlane, two former Marines, had persuaded President Reagan—over Weinberger's objections—to authorize an aerial reprisal for the truck bombing, according to a top White House official. Shultz and McFarlane wanted a joint raid on November 17, 1983, with the French, who had lost fifty-nine lives to another truck bombing. French jets from the aircraft carrier *Clemenceau* carried out the raid, but the Americans did not. Weinberger called McFarlane at about 6:30 A.M. to say, "We just weren't ready. We needed more time." General John Vessey, chairman of the Joint Chiefs of Staff, told me that he was notified so late "that there wasn't time even to write alerting messages and get them out" to the American aircraft carrier *Eisenhower*. In short, a joint raid had been impossible.[9]

Shultz and McFarlane were deeply upset. The president was apparently angered, too. "He was mad about it," a top aide told me. "But he didn't pick up the phone and say, 'What has gone wrong and why?' He was visibly sighing and head shaking, but he's not the kind of person who would ever sternly discipline anybody."[10]

Eventually, Weinberger, bolstered by political pressures from Congress, got Reagan to pull the Marines out of Lebanon while Shultz was off on a trip to Grenada on February 7.

The Shultz-Weinberger policy disputes had a personal edge—a battle for image and standing as well as policy influence. The coin of success was not only who prevailed on policy but who was closer to the president. As a Reagan confidant, Weinberger goes way back. As a San Francisco lawyer, he had been Republican party chairman in California and was named by Reagan in 1965 to be state finance director—the key figure in Reagan's California cabinet. Shultz met Reagan back in those days, but did not get seriously involved with Reagan politically until he became an economic adviser to the 1980 Reagan campaign.

Having been Nixon's budget director, Labor secretary and Treasury secretary, Shultz put great stock in direct, private access to the president. "You have to involve the president in this strategy or he won't be with you," he advised me. "I have to be with the president, have opportunities to talk with him privately, and know what his bottom line is."[11]

Shultz demanded—and got—the privilege of two private audiences a week with Reagan, on Wednesday and Friday afternoons. To build up Shultz's prestige in 1983, Mike Deaver arranged for him to be photographed often with Reagan and to take trips with the president, without Weinberger. "George feels very strongly that being with the president without the opposing view being there is always helpful," one former national security adviser said. "He believes that the president's quality of not wanting to counter anybody makes him vulnerable to collegial decision making and vulnerable to not doing what he would naturally prefer to do. And I think he's right."

On occasion, Shultz would get Reagan's assent to policy initiatives that the Pentagon would have fought, had they known about them. Weinberger was upset, for example, that Shultz got Reagan to approve his unannounced trip to Nicaragua on June 1, 1984, to negotiate with Daniel Ortega, the Sandinista leader. Weinberger was even more infuriated that in October 1985, Shultz got Reagan's approval for a proposed joint communiqué for Reagan's 1985 summit meeting with Gorbachev. When Weinberger found out, the Pentagon protested so vigorously that the draft was eventually abandoned.

Shultz's regular private access to Reagan grated on Weinberger. "The timing of meetings with Reagan is very important because everybody knows that with people he likes, the last one to see him can usually carry the day," one high Pentagon official told me. In 1986, when Rear Admiral John Poindexter became national security adviser, Weinberger established his own privilege of regular private meetings with Reagan. And in October 1986, one Pentagon official bragged to me, Weinberger used his special access to lobby Reagan not to bargain away the right to develop strategic defenses at his imminent summit meeting with Gorbachev in Reykjavík.

SALT II: Battle of the Clans

Weinberger entered the war of bureaucratic clans over the SALT II treaty with distinct advantages. He had allies strategically placed in the bureaucracy: William Casey as head of the CIA; Ed Meese as Reagan's personal counselor; first Richard Allen and then Bill Clark, as national security adviser; retired Army Lieutenant General Ed Rowny as first-term strategic arms negotiator; and first Eugene Rostow and then Kenneth Adelman as director of the Arms Control and Disarmament Agency.

Moreover, Weinberger had hired Richard Perle, one of Washington's most canny infighters, as assistant secretary of Defense for International Security Policy. Chubby and cherubic-looking, Perle was a tough, brilliant master of the intricacies of arms control. As aide to Senator Scoop Jackson of Washington, he had been a no-holds-barred foe of both SALT I and SALT II.

Weinberger's antagonism to all past arms-control treaties, especially SALT II, appealed to Reagan's gut instincts. In a debate before a president who has no taste for details, subtlety and complexity lose out. The hard-line simplifier has important advantages. Uncertainty and ambiguity do not cloud his views or slow his maneuvers. One Weinberger-Perle gambit was to establish an appealing-sounding, hard-line position and then discredit anything less as "selling out." State Department officials complained that the Weinberger-Perle terms were unrealistic because they required Moscow to restructure its nuclear forces without imposing equal burdens on Washington. State urged "negotiability," something within reach of the Russians; Perle derided negotiability as "cowardice." Weinberger hammered his line: Moscow could not be trusted to make and keep agreements, and no important American weapons system should be compromised unless Moscow gave up more. Weinberger was on the offensive.

Shultz's game was defensive, for he lacked one normal asset of the secretary of State. Usually, in the battle of policy coalitions, a secretary of State tries to position himself at the political center of the national security community—as a broker between the hawkish, hard-line right and the pro–arms-control left. In the Carter administration, Secretary of State Cyrus Vance had done that—with Paul Warnke, as the chief arms negotiator and director of the Arms Control and Disarmament Agency, on his left pressing for an arms agreement, and with Defense Secretary Harold Brown and the Joint Chiefs of Staff on his right, raising cautions and opposing concessions. In that lineup, the State Department can forge compromises for the president.

But Shultz never got that chance because the normal political lineup got switched in the Reagan administration. Instead of the Arms Control and Disarmament Agency (ACDA) advocating arms agreements, Reagan's ACDA was manned by hard-liners in league with Weinberger. That left Shultz on the left flank—not in the center, and it hurt his bargaining leverage.

Nonetheless, Shultz had important allies. At State, his arms guru was Paul Nitze, a slender, silver-haired former Wall Street investment banker who had helped negotiate Nixon's 1972 arms treaties. Initially Nitze had fought SALT II, and he had strong credentials among hard-liners; now, he wanted to save SALT II. But the critical balance was swung by National Security Adviser Bud McFarlane and the Joint Chiefs of Staff. McFarlane believed in arms control, saw value in SALT II, and did not think American security had been seriously damaged by Soviet violations of arms treaties. McFarlane's support was pivotal, for when secretaries of State and Defense disagree, the national security adviser can tip the balance with the president. It was more ticklish for the Joint Chiefs to help Shultz. Since Weinberger oversaw their budgets, they could ill afford to declare open revolt; but as careerists, they were inclined to keep SALT II. Careerists tend to favor continuity in policy, whereas in-and-outers—Reagan's political appointees in the Pentagon—were eager to make a fresh mark on policy.[12]

In a tough bureaucratic fight on arms control, the military chiefs play a crucial role. A politically astute president wants them on his side on arms issues—especially if Congress may second-guess the president. In 1979, Carter had gotten endorsement from the Joint Chiefs of Staff (JCS) for his SALT II treaty. In Reagan's first two years, military men had defended it to him: first, Haig; then General David Jones, the JCS chairman whom Reagan inherited from Carter; and later, Vice Admiral Bobby Inman, the widely respected deputy director of CIA.

After the early skirmishes over SALT II in 1981, the battle inside the Reagan administration was not seriously joined until 1985. In 1982 and 1983, the policymakers had been engaged in framing the Reagan administration's arms proposals. By 1984, President Reagan was caught up in his reelection campaign, eager to project a conciliatory image toward Moscow. In early 1985, the Weinberger faction mounted a new campaign to scrap SALT II.

A natural deadline emerged: In late 1985, the United States was preparing to launch a new Trident submarine, the U.S.S. *Alaska*, with twenty-four multiwarhead nuclear missiles. That submarine would put the United States over the SALT II ceiling on multiwarhead missiles (1,200)—*unless* Reagan retired and dismantled an older, sixteen-missile Poseidon submarine. The Pentagon hawks wanted Reagan to disavow the treaty and keep both old and new submarines.

In the foreign policy game, changing policy usually requires a powerful rationale. The Weinberger camp used Soviet bad behavior—violations of past arms treaties. For years, the American intelligence community and past administrations had been divided over whether Moscow had violated those treaties; in early 1983, a Reagan interagency task force was hopelessly mired in disagreement on that issue. Then Ken Adelman, who became director of the Arms Control and Disarmament Agency in April, 1983, bypassed the deadlock by doing a report in his agency, which found Moscow guilty.

Adelman, a thirty-six-year-old former student of and deputy to Jeane Kirkpatrick, Reagan's conservative United Nations ambassador, sensed a need for pressuring the president from the outside as well as inside the administration. Adelman had connections to the right-wing Senate Steering Committee. He teamed secretly with conservative Republican senators such as Malcolm Wallop of Wyoming, James McClure of Idaho, and Jesse Helms of North Carolina to have Congress require that Reagan make public ACDA's report.

The Kremlin inadvertently helped the Weinberger clan. In summer 1983, American spy satellites discovered a huge new radar facility—a building five football fields long and twenty-four stories high—in the Krasnoyarsk region of East Siberia. Washington objected that under the 1972 ABM (antiballistic missile) Treaty, no such radar site was permitted hundreds of miles inland. Each side was permitted big radars near its frontiers for early warning of attack. But a radar stuck deep in the country looked like battle-management radar, a facility to help direct antimissile defenses. Under the ABM Treaty, such defenses were forbidden except at one limited site. The Krasnoyarsk radar gave new ammunition to Weinberger, Adelman and company.

On January 23, 1984, Reagan sent a revised version of Adelman's report to Congress, accusing Moscow of several outright violations of treaties and agreements—using chemical warfare agents ("yellow rain") in Indochina and Afghanistan; failing to provide the West with advance notice of large-scale troop movements in Central Europe, as required by the 1975 Helsinki Accords; and unfairly encoding the telemetry (electronic messages) from its missile tests, thus impeding American efforts to check on Soviet compliance with SALT II. The

report found "likely" or "almost certain" arms violations in the Krasnoyarsk radar and the development of two new land-based ICBMs
(whereas SALT II permitted only new ICBM).

That first report was sharply disputed. Pro-arms-control moderates
and liberals, as well as some conservatives in Congress, questioned the
evidence. The report itself acknowledged the evidence was "somewhat
ambiguous." Moscow insisted that Krasnoyarsk was a space-tracking
radar facility and violated no treaty. It claimed the supposed second
new ICBM, the SS-25, was a legal modification of an earlier Soviet
missile, the SS-13. It argued that encryption of its test telemetry was
permitted. Also, State Department officials argued that Moscow had
complied with the main SALT limits, that violations were marginal,
and that SALT II was still a net plus for the United States.

The official military judgment was similar—and it had important
sway with Reagan. Since 1979, the military assessment was that the
Soviets were in a better position than the United States to "break out"
of SALT II—that is, rapidly build up their strategic nuclear forces if
the treaty were scrapped. In 1985, a White House official told me, the
Joint Chiefs of Staff estimated that Moscow had the capacity to jump
from about nine thousand strategic nuclear warheads to thirteen thousand by 1990. A CIA estimate projected up to twenty thousand by
1995. The United States could not come close to matching that. "The
JCS did not want numerical restraints taken off," one State Department policymaker told me, "for fear of a Soviet push in the arms race
over the 1985 to 1990–92 period, especially at a time when the U.S.
defense consensus was fading."

Much later, Reagan admitted that JCS estimates had jarred him. "I
learned that the Soviet Union had a capacity to increase weaponry
much faster than the treaty permitted, and we didn't," Reagan told my
colleague Leslie Gelb of *The New York Times*. [13]

In Reagan's informal, top-level caucus of the National Security
Council (the National Security Planning Group), the nation's military
leaders played a subtle game. Technically their advice to Reagan on
SALT II was neutral. Several officials informed me that John Vessey,
then JCS chairman, told Reagan that living with or without SALT II
was a "wash" militarily. Vessey's primary concern was maintaining
"our strategic modernization program." Translated, that meant: Don't
abrogate SALT II if that alienates Congress and jeopardizes our military budget; stick with it for political reasons. Beyond that, the Navy
did not want to spend $150 million to keep a twenty-year-old Poseidon
submarine in service; it wanted new attack submarines. So the Joint

Chiefs of Staff equivocated—in theory, they supported Weinberger, saying in principle SALT II should no longer be valid, but in practice, they advocated scrapping the old submarine, which meant abiding by SALT II's limits.

Weinberger played what bureaucrats call "the hundred-percent game." On tough issues, a policymaker may add up very close arguments and come out fifty-one percent pro and forty-nine percent con on some policy line. But meeting with other agencies, especially with the President, he argues his case one hundred percent, black and white, as an attorney would. To do less, so the theory goes, weakens your arguments and hurts your agency. Weinberger is at his best as a case lawyer, arguing his brief. "He wanted to drive a stake in that treaty," said a senior White House official.

Shultz's gambit was different. Like many a power-game player, he did not want to lose, for losses are a blow to prestige. So Shultz did not buck the president head on. He and McFarlane figured that Reagan would insist on taking some action to punish Moscow for arms violations; they tried a middle course. Instead of dismantling the old Poseidon submarine, they proposed drydocking it. Technically, drydocking would violate SALT II limits, but it would take the old sub out of service and give Reagan time to decide what to do with it for the long run. Shultz's gambit was a policy hedge, aiming at fuzzing the decision and winning the fight. At a National Security Council meeting on June 3, 1985, Shultz urged Reagan to "keep the high ground" politically— not be the one publicly to annul SALT II.

Following a Schattschneider strategy, Shultz widened the circle, reaching outside government for support. Events were favoring his clan. First of all, arms talks with Moscow—broken off in November 1983—had resumed in early 1985, and Reagan was pressing to meet the new Kremlin leader, Mikhail Gorbachev. Also, swing moderates in Congress, suspicious of Reagan's commitment to arms control, were demanding movement in arms talks before funding more of his military buildup. A bad time for Reagan to abrogate the SALT II Treaty.

Shultz mobilized Allied pressures on Reagan. Through its ambassadors, the State Department got European allies, especially those whom Reagan liked most, Prime Minister Margaret Thatcher of Great Britain and Chancellor Helmut Kohl of West Germany, to send Reagan telegrams urging him to stick with SALT II. Bitterly, Pentagon officials accused State of having ghostwritten the cables for Thatcher and Kohl. With Cheshire-cat grins, veteran diplomats insisted to me they had not gone that far, but they admitted that U.S. embassies were given "talk-

ing points" for Allied governments to use against the Pentagon position. In the clinches, that's how the foreign policy game is fought.

Also, Shultz and McFarlane persuaded Reagan to delay his decision
on SALT II for ten days to let Shultz sound out the Allies at a NATO
meeting in Portugal. Shultz knew in advance he had NATO on his side.
The European leaders put great stock in Soviet-American arms agreements. They were not persuaded that Soviet arms violations were
serious. They did not want the West—the United States—to take the
onus of annulling SALT II. And they wanted nothing to disrupt plans
for a Reagan-Gorbachev summit. Shultz cabled Reagan NATO's views
from Portugal, and a senior Reagan aide told me the cable had impact
with the president.

Armed with Allied support, Shultz and McFarlane shifted their
position and proposed that Reagan dismantle the submarine's missile
bays in full compliance with SALT II. In a final memorandum to
Reagan, I was told, McFarlane recommended that Reagan abide by
SALT II, call for Moscow to halt arms violations and offer to go the
"extra mile" by giving Moscow more time to reform. That is the course
Reagan announced on June 10, 1985. In sum, Shultz, backed by
McFarlane and the Joint Chiefs, won.

But a key axiom of the Washington power game is that no bureaucratic war is over *until the loser accepts final defeat.* Weinberger did
not. In fact, McFarlane, as the man in the middle, devised a compromise that gave Weinberger's clan an important consolation prize—and
a new opening. For Reagan, at McFarlane's urging, laid out tough
terms for testing Moscow's future behavior on three counts: whether
arms violations continued, how seriously the Soviets negotiated, and
whether they slowed their military buildup. Weinberger was told to
grade Soviet actions and propose "proportionate" countermeasures if
Moscow did not measure up. That set up another battle over SALT
II in 1986.

1986: Shifting Alliances Kill SALT II

Policy-making can be like a decathlon or a steeplechase: sheer endurance and tenacity pay off. That was true for Weinberger, for his
power-game style is to stake out an extreme position and ride his policy
horse without change, wearing down opponents and forcing others to
compromise. For the sake of final resolution, the heat is on them to
move toward his position.

With Congress, Weinberger's unyielding hard line backfired. But not with Reagan; for it put Shultz perennially on the defensive, trying to protect this policy from Weinberger's sallies. In 1985, for example, when Weinberger was savaging SALT II, Shultz emphasized that the timing and the politics were bad for getting out of the treaty. But by 1986, the ground had shifted.

Inside the administration, Shultz lost his clan. McFarlane was replaced by John Poindexter, his deputy, who did not favor SALT II. Poindexter was an active duty Navy admiral with an eye to becoming chief of naval operations, which made him technically Weinberger's subordinate and extra mindful of his views. In addition, there was a new chairman of the Joint Chiefs of Staff—Admiral William J. Crowe, Jr. Before he was selected, Weinberger and Perle had talked with Crowe and found that he shared their views on Soviet violations of arms agreements. Together, these shifts left Shultz isolated on SALT II in Reagan's inner circle.

On the outside, the political trends were working against Shultz, too. By late spring, 1986, Reagan was miffed at Gorbachev for not keeping his promise to set a new summit meeting in Washington. Soviet-American arms talks had not yielded any significant progress in recent months. So there was little incentive from Moscow to keep Reagan from breaking out of SALT II. What's more, Reagan was less inclined to listen to the European allies on arms issues than in 1985, because of their refusal—except for Margaret Thatcher—to support the American reprisal raid against Libya's Muammar Qaddafi for a terrorist bombing in Germany.

Finally, Weinberger declared that Moscow had failed to meet Reagan's test of its intentions on arms issues, and argued for American reprisal measures. In late March 1986, Reagan's senior advisers all agreed on the need for some American action, although Shultz's deputy, John Whitehead, had proposed American moves that did not violate SALT II limits, such as deploying more airborne cruise missiles and developing the Midgetman ICBM.

The issue of SALT II came to a head on April 16, two days after the Libyan bombing raid.[14] In a meeting of Reagan's inner circle, Shultz defended the overall SALT II limits as still in the American interest. Despite Soviet violations, he said, the overall ceilings had "taken on a magical aura." He did not want Reagan to disrupt the process of arms control.

Across the table, Weinberger slashed away. "I've never liked SALT II and neither have you, Mr. President," he asserted.

Attorney General Ed Meese agreed. "Mr. President," he recalled, "you gave a hundred speeches against SALT II and never liked it."

"Never liked it at all," the president nodded.

Weinberger favored deliberately violating the treaty's ceilings to show that it was dead. He made several proposals. Casey objected to one—encoding telemetry from American missile tests to foil Soviet eavesdropping—because he feared it would prompt Moscow to encode even more of its telemetry. Otherwise, Casey joined Weinberger and Meese on renouncing SALT II.

So did Admiral Crowe. He was bothered by Moscow's arms violations and, breaking with former JCS chairmen, he discounted the dangers of a rapid Soviet "break out" if SALT II were revoked. The Soviets already had more than enough warheads, he said. The real issue, as Crowe saw it, was Reagan's personal credibility; Reagan had to decide whether to carry out earlier warnings to the Kremlin about its arms violations. Crowe's comments were crucial, because he had moved the military hierarchy from Shultz's clan into Weinberger's clan.

Ken Adelman, head of the arms control agency, joined Weinberger, too. He reminded Reagan that SALT II was still unratified, would never be ratified, should have expired by the end of 1985, and was flawed anyway. Adelman also challenged Shultz's contention that the treaty's overall limits were "magical." He contended that Moscow had broken the overall SALT II ceilings, and pointed to a chart on an easel at the end of the table, showing a "clear violation" for overall SALT II limits.

"Every agency in town including the State Department has found it a clear violation," Adelman asserted.

Shultz reddened. He turned around to ask two questions of Paul Nitze, his arms adviser. Twice Nitze nodded. State had agreed prematurely to the arms chart Adelman was citing. (State later withdrew its assent.) The issue was intricate enough for Philadelphia lawyers— whether the Soviets were actually dismantling some old Bison bombers, as required, or merely taking them off operational bases, less than required. It was a matter of interpretation still to be finally resolved.

The Weinberger clan was exploiting a technicality, and Shultz was thrown off balance, being no master of the intricate details of arms control.

Casey pointed Reagan to another chart, showing that in the next few years SALT II would force the United States to dismantle more nuclear warheads than Moscow, a coincidence because Washington planned to retire old American submarines.

"Why should we do this when they're ahead?" Reagan demanded, his face flushed.

"That's the point, Mr. President," Casey pursued.

Poindexter, acting as a referee, interrupted to say that the American weapons were old and would be dismantled regardless of SALT II. He could have added that the American warhead total would actually rise, because new American submarine missiles carried more warheads than the old ones.

"Mr. President," Shultz objected, "We think the chart is just deceptive."

"In what way, George?" the president asked.

The answer lay in other charts provided to all of them. One chart showed that the Soviets would have to dismantle as many *missile launchers* as the United States in the coming years. Another chart showed that since 1972 Moscow had already dismantled 540 bombers and ballistics missiles in order to comply with SALT II—nearly three times the number Washington had dismantled. In sum, the charts showed Moscow making sacrifices to comply with SALT II. The Weinberger clan knew about those charts, as one member admitted to me, but they did not point them out to Reagan because that would hurt their case. Shultz was not schooled enough to cite these numbers quickly, to rebut Casey's chart.

"It's just wrong," Shultz insisted to Reagan.

"Well, in what way is it wrong?" Reagan asked.

"We don't think it's an accurate portrayal of the real case," Shultz replied.

The discussion moved on, but Reagan kept staring at the charts singled out by Casey and Adelman. The charts seemed to fix in Reagan's mind the idea that Moscow had finally breached SALT II's overall limits and that the treaty would be harder on him than on Gorbachev in the years ahead. It was a case of visuals beating oral arguments, selective facts overcoming a larger, more complex reality—and critically affecting the outcome.

To others, Reagan's mind seemed made up in principle; the question was what specific action to take. The Navy still did not want the old Poseidon submarines; Reagan was ready to dismantle them. To help him demonstrate he was disavowing SALT II, Casey proposed that Reagan break through the treaty limits in the fall by fitting out the 131st American B-52 bomber with long-range cruise missiles and not retiring some other weapon system to compensate. Reagan liked that idea.

After the meeting broke up, Shultz still had one major card to play—the reactions of Allied leaders, which had restrained Reagan in the past. Emissaries were sent to brief European leaders on a presidential decision document, NSDD-222. The problem was that NSDD-222 was fuzzy; it did not accurately convey to the European leaders just how close Reagan was to canceling the arms treaty. It left the fate of SALT II uncertain.

Thus, Shultz's political ace in the hole was wasted through confusion. The European leaders were pleased to see that Reagan had decided to dismantle the old American submarines; but NSDD-222 did not make clear what Reagan would do about the 131st B-52 bomber in the fall. Some Allied leaders were uneasy, but when Reagan met them personally at the seven-nation economic summit meeting in Tokyo in early May, they did not object strenuously enough to deter Reagan from abandoning SALT II.

Back in Washington, Reagan had some final discussions with Vice President Bush, Chief of Staff Regan, and National Security Adviser John Poindexter, but Shultz was traveling abroad. When he got home, he objected in writing to a new presidential decision document—this one with teeth in it—but his protest was to no avail.

On May 27, Reagan signalled the death of SALT II. He announced he would dismantle two old Poseidon submarines because of their inefficiency, but he would arm the 131st B-52 bomber with air-launched cruise missiles, breaching SALT II limits. Declaring SALT II null and void, Reagan said that from then on, the American force structure would be set by the "nature and magnitude of the threat posed by Soviet strategic forces, and *not on standards contained in the SALT structure. . . .*" [Emphasis added.]

The Weinberger clan had won the tribal war. Finally, on November 28, 1986, the 131st B-52 bomber was deployed, and the United States broke through the SALT II limits.

Weinberger's ultimate victory was not so astonishing. What was astonishing was that it took so long. The lesson for the foreign policy game was that Reagan had allowed prolonged maneuvers to stalemate him—and stall decision—for six years.

A more sure-footed foreign policy leader—Eisenhower, Nixon, or Kennedy—might have broken the stalemate sooner, but no president can avoid institutional deadlocks. The SALT II epic is but one of many battles that frustrated Reagan; it typifies the foreign policy game in virtually every administration.

In Reagan's case, the marathon battles between Shultz and Weinberger contributed to Reagan's eventual disaster in Iran. The frustrating paralysis of tribal warfare, added to Reagan's well-known distaste for confrontations, apparently made Reagan impatient with debating contentious issues and ready to set policy secretly, in league with one faction or another.

Some of Reagan's advisers admitted to me that the foreign policy apparatus had become so constipated that high officials felt moved to short-circuit the normal interagency process and sell Reagan privately on some policy. In other words, some gravitated toward a secretive, conspiratorial style of policy-making, not only to avoid Congress and a prying press but to bypass internal critics and paralysis. In a very real sense then, the deadlocks of tribal warfare laid the groundwork for the secretive policy-making of Reagan's fateful Iranian arms deals.

16. The Other Foreign Policy Game: End Runs and Back Channels

The trend seems to be for staff officers to consider themselves powers in their own right. The staff sometimes takes the president more seriously than the Great Man himself.
—John S. D. Eisenhower, President Eisenhower's son

As revelations of President Reagan's secret arms deals with Iran and of Lieutenant Colonel Oliver North's diversion of Iranian funds to Nicaraguan *contras* burst upon the country in November 1986, the public reacted with dismay. How could this policy cabal have happened? How could Secretary of State Shultz be so ignorant and uninvolved? How could Defense Secretary Weinberger be so opposed and distant? What murky figures were running American foreign policy? Had the system run amok?

Three months later, former Senator John Tower, head of President Reagan's special review board, called the Iran-*contra* operation "an aberration."

In one sense Tower was correct. The Iran-*contra* conspirators, as some later said, regarded themselves as above the law or the normal channels of decision. As a covert operation in fund-raising, cowboy diplomacy, gunrunning, dummy businesses, and conniving with foreign arms dealers to conceal Reagan's policies and to escape congressional law and accountability, it was an aberration for the American system.

Reagan pushed the NSC staff into covert operations, using it as his personal CIA. That raised echoes of Nixon's "plumbers"—an extralegal investigative staff unit subsidized by taxpayers but unknown to Congress. The deviation from the norm lay in the monumental deception of Reagan's declaring one policy toward Iran and following the opposite; his administration's defiance of a congressional ban on funding and arming the Nicaraguan *contras;* and the conspiracy to cover up policy through phony scenarios, false testimony, and shredding incriminating documents.

But in another sense Tower was wrong. As an example in how foreign policy can be made in secret by a small clique, short-circuiting the normal process of decision making, the Iran-*contra* affair was not an aberration. It was a case study in the "other foreign policy game"— the opposite of tribal warfare—the game of end runs and back-channels.

Part of the shock to the public of the Iran-*contra* operation was that it baldly stripped away the institutional formalities of cabinet government and exposed the great power of the national security staff. But there were precedents in Reagan's presidency for bypassing the regular policy apparatus, policy-making in secret by a small cabal, keeping most of government in the dark—not to mention Congress and the public.

At least two years before the Iran-*contra* operation began, Reagan had used his vest-pocket State Department—a small group of national security aides—to hatch one of his most important policy initiatives. In that vital sense, the Iranian operation was not unique. There is a parallel between the way it was run and the way Reagan generated his Strategic Defense Initiative (Star Wars) in 1983. SDI was hatched in conspiratorial urgency by the NSC staff and sprung on other top policymakers too late for serious debate. Like the Iran-*contra* operation, SDI was kept secret from internal critics for fear their resistance would kill it. Indeed, several high-ranking advisers were so taken aback by Reagan's utopian notions that they tried to stop him from giving his famous Star Wars speech. But just as Reagan intended, they were too late. Stealth enabled Reagan to proclaim policy suddenly before dissent could coalesce and then to force skeptical advisers into line.

Actually, the genealogy of Oliver North's rambunctious staff activism can be traced back to the Lone Ranger diplomacy of Henry Kissinger. As President Nixon's national security adviser—not as secretary of State—Kissinger circled the globe, secretly orchestrating Nixon's surprise trip to China in 1972. Then, Kissinger personally struck the most important arms deals with Moscow behind the backs of regular American negotiators. Kissinger's back-channel negotiations with North Vietnamese leader Le Duc Tho carried on the real business of American disengagement from Vietnam, supplanting the formal peace conference. No one, except Nixon, knew what Kissinger was doing. Kissinger was "end-running" the foreign policy apparatus.

There were conscious parallels between Kissinger's operations and those of Reagan's aides. Kissinger was a role model for Bud McFarlane, a principal architect of both Star Wars and Reagan's Iranian operation. McFarlane had worked on Kissinger's staff from 1973 to 1975, and he nursed a driving ambition to prove himself a new Kissinger by forging some stunning stroke of policy and by Kissinger-style personal diplomacy. As national security adviser in 1985, McFarlane persuaded the president to approve the first Iranian arms deals and guided Oliver North's operations. After leaving government, McFarlane flew to Iran in May 1986, hoping to meet Iranian leaders and bring home all six American hostages held in Lebanon. When the Iranian plot was exposed, McFarlane publicly invoked Kissinger—comparing his efforts to open up Iran for Reagan to Kissinger's China opening for Nixon.[1]

The common thread from Kissinger's secret diplomacy to Reagan's hush-hush preparation of Star Wars and the clandestine Iran-*contra* operation is the tremendous power of the White House national security staff. These episodes dramatize its capacity for initiating policy, conducting secret diplomacy, and running covert operations, unsupervised by Congress or other policymakers, except the president. The role and power of the national security staff has changed enormously since the National Security Council was first established by law in 1947.*

Well-publicized clashes between secretaries of State and Defense in several administrations obscure the fact that in the past quarter century, secretaries of State have lost less power to rivals in the Pentagon than to ambitious national security advisers. Since President Kennedy, national security advisers have moved into the terrain of the secretary of State and sometimes usurped his role as chief architect and manager of foreign policy, even as chief diplomat.

When the National Security Council was established by law under

---

*The National Security Council is the president's cabinet-level advisory group—usually the vice president, secretaries of State, Defense, and Treasury, the Attorney General, director of Central Intelligence, chairman of the Joint Chiefs of Staff, and the national security adviser. The national security staff serves the council, working under the national security adviser. Technically, the NSC is the cabinet group; but when Washington insiders refer to "the NSC," they often mean the staff.

Truman in 1947, its job was to integrate policy, to help other foreign policy agencies and departments "cooperate more effectively," and "to advise" the president. Truman's NSC began with a neutral, anonymous executive secretary, Sidney Souers, who was to sift, channel, and coordinate the flow of foreign policy advice to the president. Robert Cutler did that for Eisenhower; Brent Scowcroft, for Gerald Ford. The idea of the NSC staff was high-level civil service, not policy-making.

But over time, the NSC staff's function got turned on its head. Starting with McGeorge Bundy under Kennedy, the president's right-hand man on national security plunged increasingly into influencing policy, forcing decisions, taking initiatives, and pulling power to the national security staff. The NSC staff developed into policy managers and entrepreneurs. By the time of Nixon and Reagan, powerful national security advisers were not working as policy coordinators to cut cabinet secretaries *in* on the action, but they were cutting cabinet secretaries *out* of the action. The Iranian conspiracy was the culmination of that trend.

The Primacy of the NSC Staff

Somewhat disingenuously, given his aggressive activism as national security adviser, Henry Kissinger wrote later that the president should make the secretary of State his principal foreign policy adviser and restrict his national security adviser to a coordinating role. But then, he shrewdly added, "For reasons that must be left to students of psychology, every President since Kennedy seems to have trusted his White House aides more than his Cabinet."[2]

The power dynamic is natural enough. Presidents see their staffs, domestic or foreign policy, as extensions of themselves, whereas they look at cabinet secretaries and departments as sometimes difficult allies or even liabilities and nuisances. Proximity is one key reason. Top White House staffers orbit constantly around a president; cabinet secretaries have their own orbit. The senior White House staff, including the national security adviser, live with the President. They are constantly in and out of the Oval Office or on the phone with the president. They know his views, feel his triumphs, share his frustrations, read his moods, sense when to make a pitch and when to leave him alone. They are like family or like courtiers in royal households, contesting the power of cabinet barons.[3]

Staff aides are often true believers, their creed unsullied by the independent views of a departmental bureaucracy. Except for people of unusual self-confidence and independence, the mentality of staff aides is to see policy and politics from the president's personal perspective. Totally dependent on him for both job and influence, they rarely stand firmly against his policy impulses—even though it might be in his interest for the staff to oppose him. The natural impulse of staff is to tell the President what he *can do* and help him try to do it, not advise him what he *should not do* and try to talk him out of it. For the nearer the pinnacle of the political pyramid, the more loyalty to the boss is the vital touchstone.

The national security staff, as part of the White House apparatus, is more alert to the president's political interests than is the State Department—more sensitive to his itch for political theater. National security aides are more prone than are career diplomats to think of the domestic payoff of a foreign policy spectacular (summitry, a hostage release) or to weigh the domestic downside of a policy line (arms for moderate Arab states).

By the unwritten rules of the power game, it is practically immoral for presidents to admit that domestic politics play a role in foreign policy decisions. But everyone knows they do, and presidents listen to those who heed the political winds. That is why leaders like Reagan, Nixon, or Kennedy often lean on the advice of loyal national security advisers. Even Jimmy Carter, under pressure to silence Zbigniew Brzezinski, retorted: "I need Zbig to speak out publicly. He can go after my enemies. He can protect my flanks."[4]

By contrast, presidents from Kennedy to Reagan have felt State Department careerists were too prone to treat foreign countries as their clients. Epitomizing this mistrust, Richard Nixon told his staff that foreign policy was to be managed by the White House, "not by the striped-pants faggots in Foggy Bottom!"[5] Presidents get impatient with State's resistance to radical change, its stress on patient diplomacy, accommodation, and pursuit of long-term interests. From a presidential point of view, State is too nonpolitical and too frequently the bearer of bad news. Presidents resent the expertise of career diplomats when it challenges their own view of reality. As George Shultz learned with Reagan on Iran, the naysaying of diplomacy is a necessary check on presidential impulses, but it makes a secretary of State unpopular at the White House.

In the game of bureaucratic warfare, the national security staff has great advantages over the State Department. Proximity gives it constant contact with the president, presence in almost all high-level meetings, the chance to put in the last word with the boss. Its job is to write cover memos critiquing positions of other agencies. Moreover, somebody has to mesh the competing views and the strands of diplomacy, defense, aid, propaganda, and intelligence. State would like to do that, but State is one of the partisan tribes, and therefore unacceptable to rival tribes as the sifter of options, the arbiter. However, other agencies accept the primacy of the White House staff.

As Zbigniew Brzezinski contended, "Integration is needed, but this cannot be achieved from a departmental vantage point. No self-respecting Secretary of Defense will willingly agree to have his contribution, along with those of other agencies, integrated for presidential decision by another departmental secretary—notably, the Secretary of State. And no self-respecting Secretary of State will accept integration by a Defense Secretary. It has to be done by someone close to the President, and perceived as such by all the principals."[6]

What's more, modern technology has robbed the State Department—and the Pentagon—of important advantages in the power game. The two departments used to have exclusive global communications networks to American embassies or forces abroad. But in recent years, the White House has gained the technical capability to bypass State or Defense electronically. Its Situation Room has links to a worldwide network that lets the president get in touch with any leader in any country instantaneously. His national security staff can read the incoming electronic mail from around the globe and contact any embassy or CIA operation without ever informing State or CIA headquarters, as Oliver North often did. That means the White House can step into any issue at any time in any place.

Finally, the urge of modern Presidents to engage in personal diplomacy—summit meetings, personal visits, and a flow of private correspondence with kings and prime ministers everywhere—has enlarged the domain of national security advisers and pushed them into operational activism. They leave State the routine diplomacy, but they pull the most urgent business into the White House.

Richard Nixon's activism and mistrust of the State Department enabled Henry Kissinger to move out of the old mold of national security adviser as coordinator and honest broker for the foreign policy apparatus, and to set a new pattern, largely supplanting the secretary of State.

Under Carter, Brzezinski aspired to similar preeminence and established himself as a rival power center to Secretary of State Cyrus Vance. They battled toe-to-toe on Soviet policy, Vance handling arms negotiations, Brzezinski managing Carter's tougher line, especially after Moscow's 1979 invasion of Afghanistan. Like Kissinger, Brzezinski had his back channel to the Kremlin through Soviet Ambassador Anatoly Dobrynin. Also, Brzezinski was more of a strategist than Vance. He laid the groundwork for Carter's diplomatic recognition of China and handled crisis management when the shah of Iran was falling. Later, he and his staff were the architects of a rapid deployment force to cope with threats to the Persian Gulf.

Kissinger and Brzezinski established ample precedents for the bold actions of Reagan's national security advisers. The supreme irony is that Reagan came into office believing he would establish cabinet government and downgrade the national security staff. But Reagan's effort lasted for only a year.

What is remarkable—and significant—is that the national security job vaulted back to preeminence under Bill Clark, who had no experience in foreign affairs except one year as number two to Alexander Haig at the State Department.

Clark, who took the NSC job in January 1982, was not shy about exercising power. He projected the boyish modesty of a tall, lanky rancher who gave up a sunny life on the California Supreme Court to help his old friend Ron Reagan. Clark evoked Gary Cooper in the White House Situation Room, quiet-spoken and clad in cowboy boots. I recall Clark's constant self-deprecating litany that his NSC role was to be "referee" of the policy free-for-all and "coordinator" for the president. His stated recipe was to be invisible—not to be a policymaker but to be a lawyer insuring that all arguments were put before his one-man court, the president. Indeed, unlike most power brokers, Clark did not crave the limelight. He shied away from television appearances, made few speeches, and gave fewer interviews.

Nonetheless, within a few months he became the most influential foreign policy figure in Reagan's entourage. Clark engineered Haig's ouster and brought in Shultz. He pushed Reagan to center stage on foreign policy and encouraged Reagan's hard line. As an old Reagan crony (chief of staff in Sacramento), Clark had enough clout to muscle the cabinet barons. In mid-1982, Clark forced the brawling bureaucracies to agree on a strategic arms proposal. Without consulting Haig, he got Reagan publicly to propose an informal, get-acquainted meeting with Soviet leader Leonid Brezhnev. Later, leaving Shultz in ignorance, he prodded Reagan to make his strategic defense proposal. In 1983, Clark sent U.N. Ambassador Jeane Kirkpatrick to Central America to craft a more aggressive regional policy. Then with Weinberger, he persuaded the president to approve a huge American show of force in Central America, again with Shultz in the dark. Although State coveted the role of managing arms negotiations, Clark drew that function to himself and even toyed with setting up his own diplomatic back channel to the Kremlin.

Clark's activism demonstrated that power gravitates to the center of the administration. Even an admitted amateur such as Clark is quickly tempted to exercise broad authority in the president's name, consulting whom he will and ignoring others. With a laissez-faire president like Reagan, the latitude of the NSC staff is vast. Zbigniew Brzezinski gleefully observed that the Reagan presidency proved that it was not merely Kissinger's legendary ego or Brzezinski's celebrated instinct for the jugular which drew power to the national security staff.[7] It was the very nature of the modern foreign policy game that did it.

SDI: Short-Circuiting the System

President Reagan unveiled his Strategic Defense Initiative on March 23, 1983—intending it as a radical departure from the doctrine of nuclear deterrence by which this country had been defended since World War II. SDI marked a far more momentous shift of policy than many issues which were thrashed out for months and years in the National Security Council. Yet not a single NSC meeting was called to discuss SDI before Reagan unveiled it.

Reagan told the nation that he was announcing his bold promise to render nuclear weapons obsolete—"after careful consultation with my advisers." In fact, the consultation had been hectic, belated, chaotic, and minimal for practically everyone in Reagan's own government. The central issues raised by the president were not examined in depth beforehand by most top policymakers. The highest officials at State, CIA, and the Pentagon were shown drafts of the president's speech too late to offer more than modest adjustments.

The Joint Chiefs of Staff, though they had urged more research on defenses, were so shocked at what Reagan and his staff had done with their ideas that their chairman, General John W. Vessey, recommended that Reagan not give his famous Star Wars speech. Three military Chiefs told me they were stunned by how fast Reagan moved and how he had overstated their ideas. They had expected a serious study before the president announced a shift in policy. Secretary Shultz, fearing repercussions among NATO allies, also tried in vain to stop the speech, as did Richard Perle, then the Pentagon's top civilian thinker on arms issues. But suggestions to delay were brushed aside by the president and National Security Adviser Clark.

"Clark wanted this to be Ronald Reagan's legacy," said one high-level official. "They were far more concerned with building Ronald Reagan's image than whatever might be the losses, like Allied relationships or congressional criticism."

Star Wars epitomized an end run by the national security staff. It was a stunning example of how that staff can outgun the cabinet in making policy. Without exaggeration, Bud McFarlane, who as deputy national security adviser was midwife to the new plan, could boast to me that SDI was an "NSC creation." For years, Reagan had harbored the dream of strategic defenses; a tiny circle of staff led by Clark and McFarlane orchestrated its birth. The national security staff was not the sifter of options from other agencies but the policy entrepreneur.

Star Wars was launched in haste and intentionally sprung as a surprise, not only for dramatic political effect but to minimize internal opposition. "The impulse of other people in government would have been negative—because it would make their lives harder," one member of the policy cabal told me. Another top White House staffer candidly added: Star Wars was deliberately hatched in tight secrecy "to keep skeptics and doubters from strangling it in its crib."

The policy process was driven by Reagan's impulses. He had a personal epiphany on July 31, 1979, during a visit to the North American Defense Command, near Colorado Springs, Colorado. At the end of an all-day tour, Reagan and a domestic policy aide, Martin Anderson, were briefed on America's early-warning radar system by General James Hill, the Norad commander. Anderson asked what would happen if Moscow fired one of its big SS-18 missiles at an American city. "Well," Hill replied, "we would pick it up right after it was launched, and the officials of the city would be alerted that their city would be hit by a nuclear bomb in ten or fifteen minutes. That's all we can do. We can't stop it."

Disbelief spread over Reagan's face. Flying home to California with Anderson, Reagan talked soberly about what Hill had said. Obviously thinking ahead, he turned to the dilemma of a president once a Soviet attack was launched. "The policy options he would have would be to press the button or do nothing," Reagan said starkly. "They're both bad. We should have something in the way of defending ourselves against nuclear missiles."[8] Years later, Reagan used the dramatic image of a "Mexican standoff"—the Soviet and American leaders like two gunmen with nuclear pistols drawn "and if one man's finger flinches, you're going to get your brains blown out."

Within weeks, Anderson drafted a ten-page memo proposing that Reagan, as a candidate, come out for developing a "protective missile defense system." Reagan liked the concept but his top political handlers, John Sears and Michael Deaver, vetoed the proposal as political suicide, fearing such talk would add to jitters that Reagan was a warmonger. "Hey," Deaver told Anderson, "Ronald Reagan does not go out and talk about nuclear weapons."

After his election, Reagan was lobbied on strategic defenses by Edward Teller, a nuclear physicist who helped develop the U.S. hydrogen bomb, and by some of Reagan's "Kitchen Cabinet" and millionaire conservative financial backers (among them, Joseph Coors, the brewery owner, and Karl R. Bendetsen, a former Army undersecretary and later chairman of the Champion International Corporation). Teller, an ardent advocate of a space-based defense weapon—the X-ray laser—had first pushed space-based defenses with Reagan when he was governor of California. With support from Clark and Meese, the Bendetsen group met Reagan twice in 1982 to promote strategic defenses.

"We gave him a written proposal," Coors recalled. "We had hoped that the president would set up a separate agency outside the Pentagon and the Joint Chiefs." Coors had in mind a massive crash project comparable to the hush-hush Manhattan Project, which developed the atomic bomb during World War II.[9]

Teller's tales of the scientific potential for supermodern defense intrigued the president. Reagan questioned the Bendetsen group about the cost, duration, and technical difficulty of the project, but he was noncommittal. What really put strategic defenses on Reagan's agenda was the House vote in December 1982 blocking funds for the MX missile. That vote stymied Reagan and, according to aides, drove home to him how difficult it would be to get funds to continue a major buildup of offensive land-based missiles.

Politically, diplomatically, and militarily, Reagan needed a bold stroke to escape his stalemate and put life back into his foreign policy game. Clark saw that and favored doing something on defense, but he lacked specific knowledge. Within the NSC apparatus, Bud McFarlane became Reagan's idea man, and he put together the pieces on defense, operating secretively.

McFarlane is a quintessential staff man. New to Reagan's personal circle, he gained influence because he understood arms issues and had good links to Congress, a rare combination in the Reagan foreign policy team. McFarlane's father had been a Texas congressman, and McFarlane himself had worked on the Senate Armed Services Committee staff for Chairman John Tower. In early 1983, McFarlane was the

White House link with leading House Democrats, trying to devise a compromise to save the MX missile.

In an administration that had no high-level strategic thinkers, McFarlane knew much more about nuclear strategy and Soviet-American relations than Reagan, Clark, Shultz, Weinberger, Casey, or Meese. He had learned these issues in the mid-1970s as a staff aide to Henry Kissinger, his mentor and model.

Personally, McFarlane is a curious amalgam of boldness and insecurity. He is superearnest, methodical, and prone to bureaucratic circumlocutions about "families of options," delivered in a monotone. Yet he can be a jokester, entertaining friends with flashes of humor and hilarious spoofs of Kissinger's pompous Germanic elocution.

More than once, I heard McFarlane say he felt he was not on a par with the cabinet power brokers who had won Reagan's admiration by success in the corporate world. After McFarlane's promotion to national security adviser in late 1983, he made awkward confessions that he felt over his head in a job once filled by Kissinger. During his twenty-year Marine career, McFarlane had risen to lieutenant colonel but no farther. He is not an imposing figure—short, slight, squint-eyed—but he is ramrod straight and emphatic about duty and self-control. He was surprising in his policy and personal daring, though depressed by exposure of the Iranian arms debacle and evidently fearful of being forever a pariah in governmental circles, he attempted suicide with an overdose of Valium pills in early 1987.

Back in January 1983, McFarlane watched in dismay as Reagan's defense consensus crumbled—beset by opposition in Congress, torn by internal disagreements on the MX missile among the Joint Chiefs, under fire from the nuclear freeze movement and the Catholic bishops' berating the immorality of nuclear deterrence. Actually, the administration was pushing ahead with Trident submarines and their new eight-warhead missiles, with new Stealth strategic bombers and modernized cruise missiles. But Reagan talked incessantly about trailing Moscow in land-based ballistics missiles, as if no other weapons systems mattered.

McFarlane feared the United States could not match two new Soviet ICBMs (the single-warhead SS-25 and the ten-warhead SS-24) because both were mobile missiles and Moscow had such vast territory for hiding them. "The traditional concept of offensive deterrence was becoming less stable," McFarlane believed, "so defense was conceptually an answer"—offering some protection for America's vulnerable deterrent forces. Moreover, McFarlane reasoned that the Russians feared a technological race with the United States on defenses. Finally and "most compelling," he later told me, SDI offered "something which would leverage the Russians" to make concessions in arms negotiations.[10] As McFarlane told others, he pushed SDI with President Reagan as the best "bargaining chip" for negotiating deep cuts in Soviet ICBMs.

But it is an axiom of the foreign policy game that every major weapon system requires endorsement from the top military hierarchy. McFarlane worked "back channels" to fish for Pentagon support. Through Rear Admiral John Poindexter, then number three on the national security staff, McFarlane found a willing ally in Admiral James Watkins, chief of naval operations.

Watkins had been worrying for some time that the nation was near a dead end in the offensive arms race. Hunting for new ideas, Watkins lunched with Edward Teller on January 20, 1983. He was moved by Teller's vibrant optimism about emerging defense technologies and his worrisome assertions that the Soviets were already hard at work on strategic defenses.[11] McFarlane and Poindexter encouraged Watkins to push his views with the other Chiefs. "You can be assured that your input is always going to be welcomed" at the White House, Poindexter told Watkins.[12]

In the power game, timing can be everything—and the moment was ripe for defense. The Joint Chiefs were due to meet with Reagan on February 11 to examine the "strategic equation." At their private dress rehearsal on February 5, Watkins laid out the rationale for "forward strategic defense." He took pains to emphasize that he did not advocate scrapping the offensive side of nuclear deterrence, but he favored a new push to see how defenses could be combined with offensive deterrence. This idea was an embryo, Watkins emphasized, something that required much more study. As a devout Catholic, he added a moral argument: "We should protect the American people, not avenge them." Later, Reagan hungrily grasped that line.

The other Chiefs had reasons for liking the defense notion. They were all—especially the Air Force—exhausted by the political wrangle over the MX missile. The Army already had a $1 billion-a-year program for testing and research on ballistics missile defenses and saw a chance to do more.

On February 11, 1983, Reagan met with the five uniformed Chiefs in the Roosevelt Room. Secretary Weinberger, still bent on the offensive buildup, told the president the Chiefs had another idea. "We have not studied this," Weinberger cautioned. "It's not something I can endorse at this time."[13]

The session followed the McFarlane-Clark script. It began with a look at trends in the arms race. Then General John W. Vessey, as chairman, laid out Watkins's logic, telling Reagan the Chiefs felt the time had come to take another look at defense.

"Do you all feel that way?" the president asked.

The room got very quiet, as Reagan looked around at Vessey, Watkins, General E. C. Meyer of the Army, General Charles Gabriel of the Air Force, and General Robert Barrow of the Marines. Clark and McFarlane wanted the Chiefs on record. "It was a very, very auspicious moment," one top White House participant told me.

Each Chief endorsed the general concept. Meyer said he felt that the historic balance between offense and defense had gotten "out of kilter—whether you're talking about defense against tanks, defense against aircraft, or defense against missiles." Watkins told the president he had heard hopeful things about developing defensive technologies against missiles.

"Wait a minute," McFarlane said. "Are you saying that you think it possible, not probable but possible, that we might be able to develop an effective defense against ballistics missiles?"

"Yes, that's exactly what I'm saying," Watkins replied.

"Mr. President," McFarlane said, throwing his weight behind the idea, "the implications of this are very, very far-reaching. If it were feasible to find an alternative basis for maintaining our security against nuclear ballistics missile weapons, that would be a substantial change, obviously."

Reagan nodded, "I understand that."

The concept of stepping up research on defenses was vague, the discussion very general. The Chiefs did not make clear whether they were talking about a defense against all nuclear weapons or just ballistics missiles, whether they had in mind a defense of cities or silos, a limited defense, or a total national shield. Nor did they specify whether they were talking about building a land-based defense, permissible under the 1972 ABM Treaty, or a space-based defense, forbidden by the treaty. Nor did they examine cost, time-frame, or specific programs. Significantly, the Chiefs were not proposing an end to the doctrine of deterrence, but supplementing it with defenses.

"There was no program definition," Vessey recalled later. "It was the idea that defense might enter the equation more than in the past. It was the idea that new technologies were more promising than they had been in the past."[14]

"I don't think any of us had a clear vision of what form this strategic defense would take," Meyer added. "The issue needed to be debated at the very highest levels by people concerned with policy and people concerned with technology."[15]

"Well," the president concluded, "I would like very much to pursue this. I think we need to hear further from you on whether we shouldn't reorient our priorities and put a lot more effort behind this."

The Chiefs left expecting that there would be more study and more talk with the President before a new policy was set.

The Power Cocoon

President Reagan was exhilarated by his meeting with the Joint Chiefs and eager to declare a brand new national strategy. The Joint Chiefs had talked of research to check possibilities for combining strategic defense with the existing strategy of deterrence through offensive nuclear weapons. But the president transformed that idea into a grand vision of a nuclear-weapons-free world. His national security aides found him suddenly talking about a utopian plan to "render nuclear weapons obsolete." Evidently drawing on his talks with Dr. Teller, as well as the tentative ideas of the Joint Chiefs, Reagan conveyed to his national security aides a desire to proclaim a radical shift of doctrine away from nuclear deterrence which had protected the country and its NATO allies for four decades.

"Reagan's view of the political payoff was sufficient rationale as far as he was concerned," Bud McFarlane told me much later. "By that I mean, providing the American people with an appealing answer to their fears—the intrinsic value of being able to tell Americans, 'For the first time in the nuclear age, I'm doing something to save your lives. I'm telling you that we can get rid of nuclear weapons.'

"The president all of his adult life has operated in a universe which counts on happy endings, and I think if you count on happy endings and experience them enough, you begin to believe that's what life is like and that the job of the hero is to be Frank Merriwell (a dime-novel success story). And it will turn out, because it always has—thirty-nine times! Every time he made a picture it turned out right. I never saw the president indicate the slightest hesitation [about strategic defense]. He was all the time, foursquare: 'Let's go to it.' . . .

"He was terribly excited about that. He wanted to get it out, and he was less worried about details—such as changing strategic doctrine or how it would affect the Allies. He didn't worry about those things."[16]

Clark encouraged Reagan to move rapidly, but they needed McFarlane's expertise—and he tried to restrain the president. Reagan's MX commission was seeking bipartisan support in Congress, and McFarlane urged waiting for its report in April. With the MX campaign launched, McFarlane suggested, the president could make strategic defense the next bipartisan effort, with support from Speaker O'Neill and other congressional leaders. But Clark—eager to make strategic defense Reagan's legacy—opposed McFarlane, and Reagan sided with Clark.

Star Wars was developed secretly within a tiny power cocoon. To protect it from internal critics, Clark ordered McFarlane to have the NSC staff develop the idea on a "close-hold" basis—that is, in secret, without informing other agencies. Thus, with the Joint Chiefs unaware, McFarlane and three NSC staff aides, John Poindexter, Air Force Colonel Bob Linhard, and Ray Pollock, a civilian arms specialist, began developing options. Their work was complicated; they were not told whether to build up one specific program such as the Army's existing ballistics missile defense, to plan for more ambitious research on technologies against all nuclear weapons, or to declare a massive new Manhattan Project for all defenses.

By mid-March, strategic defense had become a crash project. Clark and Deaver felt the president needed an upbeat defense speech to revive congressional support for his military buildup. Regular White House speechwriters began to draft a major address; on his computer, McFarlane secretly wrote the "annex" to his speech—the surprise on SDI. The White House staff was kept in the dark. No contact was made with the Joint Chiefs or civilian arms experts at the Pentagon or the State Department. Secrecy insured NSC staff control of the policy.

Eventually, McFarlane felt he could not proceed without scientific advice. On Saturday, March 19, just five days before Reagan's scheduled speech, he called in Dr. George "Jay" Keyworth, the president's science adviser, and asked broadly whether Keyworth could support stepped-up research on strategic defenses. Keyworth, a nuclear physicist and former head of experimental physics at Los Alamos Laboratories in New Mexico, was sympathetic to Edward Teller's views. Teller had pushed Keyworth for the White House science post, and Keyworth told others Teller was his intellectual "father."

Coincidentally, the day before McFarlane called Keyworth, the White House Science Council had finished a meeting. Keyworth had routinely asked that group whether any technologies, offensive or defensive, held military promise over the next five years, and one participant told me the group had given a categorical no. But Keyworth himself and a smaller panel had seen long-term potential for defenses in one experiment that had bounced directed-energy beams off mirrors in space. So Keyworth told McFarlane he favored increased research on defense.

With that, McFarlane handed him the SDI bombshell and asked for help. As Keyworth read it, he was numb at the dramatic shift Reagan was going to propose. McFarlane's draft was sweeping; it declared a massive change in American nuclear strategy and proposed defense against *all nuclear weapons*.

"Hey, wait a minute, give me time," Keyworth gulped. "This is a monstrous step we are proposing to take. Basically, I'm frightened. I've never dealt with anything so encompassing in all my years of dealing with national security issues."[17]

"Bud," he said, "there are so many considerations we have not thought through here. They go from technical feasibility to implications for the Atlantic Alliance, to implications for arms control, to what the Soviets are doing in these areas, to what the reactions will be in the scientific community."

Keyworth immediately recognized the vast, intricate undertaking implied in Reagan's vision of "rendering nuclear weapons impotent and obsolete." To others, that implied a leak-proof defensive umbrella, what former Defense Secretary James Schlesinger later ridiculed as an "astrodome" defense.

It meant devising a multilayered defense that would destroy, either at launch or within their half-hour flight time, ten thousand or more Soviet nuclear warheads, as well as stopping other nuclear weapons such as bombers and cruise missiles. The ballistics warheads alone would require a complex system of satellites and sensors that could insure instantaneous detection of a Soviet missile launch, plus a command and control system that could in milliseconds begin firing particle or laser beams, operating at the speed of light, or high-speed kinetic pellets to destroy missile rocket boosters. To back that up, even more sophisticated sensors would be needed to distinguish in space between real nuclear warheads and decoys and then firing new beams at them. And to back that up, strategic defense required a terminal defensive layer that would shoot down all the surviving warheads as they plunged back into the earth's atmosphere.

The electronics were more complex than the entire American telephone communications network. The architecture and the computer programs to manage such a system had not been imagined, let alone invented or produced. It was a gigantic dream, and Keyworth knew many scientists would be dubious about it.

But McFarlane drew Keyworth into his game. They had a heart-to-heart talk, McFarlane asking Keyworth what problems he saw, how he would change the draft. Within half an hour, Keyworth said, he was enlisted in the cause, and given an "eyes only" draft, meaning he should not share it with anyone. (Even so, he called in two science advisers.) Keyworth and McFarlane talked with the president, explaining complications. The NSC's Bob Linhard also warned against exaggeration. Linhard argued that it was impossible to declare an immediate change in strategic doctrine—the defensive weapons were not at hand, and reliance on defense alone would cut the heart out of NATO's war strategy, embodied in War Plan MC 14/3, which required offensive American nuclear weapons to protect Europe.

Despite the cautions of his advisers, Reagan hewed to his line about rendering nuclear missiles obsolete. In private, McFarlane tried to talk Reagan out of this utopian view, but McFarlane later defended it as "a license he [Reagan] takes"—acceptable hyperbole for a political leader.

About twenty-four hours before Reagan's scheduled speech, Richard DeLauer, the Pentagon's top-ranking scientist with the title of Defense Undersecretary for Research and Engineering, saw Reagan's speech and exploded in disbelief at Reagan's grandiose dream.

"That's nonsense," DeLauer told Keyworth. "That can't be so."

DeLauer concluded that Reagan and other top policymakers did not understand what they were proposing. Reagan and Weinberger, for example, talked about a "nonnuclear defense," but they included Teller's pet X-ray laser, which was powered by a nuclear bomb. Weinberger, shown Reagan's speech two days before delivery, did not seem to understand the concept well.

Later, as Weinberger was heading off to brief a congressional committee, DeLauer told him bluntly that space defenses would not be nonnuclear if the X-ray laser were used. Weinberger looked crestfallen.

"Is it a bomb?" he asked.

"That's how you're going to get the X ray," DeLauer replied in his raspy voice, teaching Weinberger the ABCs of strategic defense, *after* the new policy was announced. "You're going to have to detonate a nuclear device in space."

"But it's not a bomb, is it?" Weinberger repeated, looking for a semantic loophole.

DeLauer, astonished at the high-level ignorance, offered Weinberger a euphemism. "No, it's not a bomb," he said with exasperation. "It would be a 'nuclear event.' "

Weinberger seemed somewhat relieved.[18]

As other top experts were brought in belatedly, reactions were almost universally negative. The Joint Chiefs were shocked, both that Reagan was making this speech and at Reagan's claims.

"We weren't ready to announce it yet—the necessary policy ground-work had not been laid," complained Admiral Watkins, who had only thirty minutes to go over a speech draft at Andrews Air Force Base with General Vessey, who was flying to Portugal three days before the speech. "We were not expecting the speech. It was unfortunate he gave the speech."[19]

"Everybody was shocked," added General Meyer. "I would have preferred six or seven months to study it internally. We could have started out in a more organized way. We could have outlined the technologies we wanted to go after and the benchmarks five and ten years out."[20]

General Vessey, chairman of the Joint Chiefs, urged Weinberger to try to stop the defense portion of the speech and to undertake further study of strategic defense.

"I said, 'Hold off until we have a chance to examine it more,' " Vessey told me later. "We were surprised that it went that fast. It was clear that more study had to be done. But it wasn't in the cards to stop the speech. The White House was full speed ahead."[21]

The Joint Chiefs were uneasy with Reagan's promise of a nuclear-weapons-free world. "We had not suggested that," Vessey said. "We're not going to wish away nuclear power, fusion or fission, whether for weapons or for heat."

"Knowledgeable people knew the president had gone too far" with that promise, Meyer asserted, because nuclear weapons were vital to the defense of the West.

Drafts of Reagan's speech caused similar shock waves among the Pentagon's top civilian hierarchy. Weinberger and top policymakers such as Fred Iklé and Richard Perle were in Portugal for a NATO meeting when a speech draft was first cabled to them two days before delivery. Some reportedly threatened to quit because they had been bypassed on such an overarching defense issue.

The speech draft arrived close to midnight in Lisbon and was brought to Perle in his room. Perle was stunned, he later told me, and he went down the hall to awaken Weinberger, who came to his door in a bathrobe.

"Look what they've tacked onto the end of this speech!" Perle exclaimed. Weinberger read it and seemed equally surprised.

"That's no way to surface a new policy," Perle protested.[22]

With Weinberger's approval, Perle said, he tried to delay the speech. He put in a transatlantic phone call to urge Jay Keyworth "to fall on your sword" to block Reagan from making the speech, according to one White House official. Perle wanted Keyworth to threaten to leak Reagan's plan to the press in order to kill it, if he could not stop the speech by direct appeal. Keyworth refused.

Pentagon objections did get the speech delayed for twenty-four hours as Perle and Iklé then pressed for revisions; in forty-eight hectic hours, twenty drafts and redrafts hummed across the Atlantic.

Shultz was even more explosive on seeing his "eyes only" copy just forty-eight hours ahead of time. I was told he was livid at being blindsided by the NSC's Clark and McFarlane. Twice he met with the president and strongly opposed Reagan's giving the speech, according to one official who was present.

At State, Shultz told Richard Burt, his arms strategist, "The president has this idea of a world without nuclear weapons."

Burt shot back: "He can't have a world without nuclear weapons. Doesn't he understand the realities?"

At one White House meeting, Shultz wheeled on Jay Keyworth for encouraging the president on his utopian vision.

"You're a lunatic!" he bellowed at Keyworth.

Shultz worried that shifting to a defensive doctrine would have a shattering effect on the Atlantic Alliance, because the Allies had depended for four decades on the American nuclear umbrella and the offensive nuclear standoff between Moscow and Washington. Now Reagan was moving away from that whole concept of Western security—without consulting the Allies.

From across the Atlantic came unusual Pentagon echoes of Shultz. Iklé and Perle warned that SDI looked like Fortress America protecting itself, but not the rest of the Alliance.

McFarlane urged the president to consult with Allied leaders before giving the speech, but Clark and Reagan refused. Then McFarlane inserted a passage to try to reassure the Allies. In it, the president promised that "no change in technology can or will alter" the link between American and European security. It was a verbal Band-Aid. (One high Pentagon oficial told me that after the speech was given, Weinberger had to extend his stay in Portugal to telephone European defense ministers and apologize for having been forbidden to give them advance warning of Reagan's sudden change of policy.)

Shultz also feared that Reagan's new tack would be provocative to the Soviets. If the United States were to get a strategic defense ahead of Moscow, it could theoretically launch an offensive first strike against the Soviet Union and then ward off a Soviet reprisal with a defensive system. Rather than let that happen, the Kremlin leaders might be tempted to attack the United States first. Shultz and Burt pressed McFarlane to insert some reassurance for Moscow: an acknowledgment by Reagan that if defensive systems were "paired with offensive systems, they can be viewed as fostering an aggressive policy, and no one wants that." Again a Band-Aid; the issue haunted Reagan's meetings with Soviet leader Mikhail Gorbachev.

Perle, Keyworth, and the NSC's strategic specialists warned that Reagan was promising too much: a defense against *all* nuclear weapons—ballistics missiles, cruise missiles, and long-range bombers. Perle argued that this would multiply the cost and complexity of an already staggering task, and urged that Reagan concentrate on defense against strategic ballistics missiles. In the end, Reagan trimmed back. He spoke only of destroying "strategic ballistics missiles before they reach our own soil or that of our allies."

Senior Reagan aides admitted that in the chaotic haste several major issues did not get well examined: Whether strategic defenses could be tested and developed without violating the 1972 ABM Treaty, whether the X-ray laser would violate the treaty banning nuclear weapons in space, what the cost would be, how long the research effort would take, whether the United States would give up all its ballistics missiles or keep some, and how to manage the transition from nuclear deterrence to strategic defense.

"What was wrong with the decision-making process was not that defense was a screwy idea," said one senior presidential aide, "but that the key people involved, including the president, did not understand the range of reasons to be for it, or the reasons to be against it."

"The president shocked the system," Admiral Watkins commented. "It's unfortunate it was done so piecemeal with people ricocheting off the walls. But maybe that's the only way to do it. If the president did it the logical way, he'd have been beaten by the bureaucrats. The problem in this town is you can't study anything at length, because everyone studies it right along with you, and you get defeated before you start it."

Obviously that was Reagan's instinct and Clark's as well. They clearly concluded it was better to gain surprise and establish a fait accompli than undertake careful preparation and risk deadlock. McFarlane, despite misgivings, went along.

In the short run, Reagan got his way but he paid a price for haste.

SDI's research was funded, though always at levels substantially below Reagan's requests. The real political risk to Reagan from the conspiratorial policy game was that SDI has still not gotten firm bipartisan support to insure its implementation. Broader consensus building offered a better chance to achieve the necessary support. It is impossible to bypass the political checks and balances over the long run.

Moreover, the short-circuit, NSC style of policy game put high premium on Reagan's judgment and the quality of advice given him by a very small staff. That method not only cut against the grain of Reagan's much-advertised preference for collegial decision making, but it handed great power to a small staff inclined to bow to Reagan's impulses and to filter out dissent. That pattern set Reagan up for his more disastrous plunge into clandestine arms deals with Iran.

Government Within the Government

With the White House conspiracy to sell arms to Iran and secretly fund the Nicaraguan *contras,* the national security staff became a government within the government. The Rambo exploits of Lieutenant Colonel Oliver North and Bud McFarlane's flight to Tehran were light-years from the gray bureaucratic task of sifting options that was originally conceived for the NSC staff. Gone was the role of neutral policy referee. Reagan made his NSC staff a free-lance CIA, to conceal his policies and escape accountability from an objecting Congress and to circumvent all but a tiny fragment of his own administration. National Security Adviser John Poindexter usurped the president's authority (if Reagan and Poindexter are to be believed), approving the diversion of Iranian profits to the *contras* and then keeping that secret from the president.

The Iran-*contra* operation is the most stunning case of the surreptitious accumulation of staff power in recent presidencies. It carried the long-term trend of growing national-security-staff power beyond anything previously attempted. Nixon and Carter had used their national security advisers, Kissinger and Brzezinski, to formulate policy and to conduct negotiations with Peking and Moscow. On the Strategic Defense Initiative, Reagan's NSC staff became the entrepreneur of policy. But in the Iran-*contra* operation, the NSC staff added three critical aspects of power: the power of decision, the power of operational action, and the power of curbing dissent through tight secrecy and deception.

First, the power of decision: John Poindexter's raw arrogation of presidential authority shocked the congressional investigating committee. Puffing on his pipe, Poindexter treated his explosive, on-the-spot decision to approve North's skimming profits from the Iranian arms deals to fund the *contras* as a mere "detail" of policy, implementing Reagan's general line. Invoking Harry Truman's famous quip about presidential responsibility, but with an ironic twist, Poindexter declared, "On this whole issue, you know, the buck stops here with me.

"I made the decision," Poindexter said with chilling self-assurance. "I felt I had the authority to do it. I thought it was a good idea. I was convinced that the president would, in the end, think it was a good idea. But I did not want him to be associated with the decision. . . . I made a very deliberate decision not to ask the president so that I could insulate him from the decision and provide some future deniability for the president if it ever leaked out."[23]

This deniability supplanted the principle of accountability.

Second, the power of operational actions: Well before Poindexter made that fateful decision, Reagan had made his NSC staff an operational arm of government in the new arena of overseas covert operations. In the Iran-*contra* affair, Reagan's NSC usurped not only policy-making authority but the action operations of the Pentagon, State Department, and CIA combined.

Ollie North was chief executive officer of a covert private-sector empire—known among insiders as the "enterprise"—which short-circuited the U.S. government. As Reagan's case officer for the Iranian operation and the *contras*, North built a network of former CIA officials such as Eugene Hasenfus, the cargo handler captured when his supply plane was shot down over Nicaragua on October 5, 1986, and the pilot, William Cooper, who was killed in the crash. Through former Air Force Major General Richard Secord, a specialist in covert operations, North bought arms, transferred big money, and chartered ships and planes to ferry arms to Iran and to airdrop weapons to the *contras* through a string of dummy companies (Lake Resources and Compagnie de Services Fiduciares in Switzerland and Dolmy in Panama).

By 1986, North's own diagram showed a network of twenty-eight organizations in what he called "PROJECT DEMOCRACY," or "PRODEM." He told Poindexter that it was worth "over $4.5 million," and he wanted the CIA to buy it all—including "six aircraft, warehouses, supplies, maintenence [sic] facilities, ships, boats, leased houses, vehicles, ordnance, munitions, communications equipment, and a 6250' runway on property owned by a PRODEM proprietary." In Bill Casey's words, North ran "a full-service covert operation" for

Nicaragua—but without the formal written presidential authority and notification to Congress required by the National Security Act and by Reagan's Executive Order 12333.

North's operation was an incredible end run of all governmental controls. By North's account, Casey—who hated congressional oversight—saw great potential for an even more ambitious end run. In North's operation, Casey envisioned a global clandestine service—outside of normal governmental control and perhaps without telling the president. According to North, Casey wanted to run an "off-the-shelf, self-sustaining, stand-alone entity"—a secret, self-financing slush fund for covert operations that would evade the legal controls instituted in the mid-1970s in reaction to earlier CIA excesses, such as attempted assassinations on foreign leaders.[24]

As Senator Sam Nunn observed, the NSC staff had mounted "an internal coup." The normal rules of the foreign policy game were suspended. Poindexter, McFarlane, and North went behind the backs of cabinet officers and normal chains of command. They gave secret instructions to U.S. ambassadors and flashed messages to CIA station chiefs; they commandeered planes and gave bogus stories to other government agencies to cover their real actions; they privatized foreign policy, and their commercial operatives knew more about Reagan's policy than the president or members of his cabinet. After Congress cut off aid to the *contras*, Reagan partisans raised $1.7 million for the *contras* from private donors and illegally channeled funds to North through a tax-exempt foundation. Reagan, who posed for pictures with big donors, claimed he thought their money was going for television ads, not weaponry. Saudi Arabia's King Fahd donated another $32 million, after being nudged by National Security Adviser Bud McFarlane. The president too thanked Fahd. All this circumvented Congress.

Third, the NSC staff exploited the power of information to control policy. It used the time-tested practice of bureaucrats in the power game: secrecy, keeping other policymakers in the dark. At the congressional hearings, Poindexter and North invoked the need to protect hostage lives, the Iranian channel, their clandestine agents, the covert operation itself, as the reasons for "compartmenting" information of their operation and deceiving others. But clearly one overriding imperative—especially for practicing secrecy and deception against other top officials—was control of policy. Poindexter's blunt rationale: "I simply didn't want any outside interference."[25]

Caspar Weinberger, cut out by Poindexter, observed bluntly that those who favored the Iranian operation and "who knew that I opposed it and George Shultz opposed it, did not want the president to hear these arguments after the decision had been made . . . and I think it was a very bad procedure."[26]

Moreover, the NSC staff dissembled to the president, Congress, members of the cabinet, other agencies, and other governments. When congressional intelligence committees pressed in 1985 to know what aid North was giving to the *contras,* the NSC responded with outright lies, as North later admitted. By March 1985, North had developed a plan to finance and supply the *contras* and was soon raising funds, obtaining arms and giving tactical instructions to the *contras.* But when Congress inquired, North and his NSC superiors falsely denied his activities—once in a letter to a House Foreign Affairs Subcommittee on September 12, 1985—just eight days before North gave a CIA agent in El Salvador orders for air drops into Nicaragua for the *contras.* A year later, North told Poindexter how he had lied face-to-face to the House Intelligence Committee about his operations, and Poindexter sent him a pat-on-the back message: "Well Done."[27]

Inevitably, the lies turned inward. The main plotters misled and lied to each other. North and Casey sometimes operated behind the backs of Poindexter and McFarlane. Poindexter led North to believe the president knew and approved things that Poindexter kept from Reagan. North lied to Secord about his access to the president. So pervasive were the lies that as the Iran-*contra* operation was being exposed in November 1986, a battle royal erupted in Reagan's inner circle over what had been done, what would be told to the president and the public, and who would control policy. Secretary of State Shultz, bent on shaking Reagan to face the truth, bellowed at him on November 19: "We have been deceived and lied to" by Casey and Poindexter.[28]

Secrecy had taken precedence over everything, ends justifying means. Casey lied to congressional intelligence committees, pretending ignorance about operations he had helped organize; Poindexter tore up the December 5, 1985, order signed by Reagan for an arms-for-hostage deal, supposedly to protect the president from political damage; Casey, Poindexter, and North met—in the presence of others—to concoct a cover story so palpably false that State Department legal adviser Abraham Sofaer threatened to resign if it were used; North and his secretary, Fawn Hall, shredded an eighteen-inch thick stack of documents to cover up North's Iran and *contra* operations. North kept shredding one night until four A.M. and continued the next day, even in the presence of Justice Department investigators. When Hall found other incriminating documents in the White House, she smuggled them out in her

boots and in the back of her blouse to be destroyed. When members
of Congress asked why risk violating the law, Fawn Hall replied,
"Sometimes you have to go above the written law, I believe."[29]

In sum, the Iran-*contra* operation was the epitome of the backdoor
foreign policy game. The NSC staff became the vehicle for unilateral
policy-making, avoiding checks and balances inside the administration
as well as the constitutional authority of Congress. "People [in the
administration] turned to covert action because they thought they
could not get congressional support for overt activities," Bud McFarlane explained. "But they were not forced to think systematically about
the fatal risks they were running."[30]

The impulse to turn to a clandestine power game came from Reagan
himself. The Iranian arms deals and the White House fund-raising and
gunrunning to the Nicaraguan *contras* were not two separate policies
that happened to merge in midstream through the ingenuity of Colonel
North. They were parallel elements of the same foreign policy game
undertaken by a president blocked by Congress, frustrated by divisions
in his inner circle, and determined to override all objections in pursuit
of his goals.

After the operation was exposed, President Reagan cast himself as
innocent and ignorant of the most incriminating details of the policy
cabal: the diversion of Iranian funds to the *contras*, the private donations for *contra* weapons, the efforts at covering up the Iranian arms
trade. But in October 1984, when Congress banned further governmental aid to the *contras*, Reagan had told McFarlane that he "did not
intend to break faith with the *contras*"—Reagan's signal to find the
contras other support, a signal which he reaffirmed to Poindexter in
1986.[31] Poindexter testified that Reagan had been briefed on NSC
staff actions, such as arranging for construction of a clandestine airstrip
for the *contras* in Costa Rica.

For months President Reagan and other officials claimed that the
administration did not solicit private donations for the *contras*, but in
mid-May 1987 the president did an about-face. "I was very definitely
involved in the decisions" about private covert aid to the *contras*, he
said. "It was my idea to begin with." Justifying his backdoor game,
Reagan claimed a legal loophole for the NSC staff. He argued that the
congressional ban on aiding the *contras* "does not legally apply to me"
and was "not restrictive" on the NSC staff. Although Reagan had
pushed his NSC staff into intelligence operations, he contended that
it was not—in the language of the law—an agency involved in intelligence activities, and therefore was not covered by the law.[32]

Some of his own top advisers disagreed. Bud McFarlane, then national security adviser, felt the law meant "no one in the government" could help the *contras,* beyond moral and political support. In September 1984, when North wanted to raise funds for a *contra* helicopter, McFarlane turned him down saying, "I don't think this is legal." In 1987, McFarlane said he had not known how much fund-raising and tactical guidance North had provided the *contras,* but it had clearly been illegal.[33] Similarly, Attorney General Edwin Meese testified— long after the fact—that he did not see any exemption from the law for the NSC staff.[34]

President Reagan was also the driving force behind the arms deals with Iran, which he publicly tried to justify as a bid for strategic influence with Iranian "moderates." Weinberger mocked that whole idea. "I didn't think there was anyone we could deal with who was not virulently anti-American," Weinberger told the congressional committee. "I did not think and do not think there's any moderate element that is still alive."[35]

Moreover, the record showed that Reagan's passion about the hostages kept the operation moving. The hostages became Reagan's obsession, as they had been Carter's. Other officials read his real motive as freeing the hostages. At daily briefings, the president would ask Poindexter, "John, anything new on the hostages?" From Reagan's drumbeat, McFarlane concluded, "his concerns here were for the return of the hostages." North testified that whenever he briefed the president about a strategic opening with Iran, Reagan would focus on the hostages.

In mid-November 1986, Reagan told the nation, "We did not, repeat, did not, trade weapons or anything else for hostages." But Reagan had signed an order on December 5, 1985, which approved a straight arms-for-hostages deal.[36] The hard calculus of the arms ransom was laid out baldly in North's December 4 memo to Poindexter, giving a schedule of arms-for-hostage exchanges:

H—hr: 1 707 w/300 TOWs = 1 AMCIT
H+10 Hrs: 1 707 (same A/C) w/300 TOWs = 1 AMCIT
H+16 Hrs: 1 747 w/50 HAWKS & 400 TOWs = 2 AMCITs
H+20 Hrs: 1 707 w/300 TOWs = 1 AMCIT[37]

In other words, the first Boeing 707 would arrive at "H-hour" with three hundred TOW antitank weapons to exchange for one "Amcit," (American citizen held hostage). Ten hours later, a second shipment;

six hours after that, a third shipment, a Boeing 747 with TOWs and Hawk antiaircraft missiles; and then a fourth.

Nor was this a deal foisted on Reagan from below. When other advisers favored scrapping the operation in December 1985, the president argued to keep going. Reagan feared reprisals against the hostages if the Iranian channel were broken off. Also as Don Regan told investigators, the president was worried that he would look powerless and inept, with hostages still held in Beirut. Meeting his inner circle on December 7, 1985, Reagan brushed aside objections—including questions of legality—raised by Shultz and Weinberger against the arms traffic with Iran. "The American people will never forgive me," Reagan declared, "if I fail to get these hostages out, over this legal question."[38]

Tunnel Vision: The Hubris of Landslide

There is a special political chemistry at work in the White House of an enormously popular second-term president. Call it the hubris of landslide. The pattern is familiar among landslide winners who get in trouble in their second term: Franklin Roosevelt trying to pack the Supreme Court after 1936, Lyndon Johnson deepening the war in Vietnam after the 1964 election, Richard Nixon covering up Watergate after the 1972 election. Inside the White House, a landslide is often read as a license from the electorate to the president to govern as he wants without interference from Congress. The clear danger is that the White House will overreach. After Reagan's forty-nine-state victory, his partisans urged: "Let Reagan be Reagan." The president, stymied on domestic policy, and passionate about his foreign crusades, pursued his instincts and bucked at restraints.

Presidential overconfidence gets reinforced by a zealous, loyal staff, feeling their champion invincible and hooked on the hothouse narcotic of power in the White House. Reagan's staff tried to give the president what he wanted. His daily anxieties and impulses became their catechism, their commands. Reagan's NSC staff may have been more susceptible to this virus than most, for it was heavily peopled by military staff officers conditioned to salute the commander in chief and charge the next bunker.

"We Americans have built our President into a sort of demigod," John Eisenhower observed, recalling his father's White House. "It seems that the longer a President is in office, the more headstrong he becomes. If in office long enough, he may approach the omnipotent— in his own mind. That condition would not be so serious were it not for the fact that the hubris spreads like a disease to the President's associates, both family and staff. The trend seems to be for staff officers to consider themselves powers in their own right. The staff sometimes takes the President more seriously than the Great Man himself."[39]

In the Eisenhower era, Senator Henry Jackson of Washington, a well-known foreign-policy hawk, worried about the pitfalls of excessive zeal for covert operations, with a president surrounded by policy clones. "In the best of circumstances, it is difficult for a powerful executive to escape the 'yes-men hazard,' " Jackson asserted. "The clear-eyed executive will understand that he should be concerned about the possibility that he may, with the best of intentions, misuse his power—through some lack of sophistication, mistaken judgment, or shading of the truth to protect his personal reputation."[40]

In short, tunnel vision is an occupational hazard at the White House. In 1985–86, the aggressiveness and tunnel vision of Reagan's NSC staff was fueled not only by Reagan's heady election triumph and by his obsession with the hostages and pursuing the *contra* war. It was also fed by the siege atmosphere at the White House, caused by terrorist bombings, airliner hijackings, and the seizure of the *Achille Lauro* cruise ship. The Reagan team was bent on breaking out of the diplomatic defensive, and it mounted what a congressional report called "the cabal of zealots."

Tunnel vision left the Reagan team vulnerable on the Iran-*contra* affair—without a plan for political damage control to shield the president, other than the belated firing of North and Poindexter's resignation. Those actions did not spare the president from public outrage. The scandal came as a cold shower to the public, because the plot was operated—not by the CIA—but right in the White House, under the president's orders.

The rolling disclosures of the Iran-*contra* debacle rumbled like a political earthquake through the Reagan presidency. Other presidents have been shaken by similar events: Eisenhower by the Soviet downing of the American U-2 spy plane in 1960; Kennedy by the dramatic failure of the Bay of Pigs invasion in 1961. Covert operations carry heavy costs when they fail or when their cover is blown. That is why most presidents keep covert operations at arm's length, buried deep in the CIA. It leaves room for plausible denial about the president's knowledge and involvement. But by bringing the Iran-*contra* operation into the NSC staff, Reagan had dynamite in his political household. When it exploded, he was too close to avoid serious injury.

The president's evasions compounded the damage. Three days after a Lebanese newspaper disclosed McFarlane's mission to Tehran, Reagan told reporters, "to us it has no foundation"—though Reagan himself had approved the mission. The very next day, he told reporters that Shultz and Weinberger had backed his policies ("yes, we have all been working together," he said) though Reagan knew they had vigorously opposed the Iranian deals. Next, Reagan was claiming "the modest deliveries, taken together, could easily fit into a single cargo plane." Actually, many tons of equipment had arrived on at least eight planes. At his news conference on November 19, Reagan denied Israel had been involved and had to be corrected by his staff within minutes. Testimony by Shultz, McFarlane, Poindexter, and Regan showed that Reagan knew the truth *before* he misled the nation on those points.

The real shocker was the monumental deception of Reagan's engaging in the Iranian operation at all. Having savaged Jimmy Carter in 1980 for allowing Iran to hold American diplomats hostage for fifteen months, Reagan torpedoed his own credibility. He violated his pledge never to make "concessions to terrorists," and his denunciation of Iran as part of a "new international version of Murder, Incorporated." He made a mockery of his legal ban against selling arms to Iran and made fools of Shultz and Weinberger for urging the arms embargo on other countries.

The operation exposed the traps inherent in the backdoor-policy game. The Joint Congressional Committee investigating the Iran-*contra* operation and the president's Special Review Board, headed by former Senator John Tower, documented a trail of folly—a scenario of American innocents abroad, gulled by crafty Iranians ever demanding a higher price and stalling on American demands. As the Tower board observed, the Americans proceeded "always apparently with an expectation that the process would end with the next arms-for-hostages exchange," each time drawn deeper into the morass.[41] Don Regan warned Reagan the United States was being "snookered" by "rug merchants."[42] Shultz groaned: "Our guys . . . got taken to the cleaners. You look at the structure of this deal. It's pathetic that anybody would agree to anything like that. It's so lopsided, it's crazy."[43] Weinberger said the NSC staff had laid Washington open to blackmail.

Initially, the White House was told by the Israeli government that all six American hostages in Lebanon, including William Buckley, the CIA station chief in Beirut, would be freed for just one hundred American TOW antitank missiles. That shipment landed in Tehran on August 30, 1985, and not a single hostage was released. Another shipment of 408 TOW missiles was sent by Israel on September 14, and one hostage was released, the Reverend Benjamin F. Weir. In November, another Israeli shipment; no hostages. Fed up, McFarlane tried to halt the operation and quit the government on December 11, 1985, but Poindexter and North kept it going.

"We are signaling to Iran that they can kidnap people for profit," Shultz protested to Poindexter, worried that paying arms ransoms would lead to more hostage taking.

But Reagan did not want to stop, and in his game of Persian roulette, he decided to bet more chips.

In a formal order, or "finding," on January 17, 1986, the president authorized supplying Iran with four thousand TOW missiles—forty times the original deal. That night, he wrote in his diary, "I agreed to sell TOWs to Iran."

In a memo to Reagan, Poindexter talked tough, asserting that "if all the hostages are not released after the first shipment of 1,000 weapons, further transfers would cease."[44] Those one thousand weapons went in February in two batches; no hostages were freed, but *still* the shipments went on. In May, McFarlane flew to Iran with more weapons; no hostages. In late July–early August, more weapons; one hostage freed, Father Lawrence Jenco. In late October, more weapons; one more hostage, Peter Jacobsen, freed on November 2. The next day, the whole operation was exposed by a Beirut newsweekly, *Al Shiraa*.

The Iranian middleman was Manucher Ghorbanifar, an arms merchant branded in 1984 by the CIA as a "talented fabricator." The CIA had warned its agents not to deal any more with Ghorbanifar, but the NSC staff used him. By January 1986, Casey was so suspicious of Ghorbanifar, regarding him as an Israeli intelligence agent, that the CIA gave Ghorbanifar lie-detector tests. Casey told Reagan that Ghorbanifar had flunked on several counts; but by then, the Americans were so hooked that North championed Ghorbanifar, and strangely, Casey went along.

In all, the Americans and Israelis shipped Iran two thousand TOW missiles, eighteen Hawk antiaircraft missiles, and millions of dollars' worth of spare parts. In return, they got three hostages—but three additional American hostages were taken, and Buckley was killed. The Joint Congressional Investigating Committee estimated that the Iranian government had paid at least $48 million for the arms. North's agent, Richard Secord, testified that only $3.5 million of the profits went to the Nicaraguan *contras;* $8 million remained in the Swiss bank account of Secord's partner, Albert Hakim.[45]

The back-channel operation betrayed a White House contempt for

Congress, for most of government, for procedure, and for legal processes that might interfere with what Reagan and company wanted to
do. The Tower board asserted that the "legal underpinnings" of the
Iran initiative in 1985 were "at best highly questionable." The congressional report accused the administration of "disdain for the law" in
numerous instances. The secret funding of the *contras,* it charged,
"evaded the Constitution's most significant check on Executive power:
The President can spend funds on a program only if he can convince
Congress to appropriate the money."[46]

The two arms deals carried out through Israel in the fall of 1985 were
of such dubious legality (possibly violating the Export Control Act),
that CIA Deputy Director John McMahon pressed for President Reagan to sign a retroactive order in early December to try to legitimize
them. Later, on January 17, 1986, as he ordered further Iranian arms
deals, Reagan specifically directed the CIA not to notify Congress,
although "timely" notification was required by law.

In the whole affair, Reagan comes across as eager to move and
impatient with legalities and with warring among his advisers. On three
occasions, December 5, 1985, January 6, 1986, and January 17, 1986,
Reagan signed findings—or orders—approving the Iranian arms deals
and did not inform Shultz and Weinberger, though he had almost
immediate opportunities each time to inform them. Like his NSC staff,
Reagan was content to leave these two major dissenters in the dark and
give ample leeway to the NSC staff to fill the policy vacuum. Obviously,
the president knew that Casey and his NSC staff were pushing policy
where he wanted to go.

NSC: How To Grab the Action

Even game players who know the great influence of staff aides were
stunned by the power Oliver North accumulated. He was like a poker
player with extra hole cards. Before the bubble broke, his leverage was
incredible. When Israeli planes could not get clearance in Portugal,
North got the CIA station chief in Lisbon to pressure the Portuguese
government to let the Israeli planes land. In early 1986, high-level CIA
officials repeatedly objected to North's sharing American intelligence
with an Iranian middleman, but North overruled them.

Like exploits lifted from James Bond movies, North's operations had
a fictional quality, a touch of fantasy. According to congressional testimony, one North agent picked up rolls of hundred-dollar bills in a
Chinese market; North's network built an airstrip in Costa Rica and

did "black" (disguised) airdrops of weapons; North lined up ships off Cyprus to pick up American hostages from Lebanon after Reagan agreed to pay $2.2 million in ransoms and bribes to terrorist guards of the hostages; North steered a $10 million donation to the *contras* from the sultan of Brunei, but the money got lost—mistakenly deposited in the wrong Swiss bank account; North's commercial agent told Iranian officials the United States was prepared to help Iran overthrow the leader of Iraq and "to fight Russia in Iran" if the Soviets invaded.

How this one Marine colonel got so much control of policy is a case study in the backstage power game. Early on, Shultz and Weinberger probably could have stopped the NSC staff's Iranian operation. But once it was rolling, by late January 1986, probably nothing short of their resignations could have shaken Reagan sufficiently or broken the NSC staff's momentum.

Actually, the NSC's stunning ascent had been foreshadowed by David Stockman's preeminence on the budget. Reagan's hands-off habit of delegating great authority pays a premium to aides who are sharp and aggressive. In fact, Reagan's permissive style was the most important element in the rise of his NSC staff. Ironically, in September 1986, just two months before the Iran disaster burst Reagan's bubble, *Fortune* magazine carried a flattering cover story on Reagan's management style. It promised: WHAT MANAGERS CAN LEARN FROM MANAGER REAGAN. Beside a head shot of Reagan was his formula: "Surround yourself with the best people you can find, delegate authority, and don't interfere."

That formula made a virtue out of Reagan's shortcomings. If Jimmy Carter got mired in excessive concern with detail, Reagan's weakness was being inattentive not only to detail but the whole sweep of policy implementation. Aides kept defending him as a strong leader, tenacious about his goals. But the Iran hearings in Congress underscored how lax he was, how rarely he pressed tough questions, prodded for explanations, checked the odds and consequences of failure, kept his staff on its toes. Even when the Iranian operation blew up in his face, Reagan was neither curious nor alert enough to ask Poindexter for an explanation of the diversion of Iranian funds (or so he said).

This fit Reagan's pattern on foreign affairs. He would set a general course, but his understanding was often so hazy and simplistic that he was at the mercy of aides—more than most presidents. Republican senators, coming away from the Oval Office, told me of their shock at his weak grasp of important issues. Most Reagan aides loyally defended him, but some admitted embarrassment at his gaps or his mental laziness. Others reported having to step in and handle conversations for Reagan so that he did not look stupid. McFarlane complained that Reagan sometimes did not listen and did not absorb what he was told.

One high State Department official told me of his dismay at Reagan's comments—after an hour's briefing by other officials—"that showed he simply had not understood what we had been talking about. I got the impression on that occasion and others that his knowledge is shallow and superficial. The people around him can manipulate things to get his general approval on something and then keep complications away from him."

Although Shultz, Weinberger, and Poindexter defensively disputed such a portrait of Reagan, the Tower board portrayed him as a slack, absentee boss. Former Senator Edmund Muskie, a Tower board member, said, "We were appalled by the absence of the kind of alertness and vigilance to his job and to these policies that one expects of a president." Typical was Reagan's flip-flop on whether in August 1985 he had approved in advance the first Israeli shipments of American arms to Iran. First, Reagan agreed with Bud McFarlane's version that he had orally approved the shipments; then he shifted and agreed with Don Regan that he did not approve them beforehand. Finally, he said he could not recall. "I'm afraid that I let myself be influenced by others' recollections, not my own," he confessed weakly.

Reagan's formula is made to order for an assertive, activist national security staff, taking general cues from the president and translating his wishes into orders to other agencies. That gives the NSC staff great leeway to speak for the president, leaving no one but the president in a position to challenge *its* word.

The second key ingredient in the NSC staff's ascendancy was its own boldness. Despite the publicity given North and Poindexter, the quiet-spoken McFarlane, as national security adviser in May 1985, was the one who moved in on Iran policy, just as he had on SDI. McFarlane grabbed State's normal diplomatic role after Shultz and Weinberger dismissed the idea of an opening to Iran. McFarlane had asked for their reactions to a CIA paper urging a policy shift to permit arms sales to Iran—to offset supposedly growing Soviet influence in Iran.

"Perverse," Shultz responded. "Contrary to our own interests." Prophetically, Shultz said it was wrong in principle, bound to be exposed, and thus damaging to the president.

"This is almost too absurd to comment on," Weinberger jotted in the margin.

Stymied by the normal process, McFarlane launched his own back-channel diplomacy, seeking a link to Iran through Israel. His emissary was Michael Ledeen, a Georgetown University professor and part-time NSC consultant who had close contacts with high-ranking Israelis. In early May 1985, Ledeen went to Israel with McFarlane's blessing and came back reporting that Israeli Prime Minister Shimon Peres wanted to know if the United States would approve a shipment of American-made arms to Iran.

Shultz was touchy about others invading his diplomatic turf. In 1983, he had threatened to resign when he learned that McFarlane had made a mission to the Middle East without State's knowledge. The new NSC staff initiative offended Shultz, and he protested to McFarlane, noting that Israel's diplomatic interests were different from Washington's. A channel to Iran through Israel, Shultz warned, "contains the seeds of . . . serious error unless straightened out quickly." McFarlane, playing down his links to Ledeen, replied to Shultz, "I am turning it off entirely." But in fact, McFarlane pressed ahead, spurred by the Israelis. By mid-July 1985, two Israeli emissaries had urged McFarlane to use Israel as a channel for arms deals with Iran, and McFarlane got the president to let him explore the idea.

Here was a classic pattern of bureaucratic infighting, seen again and again in the Iranian operation—the NSC staff pushing, Shultz objecting, Shultz thinking the operation had stopped, the NSC proceeding on its own. At each stage, the NSC became more ambitious. McFarlane maneuvered the NSC staff into control of an active diplomatic channel. Shultz was still wary but significantly, he did not block the effort. Instead, he left the field to the NSC, asking only that State be kept informed. Shultz's acquiescence at that point was crucial. It opened the way for the whole operation.

McFarlane grabbed the action, and within a couple of weeks, his man Ledeen was back in Israel, meeting not only with Israeli middlemen but with the Iranian arms dealer, Manucher Ghorbanifar, who put the arms-for-hostages issue on the table. Next, McFarlane jumped the chain of command and opened a back channel to the U.S. ambassador to Lebanon, without telling Shultz. McFarlane's operation led to three arms shipments to Iran but only one hostage release. When McFarlane resigned in disgust in December 1985, Poindexter took over, providing protection for North. "I never carried out a single act, not one . . . in which I did not have authority from my superiors," North told Congress.[47]

The third element in North's rise to power was Bill Casey—North's operational patron, tutor, adviser, de facto boss, and the mastermind behind North's operations in Central America, according to North's testimony. North was in awe of Casey as a spymaster and intellectual. And Casey evidently admired North's can-do daring, and saw him as a soul mate, perhaps even as a son. They thought alike, and they were in almost constant contact. Records showed they had at least thirty-five meetings, and probably many more. Casey had an office "down the hall" from North on the third floor of the Executive Office Building (next to the White House).

North said it was Casey in 1983, expecting Congress to restrict CIA operations in Nicaragua, who moved North to set up a private network for covert operations. "Casey suggested [my] setting up outside entities, and he gave me the name of General Secord as a person who could do it," North told the Iran-*contra* hearing. In 1984, Casey instructed North how to set up a revolving operational cash fund to keep North's operations secret from Congress. Casey worried about Soviet eavesdropping picking up North's phone calls and persuaded North to shift to communicating with encryption devices. Casey warned North to face the prospect of torture and to be prepared to commit suicide on a mission to Iran in early 1986. North first shared the idea of diverting Iranian funds to the *contras* with Casey. (Casey loved it, North said, thought it was "the ultimate irony, the ultimate covert operation.") In early October 1986, North said, Casey warned him that the Iranian operation was about to "unravel" and it was time to "clean things up"—meaning North should destroy his cash accounts ledger, notes, and official documents, in order to quash evidence of the "full-service covert operation."[48]

Most importantly, North filled a need for Casey. The crucial moment was October 12, 1984, when Congress passed a ban against further aid—direct or indirect—to the *contras* by the CIA, Pentagon, or any other agency "involved in intelligence activities."[49] That created a vacuum, by taking the CIA out of the *contra* war. Ahead of time, Casey and North had laid the groundwork for North to step into the vacuum and replace the CIA as point man for raising funds, organizing support, delivering arms to the *contras*—in short, running the war for Casey and the president. Once Congress voted the aid ban, North pushed the argument that the law did not cover the NSC staff because it was not an agency "involved in intelligence activities"—a euphemism for covert operations. Casey also claimed a loophole for the NSC staff, and evidently got the rationale to Reagan, who wanted a way to get around Congress.

CIA officials buttressed North's testimony that Casey guided North and gave his blessing for key CIA officials to help North, but masking the CIA's involvement to the rest of the administration and Congress. For example, Tomas Castillo (cover name), the CIA station chief in Costa Rica, provided maps and information for North's air drops to the contras, helped locate a site for a clandestine air base that North wanted in Costa Rica, and tried to shift munitions from one contra group to another.[50] North also got help from Dewey Clarridge, chief of the CIA's Central American Task Force, in arranging for planes from Southern Air Transport, a CIA proprietary firm, to fly Israeli arms to Iran and other arms back to Nicaragua. He also worked with Clarridge's successor, Alan Fiers, and Clair George, the CIA deputy director for operations.

"Bill Casey knew that he had a terminal illness as long as two years before his death [May 6, 1987]," McFarlane told me, "and I think that he was a person of such conviction and loyalty—conviction on policy and loyalty to Reagan—that he decided to take upon himself steps which he believed essential to promoting the president's interests and, he believed, the national interest vis-à-vis the Sandinistas. But as a matter of loyalty, he did these things without the president being aware of it."[51]

The fourth element in North's rise was the extraordinary leverage he gained by force of personality, by his cocksure manner, by acting when others hesitated—and that tells a great deal about the inside power game. North knew how to exploit his White House power base and the mystique of secrecy. For the messianic, gung-ho Marine lieutenant colonel with a Silver Star and two Purple Hearts from Vietnam—still boyish-looking at forty-three—ran circles around a bureaucracy often mired in red tape or endless policy disputes.

The swashbuckling Hollywood touches that were North's trademark attracted Reagan, who had played Rambo movie roles back in Hollywood, once helping free Errol Flynn from a Nazi prisoner-of-war camp. The president evidently identified with the exploits of the fervently patriotic Marine, who went by the code name of Steelhammer, who was a true believer in the Reagan doctrine of anti-Communist guerrilla wars. The day after firing North, Reagan telephoned the colonel to praise him as a hero and express gratitude. Referring to new revelations of North's channeling Ayatollah Khomeini's funds to the Nicaraguan contras, the president joked: "This is going to make a great movie one day."[52]

As his congressional appearances demonstrated, North's energy and magnetism cannot be underestimated. One colleague called him a "whirling dervish," a one-man band for the *contras.* He contacted ten or more countries to obtain arms and funds for the *contras,* flew to Honduras to bolster *contra* morale, stashed money for them in his office safe (once as much as $1 million), acted as paymaster for *contra* leaders, masterminded their arms drops, prodded them to open up new military fronts, urged them to take over a part of Nicaragua and declare their independence.

North's White House base was crucial to his power game—enabling him to act in the name of the president and to press officials in other agencies into helping him. North's formal title was deputy director of the NSC's Division of Political-Military Affairs, but that title masked his importance as an action officer. Presidents and cabinet secretaries rarely know how to get things done; they need aides to make operations click.

North was once unofficial crisis staff officer for the White House Situation Room, the President's command post and communications center. An irrepressible workaholic, North was an important figure in planning the invasion of Grenada, the interception of the *Achille Lauro* hijackers, and the curbing of death squads in El Salvador. In 1985, North was deep into counterterrorism, working on the TWA hijacking, and in 1986, he became cochairman of the "Operations Sub-Group," the NSC unit on terrorism. Those activities gave him important links in the Pentagon, State, and CIA. Moreover, having joined the NSC staff in August 1981, North lasted through four national security advisers; near the end, he knew more than his bosses about actual operations. Their dependence on him gave him power.

North cut through the bureaucracy with his own special swagger. "I just saw the boss," he would brag. In fact, by one official tally, he saw Reagan only about once a month, in briefings or National Security Council meetings. But even officials who discounted North's chesty exaggeration accepted North's authority as someone who spoke for the president. They sensed North was pursuing policies close to Reagan's heart and for all they knew, with Reagan's explicit approval.

North told congressional investigators that he wrote five proposals for President Reagan's approval, outlining arms deals with Iran and diversion of funds to the *contras.* [53] Three times, he said, he was given the go-ahead—he assumed by the president —in February, May, and October 1986. "I assumed that the president was aware of what I was doing and had, through my superiors, approved it," North asserted. "Throughout I believed that the president had indeed authorized such activity."[54] Poindexter claimed never to have seen any of North's proposals, even the one found in North's files.

Nonetheless, Poindexter backed North's contention that he had operated under orders, but Shultz and McFarlane disputed North. McFarlane said that North had gone too far and had misled him about how deeply North was engaged in aiding the *contras*. McFarlane denied agreeing to North's "creation of a separate, clandestine, and far-reaching network of private operations that involved private profits and which was to be concealed even from other members of the executive branch."[55] Shultz said that Reagan had erupted in fury at learning that one of North's agents had—with Poindexter's and North's assent—discussed with an Iranian contact the possible release of the Dawa terrorist prisoners in Kuwait, contrary to Reagan's policy. The president, said Shultz, reacted to that news as if he had been "kicked in the belly."[56]

The Power of the Secrecy Loop

Finally, the policy leverage of North and his NSC bosses is a lesson in the power of the secrecy loop—the power of classified information. To be involved in a "close-hold" covert operation is to take on an extra mystique of authority with bureaucratic peers. People in the know are assumed by other officials to have authority for what they are doing. The NSC staff, especially North, worked that angle to the hilt.

Clandestine operations are compartmented and officials regularly accept being shut out of sensitive information if they are not central players. If others know more, that alone is a badge of authority. The mentality of the covert operators is that protecting the operation is the highest need—above the law and other obligations. In the Reagan administration, moreover, paranoia about Congress caused some officials to avoid asking about things they might later be compelled to tell Congress.

"Agency people, and I would say here from the director on down, actively shunned information," CIA Deputy Director Robert Gates told the Senate Intelligence Committee in 1987. "We didn't want to know how the *contras* were being funded, in part, because we were concerned it would get us involved in crossing the line imposed by the law. And so we actively discouraged people from telling us things." That instinct went for the State Department and the Pentagon, too; it gave North carte blanche.

Secrecy becomes an important pretext for shutting out policy dissenters. By their nature, covert operations cause sharp disagreements (to wit, Shultz and Weinberger on the Iranian operation). So, advocates of covert operations use the fear of leaks as a justification for freezing out internal critics and maintaining their own exclusive channel to the president. That was Poindexter's mind-set and his favorite litany.

It is a familiar rationale in the foreign policy game, used in some notable disasters. In 1961, under President Kennedy, the CIA and top military did not want the State Department informed about plans for the Bay of Pigs invasion, for fear that State would object and block the operation. Kennedy learned the price of such self-serving secrecy. By the Cuban missile crisis in October 1962, wary of the CIA and the generals, Kennedy drew on a wide range of civilian advisers. Clearly, the same secretive motives were at work in Reagan's Iranian operation. Advocates kept critics in the dark—not only for security reasons but to avoid giving them ammunition to scotch the operation.

Given Shultz's and Weinberger's vehement opposition, many found it hard to understand why those two—as the senior cabinet officials for defense and foreign policy—could not dissuade the president. Most important, Reagan did not want to be deflected; his impulses were reinforced by Casey, Poindexter, McFarlane, Meese, and sometimes Bush and Regan.

Moreover, Shultz claimed he was crippled by secrecy. In the congressional hearings, Illinois Congressman Henry Hyde asked Shultz why he had never tried to stop the Iranian deals by threatening to resign. Shultz replied that he had never had the right information at the right time. Indeed, during the eighteen months of the Iranian operation, Reagan met only four times with his full national security circle on that issue. Each time, Shultz said, he had left with the impression that he and Weinberger had succeeded in halting the operation, only to discover long afterward that it was still going. After one session, on January 7, 1986, Shultz and Weinberger thought the operation was dead; ten days later, Reagan signed the go-ahead order. But Shultz did not learn of that order for ten months, because Poindexter kept Reagan's order in his safe and never informed Shultz.

Repeatedly, cabinet officials learned more from outsiders than from colleagues or simply stumbled onto information. Weinberger discovered that—on NSC staff orders—the Pentagon's electronic intelligence arm, the National Security Agency, cut him off the list for some Iranian intelligence. Infuriated, he ordered an aide to "remind the agency for whom they were working."[57] In May, 1986, Shultz was tipped off by the U.S. ambassador in London that a major British arms dealer had been asked for a $50 million line of credit to underwrite American arms sales to Iran. When Shultz inquired, Regan told him this "couldn't be true or shouldn't be true," though plans were then under way for another big arms deal. When North urged Poindexter in mid-May to have a top-level review of McFarlane's Tehran trip, Poindexter replied: "I don't want a meeting with RR, Shultz, and Weinberger." Ignorance kept the two cabinet secretaries from objecting.

But in June and July 1986, Shultz was tipped off by senior State Department officials that the Iranian deals were going ahead, and he made no protest. Never did he and Weinberger approach Reagan jointly—and privately—to tell him they could no longer serve in good conscience so long as the Iranian operation continued. Perhaps their disagreements on other issues hampered such collaboration. More likely, both sensed what Reagan wanted to do, and they retreated into self-protective ignorance.

By pushing his NSC staff into running covert operations, President Reagan got part of what he wanted: The *contras* were kept afloat militarily until he could press Congress in 1986 to vote for overt military aid. But the Iranian operation blew up in Reagan's face. It was both a policy and political catastrophe.

The presidency—not only Reagan's presidency but future presidencies—paid a steep price for the deliberate duplicity of Reagan's NSC staff and its contempt for the rule of law.

"The reason for not misleading Congress is a very practical one—it's stupid!" Representative Dick Cheney scolded Poindexter. Cheney was no dove; he was former chief of staff under President Ford and an ardent Republican partisan of Reagan. "It's self-defeating," Cheney insisted, "because while it may in fact allow you to prevail in the problem of the moment, eventually you destroy the president's credibility."[58]

Another high cost was the legacy of institutional mistrust left by the Iran-*contra* operation and ventilated in the long Iran-*contra* hearings, which became not only a vehicle for Congress to redress the power balance vis-à-vis the presidency but a forum for generating reforms. Secretary Shultz urged that the NSC staff be barred from covert operations, that its size be reduced, and that the CIA's intelligence-gathering function be separated from its policy advice and operations, because it was tempted to slant intelligence to fit its policy bias. The congressional investigating committee recommended new laws requiring presidents to approve all covert operations and inform Congress within forty-eight hours of such approval, and new controls to plug the escapes used by Reagan's NSC staff—any covert operations funded by foreign countries and private individuals.[59]

Congress was outraged, as Congressman Ed Jenkins, a pro-*contra*

Georgia Democrat, protested, that not a single elected official —president, vice president, or any member of Congress—knew about the *contra* fund diversion from Iran. House Committee Chairman Lee Hamilton lectured North on how he had undermined the basic philosophy of the Constitution. "If I understand our government correctly, no small group of people, no matter how important, no matter how well intentioned they may be, should be trusted to determine policy," Hamilton admonished North. "Short cuts in the democratic process, and excessive secrecy in the conduct of government, are a sure road to policy failure," he later said. "Policies formed by short cuts and excessive secrecy undermine a president's ability to make informed decisions, lead to confusion in his administration, and deny him the opportunity to gain and sustain congressional and public support."[60]

William Cohen, ranking Republican on the Senate Intelligence Committee, put the responsibility on President Reagan. "He in essence took policy underground by cutting out the State Department, for all practical purposes the Defense Department, and the CIA, and most specifically, Congress, and he placed the responsibility for this covert policy and its execution in the hands of a few individuals," Cohen protested. "Unfortunately, the President turned to amateurs instead of listening to professionals and, in my judgment, he must accept the consequences. . . . The President cannot be held accountable for those acts of agents and employes who act well beyond the scope of their authority. But he surely is responsible when he sets up a mechanism that is specifically designed to eliminate the institutional checks and balances against rash or impetuous conduct in the affairs of the Executive Branch of government."[61]

The congressional investigating committee placed ultimate responsibility with Reagan despite his claim of ignorance about the diversion of Iranian funds to the *contras*. The committee's majority judgment said, "The President created or at least tolerated an environment where those who did not know of the diversion believed with certainty that they were carrying out the President's policies."[62]

Congressional criticism of Reagan framed a basic maxim of the power game: The gravest risk a president takes in clandestinely using his NSC staff to make and carry out policy is that this policy cannot survive wider scrutiny and win sustained political support, either from Congress or the public. That risk is magnified when the policies override acts of Congress or run counter to the administration's declared policy. Reagan took that risk on the Iran-*contra* operation, bypassing Congress and internal dissenters, because he did not want to be deterred from his policy goals. Reagan played the backdoor game because, like Poindexter, he "didn't want any outside interference." And the crashing collapse of his policy and his credibility was inevitable when his deceit was exposed.

Another Reagan Pattern: Short-Circuit

However serious the political fallout from the Iran-*contra* affair, top strategists and politicians felt that Reagan raised an even graver danger with his radical, pell-mell decisions at the Iceland summit meeting in October 1986. In his meeting with Soviet leader Mikhail Gorbachev, Reagan once again showed a penchant for short-circuit decision making, working with a small group and leaving key advisers in the dark. As on SDI and the Iranian operation, Reagan's Iceland tactics betrayed his go-for-broke impulse: his tendency to improvise crucial policy on the spot, bypassing normal channels of advice that protect presidents on major decisions.

Reagan's moves in Iceland alarmed West European leaders as well as thoughtful American politicians. Intelligent censure of Reagan came from Republicans such as Henry Kissinger, Alexander Haig, Brent Scowcroft, and former Defense Secretary James Schlesinger, and from Democrats such as Senate Armed Services Committee Chairman Sam Nunn and House Armed Services Committee Chairman Les Aspin, among many others. These critics all favored workable arms control and reductions, but felt Reagan had thrown caution and realism to the winds because he was reaching too hard for an unprecedented breakthrough. They criticized him not only for what he proposed but for his impulsive style of decision-making.

Schlesinger called Reagan's "carefree utopianism" at Reykjavík a "near disaster" for Western security because it could have led to the "end of the shield that has protected the West since 1945."[63] Kissinger and West European leaders echoed that fear. "In the long run, the events surrounding the Reykjavík summit may prove to have been more damaging than Iran," he observed. "At Reykjavík—as on Iran—the President lacked a reasoned statement of options and consequences."[64]

The alarm was touched off by Reagan's unexpected and unprepared proposal to abolish all offensive ballistics missiles in ten years, a shocking shift from Reagan's own offensive weapons buildup. It was a sudden, on-the-spot modification of a much looser notion that Reagan had raised in a letter to Gorbachev in July 1986. The new version promised in a decade to sweep away the deterrent force that had protected the

Western Alliance since World War II, without studying the cost of replacement weapons and of building up conventional armies to protect the West.

The Iceland gambit represented Reagan's old pattern of end-run foreign policy-making. This time it was quite clearly the president's option, not just his staff's. Once again Poindexter was at his elbow, but this time in league with Shultz and without Weinberger or the military. Any president has the prerogative to launch policy initiatives. But nuclear issues touch so many interests, not only American but also West European and Japanese, that major changes of nuclear policy require much more advance discussion than most normal political issues. At Reykjavík, Reagan ignored long-standing custom—just as he had when he announced the SDI program.

Reagan went far out on a limb without consulting allies dependent on American protection, and he did it without consulting his military Joint Chiefs of Staff. When the Chiefs found out about Reagan's proposal, they were angered at being disregarded, horrified by what Reagan had proposed, and relieved that Gorbachev had not accepted Reagan's offer, which they regarded as unsound and unworkable. The Reagan proposal, as Les Aspin put it, "scared the bejesus out of the [U.S.] military." Admiral William J. Crowe, Jr., chairman of the Joint Chiefs, was so opposed that he advised the president against offering it formally at the Geneva arms talks. But in an echo of the SDI episode, Crowe's dissent came too late.[65]

What these episodes show is a president zigzagging between orderly process and sudden policy lurches, between burying issues with paralyzing debate—as on SALT II—and giving them quick, premature birth—as on SDI. One senior adviser summed up his erratic style: "If you're hamstrung in any kind of coherent planning, then you go for broke when you're not hamstrung." At Reykjavík, Reagan did not have a full team of advisers to bog him down, so he went for broke with the faction that was urging him on.

Some Reagan partisans justify his policy lunges by the need for secrecy, but that is only part of the explanation. By several inside accounts, Reagan not only plunges ahead when seized with ideas, but he is clearly pained by the alternative: having to deal with strong policy dissent within his official family. He sometimes found it hard to overrule his most trusted advisers face-to-face and thus delayed and delayed. But if he did not have to face them all at once, he was willing to short-circuit some important advisers. That is an essential ingredient of the Iran story and of Reykjavík.

Arms negotiations are inherently intricate and prolonged; proposals need to be checked out all around. In theory, that should make them less vulnerable to snap decisions and end runs. Typical was the six-year marathon battle between Shultz and Weinberger over the SALT II Treaty and their subsequent battle over whether the ABM treaty allowed Reagan to test and develop space-based strategic defenses. What's more, the Reagan camp was on record against arms control end runs. They had attacked Kissinger for bypassing regular channels in 1972 to achieve the SALT I and ABM treaties. Also, the Pentagon and Reagan White House were infuriated in 1983 when Reagan's arms negotiator, Paul Nitze, reached tentative agreement on limiting intermediate range missiles in Europe during his back-channel "walks in the woods" with Soviet negotiator Yuli Kvitsinsky.

Nonetheless, at Reykjavík Reagan broke some time-tested rules of the foreign policy game by improvising a major departure on the spot. With hype and confusion, the president came away hailing his new package—to eliminate all offensive ballistics missiles by 1997—as "perhaps the most sweeping and important arms-reduction proposal in the history of the world." And he blamed the summit's failure on Gorbachev's demands for strictly limiting strategic defenses to "laboratory research." Actually, Gorbachev was more sweeping than Reagan; he proposed banning all offensive strategic systems—bombers and cruise missiles, as well as ballistics missiles. Also, some Reagan advisers felt Gorbachev saved Reagan, at home and with Western allies, by not accepting the ten-year "zero BM" plan.

Because arms control is so intricate and affects such vital matters, it is a well-tested axiom of the foreign policy game is that no major arms proposal should be put forward in face-to-face summit sessions without being well studied in advance so that its ramifications are well understood. The price of mistakes is enormously high. A second cardinal rule is that no arms agreement can win ratification politically without backing from the military Joint Chiefs because Congress relies on their judgment of the nation's safety. Their disapproval is powerful—if not fatal—ammunition against a president who ignores their advice. Reagan ignored both axioms. But he was spared from disaster by Gorbachev's countermoves and because Reykjavík was overshadowed by the blowup over the Iranian affair.

Banning ballistics missiles has natural popular appeal—and great appeal to Reagan, with his urge for a nuclear-weapons-free world. Ballistics missiles are powerful, accurate, and fast. Their thirty-minute flight time, continent to continent, and the great destructive power of their warheads makes them the most dangerous of all weapons, the ones that threaten surprise attack. Obviously Americans would like to do away with Soviet ballistics missiles. But these missiles also comprise two thirds of the American deterrent force, based on land and in submarines. The third leg of the nuclear triad is strategic bombers carrying nuclear-tipped cruise missiles, but ballistics missiles are the backbone of deterrence, threatening Moscow with massive reprisal for any attack. So doing away with them is a radical idea.

But proposing a ban on ballistics missiles—*zero BM*, in arms-control shorthand—without actually having to implement the idea is a clever ploy. In early 1986, Reagan needed a gambit to match Gorbachev's call for a halt to nuclear testing and for the elimination of all strategic weapons by the year 2000. Pentagon hawks, such as Fred Iklé and Richard Perle, pushed zero BM as an American response, because it cut the heart of the Soviet nuclear arsenal (ninety percent of Soviet nuclear warheads are on ballistics missiles), but it left us with a big advantage in nuclear bombers and cruise missiles.

Zero BM was injected into Reagan's policy stream in late May 1986, when Soviet arms negotiators in Geneva began making significant concessions. Reagan wanted a deal with Gorbachev; he also felt, as one top aide told me, that he had only two years left and "needed to take steps to make sure that SDI survives this administration." Gorbachev was trying to stop SDI, pressing for American guarantees not to withdraw from the ABM Treaty for fifteen years—i.e., no deployment of SDI during that period.

After meetings with Shultz, Weinberger, and Poindexter, and reactions from a dozen other top officials, Reagan bought zero BM. He put it in a July 25 letter to Gorbachev, coupled with a promise not to withdraw from the ABM treaty for seven and a half years, provided that after that period, either side could deploy strategic defenses. Reagan's aides said the zero-BM idea was intended to meet Gorbachev's worry that Reagan wanted a strategic defense in order to mount a first strike against Moscow—to hit first with ballistics missiles and then block a Soviet reprisal with SDI. By offering to give up American ballistics missiles, Reagan felt he was showing Gorbachev that was not his intention.

What is crucially important is that the zero-BM proposal in Reagan's letter to Gorbachev was deliberately vague. Reagan did not promise to get rid of ballistics missiles or set any time frame for eliminating them. Reagan's letter, according to officials who read it, only required that the side which first wanted to deploy strategic defenses had to *produce a plan* on how to get rid of ballistics missiles, but there was *no actual commitment to get rid of them.* As one high official told me, "That's like saying I can plan how I'm gonna jump ten feet high for you—eat Wheaties every morning and all that. But it doesn't mean I actually have to jump ten feet high." Between the lines, that meant Reagan's SDI could be deployed *and* ballistics missiles could remain. That was the American safety catch. Still, Admiral William Crowe, chairman of the Joint Chiefs, and Ken Adelman, head of the Arms Control and Disarmament Agency, ridiculed zero BM as meaningless because it was so vague and as unacceptable to Moscow.

Going for Broke—Reykjavík

At the Iceland summit, zero BM surfaced again—but in dramatically different form. The differences were crucial and they were not reviewed by the same range of officials as in the summer—testimony to Reagan's bent for short-circuit decisions and "going for broke."

At Reykjavík, Gorbachev surprised Reagan and company by unveiling a full-fledged arms package and making major concessions. At his first session with Reagan on Saturday morning, October 11, Gorbachev proposed complete elimination of medium-range nuclear missiles in Europe, a fifty-percent reduction in strategic nuclear weapons in five years, a commitment not to withdraw from the ABM treaty for ten years, and restriction of SDI to "research and testing in laboratories." That night, American and Soviet teams reached surprising agreement on much of what Gorbachev had proposed. But there was deadlock on SDI and the ABM Treaty.

The issues came to a head Sunday afternoon when Shultz met Soviet Foreign Minister Eduard Shevardnadze. With Shultz were Paul Nitze, his veteran arms adviser; Max Kampelman, chief American negotiator in Geneva; NSC chief John Poindexter; the Pentagon's Richard Perle; and Colonel Robert Linhard, NSC staff expert on strategic nuclear planning and arms control. But there was no representative of the Joint Chiefs of Staff or of the Arms Control Agency.

Shevardnadze pressed for Reagan to agree not to withdraw from the ABM treaty for ten years and to accept "strict adherence" to the treaty. All Soviet concessions hinged on that, he said.

"Are you prepared to agree to ten years?" Shevardnadze asked Shultz. He needled the Americans for a counteroffer.[66]

While he was speaking, Perle and Linhard were writing in longhand on a yellow legal pad. They passed their paper to Poindexter who looked at it, nodded, and passed it to Shultz. Then, without showing it to Nitze or Kampelman, Shultz told Shevardnadze that the Americans had an idea for breaking the impasse, and he read from the Perle-Linhard paper. It reaffirmed what had been negotiated the night before—that both sides would "adhere" to the ABM treaty for five years while cutting their strategic offensive arsenals by fifty percent, and then—the new part—they would adhere to the treaty for a second five years, provided that all remaining ballistics missiles were eliminated (zero BM). Both sides would then be free to deploy strategic defenses.

Shultz emphasized that this was a conditional proposal. "I haven't discussed this with the president," he said, "and I have to consult with him to see whether he will table [offer] it formally." The session broke up without much discussion.

Zero BM had suddenly been transformed, it was no longer just a promise to produce a plan, but an actual commitment to do away with ballistics missiles. And it was no longer open-ended, but it had a ten-year deadline. Although some officials, notably Perle, Linhard, and Poindexter, had kicked around such ideas, no serious study had been done on the military impact of this radical proposal. The Joint Chiefs had never been asked to examine how it would affect the American defensive posture, military budgets, or the balance of forces in Europe. They had a representative at Reykjavík, Lieutenant General John H. Moellering, but Moellering had not been in the session with Shevardnadze, nor was he included in the subsequent policy huddle with President Reagan. The Arms Control Agency was left out, too. Weinberger, whose offensive buildup would be cut off by this plan, was traveling in Asia, unaware of the improvised proposal. His agent, Perle, did not contact him. No one consulted the European allies.

The president, meeting with Shultz's small group plus Don Regan, liked the Perle-Linhard proposal. But he wanted to know its impact on both Soviet and American arsenals, whether it was sound and practical. Would it eliminate the heavy Soviet SS-18 missiles, Reagan asked. Linhard replied that it would do away with that worry, as well as with other Soviet ICBMs and submarine-launched ballistics missiles. What's more, Linhard told Reagan, zero BM would help European and Asian allies by removing intermediate and short-range ballistics missiles.

Reagan turned to Perle: Could the United States actually eliminate its ballistics missiles in a decade? Perle thought this could be done, and said it suited American weapons trends. Not only did the United States have an edge over the Russians in existing bomber forces and air-launched cruise missiles, Perle said, but it was moving faster than Moscow on new technology—a Stealth bomber and newer, hard-to-detect versions of cruise missiles. Perle told Reagan that zero BM would return the United States to the days of the 1950s, with much less threat of surprise attack. Shultz and Poindexter added their assent. Nitze offered no assessment.

It was a small group; only Linhard, Perle and Poindexter were expert on military issues, and they had no time to consult other experts. Dissent is vital for sharp consideration of major issues, and there were no strong dissenters in the group. Shultz, whose knowledge of arms issues is limited, felt a momentous opportunity at hand and was eager to seize it. Perle and Linhard saw military advantages for the United States. What's more, Perle told another official, "The Soviets will save us, they'll never agree." In other words, it was a great debating position.

Reagan did not tip his hand before rushing into his final session with Gorbachev. Only later did the others learn that he had proposed the Perle-Linhard ten-year ban on ballistics missiles. Gorbachev countered with his more sweeping proposal, to eliminate bombers and cruise missiles, too. The summit broke up, stuck not only on offensive arms but also on the Soviet demand for restricting SDI to "laboratory" research and testing.

In the summit's chaotic aftermath, the significance of Reagan's proposal was lost. Reagan's grimness after the session and Shultz's clear disappointment focused attention on why the summit had collapsed and on Reagan's assertion that SDI was the sticking point.

Only in late October did Reagan gather his top advisers to review the Iceland summit, and then his proposal came under sharp fire from officials who saw important disadvantages in Reagan's ten-year zero-BM proposal. Weinberger, one policymaker told me, was furious at being blindsided and bawled out Perle for giving the Pentagon's blessing without consulting Weinberger. The Defense secretary told other officials he did not like the ten-year zero-BM ban, though in keeping with his policy of not openly disagreeing with a presidential decision, he did not oppose it when Reagan met with his top advisers on October 27 around the table in the White House Situation Room. The main dissenter was Admiral William Crowe, chairman of the Joint Chiefs.[64]

Shultz defended Reagan's proposal and urged that it be put forward in the Geneva talks. The public, Shultz said, would like getting rid of ballistics missiles, and Allied conventional forces could be built up in Europe. The president agreed, saying, "Yes, there is good support for this kind of arms control."

But when Crowe's turn came, the tone changed. Normally, the admiral spoke extemporaneously. But he considered the step he was about to take so grave that he had prepared his position in writing. As he read it, the room fell quiet.

Eliminating ballistics missiles is good in theory, the nation's number one military man told the president, but we're not sure we can do this in ten years. There are pitfalls, Crowe said, such as Soviet conventional superiority in Europe, as well as the enormous cost of changing American strategic force structure and building up conventional forces in Europe. A new American air-defense system would be needed to cope with new Soviet bombers. The American strategic bomber force would have to be expanded greatly. American nuclear submarine forces would have to be shifted from ballistics missiles to cruise missiles. Much more would be spent on cruise-missile development. In addition, the cutbacks in ballistics missiles would have to be very carefully phased to insure that Moscow did not gain advantage at any stage.

"You are talking about a really dramatic change in the military forces of both countries in ten years," Crowe told the president. "We didn't develop our current ballistics missile force in ten years. We didn't develop the strategy and our current posture quickly. It evolved."

Given congressional resistance to rising Pentagon budgets, Crowe was skeptical of getting enough money for the new weaponry.

"We can't do what we have to do in ten years," Crowe declared.

Crowe was also worried about Soviet cheating—a far more serious problem with zero BM than with existing arsenals. Now, with each side possessing ten thousand warheads, hiding one hundred ballistics missiles made only a modest difference. But when each side is supposed to have none, one hundred hidden missiles is an enormous threat.

Crowe read four pages of objections. Finally, he told the president somberly, "As your chief military adviser, I don't advise you to submit this proposal."

The Arms Control Agency's Ken Adelman added his dissent to Crowe's. The ten-year zero-BM plan was unwise, he said, because it would be too expensive and politically unpalatable to replace the current deterrent forces with a new weapons buildup.

"There is no way that the most massive arms-control agreement in history is going to be accompanied by the most massive military buildup in peacetime," Adelman asserted. "The two things don't go together in people's minds."

Plus, he said, Soviet cruise missiles on submarines would threaten our bomber forces and sneak in under SDI.

Poindexter cut Adelman off sharply.

"Ken, that's out of place," he chided Adelman roughly. "The president's already decided to ban ballistics missiles in ten years' time."

"Well," said Adelman, turning to Reagan, "if you don't want to walk back from what we did at Reykjavík, then at least don't emphasize it any more. Concentrate on fifty-percent cuts in offensive arsenals over five years. What we are doing, Mr. President, is setting ourselves up for a political fall. We're overpromising."[68]

The arguments clearly jolted Shultz, for he backtracked from his Reykjavík formula in mid-November, proposing that some ICBMs be retained. This country, he said, needed "insurance policies to hedge against cheating" by Moscow, requiring "an agreed-upon retention of a small nuclear ballistic missile force."[69] Prime Minister Thatcher voiced European concerns about zero BM to Reagan and got the White House to issue a communiqué on November 15; significantly, on arms objectives, it omitted the ten-year zero-BM proposal. Over time, zero BM was allowed to languish—a stillborn stepchild of haste.

Instead, Reagan and Gorbachev agreed, in December 1987, to eliminate medium- and short-range nuclear missiles—a much more modest idea, originally broached by Reagan in 1982.

On zero BM, as on SDI and the Iranian affair, vital national policy was made from the top down, bypassing the more careful, thoughtful, and sometimes deadlocked policy game. Normally, policy develops from the bottom up, a range of officials prudently examining the options, winnowing out bad ideas, gauging the consequences of better ones. The president taps every important branch of expertise, giving top policy advisers time to think things through and lay their case before him. But Reagan liked going for utopian policies with a popular ring—bypassing long internal debate—and then advertising his ideas so widely that they became hard to reverse or revise. Once Reagan proclaimed his programs, they became a touchstone of loyalty, inhibiting internal debate of pros and cons. At times, his decision-making style was more that of a king than of a late-twentieth-century president.

Whenever Reagan or some other president makes policy unilaterally, it delights his partisans and temporarily gives the president his way. But no leader can end-run the system for long. After Reykjavík, Reagan's zero-BM proposals simply withered. On SDI, the ultimate political verdict awaits the next presidency. On the *contra* war and the Iranian operation, Reagan's efforts to impose his policy by stealth—using Saudi money to finance the *contras,* and the NSC staff to avoid Congress—

ran aground. Not only did Congress chastise the president, but it stymied his new efforts to renew military aid.

No foreign policy is possible to sustain without a broad political partnership. The backdoor, end-run foreign policy game cuts against the grain of democracy, because it requires more deceit and subterfuge than our political system will tolerate—especially when covert policy directly contradicts the stated public policy.

"We cannot advance United States interest if public officials who testify before the Congress resort to legalism's and word games, claim ignorance about things they either know about or should know about, and at critical points tell the Congress things that are not true," declared Lee Hamilton, chairman of the House Committee investigating the Iran-*contra* affair. "The Congress cannot play its constitutional role if it cannot trust the testimony of representatives of the president as truthful and fully informed. The president cannot sustain his policy, if he tries to carry that policy out secretly and his representatives mislead the Congress and the American people."[70]

Significantly, an understanding echo came from a chastened member of Reagan's inner circle, former National Security Adviser Bud McFarlane. With hindsight, McFarlane explained why it had been a disastrous mistake to rely on a covert operation in Nicaragua—especially since President Reagan saw Central America as a vital arena for checking Soviet influence.

"If we had such a large strategic stake, it was clearly unwise to rely on covert activity as the core of our policy," said McFarlane. "First, you can never achieve a sufficient level of resources through a covert policy to cope with a determined effort backed by the Soviet Union. The Congress views covert actions—properly, in my opinion—as an instrument to be used with great selectivity, as an adjunct of policy, not as its foundation, and surely not as a vehicle for waging war with a Soviet proxy.

"The other reason . . . is that you cannot get popular and congressional support for such a policy," McFarlane said. "If you decide to engage in conflict with a Soviet client in whom the Russians are prepared to make a substantial investment, you must have the American people and the U.S. Congress solidly behind you. Yet it is virtually impossible, almost as a matter of definition, to rally the public behind a policy you cannot even talk about."[71]

PART IV

Governing: Why It Doesn't Work Better

Governing: Why It Doesn't Work Better

The temptation in the world beyond the beltway is to blame the failures of government on the self-serving tactics of the games politicians play in Washington, without considering larger flaws in our political system.

Clearly, the collusion of the power networks in the Pentagon Iron Triangle, the tribal warfare of baronial bureaucracies, the pull of PAC money, or the imperatives of the constant campaign often frustrate sensible and coherent policy-making.

But there are more fundamental obstacles to effective governing in the election system and in the ticket-splitting habits of modern American voters. Any president is severely handicapped when he faces a Congress controlled by his political opposition. And yet partisan divided government has become the rule for Republican presidents, because Democrats have an incumbency lock on the House of Representatives.

Beyond that, the zigzags and deadlocks of Washington reflect the ambivalence of the electorate and the lack of a clear majority party since the breakup of the old New Deal coalition. At the presidential level, there is a mismatch between the talents needed for campaigning and the skills needed for governing. Political amateurism in the White House is one product of a primary system that rewards anti-Washington showmanship more than it does a proven capacity to forge the coalitions necessary to govern.

Reforms exist for dealing with structural maladies. But they stand little chance of enactment, unless there is a national calamity that makes them imperative. Even then, improvement lies mainly in the hands of voters—voters more alert to the impact their actions have, on how our government works.

17. Divided Government: Gridlock and the Blame Game

I've never seen a Congress yet that didn't eventually take the measure of the president it was dealing with.
—President Lyndon Johnson

As Ronald Reagan took office in January 1981, it was fashionable for political commentators to cite the litany of five flawed presidencies. Five leaders had been driven from office before their time: John Kennedy assassinated; Lyndon Johnson hounded into retirement by the nation's trauma over Vietnam; Richard Nixon forced to resign because of Watergate and other abuses of power; Gerald Ford, the appointed president, doomed by his pardoning of Nixon; and Jimmy Carter, humiliated by Iran and rejected by the voters. Five political tragedies that dramatized the crumbling authority of the presidency.

But focusing on the personal misfortunes of our presidents misses the structural maladies in our system. As we have seen, any president is less powerful than his TV image suggests. Power floats away from the White House; other players in the power game steal the leadership role from time to time. In Congress, the earthquake of the early 1970s shook the old power structure. Television helped spawn a new political culture and a new breed of politician, irreverent toward the old power barons, impatient with the old channels of power. The independence of this new generation, combined with new ways of financing campaigns, fueled the explosion of special interest politics. All these centrifugal forces loosened the cohesion of political parties in the 1970s and tore at the fabric of the old system.

Voters added the most fractious division of all: the gridlock of divided government. Often they gave the White House to one party and control of Congress to the opposite party. The Constitution had ordained permanent struggle between the legislative and executive branches. James Madison justified giving the president and Congress separate powers and constituencies, arguing that "ambition must be made to counteract ambition."[1] But the conflicts built into our system of checks and balances have been exacerbated to the point of periodic paralysis in the past three decades—by split partisan control of government.

The partisan division of government is a crucible for repeated stalemate unless there emerge leaders of uncommon wisdom and political skill, both in Congress and the White House. Normally we seem doomed to inconclusive quarrels; no struggle, however great, settles policy permanently. Year in, year out, we are burdened with endless ventilation of the same spent themes: the deficit, defense versus social spending, arms control, abortion, free trade versus protectionism, military intervention abroad, the role and size of government.

"Issues are like snakes—they just refuse to die!" Howard Baker blurted out. "They keep coming back, time after time."

This pattern predates the Reagan presidency and will endure after Reagan leaves the White House. Our national political irresolution derives from the ambivalence of voters on many central issues and from the lack of an overarching political force to organize and manage government. It takes an effective, durable governing coalition to make our government work. But over the past three decades, governing coalitions have been exceptional interludes, not the norm of American politics. Our recent history is a story of episodic spurts of cohesive action followed by long periods of stalemate and disarray. Governing has become a political football game of grunting line play fought between the forty-yard lines. Touchdowns are rare.

One basic problem is that we have no majority party. The old New Deal Democratic coalition has been broken up without being replaced by a solid Republican majority. Effective political parties are vital to governing, to giving shape and coherence to policy-making. Yet the public disdains and discounts parties, the Constitution does not mention them, and the Founding Fathers were wary of what James Madison called the "dangerous vice" of partisanship and "sinister combinations." The separation of powers was devised to foil the tyranny of the majority, namely, a government in the hands of a single party.

Yet American history shows that our system of separated powers functions most effectively when there is a single party to articulate a cohesive program and carry it out with sustained majorities over several years. And in practice, even the founders divided quickly into the Adams-Hamilton Federalists and the Jeffersonian Democratic-Republicans.

In the first 160 years of our Constitutional history, responsible, single-party government was the norm eighty percent of the time. Only three presidents, John Quincy Adams in 1825, Zachary Taylor in 1849, and Rutherford B. Hayes in 1877, took office facing a different party in control of part or all of Congress, and each was hampered seriously. But mostly, our governmental system thrived on party rule—until the past third of a century.

Consider our six most recent presidents: Confronted by Democratic majorities in both houses, Richard Nixon was often embattled on domestic policy, especially on spending issues and his impounding of funds appropriated by Congress. Gerald Ford, after a lifetime on Capitol Hill, began his presidency by telling Congress, "I do not want a honeymoon with you—I want a good marriage." But Ford wound up in a war of vetoes, sixty-nine in just two and a half years, many overridden. Ronald Reagan, too, after his stunning 1981 victories, had to backtrack on taxes and job-creation bills in 1982 and 1983 and fought Congress in his second term on budgets and foreign policy, especially after the Democrats regained control of the Senate in 1986. Even Jack Kennedy and Jimmy Carter, armed with Democratic majorities in both houses of Congress, had little success in passing their programs because they were not good at coalition building.

That overall record moved Ford to write in late 1980, "We have not an Imperial Presidency but an imperiled presidency."[2]

In three decades, there were only two periods of strong president-led coalitions. One was in 1964–65, when Lyndon Johnson masterfully marshaled Democrats to pass Kennedy's unfinished legislative agenda and his own Great Society program. The other, of course, was Reagan's conservative coalition, which bent history in the opposite direction, cutting taxes and checking the growth of government. Reagan had a brief reprise with the tax-reform bill of 1986, when tax rates were cut still further. Until the Iran-*contra* scandal broke, Reagan had restored enough vigor to the presidency to rebut the Cassandras lamenting that our system of government had become unworkable.

But it is also striking that this very popular president failed to institutionalize his agenda. Reagan's great personal popularity did not engender enduring public agreement with his positions on defense spending, Social Security, military aid to the *contras,* or abortion. Indeed, opinion polls showed that Reagan not only failed to pull the public to the right during his presidency but that the electorate actually drifted leftward: The consensus for a big defense buildup melted away; support for governmental activism in areas like education rose; people came to feel that deregulation had gone too far on health, safety, and the airlines.

Unlike Franklin Roosevelt, who embedded the New Deal legacy in the American system, Reagan failed to embed the opposite legacy of erasing government programs or pushing policy into the private sector. His dream of shifting big federal programs to the states did not materialize. In sum, Reagan bowed to perpetuation of almost all government programs, and David Stockman accused him of being less radical than he sounded—of waging a "phony war on spending."[3]

Hugh Heclo, a Harvard University political scientist, rendered a more temperate verdict: "Reaganism is devoted to reducing the domestic presence of the federal government. The paradox is that Ronald Reagan's genial exertions may have served only to entrench and in some cases expand that presence. . . . Much as F.D.R. and the New Deal had the effect of conserving capitalism, so Reaganism will eventually be seen to have helped conserve a predominantly status quo, middle-class welfare state."[4]

Paul Weyrich, a leading New Right conservative, agreed that there had been "no Reagan Revolution," but he suggested that divided government was the real reason: "The Republican Party spent $1 billion on national elections during the past decade," he said. "The conservative movement spent another $200 million, and business PACs and individual contributors over $300 million, supporting national Republican candidates during the same period. That is more than $1.5 billion spent on national elections with very little to show for it. Why? The first reason is that many conservatives are monarchists at heart. They *love* the Presidency. They think that if you own the Presidency, that is all that really counts. . . . A few conservatives have now come to the conclusion that Congress is just as important."[5]

For eight years Reagan faced Democratic majorities in the House (from 51 to 103 votes), majorities largely committed to protecting the status quo or to snip government only at the margins. In Reagan's first year, Congress supported him on eighty-two percent of his issues—a high success rate, though less than Eisenhower and Johnson in their heydays. Despite his landslide reelection, Congressional support for Reagan in 1985 and 1986 fell below sixty percent, almost as poor as for Nixon and Ford at their low ebbs.[6] In retreat in 1982 and 1983, Reagan struck some one-shot bipartisan compromises on Social Security, the MX missile, and tax increases. But from then on, his ideological rhetoric and his uncompromising position sharpened the combative instincts in Congress, tightening the vise of stalemate.

My purpose is not to dwell on Reagan's problems but to suggest that they are endemic to our system. Reagan's conflicts with Congress did not originate with him, nor will they end with him. The gridlocks of divided government are now almost inevitable under a Republican president.

On January 20, 1989, Republicans will have occupied the White House for sixteen of the last twenty years. The Democrats ruled the House for that entire period. Going further back, Eisenhower enjoyed Republican majorities in both House and Senate for his first two years, and then had six years of opposition control of Congress. The pattern was the same under Nixon and Ford.

"At such times, the normal tendency of the U.S. system toward deadlock becomes irresistible," political scientist James Sundquist commented. "Harmonious collaboration, barring national crisis, is out of the question. The President and Congress are compelled to quarrel. No presidential proposal can be accepted by the legislature without raising the stature of the President as leader. Similarly, no initiative of Congress can be approved by the President without conceding wisdom to his enemies. The conflict, bickering, tension, and stalemate that characterized the 14 years of divided government were inevitable."[7]

Sundquist was writing not long before Reagan took office. Reagan's two terms made it not fourteen—but *twenty-two*—years of partisan division during the last thirty-six years, nearly two thirds of the time. Democratic presidents have other problems holding together the factions of their diverse party and forming governing coalitions. But since 1952 Republicans have been better than Democrats at winning the White House, and if that continues, the pattern of divided government is likely to persist—unless significant changes are made in our political system.

Blame-Game Politics

Divided government leaves a Republican president and a Democratic Congress with two basic options: bipartisan collaboration or partisan warfare and blame-game politics. It takes a sustained commitment to bipartisan compromise both by the president and congressional leaders to overcome divided government. During the Reagan presidency, which bears lessons for the future, bipartisanship withered and partisan divisions became more intense—hardening the arteries of government.

Politics is like physics, action begets reaction. As political scientist Thomas Mann observed, any president "shapes the climate of politics in Congress."[8] Eisenhower, as a moderate Republican, not only worked with Democratic leaders but often set a climate of tolerance and cooperation. Richard Nixon sharpened the partisan edge, Reagan even more so. As an ideological president, bent on imposing his agenda and scoring partisan points, quick to blame Congress for stalemates, and more rigid in his second term than in his first term, Reagan polarized the politics of Congress. His highly partisan style aggravated the deeper neuralgias of divided government.

But Reagan had no monopoly on partisanship. Democratic leaders on Capitol Hill struck back with partisan war cries and maneuvers aimed at blocking or embarrassing Reagan. Except for one-shot compromises on MX, Social Security, tax reform, or putting Marines into Lebanon, Speaker Tip O'Neill challenged Reagan head-on for six years. Jim Wright, as speaker in the 100th Congress (1987–88), was even more aggressive in opposing Reagan. Moreover, with Democrats back in control of the Senate, Wright had a powerful ally in Majority Leader Robert Byrd.

According to *Congressional Quarterly,* the Congress that faced Reagan in 1985–86 was the "most partisan in at least three decades."[9] Partisan majorities fought each other more frequently than at anytime since the Truman presidency. Reagan had scored well in 1981 by combining highly partisan voting by Republicans with the defections of thirty or more Democrats. But further into the Reagan presidency, fewer and fewer Democrats defected to Reagan.

The brutal 1986 battle for control of the Senate and the onset of the 1988 presidential campaign deepened the partisan divide in 1987. Whenever they could, Speaker Wright and Majority Leader Byrd garnered Republican support to override Reagan's vetoes of an $87.5 billion, five-year highway bill and a $20 billion clean water bill in 1987, to oppose Reagan on trade measures, or to press Reagan to accept a tax increase to finance his defense buildup. But the Democratic leaders also pushed partisan causes: bills to reform campaign financing or to oppose Reagan's use of the Navy to protect Kuwait's Persian Gulf shipping, or the battle over Reagan's nomination of Robert H. Bork to the Supreme Court. The Democratic leaders knew Reagan could veto their bills, but they pushed ahead anyway—just as Reagan had long pushed a constitutional amendment to balance the budget, knowing it would not pass. The purpose on both sides was less to solve the issues than to reap credit with the voters and put blame on the other side.

The very fact of divided government invites politicians to play the blame game—to engage in maneuvers which have little chance of implementation but which dramatize their side's virtue and the opposition's villainy. With power politically divided, it is hard for voters to know whom to hold responsible for failure: the president or Congress, Republicans or Democrats. In this situation, the incentives of the power game reward tactical squeeze plays, finger pointing, damage control, and partisan posturing. The temptation for both sides is to protect their sacred cows and to gore the other side's oxen. The gambits have become familiar: budgets passed at the eleventh hour, Congress forcing the president to swallow unpalatable provisions in omnibus bills, or the president melodramatically shutting down government so that TV networks can dramatize "congressional irresponsibility." These are blame-game politics staged for the fans at home.

The blame game usually distorts sensible government, because its goal is not solving problems but scoring political points. A favorite tactic is known as "positioning." It is rampant in election years. To pick one memorable example: After the highly publicized deaths of two athletes in mid-1986, the public panicked over crack, a new form of cocaine. Fighting drugs became the hot issue. All sides genuinely wanted to do something about drug abuse, but rather than jointly developing a sensible program, the rival parties maneuvered for maximum public credit. House Republicans, eager to divert attention from a sagging economy, picked the war on drugs as their campaign issue. Then Democrats, led by Speaker O'Neill, one-upped the Republicans with a bigger program. Finally, President and Mrs. Reagan tried to top the Democrats with a joint appearance on nationwide TV. The politics of fighting drugs made daily headlines in the campaign homestretch. But after the election, the issue dropped out of sight and very little new action was taken to fight drug abuse, despite all the hoopla. By early

1987, even Republicans were berating Reagan for penny-pinching on the drug war.

Obviously, blame-game tactics are not an invention of the 1980s. In an earlier era of divided government, Harry Truman won reelection in 1948 by attacking the "do nothing" Republican Eightieth Congress for refusing to cooperate on anti-inflationary measures. In the mid-1970s, Richard Nixon and Gerald Ford had blame-game spats with Democratic congresses. Ford lashed out at the "whining and whimpering" of the Democratic "can't-do Congress."

But Ronald Reagan has been the most skillful blame-game politician in the past three decades. Until the Iran-*contra* affair, he was masterful at ducking or deflecting the blame for failures, such as the breakdown of his toxic-waste program in 1982 or the forced withdrawal of American Marines from Lebanon. His cabinet officials (Interior Secretary James Watt or Chief of Staff Donald Regan) became lightning rods, absorbing public outrage. Although Reagan often delivered inaccurate or disingenuous accounts in speeches or press conferences, he was rarely blamed or distrusted by most of the public, until the Iran-*contra* affair. And he got swing Democrats to support aid for the *contras* for fear of being blamed for Communism in Nicaragua.

The normal disarray of Congress makes it a far easier whipping boy than the presidency; Reagan made the most of that. He rode into office savaging Congress for wild spending, though nonpartisan studies show that is a bum rap. Over time, deficits have been driven mainly by wars and presidential activism. (In Reagan's case, military spending, farm programs, and interest on the national debt have pushed up the deficit.)

"Historically, Congress was certainly an accomplice [in creating deficits]—but Presidents were the masterminds," asserts Norman Ornstein of the conservative American Enterprise Institute for Public Policy Research.[10]

Reagan constantly browbeat Congress, especially the Democrats, by trumpeting a constitutional amendment requiring Congress to balance the budget, though Reagan did not live by that standard himself. When Senate Democrats submitted proposals requiring Reagan and future presidents to submit a balanced budget starting in 1984, the Reagan White House fought and defeated these requirements.[11] Typical blame-game politics.

A study by Paul Peterson of the Brookings Institution shows that over a thirty-seven-year period, from 1947 to 1984, *Congress has spent less* on average than presidents requested.[12] In the Reagan years, Congress showed more political courage than the president in taking unpopular steps to curb the deficit. Despite the maxim that Congress never raises taxes in election years for fear of angering voters, congressional leaders such as Howard Baker and Bob Dole, on the Republican side, and Tip O'Neill, on the Democratic side, pushed tax increases through in 1982, 1983, and 1984—ultimately signed by Reagan—lowering Reagan's deficits by about $75 billion a year, from 1986 onward.[13]

But blame-game tactics kept both sides from later taking major steps to reduce the national deficit. Reagan scalded the Democrats so harshly as the party of "tax and tax, spend and spend" that most Democrats dared not support a tax increase to reduce the deficit. Some Republicans openly asserted that a tax increase was necessary. But Speaker O'Neill had been so burned by President Reagan that in 1985 he decreed that no Democrat could push a tax increase until Reagan took the initiative. But Reagan, stung by Walter Mondale's 1984 campaign charge that Reagan would ultimately have to raise taxes, stubbornly refused to let Mondale be proven right. The blame game dictated policy.

Democrats indulged in demagoguery, too, with exaggerated attacks on Republicans on the Social Security issue. Privately, many congressional Democrats conceded that any serious attempt to reduce the budget deficit would require cutting Social Security COLAs. But Democratic campaign ads blistered Republicans as a party bent on tampering with the financial lifeline of the elderly—Social Security—so most Republicans dared not mention Social Security as part of a budget-control package. Again, the blame game dictated policy.

Blame-game politics are not always bad. Such tactics played a constructive role in passing the major tax-reform bill of 1986. Public resentment against the existing tax code was so strong that both the Democratic House and Republican Senate were afraid to let the tax-reform bill die on their doorsteps. The tax bill was not popular with most members of Congress, but they feared the wrath of voters. President Reagan and congressional leaders such as Dan Rostenkowski and Bob Packwood used that fear to prod Congress to act at crucial moments.

The dynamics of blame-game politics also provided the stimulus for action on the federal budget deficit in late 1985. Congressional Democrats were raw from Reagan's attacks and eager to take some action. Republicans, especially Senate Republicans, were worried about being saddled with responsibility for the mounting national debt. In October 1985, the debt was going over $2 trillion—more than double its size

when Reagan took office and the Republican majority took over the
Senate, both promising to balance the budget. A vote to raise the debt
ceiling above $2 trillion would dramatize Republican failure.

Reagan too was feeling political heat. In 1984, his private polls done
by Richard Wirthlin had shown that voters felt Reagan was soft on the
deficit. But Wirthlin told Reagan not to worry, because only two to
three percent of the public listed the deficit as the nation's most
important problem. But by September 1985, Wirthlin told Reagan this
issue "just could no longer be ignored."[14] With the 1985 deficit projected at $180 billion, Wirthlin's polls found that a substantial fourteen
to fifteen percent of the public saw the deficit as problem number one.
Reagan had "very negative" ratings—the public disapproved of his
handling of the deficit by nearly 2–1.

In short, fear of political blame for the ballooning deficit propelled
all sides toward compromise.

The Double Veto and Power Karate

The congressional initiative in late 1985 to bring down deficits, later
joined by President Reagan and both parties in Congress, is a case study
in divided government and blame-game politics. A lot of serious effort
went into the Gramm-Rudman-Hollings bill, named for its main sponsors, Republican senators Phil Gramm and Warren Rudman and Democrat Fritz Hollings. House Democrats such as Whip Tom Foley and
Caucus Chairman Richard Gephardt worked hard to improve the bill.
But the blame-game climate produced false rather than genuine bipartisanship.

It was a shame, because the elements for bipartisan compromise on
the budget were obvious by mid-1985, and so was the need for collaboration. Even with three years of economic growth, government spending was 24 percent of GNP and tax revenues only 18.6 percent, leaving
a gaping *structural* deficit. The political situation dictated a "three-
legged" approach: defense, entitlements, and taxes.* The bipartisan
consensus in Washington, except for Reagan, was that a politically fair
and viable antideficit package should include a tax increase, a slowdown

---

*Entitlements then comprised forty-one percent of the budget, defense twenty-nine percent,
interest on the national debt fifteen percent. The final fifteen percent was the basic operation
of government. This portion—already squeezed hard—was for domestic spending on highways,
national parks, the FBI, customs, education, housing, border patrols, space, air safety, mass transit,
environmental protection, etc. In all, this cost $144 billion. Reagan talked as if these should be
cut more. But even if they had been wiped out—something impossible—it would still have left
a deficit of $68 billion in 1985.

in Reagan's defense buildup, plus spending caps and reduced COLAs for multibillion-dollar entitlement programs such as Social Security, Medicare, Medicaid, and government pensions.

Some congressional leaders wanted a "domestic economic summit" to join with President Reagan in forging a grand compromise. But Reagan refused, and a tricky blame-game ensued.

What emerged in late 1985 was a shotgun coalition—consummated at political gunpoint—not a durable political marriage. Instead of willing cooperation to beat the deficit, the White House, Senate Republicans, and House Democrats got into a game of political chicken. The legislation that emerged was a symbol of the impasse it was supposed to resolve. Opposing parties and factions latched onto the Gramm-Rudman scheme at cross-purposes and for conflicting motives. The 1985 Gramm-Rudman bill came to illustrate what plagues the governing of America.

The budget deficit epitomizes the main defect of divided government: the "double veto." Presidents have a constitutional veto power to block anything that does not command a two-thirds majority in both houses of Congress. But either house of Congress has the power to veto or block what a president wants. On the deficit, Reagan wanted to kill and shrink domestic programs and to keep expanding military spending, but House Democrats, and a lot of Senate Republicans, wanted almost exactly the opposite: to protect most domestic programs and stop the growth of Pentagon spending. Neither side had the political courage to make modest cuts in the big entitlement programs popular with middle-class voters.

To get around the basic deadlock, senators Phil Gramm and Warren Rudman devised a mechanism for imposing automatic cuts on all programs, regardless of their merit or the impact of the cuts. It was a desperate attempt to force all sides to take unpleasant political medicine for the good of the country.

Gramm dreamed up the scheme as a way to revive the Reagan Revolution and to squeeze down the federal government. Few modern politicians have a faster trigger finger and a more jugular instinct than Gramm has. His political game is power karate: numbing foes with an unexpected chop and then outmaneuvering them while they are still dazed. As a renegade sophomore Democrat in 1981, Gramm colluded with the Reagan team to whisk a final round of overnight budget cuts through the House of Representatives before most members could even read his package. Later, he openly defected—becoming a Republican.

Gramm's receding, mid-forties hairline, his soft Texas drawl, and his professorial theorizing belie his lust for partisan combat. But Gramm exudes energy. On his desk, he parades the symbols of a brash and aggressive political style: a miniature Texas flag, the first American flag (a curling snake and the words DON'T TREAD ON ME) and a silvered bullet made by an admirer. The bullet was inspired by Gramm's warning to the House in 1981 that the Reagan-Stockman-Gramm budget package was no paper exercise but spelled real cutbacks for many people. "We are shooting real bullets," Gramm declared dramatically, garnering big TV play.

Gramm's passion for free-market economics has never been a secret. As an economist at Texas A&M University, he described his research topic as "How to get rid of government." And Gramm is a supremely clever legislative schemer, skilled at throwing opponents into disarray. Gramm thinks harder than most politicians. ("Ideas have consequences," he is fond of saying. "Ideas dominate the agenda.") But he is no abstract thinker; he is a bare-knuckled political plotter. He ruminates powerfully on the means to his ends, ready to pounce when he spots a partisan opening, usually when Congress is mired in deadlock. "You immobilize politicians when you give them a problem without a solution," Gramm advises. "So one of the things I have always tried to do is to bring the problem and the solution together."[15]

The Gramm-Rudman plan to balance the federal budget by 1991 through legislating *automatic across-the-board budget cuts*, year by year, was intended to impose a legislative straitjacket so uncomfortable that it would force all political factions to behave more responsibly on the deficit to avoid decimation of their favorite programs. It was an ingenious mechanism. Some Democrats ridiculed it as "government by Veg-O-Matic," chopping up programs willy-nilly. David Stockman derided it as "mindless, destructive gimmickry." Defending the bill, Gramm said, "It puts the fat in the fire" and forces decisions.

In the quagmire of congressional paralysis, the Gramm-Rudman scheme caught the public's fancy. To voters uninterested in the nitty-gritty of budget priorities, Gramm's formula had the appeal of an easy solution. And with voters enamored, Congress found it well-nigh irresistible. All sides proclaimed their support and then played blame-game politics over the fine print.

Phil Gramm's timing in the fall of 1985 was brilliant. It helped extricate the Republicans from a bad political jam and put a partisan squeeze on the Democrats. Up to then, Reagan had been faring badly in his fifth year. The Reagan Revolution was mired in deadlock. Democrats were basking in Republican fratricide. Gramm saw a chance to breathe new fire into Reaganism and throw Democrats on the defensive. Although he was only eight months a senator, his elixir sold fast to his elders.

In the fall of 1985, most Senate Republicans were seething with fury at President Reagan and desperate to show action on the deficit before the 1986 election. Forty-nine Senate Republicans (eighteen up for reelection in 1986) had gone out on a political limb to fight the deficit in May 1985. They had risked angering millions of senior citizens by voting to cut COLAs for Social Security and other entitlement programs. That act of political courage was undercut by Reagan, who had endorsed it initially and then backed away. Even Reagan's closest allies felt double-crossed, and wanted to get political cover.

Warren Rudman, who has the build, bark, and tenacity of a bulldog, typified the Republican frustration. "The problem is that you have a Republican president, a Republican Senate, and a strong Democratic-controlled House, and there's nothing in there for compromise as long as you can add everything onto the deficit," he grumped. "That's what we've done the last four years." Rudman was so sick of the deadlocks of divided government and so irate with Reagan that he joined forces with Gramm.

But he was less ideological and more pragmatic than Gramm—and more intent on conquering the deficit than on reviving the Reagan Revolution. He wanted to squeeze Reagan as well as House Democrats. So he insisted that the Pentagon be included in the automatic budget cuts. His theory was that holding the Pentagon hostage would compel Reagan to raise taxes. "It will force the president to face up to the fact that if we want all of the increases that he wants in defense, we may have to have new taxes to finance them," Rudman told me.[16] That thinking appealed to both Republican and Democratic moderates, and some liberals (Chris Dodd and Ted Kennedy) who saw a chance to squeeze Reagan. House Democratic Whip Tom Foley later quipped that Congress was "kidnapping the president's favorite son [the Pentagon], and we're going to make him pay ransom."

Reagan had different motives for going along with the scheme. He was still trying to use high deficits to force Congress to cut the size of government. Many Democrats believed that Reagan had purposely built up the deficit as a leash on Congress. Indeed, Reagan compared dealing with Congress to a father cutting his son's allowance to stop him from spending money foolishly. In his 1987 budget message, Reagan bluntly declared that "the deficit problem is also an opportunity—an opportunity to construct a new, leaner, better focused, and better managed federal structure." That is, to cut programs.

By late 1985, Reagan himself looked bad on the deficit. His strategists figured that endorsing Gramm-Rudman would make Reagan look better. Moreover, his aides told me, they reckoned Congress would never pass the bill, sparing Reagan from its impact. So, faced with steamroller support for Gramm-Rudman in the Senate, Reagan endorsed the plan on October 4, though he tried to deny its intent: He barred any tax increase, excluded Social Security, and insisted that he could still get defense spending increases. Chief of Staff Don Regan, who talked the president into buying the scheme, belatedly sent him a memo on October 4 warning that it could hit the Pentagon hard.[17] But it is doubtful the president received or read that memo in time. Two cabinet-level officials told me that Reagan did not understand the bill's impact on defense spending before he endorsed it.

Typical of blame-game politics, the president and most Senate Republicans were signing onto the plan for radically different motives. This had the façade of compromise. Reagan, like Gramm, wanted the automatic slicer to chop Democratic-style domestic programs. Most Senate Republicans wanted not only to cut domestic programs but to pressure Reagan to raise taxes and trim back on defense; twenty-seven Democrats felt the same way. On October 9, the Senate passed the plan by a 75–24 vote—as part of a bill raising the debt ceiling above $2 trillion.

Escaping Blame: Reverse Houdini

When Congress gets tangled in the partisan warfare of divided government, it often ties itself in knots. All sides resort to one-upmanship. That is what happened on Gramm-Rudman. The House Democratic leadership, initially stunned by the Senate vote, eventually put a reverse squeeze on Republicans. It was a case study in the legislative power game.

Old-line Democratic committee chairmen wanted to fight. The group that Tip O'Neill nicknamed the "old oaks" (Claude Pepper of Florida, Jack Brooks of Texas, Jamie Whitten of Mississippi, Peter Rodino of New Jersey, and John Dingell of Michigan) urged the speaker to kill Gramm-Rudman—to pass the debt-ceiling bill without it. They saw it as an outrageous, unconstitutional giveaway of congressional power to the president, because his budget director would get authority to decide when and how to carry out the automatic budget cuts.

But O'Neill knew the Democrats had no chance unless they were unified, and revolt was rippling through the rank and file. Democratic conservatives liked the budget-balancing purpose of Gramm-Rudman. Moderate Democrats feared looking passive on the deficit while the Republicans were billboarding a new panacea. Whip Tom Foley told the committee chairmen they were outgunned.

"You're the toughest unit in the U.S. Army," Foley kidded them. "You're willing to take on machine-gun emplacements with your hands, kick the treads off Tiger tanks with G.I. boots." But he warned them that it would take winning all the Democrats—"and you can't get that kind of vote!"[18]

Within forty-eight hours, O'Neill had adopted a Democratic damage-control strategy: matching the Republican squeeze play. With two moderates in charge, Foley and Gephardt, the Democratic tactic was to endorse Gramm-Rudman's goals and then revise its specifics. There followed two months of tense maneuvering. House Democrats eventually got agreement from Senate Republicans to suspend Gramm-Rudman during a recession. They also inserted provisions to protect Congress. Their plan provided that the Congressional Budget Office share with the budget director the power of deciding when to activate automatic budget cuts—and empowered the comptroller general (an agent of Congress) to specify the actual cuts. Those provisions got bipartisan support.

But House Democrats also played blame-game politics: a game of political chicken. They decided to expose the Republicans by tightening the Gramm-Rudman scheme to make the public howl at the cuts it imposed. "Let's really make it hurt," was the Democratic war cry.

"There's no doubt there was a strain of partisan political vengeance," Foley told me. "The feeling was, 'Let's get revenge on those bastards. They want deficit reduction—let's give it to 'em early in the year so they're gonna have to explain to their constituents why all these programs are cut out six months before the election.' "[19]

Gramm's original bill had been a clever blame-game ploy. It gave Senate Republicans a partisan advantage—publicity for fighting the deficit in 1985 and 1986, but delaying actual cuts until after the 1986 elections. Democrats ridiculed it as a tactic to save Republican Senate seats in 1986. The Democratic countersqueeze was to make Gramm-Rudman bite into programs in early 1986, so that voters would feel the pinch before the 1986 elections and punish Republican candidates. To compound the political pain, Democrats also pushed for deeper cuts in 1986.

Foley, Gephardt, and company also made sure the axe would fall fully on Pentagon spending and fought to exempt their pet social programs from automatic cuts. In the end, the Democrats spared a string of programs from Gramm's guillotine: Social Security, veterans pensions, and such programs for the poor as food stamps, Medicaid, child nutrition, supplemental income for the elderly, and welfare for families with dependent children. Cuts on Medicare and four other health programs were limited.

Finally, the Gramm-Rudman law passed by large majorities, creating optimism in financial markets that the government was serious about licking the deficit. But the lopsided majorities were misleading. At the White House, officials admitted privately that they were counting on the law's being ruled unconstitutional. Members of Congress filed suit.

Indeed, the Supreme Court ruled the automatic cutting mechanism unconstitutional, as the canniest White House and congressional strategists had expected. The Court saved the politicians from themselves, as some had intended.[20]

The Gramm-Rudman law had a fallback procedure: The automatic budget-cutting could take effect, provided that Congress and the president agreed. But that never happened; the blame-game rivals kept on arguing. Even if the Court had upheld Gramm-Rudman, the conflicting motives of Reagan, Senate Republicans, and House Democrats suggest there would have been endless maneuvers to avoid its full and fair implementation—because a genuine budget compromise had not been reached.

In short, the 1985 Gramm-Rudman act turned out to be not a model of political responsibility but an exercise in the politics of evasion. Not that everyone's intentions were cynical. Many in Congress wanted to curb the deficit, and some worked hard to that end. But after President Reagan blocked the consensus approach, all sides vied to look good fighting the deficit, while using the fine print to protect their pet programs—thus perpetuating big deficits. Instead of the deficit declining, it shot up. The 1986 Gramm-Rudman target was $144 billion, but the deficit hit a record level of $220.6 billion.

Unintentionally, Gramm-Rudman became a metaphor for divided government. Because no one wanted to deliver any bad news to voters, the politicians invented a Rube Goldberg contraption that made the dirty work of cutting programs and raising taxes seem impersonal. Congress literally tied itself in knots. Barney Frank of Massachusetts called Gramm-Rudman a "reverse Houdini." Houdini was known for miraculous escapes from impossible predicaments; Frank felt Congress was great at the opposite—locking itself into unbreakable deadlocks, so voters cannot fault anyone in particular. That is what Gramm-Rudman did. It offered everyone from President Reagan to the most junior Democrat in Congress what politicians love—political cover: a way to look well intentioned but avoid blame for unpleasant action.

In late 1987, still at loggerheads with Reagan over the deficit, congressional leaders tried again. They revived Gramm-Rudman, but giving Reagan's budget director power to activate the automatic cutting mechanism. The deficit target for 1988 was still $144 billion, two years behind schedule. Pressure was again on Reagan to raise taxes or cut defense, and Treasury Secretary Jim Baker accused Congress of pointing a "gun at his [Reagan's] head."[21] Protesting loudly and insisting he would not raise taxes or cut defense, Reagan signed the bill. But the melodrama may have been overdone, for the bill was a watered-down version—postponing really tough action until after the 1988 election.

Conservatives such as Nebraska Democrat James Exon contended the new law was political gimmickry. "The entire Gramm-Rudman process actually delays serious action on the deficit," Exon asserted. "Rather than force action, the Gramm-Rudman process fakes action. . . . After two years of operation, by and large, Gramm-Rudman has not worked. The new version of the law does not bring with it a new promise of deficit reduction. If anything, it pushes difficult decisions away from this Congress and President Reagan onto the next Congress and the next president."[22]

Eventually, it took the 508-point nose-dive in the Wall Street stock market average to jolt Reagan into negotiations with Congress to make even a modest dent in the 1988 deficit. The long-term deficit problem was left to the next administration and the next Congress.

Gramm-Rudman remained on the books, less a solution to the problem than a symbol and symptom of divided government. It underscored the political deadlock at the heart of American government: the partisan division between Congress and the White House, created by voters. And divided government will continue to produce "sons of Gramm-Rudman" until there is leadership in both branches of government committed to genuine compromise, or until voters put a single party in charge of White House, Senate, and House for long enough to resolve such basic long-term problems as the deficit.

18. Where's the Majority Party?: No Longer the Democrats, Not Yet the Republicans

People don't want any one party to be dominant . . . they prefer divided government. They just don't want one party of scoundrels in there . . . People believe in checks and balances.
—Pollster Louis Harris

Voters like to blame politicians for the "mess" in Washington, as if voters themselves had no role in the problem. Yet obviously, what happens inside the beltway depends greatly on what the voters decide—on millions of people voting the "paralysis ticket." For the root cause of divided government is rampant ticket splitting, which paralyzes government.

Perhaps the most important fact about the American political system today is that we have no clear-cut majority party. Our history shows that it usually takes a single party with a cohesive program and dominance in both Congress and the White House to run our political system. Yet today, neither party has such command. The Democratic party's long hegemony has ended. Republicans have won four of the last five presidential elections, but no new Republican majority has replaced the Democrats' New Deal coalition, because of the rise of independent voters. Today, we have two minority parties, and the equilibrium between them works against effective government.

A Republican takeover as the true majority party would have required a sea change at the grass roots. It has nearly happened, but not quite—mainly because of split-ticket voting. It is true that America's established voting habits have changed over the past two decades, even from Reagan's first victory to his second. Important streams of voters in both North and South have defected from the Democratic party, but many of them did not become Republicans. Several times Republicans have felt a realignment within reach, but the electorate has not yet swung over. And its long hesitancy not only throws uncertainty over the 1988 election, but foreshadows more years of political muddle.

What marks the present political era is not a major political realignment but "dealignment"—the erosion of one majority without the formation of a new one, plus the simultaneous weakening of the party system.

We still use party labels as if they meant today what they have traditionally meant in American history, but they do not, and the difference is crucial. We talk about the rivalry between parties for the White House or control of Congress, as if they were solid blocs. The language is unchanged, but the reality of the party system—the nature of parties, their functions, their power, and their cohesion—has changed significantly.

American parties have always been looser coalitions than the more ideological parties of European democracies have been. Our parties are confederations of state parties, rather than unified, top-down national structures. Even in our most partisan Congresses, party-line voting does not nearly match the party discipline of major European parliaments. In America, it is considered a "party vote" when the majority of one party in the House or Senate opposes a majority of the other party. That permits large defections in both parties; by contrast, in the British House of Commons, it is quite rare to have even one defection from the governing party on a vote of consequence. Such discipline makes a vital difference for governing.

But here, as in Europe, the national parties have been essential vehicles for formulating the nation's agenda, presenting programs and candidates to the electorate, and then implementing those programs by marshaling majorities in Congress. Voters deride parties and many politicians try to walk away from them, but parties are indispensable for governing.

"The political party is the tie that binds, the glue that fastens, the bridge that unites the disparate institutions that make up the government," observed James Sundquist, a senior scholar at the Brookings Institution in Washington. "Without parties, democracy on a national scale simply couldn't work."[1]

Traditionally, parties have been the essential link between the voters and government. Elections provide people with the opportunity to send a national message to their leaders. Voting for the "out" party has long been the vehicle for registering discontent with current policies and for producing new policies and new power arrangements. Changes in the balance of power between the major parties are signals of the electorate's demand for a change in political direction.

For decades, it was primarily the role of political parties to nominate presidential candidates, raise the money and organize political campaigns, draw together the demands of diverse interest groups, and meld them into a general program, and help the public sort out its broad choices by encouraging identification with one of the two major parties.

But the primacy and the structure of our parties have been undermined by a host of changes. Presidential nomination is now determined in direct popular primaries. Party endorsement is an empty ritual. Candidates raise their own money and build personal organizations, bypassing party machinery. With the progressive reforms of the early twentieth century (referendum, initiative, and direct primaries), the public grabbed power from party bosses. In the nineteenth century, parties actually distributed ballots to voters—all straight tickets. But today, voting machines make split-ticket voting easy; only twenty-one states permit levers for straight-ticket voting.

Not only do parties no longer distribute ballots, but their historic role of dispensing patronage and social services has all but expired. The civil service has largely replaced patronage, and government programs have replaced the handouts of local party bosses and machines. Political clubs have withered as social centers, and party machines in big cities such as Boston and Chicago lack the steady infusion of new immigrants to swell the faithful party rank and file.

What is more, the parties have been shoved into the shadows by the modern technology and techniques of politics. Television, not the party network, is now the main channel of communication between candidates and the electorate. Political consultants and pollsters have replaced party bosses as the managers of candidates, the manipulators of political messages, the interpreters of the public mood. Government subsidies and PACs now compete with parties as the underwriters of campaigns. Even when parties raise hundreds of millions of dollars and support candidates with all kinds of help and advice, they act as service centers, not as hubs of power-giving direction and discipline. PACs are far more aggressive than parties are after elections, following up to see that victorious candidates attend to their pet issues.

Finally, parties have lost their strength as unifying forces across the country. Brand-name loyalty simply does not work with voters as it used to. The most important phenomenon of American politics in the past quarter century has been the rise of independent voters who have at times outnumbered Republicans. Independent voters plus millions of ticket-splitting party members, hopscotch their ballots from office to office, foiling any party's attempts to gain unified control of government for any length of time.

Political analysts such as William Schneider of the American Enterprise Institute make the point that under pressure from New Right and New Left activists, both major parties have narrowed philosophically, and this has lessened their political reach.[2] In presidential primaries, ideological activists have occasionally pushed both parties to pick ideological presidential candidates: Barry Goldwater in 1964 and Ronald Reagan in 1980 for the Republicans, George McGovern for the Democrats in 1972.

As Schneider observed, the two biggest third-party presidential candidacies in the past two decades reflected mass disenchantment with the way mainstream parties were being pushed toward extremes. In 1968, George Wallace led a revolt of conservative southern whites disgusted with the liberal civil rights policies of the national Democratic party. His bolt helped elect Richard Nixon by a minority vote. In 1980, John Anderson's independent presidential candidacy signaled the disaffection of northern Republican liberals and moderates, no longer at home in a party controlled by militant conservatives. Although Reagan won fifty-one percent of the popular vote in 1980, these two big splinter movements demonstrated the absence of an enduring majority party.

The Partisan Rhythm of History

The emergence of a new partisan majority would not only give greater coherence to American government, it would fit the patterns of the past two centuries. For our two-party system has been marked by rhythmic swings from one party to another. Every three decades or so has brought a political watershed.

The first great dynasty began in 1800 with the dominance of the Jeffersonian Democratic-Republican party. A major realignment took place in 1828 with the rise of Jacksonian Democrats battling the Whigs, the new opposition. Another major shift occurred in 1860 with the demise of the Whig party and the birth of the unionist Republican party of Abraham Lincoln. Then in 1896, after a muddy two decades of often-divided government, the Democrats swung to the western, silver-standard populism of William Jennings Bryan, while the gold-standard, probusiness Republicans gained national hegemony with the election of William McKinley in 1896. Republican dominance lasted, allowing for the interlude of Woodrow Wilson, until Franklin Delano Roosevelt forged the New Deal Democratic coalition in 1932. Then, for two uninterrupted decades, the Democrats held the White House.

This historic rhythm, with swings every twenty-eight to thirty-six years, should have produced a new watershed between 1960 and 1968 with a Republican majority replacing the New Deal coalition.

The first trumpeting of the Republican coming sounded in 1952 when Dwight Eisenhower cracked Democratic control of the West and the Solid South. Republicans, winning House and Senate as well as the White House, sensed the hinge of history opening to a new era of GOP dominance. But the Republican surge proved ephemeral. Two years later, the Democrats regained control of Congress, and despite Eisenhower's second triumph in 1956, congressional Republicans fell back. No realignment took place.

Again with Nixon, Republicans saw their dream rekindled, especially in 1972, when they made a net gain of two Senate seats and five House seats in the South. Republican strategists saw these modest but steady gains as a harbinger of a changing balance. But the Watergate scandal and Nixon's resignation in 1974 threw the Republicans off track. Kevin Phillips, a Nixon strategist who wrote *The Emerging Republican Majority,* told me years later that he believed that Watergate had blocked the normal swing of the pendulum and prevented full Republican realignment.[3] In 1974, the Democrats won the Senate for six more years, firmed up an unbeatable majority in the House, and set the stage for Jimmy Carter's unexpected victory in 1976.

But Watergate created an illusion of Democratic strength. For despite its hold on Congress, the Democratic party was losing its grip on the country and its long hegemony over national government. During the past two decades, the Democrats have suffered painful hemorrhages among traditional constituencies in both North and South.

At its core, Roosevelt's New Deal coalition was an uneasy alliance of its northern and southern wings: white southerners, mainly Protestant, conservative, largely rural and mostly native-stock Americans; and white northerners, mainly Catholic, liberal, urban, and largely ethnic immigrants. If either faction pressed its agenda too hard, the other was sure to be disaffected.

Issues of race, war, and the economy finally tore apart FDR's coalition. In two great waves, millions of voters abandoned the Democratic party. The first major defection came among white southerners from the mid-1960s onward, mainly because of their anger at the civil rights policies of the northern liberal wing but also because of disenchantment with liberal Democratic opposition to Vietnam War. The defection was especially stunning among evangelical Christians. Overall, Democrats lost more than half their strength among southern whites. Republican strength doubled among this group and independent voters tripled. In 1952, for example, seventy-eight percent of white southerners called themselves Democrats; but after Reagan's 1984 reelection, only thirty-seven percent were still self-proclaimed Democrats. In that interval Republicans shot up from eleven to twenty-four percent and independents from twelve to thirty-nine percent.[4]

The second great Democratic defection came in the North during the early 1980s among urban ethnic blue-collar voters. These were mainly the rank and file of organized labor who had long regarded the Democratic party as their bulwark against economic adversity. In the 1960s, many of these working class voters were upset with the Democratic party's stand on racial issues and foreign policy. Some flirted with George Wallace in 1968. But the Democratic record of protecting them from inflation and unemployment held their allegiance—*until* Jimmy Carter soured Democratic credibility with blue-collar voters.

Ironically, Carter fashioned the political litmus test that sealed his own fate and wounded his party. To highlight Republican economic failures, Carter invented the "misery index," which added the rates of inflation and unemployment. In 1976, Carter browbeat Gerald Ford mercilessly for a misery index of 15.3. But in October 1980, Carter's own misery index shot up to 21.3. Reagan used that miserable record, and his later success in beating down inflation, to lure away big labor's rank and file. Reagan got fifty-four percent of the blue-collar vote against organized labor's candidate, Walter Mondale, in 1984.[5]

Weakened by these two large defections, the Democrats have competed poorly for the White House in the past two decades, except for Carter's paper-thin, post-Watergate victory over Ford in 1976. The weakness of Democratic presidential candidates underscores the erosion of Democratic strength nationwide. Three times—in 1968, 1972, and 1984—the Democrats fielded variations of the same ticket: a northern liberal Protestant running for president with a northern liberal Catholic as a running mate (Humphrey and Muskie in 1968; McGovern and Shriver in 1972; Mondale and Ferraro in 1984). All three times, the Democratic ticket got only about forty percent of the popular vote, a weak race for the presidency. In 1980, Carter, as incumbent president and a southerner, got only 41.7% of the vote.

That poor Democratic record highlights one hallmark of a major realignment: the Republican "lock" on the presidency. *Lock* is the graphic term of Horace Busby, a political commentator who rose to prominence as a Texas lieutenant of Lyndon Johnson. In the last five presidential elections, Busby points out, Republican nominees have won a staggering seventy-seven percent of the nation's electoral college votes while Democrats have won just twenty-one percent. (Third parties won two percent.) Busby calls Republicans America's "presidential party," arguing that the Republican party appeals to that basic conservatism of Americans.[6]

In support his lock idea, Busby notes that in the nine presidential elections from 1952 through 1984, twenty-nine states voted Republican at least seven times—and those states cast 289 electoral votes, more than an Electoral College majority (270 votes). Twenty-three states have gone Republican the last five times in a row, while only the District of Columbia went Democratic five times. The strong pro-Republican group covers every state from the Great Plains to the Pacific Coast except Texas, Oklahoma, and Washington. In short, Republican ascendancy rides on people moving to the Sunbelt, both West and South.

Again, this fits historical patterns. Virtually every political realignment in American history has been a revolt of what then constituted the South and West against established power in the North and East—originally the Virginia dynasty against the New England and New York federalists, then the border states and Middle West against the Eastern seaboard, and so on. Nowadays, California and the Rocky Mountain West have anchored the new Republican power base, usually joined by Florida, symbol of the new Sunbelt, against established power centers in the industrial Rustbelt heartland and the old South.[7]

Reagan Tugs the Grass Roots

What the Republican drive for hegemony lacked was sufficient voter strength at the grass roots and growing echelons of Republican officeholders, from city hall and state legislatures up to Congress. No one worked harder at patient party building than former Republican National Chairman Bill Brock, a former senator from Tennessee and later Labor secretary under Reagan. Starting in 1977, Brock developed Republican fund-raising muscle and high-tech politics. With computers, well-culled donor lists, and sophisticated direct mail, the Republican party shifted financially from the party of fat-cat donors to the party of small contributors. By 1980, Republican House and Senate campaign committees were raising from five to nine times as much money as their Democratic counterparts were—and the money gave a great boost to the 1980 crop of Republican congressional candidates.

The Reagan tide of 1980 quickened Republican expectations of a full-fledged political realignment, picking up where Nixon had been blunted by Watergate. With their 1980 gain of twelve seats in the Senate and thirty-three in the House, Republicans thought they had found legs to win in Congress as well as take the White House. Exuberantly, Republican leaders such as Congressman Guy Vander Jagt of Michigan boasted they would take over the House in 1982. They ballyhooed conversions of congressional Democrats, celebrating in the White House Rose Garden when Pennsylvania's Eugene Atkinson joined Republican ranks, and jubilant at later crossovers by Phil Gramm of Texas, Andy Ireland of Florida, Bob Stump of Arizona.

Subterranean changes were also taking place at the grass roots. In opinion polls, more voters were calling themselves Republicans than previously. In the heyday of Harry Truman, and even under Dwight Eisenhower, the Democratic party had been a clear majority, with fifteen to twenty percent greater support among voters than Republicans had. After Reagan's 1980 victory, the Democratic advantage fell below ten percent in some polls. A temporary postelection surge is normal for the party that wins the presidency, but the Republican bulge persisted into mid-1981, suggesting that the long-predicted sea change among voters might be taking place. But with the deep recession of 1982–83, voter allegiances shifted back and the Democrats regained their traditional advantage.

Reagan's 1984 landslide revived the Republican dream. "We're on the threshold of a golden era in Republican politics," Senator Paul Laxalt, the party's general chairman, boasted. "We've got Ronald Reagan and the economy, plus a solid Sunbelt base, while the traditional coalitions in the Northeast are crumbling."[8]

Even more than in 1980, the statistics behind Reagan's 1984 victory showed a partisan shift among voters. The most striking evidence came in a mid-November 1984 poll for the National Republican Congressional Campaign Committee, conducted by Robert Teeter of Market Opinion Research. Teeter, a highly respected pollster, found that for the first time in half a century, Republicans and Republican-leaning independent voters actually outnumbered Democrats and Democrat-leaning independents by forty-seven to forty-one percent. Teeter cautioned that the Republican numbers would undoubtedly soften in the coming months. But he asserted that "there is no question that we are undergoing party realignment."[9]

Other polls (Gallup, *The New York Times*/CBS News) showed the Democrats still ahead, but by only three or four percentage points—almost dead even. Democratic strength among blue-collar voters had fallen dramatically since 1980.[10] Republican leaders were ecstatic about their strength among young voters, contending that allegiance won early in life could help cement a long-term realignment.

In short, even if the Republicans were not yet a majority party, there was ample evidence of dealignment—the loss of majority status by the Democrats. The two parties had become competitive, neck and neck. That in itself was a watershed.

But the Republicans could not turn this opportunity into victories up and down the ticket. A few exuberant Republican strategists called Reagan's 1984 victory a "consolidating election" on a par with Democratic gains in 1934 and 1936, which nailed down Franklin Roosevelt's New Deal coalition. But the analogy was false. Down the ballot, Republicans were still not doing well. Even with Reagan's 1984 landslide, the party was slightly weaker at the state and local levels than it had been with Eisenhower and Nixon. It still controlled the Senate, but elsewhere it lacked a springboard to convert Reagan's victory into majority control of government. His reelection brought only 182 Republican seats in the House (compared to 201 under Eisenhower in 1956 and 192 under Nixon in 1972). Similarly, in 1984, Republicans held only sixteen governorships, compared to nineteen in the Eisenhower and Nixon reelection years, and only about forty percent of the state legislative seats across the nation.

"These are not the numbers of a party achieving grass-roots realignment," Republican analyst Kevin Phillips candidly observed.[11]

The Democratic rebound in the 1986 Senate elections bore out Phillips's analysis and dealt a hard blow to Republican dreams of realignment. In 1986, Republicans scored a net gain of eight governorships, heartened especially to win in Texas, Florida, Alabama, and South Carolina. But they also lost a net of eight Senate seats—and control of the Senate.

What made the Republican setbacks in 1986 so terribly painful was that President Reagan—the party's great vote getter—had gone all out. Reagan traveled 24,800 miles to twenty-two states and raised $33 million for Republican candidates.[12] In the homestretch, the "Gipper" pleaded for voters to help him by keeping the Senate in Republican hands. He did personal appearances for sixteen Republican Senate candidates, but only four of them won. Polls showed that jitters about feeble economic growth, the skyrocketing trade deficit, and Japanese competition hurt Republicans. Bread-and-butter issues pushed the Republican dream of realignment further away, like a receding mirage.

"This year will go down in history as the year of the lost cause, when the Republicans snatched defeat from the jaws of victory," complained L. Brent Bozell, president of the National Conservative Political Action Committee. "The Republicans lost a golden opportunity in the sense that they could have solidified the Reagan Revolution."[13]

The Republican setback in 1986 may signal that their drive for realignment has crested. Obviously, pocketbook appeal to voters is crucial to long-term Republican strategy. In many opinion polls in the 1980s, Republicans have won better marks than the Democrats had for managing most aspects of the economy. Low inflation and five years of growth under Reagan have given the Republican party a good name. But the economic slowdown of the past two years, and the stock market plunge of October 1987 blurred the lustre of those GOP advantages.

To become the majority party, the Republicans must put down the image that they are the protectors of class and privilege. Reagan's tax-reform proposal, dropping six million poor off the rolls and offering everyone lower rates, was geared for populist impact. But Democrat Dan Rostenkowski shrewdly neutralized the Republican appeal by helping pass tax reform. Reagan's record leaves Republicans vulnerable to the charge that Reagan built his electoral victories on support from the economic "haves" over opposition from the "have-nots." Compared with Eisenhower, for example, pro-Reagan voting was notably more class based. Ike had majority support from all economic groups, but Reagan lost at the low end of the economic scale.[14] The economic fate of the middle class is pivotal to Republicans.

Second, Republicans now carry the onus of the "in party," which undercuts the popular appeal that Reagan and the conservative movement built by playing heavily on anti-Washington populism. Reagan vilified the Democrats as the political establishment, and alienation from establishment politics gained partisans for the Republican cause. But in the 1980s, the Reaganites became the political establishment. Investigations of influence peddling targeted such Reagan intimates as Michael Deaver and Lyn Nofziger. Also, the fresh political shock troops who mounted the 1980 Reagan campaign (Ed Rollins, Roger Stone, Lee Atwater, and Charlie Black) became $450,000-a-year political campaign consultants—the kind of affluence that robs realignment of recruits and dynamism.

There have been other signs that the original Reaganite thrust has lost élan. In 1981–82, for example, the Republican party arm that focuses on House races raised nearly $58 million. Donors were pouring money into the dream of realignment and taking over Congress. But by the 1985–86 election cycle, after twice failing to generate a majority, this same Republican committee raised just $39.8 million. Obviously some donors had lost heart. In mid-July 1987, the Republican National Committee had to fire forty of its 275 staff members, because of alienation among small donors over the Iran scandal.

Third, even if Republicans win the White House again in 1988, they have no real chance of getting control of Congress, especially without Reagan as a charismatic leader to head their ticket. Many Democrats discounted Reagan's 1984 landslide; they saw it as a personal victory, not a party victory, arguing that the pro-Reagan surge of Republicanism was bound to fade after his departure. Indeed, the bad publicity of the Iran-*contra* affair in 1987 caused a drift away from the Republican party and enabled Democrats to regain a popular advantage of several percentage points over Republicans. Looking ahead, the youth vote, a source of special Republican pride in 1984, is far from settled in its loyalties. Young voters are typically changeable. In the 1986 elections, polls showed, congressional Democrats broke even with the Republicans among under-thirty voters.

Finally, to lead the Republican party to majority status, the new standard bearer must manage the centrifugal elements in the Republican coalition: southern rednecks and country-club Republicans; supply-side tax cutters (Jack Kemp) and deficit-minded budget balancers (Bob Dole); the born-again fundamentalist followers of television evangelist Pat Robertson and high-tech suburban yuppies; corporate executives and farmers from small-town mid-America. Protectionist issues have already sown rifts in the business community. Reagan's new accommodation with Moscow and his agreement with Gorbachev to eliminate intermediate-range nuclear forces sharply split Republicans loyal to Vice President Bush and the ideological anti-Communist wing led by Senator Jesse Helms. Reagan juggled all these constituencies with personal chemistry, for example, placating the New Right with fiery rhetoric (though little action) on its social agenda. But the battle to succeed Reagan inevitably set Republican factions at odds; over the long run, the Reagan coalition is already splintering.

Indeed, some Republican strategists such as Kevin Phillips suggest that the recent Republican realignment began not with Reagan, but with Nixon in 1968, and it has already run its most dynamic twenty years. In Phillips's view, President Reagan is the end—rather than the start—of the conservative Republican trend. "Reagan may be remembered less as the engine of late 20th Century U.S. conservatism than as its jaunty, if somewhat wayward, caboose," Phillips wrote after the 1986 elections.[15] Following the old cyclical swings of the pendulum, Phillips's theory points to another national partisan watershed in the 1990s—away from the Republicans.

The Democratic Lock on the House

While the long-term Republican future is uncertain, what is well established is the unbreakable Democratic lock on the House of Representatives for thirty-four straight years.

The Senate has become the swing element in our government, going under Republican control in 1980 and switching to the Democrats in 1986.[16] The Senate shifts reflect changing voter views, rising with the Reagan tide and ebbing with that tide.

But the House has become insulated from national partisan trends. It has become the Gibraltar of the Democratic party. For seven successive presidencies—starting with Eisenhower in 1954 and then under Kennedy, Johnson, Nixon, Ford, Carter, and Reagan—the Democrats have had a majority in the House. That is by far the longest span of control in American politics since the Civil War.[17] Even New Deal Democratic control of the House, from 1932 to 1946, does not match the current Democratic hegemony.

In part, this reflects the fact that vast numbers of American voters no longer conceive of their government as a unit or vote a straight ticket for president, vice president, Senate, and member of Congress. People used to vote that way. In the nineteenth century and the early twentieth century, the custom was to vote a straight ticket. Back then, there were only five or ten congressional districts where a majority of voters selected a president from one party and a congressman from the opposite party.

By contrast, in 1984, the year of Reagan's crushing landslide, there were partisan splits in forty-four percent of the districts. In 192 of 435 congressional districts, voters chose one party for the White House and the opposite party for the House. Many people think of this as common in the South; but this is no longer a regional phenomenon; the Rocky Mountain West has many split districts as well. In fact, ticket splitting happens nationwide. The result, after Reagan's smashing reelection, was that he had only 182 Republicans in the House to carry out his program—thirty-six votes shy of the needed majority.

Walter Dean Burnham, a political scientist from MIT, pointed out that the House Republican strength after the 1984 election was the lowest proportion of party supporters ever recorded for a victorious presidential candidate in the fifty presidential elections since 1789.[18] Obviously, this outcome was a blow to Reagan's hopes for a dynamic second term; it was also a blow to a cohesive and durable governmental policy. And unless some dramatic changes are made in our election system, any Republican president will probably face a similar disadvantage.

The causes of the Democratic lock on the House are imbedded both in political habit and in how the modern power game is played. First, inertia is a powerful force for continued Democratic control. For most of the thirty-four-year Democratic reign in the House, Democrats were the majority party, demonstrating strength at all levels. They won the presidency three times, held the Senate twenty-six years, dominated state governorships and legislatures. Second, Republicans, perceived by voters and political aspirants as the minority party, had difficulty recruiting strong candidates and financing campaigns. The Republicans' losing record became a vicious cycle, until the 1980s' surge.

Some Republican officials contend the electoral system is stacked against them. They blame gerrymandering of congressional districts by state legislatures under control of Democrats and by Democratic state governors. In 1986, Republican officials charged that their party was deprived of twenty-three rightful seats in the House, by the way congressional district lines were drawn. As evidence, they asserted that the Republican share of House seats does not match the party's share of the popular vote. In 1984, for example, Republican candidates won forty-seven percent of the popular vote for the House, but only forty-two percent of the seats.[19]

In the redrawing of congressional district lines in 1981 (after the 1980 census), Republicans were probably gypped out of five seats in California, and perhaps of a couple of seats elsewhere in the country, through crafty Democratic remapping of districts. But several nonpartisan studies assert that nationwide, political gerrymandering has had minimal effect on the overall balance of power in the House. In Indiana and Pennsylvania, for example, the Republican tilt in state government in 1981 gave Republicans an advantage in drawing district lines, to balance off the Democratic tilt in California.

What is not well understood is that our electoral system of single-winner districts automatically results in a "seat bonus" for the winning party: a larger percentage of seats than votes. Members of Congress represent districts, not numbers of people. At the extreme, imagine the Democrats having a slim fifty-one percent majority in every single district: They would win one hundred percent of the seats with fifty-one percent of the votes. At lower percentages, the winner's bonus is smaller but it still exists. Republicans had a seat bonus when they had a House majority back in the early 1950s.

That inevitable result of our election system is exacerbated by the fact that, on average, the Republicans turn out more votes per winner than Democrats do. Congressional districts must all have roughly the same population. But Democrats win more urban districts—where turnout is relatively low among poor, minority voters; whereas Republicans win more suburban districts—where turnout is much higher among well educated, well-heeled voters. So on average, Republicans get more votes per House seat, regardless of who draws the lines.[20]

Above all, the Democratic lock on the House reflects the enormous advantages of incumbency. For what is striking about recent election returns is the public's tendency to reelect members of Congress. Throughout the postwar period, an average of ninety-one percent of the House incumbents who sought reelection were reelected. (In the more volatile Senate, it was only seventy-five percent.) Reelection of incumbents reached an all-time high in 1986 when 394 House members sought reelection; only nine lost. The other 97.7 percent were reelected—and mostly by overwhelming numbers; eighty-five percent of them had no serious contest. The overall trend of lopsided incumbent victories has been increasing.[21]

Most House incumbents are so well entrenched that they scare off serious opposition long before the campaign begins. Marcia Hale, former political director of the Democratic Congressional Campaign Committee, reckoned that at least 190 Democrats and 120 Republicans had safe seats going into the 1986 election. Indeed, Linda DiVall, a pollster who used to work for the National Republican Congressional Committee, estimated that in 225 districts, no Republican has won since Watergate—a pattern that guarantees Democratic control of the House.

The key lies in the enormous resources available to incumbents and their ability to localize elections, insulating themselves from national trends. The Democrats made big gains in 1974, many in suburban, normally pro-Republican districts, and then protected them shrewdly. Their cushion rests heavily on the skills of new-breed Democrats at the techniques of the constant campaign: constituent case work by their staff, campaigning at home practically every weekend, mass newsletters and sophisticated computerized direct mailings financed by taxpayers, and high visibility through radio and TV satellite feeds. In money terms, political strategists reckon the "incumbency advantage" to be worth the equivalent of half a million dollars in campaign contributions to each incumbent.

Name recognition is the first requirement for any political candidate. Most incumbents have it, and most House challengers are virtually invisible unless they get heavy TV exposure. The old-breed technique of knocking on doors is too slow and inefficient to fill that need of becoming known. The challenger desperately needs media time, and unless he is extremely adept at generating news coverage, that means lots of expensive television ads. Such media advertising has driven up the costs of congressional campaigns astronomically: from $99 million in 1976 to $450 million a decade later.

In the crucial game of fund-raising, most challengers are licked before the race begins. Political money has been a prime protector of incumbent House Democrats—Republicans, too, but mainly Democrats since they are a solid majority of the incumbents. A study by Common Cause, the public-affairs lobby, showed that in the 1986 election, House incumbents on average raised more than three times as much money as their challengers, and that in the critical two-week homestretch of the campaign their cash on hand was twenty times that of their challengers.[22] That meant the incumbents were sitting pretty to finance their final media blitzes and lock up their seats for two more years.

The greatest incumbent advantage in the money game is among Washington-based PACs, whose contributions to congressional races tripled from 1976 to 1986.[23] The continuous floating fund-raising game in Washington and the symbiotic relationships between members of Congress on one side and lobbyists and PAC managers on the other side all play to the advantage of incumbents. "PAC Money is and will remain the easiest money for most incumbents to raise," Michael Malbin of American Enterprise Institute asserts. "Tens of thousands of dollars typically change hands in any of the hundreds of Washington fund raisers held every year. . . . The members [of Congress], clearly on top of the situation, use the events to raise $250 or so in quasi-tribute fees from people who might not otherwise support them."[24] Unless an incumbent has deeply angered some group of PACs, or unless a member retires and both parties have an equal scramble over an open seat, the incumbency bias of PACs leaves all but a handful of challengers out in the cold. This is more true in the House than in the Senate. In 1986, for instance, House incumbents received six times as much PAC money as did their challengers.

In short, the cards are stacked in favor of continuing Democratic control of the House—unless changes are made in the current system of campaign financing or challengers are given some new means of access to television exposure. Democratic control of the House obviously spells divided government for every Republican president. Moreover, the existence of a permanent majority and a permanent minority in the House has a corrosive effect on the two-party system and on the process of governing. Permanent minority status is not only demoralizing to House Republicans but drives them toward the negative tactics of obstructionism, because a permanent minority scores political points with the voters by loud criticism and by playing the spoiler role, rather than by developing responsible, constructive proposals, which it cannot pass. And on the other side, being a permanent majority can make Democrats fat, satisfied, and so cocky that they do not feel pressure to work together.

"Large, stable majorities tend to become divided and self-centered," observed political scientist Thomas Mann. "They take for granted the rewards of majority status and lose sight of the importance of the party's collective performance."[25] Both tendencies reinforce the ills of divided government.

Ticket Splitters: New-Collar Voters

With Reagan's great personal appeal, the built-in advantages of incumbency would have been seriously tested if voters were still casting party-line ballots. But ticket splitting obviously helped protect House Democrats. Most political observers attribute ticket splitting to the increased independence of voters, rather than to any conscious decision by voters to keep government divided.

But some voters are quite deliberate about ticket splitting. In 1984, I heard Democratic candidates in heavily pro-Reagan districts from Texas to Pennsylvania openly appeal to voters to keep government divided, to elect Democrats to the House to "keep a check on Reagan." In two touch-and-go districts outside Philadelphia, for example, Democrats Bob Edgar and Peter Kostmayer adopted this tactic as a matter of survival, for they took President Reagan's reelection as a foregone conclusion. They also saw evidence in opinion polls that people liked

Reagan as a national leader but did not agree with all his policies and did not want to give him free rein. Edgar and Kostmayer argued that ticket splitting gave voters the best of both worlds: Reagan as chief of state with a partially Democratic Congress to restrain him. With that pitch, Edgar, Kostmayer, and slews of other Democrats stayed in office in 1984.

Pollster Lou Harris told me that his surveys found this motivation for ticket splitting as far back as the mid-1970s. Harris felt that voters had grown so wary of both parties that they were hedging their bets. "People don't want any one party to be dominant," Harris told me. "We've asked people, 'Would you rather have divided government or one party in control?' And they will say, sixty to thirty-five percent, they prefer divided government. They just don't want one party of scoundrels in there. It's born of the cynicism toward politicians. We first got that under Ford in '75–'76. The more Congress stands up to the president, the more they like it. People believe in checks and balances."[26]

Other polltakers will not go that far. They attribute divided government to the rise of independent voters who go by the code: "I vote for the candidate, not the party." That embodies the erosion of party allegiance at the grass roots. In 1952 at Eisenhower's reelection, a regular biennial nationwide survey found that only twenty-five percent of the electorate were independents, the rest identifying with one of the two big parties. In 1986, independents had risen to thirty-five percent.[12] Except for the Republican surges around Reagan's two elections, independents have outnumbered Republicans for a decade or more.

The rising mass of independent voters reflects social and economic changes in American life. For growing millions of suburbanites, well educated and well off, are issue oriented and proudly independent. Yuppies especially—young upwardly mobile professionals—do not take political cues from parties. Indeed, as life-styles and values change, even workers of the new high-tech service economy have moved away from the big-city politics of their blue-collar parents. Some sociologists have coined a term for them: *new collars.* They are neither industrial blue-collar workers nor white-collar workers, but the service technicians of the computer age. By some reckonings, they are fifteen percent of the adult population, roughly twenty-five million strong.

"You can have a picture in your mind of a guy in his early thirties— running shoes, work pants, a Miami Dolphins T-shirt, a handlebar mustache, and a baseball cap," explained Ralph Whitehead, Jr., a

University of Massachusetts political scientist. "Young enough to be influenced by baby boom culture and so roughly 45 years old or younger. A family income in the range of $20,000 to $40,000. And a job in that expanding range that stands between traditional blue collar work and a career in upper-middle management or the professions. . . . Blue collars base their identity on their work, if they've got it. New collars tend to base it on their leisure."[28]

Most new collars refuse to be pigeonholed as Democrats or Republicans, liberals or conservatives. Along with yuppies, they are among the biggest political switch hitters, who produce crazy-quilt results in elections—at the state as well as at the national level. In 1986, for example, Florida and Alabama elected Democratic senators and Republican governors. As MIT political scientist Walter Dean Burnham noted, Governor Mario Cuomo of New York easily won reelection, but his Democrats failed to gain even one seat in the Republican-controlled state senate. In Illinois, Republican James Thompson won an unprecedented fourth term as governor while the Democrats held control of the state senate.[29]

This free-floating independence of voters has encouraged the individualism of new breed politicians. Since the party brand name lacks its old punch, some candidates run away from their party when it suits them. They sell themselves, not their party. In many marginal districts, I have found plenty of candidates in both parties playing down party labels in order to woo voters across party lines. On billboards, bumper stickers, and lapel buttons, they often drop their party identity entirely, implying nonpartisanship. In his excellent book, *The Rise of Political Consultants*, Larry Sabato, a political scientist at the University of Virginia, quoted the play on words of a campaign ad for Republican Senator John Heinz: "If you think Pennsylvania needs an *independent* senator, elect John Heinz."[30]

Moreover, the new cadre of campaign consultants have accelerated the antiparty trend. The expertise for hire of strategists, pollsters, media advisers, and direct-mail and phone-bank specialists has made politicians less dependent on the party apparatus than they were in the old days. Most consultants usually work for candidates from only one party, but many of these political mercenaries have little commitment to party building or to building policy coalitions. A few firms work both sides of the street. In 1986, for example, the brassy, highly touted consulting firm of Black, Manafort, Stone and Kelly ran into bad publicity when the press learned that Democrat John Kelly and Republican members of the firm were helping raise money for the opponents in the Louisiana Senate race, Democrat John Breaux and Republican Henson Moore. But the main impact of consultants, moving in on the turf of party bosses and other party officials to run campaigns, is to help political newcomers bypass both the party apparatus and the party hierarchy, by helping them build their own individual organizations.

"We have enabled people to come into a party or call themselves independent Democrats or Republicans and run for office without having to pay the dues of being a party member in a feudal way," Republican media consultant Bob Goodman boasted to Larry Sabato. "Meaning kiss the ass of certain people and maybe down the line they'll give you a shot at public office."[31]

In turn, candidates have sometimes become creatures of their campaign Svengalis. In *The Candidate,* a movie in which Robert Redford plays a media-manufactured candidate for the U.S. Senate, Redford turns to his campaign manager the morning after his victory and asks rather pathetically, "What do I do now?"

If that lampoon was an exaggeration, real politicians have their own bitter assessments of the harvest of the current campaign system. Warren Rudman, an able and outspoken Senate Republican, offered this tart judgment: "One third of the members of the U.S. Senate know why they're here, know what they want to do, and know how to do it. The second third know why they're here, know what they want to do, but don't know how to do it. And that last third—I'm not sure why they're here."[32]

As Rudman was implying, some members just carry on campaigning in office because it's what they know how to do. No one can discipline them but the voters. And clearly, as election campaigns have become less party based and more candidate centered, the winners behave independently in office. The highly independent campaign style of the political new breed makes them less pliant to party leaders in Congress.

Finally, the centrifugal forces of PACs have helped seduce politicians away from the cohesion of political parties. The PACs are a potent force both in campaigns and in the new lobbying game. Some PACs reinforce parties, especially big-labor PACs, which regularly line up behind the Democratic party or the U.S. Chamber of Commerce, and corporate PACs, which steadily back the Republican party.

But most PACs exert cross-pressures, independent of party. They finance members of committees that are of special interest to the PACs' constituencies, regardless of party, and then lobby these members hard after the election. PAC special interest politics work against the general interest compromises and coalition building of parties.

These pressures compound the fragmentation of power in Congress created by the reforms of the 1970s. In sum, as Leon Billings, former executive director of the Democratic Senate Campaign Committee, put it: "PACs have forced members of Congress to serve too many masters in the constant search for more and more TV advertising dollars."[33]

Under such pressures and with the independent style of campaigning, new-breed politicians get more payoff with the voters by playing the media game than by being team players. The main test of success becomes exposure, not legislation. In Sundquist's telling comment the new-breed politicians are "self-selected, self-organized, self-propelled, self-reliant, with no habit of being deferential to the established and the powerful and they will not be so in Congress, either in committee or on the floor. When there were enough of this type of member in Congress, the nature of the place was bound to change."[34]

The Impact on Washington

From their nadir in the 1970s, the political parties have made a modest comeback in their national organizations, though not at the grass roots among the voters. During the Reagan era, the national parties—especially the Republicans—became big-budget service organizations for their candidates. They have raised money, financed get-out-the-vote drives at the state level, paid for opinion polling and training for congressional candidates, and mounted multimillion-dollar nationwide media campaigns. Both have erected and equipped lavish new media centers on Capitol Hill to help their incumbents play video politics. In the 1985–86 election cycle, the two major parties raised about $260 million at the national level.[35]

As a polarizing political figure, President Reagan has produced strong partisan voting in Congress at times, rallying Republicans and provoking majorities of Democrats into opposing his assaults on social programs. Reagan was confronted by two partisan speakers of the House, Tip O'Neill and Jim Wright. Moreover, the decline of the moderate wing of the Republican party once represented by Governor Nelson Rockefeller and Senator Jacob Javits of New York has given the congressional Republican party a more consistently conservative hue. Institutionally, the party caucuses—especially the House Democratic Caucus—have grown somewhat stronger than in the early 1970s.

But as many politicians and political scientists have observed, the rehabilitation of the party system has a long way to go. If parties are raising a lot of money, PACs are raising even more: $353 million in the 1985–86 election cycle, about $100 million more than the two national parties. And recently, PACs have provided a larger share of congressional candidates' campaign money (twenty-eight percent) than the national political parties (an estimated ten to fifteen percent).[36] As Larry Sabato commented in *PAC Power*, "the parties remain less influential than they would have been otherwise because alternative sources of funding are available to candidates. And the most available 'alternate source' for incumbents . . . is in PACs."[37]

In Congress, the perpetual disarray of filibustering, delaying tactics, score upon score of amendments, and turf squabbles indicates that partisan ties are insufficient for party leaders to discipline the legislative process. On spending bills, Congress gets so bogged down every year that it gives up on its regular appropriations process and resorts to one omnibus catch-all bill (in part because President Reagan contributes to the deadlock). Sometimes, Speaker O'Neill would achieve party unity less by leading than by sensing where his rebellious troops were headed (as on Gramm-Rudman) and rushing to find the front of the parade. The Senate regularly gets so waylaid by tactical quorum calls, filibusters, and delaying amendments by unruly factions that Missouri Democrat Tom Eagleton protested in late 1985 that "the Senate is now in the state of incipient anarchy."[38]

"There is a breakdown in the Congressional machinery," moaned David Stockman. "There are 100 gauntlets and 1,000 vetoes on Capitol Hill. You simply can't sustain any kind of policy through that process, whether it's the conduct of foreign affairs, the shaping of the budget or the management of the fiscal affairs of the nation, because there are 180 subcommittees with overlapping jurisdictions and huge staffs."[39]

Some experienced politicians, including former President Ford, who spent a lifetime in the House, fault weak party ties, as well as institutional fragmentation. The leaders, they say, lack the lever of party discipline to impose sufficient order.

"Today, a President really does not have the kind of clout with the Congress that he had 30 years ago, even in matters that affect national security," Ford lamented in 1980. "There is not the kind of teamwork that existed in the '50s, even if the President and a majority of the Congress belong to the same party. The main reason for this change is the erosion of the leadership in the Congress. Party leaders have lost the power to tell their troops that something is really significant and to get them to respond accordingly."[40]

The loosening of party unity hobbled President Carter too. He was constantly embattled by fellow Democrats, delaying and dismantling his energy program, pushing through costly water projects, giving him an aircraft carrier he did not want, imposing tighter budget cuts than he had planned. Theoretically, party ties should have helped Carter, but the climate of independence was at its peak in the late 1970s. Moreover, congressional Democrats felt no political debt to Carter. Many pointed out that they had run independently of Carter in the 1976 campaign, and pulled larger votes in their districts than he had. So they felt confident to defy him when it suited them.

Ronald Reagan used the appeal of partisanship more effectively than his predecessors, especially in 1981 when plenty of Republicans in Congress felt that Reagan had helped them win office. Reagan's legislative triumphs in 1981 rode heavily on the back of Republican spirit and unity. The Republican party had run an unusually unified campaign in 1980, and not only the new president but fresh Republican shock troops in the House and Senate came into office proclaiming common themes. Republican campaign unity produced cohesion in government.

But 1981 was a halcyon period; after that, Reagan had increasing troubles passing his program. In 1982, half of the House Republicans revolted against Reagan when he backed a tax increase; others helped override his veto of a supplemental appropriations bill. In 1985, the fractious House Republicans blocked Reagan's top domestic priority, tax reform, from coming to a vote. Even with a humbling personal plea, Reagan got support from well under half of his troops on a mere procedural motion. Democrats provided Reagan's victory. Year after year, his budgets were ignored or rejected by Republicans, once receiving only one Republican vote. Senate Republicans took their own budget initiatives in 1985, fighting Reagan much of that year.

The Democratic victory in 1986, regaining control of the Senate, was not only a personal rebuff to Reagan but also to his ability as president to make government work effectively, on his terms. Quite obviously, a politically crafty president can use the promise of giving or withholding campaign support as leverage with Congress. But if his campaign support does not help his partisans, as Reagan's failed to do in 1986, the president is sorely weakened in Congress, after the election is over. Indeed, in early 1987, thirteen of Reagan's Republican senators looked the President in the eye and turned him down when he wanted *just one more vote* to prevent the congressional override of his veto of an $87.5 billion, five-year highway bill. Later, nineteen Senate Republicans defied the president on a trade measure, sixty-seven House Republicans on catastrophic health care, and a handful of Republican senators helped block his Supreme Court nominee, Robert Bork. The election returns had shorn him of clout.

For the task of governing, Reagan's inability to persuade voters to put his party in stronger command—in both the 1984 and 1986 elections—has disturbing significance. "The electoral connection between Presidents and their party members in the House and Senate has been decoupled," Anthony King, an academic specialist, observed. "Members no longer believe that their electoral fortunes are closely bound up with the President's or even with their party's."[41] If that remains true for future presidents, it will compound the problems of governing.

Addressing the Senate in late 1985, Republican Senator David Durenburger of Minnesota lamented the "withering away" of political parties and appealed for steps to restore them as power centers. Durenburger linked the disunity and disarray in Congress to the highly personalized style of modern campaigns.

"As strong party loyalties have waned, the role of independent politicians, voters, and issue-oriented activists has expanded in contemporary elections," Durenburger declared. "There has been an explosion of organized interest groups, single issue politics, and new group-related sources of campaign finance. These are important and in some respects disturbing trends, with important implications for how Congress operates, for the messages we hear, and for the kinds of laws we enact."

The parties, Durenburger asserted, "play an irreplaceable role. They begin the process of building coalitions, of identifying areas of consensus, of focusing attention on priorities. Far from limiting the role of parties in our electoral process, as we have done in recent years, we should be raising and removing limitations on party contributions in campaigns."[42]

Durenburger was advocating higher campaign spending limits for parties—on the theory that if they became more important sources of funding for candidates, that would help revive the cohesive power of parties. His idea, a sound one, was that candidates more dependent on parties for campaign support are potentially more responsive to party discipline in office. Durenburger's broad goal was to rejuvenate the party system. Implicit in his comments, and those of President Ford, is the conviction that this country needs stronger parties—and particularly a single majority party—if our government is to function more effectively. The weakening of the parties, the absence of a clear majority party, and the divided government born of ticket splitting have all fed political stalemates and popular frustrations.

19. Our Political Disconnect: Campaigning vs. Governing

> Once he is elected president, the president's electoral coalition has . . . served its purpose. The day after his election, the size of his majority is almost—if not entirely—irrelevant to his ability to govern the country.
>
> —Samuel Huntington, political scientist

By now, it must be apparent that something is seriously out of kilter in our political system—between our political campaigns and the needs of government. Nowhere is that dichotomy more stark than at the presidential level. The campaign skills and forces it takes for a presidential candidate to get nominated and elected are poorly matched to what it takes to lead the government, especially a divided government.

As James MacGregor Burns, scholar of the presidency at Williams College, observed: "There's an increasing disparity between the tests for winning office and what's required in governing. The kinds of quick, dextrous ploys, mainly public relations ploys, that are called for in public campaigning are a very far cry from the very solid coalition building that is needed to make this system of ours work."[1]

Above all, a presidential campaign is an exercise in image making, in symbolic politics and the politics of personality, whereas governing is the business of decision making, the work of substance and programs, and the politics of coalition building. The campaign rewards debating skills and theatrical talents: the dashing, telegenic presence, the visual media event, the memorable one-liner for TV. But governing demands people skills: the less flashy crafts of persuasion, judgment, management, and negotiation. Campaign success often turns on exploiting temporary advantage; governing success needs patient year-in, year-out consistency and pursuit of policies. It is outside politics versus inside politics.

The contrast between the whirling, emotional world of the campaign and the unyielding, sometimes boring reality of government lies in the difference between word and deed, between the quick hit and quiet discourse: the quick hit pitched to impress a mass audience versus the quiet discourse that engages support from political peers. It is rhetoric versus reflection, polished policy recipes and clever evasions versus hard-headed ordering of priorities and uncomfortable decisions. The campaign is a fairy tale, long on promises and short on the "how" of getting there and "with whom." The campaign thrives on polarizing issues and personalities, on projecting the romantic illusion that one leader can make all the difference. It is factional, sometimes go-it-alone politics. But again, no single leader has that much power—governing cannot succeed without teamwork and compromise.

In the campaign game, the winning presidential candidate builds a personal organization, but the successful president must work effectively with other organizations. He must work with other factions in his party, his party's national structure, the leadership in Congress, sometimes the opposition. Indeed, several recent presidents failed because of their inability to deal effectively with rival power centers: Kennedy and Carter unable to forge durable governing coalitions in Congress; Nixon, Johnson and Reagan, overreaching for power, usually in disregard of Congress because they did not want to deal with organized opposition or modify their positions to gain wider support. The contrast between campaigning and governing is, ultimately, the difference between stagecraft and statecraft.

The modern campaign marathon pits candidates against each other but rarely tests the ability to govern: to manage and manipulate the multiple power centers of our system. Established power brokers are bit players in the modern presidential campaign scenario. The whole process is oriented toward television appeal, lavish media campaigns, and thematic homilies and values, rather than substantive understanding or proven prowess in moving the system. Jimmy Carter, a newcomer on the national scene, ran outside the political establishment and won the nation's top office without any track record for national leadership except one term as governor of Georgia, endless house-to-house politicking in Iowa and New Hampshire, a something-for-everyone pitch, a look of sincerity, and a memorable television smile.

It is a cliché, of course, but an important one, that the modern campaign is mass marketing at its most superficial. It puts a premium on the suggestive slogan, the glib answer, the symbolic backdrop. Television is its medium. Candidates must have razzle-dazzle. *Boring* is the fatal label. Programs and concepts that cannot be collapsed into a slogan or a thirty-second sound bite go largely unheard and unremembered, for what the modern campaign offers in length, it lacks in depth, like an endless weekend with no Monday morning. "What evidence do you have that you can get Congress or the Kremlin to deliver on your promises?" is the kind of hard-headed question that needs constant asking. Yet as Election Day approaches, charisma and choreography seem to matter more than substance and competence.

"Today choosing policy advisers is insignificant compared to lining up the right pollster, media advisers, direct mail operator, fund-raiser and makeup artist," complained former Kennedy White House aide, Theodore Sorensen. "Today policy positions are not comprehensively articulated but condensed into bumper-sticker slogans and clever TV debate ripostes that will please everyone and offend no one. Today experience and intellect are no more crucial to the multimedia campaign than the candidate's hair, teeth, smile and dog. Today volunteers have been replaced by computerized mail, automated telephone banks and other marvels of technology in an industry that has shifted from labor intensive to capital intensive. Today the news media rarely report what the candidates are saying on the issues. They report instead on a horse race—which horse is ahead, which one has the most physical stamina, which one is lame and which one is attracting the big money."[2]

Running vs. Ruling

It is ironic that Sorensen should raise this sad litany because his boss, Jack Kennedy, began the modern campaign game. In an article for *TV Guide* in November 1959, titled "A Force That Changed the Political Scene," Kennedy argued that television would alter campaigning by putting the main emphasis on the candidate's image. Kennedy proceeded to create a personal mystique. By marketing glamour, wit, and personal style and conveying a sense of vitality and elegance, Kennedy irrevocably transformed presidential campaigning and even the presidency. As a senator, he had a lackluster record. As a candidate he coined a slogan, *The New Frontier,* and then sold the gossamer promise to "get this country moving again" without signaling a clear direction or laying out a clear program. Smiling Irish Jack, with his flat Boston brogue and his glamorous youth, was the first successful presidential candidate to rely on personal appeal rather than the party organization to win the top prize.

As Bob Shogan of the *Los Angeles Times* recalled in his perceptive book, *None of the Above,* Kennedy ran an outsider strategy. He staked his race in the party primaries—not to accumulate an unbeatable number of Democratic convention delegates but to bypass the party bosses and to pressure them through his popular vote and media attention. In 1960, there were seventeen primaries, Kennedy entered eight and had only two real battles—in Wisconsin and West Virginia. Those were the forerunners of the Iowa caucuses and the New Hampshire primary today. Their impact was magnified far beyond the actual numbers of delegates. In those states, Kennedy took on Hubert Humphrey and beat him, by months of early grass-roots work, by spending plenty of money, and by cleverly daring West Virginia Protestants to prove they were not bigots by voting for a Catholic. With a victorious verdict from the voters, Kennedy forced the party's power brokers to recognize his popular appeal. His populist assault on the citadels of power was a lesson for the future.

In office, Kennedy also set a model with his ringing rhetoric, his witty televised sparring with reporters, the moving biblical cadences of speeches limned by Sorensen. He redeemed his promise to get the country moving with the bold, symbolic adventurism of a manned mission to the moon. The mystique of political Camelot, a noble time and a special grace and company, was his creation. And yet as a coalition builder moving the government to turn his visions in law, Kennedy fell short. He was not able to translate personal popularity into effective leverage with Congress. It took Lyndon Johnson, a master legislative craftsman, to pass Kennedy's tax cut and other major elements of his legislative program.

The problem is that our political system has a built-in requirement for coalitions among rival power centers. Without coalitions, legislation does not move, policies bog down in governmental paralysis, presidents fail, and the public chafes for yet another new leader. But the coalitions of government and the coalitions of electoral success are vastly different. After a marathon campaign in which television and presidential primary voters have taken over the roles once played by political organizations and party leaders, the modern president has far fewer building blocks than presidents had only a few decades back.

Writing after Richard Nixon's landslide reelection and resignation, Harvard scholar Samuel P. Huntington observed that the day after the election, the size of a president's electoral majority is "almost irrelevant" to his ability to govern.

"What counts then is his ability to mobilize support from the leaders of the key institutions in society and government," Huntington argued. "He has to constitute a broad government coalition of strategically located supporters who can furnish him with the information, talent, expertise, manpower, publicity, arguments, and political support which he needs to develop a program, to embody it in legislation, and to see it effectively implemented. This coalition must include key people in Congress, the Executive Branch, and the private-sector 'Establishment.' The governing coalition need have little relation to the electoral coalition. The fact that the President as a candidate put together a successful coalition does not insure that he will have a viable governing coalition."[3]

His comments had a prophetic ring—for Jimmy Carter. Carter's campaign strategist, Hamilton Jordan, shrewdly doped out the chessboard intricacies of the primary system. To voters sickened by the Watergate scandal, Carter sold his political innocence, his promise that "I will never lie to you." But four years as governor of Georgia had not schooled Carter for handling an assertive Congress, even one controlled by his party. Nelson Polsby, a leading scholar of elections at the University of California at Berkeley, observed that the primary process and general election left great gaps in Carter's political education. Having won the White House with a go-it-alone, outsider's campaign, Carter had no links with other Democrats. He did not know how to put together congressional coalitions to pass his programs. He was missing the linkage between ends and means. Carter did pass some legislation, and he got the Panama Canal treaty ratified. But his overall record with Congress was poor.

"Nothing in Mr. Carter's prior experience as a politician, certainly nothing in his experience of the nomination process, led him to the view that he needed to come to terms with the rest of the Democratic Party," Nelson Polsby commented.[4]

Certainly, marathon campaigns test the health, endurance, resourcefulness, plausibility, tenacity, good humor, and verbal agility of candidates, as well as their fund-raising and public relations skills. All of these, except fund-raising, are necessary in the presidency. But most tests in the campaign are rhetorical. What is most egregiously missing is testing by other politicians: not rival debaters, but powerful figures who will later affect the president's policy success or failure.

"Up until the late sixties, if you wanted to get the nomination, you had to go around and deal with the party leaders and get to know them," recalled Austin Ranney, a political scientist at the University of California in Berkeley. "That gave you something to leverage when you got into office. Now, the politics of the campaign very much go against the politics of governing. If someone is good at both, we are very lucky. The campaign is keyed to television. The person who comes off well is the 'good guy' and the guy with the little 'factlets.' And that's not the essence of good governing. That involves identifying good people, getting good information and advice from them, developing solutions. That involves quiet discussions, not quick adversarial exchanges but colloquy."[5]

Historically, the relationship between running and ruling was much closer. In Washington and across the country were the power barons in each major party—governors, mayors, senators, the bosses of city machines, big businessmen, or union leaders—who privately took the measure of the contenders. To succeed, candidates not only had to win popular approval, but they needed to gain the confidence of political peers, a valuable asset after the election. These were political pros who had a sense of what the job required and who could assess the candidate from personal experience. Making political alliances in the campaign often required a candidate to strike deals or to modify his positions on central issues. Such bargaining with established leaders tested his knowledge of major issues and his ability to forge political coalitions— not merely with a public whose interest was fleeting, whose knowledge was superficial, and whose loyalties were fluid, but with political heavyweights whose own survival was affected.

What's more, once a candidate had won the support of regional party leaders, it usually continued after the election. A president could look to regional power barons to help deliver votes from their congressional delegations. So the system of brokering for electoral support had the advantages of testing the mettle of a leader among experienced politicians he would have to lead, and of providing building blocks for a governing coalition.

Surely, the process of back-room deals had its seamy side, for like the current system, the old paths to power influenced what types of politicians made it to the top. Since the Civil War, we have had three different systems of presidential selection, each with its own type of victor, according to Samuel Kernell, a political scientist at Brookings Institution. As recently as William McKinley, it was regarded as bad taste to seek the nomination aggressively. From 1876 through 1932, Kernell explained, the party barons were looking for someone safe who would abide by the tacit rules of the game: spreading patronage, the spoils of victory, and distributing federal largesse to the states. The party power barons were not looking for greatness. Grover Cleveland was typical of the era, though the system also produced Teddy Roosevelt and Woodrow Wilson.

By Kernell's scheme, the second stage came in 1932 when the party barons shifted to picking national coalition builders. Nominations were still brokered at party conventions, not settled by primary voters, but the power barons gravitated toward nominees who could stitch together the disparate elements of the party and appeal to the nation. Roosevelt, Truman, and Eisenhower were quintessential examples. Power brokers were wary of Tennessee's Senator Estes Kefauver, with his televised hearings on organized crime or on drug abuse. Kefauver's populist style made the party barons uneasy; they preferred an establishment figure such as Adlai Stevenson.

But trends began to change with Jack Kennedy in 1960. By 1972, with the Democratic party's internal reforms, power was taken from the bosses and given to the masses. The barons were formally overthrown, the conventions virtually stripped of power, and the nominees chosen by direct primaries. The new campaign game favored image makers, not coalition builders: political individualists such as Jack Kennedy and Barry Goldwater and outsiders such as Jimmy Carter and Ronald Reagan.[6]

The 1988 race showed similar characteristics. Senator Gary Hart, an outsider in style and temperament, rose and fell in the media. The shower of media attention after Hart's modest but unexpected second-place finish in the 1984 Iowa caucuses made him a sudden contender, and he came close to the nomination. In 1986, rather than seeking a third Senate term, Hart left Washington for full-time presidential campaigning. His candidacy was initially killed by the media hunt after his tryst with actress Donna Rice fired controversy over his extramarital relations. And his chances, after his surprise reentry into the race in December 1987, depended heavily on using media coverage to reach the electorate. Three more outsiders, Bruce Babbitt, twice elected governor of Arizona; Pierre S. du Pont IV, two-term governor of Delaware; and Michael Dukakis, a third-term governor of Massachusetts, followed Jimmy Carter's route, hoping a strong early showing would vault them into the White House without Washington experience. Television evangelist Pat Robertson built his race around his mass following, despite his lack of government experience. Robertson's television appeal was enough to make him a contender, or at least an influence on Republican fortunes.

Of course, the 1988 field includes experienced Washington politicians—Republicans George Bush, Robert Dole, and Jack Kemp, and Democrats Richard Gephardt, Albert Gore, and Paul Simon. More than the others, Dole and Gephardt have proven their skill at the inside power game, garnering votes and leading coalitions.

But if mastery of the art of government were of prime importance to voters, it is questionable that Howard Baker would have quit the competition to become White House chief of staff. Nor is it clear that experienced, popular, big-state governors such as Mario Cuomo of New York and James Thompson of Illinois would have hesitated to enter the race. Similarly, in the Washington power game, senators Bill Bradley of New Jersey and Sam Nunn of Georgia are known for intellectual leadership, legislative skill, and integrity. Both have tackled tough issues—taxes and financial policy in Bradley's case, military and arms policy in Nunn's case. They are influential with their political peers because they are knowledgeable, fair minded, and skilled at turning their ideas into policies and laws. But the political book on both Bradley and Nunn is that they lack the charisma for presidential-level video politics—a likely factor in keeping them out of the 1988 competition.

Image over Issues

Governmental competence has not scored high with the voters in the past three presidential elections. After Watergate, Washington experience and connections were a definite handicap, and that helped produce the victory of Jimmy Carter—as an outsider. Part of Ronald Reagan's public relations genius has been somehow to distance himself from Washington, from the very government that he heads, and to treat the bureaucrats under his command as if he had no connection with them.

In the 1984 campaign, Peter Hart, pollster for Walter Mondale, warned Mondale not to expect much public credit for his three terms as a senator and four years as vice president. In July 1983, Hart had done a poll among prospective New Hampshire voters about the qualities they valued most in a president. The number one quality they

picked was: "A leader—can take charge and get results." Number two
was: "Compassionate—cares about people." Number three was: "Has
a plan for jobs and economic growth." Way down on Hart's list, tied
for tenth (out of eighteen), was political competence: "Capable, knows
the ins and outs of government."

"What I said to Mondale is that experience is like a pair of twos in
a game of poker," Peter Hart told me. "It's the lowest hand you can
form. It's the best there is until something better comes along, but it's
pretty easy for something better to come along." Looking back over the
past three presidential elections, Hart sized up the qualities that were
valued most by voters. "In 1976, political virginity and purity counted
much more than competence," he said. "In 1980, it was toughness that
counted—can-do, stand-up type of leadership. The 1984 election was
defined by Reagan, so toughness still counted."[7]

With the Iran-*contra* scandal, the Wall Street indictments for insider trading. and the scandal over television preacher Jim Bakker's
adultery and lavish profits, the climate changed. Peter Hart and other
pollsters found signs that voters were placing greater value on political
leaders who play by the rules of the game and who showed integrity
and a sense of community. Several presidential candidates stressed their
competence and substantive knowledge. If those assets prove decisive
in 1988, that could overturn the conventional wisdom of the past ten
to fifteen years that image matters more than issues. As one of President Ford's campaign strategists put it in an internal memo in June
1976: "The polls continue to show that issues are not a decisive campaign factor. The voters continue to react to personality traits and
themes."[8]

That echoed Richard Nixon's view that he lost to Kennedy in 1960
because "I spent too much time . . . on substance and too little time
on appearance: I paid too much attention to what I was going to say
and too little to how I would look."[9] By 1968, as Joe McGinniss
documented in *The Selling of the President 1968,* Nixon was paying
more attention to his shave and his image.

In fact, concern with measuring and manipulating image has become such an obsession of campaign strategists that they have devised
Buck Rogers gadgetry (borrowed from commercial advertising) to get
instant feedback. For example, when seven Democratic contenders
held a televised debate in Houston in July 1987, Democratic pollsters
Harrison Hickman and Paul Maslin assembled eighty-five Iowa Democrats at the Holiday Inn in West Des Moines to record their instant
reactions to the debaters. The Iowans were each given a cigarette-sized

gadget with a knob for dialing scores from one to seven. If they liked what was happening on the TV screen, the viewers dialed a seven; if their reaction was negative, they dialed a one. Their gadgets were wired to a nearby computer which compiled a running composite score. Actually, it computed more than an average; it showed whether some candidate was polarizing the audience, producing both sevens and ones, or just a lot of mushy, neutral fours. Media managers used that data to coach their candidates on how to remodel their images.

Dick Wirthlin, Reagan's pollster, showed me how he has used a similar system, not only for Reagan's campaign debates but for Reagan's presidential addresses. Wirthlin was trying to find "power phrases" and hot moments that scored well with the audience—to be sure that Reagan repeated them in future speeches.[10] Wirthlin and others chart audience reaction and then impose their graphs—like the sawtooth lines of stock-market averages—on videotapes of the candidates speaking. These reaction graphs suggest that people are often responding as much to the speaker's facial expressions, tone of voice, and body language as to content. To people who complain this technique has overtones of Big Brother, Wirthlin and others answer that reaction graphs are useful tools generated by political competition. Insuring the right emotional impression of a candidate on television may be the heart of a winning strategy, but it hardly matches the far more complex task of coalition building in government.

Like Nixon recalling the 1960 campaign, Walter Mondale acknowledged that he had been hurt in the 1984 campaign by his stiff television image. "I think you know I've never really warmed up to television, and in fairness to television, it's never really warmed up to me," Mondale told reporters. Not that Mondale was proposing to do away with television. "Modern politics requires television," he said. "I don't believe it's possible any more to run for president without the capacity to build confidence and communications every night." But from years in government, Mondale, like Nixon, was worried about the implications of image campaigning: "The thing that scares me about that, the thing that has held me back, is that I think, more than we should, American politics is losing substance. It is losing debate on merit. It's losing the depth that tough problems require to be discussed, and more and more it is that twenty-second snippet—you know, the angle, the shtick, whatever it is."[11]

Presidential campaigns are superficial because the contenders want to reach so many people so quickly. Mass rhetoric is light on substance and quick on slogans, because the public neither understands the intricacies of issues nor is willing to focus on much explanation. The frenetic pace of campaigning during the peak of the primary season makes thoughtful discussion of issues a rarity. Even with televised debates, the press often compounds these problems in the intense season of early primaries, by pouncing on the daily gaffes and stumbles of front-runners or lionizing some sudden challenger; by focusing on the narrative drama of who's ahead, behind, limping or gaining in the horse race; by its fascination with the inside baseball of campaign tactics, rather than the issue or long-term record of candidates. Actually, the past records of Carter and Reagan were better indicators than most campaign rhetoric of what was to come in the White House. In Georgia, Carter had been a loner, an individualistic moralizer; and in California, there had been two Reagans: one, a dogmatic ideologue with charm, and the other, an occasionally pragmatic compromiser.

But television is so preoccupied with the immediate and the visual that it rarely takes much time with the past or with extended substantive interviews. And when the print press examines a politician's performance, very few voters are interested in detail. The essence of the modern campaign is personality politics: the direct, gut impressions that viewers form from thirty-second daily blips on the screen. Advantage accrues to new-breed players at home with Boss Tube, preaching homilies and honing bumper-sticker themes to stick in voters' memories. Advantage also accrues to the familiar and the comfortable, and to media manipulators expert at appealing to emotions rather than to reason and at crafting events to leave calculated impressions with viewers.

Obviously, Reagan's 1984 campaign was a triumph of the modern political game—a textbook example of modern campaigning. It epitomized the disconnect between campaigning and governing; it was supremely successful despite its emptiness. Reagan was so smooth in selling his soothing reelection refrain ("It's Morning Again in America") that he lacked a clear policy mandate to use with Congress after the election. One reason Reagan had so much trouble gaining congressional support for his tax-reform bill in 1985–86 was that he had now risked putting this idea to the voters. His campaign was the quintessence of modern campaign choreography: upbeat music, feel-good rhetoric, symphonic patriotic backdrops, and occasional injections of powerful subliminal ads such as one showing a bear (obviously a Russian bear) stalking the woods in silent threat to America unless Reagan were returned to office. It was a campaign strong on symbolism and slick at sliding off hard-policy choices. It produced a massive landslide but not a clear agenda or a coalition in Congress.

Certainly, there is nothing new in politicians shying away from clear programs and promises. Platitudes and happy hokum have long been the stuff of stump politicians. But the modern campaign, with its ever-present camera and the politician's fear of video replay, has raised the politics of evasion to new heights. Campaigns that stress mood, imagery, symbolism, and personality deflect and drown out serious discourse. Their emptiness breeds voter cynicism and probably contributes to low voter turnout. But candidates find safety in vagueness.

By painful experience, many politicians have learned that candor is a liability, while evasion and hypocrisy pay off. Barry Goldwater got into hot water in 1968 by proposing to make Social Security voluntary, by advocating another invasion of Castro's Cuba by Cuban exiles—this time with open American air support, and by suggesting that American field commanders in NATO be given discretionary authority to use tactical nuclear weapons. Four years later, George McGovern suffered self-inflicted wounds by advocating unconditional amnesty for draft violators; by proposing a welfare program of $1,000 grants for every American, which the rich would return in taxes; and by announcing he would cut the defense budget by $30 billion a year and save another $222 billion by closing tax loopholes. In 1984, Walter Mondale impaled himself by declaring before a nationwide television audience that beating the deficit would require raising taxes. "Let's tell the truth," he said. "Mr. Reagan will raise taxes, and so will I. He won't tell you. I just did."

Scores of Democratic congressmen (and many Republicans) agreed with Mondale, but they ran away from his tax position. He lost, and they won. It was but one of many, many incidents that caused Christopher Matthews, Speaker O'Neill's spokesman, to note with a grin, "You never get in trouble in politics for lying. You only get in trouble for telling the truth"—or for speaking your mind.

Examples are legion of politicians who have lied, shaved the truth, or dodged honest answers and gone on to win office. As I reported, Reagan favored strategic defenses back in 1980, but his handlers considered it dynamite for him to touch the nuclear issue and he kept quiet. In 1976, Reagan had gotten in trouble for talking about making Social Security voluntary and urging transfer of $90 billion in federal programs to the states; but in the 1980 campaign, he kept mum on those items. In 1968, Richard Nixon dangled hints before voters that he had a secret plan to end the Vietnam War and resisted spelling it out, because it merely involved gradual withdrawal of American troops and turning the fighting over to the Vietnamese. Lyndon Johnson totally misled the nation about his future course in Vietnam as he rolled up his 1964 landslide. Declared Johnson: "We are not about to send American boys nine or ten thousand miles away from home to do what Asian boys ought to be doing to protect themselves." Of course, that is precisely what Johnson did.

Certainly, flip-flops and flimflam were practiced long before the advent of direct primaries and television. Franklin Roosevelt ran on a platform of cutting federal spending and did the opposite when he got into office. But the voters are more easily disarmed by candidates brought right into their living rooms by television. That causes what Samuel Taylor Coleridge called the "willing suspension of disbelief." If a candidate can produce a warm gut feeling in viewers, they are more easily gulled by vague and misleading nostrums. That wins campaigns; it does not provide effective government.

The Tail Wags the Dog

Instead of the demands of governance setting the tests of the presidential campaign, high-tech campaign P.R. has invaded the White House. Our last two presidents have waged the permanent campaign, including public relations experts and pollsters high in their councils, while engaging in the public pretense that their policies were above mere politics. Small wonder. As Michael Malbin of American Enterprise Institute remarked, "What you do to get in office affects how you behave in office."[12] Presidential behavior is shaped by the process of selection.

We have experienced what political scientists call the "rise of the rhetorical presidency."[13] The original framers of the Constitution, one scholarly article pointed out, were suspicious of mass oratory, fearing that demagoguery would undermine rational, enlightened self-interest because politicians would be tempted to pander to the public mood. In the nineteenth century, public speechifying by presidents in office was rare. From Thomas Jefferson to Woodrow Wilson, presidents did not even deliver their State of the Union addresses in person. For persuasion, they relied more on written argument or private discourse with congressional leaders. But with Theodore Roosevelt, Woodrow Wilson, and Franklin Roosevelt, the old pattern changed; Jack Kennedy established the televised presidency, which was succeeded by the public relations presidency. Listen to Richard Nixon, six years after leaving the White House:

"Television has transformed the presidential office and also the governmental process. This is dangerous and potentially disastrous. Congress may be fractionated; it may speak in a cacophonous babble of 535 separate constituencies; but at least its structure is built around the serious consideration of questions of public policy. Not so television. Television is a show-business medium. . . . More often than not, what is emotionally appealing—and therefore dramatically captivating—is intellectually vacuous and substantively wrong. What makes good television often makes bad policy. Because of the pervasive impact of television, the actions of Presidents are directed increasingly toward the omnipresent cameras, and confined within the distorting prism of television news. Public debate is conducted increasingly in slogans and one-liners. . . . Television is a fact of life, and a President in the 80's will have to use television effectively in order to govern effectively. The challenge will be to find a way to use it that enlightens rather than obfuscates."[14]

Nixon knew what Reagan proved: the enormous power of television in the hands of a skillful president. Reagan was the first president of the television age to turn the power of media leadership into the enactment of his program, something Kennedy had failed to do. As an actor used to being on stage and on camera all his life, Reagan enlarged Teddy Roosevelt's bully pulpit; he used television to humble entrenched politicians. He showed that going public, over the heads of Congress, is a powerful way to move political Washington. The opposition bent in 1981 under the avalanche of letters and phone calls that answered Reagan's televised appeals for cutting the budget and taxes.

It is important to recall that Reagan had two other vital political assets grounded in more orthodox politics. First, he was riding a national consensus of antigovernment populism and in 1980 had won support for a program of tax cutting and budget cutting. Second, he had a strong organizational base. Conservatives had built a strong mass movement over sixteen years and had taken over the Republican party. That army was ready to respond to Reagan's televised appeals to pressure Congress.

Beyond that, however, Reagan's personal popularity, built over the years on television, was vital political leverage in the Washington power game. He created a sense of familiarity and intimacy in people's living rooms that was an extraordinary political force. For the power of leadership is partly illusion and perception—in Reagan's case, the perception of popularity. Well before the Iran-*contra* scandal, other Washington politicians had grown mistrustful of Reagan's maneuvers, angry at his stubbornness, and tired of his telling anecdotes when they

wanted hard-headed talk about policies. But to the public he was as
likable as a friendly uncle, and his popularity intimidated other politicians. They shied away from taking him on head-on. Without television, he would have been far less formidable.

But over time, the practical impact of Reagan's popularity wore thin
on other Washington players. Few politicians other than Tip O'Neill
confronted him, for they feared he could engineer a public backlash
against them. But they learned to defy him indirectly, because they saw
the public was often not with him on substance. As early as 1982,
Reagan's televised appeals on budget and taxes failed to stir irresistible
public groundswells or to revive his governing coalition. His ratings
sank with recession, and the opposition made him retreat. Later, even
after his 1984 landslide and while the economy was still heading upward, Republicans as well as Democrats killed his budget, forced him
to bow on sanctions against South Africa and to bend on trade measures. And no matter how many times he addressed the nation from
the Oval Office, Reagan repeatedly failed to swing the public his way
on the *contra* war. So his presidency showed both the value of media
leadership and its limitations.

There is another—more hidden—price to the public relations presidency. The more any president is preoccupied with public relations and
ceremony, the more power over the substance of policy he must turn
over to subordinates. No president can do everything; what he chooses
to do leaves his other duties to others. Reagan is famous for leaning on
staff; future presidents excessively preoccupied with P.R. will be the
same. The same thing happens in Congress. Quite often, the most
video-minded senators and House members, even those who are substantively able, have to turn over great responsibility to staff aides so
that the celebrity politicians can claim the limelight. Think of former
Senator Paul Tsongas telling me how he had to let substance suffer, in
order to regain public visibility with his voters. That is the campaign
game stealing from the work of government.

The Negatives of the Modern Campaign

The modern campaign—with its hyped politics of personality—feeds
public cynicism about government, for the modern campaign encourages the illusion of presidential omnipotence. It purveys the false and
exaggerated expectation that the ascendance of a new leader will dissolve the knotty deadlocks that hobbled the incumbent. And it invites
the pretense that the rest of government and the realities of divided

power can be ignored by candidates, voters, and press. No president can live up to such inflated expectations, and his inevitable shortcomings fuel popular disillusionment with government.

"The regularity of disillusionment follows as the night follows the day," wrote Duke University's presidential scholar James David Barber. "Instead of miracles come halting progress and/or crashed hopes, as the President discovers how short a distance his independent powers can take him. . . . As the country runs through that cycle of uplift and downfall again and again, the force of the story wanes and skepticism sets in."[15]

Also, the campaign emphasis on each new president's promises of a fresh start and dramatic changes produces national policies that zigzag, especially in foreign affairs. Nixon and Ford did not harass the Soviet leadership on human rights, but Carter did, and then Reagan dropped the issue. Presidents from Eisenhower through Carter stood by the doctrine of offensive deterrence, but Reagan shifted to strategic defense, and almost any successor will at least partially reverse that policy.

In primary campaigns, highly organized special interest politics pressure prospective presidents into positions that limit their policy flexibility later. Ideological activists (New Left and New Right) pull Democratic candidates to the left and Republican candidates to the right, making it hard for presidents later to strike the compromises that governing requires. Litmus-test promises to special interests, or telling voters what they want to hear ("No tax increase"), can box in presidents. Indeed, most campaigns sell the notion that compromise is unprincipled, even though experienced politicians know that compromise is the lifeblood of workable government. Sometimes policies are made to be consistent with campaign imagery more than to fashion sensible policy. For example, Reagan scrapped an approved plan for the MX missile, though he had no satisfactory substitute.

Finally, recent campaigns have cut against the work of government because bashing Washington and trashing politicians was so popular. Negative campaigning, of course, is nothing new. George Washington wrote Alexander Hamilton in 1792 to lay off his negative attacks on Thomas Jefferson; Hamilton was undaunted. He fired back a reply that Jefferson was trying to subvert the government and had founded his own newspaper to publish hateful stories about Hamilton.[16]

But in the 1986 battle for control of the Senate, the barrages of thirty-second political ads, mudslinging and guttersniping hit new lows. "The nadir of nattering negativism," columnist Charles Krauthammer called it.[17] In South Dakota, incumbent Republican James Abdnor accused challenger Thomas Daschle of associating with Jane Fonda, who advocated meatless diets, an apparent offense against the state's beef-and-pork industry. In California, challenger Ed Zschau ran a low-ball TV ad—"Crack, Cocaine, and Cranston"—attacking Democrat Alan Cranston as soft on drugs and terrorism. In Maryland, underdog Linda Chavez hurled the sexual slur that front-runner Barbara Mikulski was a "San Francisco Democrat" whose views were "clearly anti-male."

The most egregious case occurred in Wisconsin. Challenger Ed Garvey accused incumbent Republican Senator Robert Kasten of drinking on the job and Kasten counterattacked with commercials charging that $750,000 in union money had "disappeared" while Garvey headed the National Football Players Association. Garvey filed a $2 million libel suit. Seven months later, Kasten had to backtrack and admit that the union's public records showed all union funds fully accounted for. "I do not suggest that Mr. Garvey did anything illegal or that union funds were spent for other than valid union purposes," Kasten said in a statement. "There was no intent to challenge his integrity."[18] Garvey dropped his suit, but he had already suffered the political damage. Kasten had been reelected.

Despite such mudslinging, campaign consultants defend negative ads as "candidate comparison" or as necessary catalysts to get out the vote. "We know from years of work in research psychology that people process negative information more deeply than positive information," Mark Mellman, a Democratic pollster, told Paul Taylor of The Washington Post. "When we ask people about negative ads, they'll say they don't like them. But that's not the point. The point is that they absorb the information."[19]

"It's much easier to be negative because of the construction of the political message," added Charles Guggenheim, a media consultant to Democratic candidates. "It's easier to hit and run and create doubt, fear and suspicion in 30 seconds."[20]

Ed Haislmaier, public relations director for the staunchly conservative Free Congress Political Action Committee, asserts that the key to winning is to paint contrasts between candidates. "You've got to show the voters there is more than a dime's worth of difference," Haislmaier explained. "That can be accomplished very effectively by doing negative advertising. It brings voters to the polls if they get mad enough."[21]

But some political scientists and voting experts contend that vicious name-calling is driving voters away from the polls. Curtis Gans, director of the Committee for the Study of the American Electorate, argues that voter turnout reached a low point of 37.3 percent of the adult population in 1986—a decline of 20 percent since 1962—because the style of campaign turned off voters. "People voted 'No' on the conduct of the campaign," Gans declared. "What the ad people do by and large is create false and trivial issues in a form and method that is irresponsible."[22]

Washington bashing is a special variation of this sport, practiced in scores of congressional races every year. It riles the blood and lets voters vent frustration with government by scapegoating the "ins" as a general class of sinners. Many incumbents use it to protect themselves by lashing others and by seeming to distance themselves from "low-life" professional politicians. Since incumbents keep getting reelected in overwhelming numbers, bashing Washington does not work too well. Its main impact is souring the sour public mood and feeding popular cynicism about politicians.

"If you are a member of Congress, the last thing you want is to be lumped in with all those creeps in Washington," observed Norman Ornstein, a specialist on congressional politics at the American Enterprise Institute. "The easiest thing to do is say, 'I'm Wyatt Earp. I'm back here trying to clean up that mess.' You distance yourself from the Washington crowd, and in the process you reinforce the public's cynicism about Washington and thus make it harder to mobilize public support for necessary programs later on."[23]

In sum, there is a cost to governance from campaigning that leaves scars and wounds without settling fundamental issues. Once the votes are counted, almost every president, senator, and member of Congress has to work across the aisle with the other party or with philosophical foes on some issue. Moreover, campaign rhetoric derogates the very skills of compromise and give-and-take that are essential to the successful functioning of government. Yet the public obviously warms to the partisan sport of black-and-white, good-versus-evil posturing, even if it defies common sense. That deliberate though artificial polarization—like personality politics, glitzy shallowness, and the lack of durable political coalition-building—is an element of the modern campaign. All these facets put the electoral process out of synch with governing.

20. *What Is to Be Done?*

> *We have to reestablish the link between the Congress, the president, and the party."*
>
> —Howard Baker

It is an old American sport to heap opprobrium on politicians. H. L. Mencken loved to beard them as "bloviating bumblers"; such scoffing derision is still in fashion. In frustration, we curse one party or the other for society's ills, as if our partisan champions had a miraculous monopoly on truth. Some Americans focus their frustration on devils in the White House, condemning the vacillating ineptitude of one president or the deceitful intransigence of the next. Others mock the entire breed in Congress for self-serving evasions and chaotic procrastinations. And there is blame enough to go around—though many individual politicians are far more serious about trying to deal conscientiously with issues than the public credits them.

What my stories from the Carter and Reagan years illustrate is that more than the personal foibles of particular politicians is to blame for failures in governing.

The past dozen years provide a particularily fruitful resource for political autopsy, because this period amply illustrates what works, and what does not work, in our system. Also, most of us can remember enough about important incidents in this period for the anatomy of achievement and the pathology of failure to emerge, carrying lessons for the future. Either we must do something to alter these patterns, or learn to accept them more gracefully, and with fewer illusions.

Most ailments in our political system are nuisances which irk us, but which we have no serious intention of curing. Typical is the compulsive reelection campaigning that makes many in Congress only part-time legislators. Even during their four-day week in Washington, they are forever distracted from the business of government by the need to curry favor with constituents or to raise money. As Will Rogers once quipped, "Politics has got so expensive that it takes a lot of money even to get beat with."

People talk about two major ways to deal with this problem. One is to change the rules for campaign financing. To end the frenzied fund-raising, the public-interest lobby Common Cause advocates full government subsidies for congressional elections. A variation, pushed by Senate Democrat David Boren of Oklahoma, combines modest private donations with a government subsidy contingent on overall campaign spending limits. The argument is that full government subsidies would weaken political parties even more and reduce the political involvement of ordinary citizens. Too low a spending limit would have the same effect. The best approach is a mix of private funds and public subsidies (TV time as well as funds).

The second, more fundamental reform would be to lengthen House terms from two to four years, as former President Nixon has proposed.[1] Stretching out the election cycle would give House members more breathing time between elections and ease the pressure to campaign constantly. But it would not eliminate the problem; even with six-year terms, some senators raise funds and campaign throughout their terms. Most, however, go lighter on campaigning for two or three years, and longer House terms should allow a similar improvement.

Another pet peeve of voters is the explosion of negative campaign advertising, in the voices of anonymous announcers and with graphic video gimmickry. One way to reduce that practice is to force candidates to deliver the attacks personally. For it is an old axiom of the campaign game that the candidate should stay as far as possible from making smear charges and let stand-ins do it for him. The logic is that if voters react negatively to mudslinging, they are less likely to punish the candidate if he does not personally sling the mud. A law requiring candidates to appear on fifty percent or more of the airtime of each of their campaign ads should make many of them pause before using smear tactics.

A third target of public griping is the disarray in Congress. Merely members cry for greater discipline. Howard Baker, bowing out in 1985 as Senate majority leader, asserted that the triple bottlenecks of budget, authorizing, and appropriating committees beg for consolidation of power in the budget process. Florida Democrat Lauton Chiles announced in 1987 that he was retiring because of frustration with the budget quagmire. Clearly, when politicians of such different stripes as liberal Democrat Thomas Eagleton and conservative Republican Barry Goldwater agree that the Senate is in a state of anarchy because of excessive filibustering, turf-fighting committees, and parliamentary stalling, the time has come to trim the capacity of the naysayers to paralyze that body. It is time to reduce the numbers of subcommittees (in both houses) and to streamline the Senate rules, to permit the majority leader to bring up a bill for debate without facing a filibuster before debate begins.

But these all involve tinkering, not tackling the primary problems in the functioning of government. Prime attention belongs elsewhere. There are two paramount problems that demand attention and some changes in public attitudes, as well as remedial action. Paradoxically, these are contrary problems—one of excessive power and the other of insufficient power.

The first, most visible problem in the wake of the Iran-*contra* scandal, is the recurring excesses of presidents—either personally or through aggressive staff activism—to grasp greater power than the laws or the Constitution grants. This is especially dangerous in the commitment of American forces abroad.

The second, more chronic ailment, is the fragmentation of power (exacerbated by the weakness of political parties and the partisan divisions in government). Fragmentation often leaves our politicians wallowing in deadlock because the government lacks the cohesion to form the durable coalitions, needed to resolve the nation's most demanding problems.

The Presidential Blowup

Presidential power is a dilemma for Americans. We look to presidents not only to lead our government but to personify the nation. We romanticize presidential power each time we select a new leader, or we berate congressional resistance when our favorite president is stalemated. We hate to see our presidency humbled. But when presidential misjudgment or deceit leads us into the bloody quagmire of Vietnam, the burning embarrassment of a Watergate, or the shocking deception of arms sold to Iran for hostages while our leader preaches against dealing with terrorists, we are deeply disillusioned. Even if grudgingly, we celebrate the independence of Congress and the rule of law.

Our most painful failures in the past two decades have arisen from presidential overreaching. It is worth recalling that this seems a special vulnerability of reelected presidents, a hubris evidently nourished by overwhelming landslide victories. Lyndon Johnson, Richard Nixon, and Ronald Reagan seemed to share a temporary illusion of presidential omnipotence, a sense that the nation had mandated them to do as they willed and a feeling that they—or their cause—somehow stood beyond law and accountability. Each time, their insistence on having their own way, overriding concerns of the opposition, and their loss of credibility were searing—both to the presidency and to the nation. Overconfidence and disdain for the premise that this is a nation of shared power humbled all three men.

"There is an axiom about the White House," the late Bryce Harlow, a confidant of Eisenhower, Johnson, and Nixon remarked to me. "The president who wins real big will blow himself up."[2]

Beyond the separation of powers and the slow justice meted out by Congress, it is hard to devise institutional fixes to protect in advance against titanic flaws of judgment and character. But some protectives are needed to check the president's de facto power to send American servicemen into battle.

The Founding Fathers, seeing the gravest potential danger in the war power, split that power between the president as commander in chief and Congress as the body with the power to declare war and to raise armies, to provide a navy, and to fund the military. But modern conditions have eroded the balance of the Constitution. From the Revolution through World War II, American armies demobilized after the conflict; with each new war, a president had to go to Congress to raise a new combat army and navy. But since the Cold War, specifically the Korean War, the country has had a standing Army and Navy in peacetime.[3] The president gained the de facto capacity to wage war— without congressional action to declare war or to raise an Army. And once American forces are committed, Congress feels powerless to deny them funds and weapons and ammunition. In short, Congress has lost its share of the war power. No war has been declared since World War II, but hundreds of thousands of Americans have fought in Korea, Vietnam, Lebanon, the Dominican Republic, and Grenada.

In the nuclear age, with a global adversary, Congress has accepted that a president must have the capacity to act quickly to deal with substantial and imminent emergencies. But alarmed by unilateral presidential actions, it has tried to restore the Constitution's partnership on warmaking by asserting its authority to approve or annul presidential action. The War Powers Resolution of 1973, requiring congressional approval of the commitment of American forces to a combat zone or their withdrawal within ninety days of American engagement in hostilities, was born of frustration over Lyndon Johnson's sending half a million American troops into Vietnam without an explicit declaration of war. Reagan's use of American Marines in Lebanon in 1983 and naval forces in the Persian Gulf in 1987 renewed the constitutional tug of war. No president, from Nixon to Reagan, has accepted the constitutionality of the War Powers Resolution. But members of Congress have filed suit to test its constitutionality, and if it is not tested and upheld in some form by the Supreme Court, a constitutional amendment may be needed to restore the original checks and balances on the presidential power to take the nation to war all by himself.

To deal with various problems of governing, Jimmy Carter and others have proposed a single six- or seven-year term for the president, but this is the wrong way to move.[4] One danger is that one term would render a president a lame-duck quite early, in terms of his capacity to persuade Congress. More important, removing any chance for a second term removes the check on a president of being held accountable by the voters in an election. In fact, the current two-term limit may remove such restraints in second-term presidents. To protect against excesses, it might be wise to go in the opposition direction: to revoke the current two-term limit. That would put all presidents on their best behavior—always thinking they could run one more time.

The Iran-*contra* affair has prompted talk of other measures: a law barring the national security staff from engaging in covert operations; tougher criminal penalties for lying to Congress or evading legal restrictions; taking the CIA out of policy-making; Senate confirmation for the White House chief of staff and the national security adviser. These steps make sense. Some political experts have proposed amending the Constitution to permit impeachment of the president for loss of the confidence of Congress—not only for "high crimes and misdemeanors," as mentioned in the Constitution. But that seems an invitation to troublemaking, especially with the frequent partisan divisions of government.

There is, however, one constitutional step worth considering: introducing a practice akin to "question time" in the British Parliament, where the prime minister is confronted by the Opposition. The idea would be to require the president to answer questions periodically before Congress, say once a month, as a means of institutionalizing presidential accountability before the elected representatives of the people. Such a political dialogue would be better than press conferences, which are irregular and lack the weight of elected leaders questioning or debating the chief executive. In good political times, regular presidential appearances could improve the links between the White House and Capitol Hill, reminding each side of the power they share. Such a practice would have the added benefit of forcing a president to be more knowledgeable and engaged than Reagan and of forcing the congressional opposition to be more organized and to speak through one or two recognized leaders.

But political retribution is probably the most pragmatic antidote to abuses of power. After the Iran-*contra* operation was exposed, Congress moved to regain lost power. The political pain for Reagan of the prolonged Iran-*contra* hearings and the prospect of tighter laws was intended as a deterrent to future adventurism. That had been a motive for the Watergate prosecutions, though sadly the memory of Watergates's excesses and punishments wore thin, evidently forgotten by some on Reagan's staff. The popular drift away from the Republican party in 1987, in reaction to the Iran-*contra* affair, was another penalty. Of course, impeachment is the ultimate sanction. But at bottom, the remedy is self-restraint: an acceptance of the limits of presidential power, the rule of law, and the need for sufficient consensus to sustain a policy without deception or end-running the system.

The Coalition Problem

The more frequent problem in American governance has been not excessive power, but weakness—a weakness not in sheer authority but in the craft of governing. What has been notably missing are political coalitions durable and steady enough to sustain policy for several years and to give continuity and direction to our government: a broadly accepted framework for taming the budget deficit without endless blame-gaming; a long-term strategy for meeting foreign competition without resorting to protectionist wars; a way to modernize our defenses steadily rather than zigzagging between excessive spurts in spending and almost vindictive cutbacks; a consensus on arms control that supports an incremental progress toward greater safety and nuclear stability through negotiation and sensible deterrence.

The fixation on the presidency of the American public and the media is so great that little attention is paid to the fact that the essence of governing is coalition making. This means looking beyond the White House for solutions. The task is harder now than in earlier eras, because of the power earthquake in Congress, the balkanizing impact of special interests, the weakened structure of political parties, the lack of a majority party, and divided government born of massive split-ticket voting. These problems are not related to one administration, one presidency, one set of political characters. They are enduring problems that have fed popular frustration for the past two decades.

What is needed are measures to give presidents more power to pull together governing alliances in Congress, to increase the cohesive force of political parties, to reduce the prospects of partisan-divided government, and to promote more collaboration across party lines. The two-hundredth anniversary of the Constitution in 1987 spawned an unusual number of reform proposals. Some dramatic reforms were put forward in January 1987 by the Committee on the Constitutional System, a prestigious group of former cabinet officials from four administrations, former and current senators and members of Congress, scholars, and private citizens.[5]

OPTION 1: SYNCHRONIZED TERMS

Their option 1 was to amend the Constitution to fix four-year terms for House members and eight-year terms for senators. The idea was to have members of Congress run for election only in the same years as presidents, in order to build closer partisan cohesion between president and Congress. In short, they proposed eliminating midterm elections on grounds that these elections pull the branches of government apart and work against presidential leadership. It is true that the president's party has historically lost strength in Congress in the midterm elections, and even his own party members often pull away from the White House as the midterm elections approach. Moreover, with fewer elections, the committee reasoned, president and Congress could focus more on the work of government and on longer-term solutions to major issues, free of House preoccupation with campaigning every two years.

"We have to re-establish the link between the Congress, the president and the party," former Republican Senate Majority Leader Howard Baker said approvingly. "A four-year term for House members, coterminous with the president, would create an astonishing togetherness between the House and the president."[6]

Even allowing for some hyperbole, this option would give all presidents somewhat more favorable balances of power in Congress than under the present system. This approach might soften the sharpest edges of divided government, but it would not eliminate the problem. Simultaneous elections alone do not guarantee unity and harmony. Eisenhower had a Republican Congress in 1952, but in the five other Republican presidential victories since then (Eisenhower once, Nixon twice, and Reagan twice), the Republican president faced Democratic control of one or both houses of Congress on the day he took office. Moreover, an eight-year term for senators seems awfully long.

OPTION 2: THE TEAM TICKET

Option 2, a more radical attack on divided government, is what Lloyd Cutler, former White House counsel to President Carter, calls the "team ticket." That means putting president, vice president, senator, and House member on a single slate and requiring a straight party-ticket vote. This revision would insure the president's party would control Congress.

A second variation, aimed at unifying party government, would give "bonus seats" in Congress to presidential winners, to assure them of a party majority in Congress.

Quite obviously, the "team-ticket" idea involves radical surgery on the Constitution, to make our system more like the British and other European parliamentary systems. As a practical matter, I doubt that either American politicians or the electorate would favor such a radical change. Sustained paralysis of American government could bring us to that. But our political predicament is not yet that dire and the European parliamentary record not that enviable. After all, Reagan did manage to pass his budget and tax cuts in 1981 and the tax-reform bill went through in 1986—evidence that major action is possible in a divided government, even if not very often. Moreover, there is a very serious drawback to the "team ticket" idea. While it makes one party more accountable for national policy, it also raises the risks of "tyranny of the majority"—a party majority—so feared by the Founding Fathers. This risks compounding the dangers of excessively aggressive presidents.

But there are less radical steps—short of changing the basic balance of the Constitution—to strengthen political parties and the links between presidents and their party members in Congress. They involve changes in the presidential nominating system and the rules of campaign financing.

OPTION 3: BRING BACK THE PROS

Option 3 is to give more say in the selection of presidential nominees to each party's leaders and officeholders across the country: senators, governors, members of Congress, mayors of big cities. The aim is to move professional politicians back into the nominating process, balancing delegates chosen in popular primaries. Under this option, the party's officeholders, and nominees for major offices, would automatically be unpledged delegates to party conventions, free to throw their weight to whichever candidate they felt best served the party. Their involvement would require the contenders to take more time to develop networks of support among professional politicians. Also, with more voice in picking the nominee, the elected politicians would have more reason to cooperate with him as president.

The Democrats have already moved part way in this direction because of their bad experience in 1980. President Carter wrapped up the 1980 nomination by winning a majority of delegates in the primaries. But by the Democratic convention in the summer of 1980, congressional Democrats felt certain that with Carter leading the ticket, their party was headed for heavy losses—and it was. Many senators and House members, fearing for their seats, wanted another nominee. But under the party rules, there was no way to pick another nominee. If there had been several hundred uncommitted delegates, mainly officeholders, change would have been possible. After this episode, the Democratic party rules were changed for the 1984 convention, so that eighty percent of the Democratic members in Congress got seats as uncommitted delegates. It would be better to make it one hundred percent, and to add governors, big-city mayors, and party nominees for important offices, perhaps giving them all double-weighted votes.

Another approach, assuming that the country is moving toward a national political primary, is to give the party pros a voice before the primary. Thomas Cronin, a Democratic activist and political scientist at Colorado College, has suggested that the parties hold national conventions in the summer of election years. At these conventions, elected politicians and party activists would screen would-be contenders and pick two or three to run in the primary. That way, the ultimate victor would have the support of political peers and of the popular vote.[7]

Obviously, such steps would make it harder for an outsider such as Carter to win the nomination. But they would help insure that any nominee had solid backing from the party network and improve the links between a president and his party leadership.

OPTION 4: STRENGTHEN PARTIES

Option 4 is to strengthen the role and cohesive force of political parties by changing campaign finance laws so that more campaign funding is routed through the parties and less through political action committees. There are all kinds of changes that could be made to achieve that. One is to restore the one-hundred-percent tax credit for small donations to parties by individual voters (up to one hundred dollars); another is to raise the current ($20,000) ceiling on individual donations to parties by individuals; a third is to raise the limit on how much parties can donate to individual Senate and House candidates. In each case, the point is to give the parties more money and more leeway in using it, to increase their importance to their candidates and their potential for cohesive influence on candidates after the election.

OPTION 5: TELEVISION SUBSIDIES

Option 5 is to use parties as the major conduits for a "television subsidy" to candidates. Television time is the gold coin of the modern campaign. Some reformers have recommended setting up a television fund: a bank of hundreds of hours of television time, gathered by a levy on TV stations across the country as a public service cost of their lucrative operating licenses.[8] To strengthen the national parties by making members of Congress more dependent on them, the Committee on the Constitutional System recommended that half of each party's television time be allotted to the national parties, to distribute among their candidates, and half given to the candidates—both incumbents and challengers.

A "television subsidy" would strike at one of the most alarming problems in our political system today: the enormous electoral advantages of incumbents, especially in the House of Representatives, an advantage heavily tilted for Democrats.

The single most important step to break the prevalent pattern of divided government is to restore genuine, two-party competition across the country for seats in the House. With good reason, Tom Mann cites the argument that a "responsive and responsible government requires at least an occasional change in party control of the House."[9]

The present incumbency advantage of House members is so great and there are so many safe seats that fewer than fifteen percent of the nation's 435 congressional districts produce a serious contest in most elections. This situation largely insulates the House from national political trends. It guarantees the continued Democratic lock on the

House—now thirty-four years in duration. Control of the House is unaffected by partisan changes in voter sentiment nationwide, and that insures a partisan divided government every time a Republican is elected president. Beyond that, the lack of authentic competition in so many elections undermines the essence of representative government.

The automatic advantages of incumbents are well known by now: large staffs, free mailing privilege, congressional radio and television studios, and TV satellite feeds. Political consultants reckon that package is worth $500,000 in campaign funds for each incumbent, not to mention the heavy pro-incumbent tilt of donations by political action committees.

If genuine competition is to be restored to House elections, some subsidies are necessary for challengers—for example, some postal privilege and a partial financial subsidy to offset the built-in subsidies of incumbents. But the single most important need of challengers is visibility—simple exposure to the voters. Without it, challengers are licked before they start.

No medium is more important to challengers than television, and probably no step would be more important in creating a genuine choice for voters than a television subsidy to challengers as well as incumbents. For example, each congressional district could be allotted a subsidy of an hour or two in prime time for each major candidate, during the final month before the election, to be used solely for live appearances (no media spots) of no less than ten minutes each, in order to insure some discourse on issues.[10]

Such an approach is especially important in the House because so few House races are real contests. If incumbents were less confident of reelection, they might be more loyal to their parties—especially if their parties had more funds and television time to spread around.

Flushing Out "Partisan Cholesterol"

The institutional fixes that I have mentioned—and of course, there are more—are unlikely to materialize soon. Even if there were a Democratic sweep in 1988, the odds are strong that the ills of divided government will resume over the longer run. In that case, the experience of the past few decades, and particularly the Reagan presidency, teaches that the vital process of coalition making requires a more genuine commitment to collaboration across party lines on the most important issues: in short, old-fashioned bipartisanship.

Bryce Harlow used to say that excessive partisanship was the "cholesterol" that clogged the arteries of the American system because of the enmities and bad tempers it produced. Harlow, a gruff, battle-scarred Texan, had personal ties across party lines with Lyndon Johnson and Sam Rayburn, the Democratic leaders in Congress. Often during Eisenhower's final two years, Harlow made a point of getting the president to invite Johnson and Rayburn for some quiet talk over a drink.

"The second floor of the White House, just the four of us," Harlow recalled to me, not too long before he died. "Yeah. I'd bring 'em down about once every six weeks to flush out the political plumbing so that the president and the leaders of Congress could do business if they had to in a crisis."[11]

Admittedly, that was the old power game, where fewer hands had more control. But the lesson of those quiet sessions in the White House is still important. During his two terms, Ronald Reagan did not huddle regularly with the House speaker or the Senate majority leader to work out genuine compromises on major issues, whether the budget or sending the Navy into the Persian Gulf. Nor did Carter or Nixon do it much. And therein lie many of our political problems: the failures of presidents more consistently to forge durable compromises with congressional leaders.

It is not sufficient, as Carter did, simply to declare an energy policy and then try to force it on Congress; or to try, as Reagan did, to impose budget priorities, Iranian arms deals, the *contra* war or strategic defenses. That merely activates political high blood pressure and blame-game politics.

Frustration with the stalemates and trench warfare of divided government prompted Theodore Sorensen, former aide to President Kennedy, to propose what he called A *Different Kind of Presidency* in 1984. Sorensen advocated bridging the stalemates of government with a bipartisan ticket in presidential campaigns: president from one party, vice president from the other party, cabinet drawn from both. As a precedent, he cited Abraham Lincoln's tapping Andrew Johnson, the Democratic governor of Tennessee, for his Republican running mate in 1864, to help heal the political schisms of that era. "Our problems require more than partisan answers," Sorensen argued. "They are more important than party labels. Both parties share the blame for our present plight. Neither can solve the problems alone."[12]

One difficulty with Sorensen's proposal is that Andrew Johnson's experiences as president, warring with a recalcitrant and militant Republican cabinet and Congress, is hardly an inspiring model. As for modern times, Republican John Anderson, running as an independent candidate, tried a bipartisan ticket in 1980, with Democrat Patrick Lucey as his running mate; they came in a distant third. Short of a national calamity as severe as the Civil War, it is hard to imagine either the politicians or the public adopting Sorensen's bipartisan ticket.

The basic notion behind Sorensen's proposal, however, is sound. The most prickly and difficult issues almost invariably require unpopular decisions, and bipartisan agreement is needed. Neither political party wants to bear the onus alone for inflicting the pain of raising taxes or for checking growth of massive, popular middle-class programs. The result is that those necessary steps do not get taken.

"Which political party, which branch of government, which president, wants to be held responsible for cutting the expansion of or eligibility for the indexed middle-class entitlement programs like Social Security and Medicare, or the funds for repairing our crumbling infrastructure, or the pay and pensions of those who serve in our armed forces?" Sorensen asked. "Who will change the popular tax and credit laws that encourage borrowing and consumption at the expense of U.S. savings accumulation and capital formation . . . ? Who will accept the domestic political pressures involved in galvanizing the industrialized nations into harmonizing their economic, monetary, trade, credit, subsidy, exchange rate and development assistance projects?"[13]

It is a truism worth remembering that the paramount national issues—American intervention abroad, curbing the federal deficit, strategic defenses and arms control, insuring American economic competitiveness—are not going to be settled by one president, by one round of congressional voting, or by one party. Very few purely partisan victories stand the test of time when no single party is predominant. The big issues take a prolonged effort, year in and year out, usually from one presidency to the next and beyond. And that requires some central consensus and collaboration *across party lines.* Even in eight years, Reagan could not guarantee the success of his Nicaraguan policy or the implementation of his strategic defense program, without the cooperation of his successors or a bipartisan consensus. But Reagan's success with the 1983 bipartisan commission on Social Security offers a model for future presidents. New York's Governor Mario Cuomo has talked of a bipartisan commission on the deficit to help the next president. On the paramount issues, such steps are necessary.

Not a Spectator Sport

In this book, my purpose is not to promote institutional remedies. We do need some reforms in campaign rules and in our governmental institutions. But tinkering with our laws and institutions will only go so far unless voters, too, accept some responsibility for the mess they blame on politicians.

My purpose is to explain the way the power game is played so that voters can see what changes, if any, they want to bring about, not only in politicians and institutions, but in their own behavior—because the problems in our government are rooted in our behavior and in our thinking about government. We blame the politicians, but by and large politicians deliver what voters collectively show they want—either by deliberate choice, by inaction or by ambivalence. We get the kind of Congress, the kind of president, the kind of campaign system that we want.

The popular gripe about presidential campaigns, for example, is that they are too long and too boring. But these problems are direct consequences of popular pressures for more democracy and for the spread of primaries. Campaigns are long because voters in so many states want to vote in primaries. The public wanted to throw out party bosses and stop having candidates picked in smoke-filled backrooms. Smart campaigners such as Jack Kennedy, George McGovern, and Jimmy Carter used that populist mood to storm the old citadels of power.

Now the 1988 presidential race has thirty-six primaries scheduled, seven more than in 1984. The money for that marathon gauntlet has to be raised by candidates well before the actual primaries begin. Once the voting starts, there is precious little time for raising money (that tripped up Gary Hart in 1984—he wasn't organizationally ready to capitalize on his early strength). The political pros have calculated that it takes from $10 million to $20 million to make a run for the nomination in all those states (plus the party-caucus states). And to raise all that money normally requires from eighteen months to four years. By law, nominations require petitions in every primary state and fund-raising in twenty states for matching federal funds. That is slow, back-breaking organizational work. Repeaters have a head start. Reagan tried three times, in 1968, 1976, and 1980, before he made it. Mondale announced his candidacy 511 days before his party's convention and later acknowledged that he had actually decided to run on January 21, 1981, the day after he left the vice presidency.

During the long preliminary work, most voters are paying little attention. The main patterns of support and public impressions are formed during the critical season from the Iowa caucuses through the cluster of primaries on Super Tuesday—one frenzied month. It may please voters to see the regional clustering of primaries, theoretically shortening the campaign, but that compressed scheduling, with candidates darting from state to state, leaves little time for thoughtful discussion of issues. The sudden publicity earned by early victory or surprise strength bestows extraordinary advantage to the candidate who gains momentum in that period, however small the margin of victory or surprise. Actually, a slower pace of the primary season would give voters more time to gauge the candidates and to make more thoughtful choices.

Another public peeve is the enormous power of television as the medium of modern campaigns and the superficiality of televised campaigns. It is a daunting problem. Certainly, the television news industry—and political reporters in general—could do better at making campaign coverage less superficial, at more analysis, and at delving more seriously into the revealing side of candidates' records, rather than focussing on visual fluff, gaffes, and the tactics of campaigning.

But unless the voters are prepared to give up political primaries as the main vehicle for nominating presidential candidates—and there is no sign of that—television will remain the principal medium for campaigns. In the old power game, local party leaders were important in picking the nominees; labor leaders, church leaders, business leaders, and civic leaders shared their assessments of the contenders with voters. Now voters want to make up their own minds, based on impressions from short snippets on television and from the print media. These gut impressions are light on the record and performance of candidates; more weight goes to wit, ease, and the appearance of sincerity on camera.

With primaries proliferating, campaigns are bound to remain superficial because a host of candidates want to reach a mass of voters quickly. Television is the fast mass medium, and the attention span of most voters is very short. Change will come only if voter groups find organizational ways of pressing candidates to be more substantive, or if voters turn away from candidates whose campaigns are superficial and evasive. Politicians will start being more honest and substantive when they see that honesty and substance pay with the voters.

This year, an experimental effort has been mounted to force the presidential candidates to inject more substance into their stump appearances at two early stops on the campaign trail. The nonpartisan, nonprofit Roosevelt Center for American Policy Studies in Washington has spent about $1 million to give "crash courses" to thousands of voters in Iowa and New Hampshire. The idea is to prep the grass-roots voters on issues such as the budget deficit, farm programs, the global spread of nuclear weapons, Central America, and international trade, so that they can test presidential candidates with tough substantive questions, rather than let the candidates merely wheel through prepared spiels. The purpose, said Roger Molander, president of the Roosevelt Center, is to "foster a far more robust election" because people were embarrassed by the shallowness of the last two elections.

But, as I have contended, our fixation on the president is exaggerated, and it is time for more people to recognize that our elections are for an entire government, not just a president. Any president has less power than most people imagine. The capacity to form a coalition is crucial. Any Republican president faces divided government and must be able to deal well across party lines in Congress. But most voters do not stop to think that divided government is their doing, that rampant ticket splitting is likely to produce shouting deadlocks and blame-game politics between Congress and the president. It is silly to call for strong presidential leadership, to vote a split ticket, and then to blame the politicians because they could not get their act together. Split-ticket voting feeds political deadlock.

By and large, politicians represent the public pretty accurately, its views and its lack of interest in the political process. Celebrity politics, feel-good rhetoric, bumper-sticker slogans, and negative commercials reflect what the candidates and their high-priced media consultants see voters responding to. The product is geared to the marketplace and unless the customers become more discriminating, they are in for more of the same.

It is time, for example, to pay greater attention to the capacity of presidential candidates for making our government work. On this, their political past is more important than their inevitably self-serving stump rhetoric. In short, it is time to stop knocking competence and experience in government, and time to stop believing that some newcomer can transform the world inside the beltway and the world at large, with an untested magic. It is time to discount Washington bashers and visionaries, and time to value the professional politicians whose records show that they can balance the issues, sort out priorities, rally their ranks, and reach across party lines—and keep reaching across—to draw support there, too. It is certainly time to put aside the hokum that either party can rule for long without help from the other.

This means casting a skeptical eye at glamour candidates, at visions of a bright American future, and at glib promises of dazzling presidential performance. Divided government and weak parties are a fact of political life. Personality politics and communications charm are a help, but they will only go so far in coping with the nation's most testing problems. Whatever their philosophies, the winning candidates on both sides in 1988, and beyond, will need the craft of sensible compromise to make our government work. All three—competence, credibility, and compromise—are crucial to governing effectively.

Finally, it must be said that the policy deadlocks in Washington over spending priorities, arms control, and Central America reflect the public's ambivalence on these issues.

The budget is symptomatic of the basic problem. People are tempted to seek solutions by imposing institutional fixes: constitutional amendments to require a balanced budget or to give the president a line-item veto. The effectiveness of a line-item veto is questionable. Governors of forty-three states have that power, seven do not, and spending levels are *lower* on average in state governments *without* line-item veto power, than in states which have it.[14] A procrustean requirement for a balanced budget could in the years ahead plunge a faltering economy into depression by killing programs or forcing massive tax increases just when the economy can ill sustain such action. Almost inevitably, a balanced budget amendment would be taken to the courts for interpretation—an invitation to judicial policy-making of the broadest sort. A safer, saner route is through gradual deficit reductions sincerely backed by both president and Congress.

The real problem on the deficit, as on other central questions, is the lack of a clear public consensus—in this case, on the size and role of government. The electorate sends politicians contradictory signals: Cut the budget, but don't cut popular programs—the ones that would have to be cut in order to cure the deficit. Opinion poll after opinion poll has shown majorities of people dislike "big government" in principle but not in practice. In the lingo of political science, such voters are "ideologically conservative" but "operationally liberal." This basic inconsistency encourages the politics of evasion and hypocrisy in Washington. It fuels the partisan blame game.

Similarily, on American policy in Central America, the message from the voters is ambivalent—"no more Cubas" (no more Communist-ruled countries in the Americas) but "no more Vietnams" (no more American intervention and defeat). Or again, on the arms race: Be strong enough, but don't spend too much; try to get the Russians to give up their most threatening weapons, but don't give up our areas of advantage.

Of course, politicians who shy away from hard decisions bear responsibility for our unresolved problems. But it is not their responsibility alone. Unlike many games, the power game is not a spectator sport. It goes without saying—yet it needs saying: In a system of direct primaries, voters must become more intelligently involved and more realistic, both about the structural problems in our system and their own role in it.

Politicians and reformers can tinker with the system, but major changes that affect both policy and the way the game is played also have to come from the grass roots beyond the beltway. When voters straddle, most politicians straddle. When the electorate does not throw its support behind a single majority party that can give clear direction to government, the government reflects that indecision in the nation. When the country lacks a consensus, the president and Congress lack a consensus. When the public has no overriding philosophy, the government lacks what Walter Lippman called a "public philosophy."

At this point, as the partisan combat rises again, it is well worth remembering that after the tumult is over, the nation needs a rejuvenated spirit of comity and compromise. It needs not only purposeful leadership but a realistic acceptance of the limits of power and insistence that the power game be played by the rules. No party, faction, president, or Congress can impose its will on this cumbersome, brawling five-ring political circus of ours, or ignore the rules for long—without being humbled. When the American power game was organized two centuries ago, the Founding Fathers deliberately spread the chips around so widely that no single political force could drive the others out of the game. The chips have been scattered even more widely in recent years—by reform, money, television, weak parties, and split-ticket voting—and we now need political leadership that can provide not only vision but cohesion.

From a leader, from all of us, what is required is a tolerance for the untidiness of democracy, even genuine enjoyment in democracy's untidiness. "Speed of action," Senator William Cohen observed near the end of the Iran-*contra* hearings, "was never the absolute goal of democracy, because a king is faster than a congressman on any given day." Our political system needs some neatening up. The power game will never be tidy. The competition will never quit. The ruckus will never quiet. But things will work better when people are encouraged to coalesce.

In his dismay over the Iran-*contra* affair, George Shultz framed the problem and the solution with simple clarity. "We have this very difficult task," he said, "of having a separation of powers that means we have to learn how to share power. Sharing power is harder, and we need to work at it harder than we do. But that's the only way."[15]

Bibliography

Adams, Henry. *Democracy.* New York: New American Library, 1963.

Alsop, Stuart. *The Center.* New York: Harper & Row, 1968.

Barber, James David. *The Pulse of Politics.* New York: W.W. Norton, 1980.

Barrett, Laurence I. *Gambling with History.* New York: Penguin Books, 1983; Doubleday, 1984.

Berne, Dr. Eric. *Games People Play.* New York: Ballantine Books, 1964.

Blumenthal, Sidney. *The Rise of the Counter-Establishment.* New York: Times Books, 1986.

Broad, William. *Star Warriors.* New York: Simon & Schuster, 1985.

Broder, David S. *Behind the Front Page.* New York: Simon & Schuster, 1987.

Brzezinski, Zbigniew. *Power and Principle.* New York: Farrar, Straus & Giroux, 1983.

Burns, James MacGregor. *The Power to Lead.* New York: Simon & Schuster, 1984.

Burns, Arthur. *The United States and Germany: A Vital Partnership.* New York: Council on Foreign Relations, 1986.

Butler, Stuart M., Michael Sanera and W. Bruce Weinrod eds. *Mandate For Leadership II: Continuing the Conservative Revolution.* Washington: Heritage Foundation, 1984.

Cannon, Lou. *Reagan.* New York: G.P. Putnam's Sons, 1982.

Cater, Douglass. *Power in Washington.* New York: Random House, 1964.

Cheney, Richard B., and Lynne V. Cheney. *Kings of the Hill.* New York: Continuum, 1983.

Chubb, John E., and Paul E. Peterson eds. *New Directions in American Politics.* Washington: Brookings Institute, 1986.

Cotton, Norris. *In the Senate.* New York: Dodd, Mead & Co., 1978.

Cronin, Thomas E. *The State of the Presidency.* Boston: Little, Brown & Co., 1980.

———, ed. *Rethinking the Presidency.* Boston: Little, Brown & Co., 1982.

Crouse, Timothy. *The Boys on the Bus.* New York: Ballantine, 1972.

Davidson, Roger H., and Walter J. Oleszak. *Congress and Its Members*. Washington: Congressional Quarterly Press, 1985.

Destler, I.M., Leslie H. Gelb and Anthony Lake. *Our Own Worst Enemy*. New York: Simon & Schuster, 1984.

Duke, Paul, ed., *Beyond Reagan*. New York: Warner Books, 1986.

Fiorina, Morris P. *The Keystone of the Washington Establishment*. New Haven: Yale University Press, 1977.

Gotlieb, Sondra. *Wife of. . . .* Washington: Acropolis Books, 1985.

Haig, Alexander M., Jr. *Caveat*. New York: Macmillan, 1984.

Halperin, Morton H. *Bureaucratic Politics and Foreign Policy*. Washington: Brookings Institute, 1974.

Harris, Louis. *Inside America*. New York: Vintage, 1987.

Heatherly, Charles L., ed. *Mandate For Leadership: Policy Management in a Conservative Administration*. Washington: Heritage Foundation, 1981.

Hess, Stephen. *Organizing the Presidency*. Washington: Brookings Institution, 1976.

———. *The Government/Press Connection*. Washington: Brookings Institution, 1984.

———. *The Ultimate Insiders*. Washington: Brookings Institution, 1986.

Hoxey, R. Gordon, ed. *Presidential Studies Quarterly*. New York: Center for the Study of the Presidency, 1977–1987.

Johnson, Haynes. *In the Absence of Power*. New York: The Viking Press, 1980.

Jones, Rochelle, and Peter Woll. *The Private World of Congress*. New York: Macmillan, 1979.

King, Anthony. *The New American Political System*. Washington: American Enterprise Institute for Public Policy Research, 1978.

King, Anthony, ed. *Both Ends of the Avenue*. Washington: American Enterprise Institute for Public Policy Research, 1983.

Kissinger, Henry. *White House Years*. Boston: Little, Brown & Co., 1979.

Luttwak, Edward. *The Pentagon and the Art of War*. New York: Simon & Schuster, 1984.

Macpherson, Myra. *The Power Lovers*. New York: Ballantine Books, 1975.

Madison, James. *The Federalist Papers* [originally published 1787–88]. New York: Bantam Books, 1982.

Malbin, Michael J. *Money and Politics in the United States*. Washington: American Enterprise Institute for Public Policy Research, 1984.

———. *Unelected Representatives*. New York: Basic Books, 1980.

Mann, Thomas E., and Norman Ornstein, eds. *The New Congress*. Washington: American Enterprise Institute for Public Policy Research, 1981.

Mayhew, David R. *Congress: The Electoral Connection*. New Haven: Yale University Press, 1974.

McAllister, Eugene J., ed. *Agenda for Progress*. Washington: Heritage Foundation, 1981.

McGuiness, Joe. *The Selling of the President 1968*. New York: Pocket Books, 1969.

McPherson, Harry. *A Political Education*. Boston: Little, Brown & Co., 1972.

Miller, James A. *Running in Place*. New York: Simon & Schuster, 1986.

Naisbitt, John. *Megatrends*. New York: Warner Books, 1982.

Neustadt, Richard E. *Presidential Power*. New York: John Wiley & Sons, 1976.

Nixon, Richard M. *Six Crises*. New York: Pyramid Books, 1968.

O'Neill, Thomas P., Jr., *Man of the House*. New York: Random House, 1987.

Ornstein, Norman J., et al. *Vital Statistics on Congress, 1984–1985 Edition.* Washington: American Enterprise Institute, 1984.

———. *Vital Statistics on Congress, 1986–1987 Edition.* Washington: Congressional Quarterly, 1987.

Palmer, John L., and Isabel V. Sawhill, eds. *The Reagan Record.* Cambridge, Mass.: Ballinger Publishing, 1984.

Palmer, John, et al. *Perspectives on the Reagan Years.* Washington: Urban Institute Press, 1986.

Peters, Charles. *How Washington Really Works.* Reading, Mass.: Addison-Wesley, 1981.

Phillips, Kevin. *Post-Conservative America.* New York: Random House, 1982.

Polsby, Nelson W. *Consequences of Party Reform.* New York: Oxford University Press, 1983.

———. *Congress and the Presidency.* Englewood Cliffs, N.J.: Prentice-Hall, 1986.

Ranney, Austin. *Channels of Power.* Washington: American Enterprise Institute, 1983.

Reichley, James, ed. *Elections American Style.* Washington: Brookings Institution, 1987.

Reedy, George. *The Twilight of the Presidency.* New York: World, 1970.

Reston, James B. *The Artillery of the Press.* New York: Basic Books, 1983.

Sabato, Larry J. *The Rise of Political Consultants.* New York: Basic Books, 1981.

———. *PAC Power.* New York: W.W. Norton, 1984.

Safire, William. *Safire's Political Dictionary.* New York: Random House, 1968; Ballantine Books, 1980.

Schattschneider, E. E. *The Semisovereign People.* New York: Holt, Rinehart, 1961.

Schram, Martin. *The Great American Video Game: Presidential Politics in the Television Age.* New York: Morrow, 1987.

Shogan, Robert. *Promises to Keep: Carter's First Hundred Days.* New York: Crowell, 1977.

———. *None of the Above.* New York: New American Library, 1982.

Sorensen, Theodore F. *A Different Kind of Presidency.* New York: Harper & Row, 1984.

Stockman, David A. *The Triumph of Politics: Why the Reagan Revolution Failed.* New York: Harper & Row, 1986; Avon Books, 1987.

Stubbing, Richard A. *The Defense Game.* New York: Harper & Row, 1986.

Sundquist, James L. *The Decline and Resurgence of Congress.* Washington: Brookings Institution, 1981.

Talbott, Strobe. *Deadly Gambits.* New York: Simon & Schuster, 1983.

Wanniski, Jude. *The Way the World Works.* New York: Simon & Schuster, 1983.

Weatherford, J. McIver. *The Tribes on the Hill.* New York: Rawson Wade, 1981.

White, Theodore H. *The Making of the President 1972.* New York: Atheneum, 1973.

Wills, Garry. *Reagan's America: Innocents at Home.* Garden City, New York: Doubleday, 1987.

Witcover, Jules, and Jack Germond, *Blue Smoke and Mirrors.* New York: The Viking Press, 1981.

———. *Wake Us Up When It's Over.* New York: Macmillan, 1985.

Young, James Sterling. *The Washington Community.* New York: Columbia University Press, 1968.

Notes

INTRODUCTION

1. Max Lerner, foreword to Niccolo Machiavelli, *The Prince and The Discourses* (New York: Modern Library, 1950), p. xxvi.

2. One of the most perceptive scholars of American government, Richard Neustadt of Harvard University, wrote: "The substance is important, never doubt it, for that is what the game is all about. But so is the personal element. . . . The personal is tightly interwoven with the institutional. It is a rare player who can keep the two distinct, much less view both apart from substance." See Richard E. Neustadt, *Alliance Politics* (New York: Columbia University Press, 1970), pp. 76, 78.

1. THE POWER FLOAT

1. John F. Kennedy, in Theodore C. Sorensen, *Decision-Making in The White House: The Olive Branch or the Arrows* (New York: Columbia University Press, 1963), foreword.

2. Howard Baker, interview with the author, January 14, 1986.

3. Larry Crowley and Charlie Welch, interviews with the author's researcher Lauren Simon Ostrow, April 22, 1986.

4. Many Americans assume this military aide is a mythical figure, but reporters traveling with the president do see him, and White House aides talk of his presence matter-of-factly.

5. *Oneida* (Tennessee) *Independent*, May 6, 1982, p. 1.

6. Strange as these security precautions may strike the ordinary reader, this account comes directly from my interview with Senator Baker, January 14, 1986.

7. These details on the size of the presidential traveling caravan came from the Reagan White House Press Office and the White House Transportation Office.

8. Michael Deaver, interview with the author, February 4, 1986.

9. Al Kingon, interview with the author, April 9, 1986.

10. Margaret Truman, *Harry S. Truman* (New York: William Morrow, 1973), pp. 551–552.

11. Richard E. Neustadt, *Presidential Power* (New York: John Wiley & Sons, 1976), p. 101.

12. Newt Gingrich, interview with the author, January 29, 1986.

13. *The Washington Post.* December 15, 1985, p. C1

14. Richard Darman, interview with the author, April 5, 1985. Walter Bagehot is a nineteenth-century British political essayist.

2. THE POWER EARTHQUAKE OF 1974

1. *The Wall Street Journal,* April 13, 1973, p. 10.

2. Stuart Eizenstat, interview with the author, August 8, 1986.

3. See Michael Malbin, *Unelected Representatives: Congressional Staff and the Future of Representative Government* (New York: Basic Books, 1980), pp. 10–19; and Norman J. Ornstein et al., *Vital Statistics on Congress, 1984–85 Edition* (Washington: American Enterprise Institute for Public Policy, 1984), pp. 116–127.

4. Richard Conlon, interview with the author, January 12, 1986.

5. After the 1986 election, Helms got himself reestablished as the "ranking Republican"—in effect, shadow chairman—on the Senate Foreign Relations Committee by invoking seniority over Richard Lugar, the Indiana Republican who had chaired the Foreign Relations Committee since 1984 when Helms had chosen to chair the Agriculture Committee.

6. Dan Quayle, *Congressional Record,* September 12, 1984 p. S10958.

7. Thomas Eagleton, *Congressional Record,* November 23, 1985, vol. 131, # 163.

8. Tommy Boggs, interview with the author, March 27, 1986.

9. Morris Udall, interview with the author, January 23, 1986.

10. Henry Brandon, interview with the author, November 4, 1985.

11. Barbara Gamarekian, interview with the author, February 18, 1986.

12. Morris Udall, interview with the author, June 23, 1986.

13. David Pryor, interview with the author, March 13, 1986.

14. Bob Rota, interview with the author's researcher Kurt Eichenwald, April 13, 1986.

15. Arthur Levitt, interview with the author, April 20, 1986.

16. Fred Wertheimer, interview with the author, March 18, 1986.

17. These figures come from the Federal Election Commission.

18. Both parties have national committees, separate campaign committees for the House and Senate, and mount special drives for presidential conventions. These figures, from a report of the Federal Election Commission, cover funds raised for the 1983–84 election cycle. Figures for the 1986 races are lower than 1984 because it was not a year of a presidential election.

19. *Studley Report,* December 1986, Washington edition.

20. Mabel Brandon, interview with the author, March 17, 1986.

21. Jerry terHorst, interview with the author, April 18, 1986.

22. William Regardie, interview with the author's researcher Lauren Simon Ostrow, April 14, 1986.

23. *Ibid.*

24. Howard H. Baker, Jr., interview with Steve Roberts, Martin Tolchin, and the author, January 15, 1985.

25. Stephen Hess, *The Ultimate Insiders* (Washington: Brookings Institution, 1986), pp. 9–19, and table pp. 140–142.

26. *Ibid.,* table on p. 138–139.

27. Michael J. Robinson, "Three Faces of Congressional Media," in Thomas E. Mann and Norman J. Ornstein, eds., *The New Congress* (Washington: American Enterprise Institute for Public Policy Research, 1981), p. 98.

28. Charles Schumer, interview with the author, April 10, 1986. Schumer made similar comments to Steve Roberts of *The New York Times* in "Phil Gramm's Crusade Against the Deficit" in the *New York Times Magazine* March 30, 1986. p. 23.

3. THE SOFT SIDES OF POWER

1. Thomas Eagleton, interview with the author, February 21, 1986.

2. This account draws heavily on the author's interview on April 8, 1986, with Mark Helmke, then Lugar's press secretary.

3. Bryce Harlow, interview with the author, November 13, 1985.

4. Warren Rudman, interview with the author, April 6, 1987.

5. Dave McCurdy, interview with the author, July 16, 1985.

6. Barry Goldwater, letter of April 9, 1984, to William Casey, printed in *The Washington Post*, April 11, 1984.

7. This account is based on the author's interviews with senators Joseph Biden of Delaware and Patrick Leahy of Vermont, as well as with intelligence committee staff members and one senior CIA official, who asked to remain anonymous.

8. George Shultz, testimony before the joint Congressional Committee investigating the Iran-*contra* operation, July 23, 1987.

9. This account comes from two high administration officials and one high Federal Reserve official, all directly involved but speaking on condition that they not be identified.

10. Robert Hormats, interview with the author, March 27, 1986.

11. Jack Albertine, interview with the author, March 31, 1986.

12. Barney Frank, interview with the author, December 11, 1985.

13. Morris Udall, interview with the author, January 23, 1986.

14. Bryce Harlow, interview with the author, November 13, 1985.

15. Lee Atwater, interview with the author, February 6, 1986.

16. Charles McC. Mathias, interview with the author, January 23, 1986.

17. Fred Dutton, interview with the author, December 5, 1985.

4. PORCUPINE POWER

1. Joseph Biden, interview with the author, March 6, 1986.

2. Farrell Guillory, interview with the author's researcher William Nell, May 6, 1987.

3. Christopher Matthews, interview with the author, August 7, 1985.

4. Howard M. Metzenbaum, "Senate Heal Thyself," *The Washington Post*, February 16, 1983, p. A19

5. Timothy Wirth, interview with the author, February 17, 1987.

6. Christopher Dodd, interview with the author, February 18, 1986.

7. Howard Baker, interview with the author, January 14, 1986.

8. Alan Simpson, interview with the author, April 9, 1986.

5. THE POWER LOOP

1. Elliott Richardson, interviewed on the PBS television documentary, *The Power and the Glory*, hosted by Paul Duke, which aired on July 22, 1982, on WETA in Washington, D.C.

2. Robert Strauss, interview with the author, February 11, 1986.

3. Clifford White, interview with the author, March 26, 1986.

4. George Reedy, *The Twilight of the Presidency* (New York: World, 1970), p. 88.

5. Michael Deaver, interview with the author, February 15, 1985.

6. *Ibid.*

7. William Sitman, interview with the author, July 8, 1985.

8. E. E. Schattschneider, *The Semisovereign People* (New York: Holt, Rinehart, 1961), pp. 1–2.

9. *Ibid.*, p. 3.

10. This historic antecedent was pointed out to me by Austin Ranney of the University of California at Berkeley.

6. LIFE INSIDE THE BELTWAY

1. Nelson W. Polsby, "The Washington Community," in Thomas E. Mann and Norman J. Ornstein, *The New Congress* (Washington: American Enterprise Institute for Public Policy Research, 1981), p. 8

2. Henry Adams, *Democracy* (New York: New American Library, 1963) p. 17.

3. Elliott Richardson, interviewed on the PBS television documentary, *The Power and the Glory* which aired on July 22, 1982 on station WETA in Washington, D.C.

4. Charles McC. Mathias, interview with the author, January 23, 1986.

5. Alexander M. Haig, Jr., *Caveat* (New York: Macmillan, 1984), p. 16.

6. Stuart Eizenstat, interviewed on the television documentary, *The Power and the Glory,* which aired July 22, 1982, on station WETA in Washington, D.C.

7. Austin Ranney, comment to the author, June 24, 1986.

8. *The New York Times,* May 31, 1984, p B8.

9. Senator Paul Tsongas, interview with the author, January 28, 1986.

10. Newt Gingrich, interview with the author, January 29, 1986.

11. Charles Peters, *How Washington Really Works*, (Reading, Mass.: Addison-Wesley Publishing Co., 1980), pp. 5–6.

12. Nelson Polsby, *op. cit.*, p. 9.

13. Edward J. Rollins, interview with the author, December 9, 1985.

14. James Sterling Young, *The Washington Community, 1800–1820* (New York: Columbia University Press, 1966), see especially pp. 98–105.

15. Barney Frank, interview with the author, December 11, 1985.

16. *Ibid.*

17. Henry Waxman, interview with the author December 12, 1985.

18. Katharine Graham, interview with the author, April 5, 1986.

19. Nancy Reynolds, interview with the author, March 31, 1986.

20. *The Washington Post,* May 8, 1986. p C1

21. Alan Simpson, interview with the author, April 4, 1986.

22. *Ibid.*

23. Joseph Biden, interview with the author, March 6, 1986.

24. Strom Thurmond, interview with the author, March 20, 1986.

25. Malcolm Baldrige, interview with the author, May 9, 1986.

26. Christopher Matthews, interview with the author, August 7, 1985.

27. David Durenburger, interview with the author, May 9, 1986.

28. John Blamphin, public affairs director of the American Psychiatric Association, interview with the author's researcher William Nell, June 17, 1987. According to APA statistics, Los Angeles and Boston were tied as the cities with the highest number of psychiatrists per capita, and New York was slightly ahead of Washington.

29. Blythe Babyak, "My Turn," *Newsweek,* January 23, 1978.

30. Sondra Gotlieb, *Wife of . . .* (Washington: Acropolis Books, 1985), p. 28.

31. Sondra Gotlieb, quoted in "Take My 'Wife of'—Please" by Sandra McElwaine, *Regardie's Magazine,* October 1985, p. 42.

32. Steven Pieczenik, interview with the author, May 5, 1986.

33. David Durenburger, interview with the author, May 9, 1986.

34. Richard Reeves, quoted in Timothy Crouse, *The Boys on the Bus* (New York: Ballantine, 1973), p. 71.

35. The Center for the American Woman in Politics at Rutgers University has compiled statistics showing that women comprised 5.6 percent of all state legislators in 1975 and 15.5 percent out of a total of 7,461 seats in 1987.

36. Ann Lewis, interview with the author, April 27, 1987.

37. Sheila Tate, interview with the author, February 21, 1986.

38. Nancy Reynolds, interview with the author, April 27, 1987.

39. Lynn Martin, statement before the House Administration Subcommittee on Accounts, March 6, 1985.

40. Katharine Graham, interview with the author, April 5, 1986.

41. Nancy Reynolds, interview with the author, March 31, 1986.

42. Ann Lewis, interview with the author, April 27, 1987.

7. CONGRESS AND THE CONSTANT CAMPAIGN

1. This account is drawn largely from films of the hearing by C-Span, the cable television networks which films House and Senate floor proceedings and many committee hearings.

2. Tabulations of TV coverage of Congress were done by Norman J. Ornstein and Michael J. Robinson, in "The Case of Our Disappearing Congress" *TV Guide*, January 11, 1986, p. 9.

3. David R. Mayhew, *Congress: The Electoral Connection* (New Haven, Conn.: Yale University Press, 1974), p. 32.

4. Marty Franks, interview with the author, February 3, 1986.

5. Newt Gingrich, interview with the author, January 29, 1986.

6. John Naisbitt, *Megatrends* (New York: Warner Books, 1984), p. 35.

7. These figures are from Robert Vastine, executive director of the Senate Republican Conference, May 14, 1987.

8. Paul Tsongas, interview with author, January 28, 1986.

9. Marty Franks, interview with the author, February 3, 1986.

10. Timothy Wirth, interview with the author, February 5, 1986.

11. An account largely derived from Bill Livingston, interview with the author, January 28, 1986.

12. Bob Vastine, interview with the author, January 14, 1986.

13. Timothy Wirth, interview with the author, May 22, 1986.

14. Richard Bolling, interview with the author, January 15, 1986.

15. Christopher Matthews, interview with the author, July 5, 1985.

16. J. McIver Weatherford, *Tribes on the Hill* (New York: Rawson, Wade, 1981), p. 69.

17. *Ibid.*, pp. 71, 73–4.

18. Thomas Eagleton, interview with the author, February 21, 1986.

19. See Christopher Maleson, "Solarz's Brash Style Tempers His Quest for Influence in the Foreign Policy Arena," *National Journal*, November 26, 1985. pp. 2413–2417.

20. Katherine Evans, "The Newsmaker: A Capitol Hill Pro Reveals His Secrets" *Washington Journalism Review*, June 1981, pp. 28–33.

21. Les Aspin, quoted in Katherine Evans, *op. cit.*, p. 29.

22. Kirk O'Donnell, interview with the author, May 28, 1986

23. Richard Gephardt, interview with the author, May 22, 1986.

24. *The New York Times*, April 30, 1987, p. 1.

25. Don Foley, interview with the author's researcher William Nell, May 15, 1987.

26. David Himes, interview with the author, March 4, 1980.

27. Marty Franks, interview with the author, January 7, 1986.

28. Robert Hacker, interview with the author, March 17, 1985

29. Timothy Wirth, interview with the author, May 22, 1986; interview with the author's researcher Lauren Simon Ostrow, May 28, 1986.

30. Roger Stone, interview with the author, February 13, 1986.

31. Paige Reffe, interview with the author's researcher Lauren Simon Ostrow, April 28, 1986.

32. *The New York Times* September 13, 1983 p. B1

33. Ed Martin, interview with the author's researcher Lauren Simon Ostrow, May 29, 1986.

34. Alan Simpson, interview with the author, April 9, 1986.

35. David Himes, interview with the author, February 5, 1986.

36. Bill Bradley, interview with the author, February 20, 1986.

37. *Ibid.*

38. David Durenberger, interview with the author, May 9, 1986.

39. The 1974 figures came from *Vital Statistics on Congress, 1984–85 Edition* (Washington: American Enterprise Institute for Public Policy Research, 1984) with assistance from editor Michael Malbin; the 1986 figures were drawn from the Federal Election Commission report on 1986 congressional spending, released May 10, 1987.

40. David Cohen, interview with the author, March 25, 1986.

41. Thomas Eagleton, interview with the author, February 21, 1986.

42. *Ibid.*

43. Charles McC. Matthias, interview with the author, January 14, 1986.

44. Patricia Schroeder, interview with the author, January 30, 1986.

45. Don Edwards, interview with the author, January 28, 1986.

8. PENTAGON GAMES

1. The nine newspapers are *The New York Times, The Washington Post, The Wall Street Journal*, the Baltimore *Sun, The Washington Times, The Christian Science Monitor, The Philadelphia Inquirer*, the *New York Daily News*, and the Chicago *Tribune*.

2. Cris Schall, interview with the author, June 12, 1986.

3. Harry Zubkoff, interview with the author, June 12, 1986.

4. Richard DeLauer, interview with the author, March 4, 1986.

5. Denny Smith, interview with the author, February 26, 1986.

6. Dina Rasor, who runs a clearing house for information on defense issues based essentially on information from internal Pentagon critics, used the term as the title of a book; see Dina Rasor, *Pentagon Underground* (New York: Times Books, 1985).

7. Dina Rasor, interview with the author, April 23, 1987.

8. Denny Smith, interview with the author, March 7, 1986.

9. Information on Divad's test-performance failure came to the author from five Pentagon officials, civilian and military, who were involved with evaluation but who wanted to remain anonymous.

10. Denny Smith, interview with the author, February 26, 1986.

11. James Ambrose, interview with the author, April 28, 1986.

12. Denny Smith, interview with the author, March 10, 1986.

13. Tom Carter, interview with the author, April 30, 1987.

14. Jim Burton, interview with the author, February 4, 1987.

15. In connection with the Pentagon, the phrase was coined by Gordon Adams in his book, *The Politics of Defense Contracting: The Iron Triangle* (New York, Council on Economic Priorities, 1981). Political scientists have used the term *subgovernments* to describe such networks in a variety of fields, not just defense.

16. Anthony Battista, interview with the author, March 7, 1986.

17. Warren Rudman, interview with the author, February 28, 1986.

18. Denny Smith, interview with the author, February 26, 1986.

19. Tom Carter, interview with the author, April 30, 1987. Other officials confirmed this but asked not to be identified as sources.

20. Gregg Easterbrook, "Divad," *The Atlantic*, October 1982.

21. Charles Bennett, interview with the author, March 6, 1986.

22. Richard Bolling, interview with the author, January 15, 1986.

23. Gordon Adams, interview with the author, February 17, 1986.

24. Joseph Addabbo, interview with the author, February 26, 1986.

25. Joseph Addabbo, interview with the author, February 20, 1986.

26. Thomas Downey, interview with the author, February 21, 1986.

27. Bill Gray, interview with the author, September 15, 1985.

28. John Seiberling, interview with the author, March 7, 1986.

29. Gary Hart, interview with the author, February 20, 1986.

30. Richard Stubbings, *The Defense Game* (New York: Harper and Row, 1986) p. xii.

31. Lawrence Korb, interview with the author, March 21, 1986.

32. Michael Gordon, "Defense Focus: Ready or Not" *National Journal*, June 8, 1985, p. 1387. Gordon kindly showed the author the handwritten text of Senator Stevens's note.

33. Lawrence Korb, interview with the author, March 6, 1986.

34. Warren Rudman, interview with the author, February 28, 1986.

35. *Defense Week*, July 19, 1982.

36. *Congressional Record*, July 21, 1982. p. S8746.

37. David Pryor, interview with the author, March 13, 1986.

38. William Cohen, interview with the author, March 12, 1986.

39. Lawrence Korb, interviews with the author, May 18 and 22, 1987. In late November, 1987, Korb filed suit against Raytheon, charging that his constitutional right to free speech had been violated.

40. John Lehman, interview with the author, March 21, 1986.

41. Lawrence Korb, interview with the author, March 6, 1986.

42. *The New York Times*, July 30, 1983, p. 1.

43. *Atlanta Constitution*, April 28, 1987, p. 1.

44. William Kaufman, interview with the author, March 18, 1986.

45. Barry Goldwater, speech on Senate floor, *Congressional Record*, October 3, 1985, p. S12533.

46. Edward Luttwak, *The Pentagon and the Art of War.* (New York: Simon & Schuster, 1984), pp. 24–28.

47. David C. Jones, interview with the author, March 13, 1986.

48. Anthony Battista, interview with the author, March 3, 1986.

49. Warren Rudman, interview with the author, February 25, 1986.

50. Sam Nunn, interview with the author, March 10, 1986.

51. Richard Bolling, interview with the author, January 15, 1986.

52. David C. Jones, interview with the author, March 13, 1986.

53. James Woolsey, interview with the author, February 14, 1986.

54. Melvin R. Laird, "Not a Binge, but a Buildup," *The Washington Post*, November 19, 1980, p. A17.

55. Dave McCurdy, interview with the author, February 26, 1986.

56. Sam Nunn, interview with the author, March 10, 1986.

57. Richard DeLauer, interview with the author, March 4, 1986.

58. Caspar Weinberger, interview with the author, March 28, 1986.

59. Robert Dole, interview with the author, February 24, 1986.

60. Les Aspin, interview with the author, August 1, 1985.

61. Sam Nunn, interview with the author, March 10, 1986.

62. William Cohen, interview with the author, March 12, 1986.

63. Pete Domenici, interview with the author, April 11, 1986.

64. This account comes from Pete Domenici, interview with the author, April 11, 1986; Steve Bell, a senior aide to Domenici, and two senior officials who were in the room with President Reagan.

65. The President's Blue-Ribbon Commission on Defense Management, "An Interim Report to the President," February 28, 1986, p. 5.

66. David C. Jones, interview with the author, March 13, 1986.

67. E. C. Meyer, interview with the author, May 22, 1987.

9. THE NEW LOBBYING GAME

1. David C. Jones, interview with the author, March 24, 1986.

2. James A. Baker III, interview with the author, April 5, 1986.

3. Howard H. Baker, Jr., interview with the author, January 14, 1986.

4. Doug Bloomfield, interview with the author, October 28, 1985.

5. Thomas Dine, interview with the author, July 3, 1986.

6. *Ibid.*

7. Doug Bloomfield, interview with the author, October 28, 1985.

8. Bob Asher, interview with the author, July 16, 1986.

9. *The Wall Street Journal,* June 24, 1987, p. 21, showed eighty pro-Israel PACs with expenditures of $6.9 million, but this includes operating expenses. The political donations were about $4 million.

10. Daniel Evans, interview with the author, June 25, 1986.

11. Christopher Matthews, interview with the author, August 7, 1985.

12. William Greider, *The Washington Post,* November 5, 1978, C1.

13. Norm Ornstein, interview with the author, July 9, 1986.

14. David Cohen, interview with the author, March 25, 1986.

15. Terry Lierman, interview with the author, July 2, 1986.

16. Tony Coelho, interview with the author, March 20, 1986.

17. Wayne Thevnot, interview with author's researcher Lauren Simon Ostrow, July 17, 1986.

18. Charles Peters, *How Washington Really Works* (Boston: Addison-Wesley, 1980), p.6

19. Anne Wexler, interview with the author, July 23, 1986.

20. Tom Korologos, interview with the author, July 11, 1986.

21. Jim Mooney, interview with the author, July 11, 1986

22. Gray's strategy was outlined by Sheila Tate, who was with Hill & Knowlton in 1979–80, interview with the author, February 20, 1986.

23. Betsy Weltner, interview with the author, February 10, 1986.

24. Roger Stone, interview with the author, February 13, 1986.

25. Robert Beckel, interview with the author, March 3, 1986.

26. Robert Beckel, interview with the author, February 5, 1986

27. Fritz Elmendorf, interview with the author, July 22, 1986.

28. Mike McAdams, interview with the author, March 19, 1986.

29. Lynn Pounian, interview with the author, March 19, 1986.

30. Samples of the material and internal memos from Matt Reese's companies were obtained from Reese's aides and other sources by the author.

31. Jonathan Perman, an aide to Percy, shared findings and letters with the author's researcher Lauren Simon Ostrow, May 22, 1986. Also see Ann Cooper, "Middleman Mail," *National Journal,* September 14, 1985, pp. 2036–2041.

32. Nicholas Bush, interview with the author, July 11, 1986.

33. Victor Kamber, interview with the author, November 18, 1986.

34. Federal Election Commission reports, May 10, 1987, p. 1, and May 31, 1987, p. 7.

35. Federal Election Commission report, May 21, 1987.

36. FEC report, May 21, 1987.

37. Barry Goldwater, testimony before the Senate Rules and Administration Committee, September 29, 1983.

38. Kenneth Schlossberg, *The New York Times,* May 14, 1986, p. 27.

39. Fred Wertheimer, interview with the author, March 26, 1986.

40. Lloyd Cutler, interview with the author, March 31, 1986.

41. Michael J. Malbin, ed., *Money and Politics in the United States* (Chatham, N.J.: Chatham House and American Enterprise Institute for Public Policy Research, 1984), 246–247.

42. Charls Walker, interview with the author, January 28, 1986.

43. Mark Green, "Eight Good Reasons for Reining in PACs," *The Washington Post,* March 23, 1987, p. A11.

44. Thomas Edsall, *The Washington Post,* January 28, 1987, p. A19.

45. Anne Wexler, interview with the author, January 31, 1986.

46. David Cohen, interview with the author, March 25, 1986.

47. Robert Strauss, interview with the author, February 11, 1986.

48. Thomas Eagleton, interview with the author, February 21, 1986. In a survey of 114 members

of Congress by the Center for Responsive Politics in Washington, released on January 12, 1988, 209 of the members admitted that campaign contributions affected their voting. Only half said that contributions did not influence them; the rest were more qualified in their assessment.

49. Mary Hasenfus, director of Political Affairs, U.S. Chamber of Commerce, interview with the author's researcher William Nell, May 26, 1987.

50. Tony Coelho, interview with the author, March 20, 1986.

51. Brooks Jackson, *The Wall Street Journal,* October 24, 1986, page 58.

52. This figure is derived from two reports by the Federal Election Commission, on campaign spending and PAC activity, released in May 1987, in which it was reported that 395 House incumbents spent $149 million, of which $67.7 million came from PAC contributions.

53. Materials from Phillip Sterns's lawsuit were obtained by the author's researcher Kurt Eichenwald.

54. Fred Wertheimer, president of Common Cause, quoted by the Associated Press in *The Washington Post,* March 21, 1987, p. A3.

55. Fred Wertheimer, interview with the author, March 18, 1986.

56. Joseph Califano, interview with the author, May 10, 1987.

57. Ed Roeder, interview with the author's researcher Lauren Simon Ostrow, August 5, 1986.

58. See Common Cause, *Financing the Finance Committee,* March 19, 1986.

59. See Common Cause, *Financing the Finance Committee,* March 19, 1986. The estimate of the Joint Congressional Committee on Taxation was that the administration's first tax proposal in November 1984, would have imposed a new tax burden of at least $51 billion on the life, health, property, and casualty insurance industries and on employer-provided, union-sponsored fringe benefits. The final Reagan plan, sent to Congress May 28, 1985, reduced that burden to about $25 billion.

60. Bob Packwood, interview with the author, July 12, 1986.

61. Daniel Patrick Moynihan, interview with the author, July 2, 1986.

62. Donald Regan, interview with the author, June 12, 1986.

63. Material on the former officials who became lobbyists for foreign governments, including Michael Deaver's contracts, was obtained from Justice Department files by the author's researcher Kurt Eichenwald.

64. Kenneth Schlossberg, *The New York Times,* May 14, 1986, p. 27.

10. SHADOW GOVERNMENT

1. David Brockway interview with the author, August 22, 1986.

2. Bob Packwood and Bill Diefenderfer interviews with the author, May 27 and July 12, 1986.

3. David Brockway, interviews with the author, June 13, August 8, and August 20, 1986.

4. Stuart Eizenstat, interview with the author, August 8, 1986.

5. Michael Malbin, *Unelected Representatives.* New York: Basic Books, 1979. pp. 30–38.

6. Bryce Harlow, interview with the author, November 13, 1985.

7. Michael Malbin, interview with the author, August 18, 1986. These figures are derived from Norman J. Ornstein, et al., *Vital Statistics on Congress, 1987–1988* Washington: Congressional Quarterly, 1987.

8. Daniel Patrick Moynihan, lecture, March 28, 1978.

9. David Aylward, interview with the author, February 4, 1986.

10. *The New York Times,* September 25, 1977, p E4.

11. This notion of tribal customs and relationships in Congress is developed by J. Michael Weatherford, an anthropologist and former legislative aide to Senator John Glenn of Ohio, in *Tribes on the Hill* (New York: Rawson, Wade, 1981).

12. William Cohen, interview with the author, March 12, 1986.

13. Tony Coelho, interview with the author, March 20, 1986.

14. Howard H. Baker, Jr., interview with the author, March 11, 1986.

15. This account, among others, is retold in detail by Rochelle Jones and Peter Woll in *The Private World of Congress* (New York: The Free Press, 1979), pp. 155–156.

16. *The Washington Post,* October 31, 1977, p.2.

17. The account of the debate comes from the *Congressional Record*, December 23, 1982, pp. S16047–S16060, and the account of the staff role comes from senators Warren Rudman, Alan Simpson, aides to Howard Baker, and from the Senate staff.

18. David A. Stockman, interview with the author, February 1986.

19. Pete Domenici, interview with the author, April 12, 1986.

20. This account was developed by interviews with these and other participants by the author's researcher Lauren Ostrow.

21. Fritz Hollings, testifying before the Senate Appropriations subcommittee on the legislative branch, April 21, 1975, p. 1241.

22. Rudolph G. Penner, testimony before the House Committee on Government Operations, October 17, 1985, hearings, pp. 156–157.

23. Ted Stevens of Alaska at hearing of the Senate Appropriations subcommittee on the legislative branch, July 1986.

24. Dave McCurdy, interview with the author, February 26, 1986.

25. *The New York Times*, June 28, 1982, p. A13.

26. Robert Dornan, interview with the author, August 13, 1986.

27. Anthony Battista, interviews with the author, March 3 and 7, 1986.

28. Thomas Downey, interview with the author, February 21, 1986.

29. Samuel Stratton, interviews with the author, December 2, 1985 and August 15, 1986.

30. Thomas Downey, interview with the author, February 21, 1986.

31. Jimmy Carter, interview with the author, August 12, 1976.

32. Ronald Reagan, interview with the author, February 28, 1980.

33. Richard Darman, interview with the author, April 5, 1986.

34. This account of the workings of the White House staff came from about twenty background interviews of the senior staff members and their aides with the author in 1981.

35. This draws on the excellent account of the evolution of the presidential apparatus during six presidencies, Roosevelt through Nixon, given by Stephen Hess in *Organizing the Presidency* (Washington: Brookings Institution, 1976). The recent staff figures came from the Reagan White House in August 1986.

36. Paul Light, interview with the author, August 15, 1986.

37. Alexander M. Haig, Jr., *Caveat* (New York: Macmillan, 1984), p. 83.

38. Michael Deaver, interviews with the author, June 10, 1985 and January 24, 1988.

39. Haig, *op. cit.*, p. 84.

40. Richard Darman, interview with the author, April 5, 1986.

41. Michael K. Deaver, interview with the author, June 10, 1985.

42. At the senior echelons of government, having cabinet rank is enormously important. After four years as White House chief of staff, Jim Baker wanted a top cabinet post to gain public authority and prestige. Jeane Kirkpatrick told friends that she probably would not have become ambassador to the United Nations if Reagan had not promised the post would carry cabinet rank.

43. Haig, *op. cit.*, p. 12.

44. Haig, *op. cit.*, p. 60.

45. This account comes from three senior White House officials and two State Department officials close to Haig.

46. Haig, interview with the author, February 20, 1985.

47. Haig, *op. cit.*, p. 17.

48. Michael J. Blumenthal, interview with the author, November 25, 1986.

49. In *Gambling With History* (New York: Doubleday, 1983), Laurence I. Barrett gives an account rich in detail on the Reagan White House in its first two years. The chapter on Meese is especially good.

50. Edwin Meese, in one of several interviews with the author during early 1981.

51. Tony Kornheiser of *The Washington Post* did an excellent story on Baker on a turkey shoot, January 18, 1981, p. G1.

52. From the author's background interviews with several of those most closely involved.

53. James A. Baker III, quoted in press conference on *The McNeil/Lehrer Newshour,* aired on the Public Broadcasting System, January 26, 1981.

54. The account that follows is drawn from background interviews by the author with five officials closely involved, all of whom spoke on condition that they not be quoted by name.

55. This account is constructed with interviews from two senior White House officials, both or whom asked to remain anonymous.

56. Richard E. Neustadt, interview with the author, November 14, 1986.

57. Ellen Hume and Jane Mayer, "The Rise and Fall of Don Regan," *Regardie's,* January 1987, p. 96.

11. THE AGENDA GAME

1. Thomas E. Cronin, *The State of the Presidency* (Boston: Little, Brown & Co., 1975) p. 84.

2. Harry McPherson, *A Political Education* (Boston: Little, Brown & Co., 1972), p. 268.

3. See Tom Wicker, *JFK and LBJ* (New York: Morrow, 1968), pp. 135–48.

4. James B. Reston, *The New York Times,* November 15, 1963.

5. Mark Siegel, interview with the author, January 2, 1986.

6. Robert Shogan, *Promises to Keep: Carter's First Hundred Days* (New York, Crowell, 1977) p. 204.

7. James MacGregor Burns, *The Power to Lead* (New York: Simon and Schuster, 1984), p. 34.

8. This account comes from both Carter and Reagan White House officials and draws on *Countdown to the White House—the Reagan Transition,* a documentary produced by WGBH-TV in Boston and Harvard University's Institute of Politics, aired on WGBH, January 21, 1981.

9. John Rogers, interview with the author, October 17, 1986, and Eugene Eidenberg, interview with the author, October 22, 1986.

10. Reagan's Chicago speech on September 9, 1980, the foundation for Reagan's agenda in 1981, had five goals: (1) controlling the growth of government spending; (2) cutting personal income tax rates and reducing business taxes; (3) trimming back government regulations; (4) sound, stable monetary policy; (5) consistency in economic policies.

11. David Gergen, interview with the author, August 6, 1985.

12. Cronin, *op. cit.,* pp. 264–5.

13. Reagan transition team, unpublished *Final Report of the Initial Actions Project,* January 29, 1981, p. 5.

14. David Gergen, interview with the author, August 6, 1985.

15. Jude Wanniski, *The Way the World Works* (New York: Simon and Schuster, 1983), pp. ix–xxxvii. His book is a supply-side bible.

16. *Ibid.,* pp. xii–xiv.

17. Burns, *op. cit.* pp. 59–62. Burns neatly divides the New Right into the market right and the moralistic right.

18. Thomas P. O'Neill, Jr., interview with the author, October 31, 1986.

19. David Gergen, interview with the author, August 6, 1985.

20. David A. Stockman, interview with the author, January 6, 1986.

21. Stuart Eizenstat, interview with the author, August 8, 1986.

22. David A. Stockman, interview with the author, January 6, 1986.

23. *Countdown to the White House—the Reagan Transition,* a documentary produced by WGBH Boston and Harvard University's Institute of Politics, aired on WGBH January 21, 1981.

24. David A. Stockman, *The Triumph of Politics: Why the Reagan Revolution Failed* (New York: Harper & Row, 1986), p. 87.

25. Richard Wirthlin, interview with the author, November 1, 1985, gave an account of the meeting and Reagan's reaction.

26. Summary of the final report of the Initial Actions Project, January 29, 1981, p. 22.

27. Stockman, *op. cit.*, p. 56.

28. Pete V. Domenici, interview with the author, April 11, 1986; and Steve Bell, interview with the author, January 26, 1986.

29. James A. Baker, III, interview with the author, January 26, 1986.

30. Howard H. Baker, Jr., interview with the author, January 14, 1986.

31. David A. Stockman, interviews with the author, January 6 and 7, 1986.

32. This account comes from interviews with six senior Reagan lieutenants, all of whom asked to remain anonymous except Stockman.

33. William Greider, "The Education of David Stockman," *Atlantic Monthly*, December 1981, pp. 46–47.

34. Christopher Matthews, interview with the author, August 7, 1985.

35. Dennis Thomas, interview with the author, January 8, 1986.

36. See Martin Schram, "GOP Shot Across Democrats' Bow Fizzles in Barrel," *The Washington Post*, August 11, 1984, p. A8. House Republican budget experts also tried comparisons with a putative Mondale-Ferraro budget, but Reagan's deficits were still roughly double potential Democratic budgets.

37. James A. Baker III, interview with the author, February 25, 1986.

38. Ed Rollins, interview with the author, December 9, 1985; and Richard Wirthlin, interview with the author, February 18, 1986.

39. Richard Wirthlin, interview with the author, February 18, 1986.

40. Ed Rollins, interview with the author, December 9, 1985.

41. Richard Wirthlin, interview with the author, February 18, 1986.

42. Kirk O'Donnell, interview with the author, June 3, 1985.

43. James A. Baker III, interview with the author, November 7, 1986.

44. Donald T. Regan, interview with the author, April 26, 1985.

45. Arthur Burns, *The United States and Germany: A Vital Partnership* (New York: Council on Foreign Relations, 1986), pp. 12–14.

46. *The New York Times*, April 18, 1945, p. 1.

47. Michael K. Deaver, interview with the author, June 10, 1985.

48. William Woessner, interview with the author, September 18, 1986.

49. William Henkel, interview with the author, September 20, 1986.

50. Hans Tuck, interview with the author, November 5, 1986.

51. Stuart Spencer, interview with the author, March 8, 1986.

52. Ed Rollins, interview with the author, December 9, 1985.

53. Frederick Ahearn, interview with the author, January 5, 1987.

54. This account is drawn from interviews with William Henkel, September 20, 25, and October 16, 1986, and from two other close Reagan associates.

55. Michael Deaver, interview with the author, June 10, 1985.

56. Richard Wirthlin, interview with the author, September 17, 1986.

57. Michael Deaver, interview with the author, September 17, 1985.

58. Stockman, *op. cit.*, p. 133.

59. Greider, *op. cit.*

60. See *Economic Report of the President* to Congress, February 1986 (Washington: U.S. Government Printing Office, 1986), p.254. Reagan's average of 2.36% and Carter's of 3.07% real growth were derived from the GNP figures year by year and matching figures from *World Economic Outlook*, April 1986 (Washington: International Monetary Fund, 1986), p. 180.

61. David A. Stockman, interview with the author, January 6, 1986.

62. David Stockman, interview with the author, January 6 and 7, 1986; account partly confirmed by other officials speaking on background. See also Stockman, *op. cit.*, p.97.

63. David A. Stockman, interview with the author, January 7, 1986.

64. William Schneider, Jr., "National Defense," in *Agenda for Progress* (Washington: The Heritage Foundation, 1981), p. 8.

65. Richard A. Stubbing, interview with the author, November 3, 1986. A high Pentagon

official, speaking anonymously, confirmed Stubbing's account. Also see Richard A. Stubbing, *The Defense Game* (New York: Harper & Row, 1986), pp. 374-5.

66. William Schneider, Jr., interview with the author, October 28, 1986.

67. Caspar Weinberger, interview with the author, March 28, 1986.

68. William Schneider, Jr., interview with the author, October 28, 1986.

69. David A. Stockman, interview with the author, January 7, 1986.

70. Stockman, *op. cit.*, p. 133.

71. Stockman, *op. cit.*, pp. 97-98.

72. David Stockman, "Postscript: Who Shot John?" in *The Triumph of Politics* (New York: Avon, 1987), pp. 446-447.

12. THE IMAGE GAME

1. Sheila Tate, interview with the author, February 14, 1986.

2. Joseph Canzeri, interview with the author, February 5, 1986.

3. Christopher Matthews, spokesman and media adviser to House Speaker Tip O'Neill, coined the phrase "Hang a lantern on your problem."

4. Fred Dutton, interview with the author, December 5, 1985.

5. Edmund Morris, *The Rise of Theodore Roosevelt* (New York: Ballantine, 1979) pp. 648-657.

6. John Gunther, *Roosevelt in Retrospect* (New York: Harper, 1950), p. 62.

7. See Samuel Kernell, *Going Public: New Strategies of Presidential Leadership* (Washington: Congressional Quarterly Press, 1986), pp. 1-5.

8. Tony Schwartz, *Media: The Second God* (Garden City, N.Y.: Anchor Books, 1983), pp. 114-115.

9. Norman Ornstein and Michal Robinson, "The Case of Our Disappearing Congress," *TV Guide*, January 11, 1986, pp. 4-10. Their study compares the coverage of the three networks in September 1985 and September 1975.

10. In *Channels of Power* (New York: Basic Books, Inc., 1983), Austin Ranney has an excellent chapter on "Bias in Television News" in which he argues that the "structural bias" of television news—the technical and dramatic demands of the medium—is more important in influencing coverage than the political ideology of network editors or correspondents.

11. Jody Powell, interview with the author, September 16, 1986.

12. Theodore H. White, *The Making of the President 1972* (New York: Atheneum, 1973), p. 245.

13. Lee Atwater, interview with the author, February 6, 1986.

14. Lloyd Cutler, "Foreign Policy on Deadline," *Foreign Policy*, number 56, Fall 1984, p. 121.

15. Chris Wallace, interview with the author, September 23, 1986.

16. David Gergen, interview with the author, February 25, 1986.

17. David Gergen, interviews with the author, September 22, 1985 and February 25, 1986.

18. Steven R. Weisman, "The President and the Press," *New York Times Magazine*, October 14, 1984, p. 37.

19. Ed Fouhy, interview with the author, March 4, 1986.

20. David Gergen, interview with the author, February 25, 1986.

21. Sam Donaldson, interview with the author, March 5, 1986.

22. David Gergen, interview with the author, February 25, 1986.

23. William Henkel, interview with the author, September 10, 1986.

24. Lesley Stahl, *CBS Evening News*, October 4, 1984. Stahl shared her script with the author.

25. Lesley Stahl, interview with the author, September 20, 1986.

26. Michael Deaver, interview with the author, September 11, 1985.

27. *A Nation at Risk: The Imperative for Educational Reform*, April 26, 1983, produced by an eighteen-member national commission appointed by Education Secretary T. H. Bell.

28. David Gergen, interview with the author, February 25, 1986.

29. Michael Deaver, interview with the author, February 4, 1986.

30. Richard Wirthlin, interviews with the author, September 17 and 21, 1986.

31. *Newsweek*, June 27, 1983, p. 61. The Gallup Organization interviewed 760 adults by telephone, June 15–16, 1983.

32. William Henkel, interview with the author, September 25, 1986.

33. Chris Wallace, interview with the author, September 23, 1986.

34. William Henkel, interview with the author, September 25, 1986.

35. William Henkel, interview with the author, September 16, 1985.

36. President Reagan, informal talk with the author and three other correspondents at the White House, May 20, 1985.

37. Lou Cannon, *The Washington Post*, March 5, 1984, p. 2.

38. George Tames, interview with the author, September 30, 1986.

39. Ronald Reagan, interview with the author, Bernard Weinraub, Gerald Boyd, and Leslie Gelb, all of *The New York Times*, February 11, 1985.

40. See Robert M. Entman, "The Imperial Media," in *Politics and the Oval Office* (San Francisco: Institute for Contemporary Studies, 1981), pp. 79–101.

41. Lesley Stahl, interview with the author, September 20, 1986.

42. Sam Donaldson, interview with the author, March 5, 1986.

43. Chris Wallace, interview with the author, September 23, 1986.

44. Sam Donaldson, interview with the author, March 5, 1986.

45. Leonard Downie, "How Britain Managed the News," *The Washington Post*, August 20, 1982, p. 15.

46. See reports of the Reporters Committee for Freedom of the Press, printed in *The News Media and the Law*, January–February 1984, pp. 4–5.

47. As secretary of State, Dean Rusk frequently met on Friday afternoons with regular State Department reporters for a background interview. As one of those reporters, I remember the occasion on February 9, 1968, when Rusk exploded with frustration at press reporting of the war, charging that reporters were more interested in winning Pulitzer prizes than helping their country, demanding, "Which side are you on?"

48. These findings are from telephone interviews of 1,249 adults nationwide taken December 8–12, 1983, by The Harris Survey.

49. Bill Plante, interview with the author, September 9, 1986, and transcript of White House Press Briefing, October 25, 1983, pp. 27–28.

50. Larry Speakes, "Bookshelf: Sam Donaldson's Own Story," *The Wall Street Journal*, March 18, 1987, p. 28

51. James A. Baker III, interviewed on the Public Broadcasting System program *Inside Story* with Hodding Carter, January 11, 1984.

52. Larry Speakes, in an interview on the Mutual Broadcasting Company, January 14, 1984.

53. See the index of administration actions compiled by the Reporters Committee for Freedom of the Press in March 1986. An earlier summary appeared in Floyd Abrams, "The New Effort to Control Information," in *The New York Times Magazine*, September 25, 1983.

54. The photographs, apparently taken by a spy satellite, showed the Soviet Navy's first nuclear-powered aircraft carrier under construction. They appeared in the August 1984 edition of *Jane's Defence Weekly*.

55. "Information and Personnel Security," published by the General Accounting Office, September 1986, p. 3.

56. Jimmy Carter, interviewed by Hodding Carter on "Whose News Is It?," *Inside Story*, aired January 11, 1984 on the Public Broadcasting System.

57. Austin Ranney, *Channels of Power* (New York: Basic Books, 1983), pp. 120.

58. Richard A. Darman, interview with the author, July 6, 1984.

59. Stephen Hess, *The Government/Press Connection* (Washington: The Brookings Institution, 1984), see Chapter 7, especially pp. 77–78.

60. James B. Reston, *The Artillery of the Press* (New York: Harper & Row, 1967), p. 66.

61. President Reagan, appearing before the American Society of Newspaper Editors on April 9, 1986. He and William Casey argued on behalf of their restrictive policies.

62. Henry Catto, assistant secretary of Defense for Public Affairs, briefing, January 14, 1982.

63. Four top officials involved in this episode spoke to the author on assurance that they would not be identified.

64. This account comes from the author's interviews with two of the participants, who asked to remain anonymous.

65. The November 1 Reagan directive said that lie detector tests would apply to "all individuals with access to United States Government sensitive compartmented information, communications security information, and other special access program information" (*The New York Times*, December 20, 1985, p. 1.). The General Accounting Office estimated that 133,781 government employes and contractor personnel held clearances for "sensitive compartmented information" and another 49,231 were in other "special access programs" for highly classified information (*The Washington Post*, December 21, 1985, p. 1, 8).

66. Bob Woodward, *The Washington Post*, October 2, 1986, p. A1.

67. *The New York Times*, November 16, 1986, p. 1

68. Arthur Miller, *Death of a Salesman* (New York: The Viking Press, 1949), p. 138. See an excellent piece comparing Reagan and Willy Loman by Philip Geyelin, "Death of a Sales Pitch: The Unmasking of Reagan," *The Washington Post*, February 22, 1987, p. C1.

13. THE COALITION GAME

1. Howard H. Baker, Jr., interview with the author, January 14, 1986.

2. Newt Gingrich, interview with the author, January 22, 1986.

3. Howard H. Baker, Jr., interview with the author, January 14, 1986.

4. Max Freidersdorf, interview with the author, July 12, 1981.

5. Douglass Cater, interviewed in *The Great Society Remembered*, broadcast on PBS, October 28, 1985.

6. James A. Baker, interview with the author, November 7, 1986.

7. William Armstrong, interview with the author, November 17, 1986.

8. Howard H. Baker, Jr., interview with the author, January 14, 1986.

9. Jack Nelson, "The Reagan Legacy," in Paul Duke et al., *Beyond Reagan: The Politics of Upheaval* (New York: Warner Books, 1986), p. 103.

10. Mark Nimitz, conversation with the author, January 17, 1985.

11. Mark Siegel, interview with the author, January 2, 1986.

12. *The Washington Post*, November 19, 1981, p. E1.

13. James Leach, interview with the author, November 10, 1986.

14. Richard Darman, interview with the author, November 23, 1986.

15. Howard Baker, interviews with the author, January 14 and March 11, 1986.

16. Pete Domenici, interview with the author, November 17, 1986.

17. Howard H. Baker, Jr., interview with the author, January 14, 1986.

18. Christopher Dodd, interview with the author, February 19, 1986.

19. Warren Rudman, interview with the author, July 30, 1985.

20. James A. Miller, interview with the author, January 13, 1986.

21. William Armstrong, interview with the author, November 17, 1986.

22. Kenneth Duberstein, interview with the author, February 3, 1986.

23. Robert Michel, interview with the author, February 6, 1986.

24. Phil Gramm, interview with the author, December 16, 1985.

25. Lee Atwater, interview with the author, July 17, 1981.

26. *The Washington Post*, May 10, 1981, p. 3.

27. Lee Atwater, interview with the author, January 14, 1986.

28. Bill Green, interview with the author, November 11, 1986.

29. Stockman spelled out his view of the numbers and his shock at the congressional action

in *The Triumph of Politics: Why the Reagan Revolution Failed* (New York: Harper & Row, 1986), pp. 194–198.

30. Several of the White House officials who took part in that meeting gave me this account at the time, and it appeared in my article, "Coping with Congress," *New York Times Magazine*, August 9, 1981, p. 12ff.

31. Stockman, *op. cit.*, p. 229.

32. Kenneth Duberstein, interview with the author, February 3, 1986.

33. James Sundquist, interview with the author, July 28, 1981.

34. Associated Press, November 8, 1984.

35. "Hill Backing for Reagan Continues to Decline," *Congressional Quarterly*, January 11, 1986, p. 68.

36. Robert Dole, interview with the author, January 11, 1986.

37. Thomas P. O'Neill, Jr., interview with the author, November 6, 1986.

38. Jack Kemp, interview with the author, March 24, 1986.

39. Donald Regan, interview with the author, April 24, 1985.

40. Thomas P. O'Neill, Jr., interview with the author, October 31, 1986.

41. Thomas P. O'Neill, Jr., interview with the author, October 16, 1985.

42. Robert Dole, interview with the author, January 11, 1986.

43. *Ibid.*

44. Slade Gorton, interview with the author, July 26, 1985.

45. John Sherman, interview with the author, September 28, 1985.

46. Dan Rostenkowski, interview with the author, January 3, 1986; and James A. Baker III, interview with the author, February 25, 1986.

47. All five participants gave similar accounts of the meeting.

48. Robert Michel, interview with the author, Dec. 5, 1985.

49. *The Washington Post*, December 10, 1985, p. 1.

50. Jack Kemp, interview with the author, March 24, 1986.

14. THE OPPOSITION GAME

1. Franklin Delano Roosevelt, quoted in Richard B. Cheney and Lynn V. Cheney, *Kings of the Hill* (New York: Continuum, 1983), p. 172.

2. John W. Finney, interview with the author, January 13, 1985.

3. Thomas P. O'Neill, Jr., interview with the author, January 2, 1986.

4. Both Speaker O'Neill and his close aides, Ari Weiss and Kirk O'Donnell, emphasized this point repeatedly in several interviews with the author.

5. Thomas P. O'Neill, Jr., interview with the author, October 16, 1985.

6. Thomas P. O'Neill, Jr., *The New York Times*, May 16, 1986, p. A35. He said many of the same things in 1981 and throughout his decade as speaker.

7. Kirk O'Donnell, interview with the author, December 12, 1986.

8. Dom Bonafede, "For the Democratic Party, It's a Time for Rebuilding and Seeking New Ideas," *National Journal*, February 21, 1981.

9. *The Washington Post*, May 8, 1981, p. 1.

10. Richard Bolling, interview with the author, January 15, 1986.

11. Thomas P. O'Neill, Jr., interview with the author, November 6, 1986.

12. Norm Ornstein, interview with the author, January 20, 1986.

13. Thomas P. O'Neill, Jr., interview with the author, November 6, 1986.

14. Thomas P. O'Neill, Jr., addressing the House Democratic Caucus, May 5, 1981.

15. Thomas P. O'Neill, Jr., interview with the author, October 16, 1985.

16. *Ibid.*

17. Dan Rostenkowski, speech to the Economic Club of Chicago, February 17, 1981.

18. Rather inconsistently, O'Neill contended both that the 1980 election had not been a mandate for conservative fiscal policies but only a repudiation of Jimmy Carter, and also that the

nation's mood was so conservative in 1981 that even Carter would have had to carry out much of Reagan's program. In an interview with the author on November 6, 1986, he said, "If Jimmy Carter had been reelected president that year, you would have had a tax cut, number one; you would have had increases in the military, and you would have had cuts across the line in the budget."

19. Thomas P. O'Neill, Jr., interview with the author, November 6, 1986.

20. Kenneth Duberstein, interview with the author, February 3, 1986.

21. Thomas P. O'Neill, Jr., interview with the author, October 16, 1985.

22. Richard Bolling, interview with the author, January 15, 1986.

23. Thomas P. O'Neill, Jr., interview with the author, January 2, 1986.

24. Christopher Matthews, interview with the author, August 7, 1985. Also, *The New York Times,* June 17, 1985, p. 1; *The Washington Post,* June 17, 1985, p. A1 and p. B1.

25. This account comes from aides to both President Reagan and Speaker O'Neill in background interviews in June–July 1981. A slightly different version appeared in Hedrick Smith, "Coping with Congress," *New York Times Magazine,* August 9, 1981, pp. 12 ff.

26. Thomas E. Mann, interview with the author, December 22, 1986.

27. Christopher Matthews, interview with the author, August 7, 1985.

28. Joe Foote of Southern Illinois University and former press secretary to Carl Albert, reported that O'Neill's TV appearances from 1979 to 1985 averaged 120 annually, compared to forty for Albert and thirty for McCormack. Robert C. Byrd, the Senate majority leader in 1977–80, had eighty.

29. Kirk O'Donnell, "Political Agenda for House Democrats," memorandum to the speaker, August 4, 1981.

30. This account comes from one of the participants, who asked not to be identified.

31. This account comes from interviews with O'Neill, Bolling, Ari Weiss, Howard Baker, Jim Baker, Stockman, Ken Duberstein, Kirk O'Donnell, Christopher Matthews, and Tom Griscom. Also see Martin Schram, *The Washington Post,* May 2, 1981, p. A1.

32. David Stockman, interview with the author, January 7, 1986.

33. *Ibid.*

34. Thomas P. O'Neill, Jr., interview with the author, October 16, 1985.

35. Jim Wright, interview with the author, December 18, 1985.

36. Thomas P. O'Neill, Jr., interview with the author, October 16, 1985.

37. Kirk O'Donnell, interview with the author, December 12, 1986.

38. Thomas Foley, interview with the author, March 22, 1986. O'Neill recalled to the author on October 31, 1986, that in early 1981 Haig had said, "We oughta be in Nicaragua . . . with our troops. No *contras* or anything else. They weren't around in those days."

39. Poll by Louis Harris, October 29–November 1, 1986, before the Iranian arms scandal was disclosed.

40. Thomas P. O'Neill, Jr., interview with the author, October 16, 1985.

41. Les Aspin, interview with the author, January 10, 1986.

42. Albert Gore, Jr., interview with the author, January 10, 1986.

43. *Ibid.,* and Albert Gore, Jr., "The Fork in the Road," *New Republic,* May 5, 1982.

44. Henry Kissinger, "A New Approach to Arms Control," *Time,* March 21, 1983.

45. R. James Woolsey, interview with the author, January 8, 1987.

46. Les Aspin, interview with the author, January 10, 1986; and Brent Scowcroft, interview with the author, March 3, 1986.

47. Brent Scowcroft, interview with the author, March 3, 1986.

48. Thomas Foley, interview with the author, January 7, 1987.

49. Norman Dicks, interview with the author, March 21, 1986.

50. Les Aspin, interview with the author, January 10, 1986.

51. Norman Dicks, interview with the author, March 21, 1986.

52. *Ibid.*

53. *The Washington Post,* January 3, 1983, p. A13.

54. William Cohen, interview with the author, January 13, 1987.

55. Thomas P. O'Neill, Jr., interview with the author, October 31, 1986.

56. Thomas P. O'Neill, Jr., interview with the author, October 16, 1985.

57. Frank Fahrenkopf, quoted in *The Philadelphia Inquirer,* May 30, 1985.

58. Dan Rostenkowski, interview with the author, January 3, 1986.

59. Henson Moore, interview with the author, December 18, 1985.

60. Dan Rostenkowski, interview with the author, January 3, 1986.

61. *Ibid.*

62. This account comes both from Rostenkowski and from high Treasury Department officials.

63. Dan Rostenkowski, televised speech to the nation, May 28, 1985.

64. Dan Rostenkowski, interview with the author, January 3, 1986.

65. John Sherman, interview with the author, October 19, 1985.

66. Dan Rostenkowski, interview with the author, January 3, 1986.

67. Thomas Downey, interview with the author, November 5, 1985.

68. James A. Baker III, interview with the author, February 25, 1986; and Dan Rostenkowski, interview with the author, January 3, 1986.

69. Dan Rostenkowski, interview with the author, January 3, 1986.

70. Marty Russo, interview with the author, December 16, 1985.

71. Dan Rostenkowski, interview with the author, January 3, 1986.

72. Marty Russo, interview with the author, December 16, 1985.

73. Dan Rostenkowski, interview with the author, January 3, 1986.

74. Thomas P. O'Neill, Jr., interview with the author, November 6, 1986.

75. *Ibid.*

76. One Washington humor group, The Capitol Steps, captured the mixed parentage of the tax bill. To the tune of "Supercalifragilisticexpialidoshus," they sang, "ReaganPackwoodRostenkowskiTaxSimplification."

15. THE FOREIGN POLICY GAME

1. Ronald Reagan, nationally televised campaign speech, October 19, 1980.

2. Alexander M. Haig, Jr., *Caveat* (New York: Macmillan, 1984), p. 12.

3. Stuart Alsop, *The Center* (New York: Harper & Row, 1968) pp. 97–98.

4. George P. Shultz, "The Abrasive Interface" in *Harvard Business Review,* November–December 1979, p. 93.

5. This line of analysis is well developed in an excellent book by Morton H. Halperin, *Bureaucratic Politics and Foreign Policy* (Washington: The Brookings Institution, 1974). Halperin's experience as a Pentagon policymaker and as a national security deputy to Kissinger in the Nixon years gave him ample opportunity to develop his theories firsthand, and they are as sound today as when they were written.

6. Michael Pillsbury, interview with the author, June 28, 1985.

7. James Sterling Young, *The Washington Community* (New York: Columbia University Press, 1968), pp. 221–222.

8. Stanley J. Heginbotham, "Dateline Washington: The Rules of the Games," *Foreign Policy,* vol. 53, Winter 83–84, pp. 157–172.

9. John W. Vessey, interview with the author, June 30, 1987.

10. The version given the author by a top national security official in three separate interviews, February 12 and 13, 1986, and June 29, 1987, was that Reagan had actually issued an order for American planes to attack, but Weinberger denied that in an interview with the author, March 28, 1986. "There was no order to me of any kind, has never been an order to me by the president that hasn't been carried out and carried out immediately," Weinberger said. Vessey also said he knew of no "execution order" or advance planning for a joint raid with the French.

11. George Shultz, interview with the author, January 27, 1986.

12. Morton Halperin in *Foreign Policy and Bureaucratic Politics* develops an analysis of the conflicting attitudes of careerists and in-and-outers. His experience as a former Pentagon and

National Security Council official in both Democratic and Republican administrations has made him a superb student of bureaucratic game playing. In an interview with the author, January 29, 1987, he admitted: "I almost called my book on foreign policy, *Games Bureaucrats Play*. But it didn't sound serious. It sounded too cute."

13. Leslie Gelb, "The Mind of the President," *New York Times Magazine*, October 6, 1985, p. 21.

14. This narrative is compiled from the accounts by three participants, each of whom spoke on condition that they not be identified.

16. THE OTHER FOREIGN POLICY GAME

1. Robert C. McFarlane, "McFarlane on Why," *The Washington Post*, November 13, 1986, p. A21.

2. Henry A. Kissinger, *White House Years* (Boston: Little, Brown, 1979), p. 47.

3. In *Our Own Worst Enemy* (New York: Simon and Schuster, 1984), I. M. Destler, Leslie H. Gelb, and Anthony Lake use the analogy of cabinet barons and staff courtiers, in examining the power struggle between the national security staff and the secretary of State. See especially chapters iv and v.

4. *Ibid.*, p. 265.

5. Richard Nixon, quoted by Jack Anderson, "Kissinger: One-Man State Department," *The Washington Post*, October 18, 1974, p. D19.

6. Zbigniew Brzezinski, "Deciding Who Makes Foreign Policy," *New York Times Magazine*, September 18, 1983, p. 62.

7. *Ibid.*, p. 55ff.

8. Martin Anderson, interview with the author, February 11, 1987.

9. Joseph Coors, interview with the author's researcher William Nell, February 11, 1987.

10. Robert C. McFarlane, interviews with the author, March 20, 1986, and June 30, 1987.

11. Edward Teller, interview with the author, February 13, 1987.

12. James Watkins, interview with the author, February 18, 1987. The interview is the basis for the following narrative.

13. This account is based on interviews with four participants in the meeting, General Vessey, and General Meyer, Admiral Watkins, and one other official who asked not to be identified.

14. John W. Vessey, interview with the author, February 15, 1987.

15. E. C. Meyer, interview with the author, February 22, 1987.

16. Robert C. McFarlane, interviews with the author, June 29, 1987, and July 3, 1987.

17. Dr. George Keyworth, interview with the author, February 16, 1987. The subsequent account of Keyworth's involvement is drawn mainly from this interview.

18. Richard DeLauer, interview with the author, March 19, 1986.

19. James Watkins, interview with the author, February 18, 1987.

20. E. C. Meyer, interview with the author, February 22, 1987.

21. John W. Vessey, interview with the author, June 30, 1987.

22. Richard Perle, interview with the author, December 5, 1987.

23. John Poindexter, testimony before the Joint Congressional Committee investigating the Iran-*contra* operation, July 15, 1987 (hereafter, the Iran-*contra* hearings).

24. Oliver North, Iran-*contra* hearings, July 8 and 10, 1987.

25. John Poindexter, Iran-*contra* hearings, July 17, 1987.

26. Caspar Weinberger, Iran-*contra* hearings, July 31, 1987.

27. *Report of the President's Special Review Board*, February 26, 1987, p. C10.

28. George Shultz, Iran-*contra* hearings, July 23, 1987.

29. Fawn Hall, the Iran-*contra* hearings, June 9, 1987.

30. Robert C. McFarlane, Iran-*contra* hearings, May 11, 1987.

32. President Reagan, press interviews, May 14 and 15, 1987, and comments to reporters at a White House reception, May 16, 1987.

33. Robert C. McFarlane, the Iran-*contra* hearings, May 13, 1987.

34. Edwin Meese III, Iran-*contra* hearings, July 28, 1987.

35. Caspar Weinberger, Iran-*contra* hearings, July 31, 1987.

36. Oliver North, Iran-*contra* hearings, July 7, 1987, and John Poindexter, Iran-*contra* hearings, July 15, 1987. North prepared the order, and after Reagan signed one copy, Poindexter kept it in his safe, until he destroyed it in November 1986.

37. *Report of the President's Special Review Board*, February 26, 1987, p. B. 36.

38. George Shultz, Iran-*contra* hearings, July 23, 1987.

39. John S. D. Eisenhower, "The White House Mystique," *The New York Times*, January 16, 1987, p. A31.

40. Henry M. Jackson, quoted by James Reston, *The New York Times*, July 23, 1987, p. A27.

41. My account draws on the *Report of the President's Special Review Board*, February 26, 1987; the *Report of the Senate Select Committee on Intelligence*, January 29, 1987; and testimony before the Joint Congressional Committee investigating the Iran-*contra* operation, starting May 5, 1987.

42. Donald T. Regan, Iran-*contra* hearings, July 30, 1987.

43. George Shultz, Iran-*contra* hearings, July 23, 1987.

44. President Reagan's Finding of January 17, 1986, and the January 17, 1986 memorandum to Reagan from National Security Adviser Poindexter were made available by the White House on January 9, 1987.

45. Richard Secord, Iran-*contra* hearing, May 5, 1987; and *Report of the Congressional Committees Investigating the Iran-Contra Affair*, November 17, 1987, p. 9.

46. *Report of the President's Special Review Board*, February 26, 1987, p. IV-9; and *Report of the Congressional Committees Investigating the Iran-Contra Affair*, November 17, 1987, p. 18.

47. Oliver North, Iran-*contra* hearings, July 7, 1987.

48. Oliver North, Iran-*contra* hearings, July 10, 1987.

49. The key passage said: "During fiscal year 1985, no funds available to the Central Intelligence Agency, the Department of Defense, or any other agency or entity of the United States involved in intelligence activities may be obligated or expended for the purposes or which would have the effect of supporting, directly or indirectly, military or paramilitary operations in Nicaragua by any nation, group, organization, movement, or individual."

50. Robert Owen, Iran-*contra* hearings, May 19, 1987; and Tomas Castillo, Iran-*contra* hearings, May 29, 1987.

51. Robert C. McFarlane, interview with the author, June 30, 1987.

52. *The New York Times*, November 30, 1986, p. 26, and July 5, 1987, p. 10.

53. Oliver North, Iran-*contra* hearings, July 7, 1987.

54. *Ibid.*

55. Robert C. McFarlane, Iran-*contra* hearings, July 14, 1987.

56. George Shultz, Iran-*contra* hearings, July 24, 1987.

57. Caspar Weinberger, Iran-*contra* hearings, July 31, 1987.

58. Richard Cheney, Iran-*contra* hearings, July 20, 1987.

59. *Report of the Congressional Committees Investigating the Iran-Contra Affair*, November 17, 1987, pp. 423–27.

60. Lee Hamilton, Iran-*contra* hearings, July 14, 1987, and August 3, 1987.

61. William Cohen, speech on the Senate floor, January 12, 1987, *Congressional Record*, S-596-7.

62. *Report of the Congressional Committees Investigating the Iran-Contra Affair*, November 17, 1987, p. 22.

63. James R. Schlesinger, testimony before the House Armed Services Committee, December 2, 1986, and Schlesinger, "Reykjavík and Revelations: A Turn of the Tide?" in *Foreign Affairs*, vol. 65, no. 3, pp. 428–429.

64. Henry A. Kissinger, "Not Its Power, but Its Weakness," *The Washington Post*, December 21, 1986.

65. This information comes from two participants in the top-level meeting of the National

Security Planning Group on October 27, 1986, called by Reagan to go over the results of Reykjavík summit and consider future negotiating strategy.

66. This account comes from two participants, two other American officials close to the negotiations, and Dr. Georgi Arbatov, an adviser to Mikhail Gorbachev and Director of the Institute of the U.S.A. and Canada. See also an excellent account, with some differences, by Don Oberdorfer in *The Washington Post*, February 16, 1987, p. 1.

67. This account comes from two participants in the meeting, who spoke on condition that they not be identified.

68. This account comes from two participants in the meeting with Reagan.

69. Speech by Secretary of State George Shultz at the University of Chicago, Chicago, Illinois, November 17, 1986.

70. Lee Hamilton, Iran-*contra* hearings, June 9, 1987.

71. Robert C. McFarlane, Iran-*contra* hearings, May 11, 1987.

17. DIVIDED GOVERNMENT

1. James Madison, *Federalist Papers* [originally published 1787–88] (New York: Bantam Paperback Classics, 1982), no. 51, February 6, 1788, p. 262.

2. Gerald R. Ford, "Imperiled, Not Imperial," *Time*, November 10, 1980, p. 30.

3. David A. Stockman, *The Triumph of Politics: Why the Reagan Revolution Failed* (New York: Harper & Row, 1986), p. 454.

4. Hugh Heclo, "Reaganism and the Search for a Public Philosophy," in John L. Palmer, ed., *Perspectives on the Reagan Years* (Washington: Urban Institute Press, 1986), p. 52, pp. 59–60.

5. Paul Weyrich, "Reagan's Illusory Revolution," *The Washington Post*, Aug. 23, 1987, p. C1.

6. See *Congressional Quarterly*, "Hill Support for President Drops to 10-Year Low, *1986 CQ Almanac*, p. 21-Cff. Eisenhower's high was 89 percent in 1953; Johnson's 93 percent in 1965. Reagan's support began with 82.4 percent in 1981 but fell year by year, to 59.9 percent in 1985, and to 56.1 percent in 1986. Nixon's low was 50.6 percent in 1973; Ford's low was 53.8 percent in 1976.

7. James L. Sundquist, "The Crisis of Competence in Our National Government," in *Political Science Quarterly*, vol. 95, no. 2, Summer 1980, p. 192.

8. Thomas Mann, interview with the author, July 10, 1987.

9. "Partisanship Hit New High in 99th Congress," *1986 CQ Almanac*, p. 29-C. *Congressional Quarterly's* figures showed that a majority of Democrats lined up against a majority of Republicans on 56 percent of all recorded votes in 1985 and 55 percent in 1986, compared to highs of 48 percent in 1975 under Ford, and 47 percent in 1979 under Carter.

10. Norman Ornstein, "The Politics of the Deficit," *Essays in Contemporary Economic Problems* (Washington: American Enterprise Institute, 1985) pp. 315–317.

11. On August 3, 1982, forty-nine of fifty voting Senate Republicans opposed an amendment by Paul Tsongas, a Massachusetts Democrat, requiring the president to submit a balanced budget starting in fiscal 1984, that is, in five months, rather than at some indefinite time, as under the Reagan-backed constitutional amendment. Senate Democrats split, twenty-two and twenty-three against Tsongas's proposal. The lone Republican supporter was William Cohen of Maine.

12. Paul Peterson, "The New Politics of Deficits," in *New Directions in American Politics* (Washington: Brookings Institution, 1986), pp 371–382. See especially the table on p. 375. Peterson asserts that Congress has followed the presidential lead on the overall budget, while being braver on raising taxes to counteract deficits. "In short, in the immediate postwar period, Congress was nearly as fiscally responsible as the President on tax matters, and recently it has shown more 'courage' than has the Executive Branch," Peterson contends.

13. Stockman, *op. cit.*, p. 455, asserts: "Ronald Reagan has no comprehension that Congress saved his fiscal lunch with this [1982 tax] measure and many more like it."

14. Richard Wirthlin, interview with the author, January 31, 1986.

15. Phil Gramm, interview with the author's researcher Kurt Eichenwald, November 27, 1985.

16. Warren Rudman, interview with the author, December 6, 1985.

17. Donald Regan, in an interview with the author, June 12, 1986, disclosed that on October 3, 1985, he had sent Reagan a memo urging him to back Gramm-Rudman. The next day, after Reagan's endorsement, Regan sent the president another memo warning that two thirds of the automatic cuts would fall on the Pentagon, but contending inconsistently that Reagan could still have three-percent real growth in military spending in his 1987 budget.

18. Thomas Foley, interview with the author, February 6, 1986. His version was confirmed by two of Speaker O'Neill's aides.

19. *Ibid.*

20. The Supreme Court struck down the enforcement mechanism in the Gramm-Rudman law by ruling that the comptroller general was an agent of Congress who could not give orders to executive branch departments to cut their budgets. For him to do so, the Court said, would violate the separation of powers.

21. James A. Baker III, NBC *Today*, September 24, 1987.

22. James Exon, *Congressional Record*, September 23, 1987, S 12575.

18. WHERE'S THE MAJORITY PARTY?

1. James L. Sundquist, "Strengthening American Political Parties," an unpublished paper presented at Brookings Institution, April 7, 1987, p. 9.

2. William Schneider, "The New Shape of American Politics," *The Atlantic*, January 1987, see especially, pp. 44–47.

3. Kevin Phillips, interview with the author, January 21, 1985.

4. See the biennial National Election Studies by the Center for Political Studies of the University of Michigan. For extensive analysis of political realignment in the South, see Ray Wolfinger and Michael G. Hagen, "Republican Prospects: Southern Comfort," *Public Opinion*, October–November 1985, pp. 8–13. When independent voters leaning to the two parties are counted, Democrats led Republicans in the South by only 46–39 percent.

5. *The New York Times*/CBS News election-day exit poll on November 6, 1984, showed that blue collar voters went 54 percent to 46 percent for Reagan over Mondale.

6. Horace Busby, *The Busby Papers*, November 14, 1984, p. 3. Busby points out that in the 128 years since the Republican Party emerged with Lincoln in 1860, Republicans have occupied the White House 80 years, or 62.5 percent of the time; and since 1860, Democrats have controlled the House roughly 60 percent of the time.

7. Horace Busby, "The Republican Lock Revisited," *The Busby Papers*, May 17, 1984, p. 3, has a state-by-state breakdown of the GOP presidential base.

8. Paul Laxalt, interview with the author, January 11, 1985.

9. *The New York Times*, December 24, 1984, p. 9.

10. See *The New York Times*/CBS News election day exit polls of 1980 and 1984 for significant shifts in the party vote of many groups.

11. Kevin Phillips, *The American Political Report*, January 11, 1985, p. 2.

12. Lou Cannon, *The Washington Post*, November 3, 1986, p. A10.

13. *The Washington Times*, November 6, 1986, p. 6A.

14. Martin P. Wattenberg, *The Decline of American Political Parties, 1952–1984* (Cambridge, Massachusetts: Harvard University Press, 1986) p. 144–145. The biannual National Election Studies show a striking contrast between the types of support won by Eisenhower and Reagan, by income brackets.

15. Kevin Phillips, *Los Angeles Times*, November 9, 1986, Part V, p. 1.

16. Actually, the swings in popular sentiment in Senate races are less dramatic than shifting control suggests. In 1980, when the Republican majority took over, a shift of 24,000 votes in five states would have left the Democrats in control. And in 1986, when the Democrats regained control, a shift of 36,000 votes in six states would have left a Republican majority.

17. Previously, the longest spans of partisan control—by the Republicans—were sixteen-year spurts from 1858 to 1874 and again from 1894 to 1910.

18. Walter Dean Burnham, "A Continuing Political Gridlock," *The Wall Street Journal*, June 24, 1985, p. 18

19. Norman J. Ornstein, et al., eds., *Vital Statistics on Congress, 1987–88 Edition* (Washington: Congressional Quarterly, 1987), Table 2-2, in Chapter 2, titled "Popular Vote and House Seats Won, by Party, 1946–1986."

20. Norman Ornstein, "Genesis of a Gerrymander," *The Wall Street Journal*, May 7, 1985, p. 30. His table for the 1984 House elections shows why Republican vote totals do not yield as many seats as Democratic vote totals. In districts with turnouts under 175,000 votes, Democrats got 37 percent of their seats whereas Republicans got only 10 percent. But in districts with turnout over 200,000, Republicans got 68 percent of their seats and Democrats only 41 percent. Republican winners got more voters than Democratic winners because they came from affluent, activist districts.

21. Thomas Mann, "Is the House of Representatives Unresponsive to Political Change?", in A. James Reichley, ed., *Elections American Style* (Washington: Brookings Institution, 1987) p. 263. Mann calculates "the value of incumbency increased by at least 5 percentage points from the 1950s to the 1970s."

22. Common Cause study, April 7, 1987, Chart VIII, and preliminary findings reported in *The New York Times*, November 10, 1986. p. A18.

23. The Federal Election Commission report of May 10, 1987, disclosed that $471.4 million was raised by House and Senate candidates in the 1986 election cycle and that PACs contributed $132.2 million.

24. Michael J. Malbin, "Looking Back at the Future of Campaign Finance Reform," in Michael J. Malbin, ed., *Money and Politics in the United States* (Washington: American Enterprise Institute for Public Policy Research, 1984), p. 265.

25. Mann, *op. cit.*, p. 11.

26. Louis Harris, interview with the author, October 20, 1985.

27. National Election Study, 1952 and 1986, conducted by the Center for Political Studies, University of Michigan.

28. Ralph Whitehead, Jr., "New Collar Americans and the Democratic Vision," paper presented to the Democratic Policy Commission, Washington, D.C., July 10, 1985, pp. 2, 4, 5.

29. Walter Dean Burnham, "Elections Dash GOP Dreams of Realignment," *The Wall Street Journal*, November 26, 1986, p.20.

30. Larry J. Sabato, *The Rise of Political Consultants* (New York: Basic Books, 1981), p. 289.

31. Ibid., p. 288.

32. Warren Rudman, interview with the author, April 6, 1987.

33. Leon Billings, "The Chaos of Congress," *The Washington Post*, December 30, 1986, p. A21

34. James L. Sundquist, "The Crisis of Competence in Our National Government," *Political Science Quarterly*, Summer, 1980, p. 198.

35. Report of the Federal Election Commission, May 31, 1987, p. 2.

36. Report of the Federal Election Commission, May 21, 1987, p. 1, gives the PAC donations as $132.2 million—28 percent of the $471.4 million received by candidates for Senate and House in 1986. The FEC report of May 31, 1987, amended, lists party donations of cash and in-kind services to individual candidates as $25.9 million, or 5.5 percent. But adding common services provided to candidates as a group, experts estimate the actual party contribution is double or triple the FEC figure.

37. Larry Sabato, *PAC Power* (New York: W. W. Norton, 1984), p. 158.

38. Thomas Eagleton, Senate speech, November 23, 1985, *The Congressional Record*, vol. 131, no. 163.

39. David A. Stockman, interview with James Reston, *The New York Times*, April 12, 1984, p. B14.

40. Gerald R. Ford, "Imperiled, not Imperial," *Time*, November 10, 1980, p. 30.

41. Anthony King, "A Mile and a Half is a Long Way," in Anthony King, ed., *Both Ends of the Avenue* (Washington: American Enterprise Institute for Public Policy, 1983), p. 249.

42. David Durenburger, Senate speech, August 1, 1985, *Congressional Record*, vol. 131, no. 106, Part II.

19. OUR POLITICAL DISCONNECT

1. James MacGregor Burns, interview with the author, October 2, 1984.

2. Theodore Sorensen, *A Different Kind of Presidency* (New York: Harper & Row, 1984), pp. 46–47.

3. Samuel P. Huntington, "The Democratic Distemper," *The Public Interest*, Fall 1975, p. 27.

4. Helson W. Polsby, *Consequences of Party Reform* (New York: Oxford University Press, 1983), p. 129.

5. Austin Ranney, interview with the author, September 12, 1984.

6. Samuel Kernell, interview with the author, April 6, 1987.

7. Peter Hart, interview with the author, July 15, 1987.

8. Memorandum to White House Chief of Staff Dick Cheney from Campaign Strategists Mike Duval and Foster Chanock, June 11, 1976, quoted in Martin Schramm, *The Great American Video Game* (New York: William Morrow, 1987), p. 93.

9. Richard Nixon, *Six Crises* (New York: Pyramid Books, 1968), p. 457.

10. Richard Wirthlin, interview with the author, January 31, 1986.

11. Walter F. Mondale, press conference, November 7, 1984.

12. Michael Malbin, interview with the author, September 23, 1986.

13. James Ceaser, Glen E. Thurow, Jeffrey Tulis, and Joseph M. Bessette, "The Rise of the Rhetorical Presidency," *Presidential Studies Quarterly*, volume XI, no. 1, Winter 1981, pp. 158–171.

14. Richard M. Nixon, "Needed: Clarity of Purpose," *Time*, November 10, 1980.

15. James David Barber, *The Pulse of Politics* (New York: W. W. Norton, 1980), p. 318.

16. Alexander Hamilton's reply to George Washington on September 9, 1792, was quoted by Herb Schmertz, "Negative Is Their Own Game," *The Washington Times*, December 3, 1986, p. 2D.

17. Charles Krauthammer, *The Washington Post*, October 24, 1986, p. A27

18. *The Washington Post*, June 30, 1987, p. A8.

19. *The Washington Post*, October 5, 1986, p. 6.

20. *The New York Times*, August 27, 1986, p. A18

21. *The Washington Times*, November 6, 1986, p. 4D

22. Curtis B. Gans, "Non-Voting: The Nature of the Problem, Its Importance to American Democracy, and Some Approaches to Its Solution," an unpublished paper given at The Brookings Institution, April 7, 1987. Gans also quoted in *The Washington Times*, November 6, 1986, p 4D.

23. Norman Ornstein, interview with the author, October 3, 1984.

20. WHAT IS TO BE DONE?

1. Richard Nixon in "Taking Another Look at the Constitutional Blueprint," *American Heritage*, May–June 1987, pp. 53–54.

2. Bryce Harlow, interview with the author, November 13, 1985.

3. Donald L. Robinson, *To the Best of My Ability* (New York: Norton, 1987), pp. 133–48, develops the case that the Constitution has been changed by the modern standing army at the disposal of the president.

4. Jimmy Carter in "Taking Another Look at the Constitutional Blueprint," *American Heritage*, May–June 1987, p. 54.

5. "A Bicentennial Analysis of the American Political Structure," report and recommendations of the Committee on the Constitutional System, Washington, D.C., January 1987. The committee is jointly chaired by Democrat Lloyd Cutler, White House counsel to President Carter; Republican Senator Nancy Kassebaum of Kansas; and Republican C. Douglas Dillon, Treasury secretary to President Kennedy.

6. Howard H. Baker, Jr., interview with James Reston, *The New York Times*, May 12, 1987, p. B6.

7. Thomas Cronin, conversation with the author, October 11, 1987.

8. See Larry Sabato, "Real and Imagined Corruption in Campaign Financing," in A. James Reichley, ed., *Elections American Style* (Washington: The Brookings Institution, 1987), p. 168. This paper was included in the recommendations of the Committee on the Constitutional System, p. 9.

9. Thomas E. Mann, "Is the House of Representatives Unresponsive to Political Change?," in Reichley, *op. cit.* p. 278.

10. All kinds of formulas are possible for levying time requirements on TV stations by the size of their listening area or audience, and granted to candidates of the two major parties. Other candidates would qualify by past voting support above a given threshold and by petitions of some fixed size.

11. Bryce Harlow, interview with the author, November 13, 1985.

12. Theodore F. Sorensen, *A Different Kind of Presidency* (New York: Harper & Row, 1984), pp. 55–56.

13. Benjamin Zycher, "An Item Veto Won't Work," *The Wall Street Journal*, October 24, 1984, p. 32. Zycher also points out that the states with the highest spending levels all have the line-item veto.

14. George Shultz, Iran-*contra* hearings, July 23, 1987.

Index

About the Author

Hedrick Smith has taken readers inside foreign countries with his best seller *The Russians* and his Pulitzer Prize–winning international reporting for *The New York Times*. Now he turns to Washington—a city he knows well. He was a member of the Pulitzer Prize–winning team that produced the Pentagon Paper series for *The New York Times* and has served as that paper's Washington bureau chief and chief Washington correspondent. Coauthor of two books on President Reagan and politics, he is a longtime panelist on the PBS program *Washington Week in Review*.